ORGANIZATIONS:
Behavior, Design, and Change

ORGANIZATIONS:
Behavior, Design, and Change

GEORGE F. WIELAND, Ph.D.
Associate Research Scientist
University of Michigan

ROBERT A. ULLRICH, D.B.A.
Associate Professor of Management
Vanderbilt University

 1976

RICHARD D. IRWIN, INC. Homewood, Illinois 60430
Irwin-Dorsey International Arundel, Sussex BN18 9AB
Irwin-Dorsey Limited Georgetown, Ontario L7G 4B3

© RICHARD D. IRWIN, INC., 1976

First Printing, March 1976

ISBN 0-256-01847-2
Library of Congress Catalog Card No. 75–28942
Printed in the United States of America

FOR

SHARON AND CELIA

Preface

Many people alive today were born before the Wright brothers took to the air from the base of Kill Devil hill. Geronimo's surrender is three generations past, and still within living memory. Six generations separate us from Washington's farewell address. The progress that placed the Wright brothers' flight and the first moon landing within the span of a lifetime is attributable in part to the growth of modern organizations. Understanding these organizations is essential—especially now, when some of the progress they achieve is offset by socially undesirable consequences. Unfortunately, such understanding is hard to come by. One problem is that these organizations are extremely complex. Yet, complexity can be mastered ultimately. More frustrating, from our point of view, are the divergent views of organizations confronting the student.

Two major, recurring themes are found in the literature on organizations. Resulting from different traditions and philosophies, they sometimes appear irreconcilable. On the one hand there is the "rational/ mechanical" school of thought which views organizations as logically-configured means for pursuing well-defined ends. On the other hand, the "natural/open system" school argues that organizations are complex social systems that respond to membership needs and environmental pressures, as well as to forces they create themselves.

In our opinion, the separation of these views is unfortunate, for they appear complementary. The concepts, models, and empirical findings presented in this text emphasize the circumstances under which prescriptions from either school may be appropriate, as well as their short-comings.

Beyond these two models, we have emphasized the social processes found in organizations. People's values and socially derived views of the world are important determinants of processes such as conflict, strategic choice, and change. We have described these processes as they are influenced by the interactions of major organizational variables which are described by both models.

Chapter 1 provides an introduction to the two schools of thought on organizations. Chapter 2 describes prescriptions and organizational designs developed by theorists and practitioners identified with the rational

school of thought. The following chapter, which begins Section II, introduces a view of organizations primarily derived from the systems perspective. The middle portion of the text, Section III, is devoted to an analysis
of processes—some of which cross organizational boundaries—and to
their behavioral and rational foundations. Section IV explores the relationship of the organization to its environment. The final section deals
with processes of organizational change.

We have emphasized the aspects of organizations that are subject to
control and manipulation by management *and* which have been studied
by one or another of the scientific disciplines. Our aim has been to
provide a text which is practical, and yet sufficiently based on scientific
evidence to provide a foundation for subsequent, systematic learning by
the student of management.

Our aim has been to describe organizations as we understand them.
Thus, we have not provided an exhaustive survey of the literature, but
have cited the major findings upon which our understanding is based. At
the risk of being repetitious, we have interrelated these findings throughout the text to describe the organization as a complex whole. Finally, we
have acknowledged the manager's need to take decisive action in areas
where the behavioral scientists would prefer to withhold judgment. In
doing so we occasionally have weighed the evidence available and advised the reader accordingly.

Every author becomes indebted for the help and kindness of others.
We shall take a moment to acknowledge our special gratitude to Larry
Cummings and Kirby Warren for their guidance and encouragement;
to Johannes Pennings for his critical commentary on our drafts; to
James V. Davis and Eugene Feingold for their organizational support
and understanding; to Betty Elder for her friendship and editorial skill;
and especially to Diane Sullivan, who has seen us through more than one
book and helped us in more ways than we can acknowledge in this
brief space.

February 1976   GEORGE F. WIELAND
                                                   ROBERT A. ULLRICH

Contents

xi

The Importance of Power in Resolving Conflict. BUREAUCRATIC CON-
FLICT: Autonomy and Conflict. Activation of Commitments and Obligations. Integrating Individual and Organizational Goals. Socialization as
a Means for Resolving Bureaucratic Conflict. Socialization of Attitudes
and Values. Leading Control Mechanisms. Selective Recruitment. Unobtrusive Cognitive Controls. Participation as a Social Control Mechanism. The Accommodation Mechanism for Individual and Organizational
Integration. Primary and Secondary Relations in Organizations. SYS-
TEMS CONFLICTS: Subgoals and Conflicts. Goal and Style Differentiation.
Superordinate Goals. Moving Conflict within Units. Incentive Systems.
Reducing Function Interdependence. Dealing with Sequential Depen-
dencies. Reducing Pressures for Compliance. BARGAINING CONFLICTS:
Limited Resources and Conflicts. Distributive Bargaining Tactics. Pres-
sure Tactics. Concessions. Tacit Communication. Informal Conferences.
Intermediaries. The Importance of Normative Structure. Integrative
Bargaining. Dealing with Conflict Sequentially. Content Specific and
Equity Norms. The Norm of Mutual Responsiveness. PARTISANS: Two
Perspectives on Conflict: Social Control and Partisans in the Sub-
system. Getting Power. Trust and Distrust. Usefulness of Distrust.
Confidence, Neutrality, and Alienation. Reactions by Authorities. Pit-
falls in Confrontation and Participation. Participation's Usefulness to
the Partisan.

IMPACT OF THE ENVIRONMENT: A Systems View of the Organization's Environment. Causal Texture of the Environment. Coping with Turbulence. Organization Sets. REACTION AND PROACTION: Organizations, Society, and the Physical Environment. Organizational Prestige Sets. Preserving Rationality. Domains. Other Bases for Exchange, Autonomy and Dependency. Managing Interdependence. Environment, Technology, and Organizational Design. Top Management and the Environment. Organizational Intelligence. Boards of Directors. Community Power Structure. Power in Boundary Roles. The Residual Meaning.

MODELS OF DECISION MAKING: Strategy. Strategy and Planning. Strategy Formulation: The Normative Approach. Descriptive Studies. Strategy Formulation: The Disjointed Incremental Approach. A Contingency Approach. Values. Processes of Strategy Formulation. Coalitions in Strategy Formulation. Rational or Natural System Model for Strategy? DECISION MAKING AS A PROCESS: The Strategic Decision Process. Identification Phase. Development Phase. Selection Phase. The Complexity of Strategic Decision Processes. The Behavior of Strategy Makers. Strategic Management. Dissonance Reduction, and the Intractability of Managers.

Case
Walnut Avenue Church, *R. W. Ackerman*, 438

DETERMINANTS OF ORGANIZATIONAL CHANGE: Some Determinants of Change in Organizations. Complexity. Centralization. Formalization. Stratification. Production. Efficiency. Job Satisfaction. Systemic Qualities of the Variables Studied. Dynamic Organizations. Static Organizations. Stable and Dynamic Environments. Diversification. Scientific Management. Organizational Affluence. "Everyday" Change. Growth. Consequence of Growth. Organizational Life Cycles. Two Stages of Organizational Change. DILEMMAS IN THE PROCESS OF CHANGE: Determining the Need for Change. Initiation of Change. Implementation of Change. Routinization of Change. Resistance to Change. Dilemmas in Perspective.

TRAINING GROUPS IN ORGANIZATIONAL DEVELOPMENT: Controversies in Organizational Development. Characteristics of Organizational Development. Normative Goals in Organizational Development. Process Consultation. Structuring Interventions. Training Groups. The Objectives of Training Groups. The Setting and Role of the Trainer. Research on the Effectiveness of Training Groups. Training Groups and Organizational Change. Research on Training Groups and Organizational Change. Criticisms of OD. ALTERNATIVE OD STRATEGIES: The Consultant-Trainer Role. Depth of Intervention. Depth of Intervention and Client Dependency. Deep Intervention Strategies and Social Norms. The Consultant's Dilemma.

section I

Background

PREMISE

Large, complex organizations constitute a familiar part of our everyday lives. IRS, IBM, I.T.T., and M.I.T. are household words. Yet, familiar as they are, these organizations are not well understood generally. Such institutions, established to fulfill both societal requirements and membership needs, exert forces in their own right. Our text begins, then, with a preliminary investigation of organizations as entities in society. Following this, we shall examine various parts of organizations—their technologies, goals, informal structures, and the like. We feel this format is useful because the parts of an organization cannot be understood fully outside of the context in which they exist.

Each chapter is introduced with an example of the organizational phenomena to be discussed. Examples are followed by questions that will aid the reader in organizing and understanding the material that follows. These questions are answered in the chapters that follow, although not always explicitly. Together with the discussion questions found at the end of each chapter, they will help to relate text material to the reader's own experiences.

1

1

Two Views of Organizations

INTRODUCTION

One of the attributes of contemporary life that sets it apart from man's earlier experiences is the degree to which we are joined together by complex, systemic organizational networks. Anyone who has a telephone is linked to a worldwide communications network that transmits information at the speed of light. Not only can we speak with colleagues half a world away, we can also gain telephone access to computing facilities, emergency counseling services, weather bureaus, and police and fire departments. Furthermore, these services themselves are organized as complex networks or systems.

Complex social systems are a phenomena of such increasing importance that understanding them is a prerequisite to the study of contemporary experience. Of even greater importance for those who will work in organizations is the need to understand how these organizations work. To this end, we shall direct our study both to the activities of individuals and groups within organizations and to the functioning of organizations as entities within society. We will attempt to view organizations as social systems that are interrelated with other elements of the environment in which they reside.

We need, then, a preliminary definition of organizations in order to set the boundaries of our text. Some contemporary theorists have defined organizations (and, in fact, all social systems) as the patterned activities of individual members (Katz and Kahn, 1966). According to Katz and Kahn, these activities are the organization, for, in their absence, the organization ceases to exist.

But this is a rather abstract concept, and one that may not be particularly clear at this point. One way to clarify the definition is to retrace the thinking that led to its development. Let us, then, review some of the more important work on organizations that evolved around the turn of the century. A good place to start is with the writings of Frederick Winslow Taylor, "The Father of Scientific Management."

From *The Principles of Scientific Management,* Taylor states:

3

One of the first discoveries which we made—and it seems an exceedingly simple one—was that if you throw a stream of water on the chip and tool at the point at which the shaving of iron is being cut off from the forging, you can increase your cutting speed 40 per cent. You have a 40 per cent gain just by doing that little thing alone. That we found out within the first six months. Mr. Sellers had the courage of his convictions; he did not believe it at first, but when we proved to him that it was true, he tore down the old shop and replaced it with another so as to get that 40 per cent increase in the cutting speed. He built a shop with water drains extending under the floor to carry off the water with which the tools were cooled to a central settling tank; from there it was pumped up again to a tank in the roof and carried from there through proper piping to every tool, so that the workman did not need to spend much time in adjusting a stream which would flow on to any tool in any position. He was a broad enough man to see that it paid him to build a new shop to get that 40 per cent.

Now our competitors came right to the Midvale Steel Works without any hesitation. They were invited to come there, and in twenty years just one competitor used that knowledge and built a shop in which it was possible to throw a heavy stream of water on the tools, and that was a shop started by men who had left the Midvale Steel Works and who knew enough to do this. That shows the slowness of men, in that trade at least, to take advantage of a 40 per cent gain in cutting (Taylor, 1960, pp. 106–7).

Chapter Guide

At the outset of each chapter we shall provide a series of questions to help in organizing and understanding the ideas that follow. Each question is answered within the following chapter, although not always explicitly. The excerpt from Taylor's work quoted above raises the following questions about organizations as systems:

1. Only one of the Midvale's competitors copied the cooling system within the 20-year period cited. Why would presumably rational, intelligent men not take advantage of the efficiencies that had been amply demonstrated to them?

2. Taylor saw organizations as "tools" for getting work done. Can you think of any misleading assumptions that this view would lead you to make about organizations and their functioning?

RATIONAL TOOLS

Frederick W. Taylor's Scientific Management

Prior to the turn of the century, work methods were passed on as part of the culture, from father to son or from craftsman to apprentice.

Each workman learned his craft or trade differently and, as a result, similar tasks were often performed in a variety of ways. Yet, it would stand to reason that some methods were more efficient than others. Taylor (1960) became convinced that efficient work methods could be identified and taught to less efficient workers, and furthermore, as the newly found increases in productivity were shared, labor and management alike would benefit. Thus, he became one of the first practitioners to advocate control of human behavior in organizations and to call attention to the importance of people in the quest for efficiency and productivity in organizations.

Taylor reasoned that logic and order existed in the apparent chaos of work organizations if only one could find them. The problem-solving style that he used to rationalize work processes follows:

1. Gather all of the rule-of-thumb knowledge possessed by the work force, classify it, and wherever possible reduce it to laws or rules.
2. Study the workmen just as you would study machines.
3. Bring scientifically selected workmen and machines together. Inspire the men to change.
4. Divide the work formerly done by workmen into two sections— one of which is turned over to management (e.g., managers assign tools to laborers).

Taylor's approach led to major advances in industrial efficiency, and his work was extended by the works of Gantt (1973) and Gilbreth (1972a, 1972b). The magnitude of his improvements led him to generalize that his principles could be applied to all social activities, including the management of homes, universities, farms, and governmental departments.

Despite its success, however, scientific management (the precursor of operations research) took only one possible view of organizations: as a means toward the attainment of specific goals; i.e., as tools. At first glance, this may seem a useful and reasonable position. Its shortcomings, however, are readily demonstrated.

Viewing the organization as a rational arrangement of means assembled in the pursuit of specific ends draws our attention directly to the productive (or throughput) process and away from other vital attributes of organizational functioning. Generally speaking, productive processes are concerned with the ratio of output to input, the criterion of efficiency. Productive efficiency is gained, in part, through the establishment of economies of scale and a stable, steady state environment. Yet, organizations reside in turbulent environments characterized by uncertainty and change. Somehow, the organization must accommodate itself to its environment and, at the same time, strive for efficiency in its use of resources. This is a major problem and one which constitutes a recurring theme in our text.

FIGURE 1–1
A Systems View of Organizations

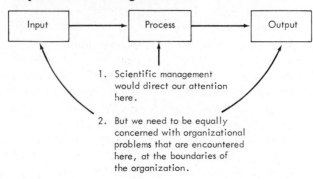

1. Scientific management would direct our attention here.

2. But we need to be equally concerned with organizational problems that are encountered here, at the boundaries of the organization.

Henri Fayol's Principles of Management

Many management experts of the day were opposed to Taylor's concepts, and others denied that principles per se were contained in his theory. They believed that Taylor was speaking, not of principles, but of a collection of axioms and an arbitrary combination of specific mechanisms, such as time study and work methods study. These critics advocated a "deeper" analysis of organizational phenomena—directed toward exposing the underlying scientific principles of management.

The Frenchman, Henri Fayol (1960), did, indeed, go deeper and developed a series of *principles of management.* These were thought to be scientific prescriptions for the body corporate which, if applied intelligently, would ensure that an organization would be managed effectively. One of the principles is elaborated below in order to provide an indication of the flavor of the times.

Order

> For social order to prevail in a concern there must, in accordance with the definition, be an appointed place for every employee and every employee must be in his appointed place. Perfect order requires, further, that the place be suitable for the employee and the employee for the place—in English idiom, "The right men in the right place" (Fayol, 1960, p. 236).

Other principles included "division of work," "unity of command" (one man, one boss), "subordination of individual interest to the interest of the organization," and "span of control" (the number of subordinates that are supervised by one person).

Limitations of the Closed-System Perspective

Although Fayol's perspective extended beyond the productive processes to more general phenomena of management, he shared Taylor's view of organizations as tools. In more recent terminology, we can say that Taylor and Fayol (and others using the rational model such as Urwick [1943] and Mooney and Reiley [1939] saw organizations from a *closed-system* perspective (Thompson, 1967). Systems are closed when they are isolated from the influences of external variables and when they are deterministic rather than probabilistic. A deterministic system is one in which a specific change in one of the system's variables will produce a particular outcome with certainty. Such a system requires, of course, that all the variables are known and controllable (or predictable). If we view an organization in this manner we will agree, as did Fayol, that organizational effectiveness will always prevail if organizational variables are held within known limits; that is, if management follows sets of rules that are assumed to maintain desired relationships among the various parts of the organization.[1]

For reasons to be elaborated below, organizations and, for that matter, all social systems are *open systems*. They are affected by changes in their environments, the so-called external variables. The environment is potentially without bounds and includes many unknown and uncontrollable variables. Rational control, with the selection of the very best means toward the given end, usually is not possible because of the limits of management's knowledge and control.

Second, the outcomes of social systems are probabilistic as opposed to being deterministic (Thompson, 1967). Human behavior is not altogether predictable. Humans are complex, responding to many variables that are not fully understood, including those pertaining to self-control. Ordering individuals to behave in a particular way or prearranging their relationships to others in the organization by no means ensures that they will act as management desires. By the same token, management cannot assume that customers, suppliers, regulating agencies and the like will behave predictably either. Obviously, consumer responses to the Edsel were very much different than those that were anticipated by the company.

Max Weber's Analysis of Bureaucracy

Another, more systematic rational view of organizations is found in the sociological theories of bureaucracy. Bureaucracy, according to German sociologist Max Weber, provides a way of consciously organizing people and activities in order to achieve specific purposes (Weber, 1958, 1964). It emphasizes the conscious, and correspondingly formal,

---

[1] The thermostat that regulates a heating system is part of a closed system. Unless the system malfunctions, a particular setting of the device will yield ambient temperatures that remain within known limits. If the temperature of the air circulating through the thermostat falls to the lower limit of this range, we can predict with near certainty that the furnace will be turned on. Furthermore, under normal operating conditions, exogenous variables (variables other than room air temperature) will have no effect on the system.

structural aspects of organizations over the "natural" and traditional forms of organization. Most importantly, bureaucracy stresses rationality and efficient organization of means toward a given end. In contrast to organizations existing prior to the Industrial Revolution, which were often governed by personality, nepotism, and various forms of capricious behavior, Weber delineated the components of bureaucracy from descriptions of large-scale organizations that were stable, enduring, and efficient. Weber proposed both to describe these very efficient organizations and, perhaps more importantly, to consider the relationship of these organizations to the status of individual freedom in society. Did the growth of large, complex, and efficient organizations foretell the curtailment of individual freedoms?

Weber developed his theory early in this century when our current research technology for studying organizations was nonexistent. The concepts of the theory and their empirical referents, therefore, were derived from the formal structure of organizations which individuals will emphasize in describing their organization to someone else. These concepts included *the hierarchy of authority, impersonality, specialization,* and *systems of rules.*

Weber contrasted *legal-rational authority* with authority that stems from either *charisma* or *tradition.* Bureaucracy is based on legal-rational authority, a formally established body of social norms designed to organize behavior in the rational pursuit of specified goals. Obedience in a bureaucracy is owed not to a person (a traditional chief or a charismatic leader) but to an office—to a set of impersonal principles. A person is selected to fill an office because of his knowledge and competence, and he acts according to the duties of the office. Bureaucracy entails a government of laws, not people.

Such legal authority is used to coordinate the specialized elements in the organization in a manner that permits efficient functioning (much as Taylor advocated, too). After a systematic division of labor based on training and expertise, the officials and their tasks are grouped in a rational way, according to technical knowledge and with the aim of attaining maximum task efficiency.

Authority is distributed in a hierarchy of positions, each successive position in the hierarchy embracing in authority all those beneath it. Authority adheres to the office or the position, not to the man. Furthermore, it is impersonal, restricted, and delimited according to the specification of the office. Rules and procedures are established to make the handling of various contingencies efficient.

Perhaps the most general way of characterizing Weber's specification of bureaucracy is in terms of *rationality:* the use of knowledge to relate various means to organizational ends in the best way possible. Rules, based on technical knowledge, are established with the expectation that they will regulate the organization's structure and processes so as to attain maximum efficiency.

People sometimes confuse bureaucracy with organizational hierarchy and consider them to be synonymous. However, not all hierarchies are bureaucratic. The rational nature of a hierarchy determines whether or not it constitutes a bureaucracy. Bureaucracies, in fact, replaced feudal hierarchies. The traditional authority of the feudal lord was replaced by legal authority, which was legitimated by a belief in the ultimate correctness of its rules. Unlike loyalty owed to the feudal lord, loyalty to the bureaucrat is oriented toward an impersonal order and a superior position, not the person holding the position.

Bureaucratic theory has also been termed a "tool" view of organizations (Perrow, 1972). Organizations are seen as the conscious, rational arrangement of means to some particular ends. Mouzelis (1968), for example, has defined formal organizations "as a form of social grouping which is established in a more or less deliberate or purposive manner for the attainment of a specific goal (p. 4)." While Weber's views are useful, a number of studies show the formal, rational elements of bureaucratic organizations to produce inconsistencies and unforeseen consequences. These consequences, furthermore, can lead to changes within the organization, which produce conflict between elements within the bureaucracy and, generally speaking, lead to inefficiencies unlike the efficiencies expected of the system.

Bureaucratic Functions and Dysfunctions

A number of criticisms and amplifications of the theory of bureaucracy arise from what is called *functional analysis*. One may view bureaucratic organization as being made up of both formal and informal social systems. The formal systems of rules, authority, hierarchies, and so on are purposively designed. In addition, various spontaneous (human) forces within the organization produce what are known as informal social systems (the informal organization). Since the elements of both the formal and informal systems interact with one another, relationships between elements can be examined in terms of their contributions to the entire organization. One may view the entire organization as having needs (or functional requirements) and any part of the organization can be viewed in terms of its contribution to the fulfillment of these needs; in terms, that is, of its *function*. Any element of the organization that hinders the fulfillment of these needs is said to be *dysfunctional*.

In a now almost classic report, March and Simon (1958) collate the accounts of a number of students of bureaucracy showing that the functioning of bureaucratic structures creates various conditions which

tend to reduce or, at least, to inhibit its expected efficiency. Merton
(1940) reasons that, over the long run, bureaucratic adherence to rules
and impersonal behavior is dysfunctional. Rules and impersonality are
desirable methods for producing reliable behavior, but ultimately they
tend to become overemphasized. Variations in the needs of clients will
render impersonal treatment ineffective, which, in turn, becomes a
source of client dissatisfaction. The bureaucrat, faced with dissatisfied
clients, will rely increasingly on rules, categorization, and impersonality
as defense mechanisms. Thus, rules and procedures become internalized and followed in an inflexible manner, especially when the ends of
the organization, to which the rules are means, are not salient. The
rigid behavior that results is not effective in dealing with individual
clients nor with changing circumstances.

Gouldner (1954) indicates the dysfunctional consequences of the
usage of rules in bureaucracies. General and impersonal rules are used
to decrease the visibility of power relations; to make power less personal and a more rational means of coordination, since it is assumed
that people work better in the absence of visible, overt power. However,
when detailed rules and regulations are specified, workers learn the
lower limits that the organization places on acceptable behavior. They
learn what is expected of them and in some cases perform only to that
level. One organizational response to minimal performance is to provide
closer supervision which, of course, makes power more visible and
creates tensions within the organization, which upsets the system.

Selznick (1949) illustrates the dysfunctional consequences of the
practice of delegating authority. Since all authority cannot be retained
at the top of a complex organization, some must be delegated to lower,
more specialized units. With the aim of increased effectiveness, these
units specialize further and use the increased delegated authority to
respond and adapt to local circumstances. However, this tends to lead to
a divergence of interests among specialized units and to the growth and
internalization of subgoals. These subgoals are appropriate for the effectiveness of specialists and local units but conflict with the subgoals
of other units and the goals of the organization as a whole.

In general, then, we see that the rational quality of bureaucracy
theory encounters problems, not only in failing to take into account the
changing environment, but also in failing to anticipate the consequences of human behavior in the organization. In attempting to gain
control over the system through utilizing rules, impersonality, categorization, and authority, the controls designed to maintain the subsystem
tend to disturb the equilibrium of a larger system, including human
behavior, with a subsequent feedback on the subsystem (March and
Simon, 1958, p. 44). Bureaucracy theory, then, falls short as an explanation of organizations because of the unanticipated consequences

which can accompany the anticipated outcomes of the rational activity.

The rational model views the organization as a mechanical arrangement in which parts may be replaced at will without repercussions on other parts, much as a physical device (Gouldner, 1959). The above examples of dysfunctions indicate the possible advantage to taking a systems view of the organization—as an organic whole composed of interdependent parts. Each of the parts contributes to the whole, and the whole, composed of other parts, contributes to the needs of each.

Bureaucracy and Individual Freedom

At this point, let us return to one of Weber's initial concerns in his study of bureaucracy. To what extent is bureaucracy detrimental to individual freedoms in society? In a study of the internal politics of large-scale organizations, a German sociologist, Michels (1915), confirmed the Machiavellian view that those with power will become an elite who dominate and prevent the practice of democracy. From his studies, Michels formulated the "Iron Law of Oligarchy": power inevitably comes to reside in the hands of a few at the top of organizations. Modern large-scale organizations are necessarily oligarchic by virtue of their very structure, even when the ideals of the organization are democratic. This phenomenon is evident, for instance, in his study of the German Socialist party which, despite its ideals, retained a facade of democracy only in its official regulations and handbooks, and, in practice, was ruled by a small elite. A more recent study of democracy and a two-party political system in a typographer's union (Lipset, Trow, and Coleman, 1956) indicates, however, that oligarchy may not be inevitable.

Oligarchy occurs because true democracy involves direct participation by the governed, and this may not be possible when their number is large and when the complexity of problems facing the organization requires the application of extensive knowledge and expertise. The absence of prerequisite knowledge and skills at lower levels in the organization will eventually force decision making to the top.

Furthermore, as the incumbents of top positions in the organization gain a near monopoly on power, power itself may corrupt them. Power obtained from hierarchical authority and concentrated at the apex of the organization makes these positions virtually impregnable. The elite can dispense distorted information or withhold information from those at lower levels, as it best serves their interests, which are not identical to those of others in the organization. Their overriding interest is to maintain the power they enjoy. Psychologically, the elite may feel that they are indispensable to the organization because of their unique knowledge and experiences. Despite beliefs they may hold about the desirability of democracy, they will find it extremely difficult to relinquish their positions and prerogatives. Even before the Russian Revolution, Michels predicted that the outcome of a socialist revolution would be a dictatorship.

At this point, whether Michels described cultural tendencies to amass power as an effort to dominate and control resources or merely as the properties of a social artifact is unclear. Perhaps the Iron Law of Oligarchy should not be viewed as the condemnation of a process that creates elite classes but as an observation of a simple fact of life: if we are to have complex organizations in society, we must be willing to live with unequal distributions of power and limitations of freedom in some areas of life. We suggest that the issue may be one of values—our priorities regarding individual freedom in comparison to the other values (such as material affluence) of individuals working in concert within organizations.

Closed-System Thinking in Contemporary Society

The ethos of closed-system thinking reflected here is not a relic of the recent past brought to light in order to place contemporary thinking in historical perspective. Rather, this school of thought is viewed as a social force that is still vital by virtue of its past successes. Consider, for example, Toffler's (1970) analysis of contemporary education.

> In stagnant societies, the past crept forward into the present and repeated itself in the future. . . . The curriculum of the present was the past.
>
> The mechanical age smashed all this, for industrialism required a new kind of man. It demanded skills which neither family nor church could, by themselves, provide. . . .
>
> Mass education was the ingenious machine constructed by industrialism to produce the kind of adult it needed. . . . How to pre-adapt children for a new kind of world—a world of repetitive indoor toil, smoke, noise, machines, crowded living conditions, collective discipline, a world in which time was to be regulated not by the cycle of sun and moon, but by the factory whistle and the clock.
>
> The solution was an educational system which, in its very structure, simulated this new world . . . the whole idea of assembling masses of students (raw materials) to be processed by teachers (workers) in a centrally located school (factory) was a stroke of industrial genius. The whole administrative hierarchy of education, as it grew, followed the model of industrial bureaucracy (Toffler, 1970, pp. 354–55).

As we have already suggested, closed social systems do not exist. However, we need to consider "closed" and "open" as extremes on a continuum rather than as mutually exclusive alternatives. In doing so, we will be able to inquire whether different parts of an organization ought to be more open or more closed. Possibly the educational system described by Toffler effectively met societal needs in years past, although it has received widespread criticism in recent times. Similarly, as we shall see, many present-day theorists advocate that specific portions of an organization should be more closed than others.

SOCIAL SYSTEMS

The Departure from Closed-System Perspectives

James Thompson (1967) suggests that open- and closed-system characteristics tend to be localized in the organization according to a scheme devised by Parsons (1960), which details three separate levels of responsibility and control: the *technical, managerial,* and *institutional* levels. The technical level, which is the lowest, is concerned primarily with the efficient operation of the organization's technological processes. For example, in a business school, those who teach students, type research reports and memos, clean and maintain the building, and those who supervise these workers perform the technical function. This is the most rational and closed level. An attempt is made at this level to exclude uncertainty and to construct a closed and deterministic system so that efficient production may ensue.

The managerial level is concerned with management or administration of the lower, technical level so as to articulate it with the environment, both on the input and output sides. In the business school example, the managerial level comprises those who deal with admissions and placement of students, purchasing of supplies, functioning of personnel, budgeting and information systems, and, in general, the planning and control systems that hold everything together.

Finally, at the top institutional level, is the function of relating the organization to its environment in terms of its "right" or legitimacy to do what it is doing and to acquire the resources that these activities require. At this level in a business school, a dean will be explaining and representing the school to the rest of the university and to the local and professional communities of which it is a part. He will be learning the needs, desires, and expectations of these in relation to his school. Functioning at this level most resembles open-system functioning.

Parsons suggests that the line of authority, assumed by bureaucratic theory to run from top to bottom, is interrupted where dissimilar levels interface with one another. Furthermore, these different levels perform different functions necessary for the system as a whole. The different levels are part of a system and are interdependent. As Thompson states, "the articulation of levels and of functions rests on two-way interaction, with each side, by withholding its important contribution, in a position to interfere with the function of the other and of the larger organization" (Thompson, 1967, p. 11). Thus, the way is open for conflict between levels of the resulting, and not very "rational," system.

Further exploration confirms our point of view that the bureaucratic model is not a completely valid description of organizational functioning. Figure 1–2 illustrates the foci of attention, operating criteria, and generalized behavior that should exist at the three major organizational levels indicated above.

Top levels of management, in relating the institution to the environment, guide the organization to appropriate changes in response to changes in the environment. Top management is change inducing. Accordingly, the criterion against which top management performance is evaluated is "responsiveness."

Supervisors, foremen, and workers are engaged in productive processes—the operation and maintenance of the organization's technical core. The criterion of effectiveness for technical and rational systems, as we have said, is productive efficiency. Since change and uncertainty are detrimental to efficiency, lower level personnel seek to maintain steady state conditions by resisting or absorbing pressures to deviate from the status quo.

Finally, according to our line of reasoning, the mission of middle levels of management is to coordinate subunits of the organization by mediating between top and lower levels in the hierarchy. These individuals, if they perceive their roles according to this logic, will serve as change facilitators, since organizational effectiveness appears to

FIGURE 1–2
Interruptions in the Line of Authority Assumed by the Theory of Bureaucracy

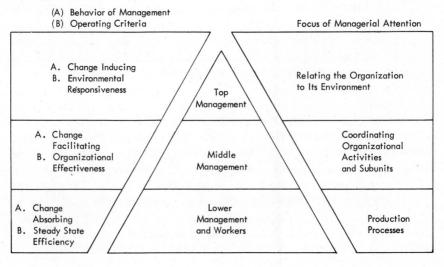

(A) Behavior of Management
(B) Operating Criteria   Focus of Managerial Attention

A. Change Inducing
B. Environmental Responsiveness

Top Management

Relating the Organization to Its Environment

A. Change Facilitating
B. Organizational Effectiveness

Middle Management

Coordinating Organizational Activities and Subunits

A. Change Absorbing
B. Steady State Efficiency

Lower Management and Workers

Production Processes

stem from the coordination of productive efficiency with environmental responsiveness.

Although this outlook describes a departure from the mechanistic, closed-system perspective, it is still essentially bureaucratic in its assumption that functional subunits can be arranged and coordinated in some rational manner to pursue known objectives. Furthermore, it suggests that the major directions and goals of the organizations flow from the top downward. Finally, this approach offers little analysis of the organizational needs that arise from the functioning of the organization, itself. These are among the major concerns of theorists using the natural-system model of organization.

The Natural-System Rationale

The "natural-system" view of organizations has three major bases in which it differs from the tool or rational model of organization (Gouldner, 1959; Perrow, 1972). We have already discussed two of these. First, we have described the view that organizations are to some degree open to the environment and to uncertainty which prevents full control of the "organizational tool." Second, we have pointed out the likelihood that the parts of the organization are often more than a mechanical arrangement in which deliberate changes can be made without affecting other parts, because each is part of an organic whole.

A third major component of the natural-systems view of organizations is that organizational structures, once created, come to have a life of their own, behaving in unplanned and spontaneous or "natural" ways. Formal structures, as we saw above in the case of delegation of authority, may lead, once created, to the generation of pressures for subsystem survival and enhancement, because the very structures that are established to fulfill both membership needs and environmental requirements exert forces in their own right.

The important focus of attention in the natural-system view is not on the deliberately created formal structure but on the actual behavior of individuals and the organization as a whole. Attention, for example, is focused on the fact that a subordinate with superior knowledge often makes suggestions to his or her formal superior that are accepted. The patterning of such behaviors comprises the organizational structure (Katz and Kahn, 1966). The structure of an organization, therefore, is inseparable from the functioning of the organization (Kahn, 1974). Viewed as a system, an organization is composed of five basic subsystems or sets of interconnected events.

The *production subsystem* operates the organization's technical core; that is, it manages throughput processes. *Supportive subsystems* secure inputs from the environment and dispose of outputs. The *maintenance subsystem* maintains the system, per se; it recruits and rewards the organization's members. Adaptation to environmental change is sought through the *adaptive subsystem*. Finally, direction and control of the various subsystems and their activities are provided by the *managerial subsystem*.

Almost inevitably these subsystems will come to operate somewhat at variance with one another; for example, the production subsystem is constrained by task requirements in meeting its objective of task accomplishment. Task requirements, however, may exclude the very attributes of work that are intrinsically rewarding to the work force, as when mass-production techniques preclude the establishment of satisfying work roles. Here, productive efficiency is gained at the expense of the objectives of the maintenance subsystem—namely, the satisfaction of workers.

The essential function of the managerial subsystem is coordination of other subsystems in situations like those above. However, rather than taking a long-run approach to reduce the sources of conflict that are inherent in the organization, management often travels the easier route of meeting problems on a day-to-day basis, making concessions first to one part of the organization and then to another. For example, a crash advertising program may be initiated to deal with a sales decline, but, at some later point, cost considerations may demand a cutback in employees, including those in the advertising section. By attending to problems sequentially (as opposed to anticipating problems and their interrelatedness with other problems), management causes the organization to move by jolts and starts, first in one direction, then in another.

However, natural-system theorists maintain that organizations react not only to external forces but to internal stimuli as well. Systems generate their own needs, and some behavior in organizations is directed toward meeting these needs and managing situations in which subsystem needs conflict.

One such system need experienced by the organization as a whole is the need to preserve the character of the system (Katz and Kahn, 1966). The structure of a social organization, as we have indicated, is based on interrelated sets of activities that are cyclical and fairly consistent over time. If these interactions are disrupted severely, the system will become disorganized and cease to exist. Hence, Katz and Kahn observe the organizational tendencies to achieve both *steady state* conditions and *dynamic homeostasis*.

Steady state, in this instance, refers to the preservation of relationships among the system's subunits and maintenance of predictable modes of cooperation within the organization. For example, faculty members in a school of management coordinate their teaching activities so that their efforts will yield an educational program with intended characteristics.

Dynamic homeostasis denotes the tendency of systems to grow, adapt, and otherwise change while maintaining the steady state characteristics indicated above. This phenomenon can be observed in a business school which grows in numbers, but preserves its system characteristics by acquiring faculty members in a way that does not upset the balance of disciplines taught.[2]

Finally, open-systems theory notes the phenomenon termed *progressive differentiation*. When an organization is formed, its mission and the roles of its members are often stated so generally that they are diffuse. As the members gain experience and strive to meet the established criteria, they focus increasingly on specialized tasks. The more specialized the requirements of tasks, the fewer tasks a single individual will be able to undertake successfully. Thus, the organization will become differentiated into subunits that have specific, as opposed to generalized, functions.

Social Systems

Our view is that a systems model of organizations is somewhat unrealistic, because it leaves out many of the social qualities of individual human beings. The analogy to dynamic homeostasis and progressive differentiation in biological organisms seems somehow inappropriate to development and change in human organizations. What is needed is a *social* systems view of organizations (Buckley, 1967; Silverman, 1970). The rational model does focus attention of the intentions of human beings and their deliberate acts. The system view of organizations may be inadequate in this regard, for in some situations there is freedom for the individual, with his or her unique combination of social characteristics, to choose to behave in ways that do not meet system needs (nor follow rational plans). Individuals and groupings will engage in conflict that is best viewed as self-serving. In short, we suggest that a comprehensive view of organizations must take into account the fact that the sometimes conflicting, sometimes congruent, and sometimes unrelated intentions of human actors are important ingredients of or-

---

[2] Katz and Kahn (1966) mention five major consequences of viewing organizations as closed systems that are avoided by the open-system perspective. First, closed-system thinking fails to recognize the full extent to which an organization is dependent upon inputs from its environment and the degree to which these inputs fluctuate over time. Second, scientific management and bureaucracy increasingly move toward tighter integration, coordination, and organizational stability. These tendencies prevail regardless of environmental conditions that may indicate increased flexibility to be more appropriate. Third, closed-system theories fail to recognize what Katz and Kahn term equifinality: the ability to reach a specific outcome through the application of numerous combinations of means. Fourth, the mechanistic views of organizations would lead us to assume that all irregularities in organizational functioning are error variances that should be treated accordingly. Finally, closed-system thinking does not give adequate emphasis to the need to develop environmental surveillance systems that will monitor environmental changes and provide feedback on organizational functioning.

ganizations. This leads us to focus on a variety of processes—i.e., conflict, decision making, and planned change, which develop as a result of rational plans, system needs, and individual choices.

The Location of Subsystems in the Organizational Hierarchy

The models presented earlier in the chapter assume that the functions of management are segregated into different organizational levels. Problems of relating the organization with its environment, for example, have been assumed to fall to top levels of management. Using implications of the open-system approach, we will begin to question this notion.

Katz and Kahn (1966) are in agreement with Parsons (1960) when they observe that, since top levels of management tend to deal solely with institutional problems, the traditional concept of unity of the chain of command is rendered invalid. They conclude, as did Parsons, that there are significant breaks in the chain of command at various levels of management.

However, we can argue that the functions of various subsystems are conducted at numerous levels in the organization's hierarchy, rather than being segregated at one level or another. Responsibilities for productive (technological) processes, for example, frequently rest at vice-presidential levels. Similarly, adaptive functions are performed by sales personnel at the bottom of the hierarchy as well as by top management. Thus, we can argue that the subsystems postulated by Katz and Kahn are located vertically in the hierarchy, as well as horizontally.

Moreover, we can argue that these subsystems consist of interrelated role requirements rather than particular organizational members. This conceptualization permits us to view the supervisor, whose primary formal responsibility is to the productive subsystem, as a member of the maintenance subsystem as well. Much of a supervisor's work consists of dealing with human problems; that is, with maintaining the motivation and satisfaction of his or her subordinates. By the same token, other organizational members perform multiple functions and operate within more than one subsystem.

This line of reasoning causes us to question the notion that institutional problems, which are resolved via strategic planning and policy formulation, are addressed by top management alone. Rather, we agree with Petit (1972) in his observation that strategies are formulated, in part, by pressures from lower levels of management. Petit suggests that the process of strategy formulation is inductive rather than deductive. Lower levels of management persuade executives to adopt policies that are designed to achieve technical rationality or uncertainty avoidance, depending on whether the managers engage primarily in the productive or adaptive subsystems. Executives, in turn, formulate organizational strategies that respond not only to environmental-institutional concerns, but that also seek to balance various policy decisions that have been urged upon them. This line of reasoning is dissimilar to the bureaucratic model and is closer, in theory, to the open-system model of organizations.

A Study Plan for Organizations

In any event, we have come a long way from the earlier bureaucratic conceptualization of organizations. Some of the generalizations that we have developed are abstract, and the student who has never had an opportunity to view organizations as social entities may be confused. New ideas and new ways of looking at complex social phenomena are often sources of confusion. As we go on, we shall clear up some of the water that we may have inadvertently muddied.

In this overview, we cannot do full justice to all theories of organizations or to their criticisms. However, we hope that our choice of substantive materials throughout the book reflects our view that useful elements exist in both the rational and the natural-system models. Any one approach is insufficient and blinds us to important aspects of organizations. Use of both approaches is better, although not fully adequate to the task either.

In the next chapter, we shall take the perspective of the rational model and focus on formal structures and organizational designs that have been developed by theorists and practitioners who are disposed toward this approach. They provide an identifiable view of the nature of the organization and its components. The reader should be cautioned however, that the rational approach is prescriptive; i.e., it is a view of the organization which may or may not be reflected in actual behavior.

In the third chapter, we begin Section II which is devoted to a view of organizations primarily according to the systems perspective, and we look in turn at the components of informal structure, technology, goals, and people. Here the view of the organization is more nearly descriptive, based on empirical study of actual behavior, which often fails to conform to the intended, rational-model prescriptions.

DISCUSSION QUESTIONS

1. Bureaucrats and bureaucracies frequently are held in contempt in our society. Is this prejudice justified? Under what circumstances would you advocate bureaucracy?
2. Is Michel's "Iron Law of Oligarchy" inevitable? What implication does your answer hold for democracy in organizations?
3. What evidence is there of conflict between the different levels of an organization (i.e., institutional, managerial, and technical)? Can you give

examples of conflict that you have experienced? How was this conflict resolved?

REFERENCES

Buckley, Walter. *Sociology and modern systems theory.* Englewood Cliffs, N.J.: Prentice-Hall, 1967.

Fayol, Henri. General principles of management. In H. F. Merrill (Ed.), *Classics in management.* New York: American Management Association, 1960. Pp. 217–41.

Gantt, Henry L. *Work, wages, and profits.* Easton, Pa.: Hive, 1973.

Gilbreth, Frank B. *Bricklaying system.* Easton, Pa: Hive, 1972. (a)

Gilbreth, Frank B. *Motion study.* Easton, Pa: Hive, 1972. (b)

Gouldner, Alvin W. *Patterns of industrial bureaucracy.* Glencoe, Ill.: Free Press, 1954.

Gouldner, Alvin W. Organizational analysis. In Robert K. Merton, Leonard Broom, and Leonard S. Cottrell, Jr. (Eds.), *Sociology today.* New York: Basic Books, 1959. Pp. 400–28.

Kahn, Robert L. Organizational development: some problems and proposals. *Journal of Applied Behavioral Science,* 1974, *10,* 485–502.

Katz, Daniel, and Kahn, Robert L. *The social psychology of organizations.* New York: Wiley, 1966.

Lipset, Seymour M., Trow, Martin, and Coleman, James S. *Union democracy.* Glencoe, Ill.: Free Press, 1956.

March, James G., and Simon, Herbert A. *Organizations.* New York: Wiley, 1958.

Merton, Robert K. Bureaucratic structure and personality. *Social forces,* 1940, *18,* 560–68.

Michels, Robert. *Political parties.* Glencoe, Ill.: Free Press, 1915.

Mooney, James D., and Reiley, A. C. *The principles of organization.* New York: Harper, 1939.

Mouzelis, Nicos P. *Organization and bureaucracy: an analysis of modern theories.* Chicago: Aldine, 1968.

Parsons, Talcott. *Structure and process in modern societies.* New York: Free Press, 1960.

Perrow, Charles. *Complex organizations: a critical essay.* Glenview, Ill.: Scott, Foresman, 1972.

Petit, Thomas A. Systems problems of organizations and business policy. Proceedings, Academy of Management, 32nd annual meeting, Minneapolis, August 13–16, 1972. Pp. 103–7.

Selznick, Philip. *TVA and the grass roots.* Berkeley, Calif.: University of California Press, 1949.

Silverman, David. *The theory of organizations.* London: Heineman, 1970.

Taylor, Frederick W. The principles of scientific management. In H. F. Merrill (Ed.), *Classics in management.* New York: American Association, 1960. Pp. 82–113.

Thompson, James D. *Organizations in action.* New York: McGraw-Hill, 1967.

Toffler, Alvin. *Future shock.* New York: Random House, 1970.

Urwick, Lyndall. *The elements of administration.* New York: Harper, 1943.

Weber, Max. *From Max Weber: essays in sociology* (trans. Gerth and Mills). New York: Oxford, 1958.

Weber, Max. *The theory of social and economic organization* (trans. Henderson and Parsons). New York: Free Press, 1964.

2

Classical Organizational
Designs

INTRODUCTION

We shall begin our study of the organization with the comprehensive treatment found in the organizational designs of the rational theorists described in Chapter 1. As noted in the discussion of bureaucracy, this aspect of organizations is perhaps more readily identifiable than any other. In addition, it is an "artifact" that has been part of our culture for thousands of years. Consider, for example, the formal organizational structure that is described in the book of Exodus (The New English Bible, 1970, p. 81).[1]

> The next day Moses took his seat to settle disputes among the people, and they were standing round him from morning till evening. When Jethro saw all that he was doing for the people, he said, "What are you doing for all these people? Why do you sit alone with all of them standing round you from morning till evening?" "The people come to me," Moses answered, "to seek God's guidance. Whenever there is a dispute among them, they come to me, and I decide between man and man. I declare the statutes and laws of God." But his father-in-law said to Moses, "This is not the best way to do it. You will only wear yourself out and wear out all the people who are here. The task is too heavy for you; you cannot do it by yourself. Now listen to me: take my advice, and God be with you. It is for you to be the people's representative before God, and bring their disputes to him. You must instruct them in the statutes and laws, and teach them how they must behave and what they must do. But you must yourself search for capable, God-fearing men among all the people, honest and incorruptible men, and appoint them over the people as officers over units of a thousand, of a hundred, of fifty or of ten. They shall sit as a permanent court for the people; they must refer difficult cases to you but decide simple cases themselves. In this way your burden will be lightened, and they will share it with you. If you do this, God will give you strength, and you will be able to go on. And, moreover, this whole people will here and now regain peace and har-

---

[1] *The New English Bible.* © The Delegates of the Oxford University Press and the Syndics of the Cambridge University Press, 1961, 1970. Reprinted by permission. (Exodus 18: 13–27.)

mony." Moses listened to his father-in-law and did all he had suggested. He chose capable men from all Israel and appointed them leaders of the people, officers over units of a thousand, of a hundred, of fifty or of ten. They sat as a permanent court, bringing the difficult cases to Moses but deciding simple cases themselves. Moses sent his father-in-law on his way, and he went back to his own country.

Chapter Guide

Similar to the bureaucratic model of organizations discussed in the last chapter, the structure proposed by Jethro implies a direct line of authority from Moses down to the "rank and file." This relationship is depicted by the organization chart in Figure 2–1.

1. Why did Jethro suggest that Rulers of Fifties have a span of control of five while Rulers of Hundreds and Rulers of Tens were provided spans of two and ten, respectively?
2. What direct authority did Jethro have over the Rulers of Thousands?
3. What differences can be seen to exist between the positions of Jethro and Solomon? Why are these differences deemed to be appropriate?

FIGURE 2–1
Exodus Reorganized

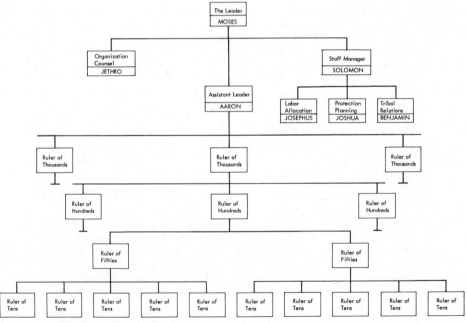

Source: Reprinted by permission of the publisher from *Organization* by Ernest Dale © 1967 by American Management Association, Inc.

4. In Chapter 1, we defined structure as patterns of interactions (Katz and Kahn, 1966). Here we use the term differently. Which use of the term is more efficacious in studying organizations? Why?
5. Would it be possible for a Ruler of Hundreds to have more influence in Moses' organization than a Ruler of Thousands?

ELEMENTS OF STRUCTURAL DESIGN

Structure

Students who have read the classical management theorists will be familiar with the description of formal organizational structure that follows. In fact, so will students who have worked in organizations that became aware of their structure through major growth, reorganization, merger, or similar problems. Formal organizational structure generally is the aspect of the organization that management seeks to change in order to alter its functioning. Attempts to change people variables, such as attitudes and motives, are less frequent because they require greater degrees of skill, time, and effort. Technology and goal changes are even less frequent as any major alterations of them may change the organization so drastically as to render it almost a new organization.

Vertical Differentiation by Authority

Organizational structure may be defined as the pattern or network of relationships that exist among various positions (and position holders). Formal structure is a pattern of relationships that has been generated through a conscious planning process. Key executives typically decide upon the basic patterns of structure that, in their opinion, will be most appropriate for themselves, their work, and company goals.

The most common organizational structure follows a hierarchical model consisting of a vertical dimension of differentiated levels of authority and responsibility and a horizontal dimension of differentiated units, such as departments or divisions. This is the pyramidal shaped organization frequently depicted on organization charts. At the apex of the pyramid are the chief executive officer (chancellor in our example) and an executive vice president or general manager (executive vice-chancellor). At the next level are senior executives, frequently called vice presidents (provost and the vice-chancellors depicted in Figure 2–4). Below the top management portion is middle management,

FIGURE 2–2
Line Management in a University's Formal Organization

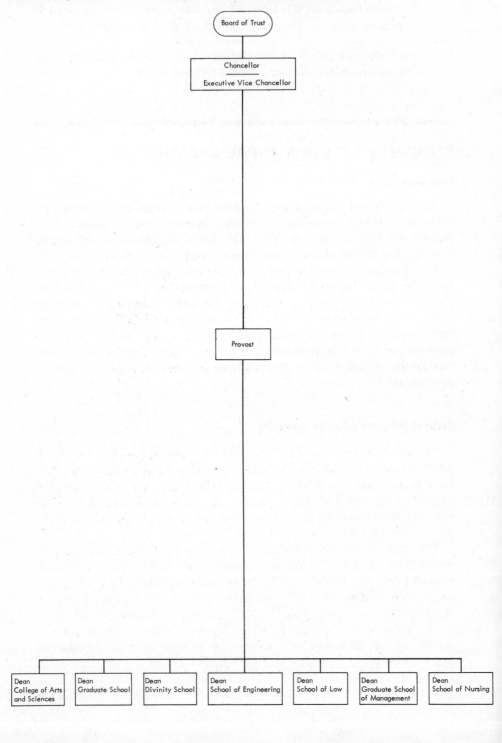

generally department or division heads or branch managers (deans). At lower levels of middle management are factory superintendents, branch sales managers, and the like (associate deans).[2] Supervisory management, composed of various supervisors and foremen (staff supervisor, assistant dean, and so on), is found below middle management. Individuals whose positions in the hierarchy fall below supervisory management are, of course, not members of management. Furthermore, as indicated in Chapter 1, each vertical level in the hierarchy embraces different amounts of authority. Those at the top have the most authority and those at the bottom the least.

Horizontal Differentiation by Specialization

The horizontal dimension of organization is *not* differentiated by degrees of authority, but rather by what is termed departmentalization —divisions of employees into groups according to some designated criteria that allow and encourage specialization. According to this reasoning, the organization will be more effective if people with similar abilities and skills work together separately from those with other abilities and skills on tasks directed toward particular problems, than if all workers are generalists and perform exactly the same set of work— a little bit of everything.

In a very small organization, the top manager may perform all major functions (e.g., purchasing, personnel activities, accounting, and supervision of production). As the organization grows, however, the manager will find his time too limited to deal with the magnitude of problems that have assumed increasing degrees of complexity, and he[3] will find that one or more of these functions demands skills and knowledge he does not possess. At this point, he will most likely *create* a position for a manager who specializes in one or more of these areas. In time he will organize his operations around these managers and the functions that they oversee.

Growth is not the sole impetus toward horizontal differentiation. Environmental change can place demands on an organization which its existing personnel are ill-equipped to meet. For instance, the advent of the union movement created the need for departments specializing in industrial relations. Similarly, technical innovations require the development of specialized subunits. Scientific management gave rise to departments of industrial engineering, and computer technology spawned today's data processing divisions.

---

[2] The formal organization of a university depicted in Figure 2–2 is incomplete in many respects. Although we will replace most of the missing positions in this chapter, we will exclude the internal organizations of individual schools, lest our example become baroque.

[3] The common pronoun "he" refers to persons of either sex and is not intended to be masculine or feminine but simply "human."

FIGURE 2–3
Line Management with Selected Staff Activities in a University's Formal Organization

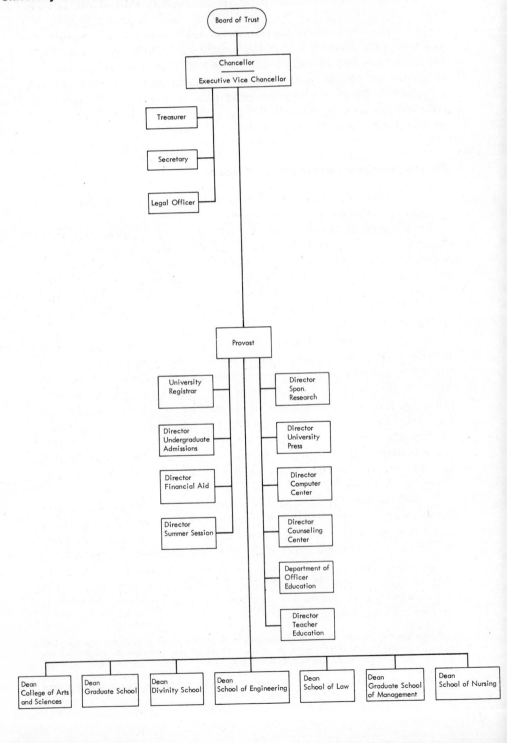

Departmentalization by Function, Process, Location, and Product

Departmentalization in organizations takes four major forms: by function, by location, by process, and by product. These four means of departmentalization (or horizontal differentiation) are usually applied in combinations. In fact, some firms are organized according to all of them simultaneously. Initially, an organization may organize its activities by product. In Figure 2–3, the various schools can be conceived to be product centers. As they grow, the schools may become organized by function. Each school, in this case, may have its own student recruiting department, placement service, and student counseling center. Alternatively, the initial organization may segregate work activities geographically, as when a university has several campuses. Within each campus, work may be further organized by product and by function within product.

Departmentalization by Function. Let us look first at departmentalization by function. In a manufacturing firm, necessary functions include production, finance, sales, personnel, research and development, and purchasing. As we have said, each function will become organized as a department as the organization grows in complexity. For example, the public relations function may be performed by sales representatives through their contacts with the environment, as well as by top managers who give speeches to service clubs and perform related activities. However, if the firm becomes large and complex enough or if special problems arise in the environment, these public relations activities will need both coordination and emphasis. These needs, in turn, provide the rationale for the creation of a separate public relations department.

Departmentalization by Process. Departmentalization by process refers to the structuring of an organization according to technological or work processes. A firm that is departmentalized by process may have shipping and receiving departments, a foundry department, a milling department, a machining department, an inspection department, and so on.

Departmentalization by Location. Organizational structures can be segregated by territories, districts, regions, countries, and the like. Where locations make a difference (where demands for educational services, products, and product characteristics vary, for instance, or where labor, energy, or raw materials supplies differ), a rationale exists for departmentalization on that basis. Sears, Roebuck has eastern, midwestern, western, and southern sales divisions each with its own somewhat different purchasing decisions. A large electrical utility with generating facilities in several cities departmentalizes accordingly. Multinational firms often divisionalize by location so that divisions operate in relatively homogeneous taxation, legal, or consumer environments.

Departmentalization by Product. Finally, departmentalization by product or product-market is characteristic of large organizations or organizations that produce a variety of products and sell in different markets. General Motors, of course, is a prime example. Chevrolet cars are produced and marketed in a division that is separate from the divisions producing Pontiacs and Cadillacs. As noted earlier, the university example provided in Figure 2–3 illustrates departmentalization by educational divisions, where ministers, lawyers, managers, physicians, engineers, nurses, and liberal arts majors are educated within separate organizational entities. In fact, an enlarged view of the university's formal structure presented in Figure 2–4 shows that the medical school bears a line relationship to the chancellor that is unique. Presumably, the problems of health care delivery and medical education are dissimilar to the problems encountered in other academic units. The dissimilarity is so great, in fact, that a separate echelon of management is deemed appropriate for the administration of this unit.

Examples from industry include firms that segregate divisions working for the government from those serving civilian markets. Presumably, meeting contract specifications, as opposed to consumer expectations, generates dissimilar managerial problems, which justify organization by product. Similarly, the quality of products manufactured or sold may serve to differentiate the organization. This is true for General Motors, as well as for department stores with bargain basements offering less expensive and lower quality products than are found in the main part of the store.

Span of Control

Next to departmentalization, span of control is probably the most important concept in understanding both horizontal and vertical differentiation. As we have said, the term refers to the number of subordinates a manager supervises. Earlier theorists attempted to define the absolute limits of span of control (e.g., five to eight subordinates). Subsequently, of course, these limits were found to be unrealistic. The number of individuals that a manager can supervise depends on the complexity of the tasks performed by subordinates, the amount of subordinate-superior interaction required by the task, the abilities of both the subordinates and their manager, and other factors (Barkdull, 1963; Udell, 1967).

The average size of the span of control bears implications for the overall shape of an organization. A large number of employees supervised by a single manager reduces the number of hierarchical levels in the organization below the number in an organization employing the same number of individuals but having a smaller span of control. If we draw organization charts for these two firms, we will find that the pyramid shape of the first organization, with a large average span, will appear rather "flat" while that of the organization with the smaller span of control will, by comparison, appear relatively "tall."

Tall department stores were compared with flat department stores to ascertain the effects of different sized spans of control (Worthy, 1950). In the tall store with a manager at the top, 5 or 6 second-level managers, and 4 to 6 department managers reporting to each of the second-level managers, the morale of personnel and the effectiveness of the store seemed poorer than in the flat store with a top manager and an assistant, and 32 department managers at the second level. In the simple, flat organization, the individual supervisor is free from close control because of the large span, and is free to develop initiative and self-reliance. We should take care in generalizing from this study, however, because we shall see in Chapter 4 that the nature of the technology and the task put some constraints on the structures, including the span of control. For example, process technologies, as in petroleum refineries, need a taller hierarchy due to their complexity and interdependency than other firms using, perhaps, a batch-technology.

Line and Staff Relationships

Let us return to the basic elements of structure and examine the concepts of line and staff. Line refers to the basic hierarchical person-boss relationship, the line of authority or chain of command, that extends from the top to the bottom of an organization. Each level of management in the line has authority over subordinates below and can command them to act in various ways.

Because special areas of competence are required in modern organizations, the line must be augmented with staff departments. Whereas "line executives are those who contribute directly to profits, either by producing the product or service or selling it. . . . The staff executives are those who facilitate the work of the line, performing services for it, providing it with advice and information, and auditing its performance in various respects" (Dale, 1967, p. 61).

As we have said, top executives frequently lack the expertise required of management. A structural solution to this problem is to provide specialists as staff assistants to the executive. Notice, in Figure 2–4, that the chancellor is provided with staff assistance from a legal officer. He can advise the chancellor and other officials on legal matters, but has no "direct" authority over individuals whose positions fall below his in the organization.

A more complex form of staff organization is illustrated by the offices of student services, alumni and development, and operations and fiscal planning (Figure 2–4). These represent fairly elaborate subunits of the organization and contain line relationships internally. Each office, furthermore, exerts authority within the limits that have been delegated

FIGURE 2–4
A University's Formal Organization

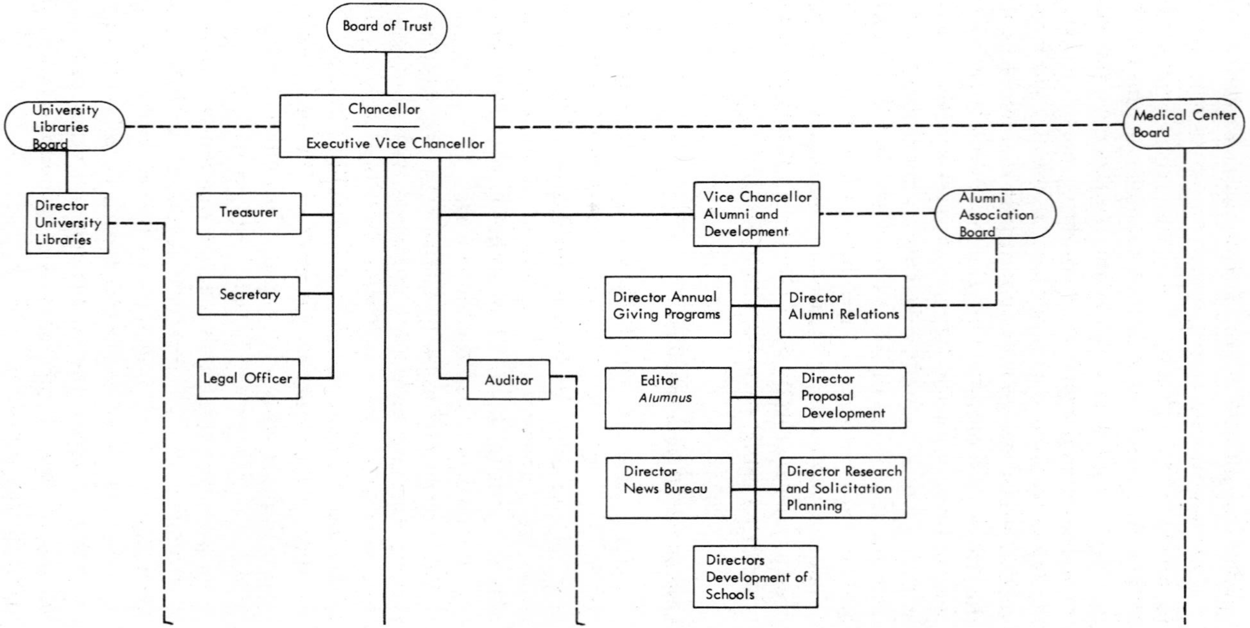

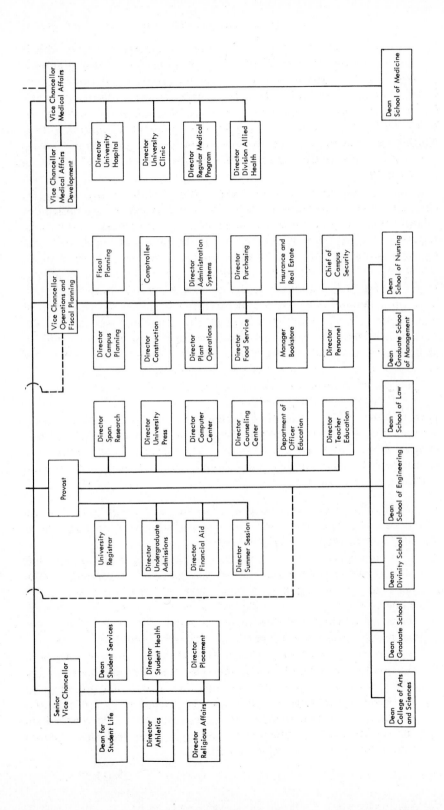

by the chief executive officer. The chief of campus security, who is responsible to the vice-chancellor for operations and fiscal planning, possesses the authority to enforce specific university regulations in each of the organizational units. That is, he has certain authority over line personnel. However, in keeping with his staff position, he may not exercise authority in other matters of the university's administration. Neither, for that matter, can the vice-chancellor for operations and fiscal planning direct the various deans in their discharge of academic responsibilities.

Large organizations may use a functional staff arrangement; for example, when a corporation decentralizes, it may experience difficulties relating staff functions at the home office to the branches and divisions. Location of executives in charge of staff functions at corporate headquarters, while assigning their subordinates to the decentralized units, might remedy this problem; for example, the vice president in charge of personnel might headquarter at the home office while those below him head up personnel departments in the firm's branches. In this form of organization, the general managers of the branches exercise autonomous control over the personnel departments in their branches, subject, of course, to corporate policy and guidance by the vice president for personnel at corporate headquarters. In general, the greater the need for certain specialized knowledge across the entire organization, the higher the staff unit will be positioned.

In practice, a whole range of authority relationships may be found between a staff specialist and members of the line who are at the same or lower levels. Hellriegel and Slocum (1974) observe at least four types of authority relationships ranging from purely advisory to command authority.

1. "Staff Advice" is purely advisory. The managers may approach the personnel department for help in recruiting a new subordinate or they may do the recruiting themselves.
2. A "Compulsory Advice" relationship entails a requirement that managers seek advice, but not necessarily follow the recommendations given (e.g., managers must have all prospective secretarial employees complete a typing test administered by the personnel department. However, they need not follow the advice that a particular typing speed is a prerequisite to employment).
3. A "Concurring Authority" relationship requires agreement by both the line manager and the staff specialist that a particular action be taken. Both must agree, for example, that a particular cutoff point on typing speed plus a minimum educational level are essential prerequisites to employment. If agreement cannot be reached on criteria for selecting prospective employees, the decision is moved to a higher level in the organization.

4. Finally, a "Limited Company Authority" relationship entails line authority by the staff unit over a particular delimited area of line functioning. In hiring practices, for example, the personnel department may be granted authority to decree unilaterally the required typing speed, and the line manager must conform to this rule, regardless of compensating or extraordinary factors. There is absolute authority in a delineated area.

Some organizations depend so much on knowledge and expertise that the staff professionals play dominant roles in the organization. In "professional organizations" such as a hospital or university, the professionals (doctors or professors) do the primary work of the organization and have both authority and responsibility for it. They are, as it were, the "line." The administrators in the hospital and university support and assist the professionals, providing facilities, resources, and personnel that enable the professionals to get on with their work. The professionals have general authority over work with their clients, and the administrators have limited "staff" authority over such matters as selection of clients and purchasing procedures.

SELECTING APPROPRIATE DESIGNS

The Evaluation of Formal Designs

As we shall see, the classical, rational approach to organizational design does not yield simple solutions to organizational design problems. What has been presented thus far is far more prescriptive than descriptive. While the language of classical design enables us to describe an organization, the organization may not behave as intended. The classical literature provides a number of useful principles (e.g., span of control, line and staff) that can be applied to the design of organizations. However, in an era remarkable for its unprecedented growth, complexity, and rate of change, we are forced to inquire about the consequences of various designs. Study of the organization chart in Figure 2–4 provokes us to ask whether the described organization functions more effectively than alternative organizational arrangements that come to mind. One must use results, rather than principles from which designs can be derived, as criteria for selection of one design over and above competing alternatives.

The problems inherent in evaluating organizational designs are nearly overwhelming, as we shall see in Chapter 8. And we must admit that an elegant, concise set of rules or formulae is yet to be found. At best, we shall develop an elaborate and somewhat sketchy approach to evaluation. That is, we will reconcile important components, such as task, structure, technology, and people, with desired organizational performance. We shall ease our entry into this admittedly difficult problem with an evaluation of a single component, structure, and its effect on organizational performance.

Consequences of Formal Structure

Ansoff and Brandenburg (1971) provide a comprehensive and systematic overview of the consequences of formal design by relating variations in design to the attainment of organizational objectives. The objective of purposive (goal and efficiency seeking) organizations is seen as maximization of the return on the resources employed. This fairly abstract objective is redefined in more practical terms: (1) the objective of maximizing near-term performance, (2) the objective of long-term growth which will develop a posture for successful long-term performance, and (3) the objective of protecting the organization from catastrophic risks.

These subdivisions of the major objective are still abstract and need reformulation into concrete measures that can be used as criteria for determining the effectiveness of a particular design. Ansoff and Brandenburg provide this reformulation through the selection of surrogate criteria that are, in their terms, "process rather than outcome oriented." What this entails, in essence, is the selection of performance measures (*process criteria*) to assess organizational behaviors that, in turn, are means to the ultimate objective. The process criteria are taken as indications that the organization is (or has been in the recent past) functioning in such a way that it is likely to reach the objective of maximization of return on resources eventually.

Process Criteria

The process criteria fall into four general categories: (1) *steady state efficiency*, (2) *operating responsiveness*, (3) *strategic responsiveness*, and (4) *structural responsiveness*. Application of the specific criteria listed under these categories, according to Ansoff and Brandenburg, will enable us to judge whether a particular organizational design is likely to be successful or not.

Steady State Efficiency.   Steady state efficiency is realized when the unit of cost of output is minimized for a given operating level. Steady state efficiency raises concerns regarding economies of scale, economies of skills and overheads ("synergy" in the terminology of Ansoff and Brandenburg), and related issues.

Operating Responsiveness.   The criteria outlined above can be contrasted with a second major category of criteria, namely, operating responsiveness which measures the organization's ability to make quick and efficient changes in the level of throughput it produces. Instead of criteria which emphasize the organization's ability to handle a specific level of throughput efficiently, these criteria emphasize the ability to change levels of production in order to respond appropriately to variations in levels of demand and competitive activity. Operating responsiveness is measured by standby capacity and information processing capacity—in other words, by the ability to balance inventories and product availability at market locations.

Strategic Responsiveness. The third major criterion is strategic responsiveness which measures the organization's ability to respond to changes in the *nature*, not the volume, of its throughput, such as the obsolescence of products, innovations in product technology, changes in markets, and alterations of the legal and social constraints under which the organization operates. Strategic responsiveness depends, in part, on the organization's ability to maintain surveillance of its environment. In addition, the organization must contain centers capable of acting on the intelligence obtained. In maintaining the ability to respond quickly to environmental changes, the organization behaves in ways that are antithetical to the maximization of steady state efficiency. We will return to this dilemma at a later point in the chapter.

Structural Responsiveness. If an organization experiences difficulty in attaining steady state efficiency, operating responsiveness, or strategic responsiveness, then a fourth set of criteria will become relevant, namely, structural responsiveness. Structural responsiveness concerns the organization's abilities to design new organizational structures and, of course, to implement them. Structural responsiveness becomes especially vital in an environment that is characterized by rapid technological innovation. As we have said, technology and structure are highly interdependent, and the nature of their interaction determines organizational effectiveness to a large extent.

Design Criteria

Ansoff and Brandenburg add to these four categories of organizational performance criteria a set of design criteria which, they argue, is independent of the particular objectives of an organization. For example, they see the quality of decisions and information as critical to organizational effectiveness regardless of the specific objectives pursued. Good decisions and accurate, timely information are always essential to effective organizational performance. Under this general category we also find criteria such as the timeliness of information, the availability of relevant information, the absence of irrelevant information, the rapidity with which decisions can be made, and the compatibility of authority and accountability.

Assumptions about Human Resources

As the preceding five groups of criteria are met by an organization's design, the potential efficiency of the organization, according to Ansoff and Brandenburg, will near optimum. In recognizing that human variables are not directly included in any of the criteria, the authors assume that the necessary individual talents are available to the organization, that individuals will accept the positions assigned to them, and that these individuals will be motivated to utilize their talents in the positions assigned. Similarly, we assume that necessary financial and physical resources are available to the organization.

At this point, we must ask whether the assumptions concerning human resources are tenable, for there is considerable evidence to the contrary; for example, reasonable organizational designs are not always accepted by managers. Similarly, organizations with similar designs are not always equally effective; some organizations within a given class of designs will be more effective than others in the same class. Then, some organizations with designs that do not seem adequate—designs judged inappropriate by experts in design—are quite effective.

Apparently the human element makes a difference in cases such as these and a motivated work force can overcome or compensate for suboptimal designs just as dissident or alienated members can thwart the objectives of even the most skillful designer. However, it will be useful to assume, with Ansoff and Brandenburg, that the organization's members will behave as they are "supposed to" in order to limit our attention to designing adequate, formal structures. In Chapter 3, we shall examine informal structures and take more account of the human element.

Structural Designs and Process Criteria

Having developed four major categories of process criteria, Ansoff and Brandenburg illustrate how contemporary designs vary in their ability to satisfy each of the criteria. In the following discussion, note the organizational forms illustrated are not necessarily mutually exclusive. In fact, we frequently find organizations utilizing a combination of two or more designs.

The Centralized Functional Form

The centralized functional form of organization gained widespread application throughout American industry during the 1920s and is still widely used today both in this country and abroad, especially in smaller firms. The design primarily consists of departmentalization by function. Activities such as marketing, manufacturing, and research and devel-

FIGURE 2–5
The Centralized Functional Form of Organization

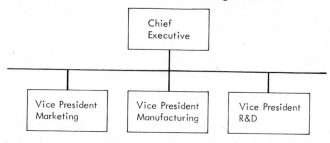

opment are grouped under functional executives who report to a central headquarters (Figure 2–5). This design is highly effective in terms of steady state efficiency. Grouping individuals by similar functions allows for economies of scale and economies of overheads and skills. Relatively high operating responsiveness also characterizes this form because of its simple communication and decision-making networks. However, beyond certain limits, increases in the organization's size, number of products or services offered, or number of product-markets served will render the organization relatively ineffective in terms of operating responsiveness.

The centralized functional design seems to result in relatively low strategic and structural responsiveness. The same individuals in top management who are concerned with operating decisions are also responsible for administrative and strategic problems. Since administrative and operating problems frequently are more pressing and visible, strategic problems are likely to suffer from neglect. Strategic responsiveness is also relatively poor because of difficulties engendered by the design in integrating the efforts of dissimilar functions, such as research and development and manufacturing. Again, operating decisions will take precedence over strategic decisions.

The Decentralized Divisional Form

As increases in both the size and complexity of centralized functional organizations caused corresponding decreases in operating responsiveness, Du Pont and General Motors pioneered a second, widely used design in the 1920s (Chandler, 1962; Sloan, 1964). Both firms, having grown quite large with expanded product lines, began to experience difficulty; that is, they found themselves making decisions for numerous different products which they were incapable of addressing. In the case of each product, relevant decisions required different information and decision criteria; in switching from one product to another, managers became confused or, at least, inefficient. Other firms abandoned the functional design for a variety of reasons, such as difficulties in developing "general" managers, too great an emphasis on vertical communications at the expense of horizontal communications needed for coordination, fragmentation of planning and control processes according to the different functions, and encouragement of conflict among functions (Carlisle, 1969). Since World War II, the decentralized divisional form has emerged as perhaps the most important design for large and complex firms.

The decentralized divisional design consists of organizational units (usually called divisions) that address a specific product-market under the direction of a manager who has complete strategic and operating decision-making authority (Figure 2–6). Thus, for a given product-market, the division is able to achieve both steady state efficiency and operating responsiveness because, *within the division,* a functional type of organization similar to that shown in Figure 2–5 exists, although some staff functions may be lodged at corporate headquarters.

Ansoff and Brandenburg reason that strategic and structural responsiveness can be attained more readily in the decentralized divisional design than in the centralized functional form in organizations of similar size. Though this appears true in principle, in fact managers in charge of specific product-markets tend to be overburdened, and their strategic responsiveness in expanding their product-market may not be very effective. Strategic responsiveness is further reduced by an inherent characteristic of the design which compels division managers to compete for limited resources (e.g., research and development) in a centralized location.

At the corporate level, reduction in top management work load as a consequence of this design may allow executives to pay greater attention to strategic decisions, as well as to problems relating to overall structure. However, in practice, corporate managements often fail to take advantage of such opportunities. Indeed, problems of strategy, being extremely difficult, are "driven out" of the decision-making process by

FIGURE 2–6
The Decentralized Divisional Form of Organization

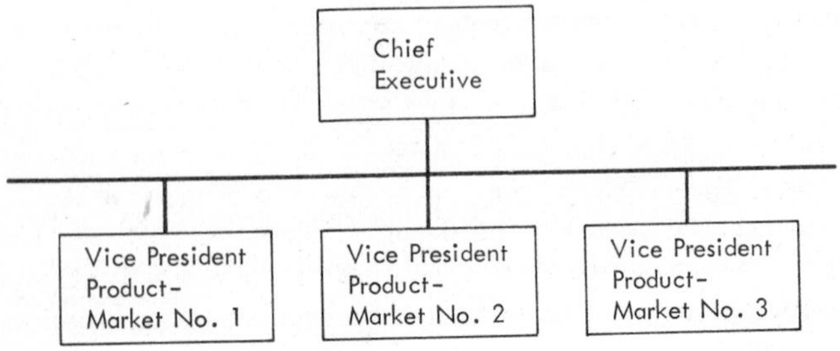

more immediate, routine, and programmable problems, *unless* management somehow creates special organizational structures for the innovative activities that strategy formulation requires. This generalization suggests that the decentralized divisional design offers only limited improvement over the centralized functional design. While operating responsiveness is added to steady state efficiency, improvements in strategic and structural responsiveness are limited.

Before moving to the next design, we should mention a fairly common variant of the decentralized divisional design, the decentralized divisional form by geographic area. Large organizations serving major geographical areas frequently decentralize by geographical subdivisions in order to achieve improved operating responsiveness. Within each geographical unit, one typically finds organization by product-market and by function within product-market; for example, the large multinational corporations often have separate companies or subsidiaries for different countries, provided the scale of operations is sufficiently large.

Adaptive Designs

A third basic organizational design evolved after World War II in response to increasing needs for structural responsiveness. Organizations, such as firms in the electronics industry, experienced rapid changes in technology, consumer and client demands, and potential demands for innovations in products and services. To exist successfully in such an environment, these organizations needed greater degrees of strategic and structural responsiveness. The project management design, or the adaptive design as Ansoff and Brandenburg call it, is reasonably well-suited to meet these organizational requirements. The Manhattan project to develop and produce the atomic bomb demonstrated the effectiveness of the design in meeting national needs during World War II. The Department of Defense subsequently required its contractors to use this structural arrangement in the 1950s when strenuous efforts were made to close the "missile gap" (Carlisle, 1969).

Much of the organizational structure in the adaptive design is flexible. The permanent parts of the organization include the corporate office and, below this, certain functional units such as manufacturing, finance, sales, and accounting (see Figure 2–7). The flexible portion of the organization consists of project units charged with specific objectives and can be disbanded once these objectives have been met. Various members of the organization are normally assigned to the permanent functional areas indicated above, but are reassigned to project offshoots upon occasion.

As management identifies problems and opportunities, it *creates a project team* (perhaps termed task force or special group) under a project manager who is responsible for attaining well-defined objec-

FIGURE 2–7
Project Management: An Adaptive Design for Organization

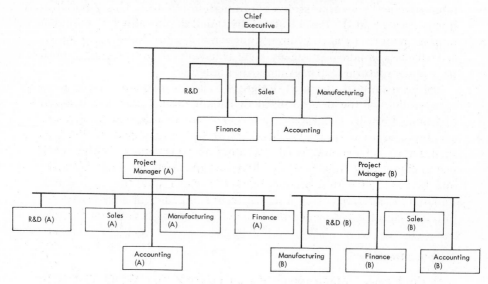

tives. For example, a project team may be established to develop and market a product. The team will continue to operate until its activities are divested by the organization, when members will return to their permanent functional areas. Conversely, a second team may be charged with developing the organization's long-range strategic plans. Typically, the project group will submit its work to corporate officers for a decision and possible implementation and then disband. Group members will then return to their functional divisions until the next planning cycle is reached. And these people may play a major role in internalizing acceptance of the plan by the organization. According to Cleland (1964), "The project manager acts as a focal point for the concentration of attention on the major problems of the project. This concentration forces the channeling of major program considerations through an individual who has the proper perspective to integrate relative matters of cost, time, technology, and total product compatibility" (p. 83). In the first example above, operating responsiveness will be increased for the organization; the latter example illustrates an attempt to improve strategic responsiveness.

Project teams can be organized in numerous ways. Members of a single function may address some objectives, while specialists from diverse functional areas are required for others. Furthermore, at different phases of the project's development, different kinds of arrangements can be introduced.

Matrix organization is a second major class of adaptive designs. This

FIGURE 2–8
Matrix Organization for Project Management

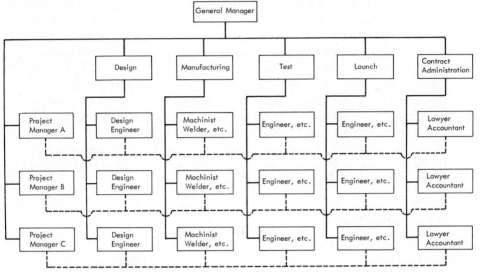

Source: Steiner and Ryan (1968).

design typically organizes personnel by their functions. For examples, an accounting unit may be established as the organizational "home" for all accountants; an engineering unit may organize the activities of engineering personnel, and so on. As projects are identified and project teams organized to respond to project requirements, specialists from the functional units will be reassigned to these teams as deemed appropriate. These individuals are subject to the authority of both their functional managers and project managers. As was the case with project management, project groups stemming from a matrix organization pursue specific objectives and are disbanded once these objectives have been met. While a traditional hierarchy of formal authority is maintained within project organizations, since project team members are subordinate to their project leader, superior-subordinate relations are less well defined in matrix organizations (e.g., individuals may be responsible to more than one superior, belong to more than one project, be shifted from one project to another as needed, and so on).

The focused concern of project managers on specific product-markets facilitates operating responsiveness and creates a vehicle for the implementation of strategic decisions. Strategic responsiveness is also improved by the organization's ability to create planning groups as the need arises and by the decreased work load of top management when project teams assume some of the existing responsibilities of these executives. The predefined cutoff points for projects also facilitate stra-

tegic responsiveness, since operating efficiency and operating responsiveness are only temporary advantages.

However, Ansoff and Brandenburg raise two major reservations concerning the limitations of adaptive designs in general. First, steady
state efficiency tends to be poor in organizations with adaptive designs
because they allow only minimal economies of scale and restrict synergy
in the functional competence groups. Each project group tends to dupli-
cate the capacities of the others. The second major disadvantage lies in
the necessity to transfer resources among project groups as projects
are created and terminated. If the major resource utilized by an organization is the intellectual capacity of its staff, as is the case, for example,
in certain research-oriented institutions, then use of an adaptive design
is clearly feasible. However, the design will not prove as advantageous
in other areas of endeavor such as heavy manufacturing.

The Innovative Design

Ansoff and Brandenburg define innovation to include both creativity
and its implementation. As we have seen, the preceding designs succeed, but only in one of the two criteria. The innovative design emerges
in the search for an organizational form that is effective in both creativity and implementation; in meeting, to some degree, all four of the
major performance criteria discussed above. Drawing from both the
adaptive and decentralized divisional (or centralized functional) forms,
this organizational design seeks to incorporate both strategic and structural responsiveness through the former and steady state efficiency and
operating responsiveness through the latter.

The innovative design consists of a current business group and an
innovative group (see Figure 2–9). The innovative group, organized
along the lines of adaptive design principles, emphasizes strategic and
structural responsiveness as essential to innovation.

Once the innovative group has demonstrated the feasibility of a project, it is transferred to the current business group, which has a more

FIGURE 2–9
The Innovative Organizational Design

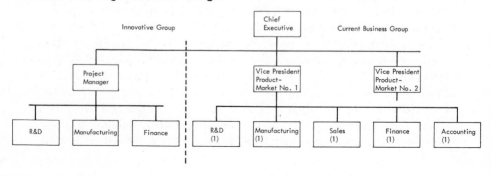

stable structure. Organized according to either the decentralized divisional or centralized functional form, the current business group is generally effective in terms of steady state efficiency and operating responsiveness. In others words, this design seeks to obtain the advantages of the strong points of the adaptive *and* more traditional designs.

According to at least one observer, the adaptive and innovative designs will receive increasing attention in the coming years:

> Three environmental influences will increasingly require the combining of specialized talents, resulting in greater use of the task force pattern of organization, or modifications of it.
>
> One of these influences is the impact of accelerating change in communications technology supported by the mathematics of operations research and rapid computation. Use of new and more precise analytical methods, aided by the computer, lies at the heart of the solution of complex operating problems that will confront business in the coming decade. An implication is that whether it is a new product to be launched or a logistics system of procurement, production, sales and inventory control, the activity will cut across the corporation's normal departmental life.
>
> A second influence is the growing acceptance by business of the need for continuous education in management development. Within the company an opportunity for management training is provided by rotating people through task force assignments, thus exposing them to different kinds of problems, as well as to different personnel with different ideas and training.
>
> The third influence comes from extending the range of corporate commitments to include *unfamiliar business and societal tasks.* Business is spreading rapidly across national boundaries to unfamiliar cultures and to global dimensions. It also is accepting functions in the community and in society at large that a decade or two ago would have been regarded as "none of its business." These commitments range from financial support of worthy causes to direct involvement and participation in the alleviation of social ills. . . .
>
> [All] . . . point to increased use of a flexible organization structure, including temporary or continuing task forces, or action groups spun off from the more routine corporate activities. They will not replace but will stand alongside the older organization structures as an expanding segment of total corporate organization (Brown, 1970, p. 46). Italics supplied.[4]

Other examples of adaptive design, found in B. F. Goodrich, are termed a "micro-company" (Miller and Wolf, 1968). Gruber and Niles (1972) suggest that an innovative type of structure be created not only for product innovation but also for innovation in management, research, development, and utilization of new management knowledge (new structures, procedures, techniques) with the targets being line managers within the firm.

We have presented an oversimplified view of formal organizational

---

[4] Reprinted by permission from *Nation's Business,* November, 1970. Copyright 1970 by *Nation's Business,* Chamber of Commerce of the United States.

structure. There are many variations of the basic forms described, as well as many more considerations involved in selecting a design. The systems view regarding "equifinality" seems appropriate—there probably are a number of ways to go from organizational structure to a particular state of organizational effectiveness.

As Drucker (1974) emphasizes, the one-best-way approach to organizational design by the classical theorists has led to many problems. Even the new "heretics" advocating "free-form" organizations make the mistake of imposing one template on everybody and every organization. This approach (as well as the earlier) ". . . misconceives an organization as something in itself rather than as a means to an end" (Drucker, 1974, p. 53).

Further Criteria for the Evaluation of Formal Designs

Although we have found criteria for selecting a formal organizational design which are, we hope, more useful than the earlier "principles of management," our criteria are by no means sufficient to the task of management. We have made the assumption, for instance, that, *ceteris paribus,* members of the organization will behave as they are "supposed to." As we know, this is not always the case. We have obviously left out the distinctly human needs that have been described by Katz and Kahn (1966) and others. Richetto (1970), for example, reminds us that "satisfied pyramid dwellers" do exist and that the new adaptive structures can induce considerable anxiety because of their ambiguity. Furthermore, we have not established criteria to assess the organization's contribution to society or its ability to interface successfully with other organizations in the environment. These important matters are examined in the following sections.

DISCUSSION QUESTIONS

1. Describe your school in terms of the concepts presented in this chapter.
2. Does the school's organization fit any of the traditional designs? Does the school have a prepared organization chart? In your opinion does the organization perform as the chart suggests it should?
3. Is the school's design appropriate according to the criteria mentioned in the chapter? Why?
4. How did the present design come into being? Has the school ever been reorganized?
5. If you were a consultant would you recommend the continuation of the present design or some modification? Why?

REFERENCES

Ansoff, H. I., and Brandenburg, R. G. A language for organization design, Parts I and II. *Management Science*, 1971, *17*, B705–B731.

Barkdull, C. W. Span of control—a method of evaluation. *Michigan Business Review*, 1963, *15*, 3 (May), 25–32.

Brown, Courtney C. Remodeling management structure. *Nation's Business*, 1970, *58*, 11 (Nov.), 46.

Carlisle, Harvard M. Are functional organizations becoming obsolete? *Management Review*, 1969, *58*, 2–9.

Chandler, A. D., Jr. *Strategy and structure*. Cambridge, Mass.: M.I.T. Press, 1962.

Cleland, David. Why project management? *Business Horizons*, 1964, 7, 4 (Winter), 81–88.

Dale, Ernest. *Organization*. New York: American Management Association, 1967.

Drucker, Peter F. New templates for today's organizations. *Harvard Business Review*, 1974, *52*, 1 (Jan.–Feb.), 45–53.

Gruber, W. H., and Niles, J. S. Put innovation in the organizational structure. *California Management Review*, 1972, *14*, 29–35.

Hellriegel, Don, and Slocum, John W., Jr. *Management: a contingency approach*. Reading, Mass.: Addison-Wesley, 1974.

Katz, Daniel, and Kahn, Robert L. *The social psychology of organizations*. New York: Wiley, 1966.

Leavitt, Harold J. Applied organizational change in industry: structural, technical and humanistic approaches. In J. G. March (Ed.), *Handbook of organizations*. Chicago: Rand McNally, 1965. Pp. 1144–70.

Miller, J. Wade, Jr., and Wolf, Robert J. The micro-company: organizing for problem-oriented management. *Personnel*, 1968, *45*, 4 (July–August), 35–43.

The New English Bible. The Oxford University Press, 1961, 1970. (Exodus 18:13–27.)

Richetto, Gary M. Organizations circa 1990: demise of the pyramid. *Personnel Journal*, 1970, *49*, 598–603.

Sloan, Alfred P., Jr. *My years with General Motors*. Garden City, N.Y.: Doubleday, 1964.

Steiner, George A., and Ryan, William G. *Industrial project management*. New York: Crowell-Collier and Macmillan, 1968.

Udell, Jon G. An empirical test of hypotheses relating to span of control. *Administrative Science Quarterly*, 1967, *12*, 420–39.

Worthy, J. Organizational structures and employee morale. *American Sociological Review*, 1950, *15*, 169–79.

Case

The Bates Company*
Lawrence M. Jones

The young man walking toward John Bates's office had joined the Bates Company a year ago after receiving a master's degree in business administration. Jack French had accepted the Bates's offer because he was interested in a career in sales administration and the company presented what he believed was an attractive long-run opportunity. His first job had been in the market research department which acquainted him with the competitive firms and the market conditions for Bates's equipment. In June 1958, he had completed the prearranged period of time in market research and was scheduled to receive a field selling assignment. Consequently, he expected the subject of his meeting with the vice president of marketing, John Bates, would involve his new job. Jack entered Mr. Bates's office and accepted a seat near Mr. Bates's desk as requested.

BATES: Jack, you've finished your time in market research, have you enjoyed it?

FRENCH: Yes, sir. You sure get a complete picture of the marketing problems in that work.

BATES: What did you learn about our marketing problems?

FRENCH: It seems to me we have three basic problems. First, our unit sales have increased for the last four years but our dollar sales have remained about the same. Second, the severe price competition that caused this development is a temporary condition. However, if we lose distributors during this period we probably will not be able to get them back when the market gets better. Therefore, the effects on our sales of this temporary price war could be somewhat permanent. Finally, it seems to me that every prime market area has its unique selling problems that can't be resolved by one standard program or policy.

BATES: Very interesting. However, aren't you speaking solely of our kitchen line?

FRENCH: Yes I am. But if Bates is going to grow significantly, the increase must basically come from our main line which is kitchens.

BATES: Well, I suppose you're anxious to get your new assignment?

FRENCH: Yes sir.

BATES: The spot we want to send you won't be open for several weeks so you will have to cool your heels for a while. Meanwhile I have another job I want you to do. As you have undoubtedly discovered, we don't have an organization chart of our sales division. That probably bothers you since you have a degree in business administration but I think they are usually a bunch of nonsense. No one pays much attention to a chart, they are seldom up-to-date, and they encourage too much functional rigidity as far as I am concerned. However, I think we've evolved a pretty poor organization in the sales division and we need to make some changes. Therefore, I would like for you to construct a chart that pictures our present organization and then reorganize the sales division as you think would be best.

FRENCH: That would be a tough job without spending a great amount of time evaluating the people.

BATES: I want you to deal only with positions and offices. I'll fit the people to the organization, change the organization to fit our people, or go outside to find the personnel we need. What I'm interested in is what structure you feel would be most effective.

FRENCH: Shall I start on this right away?

BATES: Yes. First there's a few other things you need to know. The controller has reduced our budget of operating expenses. Consequently, I'm looking for a more effective organization that will also be less expensive. You may find such a goal impossible, and that's all right. However, keep the objective in mind. Another problem is that my available time for personally supervising the organization is limited. I meet with the president's advisory committee two mornings a week and the executive committee at least once a month in addition to attending occasional industry trade associations.

FRENCH: Is this lack of time a current problem?

BATES: Yes, I think it's the main reason the organization problem seems so acute. I feel some problems demanding my attention have to be delayed too long, and I can't spend as much time with my immediate subordinates as I would like.

FRENCH: There are rumors floating around the office that we are going to open more sales branches this year. Your new organization will certainly have to reflect this if it is true.

BATES: As usual, the grapevine has it right. It's still confidential, but we will open three more sales branches this year. Your recommendations should include this change.

FRENCH: Where will you get the managers for these operations?

BATES: I hope your organization will require at least three less men for internal sales administration. But, don't let that warp your perspective. That is not the basic motivation for a change in organization, it's only a hoped for side benefit. Let me know when you have something for me to look at.

The Bates Company manufactured and marketed two major lines of product. A complete line of built-in kitchens (cabinets, sinks, and so on) had been handled by Bates since 1930. Although Bates only sold 3 percent of the total market, this product line accounted for 70 percent of the company's sales, income, and production effort. Kitchen units were marketed direct to large builders, and to appliance dealers through independent appliance wholesalers (or distributors) and company-owned sales branches. Included in the distribution system were 60 independent franchised distributors and 5 sales branches. In 1957, Bates's sales of kitchen packages were produced as follows:

Customer	Percent of Kitchen Sales
Direct to builders	10
To independent distributors	70
To company owned sales branches	20

The second line of equipment consisted of home barbecue equipment. These products accounted for 30 percent of Bates's total sales volume. Bates's barbecue products were sold to mail-order houses, hardware and household goods wholesalers and direct to large chain retail store organizations. Because of the nature of the market it was impossible to determine Bates's relative market position. However, management was convinced that the market was sufficiently competitive that Bates could increase its sales only through an uneconomical expenditure of sales effort. Therefore, sales of barbecue equipment were expected to remain about constant both in dollars and unit volume. In fact, this had been the case since 1956.

In 1959, there were over 200 wholesalers and large retail chains handling Bates's barbecue equipment. Each outlet accounted for the following share of barbecue sales:

Customer	Percent of Barbecue Equipment Sales
Direct to mail-order houses	15
To wholesalers	60
To retail chains	25

All manufacturing facilities were located in one plant in Columbus, Illinois. Except for final assembly operations, production was organized on a functional basis. During 1957, the factory operated at an average level of 75 percent of capacity producing an annual sales volume of $30 million. Sales of the end product were sufficiently level throughout the year that the problem of seasonal production was minor in nature. The Bates Company was also organized on a functional division basis. Reporting to the president were vice presidents in charge of manufacturing, sales, finance, and engineering.

After several weeks of investigation, Jack had defined the positions reporting directly to Mr. Bates:

1. Field Sales Manager—Kitchens: Mr. Johnson supervised 10 sales-men who serviced the Bates's distributors located east of the Mississippi River. Mr. Johnson spent about 40 percent of his time in the field working with his men and the remainder of his time at Bates's home office.

2. Field Sales Manager—Kitchens: Mr. Brown supervised 10 sales-men who serviced the Bates's distributors located west of the Mississippi. Because he had to cover a greater magnitude of geography than Mr. Johnson (although the number of accounts were equal), Mr. Brown spent about 60 percent of his time in the field.

3. Field Sales Manager—Barbecue Equipment: Mr. Cates supervised three regional sales managers, each of whom supervised five wholesale-retail salesmen. Mr. Cates spent about 75 percent of his time in the field because his area was used as a training ground for most company salesmen and he was continually faced with the problem of training new personnel.

4. Advertising Director: Mr. Hartley supervised 6 subordinates in the planning and execution of all company advertising and sales promotion programs. In addition, Mr. Hartley was responsible for the company's public relations activities.

5. Builder Contract Salesman: Mr. Allison made goodwill calls on the large builders and attended most of the builder trade shows and meetings. He had no subordinates and practically all of his time was spent in the field. Since Mr. Allison made no direct sales it was impossible to determine the productivity of his efforts in terms of dollars of sales volume.

6. Market Research Director: Mr. Grable supervised two subordinates and prepared statistical studies of market penetration, competitive prices, sales quotas, and consumer buying motives.

7. Sales Branch Manager: Mr. Taylor supervised the operation of five company-owned sales branches. Each branch had a manager who operated according to policy and procedure established by Mr. Taylor. The sales branches distributed only kitchen units and were dispersed in major market areas.

8. Director of Sales Administration: Mr. Ross supervised 5 subordinates who supervised a total of 25 clerks. The clerks handled order receipts, customer invoices, sales inventory records, and central correspondence files. Although sales administration was the largest wholly internal department in the sales division, its duties were largely routine and highly repetitive.

9. Field Sales Liaison Assistant: Mr. Black had no subordinates and handled many of the problems of field sales personnel. Mr. Black advised Mr. Bates on salesmen's salaries; individual sales quotas; evaluation of salesmen's performances; and the hiring, training and counseling of salespeople.

10. Merchandise Manager—Kitchens: Mr. Grey's function was to coordinate with other divisions in product design, manufacturing cost and availability, product pricing, and sales forecasting. He had two assistants and in many instances the work of his department overlapped with activities of the advertising department especially where the preparation of sales promotion programs was concerned.

11. Merchandise Manager—Barbecue Equipment: Mr. Fleck supervised one subordinate and performed the same functions as described under the title above.

12. Product and Sales Service Manager: Mr. Gage was responsible for creating installation and application literature, handling any product problems of a technical nature that occurred while the product was being used by the ultimate consumer, and administering the inventory and shipment of repair and replacement parts. In addition, this department supervised the technical product training of Bates's salesmen and wholesaler personnel. Occasionally, technical problems developed in the field which required more technical knowledge than possessed by sales personnel. Consequently, of the ten people supervised by Mr. Gage, four were constantly in the field on training or emergency service missions.

As Jack had developed these position definitions he had received several interesting observations from the people. Mr. Cates appeared convinced that the sales effort on barbecue equipment was being subverted to the kitchen units. He regarded this as an unfortunate development since in his opinion barbecue equipment was a more profitable line and with more advertising and personal sales effort it could be a fast growing business.

The merchandise manager functions seemed to be an area of considerable dispute. Mr. Fleck and Mr. Grey felt that their positions carried too little authority to affect the necessary action, and all the field managers regarded the merchandise manager as an undesirable intrusion in their areas of sales responsibility.

It also appeared that there were several instances where wholesaler sales personnel had intruded in the marketing areas reserved for a sales branch and where the reverse had occurred. These experiences had created conflict between the sales branch manager and the field sales managers. Although not a frequent occurrence, this problem was a very sensitive one because the independent wholesalers had a latent dislike of any organization that participated, even partially, in its own wholesaling process.

There were other problems of this type between the product and sales service department and the field sales managers; between advertising and market research along with normal inter-division disputes concerning schedules, prices, and design. However, Jack felt that the overall attitude of the organization was healthy and he was not sure whether the above frictions were normal or a result of poor organization structure.

The Finance Division supplied Jack with an operating budget for the Sales Division which is reproduced as Exhibit 1. With this information Jack was convinced that he had as complete a picture as the time allowed for the project would permit. As he pondered his conclusions, he wondered if it might be better to create a series of organization moves that would allow a gradual change to the final structure he envisioned. However, it seemed to him that the company's problem was an immediate one and the benefits gained from a one-shot reorganization might be greater than those of a slow evolution that would consume one to three years.

EXHIBIT 1
Operating Budget for the Sales Division

Account	Amount
Vice president	$ 52,000
Field Sales—Kitchens	
Managers	40,000
Salesmen	250,000
Field Sales—Barbecue	
Manager	20,000
Regional managers	45,000
Salesmen	150,000
Advertising	
Director	15,000
Personnel	45,000
Media and expense	865,000
Builder Contact	21,000
Field Sales Liaison	10,000
Market Research	
Director	10,000
Personnel	13,000
Sales Administration	
Director	9,000
Department heads	30,000
Personnel	100,000
Branch Management	
Manager	26,000
Branch managers	120,000
Personnel	210,000
Expense	100,000
Product and Sales Service	
Manager	11,000
Personnel	70,000
Merchandise Management	
Managers	24,000
Personnel	16,000

QUESTIONS FOR CASE ANALYSIS

1. Prepare an organization chart for the present structure. Which functions have line responsibility, staff, service?

2. What changes in the organization would you incorporate in a new structure?

3. Which of the problems uncovered by Jack would you hope to eliminate with your new organization, if any?

4. Do you agree with Mr. Bates's approach of designing an organization without considering at the same time the strengths and weaknesses of the people who will staff that organization?

5. Should a company seek people to fit the organization or the organization to fit its people?

section II

Structure and Components of Systems

PREMISE

Having introduced the notion that organizations are open systems, we can proceed to an investigation of the various components that form these systems. Leavitt (1965) suggests that the major components of organizations are tasks *(or goals),* people, technology, *and* structure. *Tasks include both the organization's purposes or* raisons d'être, as well *as the subgoals and objectives used to attain more global, long-range goals. People variables include motives, aspiration levels, mores, norms, attitudes, and other manifestations of both personality and culture. Technology is used by Leavitt in a way that subsumes both physical devices and abstract problem-solving techniques. Structure, finally, means* "systems of communication, systems of authority (or work roles), and systems of work flow" *(Leavitt, 1965, p. 1144).*

These four major components of organizational systems bear complex interrelationships with one another (they will be studied in detail one at a time in Chapters 3, 4, 5, and 6). This observation, seemingly

The Major Variables in Organizations

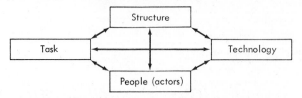

Source: Adapted from Harold J. Leavitt, "Applied Organizational Change in Industry," in James G. March (Ed.), *Handbook of Organizations*, © 1965 by Rand McNally College Publishing Company, Chicago, Figure 1, p. 1145.

obvious, has been missed by managers time and again; for example, attempts to alter organizational performance frequently deal with one of the components to the exclusion of the other three. Sensitivity training deals with people variables, sometimes to the exclusion of concern for task, formal structure, and technology. Reorganization techniques frequently do little more than change structure. Some planning efforts deal with goal-setting and not with concomitant changes in structure, technology, and human variables.

Our culture has changed dramatically over the past 25 years, and with it we note a change in people's attitudes toward work. People are beginning to expect, and in some cases demand, challenging, meaningful work. One way of meeting this demand, as we shall see, is to change the organization's technology to one that employs more of the workers' skills. However, a change in technology requires alterations of the organization's structure, and congruent architectural modifications. Even the goals of the organization may be altered in the process.

We shall begin Chapter 3 with an example of this type of change. Unfortunately, the kinds of interrelationships among components mentioned here are not well recognized in practice. We will find, for example, that the change described in Chapter 3 is reported in Chapter 6 as a failure. Thus, our major concerns in this section of the text are to convince the reader of the interrelatedness of major organizational variables and to demonstrate ways in which these variables can be made compatible with one another.

3

Informal Structure

INTRODUCTION

By 1960, American management was quite familiar with the theoretical inclinations of behavioral scientists such as Maslow, Likert, McGregor, and others. However, few of these theories found their way into accepted practice. The following story, which appeared in *Business Week* in 1965, concerns a manager who undertook a monumental gamble that traditional approaches to organization and job design are inherently inferior to participative management. Andrew Kay, president of a San Diego-based electronics firm, had read widely the literature on employee motivation and decided to put theory into practice. Here is what happened in Kay's firm when workers managed themselves.

In 1960, Kay assembled his employees and announced plans for reorganization. All workers were to be put on salary at the equivalent of $.60 per hour more than the prevailing wage rate in the area. Assembly lines were removed and replaced by 16 independent production units of 6 to 7 workers each. Each unit was to be headed by a team captain, and was free to determine its own means of production.

When put into effect, the plan yielded an immediate boost to employee morale. Productivity suffered, however, and some workers quit of their own accord. Within three months, though, productivity was at its former level. By 1965, it was 30% higher than it had been prior to the reorganization. Rejected work fell almost to nil, and customer complaints fell 70%. The job of quality control inspector was eliminated. Flexibility increased. Where it had once taken 8 to 10 weeks to tool up for a new product, it now took just 2 to 3 weeks.[1]

Chapter Guide

The report on Non-Linear Systems, Inc., raises interesting questions. If you bear them in mind while reading this chapter, you should be able to answer most of them, at least in the sense of formulating plausible hypotheses.

---

[1] *Business Week,* 1965.

1. What preconditions were essential in Non-Linear Systems' organizational culture to the workers' success in managing themselves.
2. Why did production improve above what it had been in the days of the assembly line? In tearing down the assembly line, didn't the firm move to a less efficient method of production? How can you account for this seeming paradox?

ELEMENTS OF INFORMAL STRUCTURE

Structure: Formal and Informal

Let us begin our discussion of organizations as they are seen by behavioral scientists by using Leavitt's (1965) typology of structure, technology, people, and goal.

By structure, we mean patterns of relationships among roles. These patterns comprise relatively enduring and often repeated forms of behavior which can be classified as being either formally or informally produced. *Formal* structure is planned and specified via official channels of communication with the intent that it will be used by the organization's members. *Informal* structure is unspecified, unwritten, and unplanned. Such structure can be viewed as arising out of, and in reaction to, formal structure. The early human relations movement grew in response to research findings which suggested that formally specified relationships were often amended or violated by the individuals to whom they were intended to apply. A typical example is an incentive scheme which establishes both a production standard for workers (e.g., 20 widgets per day) and a piece rate for production attained in excess of the standard amount. The intent of this type of incentive scheme is to provide workers with a measure of financial security by paying them a fixed amount for production which falls below 21 widgets per day and to motivate them to produce more than that amount by paying an incentive rate for work produced above the minimum. What often happens under such incentive schemes is that work groups decide to limit their production to 22 or 23 widgets per day because they fear that management will increase the minimum while maintaining the old base rate if it becomes apparent that the workers can produce 25 or 30 units per day. From production statistics, we find that the data cluster around 22 to 23 units of production per day and that the distribution of data appears to be similar to a normal curve. The peak of the curve describes the work group's production norm. The productivity of individual workers tends toward the norm because deviations from the norm are met with sanctions and punishments of various kinds by the work group.

FIGURE 3–1
Distribution of Individual Productivity

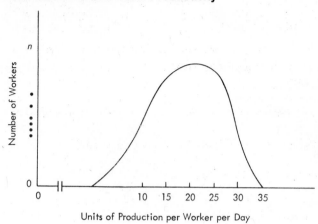

Units of Production per Worker per Day

J-shaped Distribution of Behavior

One finds normative structure in many aspects of social life. Observe, for example, the behavior of motorists at stop signs. Most people come to a complete halt and, assuming the way is clear, start up a fraction of a second later; a few come to a "moving stop"; and a few others halt for more than a fraction of a second, but the majority halt for just a fraction of a second. This, in fact, is the norm for most drivers. However, in cities where the police are unable to enforce this traffic law and where this situation is generally recognized by motorists, the norm is apt to become a "moving halt" of two to three miles per hour, with exceptional individuals either halting completely or slowing down only to five or six miles per hour. A similar phenomenon will be found when one observes arrival times at work. If the factory whistle blows at eight o'clock, people will arrive very close to eight o'clock, and only a few individuals will arrive before or after.

Actually, distributions of data around norms such as those described above are not *exactly* normal shaped. They are what we might call J-shaped (Allport, 1934). This is to say that the majority of individuals (mode) behave at the norm, and some individuals operate away from the norm in one direction, but very few individuals, if any, operate away from the norm in the other direction. Behavior tends to conform to the J-shaped distribution because sanctions are more strictly applied to one side of the range of behavior than they are to the other. If an individual is conspicuously late to work, the supervisor is likely to consult the company's rules and apply whatever sanction is appropriate. The individual who arrives at work conspicuously earlier than fellow workers risks the disapprobation and sanction which his or her peers may apply, but the sanctions in this case are not specified and tend to be applied inconsistently. What we have here, actually, is an example of how individuals shape their behavior to avoid sanctions. If sanctions are to be endured, individuals select the lesser of two evils.

FIGURE 3–2
Arrival Times at Work

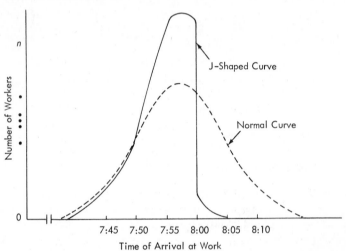

So far, we have dealt with norms which arise from reactions to formal structures such as work standards, traffic laws, and company regulations. There are also informal norms which arise directly from informal behavior, which are not triggered by formal rules or regulations; for example, work groups may decide among themselves that no more than one member of the group at a time can be absent from his or her work station during company time. Although there may be no official company regulation to this effect, workers will attempt to discipline themselves in this way if they agree that more than one of their number absent at a time makes them "look bad" in the eyes of their supervisor. Another example concerns a group of physicians who agree not to resuscitate cardiac arrest patients above a certain age. Having established an informal norm, the doctors decided to make the norm part of the hospital's formal structure. They posted the rule where it came to the attention of the general public who, in turn, fought to have it rescinded. However, this is not to say that the physicians ceased to behave according to the norm which they had established for themselves. The informal norm may still exist unless sanctions have been brought to bear against it.

Internalized Rules

Norms are internalized rules, or internalized structure, which create regularities in behavior (Thibaut and Kelley, 1959). These predictable responses are taught to give the individual an indication of how one is expected to behave in different kinds of situations. The adherence to, or the divergence from, certain social norms provides sources of information which in some elements of society are meaningful indices of an individual's background, status, and general "worth." Norms operate because of a feeling of obligation to adhere to them and a sense of guilt when one is violated. Such norms are reinforced by sanctions for nonconformity.

Roles

A role consists of a set of norms which specify the behavior of an individual within a specific position in society (Thibaut and Kelley, 1959). Viewed more broadly, a role appears as a set of norms which prescribes the expected behavior and personal relationships of an individual with respect to other individuals who maintain other, related social positions; for example, the norms which apply to leaders of small, informal groups specify not only how the leader is expected to behave with respect to other members of the group and leaders of other groups, but also how group members are expected to relate to their leader. Within a small group, roles tend to be informal. In larger organizations, informal roles are augmented by formally stated rules and regulations.

Likert's System Four Organizations

Of numerous writers in the field of human relations who have examined the phenomenon of informal structure, Rensis Likert (1967) emerges as a major contributor. In contrast to the rational model, Likert suggests that informal structure is more significant in determining organizational behavior than formal structures. Thus, we are led to view patterns of behavior as structure—patterns sometimes created by formal prescription, but often emerging, as a natural system, from a variety of forces and dynamics. Likert has articulated the important aspects of informal structure which may be used to modify, supplement, or replace the traditional formal structural designs used in businesses and other organizations. In this sense, Likert provides a bridge between the busi-

TABLE 3–1
Organizational and Performance
Characteristics of Different
Management Systems

1. Leadership processes used.
2. Character of motivational forces.
3. Character of communication process.
4. Character of interaction-influence processes.
5. Character of decision-making processes.
6. Character of goal-setting or ordering.
7. Character of control process.

ness world with its emphasis on formal structure and the academic world of the social psychologist with its emphasis on informal structure. Likert's position is most easily understood in terms of the research upon which his work is based. The research in question utilizes a questionnaire which deals with various aspects of the organizational dimensions listed in Table 3–1. Several questionnaire items are used to explore each of these dimensions. For example, one of the three items under "Leadership Processes Used" appears in Figure 3–3. Each questionnaire item corresponds to a scale which delineates the extremes of the organizational behavior in question, in this example running from "have no confidence and trust in subordinates" to "complete confidence and trust in all members."

Other questionnaire items include the following: a number of questions which are intended to indicate the kinds of motivational forces present within the organization; for example, one item determines whether the emphasis is on fear and threats (left side of the scale) or on rewards based on the attainment of group-established goals (right side of the scale). Other questions explore the nature of the organization's communication process; for example, does information flow downward only (left) or downward, upward, and horizontally among peers (right). In all, 51 items are used to examine the organizational characteristics listed above.

FIGURE 3–3
Sample Questionnaire Item

Extent to which superiors have confidence and trust in subordinates	Have no confidence and trust in subordinates	Have condescending confidence and trust, such as masters have to servants	Have substantial but not complete confidence and trust; still wish to keep control of decisions	Have complete confidence and trust in all matters

Source: Likert (1967).

Likert divides each continuum upon which responses can be made into four intervals, each of which is related to a different style of management. In completing the questionnaire, an individual is asked to place a mark on the continuum at the point which best describes the organization under investigation. Responses which fall to the left of the center of the continuum are indicative of an authoritative system of management while those which fall to the right of center indicate a system which is more participative.

FIGURE 3–4
Likert's Systems of Management

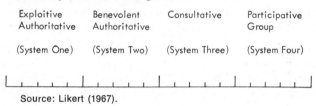

Source: Likert (1967).

Likert's respondents describe the highest producing department in their organization using the above-mentioned questionnaire. Next, using the same instrument, respondents are asked to describe the lowest producing department in the organization. Having answered each questionnaire item twice, the respondent is able to compare the patterns of responses for the lowest and highest producing units. As a rule, the lowest producing department is described by a pattern of responses which falls to the left of the pattern derived for the highest producing unit. High-producing departments usually are seen as using management systems which approach System Four. Low-producing departments, on the other hand, appear to the respondents to be using management systems which tend toward System One. This pattern has been observed consistently in experiments dealing with hundreds of managers from numerous kinds of organizations.

One of Likert's most interesting findings arises when he asks respondents to describe their own departments on the questionnaire on which they previously described high- and low-producing departments. Generally, a respondent's description of his own department will fall somewhere between the profiles for high- and low-producing units. Likert is then led to ask, "Why is it that managers use a system of management which they recognize as being less productive than an alternative system about which they know and presumably could use? Why do they not use the management as they describe it for the highest producing unit?"

ADAPTING FORMAL STRUCTURE TO INFORMAL STRUCTURE

Participative-Group Organizations

According to Likert's findings, most organizations fall in the middle of the scale, under System Two or System Three. Apparently, System One and System Four organizations are rare phenomena. Now, when Likert asks managers to describe the kind of organization they would like to have, they generally indicate a System Four style of management. They appear to want a participative group kind of organization. At this point, one is led to question whether it is entirely feasible to consider the formation of organizations which have the operating characteristics described by System Four. Is it possible, in today's society, to create an organization in which information flows downward, upward, and among peers, and in which there is cooperative teamwork throughout the organization, and in which subordinates are fully involved in decisions relating to their work? Are attempts to move in this direction bound to be met with frustration? As you might expect from having read the opening section on Non-Linear Systems, Inc., successful changes in this direction are feasible. In the next part of this chapter we will review Likert's description of experiments carried out by a team of researchers from the University of Michigan in which organizations were moved from System Two and Three to a System Four style of management.

One of the experiments took place when the Harwood Manufacturing Company, the leading firm in the pajama industry, purchased the Weldon Company, which was second in volume in the industry. The president of the Harwood company is a psychologist who had long practiced the principles of human relations. In fact, the Coch and French (1948) experiment, involving workers in planning the changeover of machinery when production runs changed, had been carried out in Harwood a number of years earlier. That experiment showed that when workers were fully involved and participated in planning the changeover, much less disruption, turnover, and reduced productivity occurred than when workers were not involved in planning. Work groups which sent delegates to participate or, even worse, work groups which were not consulted at all, experienced more disruption, more turnover of staff, and much slower rates of learning the new methods. In some cases they never regained their earlier levels of production.

As measured by the current research, the management system in Harwood was generally System Three and System Four; that is, consultative or participative management. This was not true for Weldon which was closer to Systems One and Two, exploitative authoritative or benevolent authoritative management systems. The Weldon Company had also been unprofitable for several years although Harwood had managed to show a profit during the same period.

Although Harwood personnel replaced the corporate management of the Weldon Company, the plant manager and managerial supervisory staff in the Weldon plant were retained. A training program for employees, managers, and supervisors was begun. The training consisted of learning principles and skills required by a system of management which approached System Four. The plant manager was helped to use this system and to encourage his subordinate managers and supervisors to do the same. All of these changes were initiated and supported by the new top management of the company. To use some of our earlier terminology, within the same old formal structure, a new informal structure was created; a new set of norms and roles concerning the way to manage, to communicate, to involve people, and to work together was planned and implemented for Weldon.

Measurements by the Michigan researchers showed that there were, in fact, marked changes in the management system year by year after Weldon's acquisition by Harwood. While the improvement did not reach the System Four level of functioning found in Harwood, Weldon did move to a "System Three and a Half" kind of management. As Likert expected, performance and productivity subsequently improved. The average earnings of piece-rate workers increased by nearly 30 percent in the absence of a change in the basic wage structure. At the same time, total manufacturing costs decreased by about 20 percent. Turnover dropped to half of its former level. Length of employee training was reduced substantially. Employees expressed more friendly attitudes toward the company, and finally, the organization began to show a profit. Profit as a return on investment changed from −17 percent to +15 percent and was still improving at the time of Likert's writing. A full report on how System Four was established at Weldon is found in a book called *Management by Participation* written by the psychologist president of the firm, Alfred J. Marrow, and two of the Michigan researchers, David Bowers and Stanley Seashore (1967).[2]

The Scanlon Plan, in which workers share a portion of the company's profits and are thereby motivated to work harder for the company (Katz and Kahn, 1966), provides further evidence of the feasibility of System Four. Study shows that Scanlon Plan companies differ from other companies in more than just the motivation of their workers. Workers and management operate in a System Four fashion: workers communicate upward by making suggestions for changing and improving their work;

---

[2] However, it is not clear that all improvements noted at Weldon stemmed from System Four management. Marrow, Bowers, and Seashore (1967) suggest that the bulk of these improvements may have been realized as traditional management practices were implemented.

they work together and cooperate as a team; and they are fully involved in many of the firm's decisions. Finally, the motivational system employed emphasizes rewards, not fear and threats.

Let us now look more closely at the nature of System Four management. Likert gives three basic concepts which explain its apparent success and attractiveness to managers: (1) supportive relationships, (2) group decision making and group methods of supervision, and (3) high performance goals for the organization. Each of these concepts becomes an important norm in System Four organizations.

Supportive Relationships

Likert describes the principle of supportive relationships as follows:

> The leadership and other processes of the organization must be such as to ensure a maximum probability that in all interactions and all relationships with the organization each member will, in the light of his background, values, and expectations, view the experience as supportive and one which builds and maintains his sense of personal worth and importance (Likert, 1961, p. 103).

In other words, relationships, especially between a superior and a subordinate, should be ego-building rather than ego-deflating. To test whether supportive relationships are present, one may ask the following questions: How much confidence and trust does the subordinate have in his or her superior? To what extent does the boss convey a feeling of confidence that the subordinate can do the job successfully? Is the supervisor interested in helping the subordinate achieve and maintain a good income? Does he or she try to understand the subordinate's problems and do something about them? Does the boss evidence interest in helping the subordinate perform successfully by training the subordinate, helping with problem solving in a constructive way, and providing the appropriate resources when needed? Does he or she try to keep the subordinate informed about matters relating to the work; does he share relevant information? Does he[3] ask opinions of the subordinate when a problem arises which involves the work? Does he value the subordinate's ideas and try to use them?

If these kinds of supportive relationships are established throughout the organization, then the organization will benefit through the mobilization of both the economic and noneconomic motivational forces of its members. Furthermore, the organization will benefit by the creation of cooperative action focused on achieving organization goals.

Group Decision Making and Group Methods of Supervision

The second principle of System Four management is group decision making and supervision. Likert contrasts the group form of organization

---

[3] As previously stated in Chapter 2, the common pronoun "he" is not intended to be masculine or feminine but simply "human."

in System Four with the traditional organizational structure which emphasizes a man-to-man (or line management) model of interaction; that is, a superior-to-subordinate model. In contrast, System Four requires the creation of a work group which involves a superior and all of his or her subordinates. Each subordinate may also be a superior for subordinates at the next level down in the organization and this too becomes a group, and so on down the hierarchy. The organization thus comprises overlapping groups with managers at every level, except the very highest and very lowest levels, serving as linking pins between two groups.

These groups are more than mere lines on the chart; they are more than formal groups. All subordinates in a work group, who are affected by the outcome of a decision, are involved in making the decision and carrying out its implementation. The groups function in such a way that communication is open; that problems can be fairly examined. The

FIGURE 3–5
The Linking Pin Function

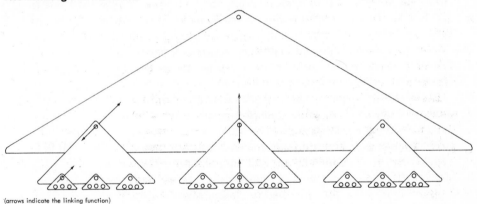

(arrows indicate the linking function)

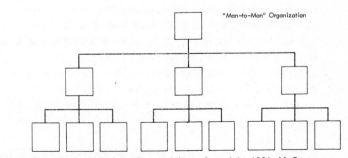

"Man–to–Man" Organization

resources of the various members are used in problem solving in a manner commensurate with the experience and requirements of all group members.

However, problems can arise with the creation of cohesive work groups. Research shows that cohesive groups can effectively mobilize their members to act in a unified fashion to achieve the goals of the group. However, if the goals of the group are antagonistic toward those of the organization, cohesiveness can, in fact, be dysfunctional and can reduce the effectiveness of the total organization.

High Performance Goals for the Organization

The third principle of System Four management concerns goals of high performance for the organization. In System Four organizations, both superiors and subordinates must have high aspirations for the organization's performance. These aspirations should, in fact, be the goals of the groups which make decisions and manage the organization as discussed in the second principle of System Four management. This combination of the first principle, which emphasizes support of the individual and his or her needs, and the second principle, which involves management by overlapping groups of individuals, provides the means by which the needs and desires of individuals can be met through the achievement of organizational objectives.

Likert shows how each of these three principles is essential to the success of System Four management. Data from a large sales organization, in which 20 high-producing offices were compared with 20 low-producing offices, showed that when sales managers exhibited both high performance goals and supportive behavior toward their salesmen, the sales office invariably performed well. High performance goals, unaccompanied by supportive behavior, were not effective, nor was supportive behavior without high performance goals.

Further examination showed that the high performing sales offices invariably used the group method of supervision. Although the salesmen in question operated within the same sales district and competed with one another for sales and commissions, they still found the group method useful and, in fact, produced more than sales representatives in other offices who merely competed against one another. A good example of the group method is the meetings in which salesmen described their selling activities so they could be analyzed by their manager and other salesmen. In these meetings, sales representatives coached one another in how to do a better job; they held group problem-solving sessions and sessions in which the group as a whole set performance goals.

High performing sales offices conducted group meetings regularly. Usually they were fairly small, consisting of no more than 12 to 15 salesmen. Typically, each sales representative, in turn, reported in detail his activities since the previous meeting, describing the number and kinds of prospects obtained, calls made, kind of sales presentations used, the closings attempted and their results, the number of sales made, and the volume and quality of the total sales. The other people in the group would then analyze the salesman's efforts, methods, and results and, from their experience, offer suggestions for improving his performance. After the analysis by the group, each sales representative, with the group's advice and assistance, proceeded to establish performance goals for the following period. These goals included both the procedures and the results he intended to realize prior to the next group meeting.

The manager or supervisor also attended the group meetings and served as chairman, but his major role was to facilitate the functioning of the group. He maintained a relationship to the salesmen as helpful, constructive, problem solver. He saw that the group remained supportive of its members and set high performance goals which served to achieve simultaneously both individual and organizational aspirations.

As the result of the meeting, each salesman felt a commitment to the group and to the manager to work to achieve the goals which he, in concert with the group, set for himself. The aspirations and implied motivation established in the meetings were often reinforced between meetings; sales representatives frequently reminded one another of the goals and commitments to which the group was dedicated. Similarly, salespeople continued coaching one another between meetings; they availed themselves of the technical knowledge and skills of both their colleagues and superiors. From an organizational standpoint, the result was a climate in which important skills and resources could be shared, regardless of the individual's position in the firm's hierarchy.

Significantly, the sales manager described above was required to go beyond his role as group chairman; he also served as a group process facilitator who was able to relate to the group as a whole. If the manager had personally analyzed each salesman's performance and results and had established each salesman's goals, a lower producing sales force would have resulted. Man-to-man interactions dominated by the manager do not, according to the study reported here, produce as much group loyalty and personal motivation as group interaction and group influence. Finally, by dominating the group, the manager would have prevented the group from making full use of the resources possessed by individual members of the group.

The manager of an effective group must do more than just act supportively during group meetings. He must see that all group members are as well trained in group decision-making and group interaction processes as they are in the technical aspects of their work. Both in group meetings and in day-to-day interaction, the manager must help the individual to maintain and realize the goals which he has set for himself. In this sense, the manager is more than just another group member; he is responsible for organizing the group effectively and for assuring that planning, scheduling, and related activities support both organizational objectives and individual goals. And, of special importance, through his membership in the group at the next higher level in the hierarchy, that is, the group composed of his peers and superior, he links his own unit to the rest of the enterprise.

Mutual Influence Systems

At this point, let us examine the influence relationships in System Four organizations. Likert found that managers who use supportive relationships and group methods of decision making possess more influence in their unit than managers who fail to utilize group resources. Moreover, the subordinates in System Four organizations enjoy a greater degree of influence within the organization than do their counterparts in organizations where the system of management is less participative. At first glance, this appears to be an anomaly. We might expect that group participation in management vests influence in subordinates at the expense of the influence possessed by superiors. Apparently, this is not the case; people at both levels of the organization experience more influence under System Four management than they do under alternative styles of management.

This is not difficult to understand when viewed within the context of research conducted on cohesive groups. Cohesive groups tend to evolve among individuals with similar values, needs, and aspirations. Because members are personally attracted to one another and because the group and the relationships within it are rewarding, they are willing to accept influence from other group members as one cost of attaining these rewards. However, since goals, values, and culture do not differ widely among group members, the cost of being influenced, in terms of loss of autonomy, is slight. Not only is the individual member willing to be influenced, he is also willing to exert his own influence on the group. Since the individual most likely values the goals of the group and the means used to attain them, he is motivated to influence and to subject himself to the influence of others. The manager and his subordinates in Likert's System Four organization create a cohesive group in which each member influences the others. The result is a mutual influence system (Wieland and Leigh, 1971). Thus, it is not surprising that under System Four management, both managers and subordinates report that they are able to exert considerable influence within the organization.

FIGURE 3–6
Influence Graph

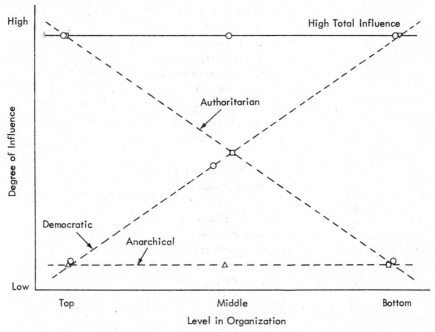

Influence Graph

Arnold Tannenbaum (1968) and his associates at the University of Michigan provide us with research findings which greatly extend our understanding of influence processes within organizations. Their research indicates an identifiable relationship between the nature of the influence process and the organization's effectiveness. Tannenbaum uses a graph to illustrate the influence process. The horizontal axis of the graph represents the organization's hierarchy of authority with the president or top manager at one end, rank-and-file members at the other, and middle managers and foremen in between. The vertical axis indicates the amount of actual, effective influence that individuals at various hierarchical levels exercise.[4] By plotting the degree of influence exercised at each level of the organization on the graph, a curve, which succinctly illustrates influence relationships within an organization, can be constructed. Such curves as this can be used to compare influ-

---

[4] A more precise term would be "control" (see Chapter 10).

ence relationships in different organizations and in a single organization at different points in time.

In practice, four different classes of curves can be identified. If top, middle, and lower management plus rank-and-file members all report they have little influence in the organization, the resulting curve has a relatively flat slope and is situated fairly low with respect to the vertical axis. Adding the degrees of influence reported by each level of the hierarchy indicates that the total amount of influence wielded within the organization is relatively low. Such an organization can be described as somewhat *anarchistic* in that individuals, regardless of their position in the organization, have relatively little influence over what others in the organization are doing.

A more common situation is one in which upper levels of management wield considerable influence, middle levels exercise moderate influence, and lower management and the rank-and-file, respectively, possess lesser degrees of control. This instance can be termed an *authoritarian* organization; the degree of influence enjoyed is proportional to the individual's status in the organizational hierarchy.

The opposite condition, in which influence is inversely related to position in the hierarchy, also exists, though much less frequently. One survey of local units of the League of Women Voters, a voluntary organization, indicated that in some units, members were able to exercise more influence than the officers. This relationship might be *democratic*, although the term is used here to describe a rather perverse democracy.

Adding the degree of influence exercised at each level of the organization, one finds that the total influence in both autocratic and democratic institutions is only moderate. This finding contrasts with the total influence found in organizations in which individuals at all levels report that they have a high degree of influence over what happens within the organization. When an influence graph for this kind of organization is constructed, the resulting curve is nearly parallel to the horizontal axis and relatively high on the vertical axis. The control graph for an organization with *high total influence,* in fact, is very similar to the curve for a cohesive group. In cohesive groups and in Likert's System Four organizations, leaders and group members alike report that they have a high degree of influence over what happens in the group.

High Total Influence Organizations

Studies of many different kinds of organizations—ranging from labor unions to industrial services firms to industrial products firms to sales organizations to voluntary organizations, such as the League of Women Voters—show that organizations with high total influence are *more effective* in achieving their goals, whatever they may be, than are organizations with lower total influence (Tannenbaum, 1968). Local

Leagues of Women Voters, for example, in which both leaders and members report that they have a great deal of influence over what happens are leagues that raise relatively more money from their community, have larger proportions of the community as members, and have larger and more active programs than leagues which have lower total influence (Tannenbaum and Kahn, 1958). Labor unions with high total influence are more effective in keeping management responsive to union-related issues than are labor unions which possess lower levels of total influence (Tannenbaum, 1961).

We saw earlier that Harwood more closely resembled System Four management than Weldon did and was, therefore, a more effective organization. Using Tannenbaum's influence graph, Marrow and the Michigan researchers found that total influence was higher at Harwood than at Weldon, substantiating the general relationship presented here between high total influence and effectiveness.

So far, we have examined groups in which members have a considerable degree of influence over one another and the leader or the manager is supportive and manages the group as a group. According to Likert, these groups tend to be highly effective. We have also discussed Tannenbaum's finding that organizations in which members at different levels all report having considerable influence over the organization tend to be effective organizations. The question then arises, "How can we translate Likert's findings about effective groups into design strategies for organizations?" We have already discussed the manner in which Likert's schemes can be used in a fairly simple organization through the use of overlapping groups. In the last part of his book, Likert shows that overlapping groups can be employed in quite complex, formal organizational designs.

In a complicated organization, horizontal as well as vertical overlapping groups are necessary. As an example, Likert describes an organization which contains both functional and product departments. In order to coordinate the activities of both, an overlapping group structure is created; for example, members of the research and development, production, and marketing segments of a firm may be organized to constitute the membership of a product development team. Their colleagues may be similarly organized into other product teams, and so on. Just as in the case of the vertical overlapping groups, members of these horizontal overlapping groups have responsibilities to two groups: one in which they are subordinates and another in which they are superiors. Likert describes how a similar setup of cross-linking roles can be created so as to coordinate geographical areas within different functions.

Now these various designs may sound similar to the matrix or project management designs discussed earlier. The important point, however, is not the formal design or the formal assignment of a manager to more than one group at a time, but the way the group is designed to operate. These groups must operate using the three principles described by Likert; namely, supportive management, management of the group, and high performance goals for the group. Groups which follow these principles will develop effective interaction-influence systems. An organization which comprises these kinds of groups will develop the capacity to exchange vital information throughout its various units, to exert influence properly, and to make decisions that take into account the needs for coordination.

Likert describes a contrasting situation in which formal group leaders use man-to-man instead of group supervision. Using man-to-man supervision, the manager will join the group as a representative of his chief. As a representative of higher management, the manager will tend to deal with differences in a polarized, win-lose fashion and, consequently, the group will not achieve appropriate cross-functional decision making and coordination.

Even if the cross-function group succeeds in getting representatives to be flexible and to think as part of the group, the representative going back to his own group will find himself in a difficult position since he will be managed "back-home" on a man-to-man basis. This means that the representative will probably lack the support of the other subordinates of the manager. In this way, Likert shows that adequate functioning of an overlapping group system of management depends on the nature of these various horizontal and vertical groups in the organization.

According to Tannenbaum's findings, organizations in which individuals at one level or another report a lack of influence and are not organized into cohesive groups with mutual influence, are in fact ineffective organizations. To be most effective, an organization must have members at all levels who are capable of influencing the organization. Likert goes beyond this to indicate how high levels of influence and, correspondingly, group management, or System Four management, must be used across functional, product, and geographical departments as well as across hierarchical levels. Only in this way can these designs achieve their potential effectiveness.

DISCUSSION QUESTIONS

1. Do you think that "high total influence" implies that all members of an organization have equal voice in all decisions?
2. How does one determine the limits of participation in organizational decision making?
3. What costs are incurred by moving to a form of organization that permits high total influence? How can these costs be justified?
4. Is the development of an informal structure harmful to the organization?

REFERENCES

Allport, Floyd H. The J-curve hypothesis of conforming behavior. *Journal of Social Psychology*, 1934, 5, 141–83.

Business Week. When workers manage themselves. March 20, 1965, *1855*, 93–94.

Coch, Lester, and French, John R., Jr. Overcoming resistance to change. *Human Relations*, 1948, *4*, 161–84.

Katz, Daniel, and Kahn, Robert. *The social psychology of organizations*. New York: Wiley, 1966.

Leavitt, Harold J. Applied organizational change in industry: structural, technological, and humanistic approaches. In J. G. March (Ed.), *Handbook of organizations*. Chicago: Rand McNally, 1965. Pp. 1144–70.

Lewin, Kurt. Group decision and social change. In G. E. Swanson, T. M. Newcomb, and E. L. Hartley (Eds.), *Readings in social psychology*. (Rev. ed.) New York: Holt, 1952. Pp. 459–73.

Likert, Rensis. *New patterns of management*. New York: McGraw-Hill, 1961.

Likert, Rensis. *The human organization: its management and value*. New York: McGraw-Hill, 1967.

Marrow, Alfred J., Bowers, David G., and Seashore, Stanley E. *Management by participation: creating a climate for personal and organizational development*. New York: Harper & Row, 1967.

Tannenbaum, Arnold S. Control and effectiveness in a voluntary organization. *American Journal of Sociology*, 1961, 67, 33–46.

Tannenbaum, Arnold S. *Control in organizations*. New York: McGraw-Hill, 1968.

Tannenbaum, Arnold S., and Kahn, Robert L. *Participation in union locals*. Evanston, Ill.: Row Peterson, 1958.

Thibaut, John W., and Kelley, Harold H. *The social psychology of groups*. New York, Wiley, 1959.

Wieland, George F., and Leigh, Hilary (Eds.). *Changing hospitals: a report on the hospital internal communications project*. London: Tavistock, 1971.

4

Technology and Structure

INTRODUCTION

Students of organizations have become increasingly aware of the impact of technology on organizational structure. The architect's observation that form follows function is mirrored in the realization that organizational design needs to respond to the requirements of technological innovations.

Before we discuss the relationship between design and technology, let us review some rather contradictory predictions and research findings on the impact of computer technology on organizational structures and processes.

Effects of Computers on Organizational Structures and Processes[1]

A. The Observers' Predictions:
   Harold J. Leavitt and Thomas L. Whisler (1958)

   1. Jobs at today's middle management levels will become highly structured.
   2. Top managers will take on an even larger portion of the innovating, planning, and other "creative" functions.
   3. The programmers and R&D personnel will move upward into the top management group.
   4. Large industrial organizations will recentralize.

   Melvin Anshen (1960)

   1. The new technology will not erode or destroy middle management jobs. Instead it will present opportunities for expanding management capacity and performance in areas that have suffered from scant attention.
   2. The tasks of middle managers will more closely resemble those of top management.

---

[1] Charles W. Hofer, "Emerging EDP Patterns," *Harvard Business Review*, vol. 48, no. 2, March–April 1970, pp. 18, 170, 171.

3. Computer personnel will not assume top management responsibilities or become the fundamental source for top management personnel.
4. The trend toward decentralization of decision making will be slowed down.

John F. Burlingame (1961)

1. If the company's philosophy is one of centralization, then the likely evolution will be along the lines predicted by Leavitt, Whisler, and others.
2. If a company's activities are centralized because of difficulties involved in achieving a harmonious unifying of individual creativity and initiative, then the computer will provide a basis for the adoption of a decentralized approach as a more desirable and more effective way.
3. If the company's philosophy is one of decentralization, then the technology should strengthen the existing decentralization of operations. Middle management should grow and flourish rather than wither and die.

John Dearden (1964, 1966, 1967)

1. The computer will have no impact on the organization of top and divisional management, relatively little impact on the ability of the top manager to control profit centers, and limited impact on management levels below the divisional manager even though there may be some centralization of data processing and logistics systems.
2. With the exception of certain routine operating control problems in such areas as logistics, production scheduling, and inventory control, it will not be practicable to operate a real-time information system, and, even if it were, such a system would not solve any of top management's real problems.

B. The Researchers' Findings:
   Ida Russakoff Hoos (1960)

1. Computer applications have led to drastic changes at the middle management level (supervisory to executive junior grade). Many jobs have been either combined or eliminated.
2. EDP [Electronic Data Processing] has systemized and standardized formal information flow and also has seemed to dam up the upward and downward flow of information through both formal and informal channels.
3. As more and more operations are programmed, the power and status of new computer personnel have been expanded, while the functions of other departments have been undercut, and the authority of their managers truncated.

4. EDP stimulates two distinct kinds of recentralization—one type referring to the integration of specific functions, the other involving regrouping of entire units of the operation and causing sweeping changes of the external structure as well.

Donald Shaul (1964)

1. While EDP has undoubtedly eliminated a vast amount of monotonous, detailed administrative work, there has been no accompanying reduction in the need for middle managers. Actually, EDP has made the middle manager's job more complex.
2. The centralization of activities has not been accompanied by an elimination of managerial positions. On the contrary, EDP and the new activities have resulted in the addition of over 50 middle management positions in the companies studied.

Hak Chong Lee (1965)

1. The nature and magnitude of the EDP impact is basically governed by the computer technology and the management attitude toward the use of the technology.
2. Drastic changes (centralization of the decision-making process and reduction in the number of middle management jobs) have not occurred to date in the companies studied during the early period of industrial experience with EDP.

Rodney H. Brady (1967)

1. Top management does not seem to use the computer directly for decision making.
2. The use of the computer by middle management permits top management to:
   a. Make some decisions at an earlier date.
   b. Gain time in which to consider some decisions.
   c. Consider more thorough analysis of some situations.
   d. Review several courses of action on many problems.
   e. Examine analyses of the impact that recommended courses of action will have on the problem or opportunity identified.
   f. Obtain additional information from middle managers concerning problems, opportunities, and promising alternatives before making decisions.

Chapter Guide

Interestingly, but not unexpectedly, a number of the foregoing predictions are contradictory. Rather than merely dismiss the variances as errors, why not analyze them in light of the following questions?

1. What assumptions do you think were made for each prediction concerning the organizations' structure (formal and informal)?
2. What sort of technology (the process for getting work done) do you think was envisioned by each forecaster?
3. Can these sets of differing assumptions account for the discrepancies in the predictions?

Even more interesting are the differences noted among the research findings on the effects of computer technology on organizational structure and process.

4. For each finding, try to imagine the kinds of technology and organizational structure that must have existed prior to the introduction of EDP systems in order for the courses of events presented above to have transpired.

RELATIONSHIPS BETWEEN TECHNOLOGY AND STRUCTURE

Mechanistic and Organic Organizations

In the last chapter, we discussed reasons for moving organizational structure toward flexibility—from bureaucratic rigidity to systems that are more open. A System Four type of management enables the organization to make fuller use of its human resources and therefore to function in a more flexible and effective manner. An interesting study by Burns and Stalker (1961) supports this point of view.

The authors investigated a number of diverse Scottish firms interested in entering the field of electronics. Most of these firms failed to enter this field successfully. Because of their reliance on formal organization, these firms exhibited a "mechanistic" organization structure, which closely followed the principles of Gulick, Urwick, and Taylor—the "classical principles of management." Typically, the businesses were unable to de-emphasize formal hierarchical structure and, in turn, develop more equality in influence relationships. Though relatively successful in previous endeavors, their attempts to enter a new field of operations were unsuccessful.

Stable and Dynamic Industries

Burns and Stalker contrasted these Scottish firms with a number of relatively successful English companies in the electronics industry. Characterized by the authors as "organic," these organizations paid less attention to formal procedures and encouraged horizontal as well as vertical communication, flexible instead of rigid roles, and decision making at all levels, including lower levels—all very much along the lines that Likert (1967) and Tannenbaum (1962) emphasized.

However, please note that the mechanistic and organic firms originated in different industries with dissimilar technologies and marketing environments. One can infer that the more informal, organic structure suits organizations within dynamic industries while the more formal, mechanistic structure is appropriate for organizations within stable industries. The results of the study by Burns and Stalker reinforce the theory that the nature of the industry (or more precisely, the nature of both the technology and the environment of the organization) determines the appropriateness of the organizational structure so as to correspond better with the technology of the new industry. Let us, then, explore the nature of technology in greater detail.

Technology

What do we mean by technology? Perrow (1967, 1970) defines technology as a means of transforming raw materials (either human, symbolic, or material) into desirable goods and services. Machines, equipment, and supplies, of course, can all be viewed as components of technology, but the most important component by far is the *process* whereby raw materials are transformed into the desired output. Technology, basically, is the technique which enables this transformation. Critical to the determination of transformation techniques is the existence of supporting knowledge. Technology may be found inside of one's head, so to speak; technology indicates the expertise that professionals bring to the job.

Perrow (1965) describes problems in structuring mental hospitals. Fundamental to these problems is the lack of an effective technology for dealing with most psychiatric illnesses. For many years, shock therapy was used to treat certain forms of psychosis though no one fully understood how or why it worked. More recently, tranquilizers have been used, and are still used today, though we lack a theoretical understanding of their effect on mental illness. In general, the same lack of understanding holds true for various forms of psychotherapy, and mental illness still remains a problem. Even though we have a physical apparatus—such as machines for giving shock therapy and pills for tranquilizing patients, the knowledge base which explains the apparatus' intervention in the process of the illness is lacking. As we shall see, the nature of the knowledge base is a critical component of technology.

Unit, Mass, and Process Technologies

This chapter will be concerned with the development of more precise measures of technology. For the moment, however, let us consider one of the initial studies of technology and structure which Woodward (1965) undertook in England. She conducted a survey of 100 firms to examine the applicability of various classical theories of management to actual practice. Woodward was concerned with the usefulness of such concepts as functional departmentalization, line-staff arrangements, the optimal span of control, and the number of hierarchical levels within an organization. After developing general measures of the effectiveness of these organizations in their industries, she attempted to correlate the occurrence of different structural forms with the degree of effectiveness. As we are learning, she found that no single form of organizational structure leads to organizational effectiveness. In fact, only after grouping the firms according to their typical mode of production did relationships between form and effectiveness become apparent.

Woodward categorized the firms according to the type of production system utilized: (1) the unit or small batch firm, which made one or at most a few kinds of products for special orders (e.g., a manufacturer of scientific instruments); (2) the large batch assembly and mass production firm (e.g., an automobile manufacturer); and (3) the process production firm involved in automated production (e.g., oil or chemicals). In Woodward's opinion, the three production systems—the unit, mass, and process systems—demonstrated increasing degrees of complexity. The survey data, thus categorized, indicated that in the unit production firms the span of control of the chief executive ranged from 2 to 9 employees, in the mass production firms from 4 to 13, and in the process production firms between 5 and 19 employees. Furthermore, the span of control for first-line supervisors also differed according to the type of production system, as did the ratio of workers to managers and other aspects of organizational structure. Apparently, the nature of the firm's technology rendered some forms of structure more appropriate than others.

Now, one might argue that these differences in structure resulted from mistakes by organizational planners—that they failed to use the appropriate, namely classical, organizational designs. However, an analysis of the various firms revealed a consistent relationship between success and particular kinds of structure. In the case of spans of control, *those firms with average spans for their type of production system were successful, whereas firms deviating from the average span in their production system were not successful.* Another way of stating this is to say that the same span of control may be successful or unsuccessful depending on whether the firm is using one kind of technology or another.

In summary then, the work of Woodward (and a corroborating replication by Zwerman, 1970) leads to a more general observation; namely, that a pattern underlying organizational structures relates to the nature of the work to be done—relates, that is, to the technology which the organization employs. The pattern or relationship between structure and technology is not only of interest in itself but seems vital in determining the effectiveness of the organization.

Technical Diffuseness and Specificity

A study by Harvey (1968) of 43 different industrial organizations used what he calls the dimension of technical diffuseness and specificity. Technical diffuseness refers to the technology of firms which employ productive processes yielding a wide range of products—a range which probably varies over time as well. Technical specificity refers to technologies wherein one product, or at most a limited number of products, is produced consistently. A degree of similarity, of course, exists between technical diffuseness and unit production, that is, "made-to-orderness," just as there are similarities between specificity and process or mass production. However, an abstraction of this dimension of diffuseness and specificity provides a finer instrument to measure organizations, even within Woodward's types. Thus, some unit production firms may be quite diffuse in their technology while others may be more specific, tending to get orders which, while they are made one by one, are fairly similar to one another.

Using the dimension of technical diffuseness and specificity, Harvey found that four structural characteristics of organizations were related to an organization's position on the dimension. Organizations characterized by technological specificity contained more specialized subunits than organizations characterized by technological diffuseness. Furthermore, in contrast with organizations which were technologically diffuse, those which were technologically specific tended to have more levels of authority, greater ratios of managers and supervisors to total personnel, and greater degrees of program specification. Technological specificity, in other words, seemed to be associated with Burns and Stalker's mechanical structure, and technical diffuseness with an organic structure.

Job Complexity and the Span of Control

Another example of technology determining organizational structure is found in the research on the effects of job complexity on the size of span of control (Bell, 1967). Bell determined that the complexity of the task in which a supervisor and his subordinates were engaged was inversely proportional to the size of the supervisor's span of control.

According to Bell, job complexity is a function of the number of tasks associated with the job, the degree of unpredictability associated with these tasks, the individuals' rights to exercise discretion in making job-related decisions, and the level of responsibility which they exercise in the performance of their work. To the extent that one or more of these factors increase for either the supervisor or his subordinates, the supervisor's effective span of control is diminished.

As the degree of job complexity, as defined by Bell, increases, a corresponding increase occurs in the amount of information which the work group will need to process. Biological systems can suffer from information overload (Miller, 1960), and only so much information can be processed by a system in a given period of time. Higher information loads cause the system to break down, to show strain (Wieland, 1965), or to engage in various coping mechanisms, producing relative inefficiency. In a relatively simple job, the supervisor and his subordinates make few job-related decisions and, consequently, process a relatively small amount of information. Under these conditions, a supervisor can manage a fairly large number of subordinates. As job complexity increases, however, the supervisor will become overloaded and eventually feel pressures to delegate some of his or her responsibility, thus reducing the span of control.

Technology, Structure, and Psychological Differences

Thus far we have been discussing organizational characteristics as if they were consistent factors within all organizations. Obviously, this is not the case. Perrow (1967) gives a graphic illustration of the differences among functional subgroups within a single organization. He describes how structural differences will accrue to the marketing, research, and production functions within an organization as a result of each function's preoccupation with different technologies and with problems characterized by different degrees of routineness. The research department generally performs less routine tasks than the marketing department, which performs tasks less routine than the production department. In consequence, departmental structures tend to vary to accommodate the degree of routineness of the tasks.

In addition to having different structures due to different classes of problems and different technologies, departments within an organization tend to vary according to the modes of thought which members typically use. Lawrence and Lorsch (1967) found that members of production departments, faced with relatively certain tasks, tended to be more task oriented and less socially oriented than sales department members who faced more uncertain tasks. Sales and production department members, who received fairly rapid feedback from actions on their jobs, tended to focus more on short-term concerns than research scientists and engineers who did not receive rapid feedback.

This finding can be explained in several ways. First, individuals who have learned to think in a particular manner may view the thought process evidenced by members of one functional specialty as more attractive than those evidenced by other specialties. Hence, departments may attract job candidates who are self-selected according to their in-clination toward a given school of thought. Second, individuals possess-ing varying thinking styles, upon entering a given department, may be-come socialized to "fit in" with other members of the department, who ultimately must fit in with the technological requirements of the par-ticular function.

The important point from the Lawrence and Lorsch study is that the structural and personality differences found among different functions must be allowed to remain if the organization is to be effective. The researchers found that effective organizations were characterized by these interdepartmental differences whereas less effective organizations tended to have people and departmental structures that were more or less homogeneous across the organization. This was especially true of organizations in dynamic environments requiring rather different tech-nologies in the functional departments. To allow these needed differ-ences to exist is not an easy task. Lawrence and Lorsch describe medi-ating devices that relatively successful organizations have used to bridge the gaps among structurally and psychologically different functional areas. While firm conclusions cannot be drawn from this study of only six organizations, there is evidence that people and structures within a given organization (and especially in dynamic industries) must be allowed to vary in ways appropriate to the tasks they face.

Technology: Certainty and Variety

Recent work by Perrow (1967, 1970) provides the means to extend our analysis of technology several steps further. Going beyond Harvey, who examined technology along the single dimension of diffuseness-specificity, Perrow makes use of two separate dimensions in his analy-sis: (1) the extent to which analyzable search can be used in problem solving (i.e., a dimension running from well-defined to ill-defined prob-lems), and (2) task variability (i.e., a dimension ranging from variety in the task to routineness).

When faced with a new problem, one for which no previously formu-lated solution exists, the individual is forced to search for feasible solu-tions. The nature of the search process will vary according to the degree to which the problem is defined. In dealing with well-defined problems, the individual can conduct the search for a solution on a logical, ana-lytical basis. This systematic search for well-established techniques or programs is typical of the problem-solving behavior of mechanical engi-neers. At the other extreme are classes of problems which are ill-defined. In dealing with ill-defined problems, the individual, lacking formal search techniques, is forced to draw upon his or her wealth of unana-lyzed experience or intuition, to rely upon guesswork and trial and error solutions. The physician dealing with a new disease or the researcher faced with a problem in basic research exemplifying this kind of problem-solving behavior, as does a glassblower or other skilled craftsman.

In addition to the problem-definition dimension, Perrow includes a second dimension, consisting of the amount of variety contained in a given job. Some jobs are routine, containing few exceptions from "normal" day-to-day practice. Assembly-line and preventive maintenance jobs are examples. At the other extreme are tasks which inherently contain numerous exceptions and deviations from day-to-day operations. The roles of an electronics repairman or a nurse in an intensive care unit exemplify this kind of work. The most variable jobs probably would include the research scientist or the top executive of a growing firm in a new or changing field. Please note some similarity between this dimension of variability and Harvey's diffuse or specific technology and Lawrence and Lorsch's stability or instability in the environment (Chapter 13).

The two dimensions of technology, postulated by Perrow, can be used to construct a 2 x 2 table. As a result, we can expect to find classes of organizations which deal with technological processes falling somewhere within the classification scheme presented in Figure 4–1. For our purposes here, we will deal only with those which fall at the extremes.

The nature of work-related problems varies considerably in some jobs. In addition, solutions to these varying problems cannot be found via logical, analytical search procedures. Jobs fitting this description are located at the upper right-hand corner of Figure 4–1. Many components of firms in the aerospace industry, for example, seem to fit this description. Jobs with these characteristics are termed *Nonroutine*.

At the other extreme are many tasks which have low variability and few exceptions, the solutions for which can be determined using logical, analytical search. *Routine* jobs, as they are called, are typified by assembly lines, and various mass-production technologies such as those used by steel mills. Routine work, to Perrow's way of thinking, is organized very much along the lines of the "mechanistic" organizations described

FIGURE 4–1
Types of Technologies

	Problem Variability	
Problem definition	*Low variability and few exceptions*	*High variability and many exceptions*
Ill-structured (*Unanalyzable search*)	Craft Industries (specialty glass)	Nonroutine (aerospace)
Well-structured (*Analyzable search*)	Routine (steel mills)	Engineering (heavy machinery)

Source: Adapted from Perrow (1967).

by Burns and Stalker (1961). By the same token, organizations which
deal with nonroutine work seem similar to the "organic" firms.

At the upper left-hand corner of Figure 4–1 one finds *Craft* industries
which deal, by definition, with problems which are fairly similar over
time—low in variability and containing few exceptions. However, the
similarity or lack of variability in tasks does not permit the use of logical, analytical search techniques, since even though the problems are
fairly similar, their solution requires the application of experience, intuition, and trial and error. Craftsmen, from shoemakers to diemakers,
fit into this quadrant of the technology table.

Finally, the lower right-hand corner of Figure 4–1 describes work
which is highly variable and which contains many exceptions. In this
case, though, the variable tasks, including even the exceptions, can be
dealt with by means of logical search processes. *Engineering* problems
are typical of this class. Every new bridge or building presents problems
different from those which an engineer has faced before, but ultimately
these problems are solved in a rational, organized manner.

Organizational Structure in Relation to Technology

In making application of two discrete dimensions, Perrow allows us
to separate technology into four different kinds and, subsequently, to
look at the kind of organizational structure appropriate for each type of
technological process. The aspects of structure which Perrow feels
should be made congruent with technology follow: (1) the amount of
discretion which can be exercised by higher and lower level staff, (2) the
amount of power held by each of these groups, (3) the extent of interdependence between these two groups, and (4) the extent to which
these groups coordinate their work using either feedback or the planning of others.[2]

Industries which engage in craft technologies, for example, are confronted with problems that require freedom for lower level personnel
to exercise considerable discretion and power in decision making. By
the same token, the activities of lower level employees will be subject
to coordination via feedback. For these reasons, Perrow suggests that
the most effective organizational structure for craft industries is one
which is *decentralized*.

---

[2] Where variability and exceptions to day-to-day operations can be handled
through routine procedures and logical, analytical search, the work of subordinates
throughout the organizational unit can be coordinated by planning. This is generally
true regardless of the rate at which exceptions arise, so long as these exceptions are
amenable to analyzable search. In cases where exceptions cannot be handled
via analyzable search, though, planning will not satisfactorily coordinate various
work activities. In these instances, the output of a work group as it is subjected to
various criteria or as it affects other groups will give rise to feedback from which
direction and coordination can be inferred. An example of an individual who derives
direction from feedback is the artist whose progress in producing a painting is
directed in part by the painting, itself, as it takes form.

Planning can effectively control work that is typified by low variability and analyzable search. An emphasis on planning requires that both higher and lower levels in the organization exercise little discretion. Furthermore, by virtue of its planning function, top management wields more power than other levels in the organization. Consequently, if they are effective, organizations which utilize routine technologies tend to evolve *formal, centralized* structures.

Nonroutine activities, typified by variability and a large number of exceptions that cannot be resolved by logical, analytical search processes, are amenable to control only through feedback. The ill-structured nature of the work requires that higher and lower levels of personnel alike exercise considerable discretion in their work. Similarly, both levels, if they are to be effective, must be free to exercise considerable power in the work situation. Because of these characteristics, organizations which engage in nonroutine activities are effective, according to Perrow, when they assume a *flexible, polycentralized* structure.

Finally, the engineering organization operates effectively when it utilizes a *flexible, centralized* structure. Engineering tasks, although associated with variability and numerous exceptions, are typified by logical, analytical search processes. Thus, the activities of lower levels of management can be controlled by planning. Similarly, lower level managers need not exercise a great deal of discretion or power. Higher levels of management, however, tend to bear the brunt of the large number of exceptions and planning activities which are implied. Hence, they should exercise significantly more discretion and power than the subordinate levels.

Technology versus Behavior: A Conflict of Ideas

Sound theoretical arguments support Perrow's analysis. In addition, empirical data bear out the model. Hage and Aiken (1969) in a study of 16 health and welfare agencies (rehabilitation, psychiatric services, and services for the mentally retarded) found considerable differences in the routine (variety or similarity) of the work performed. In one organization, the executive director said that the work is so novel and innovative that his staff doesn't even know which professional organization to join. Another staff member, in reporting his work with the highly unpredictable children, said, "We individualize very highly here; we would turn the place upside down for one child—and sometimes we do." This contrasts with an organization having less variable work, consisting mainly of a standardized interview with each client to determine eligibility for various types of governmental aid.

As expected, organizations with routine work were more likely to be characterized by centralization of organizational power. According to Hage and Aiken, "if organizational members constantly face a work

situation characterized by highly varied clients' needs, then greater organizational power will accrue to organizational members who interact
with the clients most frequently." Below we shall explain this in terms
of the power accruing to those who can absorb uncertainty for the rest
of the organizations members.

Perrow's expectations about the relationship between routineness and
discretion were not confirmed, but, as expected, they did find that routineness was associated with the formalization of roles. Formalization
was measured by the existence of rules manuals, job descriptions, and
the extent to which the job was highly specified in the description.
These are all manifestations of Perrow's "coordination by planning"
cited above. In short, Perrow's hypothesis of a relationship between the
type of technology and the nature of coordination, whether by plan or
feedback, is also confirmed.

Unfortunately, we do not have sufficient data to give us confidence
about the general validity of Perrow's model. A particular problem is
that even studies that show a certain technology to be compatible with
a certain structure fail to show conclusively that this complementarity
is essential for organizational effectiveness. Regardless, applications of
the model to specific organizations do seem to make sense. However,
the model and, in fact, most of this chapter raise design problems of
no small magnitude. Perrow, stating the implications of his model for
the design of contemporary organizations, remarks:

> Finally, to call for decentralization, representative bureaucracy, collegial
> authority, or employee-centered, innovative or organic organizations—
> to mention only a few of the highly normative prescriptions that are
> being offered by social scientists today—is to call for a type of struc-
> ture that can be realized only with a certain type of technology, unless
> we are willing to pay a high cost in terms of output. Given a routine
> technology, the much maligned Weberian bureaucracy probably con-
> stitutes the socially optimum form of organizational structure (Perrow,
> 1967, p. 204).

As logical as his conclusion seems, it nonetheless raises serious reservations when compared to conclusions implicit in the work of Likert,
Marrow, Tannenbaum, and others discussed in Chapter 3, who see
mutual influence systems, high total control, and so on, as models for
effective organizations of any kind. This dilemma is resolved in part by
the observation of Lawrence and Lorsch (1967) that individuals who
labor in different specialties tend to think in dissimilar terms. The field
of organizational behavior is subject to considerable bifurcation, as are
most other fields of inquiry. Scientists tend to view organizations differently; some define them as cooperative social systems; others approach the phenomena as decision-making mechanisms. Still others,
and Perrow is one of these, define organizations as systems for applying techniques to the problem of altering raw materials. Obviously, the

selection of any one of these premises to the exclusion of the others limits the variables which one will consider in a study of organizational behavior. Indeed, consideration of all relevant variables simultaneously is a nearly impossible task.

The student of organizations, then, is faced with "fitting together" the findings of scientists who began their investigations from different points of view. The pitfall lies in the temptation to accept one particular school of thought as valid at the expense of the others.

COMBINING TECHNOLOGY AND STRUCTURE
Changing the Fit between Social and Technical Subsystems

Examples of work successfully combining a number of schools of thought can be found in the studies of coal mining and textile manufacturing conducted by the Tavistock Institute (Trist, Higgin, Murray, and Pollock, 1963), a research organization in England. The Tavistock researchers dealt with organizations in terms of sociotechnical systems. The technical portion of the system was defined as equipment and work processes; the social portion of the system was defined as the work organization which relates to the individuals who carry out the necessary tasks of the system. As we shall see, the Tavistock work accommodates both the human needs and technological requirements which have been discussed above.

The Tavistock researchers selected the primary work group as the focus of their investigation. Within the small group of co-workers, they isolated three work-related psychological forces which the sociotechnical system could be designed to facilitate. The first of these psychological forces is *closure:* The sense of completion one feels upon having finished a meaningful unit of work. Psychological research performed many years ago by Zeigarnik (1927) showed that people become frustrated when they are prevented from completing a task and experience the motive to resume and finish the work which has been interrupted. Subsequently, it has been demonstrated (Horwitz, 1954; Lewis and Franklin, 1944) that there is a *group* Zeigarnik effect—that members of a group want to complete their task when interrupted but will be satisfied if any member of their group finishes it for them.

The second psychological force arises from the need for *autonomy* in the control of one's activities. This also has a group counterpart. The individual's need for autonomy can be satisfied provided that a trusted member of the group possesses the autonomy and decision-making authority to act in his or her behalf.

The third psychological force stems from the need for *satisfactory interpersonal relations.* At the risk of oversimplifying, we categorize this need as the workers' desire to be members of cohesive work groups. According to the Tavistock researchers, three group characteristics play major roles in determining a group's cohesiveness: (1) the range of skills required of group members in performing their task must be limited to the extent that each member of the group can understand the group's functioning with respect to the task; (2) in order to minimize barriers to communication within the group, differences in prestige and status among members of the group must be minimized; and (3) members who become dissatisfied must be provided the opportunity to leave the group in order to join another, lest frustration develop and disrupt the group's functioning.

A Tavistock study of the change in coal-mining practices from the traditional "single working" to the "longwall system" (Trist and Bamforth, 1951; Trist et al., 1963) demonstrates the importance of these three factors. In the single-working system, the primary work group consisted of six men, two of them assigned to each of the three shifts. Every member of the primary group possessed all of the skills necessary to perform the three major operations in coal mining; namely, (1) removing coal from the coal face, (2) loading and transporting coal from the face, and (3) erecting roof supports and moving up machinery as the mining proceeded deeper into the coal face. The two miners on a given shift would perform whatever operations were necessary at a given time, and the next shift would pick up the task wherever the first pair left off and carry on, as would the members of the third shift. All six men in the group were paid the same wages, the exact amount being determined by the amount of coal the group as a whole mined. Finally, the composition of the group was based on self-selection, with the men selecting their own workmates.

While the single-place working seemed to meet many of the primary group requirements as specified by the Tavistock researchers, the longwall system did not. The longwall system attempted to mechanize the coal-mining process and advance the application of mining technology and also, in a sense, to make the miners conform to the requirements of the technical system. The installation of new mining equipment required that shifts be manned by fairly large numbers of miners. The workers were divided into three shifts and, most significantly, they were assigned to specific functions. The three basic types of mining operations were separated so that the first shift cut into the coal face, the second shift moved the coal to the conveyor, and the third shift brought up the roof supports and conveyor.

The longwall system failed to meet the primary group requirements described above. First, the workers lacked a sense of closure, or completion, since each shift was performing only a fraction of the mining operation. Furthermore, since group cohesiveness was not present among workers across the different shifts, completion of the cycle of mining operations by second or third shifts did not produce the "group Zeigarnik effect." Second, workers on a given shift lacked autonomy and control over their work. Not only were the workers on a particular shift dependent on others in their large group, they were also very dependent upon the workers of the other two shifts. For example, if the first shift failed to mine a sufficient quantity of coal, the second shift would not have enough coal to load on the conveyor. By the same token, if the second shift did not finish loading the conveyor, the third shift would be unable to move the conveyor up to a new position, and so on. Third, satisfactory interpersonal relations among shift workers failed to materialize because of the existence of major differences in skills and, consequently, in status among the workers. Finally, miners who became dissatisfied with their relationship to their work group were unable to move into a more congenial setting.

As suggested above, the mutual dependency of shifts, in that the productivity of one affected the productivity of others, became a source of intergroup conflict worsened by the lack of social bonds among the groups. This psychological separation was increased by the structure of the remuneration system, since miners were no longer paid according to the amount of coal produced by the group as a whole, but rather according to differential rates for specific jobs. Thus, the three specialized shifts were in a position to compete with one another for increases in rates of pay and, consequently, were motivated to blame slowdowns and substandard output on the activities of other groups. Energy was not applied toward increasing the output of the three shifts as a whole but rather toward increasing one group's advantage relative to that of the others.

A number of coal-mining operations developed a form of compromise arrangement for using the new technology, and a study of this arrangement substantiated the analysis comparing the single-place working with the longwall method of mining. The "composite longwall system" comprised a group of 41 men who were divided into three shifts. Rather than having specialized tasks assigned to each shift, the composite longwall method provided that each shift perform all three of the major mining activities. Furthermore, the group possessed the autonomy to reassign its members as the need arose. Not only did this arrangement provide the work group with a sense of meaningfulness and closure, but, because the group organized itself, it was not dependent upon external coordination. Thus, the work group exercised considerable autonomy in making decisions which affected its functioning. Finally, the work group in the composite longwall system still selected its membership, and members were paid according to the productivity of the entire group rather than according to the types of tasks that the individuals performed.

The composite longwall system employed a larger number of workers than did the single-place working system. Nonetheless, it was designed so that the work situation reinforced the psychological and group forces which made the single-place system viable. A comparison between the composite longwall system and the conventional longwall system showed the composite longwall system had a lower rate of employee absenteeism, lower operating costs, and a higher rate of productivity.

Similar conclusions can be drawn from a study of the introduction of automatic looms to textile mills in Ahmedabad, India (Rice, 1958). In order to staff the new automatic looms, 12 different occupational roles were created and assigned among workers. The occupational roles varied from battery filler to weaver, cloth carrier, bobbin carrier, sweeper, and so on. Twenty-nine workers were assigned to the 12 roles and were responsible for the operation of 224 looms. In attempting to fulfill the requirements of the technological system, the 29 workers faced a confusing pattern of interrelationships. For example, three members of one role might serve eight members of another role, but the priorities of the eight for the services of the three were not clearly established. Furthermore, as looms were changed over to produce different types of cloth, the work load and nature of activities associated with different roles were altered. Consequently, it was exceedingly difficult to establish job descriptions for the various roles.

One way to approach the ensuing problems would have been to rationalize further the organizational structure by creating supervisory roles for individuals who would monitor performance and apply controls as necessary. Another approach, which the Tavistock group recommended to management, was to develop an internal work group structure which was related to the demands of both the social and technological systems.

The Tavistock researchers organized the workers into four groups of seven men each—four in a weaving (production) subgroup and three in a maintenance subgroup. The number of work roles was reduced further by an agreement that the new work groups would take over additional tasks previously allocated to only one or two individuals out of the whole group of 29.

Thus the work group was organized so that it bore responsibility for the completion of a meaningful unit of activity. Differences in skills, prestige, and status among the members of the work group were reduced to facilitate the establishment and maintenance of satisfying interpersonal relationships. In describing the results of the reorganization of the sociotechnical system, Rice tells how the workers now ran as they went about their work, so motivated were they by the psychological work forces. They even attempted to work throughout meal times even though Indian labor law prevents this lest it lead to exploitation of the workers. Needless to say, the reorganized portion of the mill proved highly productive, and the organizational design implemented by the Tavistock group was eventually utilized throughout the mill.

Toward the Design of Sociotechnical Systems

A fairly simple conclusion from the Tavistock research would be that the formation and nurturance of cohesive work groups is a palliative for wide-ranging organizational difficulties. Perrow's (1967, 1970) analysis, on the other hand, causes us to agree that different kinds of technologies seem to require different kinds of formal and informal structure. In fairness to Perrow's case, it should be pointed out that the coal-mining operations involved tasks which contain low variability and few exceptional problems. Solutions to these problems, furthermore, are not readily found through logical, analytical search. The natural geological occurrence of coal can require craftsmanlike skills of miners. This being the case, an organizational designer using Perrow's analytical scheme would have recommended that the mines employ a decentralized structure similar to the one which evolved in the composite longwall system.

That the textile workers were engaged in craftsmanlike activities is not clear, however, and there is considerable doubt that Perrow's analytical scheme would have suggested that management employ the form of organization which eventually proved successful. This is also true of the experiences of the Non-Linear Systems Corporation reported at the beginning of Chapter 3; that corporation replaced an assembly-line operation with a number of semiautonomous work teams. What this suggests is that some organizational designs are logically conceived to meet the technological requirements of a system while others are developed primarily around the social needs of workers.

Both schools of thought contain important elements of truth. Effective forms of organizational design are successful in dealing with organizations as sociotechnical systems; they provide an environment in which the fulfillment of the requirements of the technical system simultaneously allows for the satisfaction of social and individual needs. In Chapter 6, we examine approaches to the design process from the beginning with an emphasis on the employees' needs.

Technology and Interpersonal Relationships

We began this chapter by treating organizations as entities and then moved toward disaggregation by considering functional departments and then individual work groups. To conclude the chapter, we will closely examine an example of the subtle influence which technology can have upon relationships between individuals.

A study of restaurants (Whyte, 1949) shows a variety of ways to handle the problem of matching worker characteristics and the technology of work flow. First of all, note that the restaurant is really a rather complex organization, combining both service and production. The service end of the business requires that management discern the patrons' tastes so that menus can be constructed and foods stocked accordingly. The time factor in the kitchen is also very critical, as George Orwell so vividly describes in his *Down and Out in London and Paris* (1972).

With regard to the flow of work, Whyte found that waitresses directly initiated work orders to male countermen or cooks, often creating tensions and frictions which diminished when they gave orders to pantry girls instead. Many restaurants use barriers such as a counter (or a spindle) on which waitresses place their written orders for countermen to pick up so as to control the work to their own desired pace. Another kind of barrier is the male pantry supervisor who collects order slips from the waitresses as they come in and passes them out to the countermen.

All this may not seem very relevant to the work of the manager far removed from the handling of actual production tasks and physical materials. However, if the problem is conceptualized in terms of handling dependencies, especially dependencies arising from uncertainty in organizations, then we will find parallel phenomena at the managerial level. Uncertainties arise because environmental inputs vary, technology breaks down, or both the environment and the organization's technology give rise to problems which require unanalyzable search. These uncertainties must be handled somehow if the organization is to preserve its semblance of rationality and remain more efficient than an unorganized collection of individuals (Thompson, 1967). Those roles—managerial or worker—which absorb or buffer uncertainty are the roles on which the rest of the organization becomes dependent.

For example, Crozier (1964) describes how maintenance men in a French tobacco plant are the only individuals in the organization who can solve the problems of machine breakdowns. Thus, a situation arises in which others become dependent on them which, in turn, determines a significant portion of the power relationships in the organization. We shall see in Chapter 5 that the ability to solve critical organizational problems can be a significant element in the determination of organizational goals. However, the important point in the Crozier study is that the power enjoyed by the maintenance men did not arise "naturally." In order to meet their security needs, the maintenance workers organized themselves into a highly cohesive group which systematically disciplined any of its members who attempted to share their "esoteric" knowledge with production workers or supervisors.

In other words, social structure may play a significant part in determining the organization's means of production, the technology or analyzability of search in Perrow's terms. While many studies take a

Marxian viewpoint, one of technological determinism, the reverse is often true. Structure, both formal and informal, as well as human variables can determine technology. The important orientation for the designer of organizations is that of the Tavistock group which concerned itself with the fit or congruence between technical and social systems, not the sovereignty of one or the other.

The fit between technology and social structure is sufficient, then, to provide guidelines for an organizational design. However, two cautions are in order. First, we have been discussing both technology and structure in very general terms. For example, research findings do indicate that for a nonroutine technology an organic structure is likely to produce greater efficiency than several of the other possible combinations described above; however, within the rather global notion of organic structure and the equally global notion of nonroutine technology, certain kinds of arrangements will work better than others. The discussion of work flow patterns provides one example of such a refined discrimination. Considerable research remains to be done in this area.

Second, the process of fitting the technical system to the social system is dynamic. Depending on the nature of the original technology (or structure), a change to a subsequent technology (or structure) may not be better in spite of the intrinsic merits of the innovation. The sequencing of the technologies (or structures) is critical, too. The classic study of leadership climates (Lippitt and White, 1943) which compares the efficacy of a democratic climate following an autocratic climate with the efficacy of the democratic climate which replaced a laissez-faire climate, illustrates the importance of succession dynamics. We shall return to this point in the chapters on organizational change (Chapters 15–19).

DISCUSSION QUESTIONS

1. What sort of technology is employed by the school you attend? Do the school's design and informal structure "fit" this technology?
2. Do you think the same technologies are employed by large and small schools? By Ph.D. and undergraduate programs? By universities and junior colleges? How might these technologies differ?
3. What are some examples of technological change in higher education? What kinds of design modification do these changes imply?
4. What goals do these various educational technologies serve?

REFERENCES

Anshen, Melvin. The manager and the black box. *Harvard Business Review,* 1960, 62 (5) (November–December), 85.
Bell, G. D. Determinants of span of control. *American Journal of Sociology,* 1967, 73, 90–101.

Brady, Rodney H. Computers in top-management decision making. *Harvard Business Review*, 1967, 69 (2) (July–August), 67.

Burlingame, John F. Information technology and decentralization. *Harvard Business Review*, 1961, 63 (5) (November–December), 121.

Burns, Tom, and Stalker, G. M. *The management of innovation.* London: Tavistock Publications, 1961.

Crozier, Michel. *The bureaucratic phenomenon.* Chicago: University of Chicago Press, 1964.

Dearden, John. Can management information be automated? *Harvard Business Review*, 1964, 66 (3) (March–April), 128.

Dearden, John. Myth of real-time management information. *Harvard Business Review*, 1966, 68 (4) (May–June), 123.

Dearden, John. Computers: no impact on divisional control. *Harvard Business Review*, 1967, 69 (1) (January–February), 99.

Emerson, Richard M. Power-dependence relations. *American Sociological Review*, 1962, 27, 31–41.

Hage, Jerald T., and Aiken, Michael. Routine technology, social structure, and organizational goals. *Administrative Science Quarterly*, 1969, *14*, 366–77.

Harvey, E. Technology and the structure of organizations. *American Sociological Review*, 1968, *33*, 247–59.

Hoos, Ida Russakoff. When the computer takes over the office. *Harvard Business Review*, 1960, 62 (5) (November–December), 102.

Horwitz, M. The recall of interrupted group tasks: an experimental study of individual motivation in relation to group goals. *Human Relations*, 1954, 7, 3–38.

Lawrence, Paul R., and Lorsch, Jay W. *Organization and environment: managing differentiation and integration.* Boston: Division of Research, Harvard University Graduate School of Business Administration, 1967.

Leavitt, Harold J. Applied organizational change in industry. In James G. March (Ed.), *Handbook of organizations.* Chicago: Rand McNally, 1965. Pp. 1140–70.

Leavitt, Harold J., and Whisler, Thomas L. Management in the 1980's. *Harvard Business Review*, 1958, 60 (5) (November–December), 41.

Lee, Hak Chong. *The impact of electronic data processing upon patterns of business organization and administration.* Albany, N.Y.: State University of New York at Albany, 1965.

Lewis, H. B., and Franklin, M. An experimental study of the role of ego in work. II. The significance of task orientation in work. *Journal of Experimental Psychology*, 1944, *34*, 195–215.

Likert, Rensis. *The human organization: its management and value.* New York: McGraw-Hill, 1967.

Lippitt, R., and White, R. The "social climate" of children's groups. In R. G. Barker, J. Kounin, and H. Wright (Eds.), *Child behavior and development.* New York: McGraw-Hill, 1943. Pp. 485–508.

Marrow, Alfred J., Bowers, David G., and Seashore, Stanley E. *Management by participation.* New York: Harper & Row, 1967.

Miller, James G. Information input, overload, and psychopathology. *American Journal of Psychiatry*, 1960, *116*, 695–704.

Orwell, George. *Down and out in London and Paris.* New York: Harcourt Brace Jovanovich, 1972.

Perrow, Charles. Hospitals: technology, structure, and goals. In James G. March (Ed.), *Handbook of organizations.* Chicago: Rand McNally, 1965. Pp. 910–71.

Existing Goals	Goals That Should Be

Top Goals (*continued*)	6. Train students in methods of scholarship and/or scientific research and/or creative endeavor	6. Keep up-to-date and responsive
	7. Carry on pure research	7. Maintain top quality in those programs we feel to be especially important
		8. Assist students to develop objectivity about themselves and their beliefs and hence examine those beliefs critically
		9. Make sure the university is run by those selected according to their ability to attain the goals of the university in the most efficient manner possible

*****

*Bottom Goals**	44. Emphasize under-graduate instruction even at the expense of the graduate program	
	45. Involve students in the government of the university	45. Make a good consumer of the student
	46. Keep this place from becoming something different than it is now	46. Involve students in the government of the university
	47. Make a good consumer of the student	47. Keep this place from becoming something different than it is now

Source: Gross (1968, pp. 529–30).

Chapter Guide

Obviously, there is some congruence between existing goals and those that "should be." More revealing, perhaps, are the discrepancies between the two lists. These similarities and discrepancies begin to take on inferred meaning when the following questions are raised:

1. How are faculty/administration interests reflected in the actual and desired university goals?
2. How do you imagine students would have responded to questions about desired university goals? Board of trust members? Townspeople? Hourly paid university employees? Alumni?
3. Are the goals of a university what the faculty and administration perceive them to be, or do students, townspeople, other employees, members of the board of trust, and so on, influence the organization's behavior according to their own objectives and desires?

4. What are goals? Do organizations have goals or are we speaking of a negotiated consensus of the objectives of the organization's members?
5. What do you think is commonly done to reduce the discrepancies between actual and desired goals?
6. How do a university's goals differ from those of a business firm?
7. To what extent do your answers to the preceding questions apply to businesses? Hospitals? Churches?
8. What goals would you influence your university or college to pursue?

CONCEPTS OF GOALS

Organizational Goals

Still following Leavitt's (1965) diagram, we now turn to the study of organizational goals. We often hear an organizational goal described as the end which an organization sanctions and selects; to which it applies its energies and resources in a constructive, purposive manner. The trouble with this line of thinking is that it may conceive the organization as a sentient being possessed of a single mind. Recognition of the numbers of different constituencies to which a given organization is forced to respond renders this statement of organizational goal-setting more a fiction than a description of reality; for example, cadres of professional managers, labor unions, stockholders, and the board of directors can be numbered among the various constituencies which comprise a business firm. In addition, consumers, suppliers, competitors and regulatory agencies singly, and on occasion in concert, serve to constrain the firm's range of behavior and, consequently, its selection of goals. These goals, which the various constituencies would have the organization serve, can in the last analysis be counterproductive.

For a number of reasons, including the existence of multiple constituencies, both students of organizations and managers themselves began to turn from the notion of a specific organizational purpose or

FIGURE 5–1
The Major Variables in Organizations

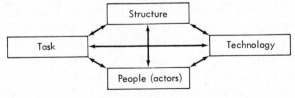

Source: Leavitt (1965, p. 1145).

purposes to the formulation of organizational objectives in broader, more global terms. Long-run profit maximization came into vogue as a legitimate goal in the profit sector. Some writers, such as Drucker (1963), began to advocate long-run survival, as opposed to profit maximization, as the ultimate objective of the firm. Clearly, if the firm survives over the long run, it will have done so because it managed to satisfy a reasonable number of the demands of its major constituencies.

As debate raged over the merits of survival versus long-run profit maximization, a third school of thought emerged. Cyert and March (1963) concluded that organizations do not have objectives; only people have objectives. Therefore, what we have been calling the objectives of the organization are, in essence, no more than a negotiated consensus of the individuals who play major roles in the organization's affairs.

Finally, a number of researchers came to view the concept of organizational goals with suspicion. Katz and Kahn (1966), for example, begin their study of organizations with the following observation:

> In fact, the classic body of theory and thinking about organizations has assumed a teleology of this sort as the easiest way of identifying organizational structures and their functions. From this point of view an organization is a social device for efficiently accomplishing through group means some stated purpose; it is the equivalent of the blueprint for the design of the machine which is to be created for some practical objective. *The essential difficulty with this purposive or design approach is that an organization characteristically includes more and less than is indicated by the design of its founder or the purpose of its leader.* . . . It would be much better theoretically, however, to start with concepts which do not call for identifying the purposes of the designers and then correcting for them when they do not seem to be fulfilled. *The theoretical concepts should begin with the input, output, and functioning of the organization as a system and not with the rational purposes of its leader* (p. 16, italics supplied).

This view flows readily from the "natural systems" model of organization described in Chapter 1. While agreeing essentially with Katz and Kahn about the problems in a purposive view of organizational goals, we shall not take quite as strong a position in support of organizations as nonpurposive or nonrational systems. The organizational designer must at least start with a view of organizational goals in terms of purposes.

We shall attempt to infer the goals of the organization from a variety of sources: Its formal goals; the actual purposive activity of members; the goals for the organization held by stakeholders; and the constraints and negotiated arrangements arising from conflict between various groupings in the organization. The notion of organizational goals is a difficult one, but with these various perspectives as bench marks, we hope to provide a more or less accurate and useful picture of the organization's goals—of where it is heading.

Formal Goals

Just as we found in Chapter 3 that the formal organization gives rise
to informal structures, so we find that an organization's formally stated
goals are interlaced with informal goals and agendas. This observation,
in fact, lends a measure of order to the apparent chaos in the literature
cited above. In contrast to Cyert and March, we contend that organizations do have goals, however ambiguously stated, which are also part of
the organization's culture and which transcend the needs and motives
of individuals and influential groups. The fact that these goals, which
are generally vague in the first place, are clouded further by informal
goals leads writers such as Katz and Kahn to despair, justifiably, of ever
understanding an organization through its stated, formal objectives.

However, we will not abandon the concept of goals as a meaningful
area of concern for the organizational designer. While the goals of an
organization are not often changed and, indeed, are difficult to change,
an understanding of the determinants of goals will enable us to take
advantage of opportunities to design new organizations with new goals
and to modify the goals of existing organizations. Obviously, changes in
goals can imply alterations to the organization's sociotechnical system
and to its design in general.

Determinants of Goals

Focusing our attention primarily on the *determinants of goals* and
the *goal-setting process* will steer us clear of normative statements—
statements about what the goals of an organization should be. We will
not concern ourselves with whether a firm ought to establish long-run
profit maximization or survival as its goal. Rather, we will attempt to
describe the manner in which goals are determined through analysis of
theory and empirical data, including case histories. By being descriptive and studying the behavior by which actual goals are set, we provide
the organization designer with the opportunity to be normative, to select
from actual goals those he or she desires, and then to implement the
means for achieving those goals that are described below.

We can begin our inquiry into the nature of goals by acknowledging
the existence of formal goals which are usually recorded in the organization's charter, annual reports, public statements by key executives, and
other authoritative pronouncements. They range, according to the type
of organization in question, from profitability in the business sector to
the "celebration of life" in one religious organization with which the
authors are familiar. Usually they are purposely vague and general,
allowing different constituencies to collaborate in the same organizational framework. Their ambiguity provides a philosophical framework

for organizational decisions rather than a system of criterion measures against which day-to-day performance and decisions can be checked. After all, how does one decide whether a particular action will eventually lead to the long-run maximization of the firm's profits?

The formal goals or purposes of an organization tend not only to be vague, but, according to a number of sociologists, may even be positively misleading. These purposes are part of the organization's culture and "are not meant to be realized" (Etzioni, 1964, p. 260). A report of over 20 women's study clubs, founded early in this century as part of the general women's suffrage movement, showed that practically identical constitutions and statements of purpose may coexist with extremely varied functioning to meet the needs of members or of their respective communities (Warriner, 1965). Sociologists have provided a number of examples of such contrasts between formal purposes and actual functioning: A community service club whose service is an incidental part of its activities as measured by allocations of time and money to these activities, with the club showing considerable financial benefits from its "services" of selling products made by the handicapped, and so on (Warriner, 1965); prisons with the stated aim to rehabilitate or "cure" but which may spend very little time or money on such services and instead primarily function in a custodial fashion, putting walls between the prisoner and society (Zald, 1963); and political organizations which espouse democracy but are internally ruled by leaders who do not countenance their replacement by any democratic procedures (Michels, 1959).

As Warriner (1965) suggests: "Statements of purpose, thus, must be treated as fictions produced by an organization to account for, explain, or rationalize its existence to particular audiences rather than as valid and reliable indicators of purpose" (p. 141). Much as some overseas companies are reputed to have different sets of accounts for the tax collector, the shareholders, and the company management, organizations are likely to have one or more sets of purposes for different constituencies.

Operative Goals

As a result of their generality, formal goals, according to Perrow (1970), are likely to obscure the operation of two major influences on organizational behavior: (1) the many decisions that must be made among *alternative means* for achieving formal goals, including the priorities which must be set in the presence of multiple goals, and (2) the *unofficial goals* pursued by groups and individual members of the organization. Perrow combines these two forces under the rubric of "operative goals"—the ends which are sought through the actual functioning of the organization.

Operative goals may specify the manner in which certain formal goals are to be attained; for example, profit goals can be met through the pursuit of operative goals such as the attainment of efficiencies of scale, market penetration, and the like. The study of operative goals is worthwhile for several reasons. First, they frequently suggest the criteria against which subsequent organizational performance is measured. Related to this is the tendency for the organization, or subunits within the organization, to embrace the operative goals as surrogates for the organization's formal goals. This phenomenon has been referred to as "suboptimization," or functioning at a less than optimal level because subgoals or a particular subset of the ultimate goal serves as a focus of efforts. The marketing department may push for a high volume of sales even though one of the items marketed may cost more to make and sell than the price at which it is sold. A production subunit comprising highly skilled craftsmen may spend a great deal of effort on finishing a product to very close tolerances and producing a "quality" product, when its use by customers does not require such high tolerances and, in fact, the product's price is more important to customers than quality. Finally, some operative goals are ties to individual or group interests and occasionally become irrelevant to, if not subversive of, the organization's formal goals; for example, a key executive may hold financial interests in an organization which is a supplier to his own. Similarly, the prestige associated with the possession of heart-lung machines and other forms of sophisticated technology has been known to lure some hospitals away from their stated goal of providing excellent patient care. In cases such as these, pressures for policies and operating decisions are based primarily on the interests of the parties involved.

Behavioral versus Rationalist Study of Goals

Perrow's view (1970) is distinctly behavioral and descriptive and can be contrasted with the rationalist and often normative approach which emphasizes the formal goals of the organization. The rational model portrays the organization as focusing its energies on the realization of desirable, although perhaps poorly defined, goals such as profit-maximization and long-run survival. In doing so, the organization's management is expected to articulate alternative means for achieving these ends. Top management selects from among the alternatives those which are most productive. The means thus chosen become the lower order goals for the next level of managers who, in turn, set means for the accomplishment of their goals. This latter set of means gives rise to a set of goals for the next lower level of management, and so on. Following this logic, many studies of organizational goals emphasize the goals which are usually formally articulated and which are consciously held by individuals or subgroups within the organization. While a social-psychological point of view describes the goals of individuals within an organization, the sum of individuals' goals may not equal the goal of the entire organization.

Here, we shall take a lead from Etzioni's (1964) definition: "An organizational goal is a desired state of affairs which the organization attempts to realize . . ." (p. 6). But *whose* desired state of affairs? We do not mean the various goals that various individuals have *for* the organization (e.g., "I think this organization should . . ."), although certain individuals or groups may have a strong influence on the goals of the organization. A view of goals as norms is not sufficient either—the view that the ". . . group goals represent an operating consensus about a desirable state of a given task" (Thibaut and Kelley, 1959, p. 257). In contrast, we emphasize goals *of* the organization which are more than the sum of private, individual goals and which are usually different from the publicly espoused purpose(s) of the organization.

Pointing the way, Warriner (1965) looks first at the behavior of the organization or at its activities. After determining the amount of member time (resources) devoted to these, he focuses on the most prevalent and important in terms of resource utilization. For Warriner, the assumed functions (i.e., the assumed consequences or results) of these activities give the purposes:

> Thus a particular mental hospital is judged to be a custodial rather than a therapeutic institution because, taking each of its activities separately, the staff attitude toward and conception of each activity is that it is designed and carried out either (1) to protect the staff, (2) to protect the patient, (3) to keep the patient manageable, or (4) to keep him physically in the institution (Warriner, 1965, p. 142).

Warriner refers to the "collective assumptions" and the "specific set of logics which members accept as the frame of reference for participating in the organization" (p. 143). As we shall see below, this concept is quite close to Simon's (1964) and Buck's (1966) "constraints." The important point, however, is that Warriner focuses first and foremost on behavior, and ascertains individuals' intentions or understandings of certain behaviors. Much as the psychologist develops the construct "attitude" from, and as an explanation of, individual behavior, we would suggest that one may observe behavior and infer a construct—not necessarily a real "intention" or "understanding," but a scientific construct akin to attitude for understanding the organization and its behavior. We would term this scientific construct for studying purposive behavior an organizational goal. In the course of this chapter, we hope to show, by examination of examples of goal behavior and the inferred organizational construct, how a suprapsychological approach to organizational goals is feasible and useful.

Output, System, Product Characteristics, and Derived Goals

Unlike Drucker (1963) and others, and more in line with the reasoning of Katz and Kahn (1966), Perrow assumes that goals can be inferred directly from the organization's behavior. In developing his study of operative goals, Perrow attempts to categorize various areas of endeavor in which organizations strive; for example, for one organization, the goal of maintaining certain product characteristics may be the single most influential determinant of the organization's behavior, over and above profit. Alternatively, another organization may take growth as its primary concern. Goals of this sort are important in that they often describe the uniqueness and "character" of the organization.

This categorization of areas of endeavor gives rise, in turn, to four distinct classes of goals.[1]

1. *Output Goals.* The kinds of output produced—such as consumer goods, services for other organizations, health care, and education.
2. *System Goals.* System characteristics such as growth, stability, profitability, decentralization, centralization, and efficiency.
3. *Product Goals.* The characteristics of goods or services produced such as quality, quantity, styling, availability, uniqueness, and innovativeness.
4. *Derived Goals.* The use to which organizations put the power which they generate such as political aims, employee development, and community service.

A brief summary of Perrow's investigation of operative goals lends interesting and provocative insights into the phenomena of organizational behavior.

Output Goals

A study of organizations' output goals directs our attention to boundary phenomena, particularly to the influence systems which exist between organizations and their environments. An historical view of universities, for example, brings our attention to changes in output goals which have occurred in response to society's shifting preferences for the output of various educational programs. Agricultural, business, and teacher-training programs have found legitimacy in academia largely as a result of society's demand for individuals who possess advanced knowledge and skills in these areas. Similarly, firms once interested primarily in the manufacture of goods have undertaken to enhance the work-related skills of individuals hitherto unemployable.

---

[1] Perrow's (1970) categorization scheme, in fact, includes five goals. We have omitted from our discussion the category of Societal Goals, which, in Perrow's words, ". . . has little to do with functioning organizations" (p. 135).

Thus, in response to perceived pressures, threats, and opportunities, organizations alter and expand their goals. In terms of expansion, law enforcement agencies may provide social services; businesses may engage in planning and developing new towns; and universities, which were once aloof and isolated centers of learning for the intellectual elite, may now supply public entertainment through their athletic departments. Yet, this tendency toward the expansion of output goals often runs afoul of the apparent societal norm which holds that output functions should be widely distributed among independent organizations (Perrow, 1965). The resistance of conservatives and business executives to the formation of the TVA was founded, in part, on their reluctance to permit a governmental agency to produce such commodities as electricity and fertilizer (Selznick, 1949). Similar fears are expressed today concerning the military-industrial complex. Such fears, no doubt, have their roots in our culture's aversion to centralized power and authority, and a concomitant belief in Adam Smith's "invisible hand."

Finally, Perrow brings to our attention the magnitude of organizational change which is implied in altering output goals. Management skills for a given type of output may not be directly appropriate to the management of production of a dissimilar type of product. Perrow cites the example in which the management and organizational skills which served Ford's purposes so well were apparently less effective in the management of the Philco Corporation, which Ford purchased in an attempt to diversify its output goals (Siekman, 1966). We recall from Chapter 4 that different technologies are likely to influence the nature of the organization's structure and behavior. Thus, the behavior which an organization finds effective in utilizing one technological process may be less than satisfactory in dealing with a different technology adopted through the introduction of a new output goal.

System Goals

System goals refer to characteristics of the organization as an organization rather than to its products or services. Organizations are systems, and in order to survive and continue to function, they must be concerned with more than output (Etzioni, 1964). Included as system goals are growth, stability, profitability, and efficiency. These refer to aspects of the system that may receive top priority beyond that of producing one or another kind of output. Growth in research funding, for example, may be a goal for a research center, rather than producing quality research. Mohr (1973) refers to these kinds of goals as "reflexive"—the referent is the organization, in contrast to the external or output referent found in what he terms "transitive" goals. By way of illustration, Perrow points to the history of Eastern Airlines and the im-

portance of efficiency. This company, which for many years held a near
monopoly on its most profitable routes, pursued the goal of cost reduction with the consequence of reducing customer service. This situation
served the company well for many years until two events transpired.
First, the Civil Aeronautics Board decided to strengthen the smaller
lines by giving them access to the more profitable routes. Second, the
newly encouraged competition began to make inroads into Eastern's
business by attracting customers with improved services. After suffering
a substantial setback, Eastern, by this time under a new top-management regime, altered its system goals to become more like its competitors.

In terms of such organizational goals as profit-maximization and
long-run survival, Eastern may have been poorly managed. Even if this
statement is true, it tells us very little. Through his analysis of operative
goals, however, Perrow lends considerable insight into the company's
history. As Perrow concludes:

> A more telling explanation would be that mismanagement was not
> the problem and that, rather, the system goal pursued by Rickenbacker
> (Eastern's Chairman of the Board) deserved analysis. Given the goal of
> maximizing profits through cost reduction, his preoccupation with fru-
> gality served the company extremely well for 25 years. Had the environ-
> ment not changed and had his successors continued his policy, there
> would have been no question that the company had been extremely well
> managed. . . . We know very little about the other companies, but it
> does not appear that they were all mismanaged while Eastern made
> money, or that they were all well managed when Eastern lost money.
> The other companies simply had different goals, and when their goals
> of growth and product innovation began to pay off, Eastern had to
> change its goals, too (Perrow, 1970, p. 150).

The point, obviously, is that an organization is open to its environment and must alter its goals and behavior appropriately as the environment changes. The study of cybernetic systems tells us that responses to feedback and other external stimuli must be dampened; that
is, restrained. Instantaneous response is something never found in
nature, and for good reason. An organism or machine that responds
immediately to each and every change in the signals to which it must
ultimately respond will quickly overload and break down. Damping allows the organism to remain unresponsive within tolerable limits. Thus,
a thermostat will allow room temperature to vary several degrees around
the desired temperature before activating the heating system.

As a cybernetic system, Eastern overdamped. Responses to changes
in the environment were delayed until a crisis became evident. In studying goals as they affect organizational behavior then, we must consider
the notion that goals may only make sense as they are related to the
environment. This not only implies that their initial formulation must
be responsive to environmental factors, but that periodic monitoring of

the environment is essential to maintaining viable goals. Furthermore, management must utilize theoretical constructs which indicate both significant variables in the environment and the kinds of effects which changes in these variables are likely to produce in the organization's relationship to the environment.

Product Characteristic Goals

That most organizations have product characteristic goals becomes most apparent when one observes the occasional organization which has none. This type of organization is typified by the firm that will handle any product as long as it is profitable, helps the organization grow, or is a means to some other kind of goal. Thus, some supermarket chains have turned to nonfood items as means to their system goal of profit. Against this kind of organization, we can contrast those whose behavior is centered around some readily identifiable product goals. The A&P nicely illustrates product goal behavior in its emphasis on the provision of high-quality, low-priced foods to the consumer. Most of A&P's capital has been invested in their own plants for producing A&P baked goods, dairy products, meats, fruits and vegetables, while competitors have been investing in larger stores to handle more profitable nonfood items and to operate more efficiently by means of higher volumes at lower overheads.

An even more striking example of an organization's behavior being shaped by its very specific product goals is Volkswagen. Early in 1972, Volkswagen's production of the familiar Beetle passed the 15 million mark and with that the long-standing record for production runs set by the Ford Model T. In observing this remarkable achievement, Ball (1972) drew other similarities between Volkswagen and Ford during the Model T era. While the buyer of a Beetle can have a choice of a variety of colors, the car's styling and its rear-mounted, air-cooled engine rendered successive years' models indistinguishable, except to the practiced eye. The company expanded its product line by the introduction of the VW Transporter in 1950, the Karmann Ghia in 1955, and the larger Type Three in 1961. The next new model, the 411, was clearly an attempt to apply the basic Volkswagen engineering and design principles to a car that would appeal to buyers in the middle-income bracket. Ball's appraisal of this tactic is that:

> By 1968, however, the auto world was becoming tired of the formula. Wags greeted the 411 with the gibe that it was so named because it had four doors and was introduced eleven years too late (Ball, 1972, p. 98).

One implication that can be drawn from Volkswagen's experience is that certain design characteristics (especially the air-cooled rear engine) of the Beetle came, in time, to assume the proportions of the design goals. Yet, as it turned out, the basic formula which served the company so well over a production run of 15 million cars appears in the process of becoming incompatible with the changing market for economy cars. Vega, Toyota, Datsun, and others have made substantial inroads into Volkswagen's U.S. market by producing economy cars which appear to come closer to reflecting today's consumer preferences. Even more apparent is that the product goals manifested in the ubiquitous Beetle were not amenable to the design of a car for today's middle-class market.

The introduction of the Audi 100 appears as a departure from Volkswagen's former product goals—but there is an interesting story behind the car. Volkswagen acquired Auto Union in order to use its productive capacity to manufacture Beetles. After the acquisition though, the Volkswagen management assigned to the company, together with former Auto Union personnel, collaborated on the design of an automobile which had been on Auto Union's drawing board prior to the takeover. Work on the Audi 100 was carried out without the direct knowledge of top management at Volkswagen. Surprisingly, Volkswagen's management approved the final design and the Audi 100 became a runaway success (Ball, 1972).

Derived Goals

Finally, it is important to recognize that organizations wield considerable influence in areas other than their marketplace, and the wielding of this interest may become a central issue for the organization, a matter of interest to management, and an organizational goal. Profit-making corporations, for example, not only contribute large sums of money to universities, public service agencies, and the like, they also may use their philanthropy as leverage to modify the organizations which they support. By the same token, lobbies, in behalf of their constituents, exert pressure on legislators in order to influence legislation which affects them.

In more subtle ways, organizations can change the quality of life around them by erecting buildings which fail to conform to the architectural themes of the locales or by altering the flow of traffic within these areas. Supporting political parties, altering the public's tastes through advertising, and providing or withholding goods and services from the marketplace are only a few of the ways in which organizations strive toward the realization of derived goals.

As important as these phenomena are to our understanding of organizations, we must conclude, along with Perrow (1970), that much ignorance still prevails in this general area of "social responsibility":

> These issues also constitute a topic which is appended to the business school training program with little enthusiasm, many generalities, and much oracular moralism. The whole question deserves better, not only because economic organizations have an enormous impact upon our

society, but because derived goals become embedded in organizations and should be closely examined if we wish to understand organizations. Neither the simplicities of the radical left nor the mushy self-congratulation of the business community will suffice (Perrow, 1970, p. 171).

MANAGING STAKEHOLDER EXPECTATIONS

Stakeholder Expectations

How can goals vary so greatly from one organization to another? How do operative goals come to be? One way of explaining the genesis of organizational goals is found in the examination of "stakeholder" expectations. By stakeholders, we mean those groups of individuals which have a legitimate interest in determining the behavior of the organizations in question. This right may be contingent on membership (e.g., managers or workers), investments in the organization (e.g., owners, benefactors of various kinds), contractual arrangements (suppliers), norms of reciprocity (e.g., competitors and other organizations in the environment), or ultimate sovereignty (the nation). Each class of stakeholders has somewhat different expectations *for* the organization, which are related to the goals and interests of the various stakeholders themselves. From the interaction of these various goals *for* the organization, the goals *of* the organization are likely to emerge.

Conflict of Expectations

The example provided in Figure 5–2 illustrates indicative, but not exhaustive, sets of expectations of some of the stakeholders in a professional graduate school. *Example (1)* brings to light a familiar illustration of the "town-gown" problem. In attempting to provide its students with a broad and objective view of current social issues, a school may invite guest speakers who, in the eyes of more conservative members of the community, are perceived as subversive of the community's values (e.g., Ralph Nader).

When the two sets of expectations come into conflict, as they do in the hypothetical example provided above, several strategies may be undertaken by both parties.

1. Initially, administrators tend to view problems such as this as the result of misunderstandings. Consequently, a "public relations" program may be undertaken under the assumption that once members of the community learn of the function which such speakers have in the educational process, they will come to view these activities in a favorable light; that is, in the same way that educators view them. Failing this, several alternative strategies can be undertaken depending on the predispositions of the parties involved.

FIGURE 5–2
Intersections of Stakeholder Expectations

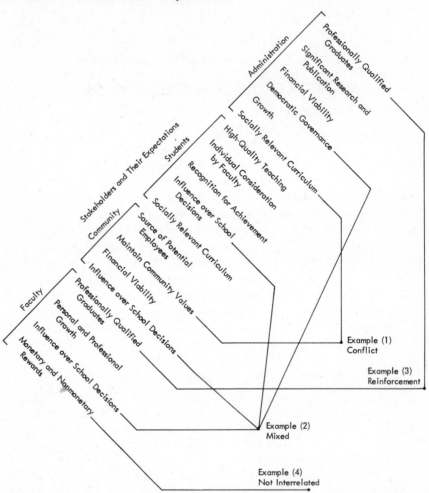

2.   Co-optation can be attempted by inviting the major critics of the school's programs to join (in limited numbers) the groups which are responsible for their planning and implementation.

3.   Alternatively, the school may withdraw from contact with the community and proceed in insularity.

4.   Other administrators may choose to meet the community's opposition with power. The authors know of one administrator who, when opposed by an influential banker in matters which affected the operation of his school, sought the appointment of one of the banker's largest customers to his advisory council. Having secured the cooperation of the latter individual and finding him to be in sympathy with the school's

aims, the administrator proceeded to arrange for the depositor to wield his influence over the banker in matters which had hitherto been sources of conflict.

Throughout dealings of this sort, the community maintains the power to withhold its support (usually financial) from the school. It is interesting to note that, while the organization is subject to threat (loss of community support), the typical responses noted above possess the common thread of altering the environment, or the organization's relationships with the environment, so that organizational goals can be attained in unaltered form.

5. It is sufficient to note here that the above responses are in counterdistinction to attempts to adapt to the environment, which is a strategy for handling conflict that should only be used with caution. Obviously, the many constituencies and interest groups which exist in the university's environment are prone to disagree on many matters. Thus, to yield to the expectations of one group is to invite the displeasure of others. More important, however, is the notion that a degree of autonomy is essential if the organization is to meet objectives which are unique to the values of higher education.

Mixed Expectations

Example (2) in Figure 5–2 provides an illustration of those instances in which the goals of a single group of stakeholders become subsumed by the entire organization. Prior to the 1960s, universities tended to make decisions which affected their members without consulting the groups so affected. However, throughout the 1960s rising expectations among members of various student bodies gave rise to the demands that student opinions and interests be included in the decision-making process. Lacking formal authority or sanctioned power, students united to bring pressures to bear on university administrators. By building cadres of supporters among sympathetic faculty members and by resorting to "direct action" politics, students were able to cause their goals to be adopted by other stakeholders in the universities. Thus, in 1975, administrators and faculty members alike give at least lip service, and, in many instances, formal organizational support, to democratic student representation in the formal decision-making machinery of the organization. This is not to say that all stakeholders in the university view student participation in decision making as a legitimate system goal. However, while certain stakeholders among alumni and community groups may abhor, for instance, the university's acquiescence to student requests for coeducational dormitories (and even student participation in the decision-making process in general), unequal distributions of power between the administration, faculty, and students on the one hand and alumni and community members on the other may virtually preclude the expectations of the later. Nor does the example suggest that all members of the faculty, administration, or student body agree with the goal of participatory democracy. As is the case with organizational norms, deviations manifest themselves throughout the institution's population.

Reinforcing Expectations

Example (3) illustrates expectations which are reinforcing in that they are shared by a number of stakeholders. The output goal of a graduate school is likely to be shared by members throughout the organization largely because it is a major determinant of individual's motivations to associate themselves with the organization. Because some goals are widely held, perhaps they tend to remain unquestioned and unaltered except in times of organizational crisis.

Unsupported Expectations

Finally, *Example* (4) provides an illustration of an expectation held by only one group of stakeholders that is, consequently, unlikely to become an organizational goal. While the faculty may view salaries and other incentives as legitimate goals, administrators tend to view them as means or inducements to other organizational ends. Students and members of the community, furthermore, may view the matter with benign indifference. Thus, unlike an entrepreneural venture, the university exists, not to provide a financial return to some of its stakeholders, but rather to view remuneration as an activity which is necessary to the accomplishment of other goals.

Propositions about Stakeholder Expectations

From the brief illustrations of stakeholder expectations provided above, we can draw a number of propositions.

1. The likelihood that a stakeholder expectation will become an organizational goal is directly proportional to the number of influential stakeholder groups that share the expectation.
2. The likelihood that a goal will be questioned or changed is inversely proportional to the number of influential stakeholder groups whose expectations are served by the goal.
3. The likelihood that a stakeholder expectation will become an organizational goal is inversely proportional to the number of influential stakeholder groups that oppose the expectation in question.[2]

---

[2] For example, when community expectations conflict with those of the organization, as can be the case in matters of racial equality, the existence of governmental and foundation support together with the diversity of racial attitudes within the community serve to limit the influence of stakeholders who oppose organizational moves toward equality. This illustration can be contrasted with the case of the student power movement, where, aside from some administrators and faculty members, few sources of influence were aligned against the cause of "student rights."

Clarity of Goals

The discussion of stakeholder expectations provides a static rather than a dynamic picture of goals; it fails to tell us of the process whereby expectations may become shared among stakeholders. A recent analysis of the determinants that clarify organizational goals contributes to the understanding of this process. Wieland (1969) defines goal clarity to comprise both (1) relatively widespread goal information and (2) agreement on the information (i.e., agreement about the goals).

In contrast, lack of clarity in goals may comprise (1) ambiguity, or lack of information in the system, or (2) conflicts between alternative goals. A lack of clarity may be undesirable for a number of reasons. Goals which are unclear may prevent members from using the organization in an efficient manner (March and Simon, 1958); the combined efforts of an organization's members may be no more productive than the sum of the efforts of the same individuals, were they not organized. Unclear goals, or what Warner and Havens (1968) have called "intangible" goals, are also subject to displacement by more tangible means. Governmental bureaucracies, which may not have clear and specifiable outcomes, may overemphasize organizational means, such as rules about how to keep records or procedures for dealing with clients, at the expense of organizational goals such as helping the client (Merton, 1957). Perrow (1970) makes the most telling point: Goals are an important resource to an organization; they are a form of structure around which efforts are organized and thereby made relatively efficient. They keep the organization from wavering because of vagrant pressures, internal or external, and keep it directed to the task. Not all goals are "good"—some may be inappropriate in terms of environmental conditions; some we may disagree with; but having a clear goal(s) means that the organization can bring its resources and organized forces to bear on the subject in an efficient manner.

Communication and Goal Clarity

A study of organizational goals in 12 liberal arts colleges (Wieland, 1969) reveals that communications and influence processes may play important roles in determining goal clarity. Communication was found to be important for clarity, but interestingly enough, the *frequency* of use of various channels of communication was for the most part not associated with clarity. The amount of contact between faculty and department heads and between faculty and the dean was not related to perceived goal clarity. However, it was found that (1) the "interest" of the dean in faculty ideas and (2) the frequency of off-campus, noncollege contacts between various ranks in the college were positively associated with clarity of the goals of the college.

If one views clear goals as organizational norms or forms of informal social structure, then the human relations literature explored in Chapter 3, particularly Likert (1967) and Tannenbaum (1968), provides an insight into the general process whereby goals can be established in an organization. Communication obviously is essential to the process. However, the sharing of information in itself is insufficient. The information which is shared must be *influential*. Individuals must communicate in such a way that they influence and convince the recipients of the communications. As we saw in Chapter 3, an organization with high total influence is one in which various groups are able to influence one another and the organization as a whole. In such an organization, one might expect to find strong social norms, including a normative structure from which we may, in part, infer a goal.

Conflicting Goals

This analysis of the determinants of goal clarity is based on an assumption that clarity is desirable to improve efficiency. However, one should not overlook the possible value of conflicting goals to an organization. In fact, conflict in goals may be consciously created to facilitate organizational performance in certain areas, particularly organizational flexibility (Wilson, 1966) and organizational innovativeness and even efficiency (Buck, 1966). Buck suggests that mutually exclusive goals may be purposefully induced by a superior. The subordinate is simply instructed to maximize every dimension of his or her job (and sufficient resources are not made available): Produce at a high level; adhere to the safest procedures; reduce wastes and other costs to a minimum; and so on. The subordinate may respond by using a sequential approach, first maximizing one, then another dimension (Cyert and March, 1963) especially if the subordinate can ascertain which particular dimension the superior is interested in at the moment. Buck (1966) describes other wasteful ways of dealing with such goal conflict: "Just in case the boss asks me" files, "boilerhoused" records, and so on. On the other hand, if the individual is capable and motivated, he may come up with a solution to the problem of conflicting goals, and thereby make the organization more efficient by means of his innovative procedures.

In our discussion of goals here we have touched several times on the existence of conflict in the goal-setting process—in discussing both stakeholders and some advantages of having unclear goals. At this point, we must introduce the view that conflict is endemic in the goal-setting process and in organizations generally. In this school of thought, we find such views as: "organization as a coalition" (Cyert and March, 1963), "goals as the result of a continuous bargaining-learning process" (Cyert and March, 1963), "organization as a system of constraints" (Buck, 1966), and finally a statement by Thompson (1967):

. . . organizational goals are established by . . . interdependent individuals who collectively have sufficient control of organizational resources to commit them in certain directions and to withhold them from others (p. 128).

On the psychological level of analysis, this view emphasizes that organizational activities are subject to a great deal of control and coordination in ways that are not immediately visible to the outside observer (Perrow, 1972). This approach suggests that the organization must control decision premises, for not only do human beings have their own interests which may deviate from others and from the organization, but they also have limited rationality.

Decision Premises

Individuals are controlled not only by rules or direct orders, but also by "decision premises" (March and Simon, 1958). As Perrow (1972) relates . . . "the vast proportion of the activity in organizations goes on without personal directives and supervision—and even without written rules—and sometimes in permitted violation of the rules" (p. 156).

To control decision premises and ultimately behavior, organizations and supervisors use a variety of mechanisms which are incorporated in members' organizational roles. For one thing, organizations have their own "vocabularies." The conventional vocabulary provides ways in which the organization can deal with environmental uncertainty and internal problems of control. The organizational vocabulary makes members "see" certain things in the environment and ignore others. In most organizations, the superior generally gives few orders but instead is a priority-setter, suggesting to subordinates that certain matters require their attention first, or second, and so on. He provides or withholds information in accordance with the attention-set he wishes to create. Subordinates may question the propriety of certain information and implied actions, but only if contradictory information is not withheld.

According to Simon (1964), an individual decision maker's behavior can also be understood in terms of the premises, or "constraints," on his decisions. Each individual is subject to a whole set of constraints which are imposed as part of his organization role and which his decision-making must satisfy. A constraint may not seem like a goal, but according to Simon: "If you allow me to determine the constraints, I don't care who selects the optimization criterion" (1964, p. 6). Thus if one can select a constraint that reduces the set of possible behaviors, he or she will have influence in directing the organization's behavior, whatever conscious "goal" the decision maker may have in mind.

Simon suggests that goals are usually multiple and such sets of goals comprise elements with two different functions; namely, (1) to synthesize proposed solutions (alternative generation), and (2) to test the quality of a proposed solution (alternative testing). The former is quite important, since alternatives must be generated before they can be tested, and the sequence by which the decision maker generates alternatives greatly affects the alternative finally chosen. However, as Simon suggests, if the constraints, or tests for quality, are set strongly enough, they can have the most influence over the direction of behavior.

Constraints

Now, the alternative generators in one part of the organization may well become the tests in another part, and vice versa. Marketing attempts to sell a high-quality product that is attractive to customers while production attempts to produce a high volume of goods at minimal cost. The marketing department's goal of high quality becomes a constraint for production, and quality controls are established so that a certain standard is reached, even though production costs are increased. The production department's goal of efficiency is likely to serve as a constraint to marketing, which refrains from promising to sell a customer a modified version of the product, requiring a costly change in production setup. The set of "widely shared constraints" becomes the goals of the organization. Thus one such constraint, profit, may not enter directly into the decision making of most members of a business organization and, yet, it may influence members either directly or indirectly and influence the behavior of the organization as a whole. If one looks only at the alternative generators, suggests Simon, one may see very different goals throughout the organization, but the behavior of individuals and the organization as a whole is determined by both alternative generators and tests, by a "widely shared set of constraints" or premises which are part of individuals' organizational roles. We shall see below that these premises pertain not only to goals but also to the means by which goals are achieved.

Conflict and Power

Building on the more psychological work of Simon, Cyert and March (1963) advocate the conflict approach to the study of goals. According to these theorists, organizations are created to be rational and to mobilize means toward certain ends, but they are subject to various problems and uncertainties which hinder this process. Resources often are inadequate to deal with the uncertainties of the environment and the task. For one thing, man is not omniscient; there are limits to his cognitive functioning, and he suffers from information overload. Often, physical resources are similarly limited. Referring to "the variable human" and the "exercise of discretion," Thompson (1967) discusses the interactions of such limitations, uncertainty, and individual aspirations, which lead to such phenomena as "evading discretion," "selecting tasks which promise to enhance scores on assessment criteria," "stockpiling," "reporting successes and suppressing evidence of failures," and, most importantly and extensively, "seeking to maintain power," and "forming coalitions." In short, the organization as a whole is not completely rational. Because of various limits on organizational members (and because of their self-interests), various interdependencies are created between them (and between members and the organization's environment), so that decision makers must take into account the power of having others dependent on themselves, as well as the power of others because of their own dependency on them (Emerson, 1964). Through the workings of these power relationships in the organization as a whole, a dominant coalition is likely to arise, and the objectives established by these interdependent individuals are likely to become the goals of the organization (Thompson, 1967).

We shall follow Cyert and March (1963) and their specification of three major ways in which the objectives of a coalition are determined: (1) a bargaining process in which the composition and terms of the coalition are set, (2) a control process for stabilizing and elaborating objectives, and (3) a learning process in which objectives are adjusted according to experience with the environment.

Earlier we discussed the goals which stakeholders or individuals might have for an organization. These goals will likely include the individual's own goals, his or her desires for pay, or other inducements. These expectations are easily met by the organization. However, because there are limits to organizational resources and to what an organization can do vis-à-vis the environment at any one time, the goals for the organization concerning its major directions are not so easily met. This is often a "zero-sum game" (my gains are your losses or vice versa) rather than a "variable-sum" game, and the mode of interaction usually includes negotiating and bargaining over the interests of the various parties, as well as problem solving in a collaborative mode (Walton and McKersie, 1965).

Stabilization of Conflict

Not all organizational life is characterized by high levels of conflict and tense bargaining, of course. To spare members negotiating every single matter, which would be very wasteful of energy, the organization creates certain relatively enduring patterns of behavior (Thibaut and Kelley, 1959). In fact, individuals' limitations require them to simplify and to accept most of their environment as given and to focus on only a few important matters at any one time. This is also true for the organization as a whole. Centralization of all problem solving in the hands of single individuals is usually not possible; organizations must be decentralized to some degree. Some decisions are made and some goals are attended to at lower levels, others at higher levels. Similarly, departments or divisions or other forms of horizontal divisions of labor attend primarily to one goal, while other subsystems attend to other goals.

While some conflict exists between these subsystem goals, it is stabilized because of the premise setting described by Simon and by the negotiated order in which some of the goals of one system serve as the constraints of another and vice versa.

Side Payments

According to Cyert and March, the goals of the organization are created by the "side payments" or exchanges made in the process of coalition formation among individuals and subsystems. A number of these side payments go beyond the simple rewards given for accepting coalition desires or rewards for the opportunity to control others; these significant side payments take the form of policy commitments. In the bargaining over side payments, Cyert and March see many of the organization's objectives being defined and established. This negotiated order does not mean complete agreement exists across the organization regarding the organization's goals. First of all, members may agree to disagree; production may allow marketing to do whatever it wants in certain selling activities as long as the volume of orders and the demands for product changes remain within certain limits; marketing also accepts "deviant" behavior on the part of production as long as their customer-determined quality standards and delivery times are met. Sometimes these agreements to disagree are not conscious. Subsystems go their separate ways within very wide overall organizational limits. In other words, there can be considerable suboptimization because of divergent subsystem goals. There is "local rationality" and, at best, only quasi-resolution of conflict. This is especially feasible, according to Cyert and March, if the organization is relatively benign. As we shall describe below, conflict between goals can also be handled by segregating them in time; i.e., by giving sequential attention to goals (Cyert and March, 1963).

Sequential Attention

With regard to the negotiated organizational objectives, Cyert and March suggest that various mutual control systems, such as budgets and allocation mechanisms, are created. The objectives of the organization, as stabilized by these structures, are generally renegotiated periodically, sometimes at certain set times. Thus, at budget-setting time, the organization reexamines past expenditures and considers whether more or less ought to be expended on each program or department. The budget-setting process either directly or indirectly questions expenditures on particular objectives and ultimately, whether these objectives should be modified in light of experience. In between the yearly budget setting, these questions tend not to be raised and there is a relative absence of conflict about the nature of the organization's goals.

Cyert and March view organizations as generally dealing with conflict between goals by using "sequential attention," much as the individual does in problem solving, first attending to one problem, then another, rather than all of life's problems at once. The organization may devote extra resources to first one department (subsystem) and its problems and goals, and then to another. The department receiving attention will attempt to enforce its constraints on other departments and its constraints on other departments will take precedence. In terms of the five usual operational goals given by Cyert and March, then, the organization may focus attention first on (1) a production (smoothing or level-of-production) goal for a time, then on (2) an inventory goal, then (3) a (level of) sales goal, (4) a market share goal, and finally, (5) a profit goal. Of course, the order of sequential attention may be rearranged, depending on the emergence of environmental or internal problems or perhaps new power coalitions.

GOALS AS DETERMINANTS OF DECISIONS

Organizational Problems and Goal-Setting

We have seen that the process of goal-setting is complicated by the influence of (as well as the organization's influence on) formal and informal structure, technology, and the predispositions of the individuals who wield the most influence within the organization. In addition, the environment and the problems created by the environment are important in the goal-setting process, as observed by Perrow (1961).

Perrow suggests that the problems currently facing an organization determine the individuals or groups of individuals who will be legitimated to dominate the organization. If power is not obtained formally, then the very fact that a group is able to handle major uncertainties for the organization (as described in Chapter 4) may provide sufficient power to dominate the organization. Furthermore, the expectations of these controlling elites, which presumably are directly related to current problems of the organization, are likely to become the goals of the organization. Perrow suggests four major problem areas which confront organizations during various stages of their existence; namely, securing capital, securing acceptance by the environment, marshaling skills necessary for the performance of organizational activities, and achieving coordination both among the activities of the organization's members and between the organization and its environment.

The relative importance of each of these problem areas is likely to vary over time. This notion becomes especially vivid when one views organizational behavior in terms of organizational life cycles. As different problem areas emerge, different members of the organization with different skills, experience, training, and outlooks acquire power, authority, and influence. They are either formally elevated to positions from which they influence the organization's goals consistent with their particular expectations or they maintain their former positions and acquire power because of their ability to handle organizational problems and uncertainty and thereby make others more dependent on them.

Perrow suggests that an organization engaged in fairly routine manufacturing, with a secure market position, may well emphasize coordination and, in doing so, yield control to an experienced administrator. Alternatively, the more an organization is engaged in research and development and, in consequence, in nonroutine production activities, the more likely it is to be concerned with the development and utilization of specific skills. Under these conditions, one would expect the organization to be dominated by engineers and other professionals. Perrow's fourfold table for different types of technology presented in Chapter 4 provides indications of the distributions of power among higher and lower levels within the organization. Although it is by no means conclusive, Perrow's analysis does lead us to consider the possibility that technology is one influence on the power structure of an organization, and the power structure, in turn, provides a major determining force in the process of goal selection.

Goals and Means as Determinants of Organizational Design

Agreement on two basic dimensions has been used (Thompson and Tuden, 1959) to characterize the various decision-making processes which organizations adopt: (1) beliefs about means—beliefs about the differential consequences of the several alternative courses of action which can be undertaken in attempting to achieve a goal, and (2) beliefs about goals—the evaluations of the potential outcomes of these courses of action on some scale of desirability. Decision making regarding means implies specific assumptions about causal relationships between activities and their eventual results. Such assumptions about causation, in turn, imply knowledge about both historical and empirical evidence concerning relationships between means and ends, as well as assumptions about the future of these relationships. The selection of goals, furthermore, indicates the preferences of individuals and groups for the various outcomes toward which their organization may strive.

In viewing organizations as decision-making entities, we can analyze the manner in which decisions are achieved by noting whether there is agreement (consensus) among the organization's members on the causal relationships and on the preferences for specific outcomes, or whether there is disagreement.

Computation

In those instances in which an organization's members agree on both causation and preferences (or the dominant coalition can get others to agree on their premises), decision making becomes a mechanical process (see Figure 5–3). In the most simple cases, decision making under these circumstances requires the application of routine formulae rather than choice. At the other extreme, data and alternatives may be so numerous that sophisticated computer techniques may be called upon to perform the required computations. In any event, when an organization deals solely with decisions which can be achieved via computation, it needs simply to identify problems according to the type of specialists required to perform the computations indicated and to route these problems to the appropriate departments.

This is the heart of what Max Weber termed the "pure type" of bureaucracy. An organization with such a computational strategy, in which decision making is merely a matter of discriminating the proper routine problem-solving sequences, is quite rare. Such an organization would have the classical pyramidal power structure, with overall coordination emanating from the omnipotent and omniscient boss at the top. There would be no question of coalitions due to the uncertainties and resulting interdependencies, or the conflicts over scarce resources which have been described by Cyert and March. But in fact, even the apparently omnipotent boss in such an organization will be subject to some uncertainties and will be dependent on outsiders, if not to someone internal

FIGURE 5–3
Goals and Means as Determinants of Organizational Design

Beliefs about causation	*Preferences about possible outcomes*	
	Agreement	Disagreement
Agreement	Computation	Compromise
Disagreement	Judgment	Inspiration

Source: Reprinted from *Comparative Studies in Administration* by James D. Thompson by permission of the University of Pittsburgh Press. © 1956 by the University of Pittsburgh Press.

to the organization, and he or she may need to form coalitions with outsiders as we shall see below.

Judgment

Where preferences for goals are agreed upon but uncertainty or disagreement exists concerning means, the decision-making process takes on more complexity. This situation may arise because it is impossible to prove that a given course of action will provide a specific outcome; the technology may comprise unanalyzable search and high variability (see Chapter 4). Some of the uncertainty regarding cause and effect relationships may come directly from the environment, as, for example, when a marketing department deals with possible reactions of competitors to a pricing change. However the uncertainty comes about, it is likely to afford opportunities for certain groups in the organization to gain power; this power may serve as entry to the dominant coalition, and may well be used then to specify the cause and effect premises of other organizational members. The organization's members are left to rely on their collective judgment in selecting the most appropriate means. Organizations that rely on their members' judgment and "get out the vote" on important issues include voluntary organizations, trade unions, and numerous forms of university governments.

While noting examples of organizations that utilize judgmental decision making is not difficult, the literature of the behavioral sciences has failed to provide a general systematic model for this type of organizational behavior. As we noted in Chapter 4 in connection with Perrow's scheme for technology, a nonroutine technology may be most compatible with a "flexible, polycentralized" structure, or an "organic" structure based on high total influence. In such an organization, individuals are likely to relate to one another in terms of a problem-solving mode with nonzero-sum outcomes (Walton and McKersie, 1965), in which there is collaboration and sharing of information so as to move from a judgmental strategy towards a computational strategy.

Compromise

In some organizations, members agree on the nature of the consequences which can be expected from the implementation of the various alternatives from which they can choose, but disagree in their preferences for these consequences. In such a case, collective judgment cannot adequately overcome disagreements, for the alternatives may be mutually elusive in that the decision to implement one alternative course of action rules out the possibility of realizing outcomes associated with other courses of action. According to Thompson and Tuden, the appropriate strategy for selecting organizational goals in this situation is compromise. Hopefully, while the rank orderings of goals differ among members of the decision-making unit, each member's set of rank-ordered goals contains at least one goal which is common to the sets of the other (or at least the majority of the other) members. Typical of formal bodies which compromise are those whose memberships are comprised of elected or appointed representatives, such as the United Nations Security Council.

Discussions of negotiation and bargaining and zero-sum games may begin to provide a structural model for this kind of decision strategy. Walton and McKersie (1965) have attempted to integrate variable-sum problem-solving processes with zero-sum bargaining to develop mixed models which reflect varying degrees of conflict in outcomes and varying opportunities for integrative problem solutions.

The dominant coalition may attempt to manipulate the premises of the parties disagreeing about goal preferences, but this is often difficult to do since many such disagreements have their basis in the external environment. The organization must interact with other organizations with different goal orderings and the manipulation of premises (creation of constraints in the other system relative to one's own goals) is rendered difficult due to both lack of trust and extended contact. Walton and McKersie similarly speak of "attitudinal restructuring" and bargaining in high conflict zero-sum games as being mutually interfering. Despite this, appropriate coalitional structures may be formed.

Inspiration

Finally, on occasion, organizations are faced with situations in which their decision makers disagree on both the nature of the consequences which can be expected from various alternative courses of action, as well as their preferences for the alternative consequences. The anomie that can easily result in this sort of setting is alleviated when inspiration, innovation, or a novel interpretation of the situation at hand restructures the situation so that overlooked alternative means, goals, or values emerge and, in so doing, facilitate agreement. This facilitating role is often filled by a charismatic leader who, according to Thompson and Tuden:

> . . . offers a new set of ideals or preferences which rally unity out of diversity, by shifting attention. Pointing to a real or fancied threat from outside is one ancient device for this (Thompson and Tuden, 1956, p. 202).

Thompson and Tuden propose that, while the situations they illustrate may occur with varying frequency, organizations, as a rule, tend not to be flexible but rather adopt one of the four decision-making strategies as their dominant strategy. Furthermore, they base their structure upon the strategy chosen despite the fact that different situations require different strategies and structures.

When one considers that the process of goal-setting can include the selection of a decision-making strategy, as well as problems of reconciling stakeholder expectations, it becomes apparent that process abounds in complexity. To add a final dimension to the process of goal-setting, we shall consider some changes over time and the phenomena which arise as controlling elites gain and lose power over the life of the organization.

Controlling Elites and Goals

Perrow (1961) provides us with an interesting description of a hospital which changed its goals (including system goals and product characteristic goals) over time. This case shows how the dominant coalitions changed as the result of changing organizational problems and the resultant ascendance in power of groups able to handle the related uncertainty. As new problems emerged, computational strategies became obsolete, and groups able to implement a judgmental or compromise strategy gained ascendance by either striving for primary leadership or joining the dominant coalition, usually replacing to some degree the formerly dominant groups.

At the outset, financial problems dominated the attention of the organization. As a result, the hospital's goals and consequent directions were subject to the control of the organization's board of trustees. Trustees of nonprofit organizations are often selected because of their ability to make financial contributions to the organization or because of their access to other individuals who enjoy considerable financial resources.

Because of their apparent ability to deal with financial problems, the trustees were able to dominate the hospital in terms of controlling the appointments of physicians and setting policies and goals. Perrow suggests that the goals of an organization can be ascertained by examining predominant characteristics of the controlling group. Since the role of the trustee requires an emphasis on community responsibility, conservative financial policies are likely to be emphasized by the trustees and, consequently, by the organization as a whole. If the trustees represent particular social groupings in the community, the provision of services for these religious, ethnic, or economic groupings may become an important goal.

These kinds of organizational goals can be contrasted with those of the hospital in a later stage of its development. With the growth of medical science early in the 20th century, it became necessary for hospitals to emphasize certain professional skills within the organization. Obviously, hospitals which failed to keep abreast of the state of the art in medical care could not expect to keep up with the competition. Because decisions increasingly were based on medical questions, trustees found themselves lacking competence in new areas of decision making. Although some equipment purchases required the skills of the trustees in obtaining appropriate financing, the most critical tasks of the hospital fell to the physicians, who solely were competent to decide the kinds of equipment and, especially, the kinds of medical skills needed by the hospital.

During this period of the hospital's development, doctors assumed dominant roles and were able to control the directions in which the hospital moved. Extensive facilities were emphasized, together with low hospital charges, both of which were in the interest of the physicians. The activities of the hospital were organized around providing services for the medical staff. High technical standards of patient care were emphasized, as well as excellence in research and medical training. Community needs and financial solvency assumed positions of lesser status in the hospital's hierarchy of goals. Preventive medicine and new forms of medical organization tended to be slighted in favor of improving the kind of medical care already provided by the hospital.

The goals of the hospital under trustee domination, and subsequently under medical domination, may be contrasted by the goals at the next stage of development. By the middle of the 20th century, the continuing growth of medical science and technology tended to overwhelm the physician to the extent that he or she was led to depend upon the services of specialized personnel, some of whose jobs were quite complex, rendering their administration beyond the competence of the physician.

In addition to changes in the technology of medicine, changes in the environment further eroded the position of the physician. Blue Cross and other prepayment schemes grew rapidly and were, at times, able to influence hospitals to improve the efficiency and economy of operation, these being in the direct interest of the former. Furthermore, the hospital became joined to other kinds of health care organizations to form a crude system for providing health care, thus requiring better cooperation and articulation beyond the walls of the hospital. For these reasons, the hospital administrator came to find himself in a critical position— able, by virtue of his specialized training, to coordinate increasingly complex hospital activities, to attend to problems of economy of operation, and to manage coordination with other organizations.

The goals of most hospitals in this third stage of development arose, no doubt, from the need to meet some of these pressures in the environment. The ascendance of this new group of personnel, with different kinds of backgrounds and interests, made it possible for a variety of new goals to emerge. Financial solvency, budgetary controls, efficiency, and a minimal development of services became the new directions for the new hospital. A professionally trained hospital manager could well emphasize the use of up-to-date computer technology, the use of human relations principles, and other elements of his training. His professional training would allow him to feel equal in many respects to physicians and, as a result, competent to interact with physicians on an equal basis about some of their covert goals—including referral systems, the lack of proper quality controls and other procedures of questionable merit. Other possible hospital goals which might emerge under the aegis of administrator domination include publicity-seeking innovations (at the possible expense of medical services), the conservative financing emphasized by the trustees, and the goal of using the hospital for career advancement to a larger hospital by expanding the hospital regardless of community needs.

One might, at first glance, view this analysis as being limited to hospital organizations where ends are multiple and vague and where numerous potential power centers exist. However, this same approach to the determination of goals can be applied to the business firm, despite its apparent emphasis on the unitary goal of profit and the apparent power of the small group at the very top of the organization. Thus Perrow indicates that the goals of a firm may change over time in much the same manner as did those of the hospital. In the beginning, the owners will be in a dominant position. Subsequently, a new generation from the founding family may rise to leadership. Eventually, professional executives with particular skills may, by virtue of their ability to solve increasingly complex problems, assume dominant roles in the firm and, in so doing, determine many of its goals. At each of these stages, one must examine the interests and backgrounds of the particular dominant group in order to learn the directions in which the organization may move. It is possible, for example, for the marketing department to play a dominant role in an organization because its skills are required at a particular stage in the firm's development. This dominance may, in fact, be a significant determinant of the behavior of other departments and of the firm as a whole. Some firms tend to select their chief executives from within the organization. Because of the chief executive's lingering identification with the goals of his or her former department, the goals of the firm overall may be similarly influenced.

This analysis of the various possibilities for different groups to dominate an organization and, consequently, to determine its goals, should be contrasted with the rational organizational theorist's view that the boards of directors or governing boards of corporations set overall policy, including the directions the organization is to take. In a study of voluntary organizations, Zald (1969) shows that the role of the board in influencing the behavior of the organization may vary considerably. It is likely that the same factors that determine the power of the board in these voluntary organizations also operate in determining the power of the board of directors of a firm—the important factors being stock ownership, community legitimation, the possession of detailed knowledge of the organization and its problems, the socioeconomic status of the individual board member, and, finally, whether the board has an opportunity to influence by virtue of certain crises or transition points arising in the life of the firm.

Conclusion

In summary, we have seen that the development of an understanding of the behavior of an organization and, correspondingly, the ability to design an organization which performs as desired, require that we look beyond the official and formal goals of the organization and focus attention on organizational behaviors and on members' expectations regarding those behaviors.

We examined operative goals categorized in terms of output, system, product characteristic, and derived goals. We have seen that one fruitful method for identifying the goals of an organization consists of identifying the stakeholders and, among these, especially the dominant individuals or groups in the organization, and determining their expectations for the organization, as well as their own particular interests and desires. An examination of the positions of such dominant groups in organizations shows that they are not invariably found at the top of the formal structure.

In looking for these dominant groups, we have seen that we ought to look at the nature of the technology of the organization, as well as the nature of its environment. We ought to look at critical problems which are presented by both technology and the environment, for these problems serve, in large measure, to determine which groups will become dominant and in a position to establish directions for the organization.

Finally, we have seen that the informal social structure is important. The distribution of power, the resulting conflict in the organization, and any tendencies to establish consensus produced by the operation of a human relations type of management are some of the major factors which may affect the form and substance of organizational goals.

From a conflict perspective, much of what may serve as organizational goals is in the nature of sets of decision premises which are negotiated between the various power centers and stabilized in the form of budgets and other forms of control mechanisms. While there may be some widely shared sets of decision premises, these may not be very evident to the outsider since they serve as constraints within which the more visible optimizing functions operate. Nevertheless, these shared sets of constraints may make up a more influential component of the organization's "goals" than the more visible optimizing functions. Furthermore, conflicting constraints or goals may coexist in an organization, through suboptimization and by segregation over time (sequential attention). With or without attempts at coexistence, such conflicting goals often are an important part of the organization's goals. The extent of agreement in an organization on means, as well as on ends, is likely to lead to distinctive patterns of decision making in the organization— computational, judgmental, compromise, and inspirational.

In what sense, then, are goals more than a summing-up of individual intentions for the organization? How do constraints created by the goals affect the power one group or individual has over another? While it is true that such intentions or constraints in part determine the organization's goals, organizational members may not be aware of them as "constraints" or "goals" for decision making.

This, in part, is what a "system" view of goals attempts to handle (Etzioni, 1964; Katz and Kahn, 1966). From the structure and functioning of organizations, theorists have attempted to specify "system needs." These are not goals in the sense of being consciously chosen (or negotiated) purposes for the organization, and yet organizations— as organizations—behave as if they have these goals; that is, if one part of the organization does not concern itself with the system need of tension reduction, then another part of the organization will—or else the organization will not survive. Many of the university goals listed in the introduction to this chapter, such as academic freedom, prestige, insuring confidence and support of contributors, are such organizational system needs which have become salient and, in fact, more important than the formal goal of producing educated graduates. We shall return to this matter when we discuss the evaluation of organizations and the problems of changing organizational character.

As we discussed technology (in Chapter 4), we found that some problems arise from the environment. Specifically, Perrow suggests that the variability of raw material inputs has a basic role in the decision processes of the organization relative to its technology. In this chapter we have had even more cause to refer to the environment, in terms of stakeholders outside of the organization having goals for the organization and perhaps even becoming part of the dominant coalition determining the goals. In the above discussion of the changing goals of a hospital, the uncertainty which arose from new problems was seen to lead to changes in the dominant coalition and to consequent changes in the goals of the organization. In another section of the text we shall take up the environment of the organization in a more systematic fashion.

DISCUSSION QUESTIONS

1. Have the goals of colleges and universities changed over the past 20 years? What changes have occurred?
2. What forces in society caused these changes? Was it in the interests of the universities to yield to these forces? Who determines the interests of the university?

3. What goals are pursued by your school now? Who set them? Are they clear? Who supports them? Who is out to change them?

REFERENCES

Ball, Robert. Volkswagen gets a much needed tune-up. *Fortune*, 1972, *85*, 3 (March), 85–105.

Buck, Vernon E. A model for viewing an organization as a system of constraints. In James D. Thompson (Ed.), *Approaches to organizational design*. Pittsburgh: University of Pittsburgh Press, 1966, Pp. 103–72.

Cyert, Richard M., and March, James. *A behavioral theory of the firm*. Englewood Cliffs, N.J.: Prentice-Hall, 1963.

Drucker, Peter F. Business objectives and survival needs. *The Journal of Business*, 1963, *31* (2) (April), 81–90.

Emerson, Richard M. Power-dependence relations. *American Sociological Review*, 1964, 27, 31–41.

Etzioni, Amitai. *Modern organizations*. Englewood Cliffs, N.J.: Prentice-Hall, 1964.

French, John R. P., Jr., and Raven, Bertram. The bases of social power. In Dorwin Cartwright and Alvin Zander (Eds.), *Group dynamics; research and theory*. Evanston, Ill.: Row, Peterson, 1962. Pp. 607–23.

Gross, Edward. Universities as organizations: a research approach. *American Sociological Review*, 1968, 33, 518–44.

Katz, Daniel, and Kahn, Robert L. *The social psychology of organizations*. New York: Wiley, 1966.

Leavitt, Harold J. Applied organizational change in industry. In James G. March (Ed.), *Handbook of organizations*. Chicago: Rand McNally, 1965. Pp. 1144–70.

Likert, Rensis. *The human organization: its management and value*. New York: McGraw-Hill, 1967.

March, James, and Simon, Herbert. *Organizations*. New York: Wiley, 1958.

Merton, Robert K. *Social theory and social structure*. Glencoe, Ill.: Free Press, 1957.

Michels, Robert. *Political parties: a sociological study of the oligarchical tendencies of modern democracy*. New York: Dover, 1959.

Mohr, Lawrence B. The concept of organizational goal. *American Political Science Review*, 1973, 67, 470–81.

Perrow, Charles. Organizational prestige. *American Journal of Sociology*, 1961, *66*, 335–41.

Perrow, Charles. Hospitals: technology, structure and goals. In James G. March (Ed.). *Handbook of organizations*. Chicago: Rand-McNally, 1965. Pp. 910–71.

Perrow, Charles. *Organizational analysis: a sociological view*. Belmont, Calif.: Wadsworth, 1970.

Perrow, Charles. *Complex organizations: a critical essay*. Glenview, Ill.: Scott, Foresman, 1972.

Selznick, Philip. *TVA and the grass roots*. Berkeley, Calif.: University of California Press, 1949.

Siekman, P. Henry Ford and his electronic can of worms. *Fortune*, 1966, *73*, 2 (February), 116–19.

Simon, Herbert A. On the concept of organizational goal. *Administrative Science Quarterly*, 1964, *9*, 1–22.

Tannenbaum, Arnold S. (Ed.). *Control in organizations*. New York: McGraw-Hill, 1968.

Thibaut, John W., and Kelley, Harold A. *The social psychology of groups.* New York: Wiley, 1959.

Thompson, James D. *Organizations in action.* New York: McGraw-Hill, 1967.

Thompson, James D., and Tuden, Arthur. Strategies and processes of organizational decision. In James D. Thompson et al. (Eds.), *Comparative studies in administration.* Pittsburgh: University of Pittsburgh Press, 1956.

Walton, Richard E., and McKersie, Robert B. *A Behavioral theory of labor negotiations: an analysis of a social interaction system.* New York: McGraw-Hill, 1965.

Warner, W. Keith, and Havens, A. Eugene. Goal displacement and the intangibility of organizational goals. *Administrative Science Quarterly,* 1968, *12,* 539–55.

Warriner, Charles K. The problem of organizational purpose. *Sociological Quarterly,* 1965, 6, 139–46.

Wieland, George F. The determinants of clarity in organization goals. *Human Relations,* 1969, 22, 161–72.

Wilson, James Q. Innovation in organization: notes toward a theory. In James D. Thompson (Ed.), *Approaches to organizational design.* Pittsburgh: University of Pittsburgh Press, 1966. Pp. 193–218.

Zald, Mayer N. Comparative analysis and measurement of organizational goals: the case of correctional institutions for delinquents. *Sociological Quarterly,* 1963, 4, 206–30.

Zald, Mayer N. The power and functions of boards of directors: a theoretical synthesis. *American Journal of Sociology,* 1969, 75, 97–111.

6

People

INTRODUCTION

Chapter 3 began with a report on the Non-Linear Systems, Inc., that appeared in *Business Week* in 1965, entitled "When Workers Manage Themselves." Below is a summary of a follow-up story that appeared in the January 20, 1973 issue of the same magazine. It provides a surprise ending to a unique chapter in management history, and one that, at first glance, seems to constitute a real-life contradiction to many of the ideas presented thus far. Whether or not this is actually the case remains to be seen in this chapter.

In the midst of a slump in the aerospace industry, NLS' revenues fell to $3.5 million in 1971; from $6 million in 1965. Major customers of NLS, aerospace firms cut their orders by half in 1970, but NLS was unprepared to respond accordingly. Six months late in reducing production, the firm accumulated a year's supply of inventory.

Commenting on these events, Kay, president of NLS, remarks that he may have lost sight of the purpose of business, which is not to develop new theories of management. Kay has returned the company to traditional budgetary and management techniques and, according to the *Business Week* article, predicts NLS will revert to its former profitability.

The management consultants who worked with Kay over the years say that the motivational programs used in NLS were sound, and that the company's misfortune stemmed from other causes. Kay feels differently. Preoccupied with behavioral techniques and long-range planning, top and middle managers lost track of day-to-day operations. Furthermore, close personal ties between management and the workforce hindered layoffs necessitated by the aerospace slump. Kay reports that when the "crunch" came he was still trying to be a nice guy. Eventually he reduced the workforce by over half.

Changes in production techniques have accompanied the implementation of traditional business practices. According to Kay, the former means of production did not accommodate individual differences in the workforce. Some workers, he suggests, need repetitive tasks. Salaries have also been brought in line with prevailing rates.

Chapter Guide

After thinking about the seeming paradox described above, the theories and research findings in this chapter may assume more relevance to one another and thus provide a conceptual framework for understanding the behavior of people in organizations.

1.   Specifically, does the recent experience of the Non-Linear Systems Company cast doubt on the validity of ideas presented in the last three chapters?
2.   Assuming that the introduction of tightened financial controls was appropriate under the circumstances, do you think it was also essential for the survival and profitability of the firm to abandon behavioral innovations? What assumptions have you made in arriving at your answer?
3.   Do you agree with Mr. Kay that some employees need to work at repetitive tasks? In responding to this question, did you refer: to research data with which you are familiar, to a theory of behavior that you have learned, to your own observations about human nature, or to your own reactions concerning working at repetitive tasks?

MANAGEMENT AND EMPLOYEE BEHAVIOR

People in Organizations

Studies of organizations and organizational behavior essentially are investigations of the behavior of people. Yet, by definition, these investigations are limited to only a portion of the activities found in the repertoire of human behavior. Furthermore, they are studies of behaviors that shape the organizational environment and, in turn, are influenced by the organizational milieu in which they occur. For these reasons, then, we postponed discussion of individual and group behavior in organizations until now in order to provide a description of some of the environmental characteristics that elicit and influence such behavior.

The Management Hierarchy and Skill Utilization

Now and then we find situations analogous to the one in which a machinist is promoted to machine shop foreman in recognition of outstanding performance in his previous job. The individual's performance as a supervisor, unfortunately, turns out to be less satisfactory than the record of accomplishments he attained as a machinist, and management is left wondering why their expectations have not been met.

An obvious explanation for incidents of this sort is that the skills and personal qualities that make for good machinists are not necessarily those demanded of supervisors. One method of determining the skill requirements of individuals who work at different levels in an organization's hierarchy is to aggregate their various activities into areas of responsibility.

Figure 6–1 groups managerial responsibilities and associated skills into three major categories: the management of (1) strategic, (2) human, and (3) physical resources. The strategic problem of an organization is to respond appropriately to a changing environment in pursuit of the organization's objectives. To this end, management has at its disposal the organization's environmental monitoring and forecasting skills, expertise in planning, and abilities to implement plans through the exploitation of existing technological and managerial resources. Essentially, these are the concerns of top management, although problems of strategic management are found to lesser extents at lower levels in the organization.

Human resource problems include forecasting work force require-

FIGURE 6–1
Skill Utilization in the Management Hierarchy

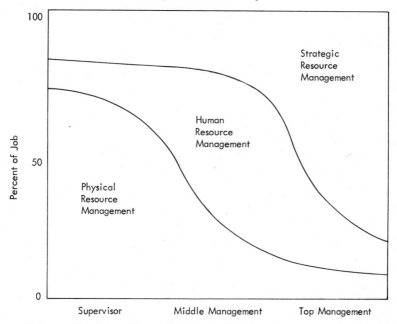

Source: Adapted from *Human Relations at Work* by Keith Davis. Copyright 1972 by McGraw-Hill Book Company. Used with permission of McGraw-Hill Book Company.

ments, training and developing personnel for advancement or lateral shifts in responsibilities, designing the organization and its internal environment so that work-related motives and satisfactions are in-creased, and similar activities, as well as interacting with employees on a day-to-day basis. These are major concerns of middle and lower levels of management. To be sure, senior executives manage relationships with people. However, these relations often are with representatives of other organizations or with officials of diverse units of the executive's own organization, and frequently concern themselves with matters that are political and strategic in nature. Similarly, foremen, who devote a considerable portion of their energies to managing day-to-day interactions with plant personnel, typically are not engaged in work force planning, career development, and organizational planning activities.

Finally, responsibilities for managing the organization's physical (tangible) assets fall to middle and lower levels of management, and engage proportionately less of the attention of senior executives.

Managerial Roles and Role Fit

Having indicated management's responsibilities vis-à-vis the organization, we have, in part, defined the roles of managers at various organizational levels. The role of middle management is defined by primary emphasis on problems of physical and human resource management. The *Business Week* article indicates that Non-Linear Systems' top management became preoccupied with improving its internal operations and long-range planning to the extent that more immediate strategic problems were obscured. That is, with the exception of long-range planning activities, top management seems to have directed most of its attention to the improvement of human resources and the productive processes, perhaps abdicating the role of senior management described here.

The Managerial Grid®

Further reflection on the role of middle management suggests that variations in managers' approaches to the human and physical aspects of organizational life give rise to a number of different managerial styles. One way to explore these variations is to examine the relative degrees of concern that middle managers give to the human and physical dimensions of their organizations. This sort of investigation led Blake and Mouton (1970) to develop the managerial grid, which is presented, along with a portion of the preceding figure, in Figure 6–2.

The grid provides a framework for identifying the major styles of management created by low, medium, and high concerns for people and production. The manager whose great concern for productivity is unmatched by a similar degree of concern for personnel (the 9,1 man-

FIGURE 6–2
The Managerial Grid®

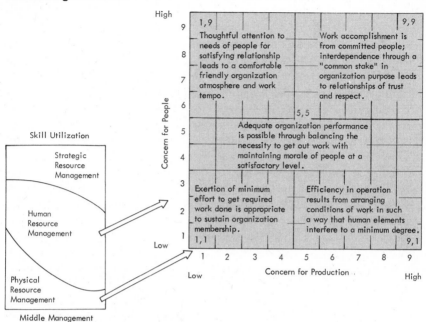

Source: The left side of the figure is a portion of Figure 6–1. The balance is The Managerial Grid figure from *The Managerial Grid*, by Robert R. Blake and Jane Srygley Mouton. Houston: Gulf Publishing Company, Copyright © 1964, p. 10. Reproduced with permission.

ager on the grid) is likely to arrange the work environment in a way that minimizes the extent to which human behavior can affect productive efficiency. Conversely, the 1,9 manager whose high concern for people is accompanied by a relatively low concern for productivity, tends to matters of employee morale, comfort, and satisfaction, often at the expense of organizational productivity. The individual whose concerns for both productivity and people are relatively low (the 1,1 manager) in essence is "retired," but still on the job. The 5,5 manager, concerned only moderately with either personnel or productivity, seeks to balance an adequate level of output with tolerable morale while maximizing neither. Finally, the most desirable managerial style, according to Blake and Mouton, is exemplified by the 9,9 individual whose high concerns for both people and tasks enable him to structure the work situation so that participants' satisfactions are contingent upon the attainment of high levels of productivity, thus enhancing each participant's "common stake" in the affairs and goals of the organization. Critical to this line of reasoning is the assumption that the manager's style is manifested in the characteristics of the organization he or she creates. Certain organizational characteristics facilitate employee motivation while others hinder it.

Dysfunctional Organizational Characteristics

Chris Argyris (1957) investigated organizations with characteristics that appear detrimental to employee motivation. He assumes individuals are predisposed to change in predictable directions as they mature. Infants are dependent, but children mature into adults with predispositions toward independence. Similarly, as life unfolds, strivings toward competence, patience, superordinancy, and permanence of interests replace the infantile predispositions of limited competence, impatience, subordinancy, and transitory interests. What occurs, then, when individuals in the process of maturation find themselves in work roles that require them to: (1) use few of their abilities, (2) work at tasks that are of limited duration, (3) subordinate themselves to management, and (4) limit their behavior to conform to predetermined norms? In other words, how do people adjust to work environments that fail to utilize their capacities as adults?

According to Argyris, placing an adult in a job that limits his or her behavior produces feelings of severe frustration and anxiety. In attempting to deal with these feelings, the individual can resort to one of three basic strategies: (1) seeking advancement, (2) quitting, or (3) engaging in defensive behavior. At first glance, advancing within the organization appears a viable remedy for the situation described. As one moves upward in the hierarchy of traditional organizations, practices of directive leadership, task specialization, and unilateral control diminish. Furthermore, seeking better, more satisfying work is consistent with American, middle-class norms. Unfortunately, the practice of hiring college-educated supervisory personnel conspires against individuals seeking to rise from the shop floor if their education ended with high school. Furthermore, the span of control employed by most organizations limits the number of job opportunities available at successively higher levels. For many individuals, then, escape through career advancement from restrictive jobs, such as those on assembly lines, is a vacuous dream.

The second alternative is quitting. However, given the education and experience of those about whom Argyris writes, it is unlikely that changing employers will result in better jobs. In addition, the longer an employee remains in an organization, the greater will be the cost of quitting. Seniority rights, company pensions, and the like may be lost in changes of employment and, consequently, serve over time to decrease the likelihood that an individual will change jobs. According to Argyris, the final and most frequently chosen alternative is to cope with feelings of frustration and anxiety through the use of defense mechanisms.

Defensive Behavior

All normal people engage in appropriate defensive behavior. People who smoke in the face of the Surgeon General's warning probably deny that *their* use of tobacco constitutes a danger to *their* health. Denial is a form of defensive behavior. We cannot hope to respond directly or effectively to all of the real and imagined physical and psychological threats that life places in our way. If we are to travel by air, we must deny the possibility that our flight will be terminated by disaster. To do otherwise would pave the way for an incapacitating fear of flying. Other defense mechanisms include: projection, the tendency to attribute one's own feelings to another; displacement, the shifting of behavior from one object to another (as is the case when the individual who is angry with the boss vents his or her rage on subordinates); and regression, the tendency to engage in behavior that was effective as a child but is inappropriate for an adult (as happens when men and women have tantrums or crying fits in the face of frustration).

As we have said, defensive behavior is both helpful and normal. However, a distinction needs to be made between the individuals who can be comfortable while in flight by denying the possibility of disaster and individuals who "take things out" on innocent bystanders or who react to difficulty with childishness. Healthy people have a repertoire of defense mechanisms from which they draw, even though subconsciously, and apply in ways that facilitate their adult behavior. Less healthy are individuals whose defensive behavior impedes their effectiveness in life or those who have learned to meet all contingencies with a limited number of defenses.[1]

Argyris contends that defensive behavior caused by certain work environments, together with apathy toward work that these defenses ultimately produce, result in phenomena such as goldbricking, restricting output, cheating, and slowing down. Furthermore, employees who engage in these practices form groups that sanction them, and eventually internalize such practices as work norms. As these norms become established, they are likely to gain recognition in the larger organization. Such norms have been termed *psychological work contracts* between supervisors and subordinates. A typical "contract" may take the form of a mutual understanding that, in return for adequate (but not outstanding) productivity and minimal dysfunctional behavior, the foreman will "stay off everyone's back"; that is, interact as little as necessary

---

[1] For a more complete description of defense mechanisms, see Sarnoff (1962).

with subordinates so as not to encroach on their apathy and desires to be uninvolved in their work.

While this definition of a fair day's work for a fair day's pay may prove mutually satisfactory for workers and their supervisor, it is liable to contradict management's expectations of the work force. Managers may diagnose such undesirable behavior as failings of their employees rather than as inevitable outgrowths of the work environment created by management. This being the case, remedies for the shortcomings of lower level personnel may take the forms of increased directive leadership, more stringent management controls, and other activities that, according to Argyris, originally caused the problems for which remedies were sought. Thus, the behavioral system described is self-reinforcing.

INDIVIDUAL NEEDS AND BEHAVIOR

Maslow's Hierarchy of Needs

The two basic premises upon which Argyris' work rests are: (1) people have an inherent need to grow along the continua he suggests and (2) the inhibition of such growth is painful and ego-threatening. Review of what other behavioral scientists have learned about human needs and the behavior that is likely to emerge when need fulfillment is thwarted will be instructive.

One of the classic theories in the field of motivation consists of the hierarchy of needs postulated by Abraham Maslow (1970). According to this theory, all people have the same set of needs. These are the needs for physiological essentials (food, shelter, sex, and so on), safety, love and belongingness, self- and group esteem, and self-actualization.[2]

Each need within the hierarchy depicted in Table 6–1 becomes prepotent when two conditions are present: (1) when deprivation of the need is sufficient for "wanting" to occur, and (2) when the needs below it in the hierarchy have been fulfilled to a "tolerable" level. With respect to the first condition, Maslow argues that needs are not likely to affect behavior until deprivation produces an awareness of them. We all need water, but do not experience constant thirst. Thirst, the wanting of water, occurs only after the body's supply of water has fallen below a threshold, and then, according to other theorists whom we shall study later, only when other conditions are present as well. Regarding the second condition, Maslow contends that unfulfilled lower order needs predominate unfulfilled higher order needs. An individual will not be

---

[2] Self-actualization, according to Maslow, is the ". . . self-fulfillment of the idiosyncratic and species-wide potentialities of the individual person." The need to self-actualize, then, is the need to become all that one is potentially. This is by no means a simple concept. The reader is encouraged to pursue Maslow's original work.

TABLE 6-1
Maslow's Need Hierarchy

Self-actualization
Self- and group esteem
Love and belongingness
Safety
Physiological

motivated to fulfill a need for safety, regardless of the state of deprivation, until his or her physiological needs have been fulfilled to a tolerable level; that is, a starving person will risk safety or physical well-
being in order to obtain food. Similarly, fulfillment of the need for love
and belongingness will be sought only after the individual's physiological and safety needs have been met to some degree. The need for esteem
becomes prepotent once the needs below it have been minimally fulfilled. Finally, the need to self-actualize will be experienced only after
some degree of success in fulfilling all the needs that precede it.

Maslow suggests that few individuals have fulfilled their needs for
self-actualization. Zaleznik and others (1958) expand on this observation by describing processes that serve to impede movement through the
need hierarchy. First, fulfillment of each successive need is likely to require the sacrifice of fulfillment of lower order needs. For example, the
quest for self-esteem may entail a loss of peer acceptance if noncon-
forming behavior is prerequisite to its fulfillment. Many individuals
seem unwilling to seek gratification of their higher order needs at the
cost of their lower order needs. Second, many of the environments that
we have created for ourselves lack the potential to fulfill higher order
needs. Similar to the organizational setting described by Argyris, these
environments thwart self-actualization and lead to elaborations of lower
order needs. Hence, individuals engage in seemingly endless pursuits of
material objects which symbolize status, group acceptance, and security. Furthermore, Maslow sees self-actualization as the work of a lifetime. It is unlikely for an individual prior to middle age to have had the
wealth of life experiences that are essential to self-actualization. If these
assumptions are correct, it should come as no surprise that self-actualization, unlike the other needs for which we have an understanding
based on our experience, is a somewhat alien concept and, therefore,
difficult to describe.

The Validity of the Hierarchy of Needs

For some reason, the work of Maslow seems to have great intuitive
appeal. Perhaps this is because the theory describes life as we have
experienced it. Certainly, we can find events in history that lend sup-

port to this view of behavior. The themes that pervade Stone Age art, for example, deal with fertility and the hunt. Given the marginal existence that prevailed in those times, we can safely assume that early man's lowest needs were rarely fulfilled to a degree that would allow him to become engrossed in more than the quest for food and the survival of his kind. Similarly, in recent times there have been instances in which individuals, faced with starvation, have resorted to cannibalism. Would not this gruesome behavior suggest that needs for self-respect, love, and so on, lose their potency in the face of the compulsion to eat and remain among the living?

As for evidence of the other extreme of the need hierarchy, we find many people experience a subtle longing for something more than what life seems to offer. Is this longing the vague and tentative perception of an emerging need for self-actualization or merely a generalized feeling of dissatisfaction? Is self-actualization a concept that is founded in reality or a part of people's wish fulfillment about the nature of humanity: a collective self-delusion of grandeur? Unfortunately, turning to empirical data is of little help in resolving the issue raised here. To date research has not yielded conclusions that would either validate or discredit Maslow's theory. Neither the hierarchy nor the need for self-actualization has been verified (Wahba and Bridwell, 1975).

But, just as some empirical events seem to lend credibility to the concept of a need hierarchy, some seem to contradict it. The social norm that women and children should receive preferential treatment in times of danger (such as on board a sinking vessel) appears to require men to act in opposition to the hierarchy. The same is true of individuals who pursue hunger strikes and even martyrdom in support of their ideals. However, neither of these examples is contrary to Maslow's thinking; his theory describes needs that are experienced rather than the behavior that these needs produce. Hence, the individual, who places his or her life in jeopardy in service of some higher goal, still experiences, and must control, strong motivations to act otherwise. If this is true, we need to give some thought to the process whereby conflicting motives are handled.

McClelland on Motivation

H. A. Murray (1938) postulated a set of needs which he felt to be generic. The set includes the needs for order, acquisition, achievement, dominance, seclusion, and others. While a proponent of Maslow's theory, on seeing an individual attempt a task, would attribute his actions to the need for self-esteem, group esteem, or security, a proponent of Murray's analysis might simply attribute the act to the need for achievement. The need for achievement can be termed an "instrumental" need learned in the service of fulfilling more fundamental needs such as those described by Maslow.

David McClelland (1955), noted for his study of the need for achievement, extended Murray's work by postulating the role of learning in the motivational process. McClelland reasoned that a motive is a strong affective (emotional) association which arises from the individual's reaction to anticipated goal attainment and is based upon past associations of certain cues with pleasure or pain. An emotion per se (e.g., fear or satisfaction) is not a motive. Neither are cues (e.g., stomach contractions which follow fasting). However, when cues are associated with changes expected to result from the pursuit of known goals, the presence of a motive can be inferred.

McClelland suggests that the persistence of a motive is a function of: (1) the frequency of the cue-pleasure (pain) association, (2) the generality of this association and the ease with which it may be extinguished, (3) the intensity of pleasure or pain experienced at the time the association was formed, and (4) the age of the individual when he first learned to make the association. We can reasonably argue that the lower order needs described by Maslow are likely to generate cues that are both more persistent and more likely to trigger associations than are the higher order needs (Ullrich, 1972). Consequently, something on the order of a need hierarchy may well evolve in the growing individual. However, the individual's attention may be engaged in the short run by associations which relate to the higher order needs to the exclusion of the formation of motives directed toward securing fulfillment of the lower order needs. Thus, we have arrived at a conceptual explanation of the hierarchical theory of needs that explains deviations from the hierarchical tendency as well.

The Two-Factor Theory of Motivation

Literature on motivation is extensive, and we have only summarized the works of a few major contributors. At this point, however, we will do well to examine more empirically based theories and determine the extent to which they are consistent with the works described above and, more importantly, their applicability to actual work situations.

Frederick Herzberg and others (1959), in a well-known but controversial study, sought to understand motivation in the workplace by asking subjects to describe their own experiences. Specifically, interviewees were asked to recall times when they felt particularly good (or bad) about their jobs and to describe these episodes. The anecdotes thus collected were found to contain three basic components: (1) job-related *factors* that led to the episodes described, (2) the *attitudes* these episodes produced in the interviewees, and (3) the *effects* that interviewees attributed to their attitudes. Factors intrinsic to the work itself (e.g., achievement, recognition, and the work itself) were more significant sources of employee motivation and satisfaction when they were present than they were sources of dissatisfaction when they were absent. Conversely, elements of the work setting that are extrinsic to the work itself (e.g., company policy and administration, technical supervision, and working conditions) were more significant sources of dissatisfaction when they were perceived as poor than sources of worker motivation and satisfaction when they were thought to be good.

To interpret these data, Herzberg utilized a variation of the psychological growth model that, as we have seen, is so prevalent in the literature. He concluded that:

> The principal result of the analysis of this data was to suggest that the (extrinsic) . . . events led to job dissatisfaction because of a need to avoid unpleasantness; the (intrinsic) events led to job satisfaction because of a need for growth or self-actualization (Herzberg, 1966, p. 75).

Thus, one finds a rationale for relating the results of the Herzberg study to Maslow's hierarchy of needs (as illustrated in Figure 6–3). Extending this line of reasoning, Herzberg suggests that the normal individual

FIGURE 6–3
A Comparison of the Two-Factor Theory*
and the Hierarchy of Needs†

Herzberg's Two-Factor Theory	Maslow's Hierarchy of Needs
Intrinsic factors Achievement Recognition Responsibility The work itself Advancement The possibility of growth	*Higher order needs* Self-actualization Self- and group esteem
Extrinsic factors Company policy and administration Technical supervision Working conditions Interpersonal relations—superiors Interpersonal relations—peers Interpersonal relations—subordinates Personal life (effects of the job on) Status Security Salary	*Lower order needs* Love and belongingness Safety Physiological (food, water, shelter, sex, etc.)

* Herzberg et al. (1959).
† Maslow (1970).

is not motivated to attain increased satisfaction from the extrinsic factors. The presumably abnormal individual who does so is:

> . . . not merely a victim of circumstances, but is *motivated* in the direction of temporary satisfaction. It is not that his job offers little opportunity for self-actualization; rather, it is that his needs lie predominately in another direction, that of satisfying avoidance needs (Herzberg, 1966, p. 81).

Herzberg's findings provide a paradox of considerable magnitude. Whereas criticisms of his work have been numerous (e.g., House and Wigdor, 1967; Vroom, 1964) and, for the most part, seemingly valid, applications of his two-factor theory in work settings have had apparent good results (e.g., Paul, Robertson, and Herzberg, 1969). Furthermore, his findings bear reasonable consistency with many of the works previously described. Then again, replications of his study and applications of his remedies frequently produce unexpected results.

Why should interpersonal relations with peers, superiors, and subordinates not produce feelings of satisfaction and motivation as does recognition for achievement when recognition stems primarily from one's interactions with others? What is so unhealthy about aspiring to work in a physical environment that is both comfortable and aesthetically pleasing? In answer to questions such as these, it has been argued that the methodology used to generate the two-factor theory is likely to bias the data upon which the theory is built (Vroom, 1964); that is, in responding to the interviewer's questioning, the interviewee is prone to exercise defensive behavior by attributing his satisfactions to his own performance and his dissatisfactions to the characteristics of his co-workers or work environment. House and Wigdor (1967), in a secondary analysis of data collected in Herzberg's study and replications, rank order the intrinsic and extrinsic factors according to the frequency with which they were mentioned as sources of dissatisfaction. Interestingly, the factors, achievement and recognition, were reported to cause more dissatisfaction than either working conditions or interpersonal relations with superiors.

Job Enrichment

Such criticisms have led to considerable skepticism about the validity of the two-factor theory. However, as mentioned above, some applications of the theory have had favorable results. According to the theory, attempts to increase the motivation (and, therefore, productivity) and satisfaction of employees will be more fruitful when intrinsic factors are improved than when extrinsic factors are. The practice of restructuring a job so that it includes more, and greater, intrinsic factors is termed "job enrichment."

A report of work conducted in Imperical Chemical Industries Limited by William Paul and others (1969) provides a lucid example of successful job enrichment. Among several experiments reported, Paul discusses job enrichment of a group of "experimental officers." These men were responsible for the implementation of experimental programs designed by scientists in a research and development unit of the firm. Basically, their tasks were to set up apparatus for experiments, record data, and to supervise laboratory assistants who carried out simpler operations. At the time of the experiment, the subjects had apparently reached a dead end in their careers. The average age of the group was advanced and approximately one quarter had reached the maximum salary for the position. They lacked the formal education and terminal degrees needed to advance into the ranks of scientists. Alternatively, promotions into the plant were unlikely due to the increasing technological complexity of the manufacturing operations. The group's morale, as measured by a job reaction survey, was low.

Paul separated the experimental officers into control and experimental groups and attempted to keep from both the knowledge that an experiment was in progress. Extrinsic job factors for both groups were held constant, while intrinsic factors were improved for the experimental group. To the existing job, the following tasks were added:

1. Subjects were encouraged to write final laboratory reports (formerly the sole responsibility of research scientists) which carried their names along with those of scientists.
2. Each officer was permitted to decide whether to have his report checked by a scientist.
3. Officers were given full responsibility for answering queries arising from these reports.
4. Officers were given opportunities to participate in the planning of projects and experiments.
5. Officers were given time, upon request, to conduct their own research, even when these projects went beyond the unit's research objectives.
6. Officers were authorized to requisition materials, equipment, analyses, and services such as maintenance.
7. The officers were made responsible for the design and implementation of training programs for their junior staff.
8. Senior officers were allowed to interview candidates for the position of laboratory assistant.
9. The officers became the first assessors of their own assistants.

As illustrated in Table 6–2, these changes restructured the officers' jobs to bring them into contact with the entire research process, as opposed to a limited segment. In addition, the subjects were provided the option to engage in creative, high-risk independent research.

As the two-factor theory predicted, the changes led to increased productivity. Laboratory research reports of both scientists and experi-

TABLE 6–2
An Example of Successful Job Enrichment

Staff Development	Production	Research and Development
Interview job candidates	Participate in planning projects and experiments	Individual research (if requested)
Devise and implement training programs for subordinates	Requisition materials and services	
Evaluate subordinates	Set up experiments	
	Record data	
	Supervise assistants	
	Write laboratory reports	
	Respond to queries	

Source: Adapted from Paul et al. (1969).

mental officers were graded by an independent authority who did not know who wrote them. All but three of the research reports written by experimental officers were within the performance range of the scientist. Furthermore, the same individual wrote all three substandard reports. Of the remaining 31 reports written by experimental officers, none was worse than the worst submitted by a scientist and 3 were judged to be as good as the best of the scientists' reports. Encouraged by their success in designing and implementing training sessions for their subordinates, the experimental officers initiated one for themselves. Finally, one of the original research ideas from the experimental group resulted in an important discovery for the company.

In order to compare the performance of experimental and control groups, members of each were requested to write monthly progress reports. These reports of activities were graded; the mean scores of the experimental group exceeded those of the control. Midway through the experiment, the control group was subdivided into two smaller groups. One of these subgroups remained as a control while the other was subjected to job enrichment identical to that applied to the original experimental group. Following this change, the mean scores on monthly progress reports of the second experimental group increased for several months until they became comparable to those of the original experimental group. Mean scores for the remaining control group declined.

Limitations to the Generality of Job Enrichment

The prediction that job satisfaction of the experimental subjects would increase significantly was not born out in the experiment. Yet, this is a minor point on which to fault job enrichment. More telling data from other studies give us reservations about the general applicability of job enrichment. More importantly, these other studies cast some doubt on the universal acceptance of the psychological growth model of motivation, at least as it is described by Herzberg.

One questionnaire survey shows that 81 percent of the firms responding were not using job enrichment (Reif and Schoderbeck, 1969). Of the 19 percent that were (41 firms) only 4 indicated "very successful" experiences. More optimistic, but in the same vein, is the finding that of 19 job enrichment studies conducted at A.T.&T., 9 were rated "outstandingly successful," 1 was considered to be "a complete flop," with the remaining 9 deemed "moderately successful" (Ford, 1969). A more recent survey (Luthans and Reif, 1974) finds that only 5 out of 132 of the top 300 firms in *Fortune's* 1,000 industrials make any formal attempt to enrich jobs.

These research findings let some questions of major importance go begging. Namely, are the observed failures of job enrichment due to inappropriate designs, implementation strategies, or measurement techniques inherent in the studies in question, or do systematic forces in the workplace render job enrichment appropriate under one set of circumstances and inappropriate under another?

Motives and Individual Differences

Turner and Lawrence (1965) lead us to conclude that, at least in some cases, such forces exist. In their study, job factors such as autonomy, responsibility, interaction opportunities, variety of task, and requisite knowledge and skill, were aggregated to provide what they term the "requisite task attribute index." The study hypothesized that job satisfaction will be high among workers whose jobs have a high index rating (that is, that are high in autonomy, responsibility, and so on) and low among workers whose jobs are low on these dimensions. Similarly, absenteeism will be low on jobs rated high on these dimensions and high on jobs rated low. The two hypotheses were generally supported, but ambiguities in the data led the researchers to pursue their investigation further.

The research sample consisted of 470 workers from 47 jobs in 11 organizations. When this sample was subdivided into subjects from *urban* or small *town* (rural) subcultural groups, the researchers found a positive relationship between job satisfaction and the task attribute score for the town subgroup, while this relationship was negative for the city subpopulation. Furthermore, index scores were negatively related to absenteeism for workers in the town subsample. For workers with urban backgrounds, no such significant relationship was found. From these findings, Turner and Lawrence reasoned that the favorable responses of town workers to complex jobs, and urban workers to simple jobs, can be explained by the observation that urban and rural workers learn different predispositions toward work. In this vein, it is postulated that the town workers in the Turner and Lawrence study held traditional values regarding work and work-related achievement and, consistent with the Protestant ethic, responded positively to more complex jobs (Hulin and Blood, 1968). Urban workers, who were perhaps alienated from these Protestant, middle-class values, did not respond favorably to complex tasks, but preferred more simple ones. More recent data indicate that the more an individual subscribes to the Protestant ethic the more he will be satisfied with his work and with life in general (Blood, 1969). Finally, in reviewing the literature on job enrichment, Hulin and Blood (1968) conclude that:

> The case for job enlargement has been drastically overstated and overgeneralized. Further, the evidence of the simultaneous effects of plant location and job size (or job level) provides a means of summarizing the literature and resolving the contradictions. Specifically, the argument for larger jobs as a means of motivating workers, decreasing boredom and dissatisfaction, and increasing attendance and productivity is valid only when applied to certain segments of the work force —white collar and supervisory workers and . . . blue collar workers [who subscribe to the Protestant work ethic] (p. 50).

However, Hulin and Blood (1968) and others recognize the tendency for dichotomies (such as urban-rural) to obscure effects of individual differences on motivation. Wanous (1974) explored differences within dichotomies by examining the contributions of: (1) urban-rural work settings of early socialization, (2) degree of adherence to the Protestant work ethic, and (3) higher order need strength to the relationship between job characteristics on the one hand and satisfaction with specific job facets, overall job satisfaction, and job behavior on the other hand. Wanous found that the relationship is explained best by higher order need strength followed by belief in the Protestant work ethic. Place of early socialization contributes least to the relationship. Wanous' interpretation of these findings is that belief in the Protestant ethic is likely to contribute to the strength of higher order needs and is more likely to be learned in rural settings than in cities. However, both are merely proximate measures of the causal variable, higher order need strength.

Contemporaneous influences on motives and aspirations are also observed as part of ongoing organizational processes. For example, Wernimont et al. (1970) report that "The supervisor seems to have an impact on motivation primarily as he modifies or intensifies 'expectancies.' " Such influences seem to align motives with opportunities in the long run, regardless of whether they are intentional or incidental. Research evidence in support of this position has been fairly consistent over time. For example, the early works of Gardner (1940), Hilgard et al. (1940), and Child and Whiting (1949) are consistent with the observation of Iris and Barrett (1972) that individuals in unsatisfactory job situations who de-emphasize the various aspects of their jobs appear to be satisfied with their jobs and life in general.

These and other studies raise serious questions about the usefulness of the so-called need or drive-reduction theories. It seems unrealistic to expect needs, even if they are universal, to produce uniform motives and behavior in the work force. Thus, we turn to a second school of thought, expectancy theory.

EXPECTATIONS AND BEHAVIOR

Work Satisfaction and Productivity

Most early research in the field of human relations focused on employee morale. At the time it was felt that improving interpersonal relations would increase morale which, in turn, would lead to greater worker productivity. Subsequent research indicates that at least two different effects contribute to feelings of morale: satisfaction with the status quo and satisfaction derived from anticipation of future rewards (Ullrich, 1972). The latter source of work satisfaction may be associated with increased productivity, but only when activities that lead to increased satisfaction also lead to greater productivity. If an individual aspires to a greater sense of accomplishment, more peer recognition, and a higher salary and thinks that greater productivity will yield these rewards at a "reasonable cost," he or she may work harder. In this case, the individual views increased productivity as *instrumental* to the attainment of these aspired sources of satisfaction. However, simply increasing the satisfaction of the work force will not necessarily improve its productivity (Kahn, 1960). This does not suggest that employee satisfaction is inconsequential. A number of studies show that dissatisfaction correlates with labor turnover, absenteeism, and other undesirable consequences (Porter and Steers, 1973). Furthermore, satisfying employees (aiding in their pursuits of happiness) may be a desirable organizational goal in itself.

Sources of Work Satisfaction

In a recent analysis of the sources and nature of work satisfaction, Strauss (1974) reports that studies almost invariably find the majority of workers to be satisfied with their work (see also Kahn, 1972). There are exceptions, of course, but according to Strauss ". . . the best evidence from psychological surveys suggests that average levels of job satisfaction in this country have remained fairly stable since the early 1960s and that satisfaction today is higher than it was during the 1940s

and 1950s" (1974, p. 23). While some observers point to recent problems evidenced by statistics on declining productivity and increasing
labor turnover, absenteeism, strikes, and accidents, Strauss argues that
these can be attributed to changes in economic conditions and occupational and demographic characteristics of the work force (see, e.g.,
Flanagan, Strauss, and Ulman, 1974; Wool, 1973).

While there has not been much recent change in levels of overall
satisfaction, there have been changes in the relative importance of specific job factors. Strauss suggests there is evidence that job security
is less important to employees than it was 20 years ago, while the intrinsic value of work has become more important. However, this generalization masks some interesting differences. For many individuals,
especially blue-collar workers, pay and job security still assume equal
or greater importance than interesting work (see, e.g., Porter and Lawler, 1965). The reasons for this are fairly obvious.

Many individuals, especially blue-collar workers, do not see their jobs
as their "central life-interest" (Dubin, 1956). Instead, they are com-
munity- and home-centered. Unlike managers and professionals who are
assumed to view work and its challenges as sources of meaning in their
lives, these individuals view their jobs as instrumental to the attainment
of security and money with which they can pursue various leisure activities (Fein, 1973; Goldthorpe, Lockwood, Beckhofer, and Platt, 1968).
Strauss (1974) carries this argument further:

> . . . much dissatisfaction is caused by low income, job insecurity, in-
> adequate fringe benefits, or tyrannical supervision. Indeed, to me, the
> evidence suggests that for many workers at all levels—even many man-
> agers and professionals—lack of challenge may be less oppressive than
> lack of income. Instrumental orientation is widespread . . . wants grow
> as fast as paychecks, and economic motivation may not atrophy as fast
> as some psychologists suggest (p. 34).

The Expectancy Model of Motivation

These statements seem to contradict theorists such as Maslow and
Herzberg. The various "need" theories typically hold motivation to be a
function of drive for need fulfillment and habit $[M = f(D \times H)]$. A
second major school of thought holds motivation to be a function of the
individual's expectation (subjective probability) that an outcome can be
attained and his valence (utility) for the outcome in question $[M =
f(E \times V)]$. This approach has its roots in the works of Lewin et al.
(1944), Edwards (1954), Vroom (1964), and others. Essentially a
theory of decision making, the approach is ideographic. Behavior is assumed to be influenced by the individual's perceptions of his environment and his ability to interact successfully therein. Need theories
direct our attention to the forces that drive behavior. Expectancy theories explore the processes by which behavioral forces are focused in

certain directions and not others (Campbell, Dunette, Lawler, and Weick, 1970).

According to Vroom (1964) and others, individuals evaluate alternative courses of action in terms of the *valences* of *outcomes* these actions are expected to produce. Valued outcomes have positive valences, while undesirable ones assume negative valences. Where the individual is indifferent regarding a potential outcome, valence is zero. A course of action produces two different kinds of outcomes: (1) *first-level outcomes* are valued for their consequences which are termed (2) *second-level outcomes* and are valued in and of themselves. Returning to our example, an individual may choose to be more productive because he or she thinks increased output will result in a sense of accomplishment, peer recognition, and a higher salary. Please note that these second-level outcomes can be instrumental to the attainment of still more outcomes. Furthermore, it is important to recall that all outcomes are not positive. Increased productivity may be associated with fatigue and foregone opportunities as well.

The extent to which a first-level outcome is seen as instrumental in producing each second-level outcome varies according to the individual's perception of the situation. Perceptions can range from complete certainty that increased recognition will follow increased productivity, through uncertainty, to certainty that the first-level outcome will not result in increased recognition. Thus, the valence of a first-level outcome is hypothesized to be the sum of instrumentality times valences over all second-level outcomes.

$$V_j = f(\sum_{k=1}^{n} (V_k \times I_{jk}))$$

where:

$V_j =$ Valence of performance
        level j.
$V_k =$ Valence of the kth
        second-level outcome.
$I_{jk} =$ Instrumentality at
        performance level j.
$n =$ Number of outcomes.

According to this logic, the individual's predisposition to achieve a certain level of performance (j) will depend, in part, on his or her perception of the valence associated with this first-level outcome.

There is an additional problem to consider. How does the individual know that his or her efforts will result in performance level (j)? The expectancy model goes on to state that the *force* on an individual to perform act (i) (invest a certain amount of effort, in this example) is a function of his *expectancy* that the act will be followed by the outcome

(j). Expectancy is expressed as a subjective probability $(P \leqslant 1)$. Thus, the mathematical statement of Vroom's model is as follows:

$$F_i = f(\sum_{j=1}^{n} (V_j \times E_{ij}))$$

where:

$$F_i = \text{Force to perform act } i.$$
$$V_j = \text{Valence of outcome } j.$$
$$E_{ij} = \text{Expectancy that act } i$$
$$\text{will be followed by}$$
$$\text{outcome } j.$$
$$n = \text{Number of outcomes.}$$

Increased effort may not always lead to an anticipated increase in performance. Reduced to its simplest terms, the model states that in considering a given amount of effort (i), the individual perceives different subjective probabilities of attaining different levels of performance (j). For example, by investing a given amount of effort the individual perceives that he or she will be able to produce no fewer than zero and no more than three wigits a day. The expectancies for each of these outcomes are as follows:

First-Level Outcome Wigits Per Day	V_j	E_{ij}	$V_j \times E_{ij}$
0	−10	0.01	− .10
1	1	0.09	+ .09
2	10	0.60	+ 6.00
3	22	0.30	+ 6.60
		1.00	+12.59

As the individual considers investing more or less effort, his expectancies associated with each first-level outcome change accordingly. The force on the individual is to invest the amount of effort that will maximize $\Sigma V_j \times E_{ij}$.

Evaluation of the Expectancy Model

Although this and similar theories have been the subject of a considerable amount of research, reviews of this research do not provide assurance that the model's validity has been confirmed. The model has been used to make reasonably accurate predictions of satisfaction (from valences), but does not fare as well in predicting the direction in which effort will be channeled (Mitchell, 1974). One problem is that no investigator has correctly tested the complete expectancy model. Tests of the model sometimes indicate that one variable (e.g., valence or expectancy) predicts just as well or better than the complete formula

(Locke, 1975). It appears to some researchers that "the theory has become so complex that it has exceeded the measures which exist to test it" (Lawler and Suttle, 1973, p. 502). Experiments designed to test the expectancy model against other models of motivation have yielded mixed results.

Further questions have been raised in terms of the model's inadequacy as a description of individual decision-making processes. (Behling, Schriesheim, and Tolliver, 1973; Behling and Starke, 1973a, 1973b). Review of the literature on decision making suggests that individuals are unable to store the amount of information the model suggests they use. Furthermore, they are incapable of making the myriad of calculations called for.

In short, while there is some empirical support for the expectancy model, the evidence is by no means conclusive. Support also exists for alternative theories, though none of these has carried the day either. Our own predelections are to keep alternative conceptualizations of individual behavior in mind.

> One suspects that the psychological forces which keep these theories separate will be found, not in the subjects whose behaviors are recorded in support of the theories, but in the experimenters, who are educationally predisposed to prefer one theory to another. If this line of thought is carried to its logical conclusion, it becomes apparent that sifting through the literature to separate "truth" from "error" will not lead us as far as will searching for an integrative model which lends order to the confusion we find (Ullrich, 1972, p. 204).

Applications of the Expectancy Model

Just as the need theories found application in practices such as job enrichment, expectancy theory has valid uses in organizations. Relatively simple situations in which behavior-reward contingencies are unambiguous are conducive to rational, cognitive behavior that may be described by an expectancy model (see, e.g., Graen, 1969). In more complex situations, where there are more unknowns and where complex social factors intervene, a less "rational" approach to understanding behavior may be appropriate (e.g., Chapter 14).

One area where expectancy theory seems particularly useful is in highlighting differences between individual and environmental determinants of motivation. Lawler (1973) has expanded the Vroom model by emphasizing the individual's expectancy regarding the consequences of his *efforts* to perform at a certain level. This "effort-performance" probability lends insight to the growing field of attribution theory—the study of psychological mechanisms by which individuals attribute their successes and failures to themselves or outsiders (Weiner, 1972). In contrast to predominantly individual, psychological views of effort-performance expectancies, Lawler emphasizes the environmental (often organizational) origins of performance-reward relationships. The latter emphasis permits us to explore the ways in which reward systems shape expectancies and motivations.

Expectancy theory is especially useful in explicating incentive plans used in industry. Such plans generally make incentives directly contingent upon the individual's performance. As Lawler (1973) indicates, individual incentive systems such as piece rates, merit raises, and the like seem to improve performance 10 to 20 percent above that experienced when rewards are not directly contingent upon performance. However, the success of such systems depend, in part, on the participants' trust in management, perceptions of a close relationship between rewards and performance, and understanding of the system (Cammann and Lawler, 1973). Group incentive plans tend not to improve performance, probably because rewards are not entirely contingent on individual performance. These schemes do tend to facilitate cooperation among group members who work at interdependent tasks and are useful in this regard. Please note that individual incentive plans may be dysfunctional when applied to group members working at interdependent tasks, since cooperation may give way to competition.

Extrinsic Motivation

Studies of expectancy theories, especially as applied to monetary incentive systems, provide a much needed counterpoise to the need theorists' apparent overemphasis of intrinsic sources of motivation. However, recent research provides a caveat for those who would rely solely on extrinsic sources of motivation such as pay and on the manipulation of performance-reward contingencies to control behavior. While contingent reward systems may be effective in eliciting immediate responses, they may also have undesirable consequences over the long run, by changing work that is intrinsically motivating and satisfying to work lacking these attributes (Greene and Lepper, 1974). Deci (1971, 1972a, 1972b), for example, found that individuals paid for correct solutions to intrinsically interesting puzzles became less interested in the task than those who were not paid. However, a fixed fee, independent of performance, did not decrease subsequent intrinsic motivation. According to Deci, the incentive reward controls the individual and makes him dependent on the reward system. Interestingly, when Deci had supervisors give verbal praise at the same time as monetary incentives were provided for correct solutions, the subjects did not lose their sense of intrinsic motivation.

The Nature of Intrinsic Rewards

It is somewhat of an oversimplification to classify only work-related outcomes (e.g., achievement, advancement, and so on) as sources of intrinsic motivation. In this text we take a social-psychological approach to understanding organizational phenomena, one in which individuals are assumed to internalize a variety of socially determined goals and values (Katz and Kahn, 1966). These goals and values become sources of intrinsic motivation (see also Wernimont, 1972). Western (middle-class) social scientists are prone to view work-related goals and values (especially individual growth and achievement) as the culmination of man's strivings. Such views may result from cultural bias. For example, reports from Communist China indicate that individuals may be socialized to value group welfare. For such individuals, service to the group is a major source of intrinsic motivation, not individual growth (Tausky, 1973a, 1973b; see also Tausky, 1975). Tausky suggests that shared meanings can endow any activity with purpose, importance, and dignity. In contrast to writers who describe routine work as inherently unpleasant and distressing, we refer to Maslow, who suggests that any activity can become intrinsically valuable if we have the wisdom to want it to become so.

> A job entered for the sake of earning a living, can be loved for its own sake. Even the dullest, dreariest job, as long as it is worthwhile in principle, can be sanctified, sacralized (ontified, changed from a mere means into an end, a value in itself) (Maslow, 1971, p. 117).

Motivation and Ability

If the concept of motivation is to be useful in understanding the behavior of people in organizations, it must be combined with individual ability, for performance is a function of motivation and ability. While a treatment of individual differences and selection techniques is beyond the scope of this book, we shall discuss various organizational characteristics that facilitate or impede the application of individual abilities.

We have seen that job enrichment, System Four management, and the like can motivate individuals to greater organizational productivity *provided that they aspire* to the opportunities for need fulfillment inherent in the respective reorganizational strategies. The managerial problem suggested here is to create a "fit" between individual members and their organizational environment. Yet, as Blake and Mouton indicate, this "fit" will be optimal from an organizational standpoint when it matches concern for individual need fulfillment with organizational productivity requirements. Furthermore, task-related needs and organizational requirements cannot be met unless the organization's design facilitates effective task accomplishment. The problem of achieving a fit among organizational tasks, organizational design, and organizational members is explored through the emerging study of contingency theory.

Contingency Theory

Although recent developments in organizational design (e.g., System Four, participative-group organizations, and high total influence systems) appear to give rise to greater productivity than do more traditional forms of organization, their advocates do not mention the conditions under which these organizational forms succeed or fail. On the contrary, they are usually presented as generally applicable. In Chapter 4, we found that other schools of thought (e.g., Perrow and Woodward) relate organizational productivity to the degree of congruence between the organization's technological processes and its structural design. Chapter 5 presented organizational goals arising from and being congruent with structural and technological arrangements. The various theories presented in this chapter agree that productivity in organizations increases with the organization's ability to satisfy the needs of its members, although these arguments generally are made in the absence of concern for variations in the goals or technologies that organizations employ. As we said, however, one of our major concerns is to understand the relationships that exist among organizational structure, technology, goals, and people.

John Morse and Jay Lorsch (1970) explored ways of improving these relationships. They observed that, in some situations, a directive, controlling approach to management works well in terms of organizational productivity, while, by the same token, some applications of employee-centered management do not produce such good results. The emergent study related organizational characteristics to productivity in four organizational units. Two organizations were used in the study: Company 1, which was engaged in the routine, predictable task of manufacturing, and Company 2, which was involved in the more unpredictable tasks of research and development. Within each of these companies, two organizational units were studied. In each pair of organizational units, one unit was more effective than the other. The Akron plant was the more productive of the two units studied in the manufacturing company, while the Stockton research lab was the superior of the two units studied in Company 2. A major finding in the Morse and Lorsch study is that the two effective performers had very different organizational characteristics.

Table 6–3 summarizes the characteristics of each organization as perceived by organizational members. Obviously, if we rated the two organizations according to High Total Influence systems, System One, Two, Three, or Four organizations, and the like, the Stockton Research Lab would score higher than the Akron plant in the majority of cases. Yet this observation is contrary to the arguments made by proponents of System Four, and High Total Influence: that organizations with these characteristics are more productive than traditional ones.

TABLE 6–3
"Climate" Characteristics in High-Performing Organizations

Characteristics	Akron	Stockton
1. Structural orientation	Perceptions of tightly controlled behavior and a high degree of structure	Perceptions of a low degree of structure
2. Distribution of influence	Perceptions of low total influence, concentrated at upper levels in the organization	Perceptions of high total influence, more evenly spread out among all levels
3. Character of superior-subordinate relations	Low freedom vis-à-vis superiors to choose and handle jobs, directive type of supervision	High freedom vis-à-vis superiors to choose and handle projects, participatory type of supervision
4. Character of colleague relations	Perceptions of many similarities among colleagues, high degree of coordination of colleague effort	Perceptions of many differences among colleagues, relatively low degree of coordination of colleague effort
5. Time orientation	Short-term	Long-term
6. Goal orientation	Manufacturing	Scientific
7. Top executive's "managerial style"	More concerned with task than people	More concerned with task than people

Source: Morse and Lorsch (1970).

Morse and Lorsch find resolution of this contradiction in the following logic. Although all people may have similar needs, it is not necessarily valid to assume that they, therefore, have similar motives (see also Graen, Davies, and Weiss, 1968). However, even where widely different motives are found, *one* motive that most people seem to share is the motivation toward competency. *Yet, given that their other motives are dissimilar, different groups will attain fulfillment of their competence motives in different organizational settings.* For example, individuals in the Akron plant appear to differ from those in the Stockton laboratory in their attitudes toward uncertainty, authority, and relationships with their peers. Because of these different need patterns, each group was able to achieve fulfillment of its need for competency in a different kind of organizational setting. Therefore, the authors conclude that an organization should be designed to "fit" both its task requirements and membership needs. In failing to accommodate the requirements of task performance, the organization will lose some of its potential to provide workers with feelings of competency. Similarly, in failing to account for the unique needs of its members, the organization will fail to provide the kind of motivational setting in which competency can be exercised.

However, while considerable attention has been paid to the problem of matching individual motives and job attributes, far less has been devoted to the measurement of organizational "needs." Sophisticated measures of individual abilities and motives found in industrial psychology are, as yet, unparalleled by techniques for making systematic appraisals of job requirements. Scientific management (time and motion study) and human factors psychology (e.g., Chapanis, 1965) have examined specific, molecular elements of jobs, but no simple, systematic taxonomy for the more molar aspects of jobs is at hand.

Consequences of Person-Job Discrepancies

A recent program of research provides information on the various strains (e.g., physiological disorders) that can arise when job requirements are ill-suited to individual motives and abilities. French and colleagues (French, 1974; French and Caplan, 1973) asked individuals to rate their jobs according to the extent selected factors were present. These subjects also indicated the extent to which they would like these factors to appear in their jobs. Factors studied included responsibility for the work of subordinates, quantitative work load, responsibility for things, utilization of abilities, and opportunities for advancement.

Responses indicating that subjects desired either more or less of a factor than their job contained were termed person-job discrepancies. Work satisfaction was found to be highest for subjects (managers and professionals employed by NASA) reporting little or no discrepancy. Similar relationships were found between degree of discrepancy and variables such as perceived threat to health and well-being, anxiety, and work-related depression. Even physiological measures such as cholesterol level, systolic blood pressure, and blood glucose level increased with extent of discrepancy.

Such research findings emphasize the desirability of increasing our knowledge of the interrelationships among people and major organizational variables. Yet here, we have reached one of the frontiers of knowledge in organizational design and behavior. How to measure and improve the "goodness of fit" remains to be seen.

DISCUSSION QUESTIONS

1. Can the same theory of motivation account for acts as dissimilar as stealing and studying?
2. What do you think would happen if interdependent team members were placed on an individual incentive payment system?

3. Is French's finding that individuals can experience more responsibility than they want incompatible with the two-factor theory?

REFERENCES

Argyris, C. *Personality and organization.* New York: Harper & Bros., 1957.

Behling, O., Schriesheim, C., and Tolliver, J. Alternate cognitive formulations of the work-effort decision. Paper presented at the Midwest Academy of Management meeting, Chicago, 1973.

Behling, O., and Starke, F. A. The postulates of expectancy theory. *Academy of Management Journal,* 1973, *16,* 374–88. (a)

Behling, O., and Starke, F. A. Some limits on expectancy theories of work motivation. Paper presented at the Midwest AIDS meeting, East Lansing, Michigan, 1973. (b)

Blake, R. R., and Mouton, J. S. *The managerial grid.* Houston, Tex.: Gulf Publishing, 1970.

Blood, M. R. Work values and job satisfaction. *Journal of Applied Psychology,* 1969, *53,* 456–59.

Business Week. Where being nice to workers didn't work. January 20, 1973, 2263, 98–100.

Cammann, Cortlandt, and Lawler, Edward E. Employee reactions to a pay incentive plan. *Journal of Applied Psychology,* 1973, 58 (2), 163–72.

Campbell, J. P., Dunnette, M. D., Lawler, E. E., and Weick, K. E. *Managerial behavior, performance, and effectiveness.* New York: McGraw-Hill, 1970.

Chapanis, A. *Man-machine engineering.* Belmont, Calif.: Brooks/Cole, 1965.

Child, I. L., and Whiting, J. W. Determinants of level of aspiration and evidence from everyday life. *Journal of Abnormal and Social Psychology,* 1949, *44,* 303–14.

Deci, E. L. Effects of externally mediated rewards on intrinsic motivation. *Journal of Personality and Social Psychology,* 1971, *18,* 105–15.

Deci, E. L. Intrinsic motivation, extrinsic reinforcement, and inequity. *Journal of Personality and Social Psychology,* 1972, 22, 113–20. (a)

Deci, E. L. Effects of contingent and non-contingent rewards and controls on intrinsic motivation. *Organizational Behavior and Human Performance,* 1972, *8,* 217–29. (b)

Dubin, R. Industrial workers' worlds: a study of the "central life interests" of industrial workers. *Social Problems,* 1956, *3,* 131–42.

Edwards, W. The theory of decision making. *Psychology Bulletin,* 1954, *51,* 380–417.

Fein, M. The real needs and goals of blue collar workers. *Conference Board Record,* 1973, *10* (2) (February), 28–33.

Flanagan, R., Strauss, G., and Ulman, L. Worker discontent and work place behavior. *Industrial Relations,* 1974, *13* (2) (May), 101–23.

Ford, R. N. *Motivation through the work itself.* New York: American Management Association, 1969.

French, J. R. P., Jr. Person role fit. In A. McLean (Ed.), *Occupational stress.* Springfield, Ill.: Charles C. Thomas, 1974. Pp. 70–79.

French, J. R. P., Jr., and Caplan, R. D. Organizational stress and individual strain. In A. J. Marrow (Ed.), *The failure of success.* New York: AMACOM, 1973. Pp. 30–66.

Gardner, J. W. The use of the term "level of aspiration." *Psychological Review,* 1940, *47,* 59–68.

Goldthorpe, J. H., Lockwood, D., Beckhofer, F., and Platt, J. *The affluent worker: industrial attitudes and behavior.* Cambridge: Cambridge University Press, 1968.

Graen, G. B. Instrumentality theory of work motivation: some experimental results and suggested modifications. *Journal of Applied Psychology Monographs,* 1969, *53* (2) (Pt. 2), 1–25.

Graen, G. B., Davies, R. V., and Weiss, D. J. Need type and job satisfaction among industrial scientists. *Journal of Applied Psychology,* 1968, *52,* 286–89.

Greene, D., and Lepper, M. R. Intrinsic motivation: how to turn play into work. *Psychology Today,* 1974, *8* (4) (September), 49–54.

Herzberg, F. *Work and the nature of man.* New York: World Publishing Co., 1966.

Herzberg, F., Mausner, B., and Snyderman, B. B. *The motivation to work.* (2d ed.) New York: Wiley, 1959.

Hilgard, E. R., Sait, E. M., and Margaret, G. A. Level of aspiration as affected by relative standing in an experimental social group. *Journal of Experimental Psychology,* 1940, *27,* 411–21.

House, R. J., and Wigdor, L. A. Herzberg's dual-factor theory of job satisfaction motivation: a review of the evidence and a criticism. *Personnel Psychology,* 1967, *20,* 369–89.

Hulin, C. L., and Blood, M. R. Job enlargement, individual differences, and worker responses. *Psychological Bulletin,* 1968, *69,* 41–55. Copyright 1968 by the American Psychological Association.

Iris, B., and Barrett, G. V. Some relations between job and life satisfaction and life importance. *Journal of Applied Psychology,* 1972, *56,* 301–4.

Kahn, R. L. Productivity and job satisfaction. *Personnel Psychology,* 1960, *13,* 275–87.

Kahn, R. L. The meaning of work: interpretation and proposals for measurement. In A. Campbell and P. E. Converse (Ed.), *The human meaning of social change.* New York: Russell Sage, 1972. Pp. 159–203.

Katz, D., and Kahn, R. L. *The social psychology of organizations.* New York: Wiley, 1966.

Lawler, E. E., III. *Motivation in work organizations.* Monterey, Calif.: Brooks/Cole, 1973.

Lawler, E. E., III, and Suttle, J. L. Expectancy theory and job behavior. *Organizational Behavior and Human Performance,* 1973, *9,* 482–503.

Lewin, K., Dembo, T., Festinger, L., and Sears, P. S. Level of aspiration. In J. McV. Hunt (Ed.) *Personality and the behavior disorders.* Vol. 1. New York: Ronald Press, 1944.

Locke, E. A. Personnel attitudes and motivation. *Annual Review of Psychology,* 1975, *26,* 457–80.

Luthans, Fred, and Reif, William E. Job enrichment: long on theory, short on practice. *Organizational Dynamics,* 1974, *2,* 3(Winter), 30–43.

McClelland, D. C. (Ed.). *Studies in motivation.* New York: Appleton-Century-Crofts, 1955.

Maslow, A. H. *Motivation and personality.* New York: Harper & Row, 1970.

Maslow, A. H. *The farther reaches of human nature.* New York: Viking Press, 1971.

Mitchell, T. R. Expectancy models of job satisfaction, occupational preference and effort: a theoretical, methodological, and empirical appraisal. *Psychological Bulletin,* 1974, *81,* 1053–77.

Morse, J. J., and Lorsch, J. W. Beyond Theory Y. *Harvard Business Review,* 1970, *48,* (3) (May–June), 61–68.

Murray, H. A. *Explorations in personality.* London: Oxford University Press, 1938.

Paul, W. J., Robertson, K. B., and Herzberg, F. Job enrichment pays off. *Harvard Business Review,* 1969, 47 (2), 61–78.

Porter, L. W., and Lawler, E. E., III. Properties of organizational structure in relation to job attitudes and job behavior. *Psychological Bulletin,* 1965, 64, 23–51.

Porter, L. W., and Steers, R. M. Organizational, work, and personal factors in employee turnover and absenteeism. *Psychological Bulletin,* 1973, 80, 151–76.

Reif, W. E., and Schoderbeck, P. P. *Job enlargement.* Ann Arbor, Mich.: Bureau of Industrial Relations, Graduate School of Business Administration, University of Michigan, 1969.

Sarnoff, I. *Personality dynamics and development.* New York: Wiley, 1962.

Strauss, G. Job satisfaction, motivation, and job redesign. In G. Strauss, R. E. Miles, C. C. Snow, and A. S. Tannenbaum (Eds.), *Organizational behavior: research and issues.* Madison, Wis.: Industrial Relations Research Association, 1974. Pp. 19–49.

Tausky, C. Meanings of work: Marx, Maslow, and steam irons. Paper presented at American Sociological Association meeting, New York City, 1973. (a)

Tausky, C. Work motivation, social control or personality? Paper presented at American Sociological Association meeting, New York City, 1973. (b)

Tausky, C. The mythology of job enrichment: self-actualization revisited. *Personnel,* 1975, forthcoming.

Turner, A. N., and Lawrence, P. R. *Industrial jobs and the worker.* Cambridge, Mass.: Harvard University Press, 1965.

Ullrich, R. A. *A theoretical model of human behavior in organizations: an eclectic approach.* Morristown, N.J.: General Learning Corporation, 1972.

Vroom, V. R. *Work and motivation.* New York: Wiley, 1964.

Wahba, Mahmoud A., and Bridwell, Lawrence G. A review of research on the need hierarchy theory. In Kenneth N. Wexley and Gary A. Yukl (Eds.), *Organizational behavior and industrial psychology: readings with commentary.* New York: Oxford University Press, 1975. Pp. 5–11.

Wanous, J. P. Individual differences and reactions to job characteristics. *Journal of Applied Psychology,* 1974, 59, 616–22.

Weiner, B. *Theories of motivation: from mechanism to cognition.* Chicago: Markham, 1972.

Wernimont, P. F. A systems view of job satisfaction. *Journal of Applied Psychology,* 1972, 56, 173–76.

Wernimont, P. F., Toren, P., and Kapell, H. Comparison of sources of personal satisfaction and of work motivation. *Journal of Applied Psychology,* 1970, 54, 95–102.

Wool, H. What's wrong with work in America—a review essay. *Monthly Labor Review,* 1973, 96 (3) (March), 38–44.

Zaleznick, A., Christensen, C. R., and Rothlisberger, F. J., with Homans, G. C. *The motivation, productivity and satisfaction of workers.* Boston: Harvard Graduate School of Business Administration, 1958.

7

Architecture

INTRODUCTION

Similar to environmentalists, who anguish over man's careless use of the biosphere and forewarn possible dire consequences, a growing number of behavioral scientists have begun to study the correlative problem of the effect on man of the environment he[1] has knowingly, but inadvertently, made for himself. Little is known for certain, and the literature is rife with contradictions. As we have seen, for example, Herzberg et al. (1967) find working conditions a source of dissatisfaction when they are poor but, when they are perceived as good, they do not affect their inhabitants positively. In contrast, R. Buckminster Fuller (1969) envisions a properly structured environment permitting man to become what he potentially is:

> Don't attempt to reform man. An adequately organized environment will *permit* humanity's original, innate capabilities to become successful. Politics and conventionalized education have sought erroneously to *mold* or *reform* humanity, i.e., the collective individual (p. 320).

Students of organizations are amply motivated to join the search for understanding in this area since the average adult spends the bulk of his or her waking hours within the physical confines of one organization or another. Beyond this, however, this area of study interests increasing numbers of scholars, presumably for its intrinsic qualities. Few other areas of study simultaneously unfold the wonderment of man's aesthetic nature on one hand and his concern for things that are mean and petty on the other. Few other topics of inquiry lead us to consider problems as complex as the design of cities, neighborhoods, factories, and schools and, at the same time, to discover phenomena of interpersonal behavior from observations of everyday occurrences such as how furniture is arranged in offices. In this light, consider the following quotation from the article, "The Top-Down Society: Spatial Decisions in the Organizational World" by F. I. Steele (1971):

---

[1] As previously stated, the common pronoun "he" refers to persons of either sex and is not intended to be masculine or feminine.

When it comes to physical facilities, the dominant pattern of decision-making in organizations is clearly a top-down, high-control one in which power is seldom shared. This is true of both large and small scale decisions. Large scale decisions about location, general layout, type of decor for offices as a whole, and relative locations of people to one another, are nearly always made at the very top management level. Most influence is exerted by the president and his staff (who control the decisions about facilities) and the maintenance staff (since a major criterion for design is usually whether something will be easy for them to clean). Those at the in-between and lower levels have relatively less influence over their own settings.

Many organizations require that members get clearance before making changes in individual offices or spaces. A case in point: a middle-level manager decided that his desk had faced the door of his office for too long. So he turned it around to face a side wall. Next day he found a memo on his desk from the president's assistant saying that it had been found that the most effective way for managers to arrange their offices was with the desk facing the door so others would feel welcome. He was instructed to return his desk to its old position, with the implied threat of no longer being considered an effective manager if he did not. He later discovered that there was only one exception to the desk-to-the-door rule—and that was the president's office!

At one level, the message our friend received was that he had encroached on the symbolic territory of the president, namely the desk arrangement itself. More importantly, however, he also received a higher-level message: "What I noticed most was not that our desks were so different, but that our freedom to arrange our desks was so different. Can you imagine him (the president) getting a memo because he moved his stuff around?"

This message of lack of control over one's own work surroundings is often institutionalized by company policy. One major national company had a famous design firm create a new building for them, including an "integrated" interior design for all executive offices. A rule was established in writing that no changes could be made in any of the executive offices without the approval of the president.

The pattern of top-down facilities decisions needs changing, because its costs to the organization and its members are relatively high. If organizational development specialists[2] fail to consider the physical system aspect of organizational change as well as the social side, their clients' physical systems may drag down efforts for necessary change rather than support them.

Chapter Guide

As indicated above, the individual in an organization frequently lacks the authority to arrange the work space to suit one's needs.

1. What reasons would management have for withholding this authority?

---

[2] Namely, change agents, behavioral scientists, and others whose role is to help organizations restructure and adapt, in order to become more responsive to changing needs, changing markets, the changing environment, and so on.

2. In what ways could the rearrangement of furniture improve an individual's performance?
3. Think of the last several offices you have visited. Can you think of reasons for their layouts?
4. Try to imagine a space in which you could perform your work (or studies) more satisfactorily than you do in the location you ordinarily use. What does this space look like? How large is it? Do you occupy it alone? What kinds of furnishings does it have? How are they arranged? How is it decorated? What kinds of equipment are present? What facilities are nearby? How is it different from the space you generally use? If you can imagine a better place in which to work, how is it that your present facilities are inferior to what they could be?

ARCHITECTURE AND BEHAVIOR

Environmental Determinism

In the preceding discussion of technology and power relationships that appears in Chapter 4, we reported that tensions arise when waitresses directly initiate work orders to countermen or cooks (Whyte, 1949). Many restaurants, it was noted, reduce the magnitude of this problem through the use of barriers such as counters or spindles on which waitresses place their written orders for the cooks, who select orders in a sequence that allows them to control the pace at which they work. What is described here, in essence, is an architectural solution to a behavioral problem. The notion that desired behavioral responses can be induced by characteristics of the fabricated physical environment is known as environmental determinism (e.g., Perin, 1970).

One of the assumptions of this school of thought is that perceived attributes of the physical environment serve as cues which evoke fairly predictable behavioral responses; for example, an individual's behavior in a church, classroom, or drugstore differs in each of these settings and, to some extent, is predictable. Similarly, one receives and interprets cues on entering nightclubs, conference rooms, and vestry rooms that rigidly define what may or may not be said or done. Ruesch and Kees (1970) explain this observation by asserting that the designers and users of settings endow them with specific meanings through what they term *object language*—"that which is communicated by the incorporation and arrangement of physical objects."

As we shall see, numerous attributes of the physical environment have the potential to influence the behavior enacted therein. At this point, however, we will deal with only two attributes: size and location.

Size is, perhaps, the most readily discernible feature of architectural structures, and one that produces easily recognizable behavioral responses. The sheer enormity of the interior space in a cathedral can give the individual a sense of his or her own insignificance or powerlessness in the broader scheme of celestial events. Hence, it is postulated, feelings of awe and wonder give rise to hushed and respectful behavior. These reactions of people who enter cathedrals are so predictable, in fact, that we have come to expect them. Now, the argument can be made that the behavior manifested is in response to religious sentiments which the place evokes rather than to size, per se. While one could argue that religious edifices evoke religious attitudes and behavior in some people, it is also true that similar behavior is evoked by monumental structures that are secular in origin. The Nazi architect, Speer (1971) made effective use of this phenomenon in his creation of a "cathedral" of searchlights under which party members were commemorated before a mass meeting.

The phenomenon described above may also account for our tendency to commemorate significant individuals in history with statues of monumental proportions. Again, size is assumed to convey a sense of the viewer's own insignificance in comparison to the individual whose likeness towers above him. Architectural design can produce similar effects. The authors are familiar with a suite of executive offices, the doors to which are 14 feet high. The impression on entering these portals is that the events that transpire within are of greater importance than the men and women who make them. These doors, as we might expect, lead to the office of the organization's top executives.

The literature provides no conclusive evidence to explain why the scale of an edifice produces the feelings and behavior indicated above, or even that such responses occur in a consistent fashion in the population as a whole; one can speculate that familiar objects constructed larger than those to which we are accustomed evoke memories and responses from childhood. We stand in relation to the 14-foot-high door as adults in much the same way that we stood in relation to ordinary doors as children. This abrupt exposure to oversized objects may serve as a source of cues which trigger the feelings of insignificance, awe, wonder, and insecurity that we felt as children but have outgrown as adults.

Size of Work Space and Group Cohesiveness

Size seems to have more complex effects on behavior than those readily observable phenomena described above. Wells (1972) studied 295 employees working in large and small office spaces of an insurance firm in Manchester, England. While all of these individuals worked on the same floor, 214 of them were housed in a single, open work area while the remaining 81 were distributed among three smaller offices. Social cohesion, one of the variables examined in the study, was measured by determining the number of reciprocal friendship choices among workers in both types of work settings. The findings showed: (1) reciprocal friendship choices were directly related to the proximity of workers; (2) workers from the small offices were more likely to prefer co-workers from the same office than from other offices; and (3) social isolates, that is, individuals who were not chosen as workmates by any of their colleagues, occurred more frequently in the smaller spaces than in the larger one. Wells suggests that, social isolates notwithstanding, group cohesion tends to be greater in smaller work spaces than in larger ones.

Research findings such as these sow the seeds of skepticism that lead us to question the validity of environmental determinism as a sole guiding principle for environmental design. The environmental deterministic school of thought, oversimplified, suggests that small work spaces foster work group cohesion, among other things, and, thus, provide us with both means and ends for office design. However, let us explore, in turn, the desirability of the ends suggested and the efficacy of the means. Does group cohesion necessarily lead to the fulfillment of individual and organizational objectives? Perhaps, but how desirable is this attribute when it is brought about in a way that limits communications among different segments of the organization and increases the percentage of social isolates? Obviously, we cannot answer these questions at this point, but only raise them in order to anticipate the direction our line of inquiry will lead. Let us return, then, to the second reservation expressed in connection with environmental determinism; namely, the efficacy of architectural means in producing desired behavioral outcomes.

Westgate and Regent Hill

A fascinating analysis of the proximity of dwelling units as a determinant of social behavior has been provided (Festinger, 1972). The foci of the studies reported here were two housing projects; Westgate, which housed graduate students, and Regent Hill, which formerly housed shipyard workers and subsequently housed a variety of different kinds of workers. The student residents of the Westgate project were enthusiastic about their environment and enjoyed an active social life. Dwellings were arranged in "U-shaped" courts leading off a road. The units at either end of the "U," being closest to the roadway, were built to face the road rather than the court, which the others faced. Friendships that developed within the housing project were influenced by two architectural factors according to Festinger: (1) the distances between houses, and (2) the directions the houses faced. People tended to establish friendships with next-door neighbors. As the distance between houses increased, the likelihood of friendships diminished; friendships between residents separated by four or five other houses were rare. Second, residents tended to interact with households that faced theirs. Consequently, individuals living in the end houses, which faced the roadway, tended to have half as many friends in the project as did those whose dwellings faced the court.

Confounding Social Variables

This finding is startling in itself. Imagine—your social life can be enhanced or diminished by a factor as impersonal as the location of your house, apartment, or dormitory room! Yet, the second study, dealing with the Regent Hill project, contains findings that weaken the case for environmental determinism and cause us to question the efficacy of purely architectural solutions to social problems. Regent Hill was constructed as a government housing project for shipyard workers in 1942. At the time of the study, 40 percent of the residents were "old timers" who stayed on after World War II. The rest of the project's inhabitants chose to live there after the war, in a time of acute housing shortage when few alternatives were available. According to Festinger, most residents felt that the circumstances that caused them to live in Regent Hill were beyond their control, stemming either from shipyard employment and other war-related conditions or from the housing shortage. Many residents reported that they expected not to like the kinds of people found living in a government housing project and assumed them to be of lower class origin. As a result, residents tended to avoid one another. Forced to choose between associating with neighbors perceived as lower class and social isolation, residents chose the latter.

We found similar dynamics in early attempts to foster better attitudes among whites and blacks by increasing their contacts with one another. At the time, many of us felt that such contacts would break down the stereotypes in which whites cast black people. We assumed that actual face-to-face contact with blacks, rather than the reliance on information from the mass media, friends, family, or white work associates, would remedy these stereotypes.

Considerable subsequent research has shown that contact alone is not sufficient for these purposes. For instance, specially created integrated housing projects did little to change attitudes concerning neighbors of different racial origins. Individuals entered into social contacts with existing beliefs and attitudes intact. Consequent interactions flowing from these social contacts tended to support and confirm existing attitudes and beliefs. This is not altogether surprising; for example, southern whites traditionally had numerous and frequent contacts with blacks without developing more favorable attitudes toward them. In the

North, increasing job opportunities and, consequently, on-the-job contacts similarly did little to change attitudes. The contact situations were predefined as interactions between high- and low-status individuals, with influence flowing one way. Only when job-related and other social contacts were established in which blacks had high status could interactions serve as an impetus for attitude changes.

Here, then, evidence suggests that proximity alone does not induce social cohesion, that architectural characteristics do not automatically determine behavioral responses, and that man is not as conditioned by his environment as some would believe. Furthermore, other individuals form part of one's environment, and the social processes which emerge between them create, as well as derive from, the environment.

Need Fulfillment in the Environment

Having expressed these reservations about the limitations of the environmental determinism school of thought, we need to affirm our view that, while physical surroundings exert something less than complete control over the individual's behavior, their influence is substantial. Proshansky and others (1970) observe that people's behavior in a given physical setting is relatively enduring and constant over both time and situation. However, changes in behavior patterns within the setting can be induced by changing either the physical, social, or administrative attributes of the setting. In addition, note that although the physical environment influences behavior, individuals also modify their physical surroundings to accommodate their own need-fulfilling activities. And yet, this distinction is not as clear as it would appear. Arranging one's work setting to enhance the likelihood of certain needs being met (e.g., the need for esteem) may create conditions that convey status symbols to others and, thus, elicit desired responses from others. Furthermore, the trappings of power, status, and authority may, in turn, affect the occupant so that he or she experiences increased esteem and status and reacts accordingly. Finally, changes in the physical environment may convey the intentions of such changes (Proshansky, Ittelson, and Rivlin, 1970); when a change in behavior follows alteration of the physical environment, we must enquire whether behavior was altered in response to the changed surroundings, per se, or in response to the actors' assumptions concerning the expected behaviors these changes might produce (Ruesch and Kees, 1970). Does the subordinate show more deference to a manager with a large office than to a second manager with a smaller one because size induces deference or because size is a symbol that "tells" the subordinate how he is expected to behave?

We need not belabor these points, but merely emphasize them as indications of the interrelationships that can exist among the physical, social, technical, and other characteristics of the work setting. Having made these points, let us explore the functions that physical environments can serve in the processes of need fulfillment. For this purpose, we will use a taxonomy of needs already described in some detail, Maslow's need hierarchy (1970).

The Physiological Needs

The observation that physical environments are designed, in part, to provide for the fulfillment of certain physiological needs is obvious. Office buildings protect inhabitants from the elements and provide adequate lighting, drinking and washing water, rest rooms, and, on occasion, restaurants and coffee shops.

Less obvious is the notion that behavior can be predisposed, in part, by the inclusion or omission of elements in the physical environment that serve the lower order needs. The exclusion of drinking fountains, lavatories, or resting places tends to limit the amount of time that an individual is willing to spend in an environment. For example, shops whose customers are expected to browse and take their time selecting purchases may include comfortable furniture and a coffee urn. Alternatively, other business establishments encourage a high turnover of clientele by eliminating access to lavatories and resting places.

The Need for Safety

Attempts to fulfill the need for safety (or security) are apparent in the incorporation of locks, fire escapes, sprinkler systems, closed-circuit television monitoring systems, and similar security and safety features in offices, schools, factories, and other places of work.

Concerns for security, however, range beyond attempts to minimize the potential for physical harm and include regard for organizational and social protections as well. For example, some factories and laboratories use elaborate security measures to protect their products and processes from industrial espionage. Similar measures are frequently used to shield certain organizational activities from clients and even other members of the organization.

There has been a growing awareness among both architects and managers of the interdependence of social and physical factors in providing protection from physical harm. Despite extensive security arrangements, banks and merchants are robbed and apartment dwellers are mugged and raped. Jane Jacobs in *The Death and Life of American Cities* (1969) discusses the need for "social density" as a protection against crime. Criminals are reluctant to act where there are many people about because of the increased likelihood of apprehension. The movement of slum dwellers from areas with small shops open at all times to antiseptic urban-renewal projects is a case in point. In the latter surroundings, there may be no shopkeeper or stream of customers to see a mugging or to notice a loitering stranger.

The importance of the "social" parts of social density—requiring both proper physical arrangements (e.g., in Westgate) and social arrangements (discussed below under "The Needs for Love and Belongingness")—has been illustrated by shocking cases of crimes observed by many people (even 50 or more in the case of Kitty Genovese in New York City), none of whom apparently was socially involved enough to help or even call the police! The high crime rates in high-rise urban renewal buildings supposedly are due to this lack of *social* density. In contrast, if a building is only four or five stories (and houses only 100 or so people), there is sufficient social density to ensure that "strangers" are noticed and that there is sufficient commitment to others to facilitate protective actions.

Erving Goffman (1959) provides a fascinating description of the elaborate measures that are undertaken to control access to interpersonal processes in physical and social settings. Part of the substance of everyday life, according to Goffman, is the management of the roles that we play in various social situations. As was mentioned in Chapter 3, social roles appear as sets of norms that prescribe the expected behaviors and personal relationships of individuals with respect to other individuals who maintain other, related social positions. The management of a role consists of controlling the ways in which we express our role to others. This expression is both "given" through verbal communications, and "given off" by the setting in which the role is enacted, mode of dress, physical gestures, and other nonverbal behavior.

Physical environments frequently are designed to provide: (1) decor and props that support (give off) the roles that are to be enacted therein, (2) segregated areas where incompatible roles can be assumed, unnoticed by the inhabitants of other areas, and (3) "backstage" areas where the "actors" can relax their roles, repair their appearances, and engage in additional behaviors unrelated to those of the "front stage." In this manner, the arrangement of physical space isolates various roles from their respective audiences and, in so doing, establishes subtle regions of security.

The Needs for Love and Belongingness

As was illustrated by the study of the Westgate and Regent Hill housing projects, the proximity and physical orientation of architectural spaces can both encourage and impede the formation of interpersonal bonds. Similarly, Wells's study of cohesion in large and small office spaces indicates that the physical dimensions of work areas may bear directly upon the social relations housed therein.

The factors in the physical environment that help and hinder the formation of social interactions may be as gross as the inclusion or exclusion of suitable places in which to congregate. Alternatively, characteristics of meeting places as subtle as the arrangement of seats and tables may, to a lesser extent, serve the same ends; for example, Robert Sommer (1969) provides evidence that individuals seated in line, next to one another, are less likely to converse than when they are seated facing one another across the corner of a table. Citing a second study, Sommer describes an old-age home in which the location of furniture required the residents to seat themselves in rows with their backs to a wall. After introducing tables and locating the chairs around them, Sommer observed that the rate of interactions nearly doubled.

However, this change, which was obviously to the benefit of the elderly residents, was resisted by staff and service personnel. The new arrangement gave the dayroom a "cluttered" look and made it more difficult to clean than it had been when the chairs were arranged in rows. Furthermore, carts and trays, which had previously been moved through the center of the room, had to be rerouted, causing the staff an inconvenience. This observation is similar to that of Steele (1971) who, at the introduction of this chapter, is quoted as follows: "Most influence is exerted by the president and his staff (who control the decisions about facilities) and the maintenance staff (since a major criterion for design is usually whether something will be easy for them to clean)."

The Needs for Self- and Group Esteem

Each of us is surrounded by an invisible sphere that Edward Hall (1966) and others call "personal space." The size of this sphere and the kinds of people admitted within it vary from one culture to another.

Beyond the sphere of personal space is another zone which we usually use unknowingly (and sometimes intentionally) to establish our status vis-à-vis second and third parties. This second space is measured in terms of "social distance" (Hall, 1966, 1972; Sommer, 1969); that is, the difference in status between two people is roughly proportional to the distance that they maintain between one another (social distance) during an interaction. Colleagues who are on good terms with one another will tend to stand closer together than will either of the individuals and his or her superior.

Office designs frequently employ social distance to regulate the status relationships of occupants. We have indicated that the size of an individual's desk relative to those of others is usually taken as an indication of status. Yet, beyond the visual cues provided by the proportions of office furniture, size provides a means for establishing social distance. The larger an individual's desk, the further the visitor to the office must remain from the officeholder, and, consequently, the greater the social distance both parties experience. The authors are familiar with the office of an executive whose desk is not only of monumental proportions, but also constructed in the shape of a hexagon with the back side removed for access. Enclosed by the desk as he is, the executive gives the appearance of being remote and unapproachable.

Height is similarly used to convey status in our culture. "Higher ups" in organizations occasionally have their desks mounted on platforms which elevate them above those who may be seated before them. The effect achieved in this manner may be similar to that described above in the discussion of the oversized door.

The more expensive the furnishings of an office, the more status we attribute to its occupant. "A title on the door rates a Bigelow on the floor." Access to "private" spaces such as executive washrooms, elevators, faculty lounges, and dining rooms renders inferior status to those denied entry. The privacy of the office itself—giving privacy and distance—is important. Finally, individuals who are free to control and manipulate their own surroundings and those of others are perceived to have greater status than individuals who lack these freedoms.

These acts, as well as others, have acquired symbolic meanings in our society and fall into the general category of "status symbols." Other status symbols include having one's own company car, secretary, titles, industry and company certificates (e.g., "one-million club," "Admiral of the Flagship Fleet"), and the like.

The Need for Self-Actualization

According to Maslow (1970), individuals who are fulfilling their need for self-actualization are engaged in the process of becoming what they are potentially. This implies that they are engaged in learning, but what is more, according to Maslow (1971):

> Self-actualizing individuals (more matured, more fully human), by definition, already suitably gratified in their basic needs, are now motivated in other higher ways, to be called "metamotivations" (p. 299).

Maslow postulates that metamotives (unlike those associated with the fulfillment of the needs described in the hierarchy below self-actualization) are experienced as metaneeds and become prepotent in the self-actualizing person. Metaneeds, or B-values as he terms them (Maslow, 1971, p. 311) include the needs for truth, goodness, beauty, wholeness, uniqueness, perfection, justice, playfulness, and self-sufficiency among others (Maslow, 1971, pp. 133–36). What sorts of physical environments are needed to permit the self-actualizing individual to experience goodness, truth, and beauty? Although we cannot answer this question directly, we can refer to the literature to learn of the effects of physical environments on learning processes and of aesthetic qualities of the environment on the average individual's behavior.

The fact that our surroundings affect our ability to learn has been demonstrated by Tognoli (1973) in a study that relates an individual's ability to remember data with attributes of the surroundings in which these data are learned. Tognoli found that the presence or absence of windows and other embellishments in a room were correlated with the occupant's ability to recall that which he had learned therein.

The effects of the aesthetic qualities of environments on the behaviors of subjects have been studied in an experiment by Maslow and Mintz (1972). The experimenters furnished three rooms rendering one of them beautiful (in the eyes of the experimenters), the second, ugly, and the last in-between or "average." Interviewers, who were unaware of the true intent of the study in question, met with groups of subjects in each of the three rooms. The interviewers showed each subject ten negative print photographs of human faces which were to be rated on two six-point scales. Subjects rated each face according to the degrees of fatigue/energy and displeasure/well-being that the face seemed to express.

The subjects in the "beautiful room" gave significantly higher ratings (that is, rated the faces as being expressive of more energy and greater well-being) than did subjects in either the "average" or "ugly" room. "Average room" scores were also higher, on average, than those obtained in the "ugly room," but not significantly so. While the findings obtained in the "average room" are consistently in the predicted directions, the lack of significance noted above leads to speculation that "average" rooms and offices produce effects that are more like those produced by ugly surroundings than by beautiful ones.

While the experiment described above was in progress, a second experiment was under way, one in which the interviewers served as unknowing subjects (Mintz, 1972). On the basis of direct observation and observational notes, it was found that interviewers spent less time in the "ugly room" (finished their testing more rapidly) than they did in the "beautiful room." Furthermore, observational notes indicated that, when working in the "ugly room," interviewers experienced monotony, fatigue, headache, discontent, irritability, hostility, and avoidance of the room. Conversely, when working in the "beautiful room" they experienced feelings of comfort, pleasure, enjoyment, importance, energy, and the desire to continue their activity. From these findings, Mintz concludes that:

> . . . visual-aesthetic surroundings (as represented by the "beautiful room" and the "ugly room") can have significant effects upon persons exposed to them. These effects are not limited either to "laboratory" situations or to initial adjustments, but can be found under naturalistic circumstances of considerable duration (1972, p. 227).

One final observation is that individuals tend to seek fulfillment of their needs in ways that are consistent with the values they hold (Ullrich, 1972). Where people are free to arrange and decorate their work spaces to suit their needs, one finds a tendency for the physical appearance of the work space to reflect the values of its occupant; for example, leanings toward the values related to power and politics will manifest themselves in furniture arrangements, posters, and the like. Similarly, the aesthetic values will become apparent in the works of art with which some people choose to decorate their offices. It may be argued that, within practical limits, individuals who are able to give expression to their values in their work will be better able to fulfill their needs consistent with these values than will those who are inhibited in such expression. Organizations that do not permit the occupant of a work space to alter its arrangement and decorum to suit one's needs and values may, inadvertently, frustrate his or her need-fulfilling activities.

DESIGNING WORK SPACES

Guidelines for the Design of Work Environments

Although it has not been possible in the limited space of this chapter to provide the reader with sufficient information to make him or her a designer of schools or factories, we have suggested ways in which intelligent modifications can be made to limited areas in the workplace. By way of illustration, we can turn to the problem of office design.

The guidelines that we suggest for making systematic use of the material presented above are relatively simple.

1. Ascertain the objectives that are sought in a given workplace (e.g., an office).
2. Determine the activities that seek to produce these outcomes.
3. Rate the physical environment according to its contribution to:
   a. Supporting these activities.
   b. Facilitating the ends to which these activities are addressed.
4. Alter the workplace so as to improve the two criteria mentioned above.

To illustrate a method for using these guidelines, we will consider some rather elementary modifications to the office space of a college professor. Professors engage in a variety of activities in their offices. Obviously, they prepare lectures, write books and articles, counsel students, give tutorial help, and collaborate with colleagues on research projects, committee agenda, and other matters of business. They also read, reflect on theoretical and practical problems, daydream, engage in informal bull sessions, drink coffee, gripe, and involve themselves in a host of other activities, some unrelated to the goals of their school. In

actual practice, we would list the objectives that are sought by the officeholder, and rank order them according to their relative importance. This
implies that the planner will work cooperatively with the officeholder, for
it is unreasonable to assume that the former will, a priori, take into
account the idiosyncratic needs of the latter.

Having rank ordered objectives, the planner in collaboration with the
officeholder will identify the activities associated with the pursuit of
each. Next, the physical attributes to the office will be rated according
to the extent to which they impede or enhance the execution of these
activities and the extent to which these activities, as modified by their
physical surroundings, serve the officeholder's objectives. Less-than-
satisfactory ratings will become the focus for office modification, with
the bulk of effort applied to the higher priority objectives.

By way of illustration, let us return to the problem of the college
professor's office. For the sake of simplicity, we will limit the number
of objectives sought at work to three: teaching, lecture preparation, and
writing.

In Figure 7–1, office layout no. 1 represents the work space assigned
to one of the authors several years ago. Office layout no. 2 represents
one possible improvement to the original layout that has been designed
to facilitate the attainment of the three objectives listed above. In
actual fact, the original layout remained unchanged by the author. This
was primarily because of two factors. At the time, the author was un-
familiar with the literature on the design of physical facilities and,
consequently, insensitive to both the limitations of the office and its
potential. Second, the author was subject to a common misperception,
namely, that of viewing the office as a "Pseudo-Fixed-Furniture Space"
(Steele, 1973). In other words, we tend to take existing furniture and
the like as fixed when, in fact, they are readily movable.

In any event, office layout no. 1 was experienced as being unsatisfactory even though no active steps were undertaken to remedy the sources

TABLE 7–1
Objectives and Activities

Rank-Ordered Objectives	*Associated Activities*
1. Teaching	Tutorial instruction Small group instruction
2. Lecture preparation	Reading Thinking Writing Preparing visual aids
3. Writing	Reading Thinking Small group discussion Writing Drawing

FIGURE 7–1
An Illustration of Office Redesign

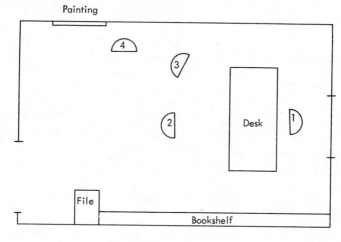

Office Layout No. 1

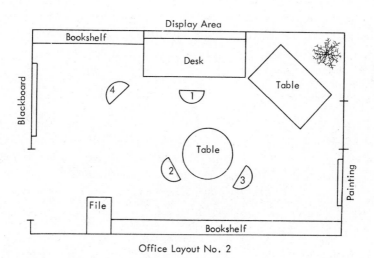

Office Layout No. 2

of dissatisfaction. In the first place, the arrangement of the furniture was unsuitable for tutorial and small group instruction. The room contained no blackboard on which ideas could be represented and explained. Students seated across the desk from their teacher could not view materials on the latter's desk. What is probably most important, a rather great social distance was established between the students seated in chairs 2 and 3 and the teacher in chair 1. Teaching consists of helping others to understand concepts and procedures. Yet, it is difficult at best to help those whom one intimidates. The prestige of a college professor and the social distance he or she maintains from students can serve to inhibit the open and free expression of ideas.

For these and other reasons, the desk has been moved in layout no. 2 to a side wall and a round table introduced. With chairs located around the table, the officeholder is afforded the following options in arranging social interactions. He or she can invite students to sit in chair 2 or 3 and move chair 1 to join them at the table. The professor can indicate to a visitor that he wishes her to sit in chair 4, placing her at a greater social distance than in the former case, or can move chair 4 up to his desk so that the visitor can look over his shoulder, so to speak. The last option provides the least social distance. A blackboard has been introduced as both an aid to teaching and thinking.

The problem of reconfiguring the environment to facilitate the preparation of lectures is addressed, in part, by the movement of the desk to the side of the room. Thinking is aided by the presence of cues that bring to mind information that is relevant to the problem under consideration. For this reason, the wall above the desk has been converted to a display area onto which can be attached charts, lists, graphs, pictures, and the like. This space over the desk, which is normally unused, thus becomes an information display area. As Propst (1968) says:

> The suppression of relevant display is one of the most serious deficiencies in our present office culture and one of the factors most assuredly due for correction. . . . An office with no relevant visual display deprives the human performer of a spectacular recall tool: the human eye as a receptor for the mind (p. 21).

A second bookshelf has been added to the left of the desk for the same reason. The spines of books bearing their titles remind the beholder of their contents. The addition of the blackboard also aids activities that support this objective. Outlines are often worked out at a board rather than on paper. For one thing, the option to work standing up is a valuable one, once discovered. Thinking may be invigorated by changes in posture and activity. Men such as Hemingway and Churchill frequently worked while standing at their desks.

A table has been added to the office to provide a second work station. Different tasks require different supporting facilities and semipermanent work stations are needed for these separate activities. The production of a book or article is a lengthy process for the author. In addition to work spaces that are used for a number of changing activities, the author requires a station that can be permanently set up with the accouterments of his or her trade—a typewriter, papers, drawing equipment, and a good dictionary.

Here, then, is a modest scheme for improving the physical environment of a college professor. Obviously, teachers pursue other activities and objectives than those used to illustrate the design guidelines put forth here. Consequently, our exercise has been less extensive than would be the case in actual practice. Yet, the point is that improvements to the design of physical facilities are well within the scope of ability of the average manager.

Physical Design in the Larger Organization

The individual manager will probably find fewer opportunities and scope in the physical design of units larger than his own office such as his department, division, or organization. Such major physical plants are often perceived as an especially visible "sunk cost." Not only is the organization viewed as being "stuck" with the present design, it is also difficult to make a strong case that a new physical design will, by itself, improve organizational effectiveness. In contrast to common beliefs in the importance of "good communications" (or good social relations, and so on), a "good" executive lounge or a "good building for a sales or marketing department is seen as less important. While we have little systematic study of the effects of physical arrangements on organizational effectiveness, we have cited some case studies as well as anecdotal evidence above, and shall attempt to provide some preliminary notes here on how physical designs may be important for the larger organization.

A Contingency Approach to Design

Here we shall assume a contingency model of the role of physical elements in relation to technology, structure, goals, or environment. An appropriate physical design matches the other impinging elements, and these relationships are conducive to effective organizational functioning. Above we suggested that physical arrangements that fit "people" variables will be conducive to effectiveness (or at least satisfactions that facilitate participation in the workplace, if not the motivation to produce more). Similarly, there must be a good fit between the physical arrangements and technological and environmental dimensions.

A major problem lies in defining the dependent physical variables—developing a taxonomy of organizational variables that have some systematic arrangement to one another. Because there is no accepted theory of physical design, we must rely on interpretations of physical variables in terms of some social variables such as communication, liking, and status. While physical size itself may not have readily understandable implications for behavior in organization, we may interpret size in terms of social cohesiveness, then discuss the fit of size with the degree of cohesiveness required for the attainment of a certain task or goal, and then judge whether the existing fit is sufficiently conducive to organizational effectiveness.

Technology clearly has implications for physical arrangements, and vice versa. A mass-production technology requires large-scale physical arrangements, while certain craft work may be undertaken in smaller facilities. Mass production or routine technologies generally have special work flow requirements, too. The programmed search and low variability that characterize routine technology enable high degrees of operating efficiency through rationalization or the systematic application of various means toward an end product.[3] In our discussions of the long-wall method of coal getting and the waitress versus cook conflict (Chapter 4), we found that such dependencies may have destructive effects on social relations if power and status are not carefully articulated with these dependencies. Alternatively, assembly-line operations have made workers dependent on their assembly line—on the *physical* work flow and only indirectly on other people. That is to say, workers on an assembly line are isolated from one another because noise and the concentration-demanding pace of work prevent communication. They coordinate their work with the activity of the conveyor belt and its materials.

At the extreme, such mass-production technology makes the worker a cog in a machine. It requires that he or she act as an object interacting with other objects, rather than as a social being with the various needs we have discussed above. Of course, these needs must be met, and it would seem that one important question is whether they are met primarily away from the assembly line (on a 5-minute coffee break or a 30-minute lunch, and so on) or whether they are met in part on the job, too. We have already discussed job enrichment as a means whereby technology can be changed to accommodate some of the "people" variables. However, the manipulation of physical variables offers an additional way in which some needs may be met, perhaps without changing the routine nature of the technology and losing its productivity advantages. The use of piped-in music, stimulating paint schemes, and alcoves for social interaction at the job place are examples.

The congruence between physical arrangements and formal (and informal) structure is important, too. In discussing formal structure, we described different arrangements of departments by function, product, process, or geography to emphasize one kind of coordination over the other. As described above, physical arrangements can facilitate organization by product by ensuring that location and distance are minimal for the members of different functions who are assigned to the same product line. Kover (1963) describes how an advertising agency reorganized from function to product. The account executives began to work with their own creative staff along "product" or account lines, and the assignment of offices was changed accordingly. Instead of working in a department consisting wholly of creative personnel, the artists and writ-

---

3 See Thompson (1967) for a discussion of "long-linked" technology.

ers found themselves parceled out to various different product lines or accounts. According to Kover, the physical inability of creative staff to interact with one another, to exchange ideas and social support, was a major factor leading to a high level of turnover. This is understandable in light of Lawrence and Lorsch's (1967) report that managers in a product-organized firm appeared to be more effective in coordinating the work of different functions around the particular product line, but showed higher levels of tension and irritation than managers in a similar, less effective firm organized by function. This firm afforded the security and support of working with members of one's own function who possessed more similar values, orientations, and styles of behaving. If, in fact, the physical arrangements in the advertising reorganization were a major factor in creating turnover, we wonder if provision of some supplemental physical arrangements, such as a lounge for coffee breaks or separate lunchrooms enabling a certain minimal amount of interaction among creative staff, might have alleviated the problems sufficiently to "save" the reorganization.

Let us examine next an example of the interrelations between technology, structure, and physical arrangements. From Perrow's analysis in Chapter 4, we recall that a nonroutine technology is postulated as requiring coordination by feedback within both middle and lower hierarchical levels, as well as interdependence within groups. This type of social system is created by means of the mutual influence found in Likert's cohesive groups (Chapter 3) or in the autonomous work groups described by the Tavistock researchers. We have seen how physical arrangements can be designed to facilitate this kind of social structure and, thereby, the functioning of an organization with a nonroutine technology. When a research institute headed by Rensis Likert was given an opportunity to design its own new building, it did, in fact, design a building with a great deal of open floor space conducive to high social density—one in which the staff could interact and get to know one another. Each floor had perhaps a dozen courtyards or open spaces around which a program director and a number of study directors or assistant study directors had offices, all facing inward onto the open space. A corresponding number of secretarial, clerical, and computational staff members had desks in the courtyard. The entire arrangement encouraged interaction across hierarchical levels within a project, as well as between staff members who were on the same level, but working on different projects. Furthermore, in walking from the central elevators to one's courtyard and workplace, one had to pass through the courtyards of other related programs. These programs comprised a research center within the institute. The arrangement, thereby, facilitated additional, but less intensive, contacts with those in related programs. Finally, all of the institute staff used the same entrance, elevators, lunchroom, library, and so on. Thus, contacts and identification with the institute were facilitated. A possibly serendipitous arrangement was achieved by locating the various business or administrative offices on the first floor, between the entrance and the elevators, encouraging contacts between administrative and professional staff and possibly facilitating harmonious relations between these two often-warring functional groups.

Physical Designs for Diagnosis

While the manager may have little opportunity to design the physical arrangements for an entire organization, knowledge and awareness of physical components are useful diagnostic tools in his or her work. We have postulated that congruency between physical arrangements and technology, structure, people, goals, and environment is likely to lead to organizational effectiveness. If this is true, it is also likely that there will be *some* existing congruency in these elements. We suggest that effective organizations will grow and acquire more resources (see Chapter 2) and will use those resources to arrange the organization in ways (including the congruencies) that are still more effective. For this reason, congruence between physical layout and other organizational variables is likely, and physical layout may provide a quick diagnosis of these variables.

Let us try out this reasoning. Take a business school. One might ask where the top executive's or dean's office is located—secluded from others at the top of a large high-rise building, similar to that of the head of a large corporation, or is it next to the main office which includes the secretarial pool and student admissions office and the like, as a chief development engineer's office might be located near the offices and workplace of the engineering staff and supporting technicians and others on the work team? The first physical layout would suggest that the former business school is structured in some ways like a business and has a relatively "routine" technology. Hierarchical differences are emphasized; students have relatively little power; analyzable search programs and a homogeneous student body may be emphasized. There will be plenty of rules and things will be done by the "book." Students may be treated more or less alike. The second school places less distance between its dean and its staff and students, and its structure and technology may render it more like a research institute than the first business school.

Of course, many of the physical accouterments have symbolic values determined by the local culture. Consequently, the outside observer cannot readily discern the meaning of all of the arrangements he perceives. However, valid diagnostic signs, other than the location of the top executive's office, can generally be found. We can cite the arrangement of parking spaces—whether assigned by name or category of staff, or first-come, first-serve, or perhaps by some differential arrangements across hierarchical levels or by departments or professional groups. The same applies to the number and arrangement of different lunchrooms (sport facilities, and the like) and their assignment.

Two interesting studies have been made of the physical diagnostic signs found in banking establishments (Coffey, Athos, and Reynolds, 1975; Wolf, 1971). Wolf describes a number of physical dimensions that enabled him to distinguish the goals and organizational character of two savings and loan associations. One was situated in a shopping center location in a modern, functional building, draped with a large banner advertising the current interest rate. The chief executive had a modern desk with a "clean" top, clear of papers. The lunchroom for the staff was small and spartan. The other savings and loan association was located in an older, downtown neighborhood and housed in an older, more traditional building relatively unobtrusive in style. The interior was richly furnished with statuary and portraits of the founders. There were flowers on desks and beautiful wood paneling on walls. Staff facilities were comfortable.

As one might expect, the former bank emphasized profitability and had a brash, growth-oriented strategy, while the latter bank had a goal of carrying on traditions with an emphasis on security. Its character included a strong component of the workplace as a "home-away-from-home." In short, we find that physical facilities tend to be congruent with goals; and technology and structure, as well as observations of such facilities, may serve as important clues about the basic nature of the organization for the management consultant.

Physical Designs in Time and Space

Finally, we may observe that physical arrangements can be designed to transcend the organization's boundaries and its present existence. Exemplifying the time dimension, Sears designed its new Chicago headquarters building, now the tallest in the world, so that it can lease out space it will need later as the firm grows in the remaining decades of this century. It has arranged office suites so that it can expand easily in a physical way, by taking over contiguous and integrated facilities from lease holders.

Geographical location, including proximity to important markets and supplies, is obviously important, too. This is even true in the mass-market publishing industry which does not rely on any geographically delimited suppliers or markets. One reason for demise of the magazine *Saturday Review* may have been its movement away from New York and the stimulation and information sources of other editorial and management personnel found primarily there. In contrast, the editor of *Transaction* (now *Society*), Irving L. Horowitz, argues that movement from Washington University, St. Louis, to Rutgers University, New

Brunswick, New Jersey, 35 miles from New York, was useful in providing physical access to New York and the relevant personnel found in sufficient and critical numbers only there.

These examples support the argument that close physical contact—face-to-face contacts, cannot be eliminated entirely by using letters or telephones. It is said that the growth of Chicago's O'Hare airport and the demise of Midway airport, despite strenuous opposition by Mayor Daley, is due to the need for executives from different parts of the country to fly in and talk face-to-face and then fly out, all in the same day. O'Hare has the airline connections plus the meeting facilities for this face-to-face contact. Midway is closer to downtown but does not have the meeting facilities and connections. O'Hare airport serves as a "conference room" for the geographically widespread firms or firms with geographically extensive contacts with other organizations. A firm with these needs does well to site its headquarters and branch operations in towns with good airline connections to a centrally located airport which may serve as its "conference room."

DISCUSSION QUESTIONS

1. What is meant by the term "object language?" Select a room such as the one in which you live or an office and prepare a glossary of the object language found therein.
2. How does the architecture of the room selected for the prior question facilitate or impede behavior? Are these intended consequences of the architecture or unforeseen results?
3. Redesign this space to make it more functional without making major structural changes (e.g., without moving walls, doors, and so on).
4. How practical are such redesign efforts in ongoing organizations? How desirable are they?

REFERENCES

Coffey, Robert E., Athos, Anthony G., and Raynolds, Peter A. *Behavior in organizations: a multidimensional view.* Englewood Cliffs, N.J.: Prentice-Hall, 1975.

Festinger, Leon. Architecture and group membership. In R. Gutman (Ed.), *People and buildings.* New York: Basic Books, 1972. Pp. 120–34.

Fuller, Richard Buckminster. *Utopia or oblivion: the prospects for humanity.* New York: Bantam Books, 1969.

Goffman, Erving. *The presentation of self in everyday life.* Garden City, N.Y.: Doubleday, 1959.

Goffman, Erving. *Asylums: essays on the social situations of mental patients and other inmates.* Garden City, N.Y.: Doubleday, 1961.

Gutman, Robert (Ed). *People and buildings.* New York: Basic Books, 1972.

Hall, Edward T. *The hidden dimension.* Garden City, N.Y.: Doubleday, 1966.

Hall, Edward T. *The silent language.* Greenwich, Conn.: Fawcett Books, 1972.

Herzberg, Frederick, Mausner, Bernard, and Snyderman, Barbara B. *The motivation to work.* New York: Wiley, 1967.

Jacobs, Jane. *The Death and Life of American Cities.* New York: Random House, 1969.

Kover, Arthur J. Reorganization in an advertising agency: a case study of a decrease in integration. *Human Organization*, 1963, 22, 252–59.

Lawrence, Paul R., and Lorsch, Jay W. *Organization and environment: managing differentiation and integration.* Boston: Harvard University, Graduate School of Business Administration, Division of Research, 1967.

Maslow, Abraham H. *Motivation and personality.* New York: Harper & Row, 1970.

Maslow, Abraham H. *The farther reaches of human nature.* New York: Viking Press, 1971.

Maslow, Abraham H., and Mintz, N. L. Effects of esthetic surroundings: I. Initial short-term effects of three esthetic conditions upon perceiving "energy" and "well-being" in faces. In R. Gutman (Ed.), *People and buildings.* New York: Basic Books, 1972. Pp. 212–19.

Mintz, N. L. Effects of esthetic surroundings: II. Prolonged and repeated experience in a "beautiful" and an "ugly" room. In R. Gutman (Ed.), *People and buildings.* New York: Basic Books, 1972. Pp. 220–28.

Perin, Constance. *With man in mind: an interdisciplinary prospectus for environmental design.* Cambridge, Mass.: The M.I.T. Press, 1970.

Propst, Robert. *The office: a facility based on change.* Elmhurst, Ill.: The Business Press, 1968.

Proshansky, Harold M., Ittelson, William H., and Rivlin, Leanne G. (Eds.). *Environmental psychology: man and his physical setting.* New York: Holt, Rinehart, and Winston, 1970.

Proshansky, Harold M., Ittelson, William H., and Rivlin, Leanne G. The influence of the physical environment on behavior: some basic assumptions. In Harold M. Proshansky, William H. Ittelson, and Leanne G. Rivlin (Eds.), *Environmental psychology.* New York: Holt, Rinehart and Winston, 1970. Pp. 27–37.

Ruesch, J., and Kees, W. Function and meaning in the physical environment. In Harold M. Proshansky, William H. Ittelson, and Leanne G. Rivlin (Eds.), *Environmental psychology.* New York: Holt, Rinehart, and Winston, 1970. Pp. 141–53.

Sommer, Robert. *Personal space: The behavioral basis of design.* Englewood Cliffs, N.J.: Prentice-Hall, 1969.

Speer, Albert. *Inside the Third Reich.* New York: Avon, 1971.

Steele, Fred I. The top-down society: spatial decisions in the organizational world. *Environment Planning and Design*, 1971, 1, Summer, 24–30.

Steele, Fred I. *Physical settings and organizational development.* Reading, Mass.: Addison-Wesley, 1973.

Thoday, J. M., and Parkes, A. S. (Eds.). *Genetic and environmental influences on behavior.* New York: Plenum Publishing, 1968.

Thompson, James D. *Organizations in action.* New York: McGraw-Hill, 1967.

Tognoli, J. The effect of windowless rooms and unembellished surroundings on attitudes and retention. *Environment and Behavior*, 1973, 5, 191–201.

Ullrich, Robert A. *A theoretical model of human behavior in organizations: an eclectic approach.* Morristown, N.J.: General Learning Press, 1972.

Wells, B. W. P. The psycho-social influence of building environment: sociometric findings in large and small office spaces. In R. Gutman (Ed.), *People and buildings.* New York: Basic Books, 1972. Pp. 97–119.

Whyte, William F. The social structure of the restaurant. *American Journal of Sociology*, 1949, 54, 302–10.

Wolf, William. Address at Southern Management Association meetings, Miami Beach, November, 1971.

8

Criteria for Evaluating
Organizational Designs

INTRODUCTION

Our interest in organizations will lead us eventually to more detailed examinations of phenomena within them. For the present, however, we shall step back and view them as complete entities again in order to gain a measure of perspective. While gaining perspective at this point will provide a framework within which later expositions on behavior in organizations can be examined, it may be difficult to accomplish. The more we aggregate phenomena (the more comprehensive our study becomes) the more abstract we must be. Furthermore, systematic, scientific study becomes more difficult as the objects of study increase in complexity. For this reason, we will marshal fewer "facts" and, indeed, arrive at fewer conclusions in our analysis of organizations as social entities than we did, for example, in our study of individual behavior in organizations.

Let us begin by asking how we can evaluate an organization as a social entity. At first glance we may respond that the successful attainment of the organization's goals is the sole criterion with which to measure effectiveness. Profitability for business firms and the delivery of quality health care for hospitals are examples of hallmarks that come to mind. For a beginning, let us test the notion that effectiveness can be measured by goal attainment. The following portion of a recent *Fortune* article will cast some doubt on the notion:

> . . . By 1970, too, the leasing companies were depriving I.B.M. of substantial rental revenues. Back in the late 1960's the lessors went on a buying spree, purchasing almost $3 billion worth of 360 computers— or about 12 percent of the 360's installed. Those purchases contributed to the big earnings bulge that I.B.M. registered in 1967 and 1968, but they came at the expense of future rental revenues. The sales-to-rental formula is generally four to one—i.e., a computer that sells for $1 million rents for $250,000 a year. In the long run, rentals obviously bring in a lot more money than outright sales. At least, that has been the experience in the past. (There are still about 3,900 I.B.M. Series 1400

computers out on rental that were manufactured in the late 1950's.) With the introduction of the 360, the leasing companies started getting under I.B.M.'s skin, and Tom Watson demanded that a strategy be formulated to combat them.

. . . The 370 [computer] was designed to accomplish a number of diverse goals, all of which would lead to restoration of I.B.M.'s customary high profitability while achieving a tightening of control over I.B.M. installations. When I.B.M. introduced its 360 computers in 1965, according to Watson, the company realized a net income gain of 20 percent on an installation basis by replacing older computers. It expected to repeat that performance with the 370. At the same time, 370 computers were designed to be compatible with the 360 machines in terms of software, so that the users' huge investment in programming would be protected. The 370 in essence was intended to make 360 programs run faster; the transition to the new machines was to be painless compared to the disruptive way the 360 had been introduced.

Because of its price and design, the 370 packed a two-pronged wallop at those old enemies—the leasing companies and the small manufacturers. To thwart peripherals makers, controls for disk drives were built into the main frames of two 370 models. And the leasing companies were surprised to find that the sales price made re-lease of the new machines unattractive. The 370 is intended to be around for perhaps a decade. So I.B.M. wanted most users to rent the machines—from I.B.M. "As long as we operate legally and fairly," says Watson, "it's not incumbent on us to price our machines to allow the leasing companies to take away our inventory." For rival main-frame manufacturers like Honeywell and Burroughs the surprise in the 370 was the use of semiconductor main memories in two of its five models. Finally, the 370 was viewed by I.B.M. as a stimulant to its own sales force. Says Watson: "You have to keep feeding them new things to keep their morale up."

This carefully laid strategy, however, boomeranged. The 370 hit hardest of all, not I.B.M.'s competitors, but I.B.M.'s own rental base. To start with, the timing of the 370 proved disastrous; announced in June, 1970, the first delivery was made in January, 1971, squarely in the middle of the recession. The timing depended to a large extent on the fact that by 1970 most of the 370 building blocks were in hand, for development had begun as far back as 1965. "We had invested a few hundred million dollars in the 370," says Watson. "Actually, we could stop any product a month before we plan to announce it. But we were reckoning that the economy was going to resume its growth, and it took us a long time to recognize that we were in a serious recession."

. . . As for those archenemies—the leasing companies—they may eventually disappear, but right now they are doing a lot of damage to I.B.M. The 370 forced the leasing firms into a scramble. Leases on many of the machines they acquired in the 1960's are now expiring, and they are eager to farm out these computers on "second" leases, usually at exceedingly low rates, or even to sell them for half their original price. "Nobody is going to rent 360's from I.B.M. anymore," says one computer user. "The leasing company now comes in and says that they'll give you the same central processing unit you are paying $15,000 for in rentals for $8,000 a month."

Similarly, the strategy against the independents turned out to be far from a resounding success, even though Learson predicts that some of I.B.M.'s competitors in peripherals will "go under." The independents haven't yet matched I.B.M.'s new 370 peripherals with their own models. But they continue to offer attractively priced devices that further enhance the value of the 360's to sophisticated users. Observing the 370 versus 360 clash, one executive remarks: "I.B.M. now has its first real competition in the computer business—and the competition is I.B.M."

Looking back, Watson says he is sure that "if we had to do it over again, I would do the same thing. We were committed and the decision had been made." As so often happens with the introduction of a new product, in the case of the 370 the marketing executives won the early round over the engineers. Technical men at I.B.M. would have preferred to have equipped the whole range of 370 computers with semiconductor memories at the same time. That would have made the 370 series more versatile, more powerful, and technologically far ahead of any other computer. But I.B.M.'s marketing men wanted to rush to the customers with the first available new product. Frank Cary puts the reasoning this way: "In the rental business, you either replace yourself or someone else will do it for you." The upshot was that I.B.M.'s two major objectives, to maintain its dominant position in the industry and to make the maximum profit while doing so, clashed painfully (Bylinski, 1972).

Chapter Guide

IBM is an unparalleled organization in many ways and has affected the lives of all of us in one way or another. As awesome as the company is, however, it resembles other organizations, even schools, hospitals, and grocery stores. Before examining characteristics that determine an organization's effectiveness as a social entity, we need to raise some questions.

1. Is continued growth a goal of the IBM Corporation? Is it a goal of all organizations? What are the limits to organizational growth?
2. In what ways does the firm's environment seem to be changing? How did the introduction of the 370 attempt to deal with this change?
3. Is the morale of salesmen a company goal? Is it a goal in the same sense that profitability may be?
4. The article observes that "marketing executives won the early round over the engineers." Are these subunits of the organization in competition with one another? Do they *not* subscribe to a common set of organizational objectives?
5. The story concludes with the statement that "I.B.M.'s two major objectives, to maintain its dominant position in the industry and to make the maximum profit while doing so, clashed painfully." Is it rational to have objectives that clash? Is this phenomenon common? How does a firm go about maximizing profits? How, in fact, does it know at any point in time that it is (or is not) maximizing profits?

6. Do similar problems exist in universities, churches, and hospitals? What are some examples?
7. Do you have conflicting objectives? How do you handle them?

INTERNAL CRITERIA

The Rational and Natural-System Models

Our earlier differentiation of two dissimilar models of organizations —the rational and the natural-system models—provides a starting point for evaluating different organizational designs. The rational model of organization, which views the organization as an instrument (or as a means toward identifiable ends) suggests an evaluation in terms of efficacy in achieving stated goals. In contrast, the natural-system model suggests that survival of the system and, consequently, the optimal articulation of efforts and resources to satisfy system needs (including environmental contingencies) are important design criteria. We will attempt to resolve these conflicting approaches to evaluating designs.

In this chapter, we shall examine the implications of the rational and natural-system models for selecting design criteria. Of course, we hope to provide criteria for selecting appropriate structures, technology, and people for specific organizational purposes. Depending on the criteria we use to judge an organization's performance, we will come up with different recommendations.

A Goal View of Organizational Effectiveness

If we follow the rational model of organizations, we must develop measures of goal attainment. At first glance, this appears a simple task. Profitability and return on investment (ROI) calculations are readily available. However, as we saw in Chapter 5, the goals of profit-oriented organizations range far beyond profitability and ROI. Some organizations are concerned primarily with stability (or risk); some want quantity of production (or quality). Furthermore, statistics comparable to profitability calculations are generally unavailable in other kinds of organizations such as hospitals, schools, and governmental agencies. For these reasons, we are impelled to learn more about other kinds of organizational goals and to develop corresponding measures of achievement.

Criterion Measures

One apparently successful method polls organizational members and qualified "outsiders" for their perceptions of the organization's goals and its performance in attaining them. One such technique was developed by Georgopoulos and Mann (1962) for a study of community general hospitals and later elaborated for use in a variety of different organizations (Price, 1972). Georgopoulos and Mann asked the following question of hospital staff members:[1] "On the basis of your experience and information, how would you rate the quality of *overall care* that the patients generally receive from this hospital?" This question was followed by seven alternative responses: (1) outstanding, (2) excellent, (3) very good, (4) good, (5) fair, (6) rather poor, and (7) poor. The researchers found that hospitals differed significantly in the quality of overall care they provided as rated by this questionnaire item, as well as in the quality of medical care and nursing care as rated in similar items for relevant groups of professional staff. In order to demonstrate that the evaluations of overall care were characteristic of the organization as a whole and not affected differentially across subgroups within the organizations, the researchers aggregated the ratings for each hospital by work group characteristics such as raters' shift of work, division where working, medical specialty, and status as full- or part-time employee. Ratings thus categorized were not significantly different from those obtained from the larger organizational unit. Therefore, answers to the questions apparently reflected organizational effectiveness as a whole and not merely subgroup effectiveness.

The Validity of Criterion Measures

The validity of this sort of measure of organizational effectiveness has been demonstrated by correlations with other volunteered comments about the organization (e.g., "I would send my family here"), as well as by correlations with other relevant questionnaire items (Price, 1972). Subsequent research shows that the measurement of medical care using these kinds of questions is significantly correlated with "harder," more objective data from hospital records. For example, the hospitals in which patients with a diagnosis of diabetes are most likely to receive a urine analysis within 24 hours of admission—a practice which experts judge to constitute good medical care (Basil S. Georgopoulos, personal communication).

Survey items constructed to elicit ratings of effectiveness may be used for a variety of different organizations. Below are examples of survey items designed for use in a governmental service agency. Bennis (1959) suggests that organizations can be assigned to four major categories according to the nature of their goals or major functions (see Table 8–1). To assess their effectiveness, one would obtain a statement of

---

[1] Hospital staff was defined to include medical staff, registered nurses, lab and X-ray technicians, various administrators, and members of the board of trustees.

TABLE 8–1
Typology of Organization

Type of Organization	Major Function	Examples	Effectiveness Criterion
Habit	Replicating standard and uniform products	Highly mechanized factories, etc.	Number of products
Problem solving	Creating new ideas	Research organizations; design and engineering divisions; consulting organizations, etc.	Number of ideas
Indoctrination	Changing people's habits, attitudes, intellect, behavior (physical and mental)	Universities, prisons, hospitals, etc.	Number of "clients" leaving
Service	Distributing services either directly to consumer or to above	Military, government, advertising, taxi companies, etc.	Extent of services, services performed

Source: Bennis (1959, p. 299).

goals or functions against which ratings and records data on actual goal attainment can be measured.

Multiple Goals

A major shortcoming of dealing with evaluation in this way is that the organization is likely to have a variety of goals rather than a single, overriding one. In a study of the goals of top executives in 145 businesses, Dent (1959) found that the goals most frequently mentioned were three: profits, public service (in the form of producing quality products), and employee welfare. It is interesting to note that only about one third of Dent's sample mentioned profits. Even when individuals who responded other than by mentioning profits, public service, or employee welfare as goals were eliminated from the sample, only half of the remaining managers cited profitability. We might infer that half of the managers in the sample did not consider profitability an important goal. As Anthony (1960) suggests, profit-maximization may be viewed by business managers as being too difficult to attain, unrealistic, and immoral.

Having been assured that their interviews would be held in complete confidence, Dent's subjects can be assumed to have been candid; their emphasis on goals other than profit can be attributed to more than platitudes in the interest of good public relations. Limiting our focus to the first three of the aims voiced by each manager, we find that nearly 40 percent of the respondents cited "providing a good service or a public service." A similar percentage of the sample cited "providing for the welfare of employees—a good living, security, happiness, good working conditions." Other important goals mentioned were growth, efficiency, meeting competition, and operating the organization. Furthermore, one sixth of the managers cited more than three goals. Clearly, there is no single goal that one can use as a criterion, even for an evaluation of a single kind of organization.

As Seashore (1965) observes:

> Most organizations have many goals, not one. These goals are of unlike importance and their relative importance changes. Problems arise because these goals are often competing (i.e., have tradeoff value), and sometimes incompatible (negatively correlated). A strategy of optimal realization of goals cannot be determined unless there exists some conception of the dimensions of performance, their relative importance, and their relationships with one another. These relationships may be of causation, of simple correlation, of interaction; they may be linear and compensatory or nonlinear and noncompensatory (Seashore, 1965, p. 26).

A further problem in effectiveness measurement in terms of goal attainment is that different individuals or groups in an organization often have different expectations concerning its goals. A study of 97 small businesses (Friedlander and Pickle, 1968) shows that the needs and demands of (1) owners, (2) employees, and (3) interested third parties (e.g., governments, customers, suppliers, creditors, and so on) generally are not fulfilled concurrently. Very few positive relationships were found among employee, owner, and societal interests (see also Pickle and Rungeling, 1973).

As we said in Chapter 5, many organizations encompass numerous different groups having goals that are incompatible or inconsistent to varying degrees. Attempts to reconcile these differences take the forms of bargaining and coalition formation, and the ensuing compromises frequently result in sets of mutually established organizational constraints that arise from these processes (Cyert and March, 1965). The use of goals as the sole criterion for evaluating organizations does not provide a simple or straightforward solution.

Empirical Approaches to Evaluation Criteria

The goal approach starts with an a priori model of organizational behavior which is used as a rationale for selecting criteria. Alternatively, we may take a more inductive approach to the problem. Starting with a great many measures of organizational performance (ratings, judgments, statistical records, and so on), we can attempt to establish the existence of functional relationships among the various measures and, possibly, correlations with some basic overall judgment.

In an early study that compared various methods of evaluation, Georgopoulos, Indik, and Seashore (1960) found that an empirically developed model predicted overall effectivenes about as well as did other, more theoretically based models. More recently, Seashore and Yuchtman (1967) studied the 11-year history of 76 different kinds of records data (taken from an original source of 200 items) which were obtained from 75 insurance sales agencies located throughout the United States. The application of a statistical technique known as factor analysis reduced these 76 categories of data to 10 general factors (see Table 8–2), which showed fairly consistent relationships to one another over the 11-year period. Seashore and Yuchtman (1967), however, did not interpret the ten factors as organizational goals, since some were

TABLE 8–2
Performance Factors in Insurance Agencies

Factor	Assigned Name	No. Assigned Variable	Indicator Variables
I	Business volume*	Ia	Number of policies in force (year's end).
		Ib	New insurance sold (dollar volume).
		Ic	Renewal premiums collected (dollars).
		Id	Number of lives insured (year's end).
		Ie	Agency manpower (number of agents).
II	Production cost	IIa	Production cost per new policy.
		IIb	Production cost per $1,000 of insurance.
		IIc	Production cost per $100 of premium.
III	New member productivity	IIIa	Average productivity per new agent.
		IIIb	Ratio of new agent versus old agent productivity. (New agent less than five years of service.)
IV	Youthfulness of members	IVa	Ratio of younger (under 35) to total membership.
		IVb	Ratio of productivity of younger members to total members of agency.
V	Business mix†	Va	Average premium per $1,000.
		Vb	Percentage of new policies with quarterly payments.
		Vc	Percentage of business in employee trust.
VI	Manpower growth	VIa	Net change in manpower during year.
		VIb	Ratio of net change to initial manpower.
VII	Management emphasis	VIIa	Manager's personal commissions.
VIII	Maintenance cost‡	VIIIa	Maintenance cost per collection.
		VIIIb	Maintenance cost per $100 premium collected.
IX	Member productivity	IXa	Average new business volume per agent.
X	Market penetration	Xa	Insurance in force per capita.
		Xb	Number of lives covered per 1,000 insurables.

* Including both accumulated volume and current increment in volume.
† Many low-value transactions versus fewer high-value transactions.
‡ Refers to maintenance of accounts, not of physical facilities.
Source: Seashore and Yuchtman (1967, p. 383).

clearly means toward other goals. The common denominator in all the factors was ". . . that they represent the acquisition of resources for organizational functioning from the organizations' environments" (p. 392).

From the vantage point of the natural-systems model, the results of the Seashore and Yuchtman study suggest that one should judge organizations, not on the basis of goal attainment, but on their performance in processes of exchange (of scarce and valued resources) with their environments. In this light, organizational effectiveness is viewed in terms of the organization's strengths in bargaining for scarce resources: "We define the effectiveness of an organization as its ability to exploit its environments in the acquisition of scarce and valued resources to sustain its functioning" (Seashore and Yuchtman, 1967, p. 393). We shall return to this definition later.

Limitations of the Empirical Approach

Other investigators have used empirical approaches to generate useful intermediate criteria. Mahoney (1967) studied 114 criteria that were developed for 283 organizational units which were subordinated to 84 managers in 13 companies. Some 24 "mid-range" criteria were found by intercorrelating (factor analyzing) the 114 items (see Table 8–3). Figure 8–3 shows the more important of these factors found in the business organization. Further analysis indicated that of these, the most important factors (the most highly correlated with ratings of overall effectiveness) were: (1) productivity-support-utilization; (2) planning; (3) reliability; and (4) initiation.

Using the 24 dimensions described above, Mahoney and Weitzel (1969) studied 103 research and development units associated with 4 companies. Ratings by 32 managers indicated a somewhat different model for R&D departments (see Figure 8–1b), with the most important dimensions being: (1) reliability; (2) cooperation; and (3) development.

Therefore, the empirical approach does not seem to yield a single, small set of criteria of effectiveness in different kinds of organizations. It may be possible to discover a small number of criteria that can be applied to specific types of organizations such as the above-mentioned types given by Bennis. However, this remains to be seen.

Efficiency

In addition to the rational, a priori approach and the inductive approach, a third approach to evaluating organizational designs, which is also derived from the rational model, used measures of efficiency as criteria. Under this rationale, one disclaims goals and attends instead

TABLE 8–3
Dimensions of Organizational Effectiveness with Standardized Regression Coefficients*

	Model	
		Research
	General	and
Dimension	Business	Development
Flexibility. Willingly tries out new ideas and suggestions, ready to tackle unusual problems.	.07	−.19
Development. Personnel participate in training and development activities; high level of personnel competence and skill.	.08	.23
Cohesion. Lack of complaints and grievances; conflict among cliques within the organization.	.07	−.00
Democratic supervision. Subordinate participation in work decisions.	.03	.01
Reliability. Meets objectives without necessity of follow-up and checking.	.13	.27
Selectivity. Doesn't accept marginal employees rejected by other organizations.	.02	−.16
Diversity. Wide range of job responsibilities and personnel abilities within the organization.	−.02	−.03
Delegation. High degree of delegation by supervisors.	.04	−.09
Bargaining. Rarely bargins with other organizations for favors and cooperation.	−.05	.01
Emphasis on results. Results, output, and performance emphasized, not procedures.	.01	.14
Staffing. Personnel flexibility among assignments; development for promotion from within the organization.	.06	.01
Coordination. Coordinates and schedules activities with other organizations, utilizes staff assistance.	−.08	−.08
Decentralization. Work and procedural decisions delegated to lowest levels.	−.01	.19
Understanding. Organization philosophy, policy, directives understood and accepted by all.	−.08	−.04
Conflict. Little conflict with other organization units about authority or failure to meet responsibilities.	−.09	−.01
Personnel planning. Performance not disrupted by personnel absences, turnover, lost time.	−.04	−.06
Supervisory support. Supervisors support their subordinates.	−.12	−.04
Planning. Operations planned and scheduled to avoid lost time; little time spent on minor crises.	.25	.31
Cooperation. Operations scheduled and coordinated with other organizations; rarely fails to meet responsibilities.	.11	.33
Productivity-support-utilization. Efficient performance; mutual support and respect of supervisors and subordinates; utilization of personnel skills and abilities.	.43	.12
Communication. Free flow of work information and communications within the organization.	−.07	−.27
Turnover. Little turnover from inability to do the job.	.01	.17
Initiation. Initiates improvements in work methods and operations.	.09	.12
Supervisory control. Supervisors in control of progress of work.	.03	.08
Multiple correlation, R	.76	.79

* Standardized regression coefficients are estimates of relationships between the dimensions and ratings of effectiveness.
Source: Mahoney and Weitzel (1969, p. 358).

FIGURE 8–1
Diagram of Relationships of Midrange Criteria of Organizational
Effectiveness to Overall Effectiveness in (a) General Business
Model and (b) Research and Development Model

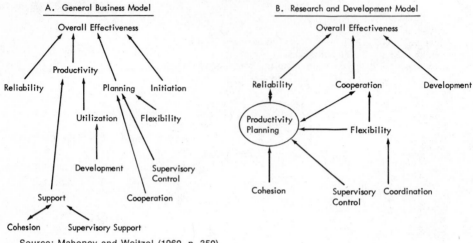

Source: Mahoney and Weitzel (1969, p. 359).

to the efficacy of organizational means in pursuing ends that are "given." Efficiency is measured by the ratio of organizational output to input. Much of the psychological literature on supervisory practices and work group arrangements uses "productivity" as a dependent variable and as an efficiency criterion of sorts. This kind of research commonly focuses on such questions as: What leadership style will allow the supervisor to get the most productivity from his work group?

Katz and Kahn (1966) speak of "energic" efficiency or the ratio of the energy produced by an organization to the energy it consumes in the process. Unfortunately, supplies, equipment, people, money, and information are not readily convertible to units of energy. Furthermore, overhead, indirect costs, and the like are difficult to measure systematically. However, Katz and Kahn argue that they can examine the relative efficiency of an organization if not its absolute efficiency; they can determine whether an organization consumes more resources and energy than another, in producing a similar level of output.[2]

---

[2] In viewing organizations as producers and consumers of information as well as of other commodities, one comes to find fault with the use of energy as an efficiency measure. If information is an output, then organizations need not run down as would be suggested by the Second Law of Thermodynamics. Culture or informational complexity may be built up, giving the organization antientropic properties (Buckley, 1967; Fuller, 1969).

FIGURE 8–2
Three Views of Organizational Effectiveness

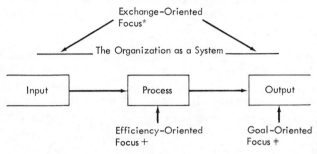

* e.g., Seashore and Yuchtman (1967).
† e.g., Katz and Kahn (1966).
‡ e.g., Georgopoulos and Mann (1962).

Potential and Actual Efficiency

A distinction between "potential" and "actual" efficiency is useful (Katz and Kahn, 1966). So far, we have described efficiency in terms of the ratio of the value of output to its costs of production. This concept can be refined by distinguishing between: (*a*) the potential efficiency conjectured for a particular design, and (*b*) the actual efficiency experienced when an organization design is implemented and operated under a variety of different conditions, including in an environment where things sometimes go wrong. Katz and Kahn suggest that some designs are more capable of actualizing their potential than others having equal potential, but which seem to be "fragile" or "accident prone." Potential efficiency is a concept with origins in the rational model of organization. The concept of actual efficiency admits to the importance of complex and sometimes unknown factors in both the organization and its environment and, in so doing, approaches the natural-system model of organization. Of the two, actual efficiency is more useful to the middle manager who deals with day-to-day problems. The concept of potential efficiency is useful to top management as an indication of the extent to which management intervention can improve ordinary practice. Potential efficiency, in short, may serve as a goal for the organization as a whole.

The efficiency approach to evaluating organizations is based ultimately on the notion that an organization of parts is better (more efficient) at producing desired outcomes than is a disorganized aggregation of the same parts. According to this logic, individuals will tend to remain organized because of the advantages of this efficiency. It is but a short step from this view of organizations to the "system" approach, a point of view that is similar to Gouldner's "natural-system" model of organizations (Etzioni, 1960).

The System Approach to Evaluation

A fourth approach to evaluating organizations, the system approach, uses "system need" variables as criteria. System analysis begins, not with organizational goals, but with a model of the system that is capable of achieving these goals. In developing a model, one identifies various independent subcomponents of the system and specifies for each a set of prerequisite operating requirements (needs). Next, one ascertains the extent to which these various system needs are being met and whether the balance of organizational effort has been optimally distributed among the subcomponents according to their specific needs. Sometimes an organization's members are not conscious of all the needs of the system to which they belong. Nevertheless, if we view organizations as natural systems rather than as rational "tools," we must argue that the fulfillment of system needs is prerequisite to organizational success. An organization that devotes all of its resources and efforts to goal attainment, and in so doing neglects some of its system needs, may eventually prove ineffectual in achieving its goals. It may even fail to survive (Etzioni, 1960).

A study of the theoretical requirements of an organization as an open system and empirical investigations of a variety of different organizations, including especially hospitals, has yielded a list of seven basic organizational "problems" (Georgopoulos, 1970):

> (1) The ability of the organization to adapt to the external environment and carry on an effective interchange with it at all times. This includes ability to respond successfully to relevant changes in the outside world; to obtain resources and personnel; to maintain advantageous relationships with outside interest groups; to project a creditable image and maintain a favorable reputation in the community; and generally to influence the environment in ways that benefit the system and its members in relation to all aspects of organization-environment articulation.
> (2) The ability of the organization to deploy and allocate available resources, facilities, funds, and personnel in the most appropriate manner; to handle related problems of access to, and distribution of, authority, rewards, and information among the participants; and to solve problems concerning work specialization and the allocation of tasks and functions among departments, groups, and members.
> (3) The ability to articulate and constantly coordinate, in time and space, the many diverse but related roles and interdependent activities of its many different staffs and members, so that the energies and efforts of all the participants always converge toward the solution of system problems and the attainment of organizational objectives.
> (4) The ability of the system to integrate itself. This includes all necessary functions associated with the problem of integrating in-

dividual members into the system and securing their cooperation and compliance, and the problem of integrating all parts of the social system with one another so that the total organization can achieve a certain overall social-psychological unity and coherence. Generally, it involves the development of common organizational values and shared norms, attitudes, and mutual understandings, which can serve to provide a common universe of discourse for the different groups and members, and to socialize and bind the members securely into the system.

(5) The ability to minimize and resolve the tensions and conflicts which arise within the organization; particularly frictions and confrontations among interacting groups, and members and among equal status participants, and to manage and control stress and strain throughout the system.

(6) The ability to reach and maintain high levels (in terms of quantity, quality, and cost) of output, e.g., patient care and health service to its clients, at all times. This involves the ability to maximize efficient and reliable performance by all departments, groups, and members, at all levels, and is in turn dependent upon maximization by the system of opportunities for personal goal attainment and job satisfaction on the part of the members.

(7) The ability of the organization to preserve its identity and integrity as a distinct and unified problem-solving system, or to maintain itself and its basic character and viability, regardless of changes which are constantly occurring within and outside it, including potential disruptions and threats to the survival or well being of the organization (pp. 65–66).

The system approach to evaluation seems to be more complex and, therefore, more difficult to apply than the goal approach described at the beginning of this chapter (Schulberg, Sheldon, and Baker, 1969). Organization theorists have not yet agreed on a single list of system needs. Furthermore, the differing lists of the various theorists tend to be quite long and complex. On the other hand, by relying on a variety of system needs, this approach may be less prone to bias than the goal approach, which uses organization-defined criteria that are based on one goal (or at most, a few) as they are reported by one or more individuals (Etzioni, 1960). In other words, the system approach seems to be more comprehensive and, therefore, more balanced. However, proponents of the system approach, who look for balance in what presently exists in an organization, are accused of being more conservative than the advocates of the goal view, who focus on ideals and the potential to improve on the status quo. But, in fact, the goal view can tend toward Utopianism or unrealistic expectations for achievement, since goals are relatively easy to state in a neat, clear, and idealistic fashion. The system approach seems more realistic in that it highlights the difficulties that can be anticipated in operating and changing the organization (Etzioni, 1960).

Our position on the matter is that although the system view is complex and unwieldy, certain basic system needs can be isolated and incorporated into the goal approach to evaluation. Later, we will pursue this notion under a discussion of the "system resource" approach to evaluating organizations.

EXTERNAL PERSPECTIVES

Profit: Efficiency and Political Effectiveness

For the most part, our discussions of efficiency and system need criteria have focused "inside" the organization, so to speak. The efficiency model, of course, is most useful internally, where management has sufficient control (through the buffering out of external uncertainties) to attempt a "rational" arrangement of means in the service of known ends (Thompson, J., 1967). The natural-system model directs our attention toward prerequisites for system survival and the attendant needs for organizational adaptation. However, the specific elements in most of these models tend to describe characteristics of the internal organization. Next we look at profit and explicit considerations of the organization's relationships with other entities in the environment as evaluation criteria.

Our earlier discussion of the concept of energic efficiency becomes relevant here. An inefficient firm can be profitable, but not as profitable as another firm which is similar to the first in all other respects, but more efficient. However, profit is determined by more than efficiency.

Some costs of production will be born by the organization, but "profitable" management sees to it that as many costs as possible are born by its personnel and outside groups—not by the organization per se. Costs born by outside groups include pollution and degradation of the environment, which are costly to undo or repair. These are termed "externalities" by economists. Employees also bear costs of production, such as tensions, frustration, and the psychosomatic illnesses that production can bring on. In dealing with externalities and human costs so as to strike an advantageous balance between costs born by the organization and by others, management evidences what is termed "political" effectiveness (Katz and Kahn, 1966).

Management also exercises political effectiveness when it persuades or influences suppliers and customers (or clients) to enter into transactions that are to the advantage of their organization. The value of the organization's outputs is thereby enhanced. Additional ways of increasing political effectiveness include advertising and lobbying for fair-trade legislation, subsidies, and tariffs (see Figure 8–3).

Through various forms of persuasion, negotiation, and the exercise of influence, the organization maximizes its return at the expense of other organizations or individuals. These political means of gaining advan-

FIGURE 8–3
A System View of Organizations

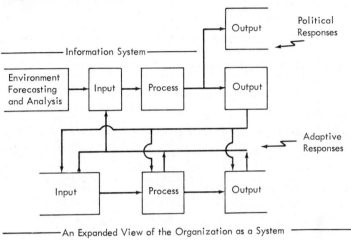

—————An Expanded View of the Organization as a System ———

tages entail shifting costs to other entities; efficiency involves gaining advantages through shifting internal arrangements to reduce costs and increase outputs. Both approaches contribute to profitability: return to the organization by (1) economic and technical means (efficiency) and (2) by political means.

Long-Run Efficiency

In observing efficiency and political effectiveness, we must also note how these attributes affect the organization over time. Attempts to increase efficiency may entail the creation of inventories, the acquisition of advanced technology, or organizational growth undertaken to achieve economies of scale. These strategies are clearly geared to long-run efficiency. Similarly, attempts to apply political pressure to outside groups and organizations may result ultimately in a measure of control over the environment. These outcomes of long-term political effectiveness and efficiency will enhance the probability of the organization's *survival,* which is often used as an ultimate criterion for organizational functioning. (See Figure 8–4.)

Organizational Effectiveness from the Perspective of the Larger System

We have viewed the transactions between an organization and its environment primarily in terms of advantages to the organization. Study of the problem at a higher level of aggregation is also useful. For the moment, let us inquire about the kinds of organizational designs and

FIGURE 8–4
Economic Efficiency and Political Effectiveness: Vehicles for Profit and Survival

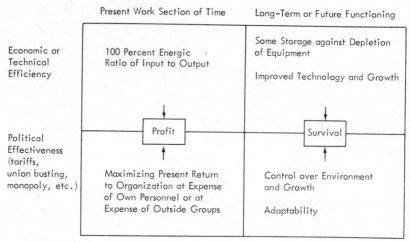

Source: Katz and Kahn (1966, p. 166).

organizational functioning, including the nature of exchanges with the environment, that are most efficient for the larger system (organization and relevant environment) *as a whole.*

There are a number of valid reasons for studying the larger system of which the organization is merely a part or subsystem. We are becoming increasingly interdependent with organizations in our own society, as well as with various segments of other societies. Increasing differentiation and specialization of social units constitute a major impetus toward interdependence (Durkheim, 1947). Also, in the near future at least, competition for natural resources may tend to assume the characteristics of zero-sum games rather than variable-sum or increasing-sum situations (Meadows, Meadows, Randers, and Behrens, 1972). This appears particularly valid due to rising expectations of lesser developed countries. Furthermore, individuals throughout the world are increasingly aware of the larger system through mass media, with the result that both interdependence and expectations for social progress are increased (see, for example, McLuhan, 1967).

If we adopt a larger system, perhaps societal, perspective, we will consider whether the organization is effective *as a component of the larger system.* Following the thinking of Katz and Kahn (1966), we can inquire whether the organization contributes to the efficiency, environmental control, and survival of the total system, which includes the organization in question. We might ask whether the functioning of General Motors, IBM, The League of Women Voters, and the Committee to

Re-elect the President, each of which may be an effective organization, also contributes to the efficiency of the United States of America of which these organizations are a part. In short, the criteria developed by Katz and Kahn can be applied, at least in theory, to the organization's contribution to the larger system.

The goal approach to evaluating organizations also corresponds to the larger system level. Parsons (1956) suggests that we try to analyze the special functions or contributions of the organization as they apply to the larger society. For example, we saw in Chapter 5 that a sample of university administrators and faculty members believe that the top two goals of the university ought to be to: (1) protect the faculty's right to academic freedom and (2) train the students in methods of scholarship and/or scientific research and/or creative endeavor. However, we cannot accept these stated goals without question. The university contributes differently to different segments of the larger system. For instance, the local business community may view the historical contribution of the university as providing a pool of well-trained young people for entry level managerial and professional positions. The business executives may see the university as most useful in training students for positions in a business organization and less useful in educating for scholarship or scientific research, as the faculty see it. Because these conflicts are perceived by different groups, we argue that the goal or function of a subsystem in relation to the larger system can be identified most readily in terms of the mutual expectations that system components have of one another.

Domain Consensus

Transactions with the larger system can be identified where these contributions have been "legitimated" (Parsons, 1956)—that is, where consensus exists among organizational members and members of the public at large that the organization "ought to be doing one thing or another." James Thompson (1967) refers to this state of affairs as "domain consensus." In studying relationships among health care agencies in the community, Levine and White (1961) refer to domain as the "claim which an organization stakes out for itself in terms of: (1) diseases covered, (2) population served, and (3) services rendered." The notion of domain can be applied to other organizations; for example, A&P produces and sells high-quality basic food products at relatively low prices. To the extent that other organizations or units in the environment accept this organization's domain, domain consensus exists. A hospital may stake out a domain of certain kinds of patients, who receive certain kinds of treatment, and who are drawn from a certain portion of the community. Physicians, other hospitals, and health care agencies support the hospital's domain by referring to it appropriate patients, rerouting inappropriate patients, providing backup support in emergencies, loaning equipment or staff, and so on. The important point here is that domain consensus can be used to identify the criteria by which an organization is judged—criteria regarding contributions to the larger system.

Domains as Subsystems

Given the great complexity of the larger system (society), legitimation of goals, or domain consensus, may be relatively circumscribed—that is, limited to a portion of the larger system. In a particular community, only other hospitals, physicians, welfare agencies, and the like will clearly recognize the domain of a particular hospital and refer patients to it appropriately. If this is true, then one is still left with primarily a subsystem frame of reference, as provided by Katz and Kahn. In this case, the subsystem is larger than the organization under study, but considerably smaller than the entire system. A domain may consist of little more than a federation or combination of organizations, and one may consider the effectiveness of a member organization in relation to its contributions to the confederation.

At a higher level of aggregation, one may also consider the effectiveness of the designs of organizations that comprise the federation vis-à-vis the federation's environment; namely, other organizations, groups of organizations, and unorganized groups in the still larger social system. For example, instead of evaluating a municipal hospital on the basis of the number of patients it handles for the city welfare department, one may evaluate the city's combined health care delivery systems to determine how they enable the city to compete with other cities for new industry. Competition will be based, in part, on the quality of health care that the city provides. Success in attracting new industry may increase the city's tax base and, in turn, provide additional resources for the improvement of existing health care delivery systems as well as other services. Thus, we have evaluated the municipal hospital in terms of its contributions (both legitimated and not legitimated) to the city which comprises the municipal government, city dwellers, private industry, and so forth. Obviously, a large system perspective is essential for certain planning purposes.

Organizational Contributions to the "General Good"

Extending the direction of our line of inquiry, we can examine the role of a particular organization in terms of its contributions to the effectiveness of the "largest system," the society of which it is a part; for example, we may inquire whether the organization in question specializes appropriately vis-à-vis other organizations, given their respective capabilities, opportunities, and the like. Inquiry such as this, in the largest sense of the word, led the Soviet Union to request that Romania emphasize agricultural production and that East Germany (German Democratic Republic) focus on industrial production for the good of the Soviet bloc (Comecon) nations as a whole. From this perspective, a single organization's political effectiveness (in Katz and Kahn's sense of the term) is not relevant. Success in forcing others to bear costs is not efficient for the system as a whole. This assumes, of course, both the presence of an overall goal for the society in question and the opportunity to arrange means toward that end. However, political effectiveness defined in terms of an organization's ability to force costs on organizations that are *outside* of the society in question can contribute to the political effectiveness of the larger system.

However, there is no consensus about the "general good." There are no agreed goals for systems larger than the single organization; for example, Romania has taken a more independent stand than other members of the Soviet bloc and turned to advanced industrialization. In fact, as we saw in Chapter 5, clearly defined goals are often lacking at the organizational level as well. Rather, what we find in society is a concern for the politics of subsystems, a concern for who gets what, when, and where (Lasswell, 1936). This observation is not merely a reflection of Western values and their emphasis on the individual or the subsystem; it is a reflection of fact and a result of the descriptive analysis of current behavior around us.[3]

The normative point we raise here is that a larger system perspective is undesirable as long as there are major disagreements and conflicts over the distribution of valued resources. A rational approach which evaluates an organization in terms of its contribution to the efficiency or effectiveness of the larger system assumes that there is some ultimate goal in relation to which relative efficiency is appropriate. At the subsystem level, one would evaluate a university in terms of the numbers and quality of educated students graduated. But, at the larger system level, government officials must decide on the goals of society, and it is not yet clear how much education, not to mention how much good health, we should enjoy. If the "pursuit of happiness" is our goal, perhaps good health is more important than education. If this is the case,

---

[3] It has been observed that much of present-day descriptive sociology provides an invitation to join the conservative party (Dahrendorf, 1958). Considering whether subsystems or supersystems should be given top priority involves us, among other things, in assumptions about human nature. Given the pessimistic, Hobbesian view of man's potential, one becomes concerned about the possible harm which can befall individuals if human nature is not constrained. Hence, one will be led to focus on the subsystem and its protection. A more liberal view of the inherent goodness of human nature will lead one to speculate about the gains that will be realized from the actualization of human potential. Here, one will be led to stress the advantages of joining together and working in trusting collaboration. One's focus will become the supersystem so as to enhance outcomes for all and ultimately for each individual, too.

we should have fewer universities and more hospitals. But how many hospitals and how few universities? Later on in Chapter 14 we will suggest that instead of a rational approach to these matters, a "muddling through" approach may be better. At this point it is sufficient to observe that the larger system viewpoint seems to raise more questions than it answers.

A FRAMEWORK FOR EVALUATION

Operative Goals and System Needs

This is all quite complex. The goal approach leaves questions of efficiency begging. Furthermore, official goals may not be the "real" goals of the organization. Different groups within an organization may profess different, often conflicting goals. The efficiency approach attends to a very limited portion of the organization's behavior. The system need approach is complicated and quite difficult to pursue if one is to evaluate the performance of an actual organization rather than an abstract "system." Finally, the larger system perspective raises the question of *which* larger system one should select for evaluation: The organization's domain, some related subset of society, or society at large?

An increasingly common response in the literature (Ansoff and Brandenburg, 1971; Hall, R., 1972; Mott, 1972; Perrow, 1971; Yuchtman and Seashore, 1967) is to throw up one's hands in the face of these problems and to settle for some set of "operative" or intermediate goals which correspond fairly well to some basic system needs. Yuchtman and Seashore (1967) have proposed a "system resource" approach which builds on the Katz and Kahn view that organizations are open systems which must be politically effective and thus compete and bargain for resources with the environment. In this sense, an organization is effective according to its "ability . . . in either relative or absolute terms, to exploit its environment in the acquisition of scarce and valued resources" (Yuchtman and Seashore, 1967, p. 898). However, Yuchtman and Seashore differ from Katz and Kahn in postulating that only the "ability to exploit the environment" is maximized, not the actual resource acquisition, since the latter might lead to dangers of various kinds. The organization attempts to optimize (rather than maximize) its resource procurement so as to avoid "depletion of its resource-producing environment or the devaluation of the resource, or . . . stimulation of countervailing forces within that environment" (p. 902). It will be recalled that the Standard Oil Trust tried to maximize resource procurement, with the result that the government attacked and broke it up with antitrust legislation.

We can simplify the views of Yuchtman and Seashore (1967) and postulate that organizations are effective to the extent that they acquire power over their environment. Organizations must engage in transactions with the environment to acquire resources which, in turn, facilitate the organization's goal attainment. The needed resources may be of various kinds, and the kinds of relationships in which power can be used to acquire them are many. Hence, there is no single criterion with which to measure effectiveness. However, according to this line of reasoning, all of the relevant measures of effectiveness fall under the general rubric of power to acquire resources. As Yuchtman and Seashore (1967) argue, factors such as business volume, market penetration, productive efficiency, and member productivity are all either resources obtained from the environment or means to attain such resources.

A number of other investigators have proposed operative goals which also seem to fall under the general rubric of power. We saw in Chapter 2 that Ansoff and Brandenburg (1971) describe an evolution of the organizational designs of business firms undertaken to meet the following "process" criteria: (1) steady state efficiency, (2) operating responsiveness, (3) strategic responsiveness, and (4) structural responsiveness. Mott's (1972) concept of organizational effectiveness is similar: ". . . the ability of an organization to mobilize its centers of power for action—production and adaptation" (p. 17). He suggests that effective organizations "produce more and higher-quality outputs and adapt more effectively to environmental and internal problems than do other, similar organizations" (p. 17).

These are all rather general statements of commonly articulated goals for the ongoing operations of organizations (operative goals). They are also examples of commonly stated system needs, although they do not by any means comprise the full list of such needs usually given by system theorists. This apparent convergence between the goal and system approaches to evaluation argues that a combination of the approaches will yield a practical means for evaluating organization designs.

Some Suggestions for Evaluating Designs

Let us spell out a full-fledged goal model for evaluating organizations, then add elements from the system model; this combination then provides a comprehensive, although unwieldy approach to evaluating designs. Suchman (1967) makes use of a "process" model in his evaluation of various social change programs, such as Headstart and X-ray screening programs for tuberculosis. An important component of the process model is the concept of a sequence of goals—immediate (or short-range), intermediate, and ultimate (long-range) goals (see Figure 8–5). Immediate goals or sets of goals result from attempts to implement various elements of a project. The immediate goals, in turn, have conse-

FIGURE 8–5
The Goal Sequence in a Process Model of Evaluation

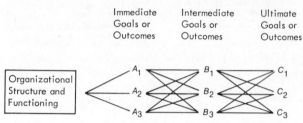

quences for the achievement of intermediate and ultimate goals; for example, in pursuing an immediate goal such as increasing *the productivity and efficiency of subordinates,* a manager may alter some of the characteristics of the organization that are under his control (e.g., the degree to which he is supportive of subordinates). Such actions and results, in turn, can affect an intermediate goal such as *profitability.* Changes in the organization's rate of profitability, furthermore, can affect one of the firm's ultimate goals, *survival.*

Relevance of Selected Criteria

A common error in managerial thinking is the assumption that the attainment of an immediate goal will lead automatically to the realization of subsequent goals in the hierarchy. For this reason, managers must examine and assess goal relationships as far down this entire hierarchy as is possible. Many of the earlier human relations studies focused on the satisfaction of individual workers under the assumption that productivity is a function of work satisfaction. Subsequently, this assumption proved valid only under very special conditions (Kahn, 1956). In light of such observations, we clearly ought to verify the assumed causal relationships among goals at various points in the hierarchical sequence. This line of questioning, furthermore, should be pursued until a goal state is reached that is of unquestioned value in and of itself, rather than being valuable only as a doubtful means to some even further end. If an ultimate goal of a hospital tuberculosis screening unit is detection of cases in the community, an evaluation of the unit based on numbers of cases may be insufficient. The assumption that the cases found at the hospital will reduce the community TB rate may be false. The cases turning up at the hospital may be ones readily found by a number of procedures and the "hardcore" TB population in the community—the ultimate criterion—may not be affected at all.

Furthermore, the stated "official" goals of the organization cannot always be taken at face value as criteria. Rather, we would do better to study the organization's actual behavior and infer its "real" goals from the ways in which it acts. These actions may only be means toward the ends of particular individuals or groups, but, as Simon (1964) suggests, such means or agreed constraints for interactions between groups may serve to guide the behavior of the organization as a whole (see Chapter 5).

As part of the process of relating organizational means to ends (immediate to ultimate outcomes), we might also consider whether there are alternative means to these ends, including alternative organizational designs. This is a matter of "efficiency." Some of these alternatives may be unknown to members of their organization. The analyst, however, through his or her ability to conceptualize organizations as systems and, in so doing, to identify requisite system needs, views the organization as flexible in some areas and thus capable of altering its structure and functioning and of using alternative means in the pursuit of particular ends.

In developing this model, we must accept no single criterion for assessing the performance of an organization. An ultimate criterion may exist in principle, but it would measure performance over such a long period of time that we must settle for more intermediate criteria, or what have been termed "midrange" criteria (Mahoney, 1967). If we used still more immediate criteria, the task would become quite complex, involving a great number of variables in complicated and dynamic relationships (Seashore and Yuchtman, 1967). Our assumption is that intermediate criteria consist of several indicators that are generally useful across different organizations and over time, as well.

As we saw above, Seashore and Yuchtman (1967) derive a relatively small number of criteria from their study of insurance agencies, as did Mahoney (1967) in his study of units in a business firm. However, no single, small list of criteria is available at this time for use across a variety of different organizations. At this point, it is partly a matter of choice which of several lists of penultimate criteria to use. We feel similarly about the use of the goal or system approach to evaluation. The goal approach allows specific tailoring of criteria to the characteristics of the organization under study. The system need approach is more general and may force one to recognize some critical but often overlooked dimensions. A combination of criteria from both approaches appears most useful at this time.

Some Operative Criteria

For this reason, we suggest that one evaluate alternative designs (including both structure and functioning) in terms of a small number of intermediate outcomes which are selected from both operative goals and system characteristics—outcomes such as efficiency, productivity, adaptability, and innovativeness. We expect that performance in these areas will contribute to the organization's ultimate effectiveness, including especially the organization's system-resource position (or its power position vis-à-vis the environment) as we have termed the Yuchtman-Seashore view.

Mott (1972, p. 20) provides a useful outline of criteria of the kind we have proposed:[4]

A. Organizing centers of power for routine production (productivity)
   1. The quantity of the product.
   2. The quality of the product.
   3. The efficiency with which it is produced.

B. Organizing centers of power to change routines (adaptability)
   1. Symbolic adaptation
      a. Anticipating problems in advance and developing satisfactory and timely solutions to them.
      b. Staying abreast of new technologies and methods applicable to the activities of the organization.
   2. Behavioral adaptation
      a. Prompt acceptance of solutions.
      b. Prevalent acceptance of solutions.

C. Organizing centers of power to cope with temporarily unpredictable overloads of work (flexibility)

Productivity, Adaptability, and Flexibility

Each of these three areas of concern is a basic component of the list of operative criteria we wish to propose. We have discussed *productivity* in the first section of this chapter under "a goal view," and it was illustrated by the questionnaire items used by Georgopoulos and Mann to measure the quality of patient care in hospitals. Also relevant to productivity is the subsequent discussion based on the Katz and Kahn view of efficiency as the ratio of output to input. Our second operative criterion, *adaptability,* was touched on when we mentioned the Seashore and Yuchtman view of organizations engaging in exchanges with the environment and, more importantly, when we discussed the Katz and Kahn view of political effectiveness. These often require the organization to make internal changes as well as external changes. Adaptability may be viewed as synonymous with problem-solving ability. As indicated by Mott's breakdown of adaptability into two parts, the organization must first become aware of problems and formulate solutions, and second, implement these solutions in a timely fashion and with sufficient breadth and depth of adjustment. *Flexibility* is a special case of adaptation. It is an unpredictable and time-limited (or temporary) adjustment that must be made.

---

[4] Questionnaire items used by Mott to measure these criteria of effectiveness are found in Figure 8–6. An earlier version of this kind of approach may be found in Georgopoulos and Tannenbaum (1957).

In addition to Mott's list of productivity, adaptability, and flexibility, there are two other major sources of operational measures that we wish to cite. Price (1968, 1972) provides a useful list of measures of organizational effectiveness which includes "productivity," "morale," "adaptation," and "innovation." Second, Ansoff and Brandenburg (1971) provide broad categories of criteria with which to measure "steady state efficiency," "operating responsiveness," "strategic responsiveness," and "structural responsiveness" in business firms.

Price (1968) defines "productivity" in much the same manner as Mott (see Figure 8–6). Price defines "morale" as the degree to which individual motives are gratified. Absenteeism and turnover rates can be used as indicators of morale (see also Lyons, 1972). A number of investigators (e.g., Price, 1972; Ullrich, 1972; Vroom, 1964) have dif-

---

FIGURE 8–6
Mott's Questionnaire Items Used to Measure Criteria of Effectiveness

Every worker produces something in his work. It may be a "product" or a "service." But sometimes it is very difficult to identify the product or service. Below are listed some of the products and services being produced in the Office of Administration.*

Typed pages	Recommended policies and
Delivered mail	procedures
Dispatched automobiles	New programs
Staff papers and studies	Classified jobs
Coding systems	Supplying new equipment
	Contracts

These are just a few of the things being produced.

We would like you to think carefully of the things that you produce in your work and of the things produced by those people who work around you in your division.

(Production: Quantity)
Thinking now of the various things produced by the people you know *in your division*, how much are they producing?
_____(1) Their production is very low.
_____(2) It is fairly low.
_____(3) It is neither high nor low.
_____(4) It is fairly high.
_____(5) It is very high.

(Production: Quality)
How good would you say is the *quality* of the products or services produced by the people you know *in your division*?
_____(1) Their products or services are of poor quality.
_____(2) Their quality is not too good.
_____(3) Fair quality.
_____(4) Good quality.
_____(5) Excellent quality.

---

* The names of other agencies were substituted when appropriate.

FIGURE 8–6 (*continued*)

(Production: Efficiency)

Do the people in your division seem to get maximum output from the resources (money, people, equipment, etc.) they have available? That is, how *efficiently* do they do their work?

_____(1) They do not work efficiently at all.
_____(2) Not too efficient.
_____(3) Fairly efficient.
_____(4) They are very efficient.
_____(5) They are extremely efficient.

(Adaptation: Anticipating Problems and Solving Them Satisfactorily)

How good a job is done by the people in your division in *anticipating* problems that may come up in the future and preventing them from occurring or minimizing their effects?

_____(1) They do a poor job in anticipating problems.
_____(2) Not too good a job.
_____(3) A fair job.
_____(4) They do a very good job.
_____(5) They do an excellent job in anticipating problems.

(Adaptation: Awareness of Potential Solutions)

From time to time newer ways are discovered to organize work, and newer equipment and techniques are found with which to do the work. How good a job do the people in your division do at keeping up with those changes that could affect the way they do their work?

_____(1) They do a poor job of keeping up to date.
_____(2) Not too good a job.
_____(3) A fair job.
_____(4) They do a very good job.
_____(5) They do an excellent job of keeping up to date.

(Adaptation: Promptness of Adjustment)

When changes are made in the routines or equipment, how *quickly* do the people in your division accept and adjust to these changes?

_____(1) Most people accept and adjust to them very slowly.
_____(2) Rather slowly.
_____(3) Fairly rapidly.
_____(4) They adjust very rapidly, but not immediately.
_____(5) Most people accept and adjust to them immediately.

(Adaptation: Prevalence of Adjustment)

What *proportion* of the people in your division readily accept and adjust to these changes?

_____(1) Considerably less than half of the people accept and adjust to these changes readily.
_____(2) Slightly less than half do.
_____(3) The majority do.
_____(4) Considerably more than half do.
_____(5) Practically everyone accepts and adjusts to these changes readily.

FIGURE 8–6 (*concluded*)

(Flexibility)

From time to time emergencies arise, such as crash programs, schedules moved ahead, or a breakdown in the flow of work occurs. When these emergencies occur, they cause work overloads for many people. Some work groups cope with these emergencies more readily and successfully than others. How good a job do the people in your division do at coping with these situations?

_____(1) They do a poor job of handling emergency situations.

_____(2) They do not do very well.

_____(3) They do a fair job.

_____(4) They do a good job.

_____(5) They do an excellent job of handling these situations.

Source: Mott (1972, pp. 21–24).

ferentiated several kinds of behavioral criteria for organizations, with *work satisfaction* or an emotional state (indicated by turnover and absenteeism) differentiated from "motivation." *Motivation* usually is measured by the amount of effort (e.g., performing extra work or working harder) put forth by workers or by their degree of commitment to the organization and its goals (Lodahl and Kejner, 1965; Patchen, 1965).[5]

We have already discussed what Price terms "adaptation," including Mott's adaptability and flexibility measures cited above. A somewhat related and important criterion from Price, but one not often treated because it presents both conceptual and measurement difficulties, is *innovation*. Innovative behavior is change inducing, as is adaptive behavior, but the change, in the former case, is in a novel direction. Forehand (1963) suggests that "innovative behavior includes the development and consideration of novel solutions to administrative problems, and evaluation of them in terms of criteria broader than conformity to preexisting practice . . ." (p. 206). Price (1972), following Becker and Whisler (1967), defines innovation as "the degree to which a social system is a first or early user of an idea among its set of similar social systems" (p. 118). Examples of measures of innovativeness include questionnaire items which are designed to determine workers' interests in work-related innovation and their attitudes toward changes introduced to their jobs (see Patchen, 1965).[6]

---

[5] Related to the study of satisfaction and motivation, mainly by psychologists, is the study of "alienation," or the extent to which work entails a feeling of meaninglessness, separation, isolation, powerlessness, or apathy (Blauner, 1964; Miller, 1967; Pearlin, 1962; Seeman, 1959).

[6] Of related interest as sources of criteria for innovation are the many studies of scientists and engineers that use as criteria such things as patents, publications, and ratings by peers or superiors. However, inventiveness and creativity do not always lead to innovation at it has been defined here (Doctors, 1970). See Pelz and Andrews (1966), Smith (1970), Andrews and Farris (1967), Gordon and Marquis (1966).

Until recently, relatively few scientific and systematic studies have been conducted at the organizational level of analysis, wherein the organization, per se, is evaluated as a source of innovation (*Transaction*, 1970). Much of the extant work is based on analogies with creativity in small groups of scientists (Steiner, 1965). However, a useful discussion of bureaucracy and its effects on innovation is presented by Victor Thompson (1965). The literature on diffusion of new technologies (hybrid seed corn to farmers, drugs to physicians, and so on) is also useful (Coleman, Katz, and Menzel, 1966; Havelock, 1971; Rogers, 1962; Rosner, 1968). Finally, we will describe a study by Hage and Aiken (1970) in which 16 health and welfare agencies were examined in terms of their additions of new programs to existing activities (Chapter 15). From one perspective the latter is simply a study of organizational growth, but we suggest that it is a study of innovative growth, or growth in "new" directions.

Further Criteria

Many of the criteria discussed above are found as overt organizational goals, or at least as subgoals of individuals within the organization. However, as one becomes more specific in defining these criteria, they shade off into the system needs described by Georgopoulos. When evaluating an organization, it is useful to view these criteria as an additional checklist for matters that are vital to the organization over the long run, but that may be, and often are, overlooked in the short run. It may be recalled that the Georgopoulos list included (1) adaption, (2) allocation, (3) coordination, (4) integration, (5) tension management, (6) productivity, and (7) integrity. As we have indicated, consensus does not exist among students of organizations on the exact nature of these critical system needs. Be that as it may, the Georgopoulos list seems both comprehensive in terms of existing theoretical models and also relatively practical, as is indicated by its usefulness in studies of hospitals (Georgopoulos and Mann, 1962; Georgopoulos and Matejko, 1967; Georgopoulos and Wieland, 1964).[7]

Another potentially useful set of operational criteria is found in the Ansoff-Brandenburg (1971) lists of measure for evaluating organizational designs. It is of interest to note the parallels that exist between these and Mott's operational criteria. Of further interest is the fact that Ansoff and Brandenburg point to an additional criterion which can be added to those of Mott.

---

[7] Examples of other criteria of effectiveness include: Price's (1968) "conformity" (the extent to which performance corresponds to institutional norms or the extent to which organizational decisions are supported by the environment), Georgopoulos and Tannenbaum's (1957) criterion of the absence of intraorganizational strain or tension, and, similarly, Caplow's (1964) "integration" ("the organization's ability to maintain or increase the total volume of interaction among its positions or, negatively, to control internal conflict") (p. 123).

Ansoff and Brandenburg's (1971) concepts of "steady state efficiency," "structural responsivness," and "operating responsiveness" are assumed to be included under Mott's criteria of "productivity," "adaptability," and "flexibility," respectively. The concept of *strategic responsiveness* is novel. We shall add this to our list of six operative criteria discussed above. It may be recalled that this criterion refers to an organization's . . . "ability to respond to changes in the *nature* (rather than volume) of its throughput, such as obsolescence of products, changes in product technology, emergence of international markets, opportunities to enter new lines of business, [and] changes in legal and social constraints under which the organization is forced to operate. Firms typically respond to these by changing [the] composition of their products and markets, acquisition of other firms, or divesting from parts of existing operations" (Ansoff and Brandenburg, 1971, p. 711).

External Criteria

Most of the criteria examined so far concern internal organizational functioning. This is particularly true of efficiency (or productivity) criteria, which assume external goals and direct our energies toward the optimal, rational arrangement of means toward these ends. Criteria that are concerned with adaptation or flexibility are less "internal" since they deal with the organization's behavior in relation to a dynamic and changing environment. However, these models essentially view the organization as adapting in a reactive way to the environment. Characteristics of the organization, rather than the organization's effects on its environment, serve as criteria.

A further task for the evaluator is to operationalize what Yuchtman and Seashore have termed the system-resource position vis-à-vis the environment. We shall refer to the *political effectiveness* of the system, for this eighth and final addition to our list of operative criteria (see Figure 8–7). Relevant here are the organization's exchanges with the environment including, in the case of business firms, profitability as a measure of the efficacy of these exchanges.

It can be argued that even the system-resource view of organizational effectiveness focuses attention within the organization. Admittedly, our attention is drawn to the organization's power to act and to its history of past interactions. For this reason, we propose the use of operative goals as criteria that will serve as "correctives" in the process of evaluation. Operative goals of interest to the evaluator include those of the dominant coalition in the organization and also those of groups in the environment which control crucial contingencies. The groups upon which the organization is dependent for resources, for supplying inputs or taking outputs, are groups with significant power over the organization. The degree to which exchanges are advantageous for the organiza-

FIGURE 8–7
Evaluating Organizations: Operative Criteria,
System Needs, and Values

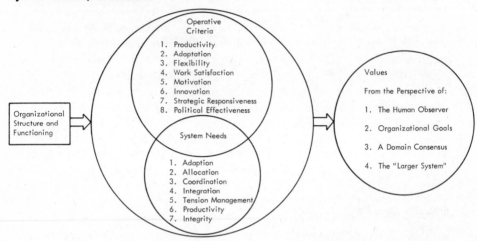

Note: The above list of operative criteria and system needs provides a set of overlapping criteria which measure outcomes of the structure and functioning of the organization. The outcomes, furthermore, have implications for the organizational values; values taken from a variety of perspectives—the individual, the organization's goals and domain, and the larger system.

tion (and the extent of the organization's political effectiveness) will be determined by the extent to which organizational goal attainment is congruent with the expectations that these groups have of the organization. We have discussed this in Chapter 5 on "Goals" and shall elaborate further in Chapter 13 on "The Organization's Environment."[8]

No Single Criterion: Trade-offs and Suboptimization

Different organizational arrangements may be needed to meet the two basic kinds criteria we have discussed—efficiency criteria (for internal functioning) and political criteria (for relations with the environment). Any single arrangement may have to be chosen on the basis of the trade-offs one desires to make. Certainly there is evidence that some of the criteria we have discussed are in conflict; for example, Ansoff and Brandenburg's operating responsiveness conflicts with organizational at-

---

[8] Also of possible use in viewing the organization in its environmental context are several criteria suggested by Bennis (1966). These criteria are derived from the study of psychological mental health of the human being as a system:

1. *Adaptability* of the organization—actively mastering the environment using problem-solving ability and flexibility to change with changing internal and external circumstances.
2. *Identity*—goals understood and accepted and perception of the organization by personnel.
3. *Reality*—Testing—accurate perception of the environment.

tempts to achieve steady state efficiency. Mott (1972) provides empirical evidence that flexibility (responsiveness to emergencies in hospitals) is negatively associated with adaptation or problem solving in these hospitals. Walker and Lorsch (1968) find that two closely matched factories differ primarily in whether they were organized by product or function. The result they found is a trade-off between productivity and manager satisfaction. The product structure yields more conflicts between managers and a high level of stress in exchange for a more dynamic, increased level of productivity compared to the functionally organized plant.

In view of these conflicts, we suggest that the evaluation of organizations take a leaf from the Lawrence and Lorsch (1967) study of differentiation and integration in organizations. According to this study, effective organizations have subsystems (such as manufacturing, marketing and R&D) that differ from one another in their goal orientations. Despite the conflict produced by dissimilar goal orientations, or, in fact, because of it, the organizations are effective (in terms of growth of profits, sales volume, and new products). Effectiveness, however, is achieved through the incorporation of various special means for integrating the dissimilar subsystems. Thus, efficiency alone, or some rational configuration of organizational parts to achieve system needs, is insufficient to realize overall effectiveness. What is needed, in addition, is a certain amount of tension or conflict between subsystems and operative goals and organizational practices that allow the optimization of conflicting goals to be realized through various integrating mechanisms.

Suboptimization as a Virtue

In a study of universities in which he illustrates the rather different goals held by different subgroups or stakeholders, Gross (1968) suggests that such conflicts are similar to the phenomena economists have termed suboptimization. Suboptimization occurs when subsystems attempt to optimize their own particular subgoals rather than the overall goal of the system to which they belong. This is often found in organizations that include groups of craftsmen or professionals. Similarly, Merton (1957) describes the bureaucratic personality which rigidly adheres to a rule rather than to the end which the rule addresses. A certain amount of this, however, may be desirable. Oftentimes, considerable attention must be given to activities which are indirectly related (or even unrelated) to overall organizational goals. Gross thus introduces the notion of "support goals," or what we have termed system needs. If the plumbing of a university is so much in need of repair that the health department is threatening to close it down, then some organizational unit (plant operations) must devote its entire attention to the task of improving the plumbing system, even to the extent that concerns for efficiency are temporarily cast aside.

Suboptimization is not necessarily a temporary matter. After the university in our example encourages plant operations to suboptimize at the possible expense of faculty and student needs, it may encourage the engineering school to do so because of falling student enrollments, and so on. But the actual situation is often worse than the one we have described. Beside sequentially attending to matters that seem to require suboptimization, the university devotes major resources to a number of efforts that conflict with one another. Attempts to meet support or maintenance goals (our "system needs") frequently conflict with attempts to achieve output goals. This can be the case when athletic programs which are intended to promote alumni loyalty and, consequently, financial support for the university compete with academic programs for the organization's limited resources. Although suboptimization in the extreme is clearly dysfunctional for the organization, we would argue that limited and intelligently managed conflict must be determined in part by the ultimate values of the organization and its top management (see, for example, Guth and Tagiuri, 1966; Miner, 1968).

Values

This leads us to a final set of criteria for organizational effectiveness. We have seen that criteria for internal functioning (efficiency criteria) must be supplemented with criteria for the relationship between the organization and its environment (political effectiveness criteria). But, efficiency and power over the environment are only means to an end(s). They may be sufficient to allow us to make judgments about the "effectiveness" of an organization if we accept a machine model of organizations, but not if we are to deal with them as social entities. People are the essential components of organizations, and people may concern themselves with alternatives over and above those that deal with efficiency and power over the environment.

We submit that the latter criteria are necessary, but not sufficient, to the task of judging an organization to be "effective" or "ineffective." We must also subject organization designs and behavior to criteria derived from human values. A tree is a tree and, as such, is neither good nor bad, effective nor ineffective. An organization, though, as a creation of society, is subject to evaluation in terms of the values of the society in which it resides.

This point becomes clear if we envisage an Englishman in 1940 contemplating the very efficient and politically effective Third Reich across the English Channel—an organization which stood for values antithetical to his own. A more problematic situation—one which calls for a very careful examination of our values and the trade-offs and risks that we are willing to undertake—confronts us in evaluating an organization that realizes enviable profits through the production and sale of hard-core pornography. Such is also the case with arms manufacturers who, while improving our balance of trade, sell their merchandise to under-developed nations that cannot really "afford" them. Finally, if one values the compact car because of its conservation of materials and energy, should one not judge the less profitable and less powerful (in system-resource terms) American Motors to be more effective than the more profitable and powerful General Motors? In this connection, our earlier discussion of contributions to the larger system is appropriate.

While the concepts of efficiency and power over the environment are useful in evaluating organizations, values play a major, but frequently overlooked, role in the process whereby means are configured to achieve organizational purposes. We find this situation in microcosm in the creation of computerized information systems. Often a manager may allow the computer expert to create an "efficient" system, and, lacking the proper computer expertise, will delegate, by default, important decisions to the technical expert. One important decision so delegated may be to make assumptions about the end uses to which data will be put. These decisions may be made in terms of the values of the computer expert rather than those of management (Boguslaw, 1965).

As we shall see in our discussion of leadership (Chapter 12), a vital function of top management is to decide the directions that the organization takes and, consequently, to mold its character, including its values. If this is not undertaken consciously, a diffuse, confused, or even undesirable organizational character may result. In short, a considerable amount of an organization's activity is directed toward matters that are not envisaged by the rational model. An organization is far more than an efficient arrangement of means or even an effective source of political power. It has implications for human values and for the values embodied in organizational goals, in the organization's domain, and in the "larger system" (see Figure 8–7).

We argue that the evaluator must go beyond mere technicism. Organizations, whether by design, error, or oversight, reflect value choices that bear directly on the lives of people (including you and me) and on what these people want, cherish, and esteem.

DISCUSSION QUESTIONS

1. How do the concepts of effectiveness and efficiency differ? Can an organization be efficient but ineffective?
2. What are system needs? What are some examples?
3. Under what circumstances would you be willing to sacrifice organizational efficiency for flexibility? Are there limits to such trade-offs?

REFERENCES

Andrews, Frank, and Farris, George. Supervisory practices and innovations in scientific teams. *Personnel Psychology*, 1967, *20*, 497–515.

Ansoff, H. Igor, and Brandenburg, Richard G. A language for organization design. *Management Science*, 1971, *17*, 705–31.

Anthony, Robert N. The trouble with profit maximization. *Harvard Business Review*, 1960, *37*, 126–34.

Becker, Selwyn W., and Whisler, Thomas L. The innovative organization: a selective view of current theory and research. *Journal of Business*, 1967, *40*, 462–69.

Bennis, Warren G. Leadership theory and administrative behavior: the problem of authority. *Administrative Science Quarterly*, 1959, *4*, 259–301.

Bennis, Warren G. *Changing organizations*. New York: McGraw-Hill, 1966.

Buckley, Walter. *Sociology and modern systems theory*. Englewood Cliffs, N.J.: Prentice-Hall, 1967.

Bylinski, G. Vincent Learson didn't plan it that way, but I.B.M.'s toughest competitor is—I.B.M. *Fortune*, 1972, *85* (3), 55–61, 145–50.

Blauner, Robert. *Alienation and freedom: the factory worker and his industry*. Chicago: University of Chicago Press, 1964.

Boguslaw, Robert. *The new utopians: a study of system design and social change*. Englewood Cliffs, N.J.: Prentice-Hall, 1965.

Caplow, Theodore. *Principles of organization*. New York: Harcourt, Brace & World, 1964.

Coleman, James S., Katz, Elihu, and Menzel, Herbert. *Medical innovation: a diffusion study*. Indianapolis: Bobbs-Merrill, 1966.

Cyert, Richard M., and March, James G. *A behavioral theory of the firm*. Englewood Cliffs, N.J.: Prentice-Hall, 1965.

Dahrendorf, Ralf. Out of utopia: towards a reorientation of sociological analysis. *American Journal of Sociology*, 1958, *64*, 115–27.

Dent, James K. Organizational correlates of the goals of business management. *Personnel Psychology*, 1959, *12*, 365–93.

Doctors, Samuel I. *The management of technological change*. New York: American Management Association, Extension Institute, 1970.

Durkheim, Emile. *Division of labor in society*, trans. by George Simpson. Glencoe, Ill.: Free Press, 1947.

Etzioni, Amitai. Two approaches to organizational analysis: a critique and a suggestion. *Administrative Science Quarterly*, 1960, *5*, 257–78.

Forehand, Garlie A. Assessments of innovative behavior: partial criteria for the assessment of executive performance. *Journal of Applied Psychology*, 1963, *47*, 206–13.

Friedlander, Frank, and Pickle, Hal. Components of effectiveness in small organizations. *Administrative Science Quarterly*, 1968, *13*, 289–304.

Fuller, R. B. *Utopia or oblivion: the prospects for humanity*. New York: Bantam Books, 1969.

Georgopoulos, Basil S. An open-system theory model for organizational research. In Anant R. Negandhi and Joseph P. Schwitter (Eds.), *Organization behavior models*. Kent, Ohio: Comparative Administrative Research Institute, Bureau of Economic and Business Research, Kent State University, 1970. Pp. 33–70.

Georgopoulos, Basil S. Indik, Bernard P., and Seashore, Stanley E. Some models of organizational effectiveness. Mimeo. Ann Arbor, Mich.: Institute for Social Research, University of Michigan, 1960.

Georgopoulos, Basil S., and Mann, Floyd C. *The community general hospital.* New York: Macmillan, 1962.

Georgopoulos, Basil S., and Matejko, Alexander. The American general hospital as a complex social system. *Health Services Research*, 1967, *2*, 76–112.

Georgopoulos, Basil S., and Tannenbaum, Arnold S. A study of organizational effectiveness. *American Sociological Review*, 1957, *22*, 534–40.

Georgopoulos, Basil S., and Wieland, George F. *Nationwide study of coordination and patient care in voluntary hospitals.* Ann Arbor, Mich.: Institute for Social Research, The University of Michigan, 1964.

Gordon, Gerald, and Marquis, Sue. Freedom, visibility of consequences, and scientific innovation. *American Journal of Sociology*, 1966, *72*, 195–202.

Gross Edward. Universities as organizations: a research approach. *American Sociological Review*, 1968, *33*, 518–44.

Gross, Edward. The definition of organizational goals. *The British Journal of Sociology*, 1969, *20*, 277–94.

Guth, William D., and Tagiuri, Renato. Personal values and corporate strategy. *Harvard Business Review*, 1966, *43*, 5, 123–32.

Hage, Jerald, and Aiken, Michael. *Social change in complex organizations.* New York: Random House, 1970.

Hall, Peter. Waiting for 1982. *New Society*, 1972, *19* (493), 504–5.

Hall, Richard H. *Organizations: structure and process.* Englewood Cliffs, N.J.: Prentice-Hall, 1972.

Havelock, Ronald G. *Planning for innovation through dissemination and utilization of knowledge.* Ann Arbor, Mich.: Center for Research on Utilization of Scientific Knowledge, Institute for Social Research, University of Michigan, 1971.

Kahn, R. L. The prediction of productivity. *Journal of Social Issues*, 1956, *12*, 41–49.

Katz, Daniel, and Kahn, Robert L. *The social psychology of organizations.* New York: Wiley, 1966.

Lasswell, Harold D. *Politics: who gets what, when, and how?* New York: Peter Smith, 1936.

Lawrence, Paul R., and Lorsch, Jay W. *Organization and environment: managing differentiation and integration.* Boston: Division of Research, Graduate School of Business Administration, Harvard University, 1967.

Levine, Sol, and White, Paul E. Exchange as a conceptual framework for the study of interorganizational relationships. *Administrative Science Quarterly*, 1961, *5*, 583–601.

Lodahl, Thomas M., and Kejner, Mathilde. The definition and measurement of job involvement. *Journal of Applied Psychology*, 1965, *49*, 24–33.

Lyons, Thomas F. Turnover and absenteeism: a review of relationships and shared correlates. *Personnel Psychology*, 1972, *25*, 271–81.

Mahoney, Thomas A. Managerial perceptions of organizational effectiveness. *Management Science*, 1967, *14*, 76–91.

Mahoney, Thomas A., and Weitzel, William. Managerial models of organizational effectiveness. *Administrative Science Quarterly*, 1969, *14*, 357–65.

McLuhan, Marshall, and Fiore, Quentin. *The medium is the message: an inventory of effects.* New York: Bantam Books, 1967.

Meadows, Donella H., Meadows, Dennis L., and Randers, Jorgen, and Behrens, William W., III. *The limits to growth.* New York: Universe Books, 1972.

Merton, Robert K. *Social theory and social structure.* Rev. ed. Glencoe, Ill.: Free Press, 1957.

Miller, George A. Professionals in bureaucracy: alienation among industrial scientists and engineers. *American Sociological Review*, 1967, 32, 755–68.

Miner, John B. Bridging the gulf in organizational performance. *Harvard Business Review*, 1968, 46, 102–10.

Mott, Paul E. *The characteristics of effective organizations.* New York: Harper & Row, 1972.

Parsons, Talcott. Suggestions for a sociological approach to a theory of organizations. I. *Administrative Science Quarterly*, 1956, 1, 63–85.

Patchen, Martin. *Some questionnaire measures of employee motivation and morale.* Ann Arbor, Mich.: Survey Research Center, University of Michigan, 1965.

Pearlin, Leonard I. Alienation from work: a study of nursing personnel. *American Sociological Review*, 1962, 27, 314–26.

Pelz, Donald C., and Andrews, Frank M. *Scientists in organizations.* New York: Wiley, 1966.

Perrow, Charles. *Organizational analysis: a sociological view.* Belmont, Calif.: Brooks/Cole, 1971.

Pickle, Hal B., and Rungeling, Brian S. Empirical investigation of entrepreneurial goals and customer satisfaction. *Journal of Business*, 1973, 46, 268–73.

Price, James L. *Organizational effectiveness: an inventory of propositions.* Homewood, Ill.: Irwin, 1968.

Price, James L. *Handbook of organizational measurement.* Lexington, Mass.: D. C. Heath, 1972.

Rogers, Everett M. *Diffusion of innovations.* New York: Free Press, 1962.

Rosner, Martin M. Administrative controls and innovation. *Behavioral Science*, 1968, 13, 36–43.

Schulberg, Herbert C., Sheldon, Alan, and Baker, Frank. Introduction in H. Schulberg, A. Sheldon, and F. Baker (Eds.), *Program evaluation in the health fields.* New York: Behavioral Publications, 1969. Pp. 3–28.

Seashore, Stanley, E. Criteria of organizational effectiveness. *Michigan Business Review*, 1965, 17, 26–30.

Seashore, Stanley E., and Yuchtman, Ephraim. Factorial analysis of organizational performance. *Administrative Science Quarterly*, 1967, 12, 377–95.

Seeman, Melvin. On the meaning of alienation. *American Sociological Review*, 1959, 24, 783–91.

Simon, Herbert A. On the concept of organizational goal. *Administrative Science Quarterly*, 1964, 9, 1–22.

Smith, Clagett G. Consultation and decision processes in a research and development laboratory. *Administrative Science Quarterly*, 1970, 15, 203–15.

Steiner, Gary A. Introduction in G. A. Steiner (Ed.), *The creative organization.* Chicago: University of Chicago Press, 1965. Pp. 1–24.

Suchman, Edward A. *Evaluative research: principles and practice in public service and social action programs.* New York: Russell Sage, 1967.

Thompson, James D. *Organizations in action.* New York: McGraw-Hill, 1967.

Thompson, Victor. Bureaucracy and innovation. *Administrative Science Quarterly*, 1965, 10, 1–20.

Trans-action. A symposium: the innovating organization. In Warren G. Bennis (Ed.), *American Bureaucracy.* Chicago: Aldine, 1970. Pp. 135–63.

Ullrich, Robert A. *A theoretical model of human behavior in organizations: an eclectic approach.* Morristown, N.J.: General Learning Press, 1972.

Vroom, Victor H. *Work and motivation.* New York: Wiley, 1964.

Walker, Arthur H., and Lorsch, Jay W. Organizational choice: product versus function. *Harvard Business Review*, 1968, *46*, 129–38.
Yuchtman, Ephraim, and Seashore, Stanley E. A system-resource approach to organizational effectiveness. *American Sociological Review*, 1967, *32*, 891–903.

Case

Hastings Electronics Company[*]
Albert H. Rubenstein

"Now that our decentralization and profit-center setup is beginning to shake down, I would like to devote some attention to developing a more uniform way of appraising our research and development projects and new business ventures." The speaker was Warren Long, recently appointed president of Hastings Electronics. "It's fairly difficult," he continued, "to compare proposals from the four product divisions and the research division for the purpose of allocating our limited resources. Some of the proposals I get are backed up by estimates of cost savings, others by predictions of new business, and still others by nothing more than an interest on the part of some members of one of the various laboratories."

"I agree," replied Arnold Green, executive vice president, "but we have to be careful about how much control we try to exert over these division managers. After all, they have only been in office two or three years and are just beginning to act like all-around businessmen. It wouldn't do to hit them with a set of detailed procedures at this point that might be viewed as encroaching on their prerogatives as managers."

"That's right, but we do need some way of choosing between research projects or other opportunities in businesses as diverse as those represented by our current product lines and the several potential ones that have been suggested already by our new business development group."

For several months Long and Green had been aware of the necessity to do something about this situation, but both clearly recognized (and

* All names disguised.

This case was made possible by a grant from the Industrial Research Institute which was extended to provide case material for the first seminar on the Management of Industrial Research. It was prepared by Albert H. Rubenstein of the Department of Industrial Engineering, Northwestern University as a basis for class discussion rather than to illustrate either effective or ineffective handling of an administrative situation.

were continually reminding each other) about the potential dangers of interfering directly in the decision making of their division managers. The profit center arrangement, backed up by a substantial bonus system, appeared to be working very well and they were anxious to avoid anything that would interfere with its efficient operation.

Pressures had been building up, however, to make certain choices between proposed business ventures—some generated from within the company's laboratories and some from acquisition opportunities. As long as the choices involved alternatives within an existing line of business, they could rely fairly well on the company's experience in that line of business to provide clues to the better bets. Where the alternatives involved radically different lines of business, however, there was no systematic way of choosing projects.

The new business development group had come up with a number of acquisition possibilities as well as some suggestions for extensions of existing product lines into new markets or for developing new products to fix existing company markets. Several dozen such proposals were being examined currently, but the company lacked an adequate set of criteria or systematic method of comparing them and assigning priorities.

Some preliminary analysis of the profit and share of the market trends in several of Hastings' current lines of business had revealed radical differences between product lines even within a given division. Instruments Division, for example, had found that one of its major product lines was in a declining market that offered little opportunity for increases in profits. Price competition—a phenomenon this product line had not faced before—was becoming severe. New models of these instruments did little except to compete with Hastings' own existing models and to decrease the margin through heavy development expenses.

In another product line in the same division, it was clear that a larger expenditure for research and development could help the company stay in the lead in a growing market where radically new instruments could command a high enough price to pay for R&D expenses in a very short period.

The problem in these two situations was that the older, declining product line was still profitable and could apparently support heavy R&D costs, while the new product line was not yet at break even and could not support a heavy R&D load based on current volume or profits. At least this is the way the situation appeared when viewed through the eyes of the division managers who had to report profitability on their current operations on a quarterly basis.

Hastings Electronics had always depended on a strong R&D program to keep it ahead of competition. They had traditionally spent 4–5 percent of sales on R&D, on a sales volume of $50–75 million. When the company had been decentralized, the research division had been established to ensure that the long-run possibilities for technological progress would be looked after. It was recognized in the company that the product division managers, operating close to the current market and evaluated primarily on the basis of current earnings, might not be in a position to carry on much long-range research. In addition, it was recognized that the company currently operated in only a fraction of the potential markets open to a company with its background and potential, and that the most promising future lines of business might not evolve logically from any of the existing product lines or divisions.

In addition to the establishment of the research division, several other moves had been made to help deal with these problems. The first had been a new business development group which was charged with investigating the various merger and acquisition possibilities that were continually popping up in this dynamic industry. Several of these had survived initial screening and were being analyzed for their potential technical and economic impacts on Hastings Electronics.

A second device had been tried in the specific area of new product development. A task force composed of members of two of the product division laboratories and the research division were using "brainstorming" and other idea-generation techniques to develop a list of ideas for new products which, upon screening, might provide the basis for new product lines or whole new areas of business.

A third group—the Product Planning Task Force—had been assigned to examine the existing product lines of the company and to evaluate their strengths and weaknesses. This activity was also generating some ideas for potential research and development projects.

All of these ad hoc groups, plus the several division labs and the research division, were actively generating ideas for R&D projects. The proportion of the R&D budget available for initiating new projects was limited, due to the continuing nature of much of the work in the laboratories—studies of materials, product improvement studies, programs of testing and evaluating components, etc. This was not the major concern of the company management, however, for Hastings had always been able to find some extra R&D money for very promising projects. The primary concern was with the more expensive, later phases of those projects which would prove successful in their initial R&D phases and which would look promising for full-scale exploitation.

Both Long and Green were anxious to find or develop a systematic method for estimating the long-run profit potential of projects that had been and would be proposed as part of the R&D or acquisition program. In order to satisfy themselves that a particular project A was more desirable than another project B, they wanted to have some idea of what would be involved in A and B if they were successful in the long run and actually succeeded in establishing a new product, a greatly improved one, a brand new product line, or a new market for their existing products or technology. One of the problems which kept arising was that some of the most appealing ideas for research projects were often proposed by the operating departments least able to afford them from the viewpoint of budget and available technical skill. Top management wanted to be sure that, from the overall company standpoint, the best ideas were getting adequate backing and the ideas that were not so good were being dropped.

Although each division manager was autonomous, in the sense that he could spend his own budget in the manner he considered best, top management was responsible for overall coordination of the expenditures on technology and new ventures in the company. They wanted to have available a systematic method of comparing the many proposals from the divisions and the various task forces. They would then be in a better position to advise division managers on their R&D programs, and to make better decisions in the allocation of capital funds for exploitation of research results and expansion of facilities for current product lines. They felt that some continuing programs in all of the laboratories could stand some economic review to see whether they were contributing to the long-run profit position of the company.

Green had had an opportunity to discuss one particular aspect of the problem with several of the division managers, and found them quite willing to admit that sometimes they were not making "cut-off" decisions on a long-run, companywide basis. Will James, of Industrial Equipment, had been frank, "It is certainly not a matter of failing to recognize the importance of longer range research, aimed at entirely new products and businesses. But our bread and butter comes from a program of continual minor improvements in our present equipments and we must devote a major share of our technical effort to customer service and helping to keep their equipment operating." George Leahy, of Components, replied to Green's question by saying, "When we have to watch profits closely, we don't do so much long-term work. Right now, I am concerned about profits in the current quarter and I have had to terminate a long-term project my lab director had his heart in. If things look better next year, I may reinstate it."

Bob Gordon, of Instruments, was even more direct. "It takes guts to cut off a project that still shows some promise. In the absence of a systematic way of evaluating the potential of such projects, the easier way out is to accede to the pressures from my laboratory people, who are competent in their fields, and let them drift on another few months. I would welcome a better way of reviewing current projects that would make the cut-off decision more objective and get me off the hook with my people."

In two of the divisions (including Bob Gordon's, despite his comments) some straightforward economic evaluation was being applied with an increasing ability to kill off really bad projects and to spot new ones with high potential. The methods used were not uniform and were unknown to the other divisions. In addition, the situation in the research division was very unsystematic. Most of the people in the research division (which included most of the Ph.D.'s in the company) were not particularly interested in economic and management problems and were not reluctant to say so. They had been impatient with several previous attempts to develop a "project selection formula." One such formula had turned out to be both mathematically wrong and conceptually unattractive to them. They continued to argue for project proposals primarily on their technical merits.

Management was faced, on the one hand, with a researcher whose only argument for a new project was, "This has great potential for a major technical breakthrough," and, on the other, with a salesman who could "sell a million of them." Neither of them generally tried to determine how much profit could be made from a particular project. Under these conditions, the need for more systematic methods was clear. What was needed was a procedure, not necessarily a formula, which would take into account all of the important considerations in project selection, and would generate the kind of information necessary for a good decision.

As an initial step, Green asked Hastings' controller, George Horn, to set up a committee to look into the possibilities of evolving a project selection procedure. Initially the committee consisted of nine members: Horn; Don Edwards, the market research director; Paul Baird, assistant to the president (who had been doing some economic analysis of company operations); Sam Davis, head of new business development; and representatives of the four divisional laboratories and the research division (Exhibit 1 gives the names of these five representatives.)

After two meetings of this committee, it was agreed that it was too large to accomplish specific results, and that it would tie up a large number of man-hours in general discussion. In the two sessions, however, a general discussion was held on the problems of project selection and some of the approaches to it. The discussion followed a lecture by a faculty member from the local university who had been active in the field of research economics for some time.

The discussion brought out the differences in practice between the several divisions and also some of the technical differences between their business and the kinds of R&D projects they customarily carried on.

Following the second meeting, George Horn reported back to Arnold Green and suggested that a working group of four people who would devote a significant portion of their time to the project over a few weeks might be the best approach. He further suggested that the work of the four-man group could benefit from several more, carefully focused, lec-

EXHIBIT 1
Hastings Electronics Company

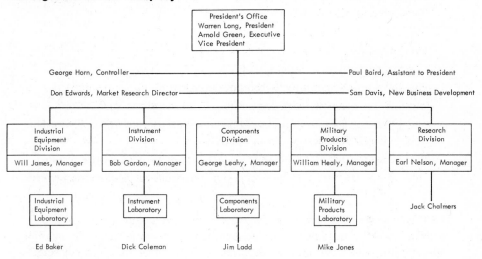

ture-discussions with Professor Royce. Following these sessions, the group would work out procedures and formulations for project selection. When the group was satisfied that it had a workable and useful system developed, the original committee of nine would be called in and asked to comment and suggest improvements. After that a method would have to be worked out for introducing the new system to the operating divisions and for followthrough to see that the procedures and formulas were properly adapted to the circumstances of each division. There was some uncertainty at the outset as to the best method of doing that, due to the decentralization of the company and the strong autonomous position of the operating divisions. In George Horn's words, "A real selling job would have to be done in presenting the new system to the operating divisions."

The working group of four was established within the next two weeks. It included George Horn, as chairman; Paul Baird, assistant to the president; Dick Coleman, of the Instruments Division laboratory; and Jack Chalmers, of the Research Division. The four had been with Hastings for a total of over 30 years and combined a broad knowledge of the company's lines of business, its technical programs, and its financial situation. After several more sessions with Professor Royce, the group met several times a week for the next two months. In their first few sessions they discussed a number of aspects of the general project selection problem as well as the specific circumstances in Hastings that would affect the success of any given system. Among the topics covered in these discussions were:

General criteria for the size of an R&D budget.

Formulas that had been presented in the literature for selecting between technically feasible projects.

Specific criteria for comparing projects.

The "pay-off period" and the rate of profit.

The return on investment concept.

The discounted cash flow method of determining present value.

Methods for after-the-fact evaluation of the results of specific projects.

Checklists for factors that should be considered, regardless of whether they could be inserted into a formula.

The combination of qualitative criteria into "project worth profiles."

Procedures necessary to generate the information needed for project selection.

Throughout the discussions, it was emphasized that a workable procedure must be acceptable to the operating divisions, as well as reasonable and valid mathematically. Several objectives of a project selection procedure were stressed, in addition to the original one of providing a better basis for top management choice of business opportunities:

A stimulus to careful estimates and reestimates of the probabilities of factors such as technical success and particular sales volumes.

The integration of such estimates and all other relevant information into a companywide framework, related to the company's business objectives.

The opportunity to learn by experience, through constant reexamination of estimates and ultimate checking of estimates against actual results.

A decision program for generating estimates, reestimates, and investment decisions.

At the end of the two months, the working group had drawn up a procedure which included a "Project Evaluation Checklist" for use by people proposing new projects and for use in periodical reevaluations of existing projects. The other major aspect of the procedure was the recommended use of the Discounted Cash Flow method for evaluating the economic returns from a project and for comparing alternative projects or business opportunities. These two devices, plus an outline for stating business objectives and the groups suggested plan for selling the new techniques in the company, were presented to Arnold Green for the approval of top management.

"This looks fine," said Green, as he examined the portfolio of material presented to him by Horn. "Now all we have to do is to sell it to the operating people."

section III

Organizational Dynamics and the Functioning Organization

PREMISE

The organization is more than a relatively static combination of structure, technology, goals and people. For one thing, these are not often compatible. Thus, we introduced Chapter 8 of the last section with an example of conflict between the engineering and marketing functions in a successful, presumably well-designed organization. In fact, the very nature of structure, technology, and so on, may be viewed as patterns of recurrent behavior, with relative invariability at times providing an illusion of the organization as a "thing," but variability, including conflict, at times emphasizing the dynamic processes comprising the organization.

Following this lead, we turn our attention in this section to processes involved in roles and norms, such as conflict, control, and leadership. Roles and norms, for example, when viewed closely may be seen to be in a state of almost constant flux of affirmation or change. Power-seeking, influence attempts, and conflict are also important aspects of the organization, as are attempts to manage and control behavior, including especially leadership.

9

Organizational Roles and Norms

INTRODUCTION

In the last section, we described organizations in terms of four major dimensions and attempted to explain how organizations are far more dynamic and complex than classical schools of thought would have us believe. And yet, something in our backgrounds still would have us ascribe more logic and programmed rationality to organizations than actually exists.

Imagine, for the moment, a psychiatric hospital. We see psychiatrists interviewing patients and diagnosing illnesses. Years of scientific training and experience permit the physicians to choose a course of therapy suited to the etiology of each patient's illness. Acting as a team, the physician, nurses, aids, orderlies, and housekeeping staff coordinate their activities to facilitate a comprehensive, rational treatment program. The organization, in fact, is a smoothly functioning system structured by means of formal rules and regulations and dedicated to meeting the patient needs determined by the application of modern science.

In any event, that is what we may think goes on in a psychiatric hospital. In actuality, according to sociologist, Anselm Strauss, the functioning of such an organization is considerably less structured, orderly, or rational; for example, consider the following quotation from his article, "Healing by Negotiation: Speciality of the House":

> Some psychiatrists in Michael Reese Hospital have established long-term understandings with certain head nurses, who know, almost without words, what is expected of them. A neurologist-psychiatrist generally tries to get his patients into the two wards where most electric shock treatment is done—and "his" nurses take it from there. We called this "speciality of the house"—as opposed to "a la carte"—treatment.
> Once the negotiated arrangements are relatively stabilized, certain responses become almost automatic. Woe to the psychiatrist whose ideas of treatment are very troublesome to established routine and understandings, and who gets stubborn about it! He may suddenly find himself

surrounded, perhaps hopelessly enmeshed, by an increasingly tight web of negotiation woven back and forth among nurses, administrators, and aides. When the furore in the ward is the greatest, the negotiation is most visible. Unless he has very powerful administrative support, he will sooner or later have to sue for peace (Strauss, A., 1964, p. 15).[1]

Chapter Guide

1. How can it be that lower level personnel negotiate therapeutic matters with physicians, who presumably are solely competent to deal with these matters?
2. What are the "long-term understandings" mentioned in the quotation? How do they develop? Are they detrimental to health care over the long run?
3. What similar kinds of experiences have you had in other organizations with which you have been affiliated?

ROLES, NORMS, AND INDIVIDUAL BEHAVIOR

The "Fluid" Nature of Organizations

In earlier chapters, we discussed the "substance" of organizations, in terms of structure, goals, and technology. To be sure, these elements of organizations do much to shape the behavior that occurs within them. Yet, neither these elements nor the behavior that they shape is fixed. Rather, they are fluid, in the nature of processes; for example, goals may be formally stated and written down, but decisions frequently are made in the context of a variety of operative (sometimes conflicting) goals. Coalitions form and dissolve around important issues. The organization as a whole behaves differently over time as existing, internally established constraints are overcome and new ones are met.

A Negotiated Order

Strauss and colleagues (1963) developed a model that portrays behavior in organizations as a *negotiated order*. Order, or a stable pattern of behavior, does not evolve solely because of formal organizational elements such as job descriptions, rules, and regulations. Order is something that must be "worked at" and continually created and recreated. Certainly, rules and organizational goals facilitate agreement among an organization's members. Even so, disagreements arise due to differences in occupational roles, individual attitudes, goals, and styles of behavior.

In the psychiatric division of the hospital studied, Strauss and his colleagues found few formal rules. The rules that did exist were neither clearly stated nor seen as binding. Yet, work did go on; the staff was able to cite the kinds of behaviors that were likely to be encountered in the division and the consequences that these behaviors were likely to evoke, as if rules did, indeed, exist. Behavior within the division consisted of complex, although fairly predictable, activities.

This is not to say that rules were nonexistent; personnel did call upon certain rules from time to time when such resort was to their advantage. Similarly, some rules and agreements between personnel were created as the situation warranted. But, while these rules may have been useful in a particular situation, they were not useful when the situation changed, rendering a rule less appropriate than before. At a later time, the same rule might be reestablished (perhaps in a modified form) by one or another of its authors, in response to some new crisis situation. In general, rules were cited selectively, broken, or ignored to suit the particular situation at hand or the needs of personnel. Even the hospital's administration did not rely on rules and regulations. Requests by new physicians for clarification and formalization of the hospital's regulations were resisted by the administrators, for fear that overreliance on regulations would impede the innovation and improvision believed essential for effective patient care.

Shared Understandings

In the absence of formally stated rules, researchers found longstanding, shared understandings, or general "house rules" which were fairly clear. In addition, the general goal of the organization, which was to discharge patients in better health than they enjoyed when admitted, existed; however this goal was admittedly ambiguous. The time-honored understandings that develop between personnel are essentially what we have termed *norms* in Chapter 3. These expectations about behavior lead to more or less regularized behavior; for example, certain nurses, who interacted with certain physicians, in time came to understand what was expected of them. The physicians, in turn, came to know that their nurses knew what was expected of them. This state of events arose more or less informally. In fact, a physician might merely say, "Do the usual," though the usual had never been formally enunciated.

Understanding of this sort must be "worked at" but not always through conscious, formal action. The socialization experienced by organizational members often results from unconscious social process wherein certain behaviors are reinforced and others are not; some are even met with negative sanctions (see Chapter 3). However, the socialization process does not automatically produce "cogs" that fit the "organizational machinery." Individual personality differences, turnover among staff members, and changing situational variables limit the extent to which socialization can produce homogeneous behavioral patterns.

Negotiating Agreements

For this reason, explicit, temporary agreements and compromises become essential to the organization's functioning; for example, the staff may not wish to keep a troublesome, hyperactive patient on the ward, but may agree with the physician to try a new course of treatment for a limited period of time. If the treatment does not seem effective by the end of the set period of time, both sides may agree to negotiate further, possibly deciding to change the treatment in some way. However, the temporal aspect of such an agreement allows the physician and the staff to compromise.

In addition to explicit agreements, a great number of tacit contracts exist in the form of understandings, as we indicated above. For example, a registered nurse may suggest to a practical nurse that she administer a treatment not permitted by hospital rules, with the implicit understanding that the registered nurse, who is the superior, will take the blame if this infraction of the rules is discovered. In the absence of such an understanding, the subordinate may press her superior, through indirect or even explicit questioning, about how the consequences will be borne if the infraction is discovered.

A minimum amount of trust and a minimum number of "tacit understandings" are necessary if the organization is to run smoothly. In their absence, complicated negotiations and clarifications of intentions are required each time a new activity is encountered. Trust and understanding are especially needed in organizations, like hospitals, which bring the talents of diverse professionals and technicians to bear on specific tasks.

Strauss and colleagues suggest that this process of establishing order, by negotiating and reaching agreements, applies particularly to organizations with vague goals or a multiplicity of purposes. We argued in Chapter 5 that most organizations, in fact, fit this description. Consequently, we expect to find this dynamic, processual phenomenon in most organizations. The extreme example described here exists where different professionals strongly adhere to specific subgoals and to different means for their achievement.

However, as organizations increase in complexity and employ staffs with diverse professional backgrounds, they tend to use processes and negotiated orders more and rely less on the kind of mechanical, formally structured order described in Chapter 2. We argue that most organizational behavior is processual, and whatever formal structure exists serves mainly as a constraint to prevent the process from destroying the organization by moving it too far in one extreme direction or another. However, we will move into a discussion of roles and power at this point, since such concepts provide a foundation for further discussions of organizational processes.

Roles, Norms, and Role Senders

We shall use the term *role* to mean expectations, or norms, about the behavior of the occupant of a position. Following Kahn et al. (1964) and Katz and Kahn (1966), we shall describe a model for understanding how roles function, how shared understandings are created, how conflicts arise, and how a negotiated order develops.

Organizations consist of numerous different positions or offices that are related to one another according to work flow, technology, and authority. The positions that are related directly to a particular role (the *focal role*) are said to comprise the *role set* of the focal role. The various members of an individual's role set depend upon his or her performance in some way: (1) they expect the individual to use what they produce, (2) they themselves use what the individual produces, (3) they are subordinate to the individual and are expected to follow his or her orders, (4) they are at the receiving end of the individual's reward system, and so on. The various members of the role set have expectations and attitudes concerning what should or should not be done by the occupant of the focal role. These expectations may be idiosyncratic or they may be agreed upon by several individuals—i.e., they may be group or even organizational norms.

The expectations that are communicated to the occupant of the focal role are termed the *sent role*. Organizational members holding and communicating these expectations are called *role senders*. In other words, role senders communicate their expectations and thereby try to influence the behavior of the occupant of the focal role in specific ways; for example, a young faculty member will learn her occupational role, or set of appropriate norms, from both the senior faculty and her students. Both groups communicate their expectations, which sometimes conflict, concerning the manner in which the new instructor is supposed to behave.

The occupant of the focal role, however, perceives the sent role with varying degrees of accuracy. Her perceptions of the sent role, called the *received role,* are prone to be conflicting and to some extent inaccurate. For example, a professor, acting as a role sender, may expect the students to defer in speaking and be attentive. The student who perceives his or her (received) role in this way will be deferent and attentive. The student who does not may appear pushy, arrogant, or insubordinate to the professor. As we shall see, roles can provide the basis for conflict when not agreed upon.

The Structure of Norms

An *occupational role* consists of the set of norms that apply to a particular position in an organization. In Chapter 3, we presented the J-curve as reflecting the distribution of employee behavior in response to a formal, prescribed rule such as the time for arriving at work. When we examine norms more thoroughly (including behavior that is not formally prescribed) we find a great variety of distributions of behavior in addition to the J-shaped curve.

Jackson (1966) provides a model, called the *return potential model,* which represents some of the more important structural aspects of norms. We can illustrate the model through a familiar example. Friendliness is expressed in varying degrees depending, not only upon personal feelings of affection, but also upon the norms that govern this kind of behavior in specific social settings. In many situations, established norms limit what are felt to be excessive displays of friendship as well as unfriendly behavior.

For the moment, let us imagine a continuum of behavior which ranges from overt hostility (unfriendliness) at one extreme to effusive demonstrations of affection at the other. On an 8-point scale, the former behavior can be placed at 0 and the latter at 8. The midpoint of the scale, 4, will represent the absence of any particular social affect, or indifference. Now, in a given social setting the behaviors described by different points on the continuum will be evaluated differently. Generally speaking, friendly behavior will be evaluated positively and hostile behavior negatively. These two dimensions, range of behavior and evaluation of behavior, provide the basis for Jackson's return potential model. Interestingly enough, we will find that not all *friendly behavior* is received with enthusiasm.

Using the two dimensions, we can plot a return potential curve which shows the extent to which approval or disapproval for different kinds of behavior registers along the entire range of possible behaviors. The curve in Figure 9–1 can be used to illustrate the hypothetical norms concerning friendliness between students and faculty members at a particular university.

The curve suggests that an hostile response on the part of students, no matter how slight, will be met with disapproval by faculty members. Students giving neutral, indifferent responses to faculty members (point 4 on the scale) will be met with a neutral response. Faculty members, however, will show approval of moderately friendly gestures on the part of students (around 5 and 6 on the scale). These might consist of short exchanges of pleasantries that are sufficient to display one's genuine sincerity and pleasure at meeting. More effusive displays (points 7 and 8), however, will be disapproved, for at this point the student will have

FIGURE 9–1
The Return Potential Model of Norms

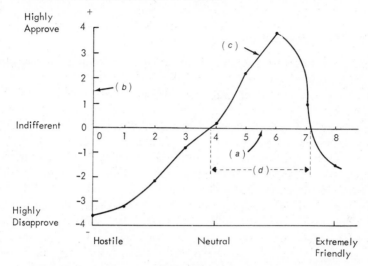

Schematic diagram showing the *Return Potential Model* for representing norms. (*a*) A *behavior dimension;* (*b*) an *evaluation dimension;* (*c*) a *return potential* curve, showing the distribution of approval-disapproval among the members of a group over the whole range of behavior; (*d*) the range of tolerable or approved behavior.

Source: Jackson (1966, p. 114).

transgressed a social barrier that maintains differences in status within the organization and will have acted out of keeping with his or her sent role.

The return potential model also shows that the norm of friendliness between students and faculty members confines the members to a relatively small range of acceptable behavior; that is, only a small portion of the horizontal dimension of behavior is approved. In addition, the norm is associated with considerable intensity of feeling, since much of the possible range of behavior is either highly approved or highly disapproved, rather than being met with milder reactions or indifference. Such norms concern matters of considerable importance in the organization. Similar norms might be found in organizations in which interpersonal relations bear directly on task accomplishment; for instance, in "people processing" organizations, such as schools and churches, relations among staff members and between staff members and "clients" are critical means to the organizations' ends. In contrast, norms concerning behavior which is less vital to the organization will be flatter, when diagrammed, illustrating less intense feeling about wider ranging behavior.

Effects of Normative Situations

Jackson also describes norms in terms of their "approval-disapproval ratio," which is the ratio of the range of behavior that is approved to the range of behavior that is disapproved. Where norms constrict the range of tolerable behavior, an organization in which learning opportunities are constrained probably exists. In this kind of organization, one attends continually to one's behavior and limits it to a narrow range of variation, rather than be exposed to disapprobation. Consequently, we find that initiative, the willingness to experiment, and creativity will be diminished by excessive concern for what others think of one's behavior.

Another interesting characteristic of norms is their tendency to *crystallize*. The return potential curve illustrated in Figure 9–1 represents average responses to behavior in the organizational unit under study. Although not shown by the curve, individual differences undoubtedly yield variations around the average. The average response to behavior described by point 3 on the friendliness behavior scale in Figure 9–1 will be mild disapproval (−1 on the vertical approval scale). However, the individual reactions from which the average is computed may range from indifference (0 on the scale) to relatively intense disapproval (−2 or −3). To the extent that the return potential curve depicts consistency (or low variation) around the average, the normal is said to be crystallized. The opposite of crystallization—where reactions to a particular behavior are random and, in the aggregate, lack a central tendency—implies a situation in which a norm does not exist.[2] The presence of a norm implies some regularity in expectations.

Ambiguous Norms

In instances where the central tendency is weak and considerable variation is experienced (i.e., the return potential plot curve shows a scatter or is "fuzzy"), the norm is said to be ambiguous. This can occur when members of the organization fail to communicate their expectations effectively or when some members do not feel strongly about the behavior in question and, consequently, do not communicate their expectations.

Another form of unclarity results from conflict among members of the organization regarding the behavior in question. We alluded to this in remarking that the young instructor sometimes receives conflicting

---

[2] Measures of *central tendency* seek to measure some central value of a distribution that is "characteristic" of it.

FIGURE 9–2

The Return Potential Model of Norm Ambiguity

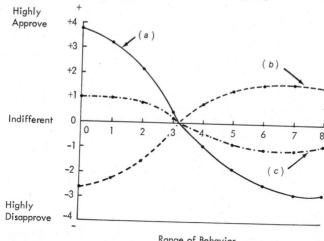

Range of Behavior

Schematic diagram for representing the *ambiguity* of a norm. In this situation there are two distinct return potential curves: (*a*) curve representing feelings of one subgroup; (*b*) curve representing feelings of a different subgroup; (*c*) return potential curve for a total group where norm has high ambiguity.

Source: Jackson (1966, p. 118).

sent roles from the student body and senior faculty. In situations of this kind, there may be a high degree of consensus within each subgroup. Considered singly, the subgroups will have fairly crystallized norms and the return potential curve for each subgroup will be distinctive. However, when the curves for both subgroups are averaged (see curves (*a, b,* and *c* in Figure 9–2), the resulting curve may be relatively flat. The latter curve, *c*, would seem to indicate a norm lacking in specificity and intensity of approved behavior. In fact, this average curve masks considerable intensity and specificity which vary according to subgroups. To the receiver of such sent roles, the norm will seem unclear, not because of ambiguity or a lack of information, but because of conflicting information.

Variance in expectations about behavior is likely to be substantial in the early stages of development of a group or organization. However, the development of some shared norms is likely with the passage of time. The negotiated order that was discussed earlier results, in part, through the establishment of clear and unambiguous norms.

A final source of influence that helps shape a role is found in the expectations that the individual in the focal role has for his or her own behavior. These expectations are the basis for what is termed the *own role*. The focal role holder's own role comprises his expectations about how he ought to behave in the pursuit of organizational goals, his own personal goals, or some combination of the two. According to Katz and Kahn (1966), each individual is a *self-sender*, a role sender to himself. Gross et al. (1958), for example, showed how the "moral" or "expedient" role orientation of school superintendents led them to favor either the parental or school board expectations, depending on who thought they had more legitimacy or stronger sanctions, and which of these was more important to their own self-conception. Understanding the various sources of the received role is important; the focal person will process these perceptions and, on the basis of this process, conform to (or react against) particular aspects of the sent role.

The Role Episode

The expectations of role senders and the means by which they are communicated, together with the focal person's perceptions of these communications and his or her consequential behavior, can be viewed as a sequence or, as Katz and Kahn (1966) term it, a *role episode*. The nature of this sequence is illustrated in Figure 9–3.

The left half of the diagram represents the role sender and the right half the focal person. The left half of each box (sections I and III) represents the individual's perceptions, concepts, and motives. The right segment of each box (sections II and IV) portrays the individual's overt responses.

The direction of the arrow from the role sender to the focal person is quite temporary, for the next role episode may well consist of the original focal person acting together with his or her colleagues as a role sender to a focal person who had originally served in the other capacity. Thus,

FIGURE 9–3
A Model of the Role Episode

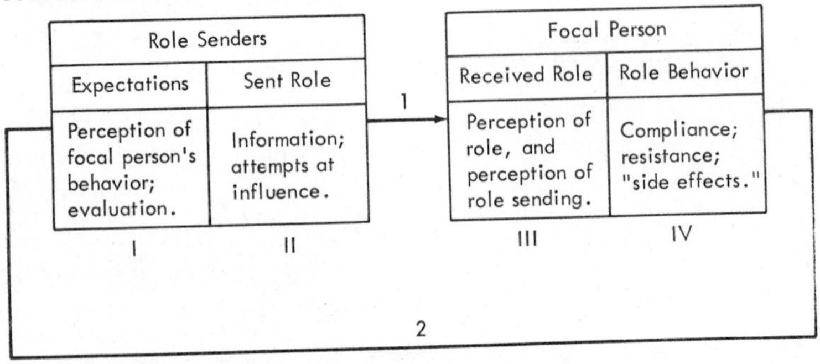

Role Senders		Focal Person	
Expectations	Sent Role	Received Role	Role Behavior
Perception of focal person's behavior; evaluation.	Information; attempts at influence.	Perception of role, and perception of role sending.	Compliance; resistance; "side effects."
I	II	III	IV

Source: Katz and Kahn (1966, p. 182).

an individual occupies a focal role during the time he[3] receives role expectations from other members of his role set. In the next instant, he may, himself, become a role sender. According to Katz and Kahn, "the on-going life of a large organization involves many continuous cycles of sending, receiving, responding, evaluating, and sending again by persons in many overlapping role sets" (1966, p. 183).

In Figure 9–3, the short arrow between the sent role and the received role indicates the process of role sending. The long feedback loop between the role behavior of the focal person and the expectations of the role sender indicates the process whereby the role sender considers how much compliance has been gained in response to the sent role, as well as the process by which he prepares to initiate another cycle of sending and hoping for compliance. Katz and Kahn have articulated a succinct overview of role episode:

> . . . the role episode is abstracted from a process which is cyclic and ongoing: the response of a focal person to role-sending feeds back to each sender in ways that alter or reinforce his expectations and subsequent role-sending. The current role-sendings of each member of the set depend on his evaluations of the responses to his last sendings, and thus a new episode begins (Katz and Kahn, 1966, p. 183).

Role Conflict

In addition to oversimplifying an ongoing process by describing a single episode, Figure 9–3 understates the complexity of the situation by omitting the fact that numerous role senders may have inconsistent and conflicting expectations of the focal person. Katz and Kahn define *role conflict* as the "simultaneous occurrence of two (or more) role sendings such that compliance with one would make more difficult compliance with the other" (1966, p. 184).

Four important types of role conflict are described: (1) *Intra-sender conflict* occurs when a single role sender communicates incompatible expectations to the focal person. (2) *Inter-sender conflict* results when two or more role senders communicate incompatible expectations. (3) *Inter-role conflict* is experienced when the expectations for one role played by the focal person are in conflict with one or more of his other roles (e.g., an individual's work role may conflict with the roles that arise from his home life). (4) *Person-role conflict* arises when sent roles are in conflict with the individual's own needs and values.

Occupational role conflict is a major problem, according to a survey conducted by Kahn et al. (1964). Interviews were conducted with a probability sample of some 725 adults representing the labor force in the United States. Forty-eight percent of the sample reported being "caught in the middle" between two sets of people who had conflicting

---

[3] As previously stated, the common pronoun "he" refers to persons of either sex and is not intended to be masculine or feminine.

expectations of them. Fifteen percent reported this to be a frequent and serious problem. Thirty-nine percent said that not being able to satisfy these conflicting demands "bothered" them.

Furthermore, the investigators linked these subjective feelings of conflict to various affective and overt responses. Role conflict was associated with low job satisfaction, low confidence in the organization, and a high degree of job-related tension. Workers experiencing role conflict frequently attempted to withdraw from the perceived sources of conflict.

Role Ambiguity

In connection with our preceding discussion of the clarity of norms, it is interesting to note that Kahn and associates also found considerable role ambiguity reported by their survey respondents. Four different kinds of ambiguity were cited as being disturbing and troublesome to focal persons. These consisted of uncertainty about: (1) the way one's work would be evaluated by a supervisor, (2) opportunities for advancement, (3) the nature and extent of one's responsibilities, and (4) other people's expectations for one's performance.

The study showed that each of the four areas of ambiguity presented a problem for about one third of the respondents. Approximately 40 percent of the focal persons felt that they possessed insufficient information to perform their jobs adequately. Ambiguity produces significant undesirable results similar to those associated with role conflict; namely, low morale, job satisfaction, and self-confidence, and high feelings of futility and levels of tension.

Sources of Role Ambiguity

Kahn and associates (1964) observe that three general conditions contribute to role ambiguity. First, modern organizations have grown in size and complexity to the extent that a single employee cannot comprehend more than a small portion of the organization's functioning. Second, the rate of organizational change is increasing as a result of growth (and various attendant kinds of structural changes such as reorganization), changes in technology, and personnel turnover. Third, ambiguity is often associated with a managerial philosophy which restricts communication. The rational model of organization suggests that individuals specialize, learn only their own jobs, and look to their superiors for coordination. Even when interdependencies between jobs are recognized by management, communication is based primarily on what subordinates *need* to know rather than on what they would *like* to know. This is not to say that subordinates do not also restrict information since this is one of the few techniques available to them for influencing their superiors.

Some writers have specified a general psychological need for clarity (e.g., Cohen, Stotland, and Wolfe, 1955; Kahn, Wolfe, Quinn, Snoek, and Rosenthal, 1964). The survey by Kahn and associates, as well as a more recent study of registered nurses (Lyons, 1971), show that even individuals having relatively low needs for clarity experience less tension in jobs which are unambiguous than in those which are not.

MANAGING ROLE CONFLICT

Organizational Roles, Innovation, and Adaptation

In our description of role conflict and ambiguity we cited consequences for the focal person. It seems that low levels of tension are found where roles are clear. However, a number of theorists suggest that motivation and satisfaction increase as organizational roles become less specific (Argyris, 1960; Likert, 1961; McGregor, 1960). Less role specification may allow individuals more discretion to work in ways that allow them to meet their own needs as well as those of the organization. An even stronger argument for the importance of discretion is provided by Frank (1963–64), who suggests that ambiguous and conflicting role definitions are useful in organizations that emphasize initiative and innovation.

Frank (1963–64) differentiates organizations according to whether they are: (1) underdefined, (2) well-defined, or (3) overdefined. The classical formal approach to organizational design described in Chapter 2 typifies the well-defined organization (which comprises well-defined roles). Frank suggests the Hoover Commission Report on Organization of the Executive Branch of the Government as a typical example, advocating an orderly, clear grouping of government functions into major departments and agencies, the establishment of clear lines of control from the chief executive to department and agency heads and thence to their subordinates, and so on. Managers who complain of overlaps between roles or lack of clear assignments of responsibility, and who long for clearly defined roles, are acting in this tradition. However, it is not well-defined roles but rather those that are under- and overdefined that lead to adaptability and innovation in organizations.

Underdefined roles permit individuals to take initiative and define roles for themselves or others. This, of course, leads to a changing, adapting and innovating organization. Underdefined roles typically are found in new organizations and at topmost levels of management (see Chapters 12 and 14). With the passage of time, of course, the tendency is for underdefined roles (and organizations comprising these roles) to become either well-defined or overdefined.

The well-defined role limits individual initiative and facilitates ritual performance. The organization with well-defined roles appears bureau-cratic and tends to be stable when compared to an under- or overdefined role configuration. It follows that to have an organization which is creative or innovative, one ought to create a new organization com-prising underdefined roles, rather than attempt to change a well-defined role configuration; for example, Frank describes how his university attempted to foster research and innovative teaching, which required underdefined roles, by setting up an entirely new college rather than changing roles in the ongoing organization.

The third kind of role configuration is the overdefined role. Excessive role expectations, or role overload, comprise one form. The other, more common, type is role conflict, in which conflicting standards or norms prevent complete role performance. Excessive and conflicting role ex-pectations allow the incumbent discretion in defining his role, since he obviously cannot perform the entire set of role requirements. In this respect, the overdefined role is similar to the underdefined role.

Sources of Role Conflict

Kahn and associates found three types of roles that were often char-acterized by conflict; namely, *boundary roles, innovative roles,* and *supervisory roles.*

Boundary roles place the individual in contact with role senders out-side of the organization. Generally, the more frequent and important an individual's contacts outside of the organization, the more role conflict he or she experiences, although this was not true at the extreme. For those individuals having continuous outside contacts, some compensat-ing factors served to ameliorate role conflict.

In any event, the focal persons have limited influence over the out-siders with whom they interact. Despite this, they are likely to be blamed by their co-workers for problems created by these outside contacts. Similarly, their outside contacts are likely to blame them for the short-comings of others in their own organization. The study also showed that internal boundaries (boundaries between departments and divisions) also had implications for conflict and tension.

Roles demanding innovative problem-solving techniques were the sec-ond major source of role conflict and tension. Such *innovative roles,* in which one attempts to bring about change, place one in conflict with those who stand to profit from maintaining the status quo (who in addition, often enjoy greater seniority and power than does the change agent). Furthermore, change agents experience conflicts arising from their involvement in nonroutine activities, as this involvement competes with their routine, administrative activities.

Supervisory roles were the third major source of role conflict. The common belief that the foreman is the "man in-between" and subject to unparallelled conflict was not entirely borne out by the study. Instead, Kahn and associates found that the higher they looked in an organization, the more conflict they found. This is because increased status usually requires the manager to have more contacts outside his or her department, to assume more supervisory responsibility, and to engage in more innovative problem solving. This increasing stress continued through the middle-management level, where conflict tended to be highest. Kahn and associates suggest that the somewhat lower level of role conflict experienced by the highest levels of management is due, in part, to the fact that those executives had already achieved their career aspirations.

The more immediate causes of role conflict and tension were examined in the context of interpersonal relations. Specific kinds of relations with role senders (or sources of power) were found to be associated with high levels of conflict. In general, high pressure and high conflict were generated by individuals who were: (1) in the same department as the focal person, (2) superior to the focal person, or (3) sufficiently dependent upon the focal person to worry about his performance, but not so dependent that they were unable to influence him. The focal person's colleagues, who were some distance from him in the organization, applied the least amount of pressure.

Kahn's study also shows that different kinds of pressure are applied by different kinds of role senders. Superiors in the organization use (*a*) legitimate power or authority, (*b*) rewards, and (*c*) coercive power or negative sanctions. However, coercive power is used sparingly, since its application produces undesirable consequences which, over time, come to reflect poorly on the superiors, themselves. In contrast, subordinates tend to use coercive power since they lack both legitimate power and rewards. The coercive power indicated here includes withholding of assistance and information both of which can have detrimental effects on organizational performance.

Close ties between the focal person and role senders (in terms of work dependence, power, and communication) intensify the effect of an existing conflict. Withdrawal from the conflict by reducing the amount of communication or denigrating the power of role senders is a common, but not particularly effective, coping mechanism. Avoidance of conflict may not only fail to eliminate its causes, but also lead to increased pressures by role senders, leading ultimately to even more conflict.

Managing Role Conflict

Kahn et al. (1964) suggest measures that managers can employ in dealing with role conflict and ambiguity. This is not to suggest that either can be eliminated in an organization. Rather, they argue that some degree of role conflict is inevitable. The manager's options, then, are limited to reducing levels of conflict so that they become tolerable or channeling the conflict in directions that are more positive for the organization and the individuals involved.

Four different approaches to reducing conflict and ambiguity are suggested: (1) Structural changes can be made within the organization. Some of these changes, discussed below in some detail, will produce configurations that are similar to Likert's "linking pin" structure (Chapter 3) and are termed *role-set management*. (2) Criteria for the selection and placement of personnel can be redefined to improve the "fit" between the requirements of a particular role and its incumbent. (3) Programs designed to increase the coping abilities and tolerance levels of employees in particularly stressful roles can be undertaken. Typically, these programs require the expertise of professional counselors. (4) Finally, similar programs can be employed to change and strengthen the interpersonal bonds among personnel (e.g., see Chapter 16 on "Organizational Development").

According to Likert's linking pin theory, the stresses that are experienced by the incumbent of a particularly difficult role can be dealt with effectively through the joint efforts of his or her overlapping groups of peers, subordinates, and superior. An even better approach, according to Kahn and associates, begins with the identification of the incumbent's role set. A group can be assembled from the incumbents of roles that are interdependent with the focal role (in terms of either work flow or hierarchical structure), and this group will probably be competent to deal with the problems of the focal role. This is not to say that the full set of role senders ought to convene to consider all problems relating to the focal role. "Whether a meeting of the entire set, consultation with subsets, or mere information will suffice depends upon the significance of the proposed action for their own needs and behavior" (Kahn et al., 1964, p. 391).

Given this strategy, which particular positions within the organization should be identified as candidates for attention and, perhaps, modification? As we have seen, boundary or liaison positions, supervisory and middle-management positions, positions that require innovation, and those that are functionally related to and interdependent with other positions are all significant sources of role conflict and ambiguity.

What is suggested is a balanced approach in dealing with the dilemmas that are always present in organizations. In Chapter 8, we elaborated the dilemma of conflicting criteria for organizational effectiveness. If one does not always expect optimum performance on all criteria, then perhaps extreme stress can be avoided. Another dilemma exists in the choice between concentrating and containing sources of stress within one or a few roles or attempting to spread them out over a number of positions. A third dilemma cited by Kahn and associates arises in choosing between one stress and another since eliminating a particular source of stress often produces side effects in the form of new tensions elsewhere in the organization.

Managing Stress in Boundary Roles

Kahn and associates suggest that boundary roles be made explicit and that their importance be emphasized within the organization. In addition to organizational recognition, such positions must have power and auxiliary services that are commensurate with the responsibilities that they bear. Wherever possible, multiple rather than single boundary and liaison roles should be established to diffuse role conflict and avoid focusing what may be crippling stress within an important organizational function.

It is also suggested that formal procedures be established for maintaining agreement and understanding between the incumbents of boundary and more internally focused roles. The means toward this end suggested by Kahn and associates include job rotation schemes wherein role senders within the organization are exposed to the received roles of boundary positions; for example, a dean may encourage faculty members to serve rotating tours of duty as associate deans in order to learn of the pressures that arise from attempts to mesh the expectations of faculty members with those of a university's administration. George Strauss (1962), in another example, explains how active and aggressive purchasing agents maintain and even expand their functions and responsibilities by bringing holders of internal roles, such as engineers, into contact with sales personnel from external vendor organizations.

Role stress tends to increase as the size of the organization increases (Kahn et al., 1964). Organizational growth increases the requirements for coordination, since the number of subunits and relationships between subunits increase with size (Graicunas, 1937). Thus, requirements for coordination can be minimized by making organizational subunits as independent of one another and of top management as possible.

Of course, the very nature of organizations requires connected and coordinated effort, but such connections between positions in subunits must be examined carefully to determine that they are essential to effective performance. If centralized leadership is advocatd merely because it is a "principle" of good management, an investigation of a more decentralized structure as an alternative would be in order. Similarly, flat rather than tall organizational structures and laterally autonomous or federated units rather than integrated units may be preferred, assuming that their introduction will not hinder the productive processes.

Influence, Power, and Bases of Power

Modifying another person's behavior through role sending implies that the role sender wields power, of one sort or another, over the focal role. By *influence,* we mean an interpersonal relationship in which one actor affects the behavior of a second actor to cause a change that would not have occurred otherwise. *Power* refers to the ability to influence. To have power is to have the capacity to influence. Below, we shall speak of "bases of power," which are various means that may be employed to influence and, thereby, cause compliance. *Authority* refers to legitimate power that is vested within a role or office; it is lawful power that is recognized by others in the organization. In contrast, one has *control* over another to the extent the other behaves as one desires, and influence attempts are successful. Not only does one influence the other, but the influence is sufficiently strong so that counterinfluence, resistance, and external forces are overcome (e.g., see Katz and Kahn, 1966).

Power may be achieved through various means. French and Raven (1959) described five "bases of power." *Legitimate power* is based on the authority vested in a role or office. Such power is lawful and is accepted and recognized as such by others in the organization. *Reward power* is based on the various positive rewards or sanctions that an individual may employ in the pursuit of influence. *Coercive power* is based on negative sanctions or threats of harm or punishment. *Expert power* is based on knowledge or information which is accepted as accurate and correct. Finally, *referent power* is based on attractive personal characteristics which may lead others to like and emulate the attractive, referent person.

This categorization seems to indicate that power emanates from the possession of one or more bases. However, power and influence are characteristics of relationships. It is an oversimplification to speak of bases of power which the power wielder possesses (Patchen, 1974); for example, expert power requires both an individual possessing expert information and a person who lacks and needs this information. Similarly, the wielder of referent power possesses characteristics which are attractive to another individual. In similar fashion, the rewards, sanctions, and legitimate authority of the power wielder are only of value when the target of influence, respectively, desires and lacks certain rewards, wishes to avoid certain punishments, and has internalized a moral obligation to obey the authority and wishes to fulfill that obligation.

Bases of Compliance

It is useful to speak not only of bases of power, but of bases of compliance (Bachman, Bowers, and Marcus, 1968; Etzioni, 1961). This distinction is useful because attempts at influence, in which the power wielder consciously mobilizes particular bases of power, may be successful because different bases of compliance are operating. For instance, one may attempt to influence by offering rewards, but influence may be gained because of some attractive characteristic of the power wielder, because of his or her referent power. In this case, one would speak of an attempt to influence on the basis of reward power and compliance gained on the basis of referent power.

Table 9–1 provides a separate listing of the characteristics and resources of persons exerting influence, as opposed to the characteristics and needs of the targets of influence. In this table, Patchen (1974) provides a systematic description of the French and Raven bases of power and the corresponding bases of compliance: expert, reward, coercive, referent, and legitimate, respectively. To this list is added power based on being a "stakeholder" (Chapter 5) and the corresponding compliance based on organizational norms that stakeholders have some influence over decisions affecting them. This notion is discussed in greater detail below.

The Power of Lower Participants

In a paper entitled "Sources of Power of Lower Participants in Complex Organizations," Mechanic (1962) describes commonly found situations in which authority does not suffice to explain the power and influence relationships in organizations. Certainly, supervisors and managers use their legitimate power to control the behavior of subordinates. However, lower participants circumvent or manipulate the organizational hierarchy by using various forms of power that are not legitimate. A major source of such power is the control of resources upon which others are dependent; for example, members of a planning staff possess important information about potential future directions for the organization and are able to parlay this information into a variety of forms of influence. An executive's secretary controls access to an important individual and can use this resource to influence others. Mechanic also cites attributes such as likability, attractiveness, and charisma as sources of power. Finally, lower level personnel may obtain power through the control of instrumentalities or various aspects of the organization's physical plant or resources (e.g., equipment, machines, cash, and so on).

Our analysis here follows that presented in Chapter 5 where power was viewed as the obverse of dependence. To the extent that a person is dependent upon another, he or she is subject to the other person's power. One can make others dependent on oneself by controlling their access to information, persons, and instrumentalities, as defined here.

Mechanic describes how the secretarial staff in a university often

Table 9–1. A Framework for Analyzing Social Influence,* with Some Examples

Kinds of Influence	Person Exerting Influence			Target(s) of Influence			
	Characteristics	Resources	Decision Role with Respect to Target	Characteristics	Needs	Decision Role with Respect to Influencer	Effect of Influencer on Target
Expert . . .	Expertise: special training, special experience, etc.	Knowledge about how to reach certain goals.	Investigates, makes tests, gives information to others.	Unexpert.	Wants to find best ways to reach goals.	Reviews information presented by experts.	Sees new options; sees new favorable or unfavorable consequences following various actions.
Reward . . .	Occupies important position in hierarchy.	Control over material rewards (money, promotion, etc.).	Makes request, coupled with promise of reward for compliance.	Occupies less important position in hierarchy.	Wants rewards controlled by influencer.	Decides whether to accede to request of others.	Compliance seen as means to rewards.
Coercive . .	Occupies important position in hierarchy.	Control over material penalties (fines, demotions, etc.).	Gives order, coupled with threat of punishment for noncompliance.	Occupies less important position in hierarchy.	Wants to avoid punishment but maintain self-esteem.	Decides whether to accede to order.	Compliance seen as way of avoiding penalty but may be seen as blow to self-esteem.
Referent . .	Strong; successful; has attractive qualities.	Approval.	States own opinions, preferences.	Less strong, less successful.	Wishes to be similar to, approved by, influencer.	Hears opinions, preferences of influencer.	Sees compliance as way of being similar to, approved by, influencer.
Legitimate .	Occupies legitimate position of authority; secured position by legitimate work methods.	Symbols of legitimacy; label of others' action as right or wrong.	Announces decision; asks for support.	Occupies position of subordination; accepts legitimacy of other's position.	Wishes to fulfill moral obligations.	Gets request from authority.	Sees conformity to requested action as morally correct.
Stakeholder	Is affected by certain decisions (by virtue of work needs, responsibilities, etc.).	Own cooperation; (may also have some resources listed in other rows).	Vigorously makes preference known to others.	Peers or final decision-making authority.	Wants high level of cooperation from influencer.	Decide whether to accept recommendation.	See accepting recommendation as leading to future cooperation by influencer.

* This framework may be expanded to include (a) the motivation of the influencer to use his resources and (b) the perception by the target
 ̶t̶h̶a̶t̶ ̶t̶h̶e̶ influencer will use his resources.

enjoys considerable power to make decisions about the purchase and allocation of supplies, the allocation of secretarial services, the scheduling of classes, and so on. Some of these powers may have been formally delegated, but often they exist because the secretarial staff takes initiative and exerts effort in areas where other, higher ranking participants are reluctant to act. A department leader may easily remove the scheduling activity from the jurisdiction of a secretary, but this can only be done at the cost of performing the scheduling activities himself.

Generally, evidence that lower level personnel are wielding illegitimate power to obstruct or frustrate certain higher level personnel is difficult to find since these obstructive activities are usually not covered by specific rules. If the worst occurs and conflict emerges between higher and lower level participants, the lower level staff may resort to "working to rule" or following to the letter those rules that do exist and thereby create mild chaos and a major backlog of work. Finally, since the process of gaining access to information, persons, and instrumentalities is time consuming, we can generalize that the power obtained by lower level participants increases with the amount of time the employee spends in the organization.

Even in prisons, the lower participants, or prisoners, have sufficient power to create difficulties for prison guards when they choose to do so (Sykes, 1958). Human behavior is complex, and every single move cannot be anticipated or controlled, even by a prison guard. Guards depend on the inmates to show initiative in activities such as working in the prison shop, cleaning their cells, and even moving from place to place in the prison according to the daily routine. Of course, it is possible to use formal sanctions against inmates in order to force compliance. However, extended use of these sanctions would make the guards "look bad" in the eyes of their superiors. For these reasons, then, exchange relationships develop in which guards give favors and overlook infractions of certain rules in return for the inmates' cooperation.

Interestingly enough, these exchange relationships seem to be inflationary in that more and more favors and increased immunity from rules are expected by prisoners in return for their cooperation. This inflation persists until the inmates have parlayed their power to the extent that the guards would lose their jobs if it were recognized by higher ups in the organization (or to outsiders, such as the press). At this point the guards "crack down," sometimes at the risk of provoking a prison riot. Such is the power of lower participants, even in prisons.

It is useful to relate the foregoing discussion to the taxonomy devised by Etzioni (1968) who speaks of "remunerative-calculative" relationships characterized by "a complementary of interest; [in which] the actors treat each other as means, and commitments are rational" (p. 96). Relationships similar to those found in a prison are termed "coercive-alienative" and are characterized by "the use, or threatened use, of means of violence by one actor against one or more other actors. Actors treat each other as objects, and the commitment may be either rational or nonrational" (p. 96). In some contrast we can observe "normative-moral" relationships characterized by "shared values and norms; [in which] the related actors treat each other as goals, and their mutual commitments are non-rational" (p. 96). We suggest that in some organizations (and quite often at higher levels of these organizations) influence relationships are based on organizational norms rather than (or in addition to) individualistic calculation or relations in which people are treated as objects. In the normative-moral relationship individuals act on the basis of expectations of others which have been internalized and also on the basis of norms. When moral considerations are taken into account, individuals act one way or another because "It is right."

The Normative Element and Power

In addition to power that is purely normative, we find that other bases of power (e.g., expert, reward, referent) have normative elements. Norms may play an important part in causing compliance to influence attempts based on more rational and coercive bases of power. We may be influenced by an expert, not only because we need his or her knowledge, but also because the influencer *is an* "*expert*." We may even accept expert advice that does not make sense to us. We are influenced by the norm that expert advice is to be followed.

Etzioni (1961) provides a list of normative organizations in which influence relationships are typically normative-moral, and individuals influence and accept influence on the basis of internalized standards of what is right. Religious organizations, political organizations, general hospitals, universities, and voluntary associations are primarily characterized by normative influence relations. Predominantly utilitarian organizations or organizations based on renumerative-calculative orientations include most business organizations. Coercive organizations, of course, include prisons, most correctional "institutions," custodial and mental hospitals, and concentration camps.

The normative-calculative-coercive distinction is useful in reminding us of the different possible ways of organizing. Any particular situation, including even the organizations listed above, will probably yield a combination of different kinds of power orientations. Azim (1973), for example, studied doctoral candidates and their relations with faculty members in a university department. The power applied by faculty members was perceived by the doctoral candidates as being both normative and renumerative. Similarly, Peabody (1962) found that police officers described influence relations in their departments more frequently in terms of the power of the person (referent power) than the legitimate power found in the office. Social workers who were expected to be compliant primarily on the basis of expert power (power based on technical competence and experience) actually gave more importance to legitimacy in departmental relations. Finally, elementary school employees (principal, teachers, and supporting staff) stressed professional competence as was expected.

In summary, then, influence and compliance may be based on a variety of different bases, not always those one might expect from the kind of organization in question. Included in this variety is a normative element which will be studied in more detail as we turn to an examination of the influence of norms on decision making.

NORMS AND ORGANIZATIONAL BEHAVIOR

Power and Decisions

Of particular interest are the ways in which norms and influence processes affect decision making in organizations. Do decision makers gather all available information and base their decisions primarily on the weight of such evidence? Certainly, the formal hierarchy of authority in organizations permits this. Or, is the decision maker moved by the power of various role senders in the organizations? If the latter is the case, what norms determine who is to have power in a particular decision?

Patchen (1974) explored these questions by examining nonrepetitive purchasing decisions made in 11 different manufacturing firms. On the average, 15 different individuals had some role in a typical decision; for example, in a company manufacturing automobile parts, the decision to use zinc rather than aluminum for a particular product involved personnel from engineering, sales, manufacturing, and purchasing, as well as other organizational units.

An attempt was made to discover the systemic bases for power in the decisions studied. The individuals involved in specific decisions were unable to agree on who had the most power. Generally, no single decision maker was identifiable. Decisions were formed through processes of accommodation and consensus. Power was rarely attributed to the sanctioning power of an individual—to his or her ability to reward or punish others. Formal authority was mentioned by respondents, but not very frequently (about 5 percent of the time). In addition, there was an almost total lack of reference to bargaining or coalition formation.

Power of Stakeholders

As one might expect, power was attributed to expertise but only by about 22 percent of the respondents. However, individuals were often seen as having power either because they would be affected or were responsible in some way. They were "stakeholders" in the outcome of the decision.

Equally important as expertise as a source of power was the extent to which an individual would be affected by the outcome of the decision in question; for example, the traffic supervisor in one firm had influence over the decision to purchase a tractor truck. In addition, individuals had power because they were responsible for a product which involved the use of the item under consideration. In one company, the plant engineer cited the sales manager as the most influential in the decision to buy a new piercing press for manufacturing because he could not have fulfilled his sales goals without it. Please note that the power described here was by and large independent of formal authority to make the decision.

Finally, some individuals were seen to have power over decisions because these decisions were their "responsibility." The buyer in a firm that manufactures musical instruments was seen as influencing the choice of a mold used in making organ parts because it was his function to influence these kinds of decisions, given the way the firm operated. Patchen suggests that such responsibility may be delegated as a way of dividing up the work, but that it is unlikely that individuals having power because of delegated responsibility will override the power of those having a stake in the decision's outcome.

Decision making, then, should be viewed as a *process* involving a variety of individuals having varying degrees of power over the decision. Although how this process develops among different individuals and under a variety of circumstances is still unclear, it is evident that the problem goes far beyond the phenomena described by the "informal structure" as we initially presented it in Chapter 3.

Normative Power and Decisions

Of special interest to us are the ways in which structure (norms regarding the power of stakeholders) begins to stabilize a process that is both dynamic and complex. The most dynamic kind of decision-making process can be characterized as including extensive bargaining, coalition formation, and direct influence by means of persuasion, threats, and the like. But Patchen's study showed that "understandings" were found in place of conflict. As we indicated, norms can arise in dynamic situations because negotiating and bargaining are time consuming and disagreeable because of the conflict and hostility they are likely to generate. In making behavior more "automatic," norms save time and energy and reduce interpersonal strife (Thibaut and Kelley, 1959).

The norm that provides stakeholders with power in the decision-making process is useful because it conserves the effort involved in negotiating a decision *and* because it has the potential to add to the satisfaction of those who will be affected by the decision. The stakeholders, who have desires and feelings about the outcome of a decision, will also possess information that is useful (and sometimes vital) to the success of the decision-making process. As we indicated in Chapter 3, participation in decision making is desirable, not only for motivational reasons, but also because it allows the specialized knowledge of subordinates to be incorporated in the process. Perhaps the most important reason for advocating this norm is enlightened self-interest. When the time comes for decisions that will affect my performance and satisfaction, the norm will protect my own interests. As Patchen suggests, it is a simple matter of "log-rolling"; if I back you on what is important to you, you are likely to back me on what is most important to me.

Where several individuals have strong interests in a decision, their abilities to influence will probably depend on their respective intensities of interest as well as their degrees of power. Jockeying for position and negotiation will be common, depending on the amount of effort each participant is willing to expend and the kinds of sanctions that are available.

Where strong sanctions exist—sanctions such as the ability to withhold cooperation, needed resources, or one's services through terminating one's employment—norms are quite likely to emerge over time. Individuals may come to *internalize* the threat of sanctions and to behave as if the sanctions would follow if desired behavior was not forthcoming (Kelman, 1961; Thibaut and Kelley, 1959). Similarly, rewards may lead to the emergence of norms. Individuals may behave in ways that are rewarding (e.g., in mutually satisfying exchange relationships) which, in time, become normative.

As indicated above, the extent of interest in a particular decision helps to determine whether or not one will try to influence the process. We cannot influence each and every decision in our organization. Those that are unimportant to us may be treated as "give-aways." In others, we may wish to stake our claim. Bauer (1968) makes the point as follows:

> In any ongoing institution, the ability to get important things done is dependent on maintaining a reservoir of good will. The person who fights every issue as though it were vital exhausts his resources including, most especially, the patience and good will of those on whom he has to depend to get things done. Therefore, it should be considered neither surprising nor immoral that, when an issue is of low salience the sensible individual may use it to build good will for the future, or pay off past obligations, by going along with some individual for whom the issue is of high salience (p. 17).

Normative Structure and Political Processes

This study of purchasing decisions in business organizations shows normative structure to be important for organizational functioning. The psychiatric hospital described in the "Introduction" above was less stable and illustrated more conflict and bargaining along the path to a negotiated normative order. Professional organizations are likely to display political processes in the service of norm-building. This is because professional organizations, such as the psychiatric hospital, serve a multiplicity of purposes and employ nonroutine technologies requiring the exercise of judgment and compromise. In addition, their external environments are constantly changing. In light of these problems for normative development, how do professionals organize?

Professional norms are found in these kinds of organizations, but in point of fact these norms are quite limited. There are norms regarding standards of expertise and knowledge and norms about using such knowledge/expertise in the client's service. However, while professional knowledge "tells" practitioners how to do their jobs, it does not tell them how to organize or how to structure their relations with others. Furthermore, professional knowledge is continually changing. Even at a given point in time there are differences in the distribution of knowledge across professionals, even within the same organization. Professional knowledge, then, cannot be relied upon to provide guidelines for organizing professionals and their interactions. Bucher and Stelling (1969) suggest that when professionals are in control, they create distinctive social organizations quite different from those described by bureaucratic theory. On the basis of their observations of various kinds of hospitals and professionals, they describe the professional organization in terms of "political" processes and emphasize negotiation and shifting alliances as concepts for understanding the nature of these organizations.

Role-negotiation

Professionals make "claims" to competence in particular areas. Professional expertise is not acknowledged automatically by others, but, rather, must be demonstrated in relation to others of one's own profession and of other professions. The professionals must show that they possess skills for defining problems, determining means for their solution and judging the success of actions undertaken in their area of expertise. To the extent that he or she is able to substantiate such claims in relation to other professionals, autonomy and influence are achieved.

Professionals typically must build their roles in the organization as opposed to taking up a previously defined role. Role-creation proceeds through negotiation with relevant individuals in the organization. For instance, Bucher and Stelling (1969) note that:

> In the medical school . . . we have never seen a case in which a new faculty member took over the role of his predecessor. Even within the same discipline, faculty members differ in their conceptions of

their responsibilities, their interests, and their ways of organizing their time. . . . One of our respondents requires a room in which temperature can be held constant. Another needs animal quarters where light can be held constant or varied by design. A third, engaged in dream research, needs a suite of rooms, *and* control of temperature. In all three of these cases, also, the researcher must have control of his time once the research begins—else the experiment is lost. Hence the new faculty member negotiates for work space and resources, and proceeds to set up his work as he conceives it (page 5).

Professionals differ from others in this negotiating behavior in that it is often conducted covertly. The negotiation is likely to be based on professional considerations. Even in the cases where one professional has authority over another, the superior will deal with the subordinate, not in terms of orders or directions, but rather in the guise of professional or technical considerations. The technically "right" thing will be discussed and argued for. The same kind of negotiation is found in the "negotiated order" in the psychiatric section of the hospital described above. In that setting, much of the negotiation took place between different kinds of professionals, especially in the context of "teams" of different professionals.

In such teams of different but interdependent professions, negotiation may become quite intense. Despite appeals to "the good of the patient," it may be that different professionals lack common goals and are interested in doing different things for different "parts" of the patient. In terms of the paradigm of Thompson and Tuden (1959), lack of agreement on goals leads to decision making by bargaining and compromise (see Chapter 5).

Participation in a team can be fateful for the professional. It is an arena of action in which the work spaces of the different team members overlap. The work of one person is likely to affect that of another. In contrast to the bureaucratic organization, these groupings emerge from the impetus of the professionals themselves as they define roles and groups of roles.

This differentiation, of course, can generate competition and conflict in the organization. The emerging groups require resources which are always limited. Consequently, there will be competition and conflict over the budget and other resources such as space. Bucher and Stelling describe how the curriculum in a professional school becomes an important arena for competition. Emerging specialities attempt to require students to devote time to their areas and are resisted by the more traditional specialities. In Chapter 14 on "Strategy Formulation," we shall describe political processes involved in strategic decision making—processes occurring at higher levels of all organizations, in which the ill-structured problem of establishing directions for the organization is debated, causing different groupings to take positions and attempt to influence one another appropriately. Our discussion of coalition formation and bargaining, found in Chapter 5, is relevant to the present topic as well.

Political Processes

Of course, interaction among professionals comprises more than conflict and competition. Structure does develop, for the organization must mobilize its resources in a coordinated effort. While large, complex organizations such as medical centers may appear to be congeries of feudal fifedoms, they do, in fact, maintain some semblance of integration with regard to organizational goals. In Chapter 14, we shall describe how coalitions and (in the case of large coalitions) "inner circles" develop to facilitate decision making. The point made by Bucher and Stelling and others (e.g., Baldridge, 1971) is not that professional organizations are disorganized, but that these organizations must be understood in terms of political processes. A chief executive does not give orders which are obeyed automatically. Rather, political parties or similar groupings develop. Professionals sound out colleagues within their department and other departments on proposals for alliance with regard to particular issues. Bucher and Stelling (1969) provide the following example of this phenomenon:

> One of our major informants in the medical school who was a department head has told us, on a series of occasions, how he has been approached by the head of medicine, the head of surgery, the head of preventive medicine, etc. In each instance, they were sounding him out as to his views on issues, and whether they might make common cause. This informant frequently alluded to the norm of *pro quid quo* in describing these encounters—if he could help out the head of medicine in something of importance to that department, he would expect similar assistance when he needed it. . . . As faculty members, we have engaged in numerous "deals" with trusted colleagues from other sectors of the university in faculty elections, and it is clear that others are doing this also. . . . This seeking of allies leads to the growth of parties, or factions. . . . Such factions represent groups of people who, perhaps only temporarily, share perspectives, who see common problems and common consequences of events (pp. 10–11).

Rather than authority, power is critical in professional organizations. Most critical is the process—the different tactics used at different points in time in cooperating and competing with other organizational members. In short, we suggest that the professional organization and also other organizations with multiple goals and nonroutine technologies are characterized by processes in which roles emerge and are created through negotiation and differentiation, by competition and conflict, with integration arising from the political processes.

Organizational Culture and Character

Several reports describe *organizational culture,* the organizationwide, relatively enduring set of beliefs or cognitions that often become normative and play an important part in determining the perceptions and actions of employees. *Organizational character* refers to the unique normative structure of the organization that provides it with a (moral) identity.

Anthony Jay, in *Corporation Man* (1971), discusses organizational "folk culture" and describes his return to a school 20 years after leaving it. He found that despite a move to new buildings in a different part of London and the influx of new teachers and students, it was still recognizable as the school he had attended. The school had maintained the same general curriculum, the same attitudes toward learning, the same academic reputation, the same tolerance of eccentricity, and the same relationship between boys and teachers.

Giving the school its continuity, group identity, and appearance of tradition is what Jay terms the "cultural tradition," or what we prefer to call organizational character—the basic identity of the organization. He suggests that the elements of cultural tradition:

> . . . give unique identity to a larger company, to a giant corporation, or even to a nation. When we say "What is Ford like to work for?" "What is IBM like to deal with?" "That's typical of DuPont," we are assuming a continuing identity going right through the corporation and back over many years. Insofar as we can generalize about nations—"just like the Italians," "typically German"—it is the same cultural condition, not a specifically German or Italian combination of genes, that we are referring to. It is something you build up over many years, and can destroy overnight. It is what you have to change if you take over . . . it is almost impossible to teach, and almost impossible not to learn (p. 176).

Elements of this culture include "external identity," the niche an organization occupies. Please note the similarity of this concept to "domain consensus" (Chapter 8). A new restaurant, for example, can decide the kind of food, prices, and atmosphere it will offer, and in time, its clientele will come to accept these. Suppliers, too, will develop an understanding of the restaurant's external identity and will offer management products and services that complement it. Even competitors, in recognition of the identity, may decide to compete by offering different kinds of foods, price ranges, or atmospheres.

Other elements of the culture described by Jay include the internal status system, the informal organization (especially leadership style traditions), shared concepts of right and wrong ways of behaving, and the internal communication system. Most important for our purposes are the elements of culture Jay terms the "central faith":

> Whereas the other elements take time to grow up, the central faith is there from the start. It is the belief at the root of the business, and I call it faith because it rests on a number of unproved assumptions. "People want quality," "If you can make a better mouse trap the world will beat a trail to your door," "It's not the product that matters, it's how hard you sell it," "If you want to stay in business, you've got to deliver on time"—all these expressions of commercial and industrial dogma spring from the central faith. . . . A good way to find the central faith of (an organization) is to get its members to see who can formulate the biggest blasphemy. . . . In the BBC: "I admit it wasn't really true, but the Home Secretary was very keen we should say it." In Rolls-Royce: "It's a lousy bit of engineering but it will sell like hotcakes" (pp. 182–83).

In short, culture includes belief systems which influence the ways in which we perceive and conceptualize reality. The latter, in turn, affect specific activities, attitudes, and predispositions to render them consistent with the organization's culture. For example, supportive behavior on the part of a superior may be interpreted as an indication of weakness in a power-ridden work culture. Identical behavior may be viewed as a sign of strength in an organization practicing System Four management (Chapter 3).

Character: Power, Roles, Tasks, and People

Harrison (1972) describes organizational character as the ideology or beliefs upon which behavior in the organization is based. He distinguishes four different ideologies which determine basic tendencies of many organizations: (1) power orientation, (2) role orientation, (3) task orientation, and (4) person orientation.

The *power-oriented* organization attempts to dominate its environment and overcome opposition. Those who are powerful attempt to maintain absolute control over subordinates. Harrison states:

> Some modern conglomerates project images of power ideology. They buy and sell organizations and people as commodities, in apparent disregard of human values and the general welfare. They seem to have voracious appetites for growth, which is valued for its own sake. Competition to acquire other companies and properties is ruthless and sometimes outside the law. Within the organization, the law of the jungle often seems to prevail among executives as they struggle for personal advantage against their peers (p. 121).

The *role-oriented* organization emphasizes rationality and order. Legality, legitimacy, and responsibility are emphasized partly in response to the power orientation and the resulting competition and conflict which are viewed as undesirable. Agreements, rules, and procedures are specified. Stability and respectability are often valued. "The correct response tends to be more highly valued than the effective one."

The organization which is *task oriented* emphasizes achievement of a superordinate goal—whether it is making a profit, winning a war, or helping the poor. Behavior is judged in terms of its contribution to the goal. If authority gets in the way or if rules and regulations become hinderances, they are eliminated. Individuals lacking confidence or information will be retrained or eliminated, too. Emphasis is "getting on with the job."

Harrison suggests that aerospace firms typify the task orientation:

> Companies involved with dynamic markets or fast-changing, complex technologies frequently established project teams or "task forces." These groups of specialists are selected to solve a particular problem and often operate in a very flexible and egalitarian manner until the problem is solved. The units are then disbanded, and the members join other teams to work on new problems. Although the larger organization in which it operates may be basically role or power oriented, the project team or task force often exhibits a relatively pure orientation. Moreover, these groups have been so successful that some organizations are trying to install a task-oriented ideology throughout their operations (p. 122).

The *person-oriented* organization emphasizes the needs of its members. The organization's purpose is not to achieve a goal but, rather, to satisfy its members. Individuals are not evaluated in terms of their contributions to goal achievements. The organization is evaluated in terms of its ability to satisfy individuals. Authority and power are discouraged. Instead, individuals are expected to influence one another through example, helpfulness, and caring. Consensus decision making is emphasized.

> Illustrations of person orientation are small groups of professionals who have joined together for research and development. Some consulting companies, too, seem to be designed primarily as vehicles for members. It is typical of such organizations that growth, expansion, and maximization of income and profit are not primary considerations. Rather, the organizations, hopefully, are conducted to make enough money to survive and provide their members with a reasonable living as well as an opportunity to do meaningful and enjoyable work with congenial people (Harrison, 1972, p. 123).

Ideological Fit

Ideologies or basic belief systems are important since the cognitions and perceptions of individuals will determine their decision making and functioning both within the organization and in relation to its external environment. To the extent that the organizational ideology fits individual needs (which is to say, provides the kinds of incentives and satisfactions desired), the ideology is internally viable. Similarly, in relating to its environment the organization responds according to its beliefs or ideology. The fit between ideology and the corresponding behavior, needs, and desires of the environment will determine the extent to which the organization itself is viable.

Harrison distinguishes between the needs or interests of individuals and the needs and interests of organizations and suggests that the four basic ideologies should be examined with regard to their ability to meet the needs and interests of both individuals and organizations. For example, an organization employing individuals with high growth needs might utilize the person orientation, while an organization with high needs for effective response to a threatening environment might utilize a power orientation.

Unfortunately, there is no best ideology for most organizations since the interests of people and the organization are not likely to match perfectly. Combinations of several ideologies might appear appropriate to particular sets of interests. However, the nature of ideologies seems to be such that they cannot be mixed. Ideologies tend to be systematic and rational; therefore dissimilar ideologies are difficult to combine. Furthermore, sociological and historical study indicates that social groupings which gain ascendency in a social system tend to eliminate minority ideologies which conflict with the prevailing ideology of the dominant group. There is a "snowball" effect in which the acquisition of power leads to instability and a dynamic situation in which less powerful groups with opposing ideologies are eliminated (Schulze, 1969).

This analysis of culture in organizations (including both belief systems and norms) has several implications. It would seem that cultures are relatively impervious to change or at least to planned change. The change agent or management consultant must diagnose the culture and decide whether his or her recommendations are congruent or in conflict with the culture. Similarly, existing conflicts in organizations may be due to the existence of different groups which have incompatible cultures and vie to impose these cultures upon others. Harrison suggests that there may be merit in dealing with such conflicts openly and increasing awareness of the culture and how it colors basic perceptions and thereby affects behavior.

In conclusion, then, we have discussed a variety of phenomena, including norms, roles, culture, and ideology. Their generation, the conflict that arises among them, and its dissolution comprise major parts of the process of organizational functioning.

DISCUSSION QUESTIONS

1. What do we mean by role conflict? In what sense is it inevitable?
2. What role conflict have you experienced?
3. What sort of power do students have vis-à-vis the university or college they attend?
4. To what extent do norms enter into decision making in a university?
5. How might decision making in a university differ from similar activity in a business firm?

6. Compare the cultures of two different organizations with which you are familiar.

REFERENCES

Argyris, Chris. *Understanding human behavior*. London: Tavistock, 1960.

Azim, A. N. Lower participants' perception of power as a determinant of their organizational behavior: an empirical study. Manuscript. Calgary: University of Calgary, 1973.

Bachman, Jerald G., Bowers, David G., and Marcus, Philip M. Bases of supervisory power: a comparative study in five organizational settings. In A. S. Tannenbaum (Ed.), *Control in organizations*. New York: McGraw-Hill, 1968.

Baldridge, Victor J. *Power and conflict in the university: research in the sociology of complex organizations*. New York: Wiley, 1971.

Bauer, Raymond. The study of policy formation: an introduction. In R. Bauer and K. Gergen (Eds.), *The study of policy formation*. New York: Free Press, 1968.

Bucher, Rue, and Stelling, Joan. Characteristics of professional organizations. *Journal of Health and Human Behavior*, 1969, *10*, 3–15.

Cohen, A. R., Stotland, E., and Wolfe, D. M. An experimental investigation of need for cognition. *Journal of Abnormal and Social Psychology*, 1955, *51*, 291–94.

Etzioni, Amitai. *A comparative analysis of complex organizations*. New York: Free Press, 1961.

Etzioni, Amitai. *The active society*. New York: Free Press, 1968.

Forehand, G. A., and Gilmer, B. V. H. Environmental variation in studies of organizational behavior. *Psychological Bulletin*, 1964, 62, 361–82.

Frank, Andrew Gunder. Administrative role definition and social changes. *Human Organization*, 1963–64, 22, 238–42.

French, John R. P., Jr., and Raven, Bertram H. The bases of social power. In D. Cartwright (Ed.), *Studies in social power*. Ann Arbor, Mich.: University of Michigan, Institute for Social Research, 1959.

Graicunas, V. A. Relationship in organization. In L. Gulick and L. Urwick (Eds.), *Papers on the science of administration*. New York: Institute of Public Administration, 1937. Pp. 183–87.

Gross, Neal, Mason, Ward S., and McEachern, Alexander W. *Explorations in role analysis*. New York: Wiley, 1958.

Harrison, Roger. Understanding your organization's character. *Harvard Business Review*, 1972, 50 (May-June), 119–28.

Jackson, Jay M. Structural characteristics of norms. In B. J. Biddle and E. J. Thomas (Eds.), *Role theory: concepts and research*. New York: Wiley, 1966. Pp. 133–36.

Jay, Anthony. *Corporation man*. New York: Random House, 1971.

Kahn, Robert L., Wolfe, Donald M., Quinn, Robert P., Snoek, J. Diedrick, and Rosenthal, Robert A. *Organizational stress: studies in role conflict and ambiguity*. New York: Wiley, 1964.

Katz, Daniel, and Kahn, Robert L. *The social psychology of organizations*. New York: Wiley, 1966.

Kelman, Herbert C. Processes of opinion change. *Public Opinion Quarterly*, 1961, 25, 57–78.

Likert, Rensis. *New patterns of management*. New York: McGraw-Hill, 1961.

Organizations: Behavior, Design, and Change

Lyons, Thomas F. Role clarity, need for clarity, satisfaction, tension, and withdrawal. *Organizational Behavior and Human Performance*, 1971, 6, 99–110.

McGregor, Douglas. *The human side of enterprise*. New York: McGraw-Hill, 1960.

Mechanic, David. Sources of power of lower participants in complex organizations. *Administrative Science Quarterly*, 1962, 7, 349–64.

Patchen, Martin. The locus and basis of influence on organizational decisions. *Organizational Behavior and Human Performance*, 1974, 2, 195–221.

Peabody, Robert L. Perceptions of organizational authority: a cooperative analysis. *Administrative Science Quarterly*, 1962, 6, 463–72.

Schulze, Rolf. Some social-psychological and political functions of ideology. *Sociological Quarterly*, 1969, 10, 72–83.

Strauss, Anselm. Healing by negotiation: specialty of the house. *Transaction*, 1964, 1 (6), 13–15.

Strauss, Anselm, Schatman, Leonard, Ehrlich, Danuta, Busher, Rue, and Sabshin, Melvin. The hospital and its negotiated order. In E. Freidson (Ed.), *The hospital in modern society*. Glencoe, Ill.: Free Press, 1963.

Strauss, George. Tactics of lateral relationships: the purchasing agent. *Administrative Science Quarterly*, 1962, 7, 161–86.

Sykes, Gresham M. *The society of captives*. Princeton, N.J.: Princeton University Press, 1958.

Thibaut, John, and Kelley, Harold H. *The social psychology of groups*. New York: Wiley, 1959.

Thompson, James D., and Tuden, Arthur. Strategies and processes of organizational decision. In James D. Thompson et al. (Eds.), *Comparative studies in administration*. Pittsburgh: University of Pittsburgh Press, 1959.

Warner, W. Keith, and Havens, A. Eugene. Goal displacement and the intangibility of organizational goals. *Administrative Science Quarterly*, 1968, 12, 539–55.

10

Power and Conflict

INTRODUCTION

When one of the authors took his M.B.A. some ten years ago, the behavioral portion of the curriculum was called "Human Relations." Surprisingly, the text used then made no references to problems associated with power and conflict in organizations. Why do you think that might have been?

As nearly as we can tell, no human organization has ever avoided conflict in one form or another nor has one existed in the absence of power. Although humans have always sought and used power, these activities are somehow viewed as antithetical to deep-rooted American cultural norms. We sometimes pretend that they do not exist.

Niccolò Machiavelli was born before Columbus sailed for America. He wrote a handbook for those who seek practical means for increasing their power. According to Gauss (1952), Hitler read the book at bedtime and Mussolini chose it as the subject of his doctoral thesis. Lenin and Stalin, too, were versed in Machiavelli.

Although the present decade has seen a revival of interest in *The Prince*, most of us look askance at Machiavelli's advice. To be sure, the book is bitter, reflecting the author's failure and 15 years in exile. What seems worse, however, is his candid discussion of power and self-interest. It is almost as if the practices Machiavelli describes are unfit for public discussion, even though we recognize that they still are the substance of human affairs; for example, note below that Machiavelli would have us manipulate those whose advice we seek.

> . . . by taking counsel with many, a prince who is not wise will never have united councils and will not be able to bring them to unanimity for himself. The counsellors will all think of their own interests, and he will be unable either to correct or to understand them. And it cannot be otherwise, for men will always be false to you unless they are compelled by necessity to be true. Therefore, it must be concluded that wise counsels, from whoever they come, must necessarily be due to the prudence of the prince, and not the prudence of the prince to the good counsels received (1952, p. 117).

Chapter Guide

1. A contemporary analogy to Machiavelli's statement is that the quality of advice received from subordinates is a function of the executive's skill in manipulating the way in which such advice is given. Do you agree?
2. Elsewhere, Machiavelli suggests that we seek advice, but only when it is our wish to be advised, not when others wish to advise us. Why do you think he recommends this?
3. In what sense is this ancient writing relevant to life in contemporary organizations?

SOURCES OF CONFLICT

Power as a Source of Conflict

Conflict is intimately related to power. It is said that "Power inevitably begets conflict, in some form and in some degree" (Kahn, 1964, p. 2). But we argue that the link between power and conflict is not necessarily inevitable. The exercise of power may produce cooperation, circumvention, or withdrawal, as well (Halpert, 1974). The manner and degree in which conflict is expressed depends upon the reciprocal power of the person who is the target of the initial change attempt. For example, the target may use his power to resist attempts to change his behavior. Alternatively, if his own power is great enough, he may "counter" with an attempt to change the other person.

Another source of conflict is found when individuals are dissatisfied with the status quo, but disagree on either the means for changing the organization or the ends these changes would produce. The greater the conflict in a situation of this sort, the more the individuals will desire power to render the particular change that they deem appropriate.

Are there not some organizations in which the seeking of power and the resultant conflict are mostly absent? Are there organizations in which individual members tend to think alike and go about their pursuits without resorting to the use of power and inadvertently producing the conflict that ensues?[1] Kahn (1964) suggests that disagreements over goals and means are typical of human organizations, and it is only because power is unequally distributed among members that the organization is able to function by suppressing, containing, and in other ways managing potential conflicts that would otherwise lead to anarchy.

---

[1] We can note that friendship groups and families, which might be assumed to be relatively free of the exercise of power and the experience of conflict, in fact, provide the sources and victims of an appalling amount of conflict and even violence.

Power enables the control of organizational resources and, consequently, the control of people. As we indicated earlier (Chapter 5), one person has power over another to the extent that the former possesses resources upon which the latter is dependent. Because of asymmetries in dependence and power, some members are able to control the organization in a relatively systematic fashion, free from resistance and diversions by those who would exercise autonomy and possibly create anarchy.

Now, it is often the case that power, which was initially sought as an instrument, or means toward the attainment of specific and limited ends, becomes valued for its own sake and becomes an end. Power is generally found to be so useful that, with the passage of time, it may become sought in its own right.

> If a person seeks power only for instrumental purposes, we can predict that his search will be bounded; he wishes to control other people only in so far as that control will contribute to the attainment of other goals. If, on the other hand, he finds the experience of controlling others intrinsically rewarding, there may be few limitations on the number of people over whom he will strive for power, the magnitude of power to which he will aspire, or the kinds of activity over which power will be sought (Kahn, 1964, pp. 5–6).

We may distinguish between *specified* and *relative* power (Kahn, 1964). An individual may seek specified power as an instrument with which to attain defined and limited aspirations. Alternatively, the individual may seek power that is greater than the powers possessed by certain other individuals. This is relative power, the quest for which maximizes potential for conflict. In turn, this gives rise to the need to distinguish between influence and control.

Having specified power, an individual can attempt to influence the behavior of another, although the other individual's reciprocal power may be sufficient to enable him or her to resist the influence, seek a compromise, or act in some other way that the power-willer did not intend. The target's behavior is still said to be "influenced," although not wholly or perhaps even partially as intended. However, given sufficient relative power, the power-willer may overrule, or "control," the other person. The target is influenced wholly in the direction desired by the power-willer. The threat of such loss of autonomy is likely to provoke extreme conflict.

Conflict also arises because organizations typically lack a single goal to which all members subscribe. Not only do members of a single organization strive toward different goals, they may also have different values and different perceptions of the means appropriate for realizing even goals and values that they hold in common. Thus, power is employed as a means for coordinating activities that would otherwise be conflicting and, perhaps, chaotic.

The Process of Conflict

Conflict can be viewed as a dynamic process consisting of a sequence of episodes (Pondy, 1967). These conflict episodes tend to follow a format: (1) Conditions arise having the potential for conflict; (2) these conditions and their implications are perceived by participants; (3) perceived conflict results in felt conflict in which emotional reactions take place; (4) emotions give rise to overt behaviors of various kinds; and (5) finally, the episode reaches some conclusion that affects the course of succeeding conflict episodes.

According to Pondy, the first stage of the conflict episode, *latent conflict,* is thought to arise from three major sources: (1) drives for autonomy, (2) divergence of subunit goals, and (3) competition for scarce resources. These three basic sources of conflict have been termed, respectively: (1) *bureaucratic,* (2) *systems,* and (3) *bargaining conflicts.* We shall discuss each type in the remainder of the chapter.

The second state, *perceived conflict,* is comparable to role conflict (Chapter 9) in which the incumbent of the focal role perceives some variance between his self-role and the roles and norms that are sent to him by others. Two types of misperception are possible here. First, conflict may be perceived mistakenly where none exists, as happens frequently when people do not communicate effectively. Second, the opposite may occur. Real conflict may be denied or otherwise kept from recognition as a result of various defensive behaviors. Even when perceptions of conflict are realistic and accurate, an organization typically contains too many sources of conflict to be dealt with effectively, given the time and resources available. Hence, Pondy suggests that the manager's normal reaction is to focus on only a few of the existing conflicts at any one time, and to limit his focus to those for which short-run, routine solutions are available.

The third state, *felt conflict,* is one in which individuals sometimes deal with perceived conflicts in a relatively rational manner, without what Pondly calls "personalization," or the experiences of conflict-related anxiety, tension, or affect. However, feelings *are* brought into conflict situations frequently. These may stem from a condition of basic anxiety from which the individual suffers or from frustrations and hostilities that have developed in the context of other interpersonal relations unrelated to the present conflict; that is, feelings are *projected* from one source of conflict to another. Obviously, these feelings may also result from frustrations that are a direct result of the conflict situation in question.

The next stage, *manifest conflict,* is sometimes characterized by overt behaviors such as verbal or physical aggression. In organizations, however, the manifestations of conflict are more likely to be covert. Examples of these covert behaviors are apathy and the ploy of "working to rule" discussed in Chapter 9 in connection with the power of lower participants. They serve to thwart aspirations of others without appearing aggressive. In any event, when conflict becomes manifest and apparent to other members of the organization, interventions are made in an attempt to resolve, or at least to confine, the issues.

Finally, *conflict aftermath* sets the stage, as it were, for subsequent conflict episodes. Whether the initial conflict is genuinely resolved or merely suppressed and unresolved will bear on the nature of subsequent episodes. This notion is similar to the role-conflict model presented in the last chapter. As we saw, behavior emerges from perceptions and feelings and is perceived and acted upon by role senders in yet another cycle of events. Depending on the behavior emitted and its effect on interpersonal relations or organizational conditions, the role sender will act somewhat differently in the next cycle of role sending.

Effects of Conflict

Before examining sources of conflict and some mechanisms for its management, it will be useful to gain an appreciation of the effects of conflict. Traditionally, conflict has been viewed as undesirable. It is unpleasant for most individuals and leads toward psychological withdrawal or aggressive and hostile behavior. It may also lead to the falsification of data and distortion of reality. The effects on organizations have been viewed as negative, too. The rational, classical approach to management advocates that organizations be designed and managed in a way that limits conflict. The epitome of this approach is a clearly stated organizational objective pursued by means of logically articulated, harmonious tasks. The organic or open-systems model, too, with its stress on dynamic homeostasis views conflict as a temporary disequilibrium to be rectified. Conflict between the system and its environment is ameliorated through adaptation. Finally, the human relations approach, growing out of the classical and rational theories, recognizes the continuing existence and great importance of conflict and seeks to reduce its toll on members of the organization.

In some contrast, however, recent views of motivation indicate that mild levels of stress or conflict are more desirable than the complete tension reduction suggested by the attitude balance, classical drive reduction, and learning theories. McClelland (1951) suggests that mild stimulation has positive emotional effects, and White (1959) tells us that the competence drive and curiosity compel individuals to submit themselves to new tension-arousing stimulations.

Furthermore, some individuals even come to enjoy high levels of conflict. Conflict may remove boredom, and, in extreme cases, may be exhilarating and provide meaning to the individual and his life (Fanon,

1967). Conflict may also be valued as a means toward specific ends. As Pondy (1967) suggests:

> One of the tactics of successful executives in the modern business enterprise is to create confusion as a cover for the expansion of their particular empire, or, as Sorenson observes, deliberately to create dissent and competition among one's subordinates in order to ensure that he will be brought into the relationship as an arbiter at critical times, as Franklin D. Roosevelt did. Or, conflict with an out-group may be desirable to maintain stability within the group (p. 310).

Finally, conflict may be viewed as an unavoidable cost of the pursuit of one's aspirations. Where the net result of this pursuit is perceived to be positive, conflict will be endured as a "necessary evil."

On the whole, our culture views conflict as undesirable, to be avoided whenever possible. Harmony and uniformity tend to be valued highly, and tolerance for divergence is generally lacking. And yet, recent works have challenged these cultural assumptions. While conflict is stressful and dissatisfying for most individuals, greater openness to conflict and confrontation has developed in organizations and in our society generally. Bach's book *The Intimate Enemy: How to Fight Fair in Marriage* (1969), as well as Sennett's book *The Uses of Disorder* (1970), and Alinsky's various works (1946, 1971) exemplify this trend. Confrontation is seen to be valuable. The question is, how to manage conflict rather than "sweeping it under the rug" on one hand or allowing it to run to pathological extremes on the other?

The Effects of Bureaucratic Conflict in Different Organizations

There is some interesting evidence, provided by Smith (1966), that bureaucratic conflict, that is, conflict between organizational levels, may produce different effects in different kinds of organizations. He found that conflict was negatively associated with effectiveness in three out of four kinds of business organizations studied. Following Litwak (1961), Smith argues that conflict in the traditional bureaucratic, or hierarchical, organization (such as those studied) detracts from effectiveness by making coordination more difficult. This is especially true in organizations that are complex and differentiated, requiring considerable coordination from top levels of management. In this kind of organization, conflict, particularly between different echelons in the organization (e.g., conflict due to lack of compliance), will impede coordination and, therefore, effectiveness.

In contrast, a study of 4 union locals and 112 units of a voluntary organization revealed conflict to be positively associated with effectiveness. Smith suggests that these organizations, unlike business firms, are typified by basic agreements among members, and among different echelons, regarding the interests and goals of members and of the organization as a whole. Conflict between members of different echelons tends to be constructive because it centers around means more than ends. Such conflict causes periodic reevaluation of means and facilitates the selection of alternatives, for individuals and the organization as a whole, for the pursuit of agreed-upon ends.

More importantly, Smith argues that the consequences for organizational effectiveness are dependent upon the techniques used to manage conflict. Whatever the amount of conflict in an organization, the use of certain techniques such as the appeal to general rules, will detract from effectiveness. Other mechanisms for resolving conflict (e.g., initiating structure (Chapter 12), supportive leadership, or mutual influence systems) permit conflict to have positive effects.

A Study of Conflict in Top Management

Before studying conflict in further abstract detail, we shall pause to examine the phenomenon as it arises in one portion of an organization. How do top executives in major corporations (2,000 to 50,000 employees) handle differences that arise in making policy decisions? Stagner (1969, 1970), in a study of corporate vice presidents, provides a description of a decision-making process that contrasts with Patchen's report of decision making at lower levels in the organization, where norms about stakeholder influence were common.

From Stagner's study emerges a view of decision making in the context of conflicting pressures. It should be emphasized that the observed conflict was dissimilar to that usually found in "small group" settings, wherein individuals react solely to each other and to their immediate setting—to communications, aggressive persuasion, personal likes and dislikes, and perceptions of confidence. This dissimilarity is due primarily to the fact that top executives, unlike subjects in small group studies, represent, depend on, or make use of outside individuals and their goals and resources.

By the same token, Stagner found that the economic or rational model of decision making did not apply to his findings either. Economic considerations such as increased profits did not play major roles in either decision making or the resolution of conflict. Although economic terminology was used to frame the arguments of both parties to controversy, it was found to serve primarily as a "cover-up" for other, noneconomic criteria. Profit projections, for example, are not precise; the trade-offs between short-term and long-term profitability are virtually unknowable. Stagner suggests that conflicts are resolved, not by appealing to the logic of economics (i.e., expert power), but by resorting to power based on rewards, authority, and so on. Individuals having common interests form coalitions which pursue their own interests first, and those of the firm second.

Observing the behavior of decision-making groups, Stagner found that problems were discussed partly in terms of economic considerations, but also in terms of the ways in which the different executives perceived each situation. The functions (e.g., marketing or production) and the disciplines (e.g., accounting or law) in which participants were trained, determined whether they shared a common frame of reference. A chief executive with training in economics seemed to agree with the points of view of his economists rather than those of individuals whose backgrounds included training in other functions or disciplines.

These differences in perceptions, and potentials for conflict, are likely to diminish as individuals come to know each other better. Socializing outside of office hours helps improve communications and subsequently, mutual understandings. As we saw in Chapter 5, the clarity of goals is enhanced by social contact. Yet, the socialization process is lengthy. This accounts for Stagner's observation that in one of the companies studied, it took about five years for an individual to become a member of the management team.

The Power of the Boss

Stagner found the power of the chief executive to be the most potent and widely recognized influence in the settlement of conflict. Despite decentralization and democratization, the boss is still the boss. Executives reported that when a conflict attained certain proportions, they would take their disagreement to the boss for his decision.

There are, however, several roles that the chief executive can play in attempting to resolve organizational conflict. Some chiefs act as mediators (go-betweens), others as arbitrators (judges). Stagner reports that mediation facilitates an open expression of views, helps conflicting parties seek agreement, and is generally effective. The chief executive using this technique effectively will conceal his own preferences, lest he be perceived as an arbitrator.

In other instances, the chief executive, serving purely as an arbitrator, hears out the principal contestants separately and decides the issue himself. Arbitration seems to provide the advantage of avoiding open confrontation and unpleasantness and offers opportunities to apply "behind-the-scene," face-saving techniques. However, the "losers" can be left with the feeling that they did not have a fair hearing.

A variation of this technique was found in the practice of having the executive vice president serve as mediator. This allowed the chief executive to play the role of referee in the event that one of the parties to the arbitration challenged the decision and requested an appeal. Both approaches, however, seemed to give less satisfaction to participants than the open hearing with participatory decision making.

The power of the chief executive seemed to be the most effective pressure for securing agreements in the organizations studied. Direct appeals to authority were common occurrences. Subjects told Stagner: "When we could not agree, we took it the president and he settled it." Also prevalent was the indirect pressure of authority which caused individuals to anticipate actions of higher-ups and perhaps the embarrassment of having to resort to arbitration, and in so doing contained their conflict.

Shared Goals and Pressures for Conflict Resolution

The second most important approach to resolving conflict, according to Stagner, is the development of shared goals, especially superordinate goals. If contestants share a superordinate goal, one which embraces both their departmental or individual goals, a basis for compromise or other form of agreement exists. Superordinate goals include the profitability and viability of the firm; for example, the heads of production and marketing will agree that, whatever their particular interests, these interests are subordinate to the goals that they hold in common.

Peer pressure is reported to be the third most effective impetus to conflict resolution. In addition to managing separate departments, the executives in Stagner's study also functioned as a team. An example of peer pressure was found in a situation in which the chief executive requested his vice presidents to submit their proposed budgets. Consolidation of the departmental budgets revealed that their total exceeded the total budget of the firm. Rather than confront each vice president with the need to pare his budget, the president asked the vice presidents to solve the problem as a group. In this way, each executive was exposed to the pressures of his peers as his inflated budget constrained the resources available to others.

Individual persuasion was found to be the least effective of the four means of resolving disagreements. "Are vigorous, aggressive, persuasive individuals more likely to 'win' controversies than less colorful persons? The consensus was negative. Two executives estimated that such personalities might be effective 20 percent of the time, but in 80 percent of the cases power of the division or status in the company would decide the issue. All respondents agreed that it would be rare for a persuasive man in a lower echelon to win out over a less fluent but higher placed objector" (Stagner, 1970, p. 94).

The Importance of Power in Resolving Conflict

Stagner's findings argue that to be effective in resolving high-level conflict, one ought to rely primarily upon the power of the chief executive; second, on one's ability to highlight or create shared goals; third, on available peer pressure; and lastly, on individual persuasion. According to the role-sender model, a focal role must cope with the demands of many different role senders. It seems that a single role sender is not very potent—unless he is the boss. One way to understand Stagner's findings is to note that in the ten major corporations studied, power seems to reside primarily in the chief executive's office. At lower organizational levels, power is more diffuse and equal among members of the same rank. Presumably, this is not true for all organizations. Sensitivity to the locus of power in an organization should provide the observer with working hypotheses about the ways in which conflict is resolved.

Conflict among Stagner's executives was resolved with hierarchical power (with authority) and the various other mechanisms discussed above, as if the nature of the organization did not permit lateral conflicts. Although coalitions and pressure groups did form around important issues, Stagner notes that factionalism was muted for the most part. These findings lead Stagner to view the corporation as ". . . a collection of pressure groups trying to arrive at compromise solutions. . . . For the most part, however, overt 'factionalism' in top management is muted. It is perhaps significant that in the only company in my survey where two vice presidents were known leaders of competing factions, one was fired before the year was out. This suggests that covert power struggles are permissible but open conflict is settled by eliminating the weaker" (Stagner, 1970, pp. 90–95). In short, the corporations studied appear to be rational, hierarchically coordinated organizations, but in reality are collections of conflicting, competitive fiefdoms held in check by hierarchical power.

Earlier, we mentioned Pondy's (1967) three models of organizational conflict: the bureaucratic, systems, and bargaining models. Stagner undoubtedly observed mostly bureaucratic conflict—conflict arising from attempts to obtain compliance with rules, orders, and organizationally prescribed attitudes, and behaviors. This is our next topic for discussion.

BUREAUCRATIC CONFLICT

Autonomy and Conflict

Members of an organization may come into conflict with their superiors for various reasons. Generally speaking, we find that the individual's desire for autonomy conflicts with the organization's need for coordination. Organizations can legitimize their requests for coordination through the use of authority, and subordinates generally accept requests that appear legitimate. However, superiors sometimes overstep their limited authority and engender resistance in their subordinates. In the next chapter we shall see that rules can be used as impersonal means of coordination. However, because they are impersonal and inflexible, they may also engender conflict. Let us examine a number of mechanisms for dealing with subordinates' resistance and their drives for autonomy and power. These are part of what sociologists term "mechanisms for social control," since they are means employed by those in authority to control deviations and to maintain the social system at the status quo.

Activation of Commitments and Obligations

Some elements of authority are not utilized fully by managers. Gamson (1968) speaks of commitments or obligations to the system (i.e., organization) as a whole. We generally feel some commitment and sense of obligation to those for whom we work. Superiors can tap this commitment to gain compliance and resolve conflicts. Commitment and feelings of obligation are especially evident in the "normative organizations" described in Chapter 9, but are present in most other organizations as well.

The existence of such commitments has been demonstrated by attempts to cause individuals to violate them; for example, Frank (1944) designed a series of experiments which had subjects perform disagreeable and nonsensical tasks. For instance, subjects were asked to balance a marble on a small steel ball. They continued to attempt this impossible task for an hour without demonstrating overt resistance. Pepitone (1958) had experimental subjects sort the contents of a wastebasket (cigar butts, dirty paper and rags, pieces of glass, damp kleenexes, and the like). Subjects performed the task without strong protest. More recently, Orne and Evans (1965) asked experimental subjects to pick up a harmless lizard, a harmless green snake, a poisonous snake, and even a coin which was in acid. Many subjects complied fully. Milgram (1963, 1964, 1965), in a widely publicized series of experiments, had subjects administer electrical shocks (ranging from 15 to 450 volts) to another "subject." Even when the "subject," who was not really shocked, pounded on the wall after an "application" of high voltage, the experimental subjects continued to honor their presumed obligation to the experimenter, despite their own obvious distress. Milgram reports[2]:

> I observed a mature and initially poised businessman enter the laboratory smiling and confident. Within twenty minutes, he was reduced to a twitching, shuddering wreck who was rapidly approaching a point of nervous collapse. He constantly pulled on his earlobe and twisted his hands. At one point, he pushed his fist into his forehead and muttered, "Oh, God. Let's stop it." And yet he continued to respond to every word of the experimenter and obeyed to the end (1963, p. 373).

An explanation of these observations is that people feel general obligations to "research" and "science," and when students are used as experi-

---

[2] What ethical considerations arise in experiments such as this?

mental subjects, to the expectations of faculty members as well. As Gamson suggests:

> Perhaps the most powerful and common means of social control is simply the conveying of expectation with clarity and explicitness coupled with clear and direct accountability for the performance of such expectations. As long as legitimacy is accorded in such situations, individuals will regard their noncompliance as a failure and any interaction which makes such a personal failure salient is embarrassing, unpleasant, and something to be avoided (1968, p. 134).

Integrating Individual and Organizational Goals

As we have said, bureaucratic conflict arises when individual and organizational goals (or means) are in conflict. Barrett (1970) describes three mechanisms for achieving integration of these goals: *socialization, accommodation,* and *exchange* mechanisms. In socialization, integration is achieved by moving the individual's goals toward those of the organization. Socialization is a long-term process wherein individuals come to value what is valued in their environment. Goals that are in conflict with those of the organization are given up by the individual. If socialization is effective, the individual learns to want to perform activities that are required of him. Matters that once were external, rational, and calculative are internalized by the individual and take on moral connotations. The organization's objectives and the individual's values become congruent.

Accommodation is a process in which the individual's goals are incorporated into those of the organization. Thus, Barrett describes how some attempts at job design configure technology and structure in ways that are compatible with the worker's objectives. Obviously, participative management is required if personal goals are to be introduced into decision-making and policy-formulation processes. As individuals participate and determine the organization's goals, these goals become their own goals.

The third mechanism, exchange, places less emphasis on goal integration than the other two. The organization offers incentives related to the individual's personal goals in exchange for performance of activities that contribute to organizational objectives. Rather than integration, this mechanism seeks a quid pro quo. Conditional reinforcement and extrinsic reward models are pertinent here. Frederick Taylor's advocacy of a piecework incentive system of payment (Chapter 1) and March and Simon's (1958) *inducement-contributions* theory are examples.

Socialization as a Means for Resolving Bureaucratic Conflict

Socialization is a pervasive and essential societal process. Through this process the child becomes a social being, learning the proper habits, skills, beliefs, ethics, and morals of culture, as befitting his or her social class, ethnic group, and even local community. Parents as well as other family members, schools, and churches aid in this process.

Organizations, too, engage in socialization of their members. This may be seen quite clearly in the purposeful way medical schools go about inculcating an impersonal and objective approach in their medical students' dealings with patients. Students are shocked by their first view of a cadaver but soon come to be fairly unemotional and objective in dealing with the human body. It is essential that their professional judgment remain unclouded by emotions. In the same way, nursing schools emphasize different attitudes toward physicians, universities emphasize academic honesty, and research laboratories emphasize standards of careful, systematic, objective reporting of experiments. In all of these examples, the organization, and particularly superiors within the organization, purposefully and consciously create a system whereby members are socialized to have the proper attitudes, values, and habits.

Socialization of Attitudes and Values

Organizations engage in socialization of rank-and-file employees, too. Such socialization may be purposeful and conscious (as in training courses) but usually is informal and even unplanned. Sigelman (1973) and Breed (1955) describe the process whereby journalists come to report the news more or less in the way their paper's owner and publisher see it. This is a most interesting example of socialization because the superiors in this case of bureaucratic conflict (namely the publisher and the editors) adhere to an ethical standard which prevents them from commanding subordinates to follow policy. Journalists, too, subscribe to ethical journalistic norms regarding objective reporting. How is it, then, that journalists whose attitudes and values vary and who are also somewhat more "liberal" than their publishers (Breed, 1955), come to subscribe to their newspaper's policies?

As Sigelman and Breed describe it, there is a subtle but pervasive socialization process at work. First of all, "anticipatory socialization" causes the new reporter, who is desirous of "getting on," and perhaps even moving up, to focus on role models provided by veteran reporters. The new reporters will say to themselves, "The senior reporters behave in certain ways and that's the way I'll behave when I have made it." The roles are learned as they interact with senior reporters and read their own newspaper everyday and note the approach taken to reporting.

Leading Control Mechanisms

Editorial actions and especially revisions are useful mechanisms for controlling reporters' deviations from the attitudes and values of the organization. Reporters may submit what they feel is a fair and accurate account of events, but find that there are consistent blue pencil changes in their copy. After some time they come to anticipate the kind of reporting that will avoid editorial revision. The editorial conference, open usually to the most senior, most experienced reporters, also provides an opportunity for socialization. Veteran reporters and management discuss news coverage at these meetings. Here the desired approach to reporting is made quite clear, but for veterans, of course, years of socialization probably render much of the conference material superfluous.

Management, including the newspaper reporter's direct superiors, does not tell the reporter how to bias the news, but in a myriad of ways the news does become reported according to the policies of the newspaper. Superiors decide which stories will be covered, and therefore which will not. They decide which particular reporter will cover the story. Furthermore, an assignment often specifies not only what will be covered and who will cover it but also the degree of importance the story will merit and the perspective from which it will be reported. Add to this the built-in "quality control check" in which editors examine and edit submitted copy (which most reporters argue entails only stylistic and not content changes), and one obtains a fairly tight system to control subordinate deviation from newspaper policy.

These control mechanisms are imbedded in the socialization process to the extent that it is difficult for newspaper reporters to perceive major conflicts between the policies of their publisher and editors and their own views. As Sigelman sees it, the news reporter–newspaper relationship is not antagonistic or inherently conflict ridden. He suggests the relationship entails a tension-avoidance process. Sigelman emphasizes that these processes are structured so that senior newspapermen and reporters can interact in ways which avoid conflict.

The job of news reporting requires expert judgment and, as Perrow would indicate (Chapter 4), autonomy. Despite autonomy and resulting possibilities for deviation from newspaper policy (according to professional standards or the individual goals of particular journalists) socialization and the associated mechanisms for social control help eliminate conflict.

Selective Recruitment

The relative ease with which the socialization process appears to work is somewhat misleading. Additional mechanisms facilitate integration of the individual's goals with those of the organizations. As Sigelman indicates, the employee selection process ensures that certain reporters will join certain newspapers. Sigelman found that reporters employed by two politically dissimilar newspapers tended to have the same political views as their employers. Despite the fact that the newspapers were located in the same building and were similar in other ways, only those reporters who were amenable to the policies of the newspaper joined its staff. Hence, the socialization and social control mechanisms were not required to completely overhaul the recruits' values or political beliefs. Socialization was limited to "cueing the recruit to matters of organizational style—developing in him a sense of limits of organizational tolerance, a more or less explicit theory of how people 'make it' in the organization, and a general conception of organizational purposes or methods . . . along with building the recruit's sense of belonging, of group solidarity" (Sigelman, 1973, p. 140). Interestingly, the selection process mentioned was neither formal nor purposive. It consisted of self-selection by the recruit. Those who were politically inclined to the left tended to gravitate to the leftward leaning paper and vice versa. Thus, as in the case of socialization, the selection process made no overt attempt to manage or bias news reporting arrangements. In point of fact, though, the newspaper organization developed in such a way that subordinates came to have values, goals, and attitudes congruent with those of top management.

Unobtrusive Cognitive Controls

A general statement of the kind of control described above is provided by Simon (1957). This view is highlighted by Perrow (1972) in a review of the contributions to organizational theory made by Simon (1957) and March and Simon (1958).

The model which emerges includes the following:

> . . . satisficing behavior; sequential and limited search processes that are only mildly innovative; specialization of activities and roles so that attention is directed to "a particular restricted set of values"; "attention-directors that channelize behavior"; rules, programs, and repertories of action that limit choice in recurring situations and prevent an agonizing process of optimal decision making at each turn; a restricted range of stimuli and situations that narrow perception; training and indoctrination enabling the individual to "make decisions by himself, as the organization would like him to decide"; and the factoring of goals and tasks into programs that are semi-independent of each other so as to reduce interdependencies. Most organizational activity takes most of the conditions as given; "only a few elements of the system are adaptive at any one time."
>
> . . . The superior has the power or tools to structure the environment and perceptions of the subordinate in such a way that he sees the proper things and in the proper light. The superior actually appears to give few orders . . . instead, he sets priorities ("we had better take care of this first"; "this is getting out of hand and creating problems, so let's give it more attention until the problems are cleared up") and alters the flow of inputs and stimuli (pp. 151–52).[3]

---

[3] From *Complex Organizations: A Critical Essay* by Charles Perrow. Copyright © 1972 by Scott, Foresman and Company. Reprinted by permission of the publisher.

Communication is critical in this model of organizational control—not so much clear communication, but, rather, information that is used as a tool. For control purposes, information is channeled very selectively; even vocabulary is used selectively to emphasize certain realities and make other parts of reality invisible.

As Perrow (1972) states: "An organization develops a set of concepts influenced by the technical vocabulary and classification schemes; this permits easy communication. Anything that does not fit into these concepts is not easily communicated" (p. 152). But this *uncertainty absorption* is used purposefully. Those in control of communication may affect its recipients through their choice of terms used to describe "reality." In sociological terms, the "definition of the situation" determines behavior, and this definition is created in part by the expectations and standards created within the organization through its communication system. Perrow continues:

> The tendency to tell the boss only what he wants to hear, so well noted in the literature, is probably not as important as the tendency to see things only in terms of the concepts reflected in the organization's vocabulary" (p. 153).
>
> The conventional, structural viewpoint says that rules direct or control behavior. You tell a man what the rule is and he follows it or is punished. Or, we say that authority is vested in the office, and the commands that issue forth tell people what to do. Coordination is achieved by having one person or group find out what two other groups are doing and direct them to do it in such a way as to make their efforts fit together. Yet, the vast proportion of the activity in organizations goes on without personal directives and supervision—and even without written rules—and sometimes in permitted violation of the rules. We tend to pass over this "residue," which constitutes perhaps 80 percent of the behavior. . . .
>
> Involved are such things as uncertainty absorption, organizational vocabularies, programmed tasks, procedural and substantive programs, standardization of raw materials, frequency of communication channel usage, interdependencies of units and programs. Such mechanisms affect organizational behavior in the following ways: they limit *information content and flow*, thus controlling the premises available for decisions; they set up *expectations* so as to highlight some aspects of the situation and play down others; they limit the search for alternatives when problems are confronted, thus insuring more predictable and consistent solutions; they indicate the threshold levels as to when a danger signal is being emitted (thus reducing the occasions for decision making and promoting satisficing rather than optimizing behavior); they achieve coordination of effort by selecting certain kinds of work techniques and schedules (Perrow, 1972, pp. 156–57).[4] Italics added.

Such control is insidious, since individuals are aware neither of its existence nor of alternatives. The limited information available pre-

---

[4] Ibid.

cludes knowledge of alternatives, and, consequently, precludes choice of alternatives to the behavior constrained by the control system. Furthermore, this is not a visible, external control system which may be easily resisted by organizational members. An effective control system of this kind operates as do the internalized controls of professionals. With passage of time, professionals commit themselves to professional standards, rendering alternative (unprofessional) behavior inconceivable. It would seem that the same control results for nonprofessionals in organizations which effectively create a systematic organizational "definition of reality" and maintain tight control over their communication systems. The difference is that the nonprofessionals may "buy into" such internal controls unknowingly. These control systems are difficult to change since they may not be recognized as such.

Participation as a Social Control Mechanism

Participation in decision making is a double-edged mechanism of social control. Participation, of course, has been advocated on the basis that it improves the motivation, understanding and commitment of participants in the decision-making process. But there is a social control aspect to participative decision making as well. By participating in decisions about proposed alternatives, one becomes vulnerable to persuasive techniques. As Mulder (1971) suggests, when individuals participate but lack adequate information or expert power, their participation causes them to lose power (by being "open" and subject to influence), and they are worse off than had they not participated.

Just as in the case of co-optation there is a mixture of influence and social control in the process of participation. Increased access to decision making may result in actual influence being given to those participating. Such participation may lead to deviation from the goals desired by authorities. On the other hand, if participation is more a matter of appearance than actual influence, participating individuals are likely to regard the process as manipulative and are likely to withhold their commitment to the results.

Gamson suggests that one ploy used by hard-pressed authorities is to involve a number of groups in participation, particularly rival groups. Such participation may appear to give increased influence to each group, but authorities can point to the increased influence of one rival group and say to the other group that pressures from the first group prevent them from taking action desired by the latter group and vice versa. Each group can be led to appreciate the constraints applied by the other group. It is said that President Roosevelt used this ploy with his cabinet members. He involved them in various (conflicting) assignments, thereby obtaining more information from a broader perspective, but at the same time maintaining control and influence for himself.

The Accommodation Mechanism for Individual and Organizational Integration

Interestingly enough, Barrett (1970) found in his study of 1,700 managerial and nonsupervisory employees in a large refinery that accommodation was most highly associated with integration of individual and organizational goals. The socialization approach was less highly related, and the exchange approach was generally ineffective in creating high levels of integration. The organization that moves toward the individual creates the most integration, as indicated by survey questions measuring the extent to which individuals satisfy their personal needs and meet organizational objectives simultaneously.

According to the data, the socialization approach to integration was nearly as successful as accommodation. The combination of socialization and accommodation reminds one of the mutual influence system described in Chapter 3. Barrett suggests that these approaches to goal integration are compatible with the "participative" or "democratic" management systems proposed by Argyris, Likert, and McGregor (Chapter 3). In contrast, the delimited, exchange approach to integration seems most compatible with the classical or traditional method of organization advocated by Gulick, Urwick, and Taylor (Chapter 1). Barrett provides evidence that participative-democratic management is more effective, if one takes as one's criteria of effectiveness the integration between individual and organizational goals.

The importance of Barrett's study can be ascertained by recalling our discussion of normative organizations in Chapter 9. Members make significant, encompassing emotional investments in such organizations. In addition, influence, coordination, and organizational functioning in general are based on the norms, values, and goals that members hold in common. Normative organizations can be contrasted with more rational, calculative organizations which are typified by segmented, delimited relationships with their membership. Barrett describes such relationships in his exchange approach to integration. These two kinds of organizations correspond to a basic distinction made in sociology regarding societal relations.

Primary and Secondary Relations in Organizations

Primary relations (diffuse, whole person, emotional relations) are found in primary groups such as families or friendship groups. Secondary relations are more rational, cerebral, and calculative. Typically, they involve individuals interacting contractually or segmentally, with regard to specific interests. A number of sociologists have used variations of this distinction to describe different social relations: Toennies (1940) referred to "community" and "corporation," Durkheim (1947) to "organic" and "mechanical" solidarity, for example.

If one values primary relations as ends in themselves, one will prefer organizations which emphasize integration based on participation and socialization. This is not to say that these organizations necessarily are more effective in terms of productivity.

In point of fact, we suggest that much of the controversy in the study of organizations arises from the value orientations of theorists. Some value primary relations as ends in themselves while others do not. However, the trade-offs between primary relations and productivity or survival are unclear (Chapter 5). Related to this distinction between primary and secondary relations is a general distinction between, respectively, internal and external mechanisms for control. This distinction will be important in Chapter 11 on "Controls."[5]

SYSTEMS CONFLICTS

Subgoals and Conflicts

The systems model of conflict derives from the observation that organizations are differentiated—that division of labor and task specialization are employed as means toward increased efficiencies and economies of scale (see March and Simon, 1958, p. 112–35). The systems model explains conflict arising among functionally interdependent units that pursue conflicting goals or activities instead of acting in a coordinated fashion. As we have said, the epitome of the rational model is an organization having a single, clearly stated goal that is pursued by means of logically articulated, harmonious tasks. Attainment of these tasks, or means, becomes the goal of lower echelons of the organization.

However, because work flows laterally in an organization, the goals of one subunit may serve as constraints for another and vice versa. Furthermore, rather than adhere to the constraints of another unit, a particular unit will often emphasize its own goals at the expense of

---

[5] Barrett found that the mechanisms for integration did not work equally well for all individuals. This was least true of the accommodation model, which facilitated individual-organizational goal integration regardless of employees' individual differences (e.g., differences in educational level, tenure, rural or urban background, managerial or nonmanagerial status, or production-administrative-research function membership). Socialization, however, showed the most effectiveness in creating goal integration in organizational units employing mostly rural workers. While the exchange model did not have much effect on the level of goal integration achieved, it did have some positive effect in units employing individuals of lower social status, low educational attainment and nonmanagerial status. These findings remind us of the points made in Chapter 6 regarding individual differences, motivational structure, and the need for corresponding organizational practices.

meeting these constraints. In Chapter 1, we described Selznick's criticism of the bureaucratic model, which suggests that delegation leads to local adaptions and, ultimately, to conflicting subgoals and suboptimization. This is what is meant by systems conflict.

Thus, the two major approaches to reducing conflict in lateral relationships, according to Pondy (1967), lie in (1) reducing goal differentiation by modifying incentive systems or selection, training, and assignment procedures, and (2) reducing functional interdependence arising from competition for resources, from scheduling and sequencing problems, and from requirements for consensus among subunits.

Goal and Style Differentiation

In addition to conflicting goals and competition for resources, one finds that the modus operandi of many subunits vary, and that these different "styles" often become ends in themselves and, therefore, sources of conflict within the organization; for example, college professors may come to view scholarly activities as the bases of a meaningful way of life instead of as means toward the acquisition of knowledge. This is not to say that they cease to produce knowledge, but rather that the activities can become as highly valued as the knowledge they seek. In Chapter 4, we discussed the structural requirements of different kinds of technologies. These ranged from structures that were bureaucratic and achieved coordination via plans and rules to those that were "organic," and vested more authority in lower levels and achieved coordination via feedback. The problem is that most large organizations have both routine and nonroutine tasks to perform, and the structures, interpersonal relations, and modes of cooperation associated with each must be combined and articulated somehow.

Lawrence and Lorsch (1967), also cited in Chapter 4, found that subunits such as R&D, sales, and production differed in their attitudes toward the environment and orientations toward time, as well as in terms of their requirements for different kinds of organizational structure. If they are to be effective in performing their allotted tasks, these departmental units *must* be differentiated. However, the differences must also be articulated if the organization is to be effective in performing all of its allotted tasks—e.g., in performing R&D functions as well as manufacturing and selling goods. Below, we shall describe the use of various integrative techniques such as "go-betweens" which enable an organization to differentiate and specialize effectively while avoiding the conflict that differentiation is likely to product.

Superordinate Goals

Hampton and colleagues (1973) advocate the introduction of *transcendent objectives* which are goals that are more important to members of the organization than those of the subunits to which they belong, and which require the cooperation of the subunits for their attainment. Sherif (1958) describes superordinate goals as goals that are highly appealing to two or more subunits in conflict and that cannot be realized by the efforts of any individual subunit. A related means of unifying the goal-directed activities of subunits is found in the use of scapegoats or external enemies. Similarly, a leader may highlight serious internal problems common to conflicting subunits and severe enough that the long-term viability of the organization is dependent upon their resolution.

Katz (1964) argues that the larger structure of the organization and its goals should be made to appear more salient when decisions that have organizationwide implications are pending.

> In setting up committees to handle an organizational problem, a common procedure is to name members who report to some top officer rather than to their department heads. In this way, the context of the committee's operation is the organization's problem, not the specialized interest of competing sub-groups. The members thus assume a set of responsibilities as citizens of the larger structure. It is not so much that there is communication across people from subgroups with varying specialized backgrounds as it is a matter of communication on issues essential to the goals of the organization (p. 112).

Moving Conflict within Units

The differentiation of goals by subunits and the resulting conflict between units may also be handled by moving conflict down to lower levels in the organization, according to Katz (1964). Goal differentiation may be increased so that the differentiation occurs *within* groups or even within individuals rather than between groups, thus avoiding polarization at the higher level. Conflict between two units is dependent upon each unit mobilizing the efforts of its members in a unitary fashion. This cannot be done if there is internal conflict within the warring groups (March and Simon, 1958).

Katz describes how an organizational structure based on process (functional) specialization can obscure the purpose of the organization because each process unit identifies with its own particular concerns, rather than with the organization as a whole. It is suggested that departmentalization by purpose (i.e., product) as well as multiple group membership for individuals in the various process specialties be incorporated in the organization's design.

The general point is that the structure, and, thus, the arrangement of power, should not be congruent with any particular kind of task specialization. Rather, decision-making power should be based across several specializations. For example, Walker and Lorsch (1968) provide evidence that reorganization from a functional to a product structure will reduce the amount of conflict between functions, but increase the amount of conflict faced by each individual manager within a product department, since each manager will need to relate to other functional managers in working on a particular product. The question here, as we mentioned earlier, revolves around the manner in which one redistributes conflict. Conflict at very high levels will have direct, critical effects on the organization's effectiveness, while lower level conflict can be compensated for, and dealt with, as the efforts of lower level units are coordinated in the directions set by higher levels of the organization.

The crisscrossing of membership advocated by Katz has been cited as one of the reasons for the relative lack of severe political conflict in the United States. The major political parties consist of both Protestants and Catholics, "WASPS" and other ethnic groups, members of every economic class, and so on. Thus, when an issue arises, it is not dealt with by members of a single economic class, a single ethnic group, or a single religion, but by a heterogeneous membership. This may be contrasted with the situations in Quebec and Belgium where political conflicts can become quite polarized. In Quebec, the Catholic, French-Canadian, and generally lower class population is sometimes arrayed against the Anglo-Protestant, middle- and upper-class population. In Belgium, the Flemish-speaking, Catholic, lower income population in Flanders is often arrayed against the Walloons—the French-speaking, anticlerical, higher-status population in the south of the country.

The analogy can be extended readily to business organizations. If there is excessive conflict between functional departments, reorganization to a product structure should be considered as a way of reducing the polarization in which, for example, manufacturing personnel see themselves in conflict with members of the sales department. In a product structure, production experts will find themselves arrayed against other production experts from time to time when problems arise in allocating resources among different products. At other times, however, they will find themselve in conflict with members of other functional specialities (sales or R&D, for instance) within their own product group. Such conflict will not tend toward polarization, but will be more diffuse, sometimes in relation to one manager and sometimes in relation to another. Thus "ingroups" and "outgroups" tend not to develop. Since problems arise in relation to specific issues, conflict tends to remain limited.

Incentive Systems

Goal differentiation can also be reduced through the use of incentive systems designed to reward activities that benefit the larger system, as opposed to those that are primarily in the interest of subunits. It may be recalled from Chapter 4 that the longwall, mechanized approach to coal mining utilized three different shifts of workers who specialized in mining, loading the conveyor, and moving the equipment up to the coal face. Each of the three shifts was paid separately according to a criterion appropriate to the shift's task. The resulting conflict was due in part to the reward system which encouraged suboptimization.

In contrast, the shortwall method of coal getting employed a small group of six men, two to a shift, who were effective in coordinating activities across shifts. In part, this was thought to have come about because they were paid as a group, rendering it in the interest of each member to do whatever was necessary on his shift to coordinate his own efforts with those of other shift workers, and in so doing to facilitate the group's productivity. The Tavistock researchers recommended the composite longwall arrangement which coupled the advantages of mechanization with the behavioral attributes of the shortwall method. Most importantly for our purposes here, the researchers proposed a group incentive system which treated all three shifts as members of one group. It should be noted that the voluntary participation of workers in the composite longwall system together with the elimination of status differences among workers complemented the incentive system in reducing conflict between shifts. Groups, too, can be effective in socializing their members to desirable norms and obtaining conformity to superordinate goals.

Of course, there is a limit to the applicability of group incentive systems (Marriott, 1949). In large, complex organizations, the individual, or small group of workers may feel that their contribution is insignificant to the attainment of major objectives. They fail to see relationships between their efforts and the unit's effectiveness. Since increased productivity on the part of a single individual will have an imperceptible effect on organizational performance, company-wide incentive systems may not generate intended increases in motivation. Furthermore, task complexity, intangible results, and changing interdependencies hinder the development of criteria for assessing worker performance. When this is the case, it is difficult for the individual to understand, let alone evaluate, his or her efforts as they relate to the goals of the larger system.

Perhaps the most to be hoped for in introducing incentive systems to reduce conflict is the elimination of existing (frequently individual-based) reward systems that inadvertently produce conflict of an unproductive nature. It is not uncommon to find situations in which two individuals or subunits have goals that cannot be met simultaneously. These are called *zero-sum or win-lose situations* (Litterer, 1966). Quality control inspectors, auditing departments, police departments, and the like are commonly subject to win-lose episodes. The job of quality control inspectors, for example, is to find errors, and they are rewarded accordingly, but the errors they find are potential sources of negative sanctions for another person.

Litterer makes the general point that win-lose situations exist where the reward system is based on individual performance which is contingent upon interdependencies. He cites, as an example, a conflict between two managers in a major airline. In this case, the sales manager tried to increase sales volume by providing additional services for customers. His incentive was to achieve a bonus computed from sales volume. These efforts to increase services were resisted by the service manager, since they would add to his budget. Ironically, the service manager anticipated a bonus that was based on cost reduction.

Another possible approach to reducing conflict that attends goal differentiation is found in the work of Likert (Chapter 3). Group management in an organization made up of overlapping groups may avoid the extreme individualism and conflict sometimes found in more traditional organizations. Overlapping membership between groups may serve to reduce between-group competition. In fact, this aspect of Likert's work is very similar to the "crisscrossing" of membership advocated by Katz.

Because organizations must perform a variety of activities in order to fulfill system needs (or to pursue conflicting operative goals, depending upon one's point of view), no *single* incentive or reward system is likely to be effective. For that matter, as we have said, conflict cannot be avoided in its entirety. Landsberger (1961) identifies several basic dilemmas which provide unavoidable conflicts: The need for flexibility and stability; the importance of both measurable and intangible results; the importance of short-run productivity; and the need to trade off short-term gains for long-term efficacy. Thus, the problem is not to select an incentive system that will eliminate organizational conflict, but rather to decide which specific areas of conflict deserve attention and then to design the incentive system accordingly.

Reducing Functional Interdependence

In addition to the reduction of goal differentiation, a second general approach to dealing with the causes of systems conflict is to reduce functional interdependencies. We have already mentioned one source of interdependency which stems from sharing limited resources such as physical space, equipment, personnel, or funds. In competing for limited resources, interdependent units focus on the accomplishment of their unique tasks, sometimes to the exclusion of realizing concern for larger organizational objectives. Such competition is likely to "poison" relationships between subunits and lead to conflict in still other areas. In short, the net result is suboptimization rather than coordinated, joint problem-solving endeavors.

A simple, although not always feasible, solution for conflicts arising from dependence on limited resources is to establish "slack"—to provide a supply of resources that is at least adequate to the needs of both subunits. Also possible is mediation of conflict by a third party, leading perhaps to the establishment of rules and agreements for equitable sharing. By their impersonality, rules so established may alleviate the more damaging, personal effects of conflict.

Interdependencies based on sequential work or information flows are somewhat more complex. Walton and Dutton (1969) discuss them in terms of *task-related symmetries and asymmetries.* In Chapter 9, we mentioned that the dependency of purchasing agents on engineers led them to attempt to influence the requisitions made by the latter individuals. In this manner, the agents developed symmetrical dependencies, wherein mutual influence was exerted. Asymmetrical interdependencies arise when the individual who is depended upon has little incentive to cooperate or coordinate his or her activities with those of the dependent individual. Such situations are likely to have adverse consequences for the organization.

Dealing with Sequential Dependencies

One approach to reducing sequential interdependencies is to loosen schedules. Another is to introduce buffers such as inventories or contingency funds. Where the output of one unit flows directly into another, the latter unit's work is subject to initiation by the former unit. This dependency is ameliorated when the first unit's output flows into an inventory from which the second unit draws. When maintained at a sufficient level, the inventory will buffer the second unit against variations in the quantity of output of the first unit. Another example is found in Whyte's (1949) order spindle (Chapter 4). Please recall that the spindle buffered higher status, male cooks from work initiated by lower status, female waitresses, thus reducing the dependence of the former on the latter and the conflicts which the initial situation created.

Just as dependence on a common pool of resources can be reduced by rules or resource duplication, so sequential interdependence can be reduced through facility duplication. For example, R&D can be provided with its own small production plant for pilot runs as an alternative to depending on the whims of the production department for access to facilities. Similarly, production can be provided with its own engineers for developmental projects and troubleshooting instead of depending upon the goodwill of the engineering department.

Occasionally, sequential conflicts are reciprocal, consisting of two-way dependencies. Rather than duplicating facilities or investing in inventories, a somewhat more effective barrier to these kinds of work flow conflict is established through the use of mediators or liaisons, who can eliminate personal contact between conflicting parties. The cost of hiring such buffer personnel may be considerable, but given the cost of major conflict between groups adjacent in the work flow, the expense may prove worthwhile. Sometimes, a low-status (and fairly passive) individual or group may serve as a communications link between conflicting units. For example, the go-between may be an individual who is near retirement age, and having little possibility for promotion, he or she presents no threat to either of the conflicting parties. Examples of liaison personnel are: (1) field engineers who come between customers and design engineers, (2) development engineers who buffer research scientists and design engineers or production managers, and (3) public relations representatives who come between political leaders and the press or public (Hampton and colleagues, 1973).

A more extreme approach to reducing functional interdependence is decentralization. This provides for a more complete separation of formerly pooled resources and jointly held goals. Of course, decentralized units must be integrated by top management and through the efforts of liaisons. When this is accomplished, suboptimization may be transformed into a virtue. Furthermore, Katz (1964) suggests that the assignment of overall coordination to top management directs attention to major issues and avoids overloading top-level staff with problems arising from minor, less important conflicts.

Reducing Pressures for Compliance

A final approach to reducing the causes of systems conflict lies in reducing the functional interdependence arising from various pressures for compliance. Not all of the compliance required in organizations is essential to effective operation. Even in cases where compliance is essential, the pressures generated can be reduced by giving those expected to comply a share in the formulation of a situation to which their conformance is sought. Participative decision-making permits subordinates to suggest the means for compliance that are consistent with the constraints under which they function.

Most of the solutions suggested for the problem of excessive functional interdependence have consisted of various forms of structural changes. An alternative approach is found in staff development. Victor Thompson (1961) speaks of *person specialization* as opposed to task specialization. Task specialization leads to differentiated tasks that are linked systemically, and thereby generate functional interdependencies. Person specialization leads to the training and education of individuals who can deal with an entire task, thereby eliminating some of the interdependencies mentioned above. Job enrichment, as discussed in Chapter 6, is one approach to this end. Participative management is another.

BARGAINING CONFLICTS

Limited Resources and Conflicts

We move now to the *third* conceptual model of organizational conflict, the bargaining model. Rivalry and the potential for conflict will arise among interested groups that compete for scarce resources. Typical of these are labor-management relations and the processes of capital and governmental budgeting (Pondy, 1964; Walton and McKersie, 1965; Wildavsky, 1964). Conflict in the bargaining model takes the forms of *integrative and distributive* processes. Integrative bargaining seeks to increase the total amount of resources available to competing factions. Distributive bargaining engages participants in the division of whatever resources are available.

Bargaining may be either explicit or implicit (Hampton et al., 1973). In contrast to explicit bargaining wherein both parties are aware that each is attempting to influence the other, implicit bargaining occurs when at least one party is unaware of the process. In a typical case, the manipulator will try to create a situation in which he or she is of service to the second party and then takes advantage of the situation by threatening to withdraw from it. Implicit bargaining may also be used as a supplement to formal authority. "A paternalistic manager who gives turkeys and bonuses at Christmas or builds an employee recreation park is often, consciously or unconsciously, attempting to manipulate subordinates into giving the firm greater loyalty" (Hampton et al., 1973, p. 758).

In distributive bargaining, one uses threats and bluffs, and presents the image of being immune to the power and threats of the other party. One withholds information about one's real strength, real desires, and minimum requirements. At the same time, one attempts to acquire valid information on the strengths and desires of one's adversary.

This is in contrast to the process of integrative bargaining wherein a free exchange of information is essential to solving the problem at hand. Here, the emphasis is not on using power to increase one's share of limited resources, but on cooperative problem solving that is intended to increase the resources available to all parties. This, in fact, was the idea behind Frederick Taylor's scientific management, which attempted to improve worker efficiency in order to increase productivity and, thereby, the returns to both management and labor.

Distributive Bargaining Tactics

As Pruitt (1972) sees it, the most general approach to bargaining is coercion of one's opponent into granting concessions while conceding as little as possible oneself. Two basic motives seem to affect all who engage in bargaining: (1) to win concessions from the opponent and (2) to resolve dispute by reaching some kind of agreement. Furthermore, he suggests two basic dilemmas that arise from various tactics used in bargaining: (1) the tactics used to resolve dispute frequently are incompatible with the aim of gaining concessions, and (2) tactics adopted to elicit concessions often subvert the aim of resolving dispute. As we shall see, these dilemmas encourage parties in conflict to rely on norms.

Pressure Tactics

Pruitt categorizes pressure tactics as: (1) threats, (2) punishment sequences, and (3) positional commitments. *Threats* are understood generally. Bargainers frequently attempt to enhance their credibility, since the party to be influenced must believe that punishment will follow noncompliance. To make a strike threat credible a union may make ostentatious arrangements for strike funds. At the same time, the party threatened may attempt to reduce the credibility of the threat. For example, management may arrange for supervisory stand-ins for striking workers, demonstrating that they cannot be hurt by the threatened strike.

A *punishment sequence* occurs when a party in conflict applies a negative sanction and promises to stop when compliance occurs. A student sit-in in the administration building, with an offer to move out when negotiations begin, is a punishment sequence. Pruitt suggests that punishment sequences are threats to continue punishment in the future.

Punishment sequences are more credible than ordinary threats because they are evidence of harm which can be continued. However, by giving the opponent a "taste" of what is in store for him if he does not comply, this tactic also gives the opponent an opportunity to learn from the experience how to cope with the punishment and thereby blunt its effect.

The third pressure tactic described by Pruitt is *positional commitment,* a commitment to a specific position. By making a commitment and indicating inflexibility (by specifying "nonnegotiable demands"), one may pressure one's opponent into conceding, provided the demand is in an area where the opponent is willing to make concessions. The problem, of course, lies in determining whether the opponent's area of acceptable concessions includes the nonnegotiable demand.

But pressure tactics often are only partially successful. They may merely serve to delimit the outer boundaries of a solution to the problem —to delimit the points beyond which each party cannot be pushed. They rarely lead to specific solutions.

Concessions

Pruitt suggests that the next action in the bargaining process may be a substantial, unilateral concession or series of concessions. The problem here is that although a concession may move the dispute toward resolution, it usually requires that one move away from one's own position. In addition, concessions imply giving up something which could be used later in the process as part of a trade. Finally, a concession may be interpreted as a sign of weakness and may thus encourage the adversary to take a more rigid stand or to use pressure tactics even more vigorously. Because unilateral concessions are weighted toward resolving conflicts instead of winning concessions, one may attempt other tactics which are more balanced with respect to the dilemma of seeking concessions and ending the controversy; for example, one may attempt an exchange of concessions (i.e., a compromise). Pruitt suggests that most exchange-oriented tactics can be useful in resolving conflicts. If concessions are exchanged, fears of seeming weak, or of rigidity on the part of the opponent, are mitigated, since both parties appear "weak" and both are flexible. A proposal to exchange concessions may not resolve the bargaining dilemma, however. The proposal to start a negotiated exchange may be interpreted as a sign of weakness. Thus, indirect communication and the use of intermediaries may be appropriate to mitigate the risks of appearing weak or being rejected.

Tacit Communication

Tacit communication, a type of indirect communication, takes a number of forms; for example, a negotiator may take too many words to say "no." This can be interpreted as a signal that the "no" will become a "yes" if a particular concession is forthcoming from the opponent. Other forms of tacit communication are more direct. A negotiator may tell the opponent: "This is the way we look at it. If we find something wrong with our position, we will change it. We will negotiate." The advantage of tacit communication is that an offer of flexibility and concession is ambiguous and may be withdrawn. The negotiator's image can be protected by giving contrary signals later.

Informal Conferences

If the issues in conflict are particularly complex and ambiguous, an informal conference (e.g., discussion over a cup of coffee) may facilitate movement toward compromise. Informal conferences give negotiators freedom to express their ideas. They may propose concessions informally, without risking loss of position if agreement does not result because of the norm that negotiators will return to the originally stated positions in the formal meeting. Such conferences may entail some loss of image in terms of flexibility but such losses are suffered by both sides equally.

According to Pruitt, the norms governing informal conferences are: (*a*) what is said in conference will be confidential, (*b*) it will *not* be necessary to adhere to the rule that concession cannot be withdrawn, (*c*) parties will be willing to make concessions if the opponent makes them, and (*d*) agreements reached in informal conferences will be honored when the formal meetings reconvene. Negotiators typically make use of informal conferences if they trust their opponent to adhere to these norms. The more trustworthy the opponent seems, the more open a negotiator can be in such informal conferences. Pruitt suggests that informal negotiation (in which there is open discussion of goals, interests, flexibility, and possible concessions), seems to resemble the bargaining between friends or family members. It is a form of bargaining that develops over time, as one comes to know one's opposite number well and develops mutual trust.

Informal meetings may be held between subordinates of the negotiators or between intermediaries. In both cases, failure to reach agreement will lead to "disowning" the actions of subordinates or intermediaries, thus saving the negotiators from loss of position or image. If parties are hostile, suspicious of each other, or likely to be embarrassed by mutual contact, intermediaries are particularly useful since face-to-face meeting will be unlikely to be productive in such cases.

Intermediaries

A mediator is a neutral figure who communicates with both parties and tries to find a formula for agreement. These individuals can be useful in a variety of ways. "They can educate an inexperienced negotiator, arrange a meeting, give strategic advice, aid in reality testing, urge that a concession be made, recommend a known option, devise a new integrated option, guarantee compliance to an agreement, or help undo a commitment" (Pruitt, 1971, p. 229). Mediators can serve as channels of indirect communication between the negotiators. The mediators may interview the negotiators to determine concessions each is able to make and the conditions governing them. They will use this information to persuade each party to accept the largest concession the other seems willing to make. Since the negotiators themselves are not offering to make the concessions, they risk no loss of position or image. A mediator typically presents a possible concession in terms of his or her own prediction of what the opponent will accept saying: "If you will take this position, I think I can sell it to them." Anyone who has dispensed with a realtor and tried to buy or sell his own house will appreciate the services of an intermediary. Just as there are important norms in tacit communication and informal conferences, mediations are governed by norms as well. These norms typically require the mediators to be impartial, to respect confidences, and to avoid publicizing their dealings with negotiators. Reciprocal norms require negotiators to be honest with mediators when indicating readiness to make concessions (Peters, 1955) and to have the flexibility to make concession when agreeing to employ a mediator (Stevens, 1963).

The Importance of Normative Structure

While there is less risk of loss of position and image in indirect communication than in direct communication, a negotiator must still exercise caution, since these exchanges are dependent on the normative structure in the situation. Regardless of whether tacit communication, informal conferences, intermediaries, or mediators are employed, relevant norms must exist to provide security and channel interactions so that the probability of successful compromise is sufficiently high to compensate for the risks involved. Norms are built up over time and through repeated interactions between individuals. Pruitt emphasizes the importance of having skilled negotiators on the opposing side.

> . . . a poorly qualified opponent will often not understand, and hence not respond to, a negotiator's efforts to coordinate an agreement. [In addition] . . . such a negotiator can often not be trusted to observe the norms that regulate tacit communication because he doesn't know them or the implications of breaking them. The practical advice to which this reasoning leads is threefold: (a) be wary of making accommodative moves when the opponent is untutored, especially if he is anxious to win and thus likely to take a short-sighted exploitative outlook on these moves; (b) when ready to move toward accommodation, insist that an experienced negotiator . . . represents the opposing side; (c) if the just prior advice seems unrealistic, take steps to *educate* one's opponent and make him into a skilled negotiator (Pruitt, 1971, pp. 237–38).

In conclusion, the indirect approaches to coordinating exchanges are useful because they reduce the risks of image and position loss in attempts to coordinate exchanges and also because they help begin the whole process of compromise and conflict resolution. In the final stages of bargaining, when there is considerable pressure for resolution of the conflict, when available pressure tactics have been tried, and especially when there is evidence that the adversary is ready to exchange concessions rather than exploit evidences of weakness, then one or more of the exchange-oriented tactics may prove successful.

Integrative Bargaining

A mutually acceptable compromise, however, must be available if agreement is to be reached. If no such compromise is available, new options must be found. The concept of *integrative bargaining* (Walton and McKersie, 1965) is appropriate here: (1) state one's position in terms of a problem to be solved rather than a solution to be accepted by the adversary, (2) retain one's flexibility by refraining from commitment to a fixed position, (3) make every effort to understand the adversary's viewpoint, and (4) present an accurate picture of one's needs and motives to the adversary so that he can derive options that satisfy the needs of both parties.

The problem, of course, is that while each of these tactics may facilitate resolution of conflict, it may also thwart the second aim of the bargainer, namely eliciting concessions from the adversary. Tactics (1) and (2) prevent the negotiator from commiting himself to a position favorable to his own interests. Tactic (3) is incompatible with the use of an intermediary, who knows little about the issues and has no authority to make concessions. Tactic (4) gives away the negotiator's minimal aspirations.

Just as integrative tactics favor the solution of conflict at the expense of eliciting concessions from the adversary, the reverse is true of pressure tactics which tend to lend more weight to getting one's way than to resolving the conflict. Pressure tactics tend to interfere with integrative bargaining which may facilitate resolution of the conflict by obtaining a mutually acceptable solution.

Dealing with Conflict Sequentially

There may be some value in attempting to sequence integrative and distributive bargaining over time. According to Walton and McKersie (1965) this approach works in union-management negotiations. A cooperative attempt to enlarge the pie is made *first* (e.g., an attempt to develop new work arrangements benefiting both the company and workers). Then competition emerges in which participants vie to split the enlarged pie. The reverse of the mixed model sequencing does not seem to work as well, since the initial competition tends to "poison" further negotiations and relations.

A similar kind of sequencing entails combining attitude change with distributive bargaining (Walton, 1969). Instead of relying solely on distributive bargaining (building power, using threats, and conveying misleading information), the participants build on possibilities for mutual attraction and trust, to establish more cooperative attitudes. This strategy entails: minimizing perceived differences between the groups in conflict and their goals; avoiding threats and harmful actions; empha-

sizing mutual dependence; building positive, rewarding contacts between as many members of the groups as possible; and being trustful
and trying to empathize. In short, one attempts to socialize the opponent.

The attitude change strategy can be made compatible with distributive bargaining through sequencing. For example, Soviet and U.S. relations have vacillated, freezing and thawing, apparently as a result of
this dual strategy. Threats and warnings are followed by positive approaches (trade concessions, cultural exchanges, and negotiations aimed
at relationship building). Walton indicates that the leader can engage
in both kinds of behavior and still be credible so long as the cycle
is sufficiently long and his initiatives and overtures are perceived
to be genuine. The agreeable, paternalistic supervisor who from time to
time reminds workers of his legitimate authority and potential for coercive sanctions uses this alternating approach.

Second, these contradictory strategies can be implemented by different groups. Emissaries for scientific and cultural exchange may pursue
harmony, while government representatives in Berlin issue threats and
warnings. Finally, one may select particular actions with regard to their
impact on the alternative strategy. One may issue threats strong enough
to win concessions, but not severe enough to rupture relationships. One
may provide concessions for relations building, but with the clear signal
that these are not to be taken as a sign of weakness. In other words, one
always remembers to negotiate from a position of strength, not from
pure trust which prevents subsequent use of the distributive strategy.

Content Specific and Equity Norms

We can argue that both distributive and integrative tactics are inadequate (when used singly or jointly) to deal with dilemmas and problems
that arise in attempts to resolve differences of interest. Pruitt suggests
that bargaining has other drawbacks as well, which include the time and
effort required and the uncertainties entailed. Norms of various kinds
reduce the severity of such drawbacks.

Content specific and equity norms serve this purpose. *Content specific
norms* specify the nature of specific issues in question. For example, in
some families the husband takes out the garbage. Norms that assign
such unpleasant tasks to various household members eliminate the need
to argue over who is to do what. *Equity norms* bring fairness and reciprocity to the bargaining process. The family in our example may have
a norm that dessert is shared equally among members.

The problem with equity norms, according to Pruitt, is that although
we all favor "fair play," we have difficulty operationalizing the concept.
We may differ in our opinions of what is fair. In addition, these norms
may be insensitive to the needs of the parties. For example, a norm specifying a 50–50 split is not very helpful when one party needs the thing

to be divided more than the other. A norm based on reciprocity will not be of much use to those who have little to give. The problem with content specific norms is that they tend to become "sacred" and inflexible, and may lag changes in the needs of the parties.

The Norm of Mutual Responsiveness

In answer to some of these problems, Pruitt suggests the *norm of mutual responsiveness*—the willingness to help the other party satisfy his needs. The norm involves ". . . a kind of unwritten contract which [one individual] may have with [another] that requires each party to exhibit a certain level of responsiveness to the other's needs" (Pruitt, 1972, p. 147).

While norms of mutual responsiveness avoid the dilemmas involved in bargaining, they require certain preconditions. Pruitt suggests that both parties must feel *dependent* upon one another—that each must believe the other capable of providing favors in the future. In addition, *trust* must be sufficient to allow the other party to be viewed as *willing* to provide these favors and to *represent his own needs honestly.*

PARTISANS

Two Perspectives on Conflict: Social Control and Partisans in the Subsystem

In this last section, we turn to a rather different view of conflict. Gamson (1968) suggests that there are two different perspectives in behavioral science theory and research on conflict. One view, the one presented here (which is most popular in recent decades), is that of the "authorities." This viewpoint, which subsumes most of our discussion of systems, bureaucratic, and bargaining conflict, emphasizes the process by which goals of the system as a whole are achieved through the compliance of lower level individuals.

The second, less common, view is that of "potential partisans"—the point of view of those without power who attempt to organize and thereby influence the decisions of authorities. This view is also characterized as a conflict view of society. It is derived from Marxian theory which describes the different interests of different groups in society and the resulting pervasive conflict (the dialectic). Rather than ask how conflict can be reduced and harmony and effectiveness achieved in the system, Marxian and conflict theorists focus on subsystems and their strategies for achieving their own ends. Conflict is viewed as an opportunity, rather than as a danger to the system as a whole. This view is the antithesis of the former social control perspective which views conflict as something to be managed and contained in the interest of organizational effectiveness.

Getting Power

We turn now to an examination of conflict from the perspective of the *partisan*—the individual or group desiring to obtain power. *How does one obtain power and use it effectively, to get what one wants?* Such aspirations may, and probably will, create conflict. Gamson (1975) studied 53 groups (including The American Federation of Teachers, the National Urban League, The Bull Moose Party, and the American Student Union) which attempted to gain recognition and various political ends. Activist groups which were willing to use violence (either to initiate, or to fight back) were more successful than those that were passive. However, it should be added that violence was usually an ancillary part of a program that included strikes, bargaining, and propaganda. Furthermore, willingness to fight had to be supplemented by ability to fight, namely organization and discipline (centralization and bureaucratic structure) if the group was to be successful in achieving acceptance and advantages for its members. Bureaucracy in these groups was indicated by the existence of: (*a*) a constitution or charter with purposes and rules, (*b*) a formal membership list, and (*c*) at least three structural subunits. Centralization was indicated by a single leader or central committee, and local chapters having little autonomy. The anarchist's dream of organizational life, free of structures and authority, was not conducive to gaining power and implementing the group's ends.

Discussing power in more conventional organizations, McMurray (1973) says, "He [the executive] must stay in power by tactics that are mostly political and means that are in large part Machiavellian" (p. 140). McMurray provides a number of recommendations based on what he terms the "fruit of thirty years of observation of a great number of executives managing a variety of enterprises" (p. 141).

(1) The executive should employ subordinates who combine technical competence with reliability, dependability, and loyalty to guard against vulnerability to sabotage by underlings. In theory, he should be backed up by a competent "number two" man who can move in if the manager is promoted. Of course, a strong "number two" man is a threat. Instead, McMurray suggests that the politically astute top executive seeks *subordinates who are loyal.* Such individuals tend to be security conscious and dependent on their chief. (2) It is useful for the executive to have a *compliant board of directors.* Inside directors are better than outside directors since they are more malleable. (3) As in diplomacy, the most important stratagem of power in business is to *establish alliances.* The more alliances the better. Thus the executive should establish alliances

with superiors, peers, and subordinates. (4) The *power of the purse* should be recognized. Thus, the astute manager "seeks as quickly as possible to position himself where he approves all budgets." In addition, McMurray enumerates supplementary ploys—personal styles utilized by politically astute executives. (Please note the similarity of this advice to that of Machiavelli presented in the introduction to this chapter.)

1. Use caution in taking council. Advice can be useful, but can easily become pressure.
2. Avoid too close superior-subordinate relationships—the door may be "open," but not too far.
3. Maintain maneuverability—don't commit yourself completely and irrevocably.
4. Use passive resistance when necessary. Stall or initiate action in such a way that the undesired program suffers delays and ultimately fails.
5. Don't hesitate to be ruthless when to be so is expedient—"no one really expects the boss to be a 'nice' guy at all times. If he is, he will be considered to be a softy or a patsy and no longer deserving of respect" (McMurray, 1973, p. 144).
6. Limit what is to be communicated. Many things should not be revealed if they will create anxieties or conflicts between parts of the organization.
7. Recognize that there are seldom any secrets. Don't reveal matters "in confidence."
8. Don't place too much dependence on a subordinate unless it is clearly in the latter's personal advantage to be loyal.
9. Compromise on small matters to obtain power for further movement.
10. Be skilled in self-dramatization and salesmanship. Be an actor, capable of influencing audiences emotionally as well as rationally.
11. Radiate self-confidence.
12. Give outward evidence of status, power, and material success.

Trust and Distrust

A key to understanding the use of influence against those who are more powerful and the responses of those in power is the nature of the trust relationship between authorities and partisans (Gamson, 1968). A climate of *trust* or confidence, support, allegiance, and satisfaction may be contrasted with one of *distrust*, discontent, alienation, dissatisfaction, or disaffection. Trust is essential in social systems. Decisions must always be made under uncertainty. Therefore, if authorities are to act effectively (without engaging in constant negotiation with subordinates), the trust and commitment of those in the social system are essential. "In war time," Winston Churchill told his critics, "if you desire service, you must give loyalty" (Churchill, 1962, p. 352). As Gamson says,

> . . . for authorities to be effective, they must have a good deal of freedom to commit resources without the prior consent of those who will be called on ultimately to supply those resources. Such freedom to invest or spend the resources they have "borrowed" from members allows leaders to generate additional resources and thus, in theory, provide the lenders with a generous return in the form of public goods or increased resources. . . . Within certain limits, effectiveness depends on a blank check. The importance of trust becomes apparent: the loss of trust is the loss of system power, the loss of a generalized capacity for authorities to commit resources to obtain collective goals (1968, p. 43).

Gamson provides an example of the use of such power and the consequent loss of credit resulting because power was used unwisely. In 1964, the Johnson administration enjoyed a great deal of trust and credit. As a result, Congress gave President Johnson considerable authority to commit the United States to war in Vietnam. The President made use of this credit and his ability to make commitments and involved the United States in a war which ultimately led to a loss of confidence by Congress and others. As a result, the President became increasingly constrained in his freedom to take action. He lost trust and credit and, paradoxically, lost power which would have enabled him to regain trust and credit. Distrust created powerlessness and, as a result, conditions engendering further distrust.

A well-functioning government is like a well-functioning bank. Both would prove insolvent at any given moment if individuals insisted on their formal rights. However, both are trusted, because individuals do not demand immediate delivery of that which is owed them. But let there be a loss of confidence or trust and one will observe a run on the bank.

Usefulness of Distrust

From the partisans' point of view, trust is less desirable. Trust seems to indicate that individuals are satisfied and unmotivated to change the status quo. Voting research, for example (Lipset, 1960), shows that as German voters became increasingly dissatisfied with the Weimar Republic, voter participation increased and led to the electoral victory of Hitler. Apparently some people did not vote earlier because they were satisfied with things. It seems that trust in authorities implies a lack of motivation to influence them. With this in mind, organizers of revolutionary groups attempt to create dissatisfaction, distrust, and readiness to organize among potential members. Much of the activity of community organizers (such as Alinsky), which is seemingly bent on stimulating the powerless to make useless, ineffective attempts to influence authorities, is really aimed at increasing their dissatisfaction and polarizing the situation. This, in turn, may lead to mobilization of support for the activist organization.

Sometimes, these influence attempts are successful, providing rewards to members, encouraging them to further influence attempts, and contributing to group cohesiveness. However, in the case where partisans are not well organized, it may be that successful influence and successful organizing efforts are incompatible. In this case, the community organizer attempts to organize individuals by these apparently defeatist actions, and, having organized them, to use the power of his organization to influence authorities. The university student dissidents during the 1960s (who lured university administrations into calling police onto the campus—police who used violence against neutrals as well as dissidents) were using the police to create distrust and to help organize students generally. Clearly, then, for those attempting to influence authorities, distrust is useful.

Confidence, Neutrality, and Alienation

Gamson suggests that trust (distrust) relationships take three distinct forms. We have *confidence* in authorities when we trust them to have our interests at heart. *Neutrality* arises from the belief that in any decision the authorities have a 50–50 chance of deciding in our favor. Finally, *alienation* stems from the perception that authorities are *not* going to decide in our interest.

According to Gamson, a *confident* group tends to rely on *persuasion* as a means of influence. Authorities are assumed to be committed to the group's goals. Thus, influence is achieved by appealing to the authorities' goodwill by presenting information and arguments, by drawing on existing friendship and loyalty, and by activating commitment to the values shared by the authorities and the group. In short, goal congruence and trust permit a psychological approach to influence to be used. Other means of influence are avoided, since they will have adverse effects on the relationship between a confident group and authorities; for example, inducements may be defined as "bribes." Gamson makes an analogy to the relationship between close friends. Such relationships entail diffuse, reciprocal obligations, and any particular action carried out in the spirit of friendship does not imply a quid pro quo. To offer a specific inducement to a friend is to violate the norms of friendship. "If one offers a quid pro quo for a favor, it implies that one also expects a *quid pro quo* when he performs a similar favor. In general, it implies a different relationship in which each act of influence becomes a separate transaction creating credits or debits for the parties involved" (Gamson, 1968, p. 167). Thus, if a partisan offers an inducement to authorities, the latter's expectations may be that in comparable situations additional inducements will be forthcoming.

In other words, the situation may become more nearly that of a *neutral partisan group* attempting to influence authority with inducements, which is appropriate under neutral circumstances. In this situation, authorities *do not* share the goals of the group but have their own set of goals which may conflict with or complement those of the group. The partisans, however, do not perceive a systematic bias against them. Here it will take more than information to influence authorities to act in one's favor. *Inducements* are necessary. In the absence of common goals, influence has to be active, and focused on the desired behavior. But influence should not be violent or coercive and unnecessarily antagonizing to the authorities. Because they are neutral, a properly selected inducement may do the job—even in the face of differing or conflicting ends. Instead of normative integration as in the case of the confident group, an exchange relationship is used to create integration and influence.

Finally, a partisan group which is *alienated* from authorities will tend to rely on coercion as a means of influence. Such groups, unlike the others, have little to lose by coercion. The probability of favorable outcomes is already low, and the resentment of authorities is of little consequence. In such situations, the prevailing sentiment may be that "the only thing they understand is force."

Reactions by Authorities

We have seen that a partisan group is liable to use different influence strategies according to its trust relationship with authorities. The tactics used will involve the various bases of power described in Chapter 9. How, then, will authorities react?

Reactions depend on the relative strengths of the two parties. The discussion of bureaucratic conflict earlier in this chapter may be recalled. Accommodation may be in order if relatively weak authorities are faced by a strong, organized partisan group. Alternatively, the authorities may appear to yield, but really stall until the situation is calmed down, the resources and organization of the partisans dissipated, and the strength of the authorities regained. Conflicts occurring in a university near the end of the school year may be handled in this fashion.

When the balance of power is reversed, bureaucratic conflicts may be handled by mechanisms of social control in which those in power (the authorities) influence those without sufficient power to force changes. All other things being equal, the existence of high levels of trust is desirable from the authorities' point of view. Trusting subordinates give authorities the power to mobilize resources in the directions they select.

In contrast, under conditions of neutrality, authorities will tend to rely on sanctions and, particularly, inducements as means of social control. Although desirable, persuasion is difficult to use with a neutral group. Constraints, if used, might alienate the group and induce reciprocal actions.

Finally, Gamson suggests that authorities tend to rely on insulation to control alienated groups. By insulating an alienated group, authorities are protected from its use of constraints. Authorities will find such groups unreasonable to bargain with and insatiable with respect to inducements. " 'Give them an inch and they will take a mile,' is the classic expression of such attitudes toward alienated . . . groups" (Gamson, 1968, p. 182).

Pitfalls in Confrontation and Participation

To continue our analysis of the partisan's role in conflict episodes, we would suggest that attempts at conflict resolution which involve openness and participation as advocated by Likert and others are fraught with dangers. When subordinates deal with their superiors, interests clash (Dahrendorf, 1959). The superior's formal authority generally is unmatched by the bases of power on which subordinates rely. Even more important is the unequal distribution of knowledge and information between the two parties.

Mulder's (1971) research illustrates how participants in problem-solving situations suffer loss of influence and are persuaded to change their positions when they possess substantially less relevant information than others. Individuals who are disadvantaged by relative ignorance find that the decision to enter into participative decision making is harmful to them, in terms of their subsequent loss of influence. A comparable situation is found in the Yugoslav Workers Council, a formal arrangement in which workers (who are relatively disadvantaged in terms of expertise and information) participate with top executives in the management of their organizations. Observations of council meetings show that the executives retain the bulk of power, even though they are elected by the workers and bound by law to share decision-making authority with them. The proposals of executives, rather than those of workers, tend to be accepted by the council (Kolaja, 1965). In the vernacular: "Them as has, gets."

Our earlier discussion of the premise-setting behavior of top management may be recalled at this point (Chapter 9). The lower level participants in decision making may be ignorant of potential alternatives. The premises they have come to accept may limit their exploration of feasible decisions. The relative ignorance produced by these premises must be remedied if participation is to be used as anything more than a mechanism of social control. It is interesting to note that blue-collar workers appointed to the boards of directors of some Swedish firms are now being sent to management schools (*Business Week,* 1973).[6]

In any event, we are led to suggest that participation be limited to the areas of decision making in which all participants enjoy knowledge and expertise. Otherwise, lacking the ability to contribute to decisions, the participant will find his or her future potential to influence eroded. Workers can participate effectively in shop floor matters, but not in those concerning the board of directors (Mulder, 1971). Similarly, managers can contribute to decisions related to their jobs, about which they possess knowledge and expertise. To extend participation to areas in which some participants are disadvantaged by virtue of their training and experience is unsound on purely logical grounds and, as we have seen, not in the best interests of the disadvantaged.

Participation's Usefulness to the Partisan

In Chapter 3 we saw that participation is conducive to organizational effectiveness. Organizations having high total influence were found to be more effective than those characterized by low total influence. Presumably, influence was enjoyed within areas of the participants' competencies. Otherwise, we would expect participation to have left lower level members without influence, as Mulder's reasoning suggests.

Thus, we are moved to advise members of organizations (potential partisans), who are faced with opportunities to participate with superiors in problem solving and decision making, to assure themselves that the areas within which they will participate fall within their competencies. Failing caution in this regard, the partisan may lose whatever potential to influence he or she enjoyed prior to becoming a participant.

A similar caution can be raised with regard to what Gamson terms "confidence," where goal congruence is assumed. If the partisans feel confidence in those with whom they will participate, relatively trusting behavior would appear in order. In Chapter 5, we suggested that various organization members and shareholders often have different and sometimes conflicting goals. Here, authorities are likely to use socialization and participation to control lower level members. In a general way, then, individuals must consider the trade-offs involved: Are they prepared to be socialized (how much?) in order to share in the rewards (how much?) of membership? Alternatively, the organizational model used by authorities may be on the order of Barrett's exchange model described above. Here the lower level participants must weigh the specific contributions they make against the inducements they receive. (In the

---

[6] One is led to speculate, however, whether these workers, as business school alumni, will continue to represent the work force. It is conceivable that their education will socialize them according to the values and attitudes of management.

next chapter we shall have more to say about these two different kinds of control, which use internal and external controls, respectively, to regulate the behavior of members.)

More specifically, individuals must weigh the extent to which opening themselves to influence will lead to: (*a*) the danger of being influenced in directions they do not want to go, and (*b*) (from Mulder's experiment) the danger of losing power and subsequently being less able to prevent undesirable influence in the future. However, participation may prove worthwhile even after the subordinates weigh the (usually unnoticed) effects noted above.

Many studies of participation have focused only on its benefits for the organization or on satisfactions reported by workers, and do not include a thorough analysis of the gains and losses of the individual worker. One wonders whether the Coch and French (1948) study of women machine operatives at Harwood (Chapter 3) fully accounted for possible losses of power of the participating workers. As Mulder observes:

> When someone's boss gives orders to him, he can resist. He can think, "what the boss doesn't see won't hurt him," or he can prevent the order from being carried out. He can also critically talk with others about it. But the mechanisms of resistance, obstruction, and catharsis are excluded from the participatory group after the decision has been made. The person is committed to the decision, and has to follow it without reserve (1971, p. 36).

The lower partisan will do well to determine whether structured protections are available to prevent his being manipulated. If the women in the Coch and French experiment had been represented by a union, the result might have turned out more like the French and associates (1960) study, in which participation was rejected (by a union). Scott (1965) proposes the creation of formal appeals systems for white-collar workers—systems in which grievances regarding unfair behavior of supervisors are taken up the managerial hierarchy. As we shall show in the next chapter, rules and impersonality, as found in bureaucracies, may serve to protect the individual, just as informal norms (Chapter 9) can structure behavior and provide security through predictability and through the legitimacy inherent in such structured expectations.

A study by Kohn (1971) supports the argument that formal structure provides protection against "premise setting" and other forms of manipulation of the participating organization member. He found that bureaucrats enjoyed more protections in terms of tenure, seniority guarantees, and formal grievance procedures, than non-bureaucrats. Consequently, the former (especially the blue-collar workers in bureaucracies) were more open to change, felt more personal responsibility, and were more intellectually flexible.

The prospective partisan must look beyond formal protections for participation. Tannenbaum et al. (1974) found higher total influence in Yugoslav firms having worker's councils than in firms in Italy or Austria (which lacked workers' councils). However, influence curves were still higher for U.S. firms. The latter curves were high, despite the lack of formal provision for participation at the board level, because informal relations between superiors and subordinates were conducive to openness and enabled relatively high degrees of influence and participation by subordinates.

The prospective partisan must consider the expected degree of influence to be gained by participation. Some of these rewards take the form of shares taken from someone else (from distributive bargaining conflicts). This suggests the need for a careful diagnosis of the situation. In addition to considering one's own preferred goals and means, and those of authorities, the potential partisan must consider where rewards are to come from. A possible bigger pie is one thing, and a zero-sum situation (such as a cutback in jobs or budget) is another.

In conclusion, we have raised these issues in part to redress what appears to be an imbalance in the literature. Participative management sometimes is advocated without due regard to the well-being of either the organization or its participants. As we shall see, this is also the case with some organizational change techniques. As we move on to even more controversial topics, please bear in mind that theoretical positions often are based on political predispositions which sometimes bias perception and reason. This phenomenon applies to all of us to one extent or another. We have our biases, too. Please bear this in mind as well, as we continue our study of organizations.

DISCUSSION QUESTIONS

1. List some of the more apparent sources of conflict for faculty and students in your school.
2. Can you categorize them as bureaucratic, systems, or bargaining conflict?
3. Are these sources of conflict unavoidable? If not, how can they be avoided?
4. Describe the power of the student body, the faculty, and the administration.
5. How are these different forms of power exercised?
6. Americans seem prone to meet conflict with violence. Is the rate of violent crime higher in America than in England? How do you account for your answer?

REFERENCES

Alinsky, Saul. *Reveille for radicals.* Chicago: University of Chicago Press, 1946.

Alinsky, Saul. *Rules for radicals.* New York: Random House, 1971.

Bach, George R., and Wyden, P. *Intimate enemy: how to fight fair in love and marriage.* San Diego: Morrow Pubs., 1969.

Baldridge, Victor J. *Power and conflict in the university: research in the sociology of complex organizations.* New York: Wiley, 1971.

Barrett, Jon H. *Individual goals and organizational objectives: a study of integration mechanisms.* Ann Arbor, Mich.: Institute for Social Research, 1970.

Breed, Warren. Social control in the newsroom: a functional analysis. *Social Forces,* 1955, *33,* 326–35.

Burke, Ronald J. Methods of resolving superior-subordinate differences and disagreements. *Organizational Behavior and Human Performance,* 1970, *5,* 373–411.

Business Week. When workers become directors. *Business Week,* 1973, 2297, (September 15), 188–96.

Churchill, Winston. *The second world war.* Vol. 4. New York: Bantam Books, 1962.

Coch, Lester, and French, John R. P., Jr. Overcoming resistance to change. *Human Relations,* 1948, *1,* 512–32.

Dahrendorf, Ralf. *Class and class conflict in industrial society.* Stanford, Calif.: Stanford University Press, 1959.

Durkheim, Émile. *The division of labor in society.* (G. Simpson, trans.) Glencoe, Ill.: Free Press, 1947.

Fanon, Frantz. *The wretched of the earth.* Harmondworth, Middlesex: Penguin Books, 1967.

Frank, Jerome D. Experimental studies of personal pressure and resistance. *Journal of General Psychology,* 1944, *30,* 23–64.

French, J. R. P., Jr., Israel, J., and Ås, D. An experiment on participation in a Norwegian factory. *Human Relations,* 1960, *13,* 3–19.

Gamson, William A. *Power and discontent.* Homewood, Ill.: The Dorsey Press, 1968.

Gamson, William. *Strategy of social protest.* Homewood, Ill.: The Dorsey Press, 1975.

Gauss, Christian. In Niccolo Machiavelli, *The prince.* New York: New American Library, 1952.

Georgopoulos, Basil S., and Mann, Floyd C. *The community general hospital.* New York: Macmillan, 1962.

Halpert, Burton P. Interorganizational relationships: some theoretical and empirical notes on power, conflict and cooperation. Paper presented at The American Sociological Association meetings, Montreal, August 1974.

Hampton, David R., Summer, Charles E., and Webber, Ross A. *Organizational behavior and the practice of management.* Rev. ed. Glenview, Ill.: Scott, Foresman, 1973.

Kahn, Robert L. Introduction. In R. L. Kahn and Elise Boulding (Eds.), *Power and conflict in organizations.* London: Tavistock, 1964. Pp. 1–7.

Katz, Daniel. Approaches to managing conflict. In R. L. Kahn and E. Boulding (Eds.), *Power and conflict in organizations.* London: Tavistock, 1964. Pp. 105–114.

Kohn, Melvin L. Bureaucratic man: a portrait and an interpretation. *American Sociological Review,* 1971, *36,* 461–74.

Kolaja, Jiri. *Workers' councils: the Yugoslav experience.* London: Tavistock, 1965.

Landsberger, Henry A. The horizontal dimension in bureaucracy. *Administrative Science Quarterly,* 1961, *6,* 299–322.

Lawrence, Paul R., and Lorsch, Jay W. *Organization and environment.* Boston: Division of Research, Graduate School of Business Administration, Harvard University, 1967.

Lipset, Seymour Martin. *Political man.* Garden City, N.Y.: Doubleday, 1960.
Litterer, Joseph A. Conflict in organization: a re-examination. *Academy of Management Journal,* 1966, 9, 178–86.
Litwak, Eugene. Models of organization which permit conflict. *American Journal of Sociology,* 1961, 67, 177–85.
McClelland, David. *Personality.* New York: Holt, Rinehart, and Winston, 1951.
Machiavelli, Niccolò. *The prince.* New York: New American Library, 1952.
McMurry, Robert N. Power and the ambitious executive. *Harvard Business Review,* 1973, 51, 6 (November–December), 140–45.
March, J. G., and Simon, H. A. *Organizations.* New York: Wiley, 1958.
Marriott, R. Size of working group and output. *Occupational Psychology,* 1949, 23, 47–57.
Milgram, Stanley. Behavioral study of obedience. *Journal of Abnormal and Social Psychology,* 1963, 67, 371–78.
Milgram, Stanley. Group pressure and action against a person. *Journal of Abnormal and Social Psychology,* 1964, 69, 137–43.
Milgram, Stanley. Some conditions of obedience and disobedience to authority. In Ivan D. Steiner and Martin Fishbein (Eds.), *Current studies in social psychology.* New York: Holt, Rinehart, and Winston, 1965. Pp. 243–62.
Mott, Paul E. *The characteristics of effective organizations.* New York: Harper & Row, 1972.
Mulder, Mauk. Power equalization through participation. *Administrative Science Quarterly,* 1971, 16, 31–38.
Orne, Martin T., and Evans, Frederick J. Social control in the psychological experiment. *Journal of Personality and Social Psychology,* 1965, 1, 189–200.
Pelz, Donald C., and Andrews, Frank M. *Scientists in organizations: productive climates for research and development.* New York: Wiley, 1966.
Pepitone, Albert. Attributions of causality, social attitudes, and cognitive matching processes. In Renato Taguiri and Luigi Petrullo (Eds.), *Person perception and interpersonal behavior,* Stanford, Calif.: Stanford University Press, 1958. Pp. 258–76.
Perrow, Charles. *Complex organizations: a critical essay.* Glenview, Ill.: Scott, Foresman and Company, 1972.
Peters, E. *Strategy and tactics in labor negotiations.* New London, Conn.: National Foremen's Institute, 1955.
Pondy, Louis R. Budgeting and inter-group conflict in organizations. *Pittsburgh Business Review,* 1964, 34 (April), 1–3.
Pondy, Louis R. Organizational conflict: concepts and models. *Administrative Science Quarterly,* 1967, 12, 296–320.
Pruitt, Dean G. Indirect communication and research for agreement in negotiation. *Journal of Applied Social Psychology,* 1971, 1, 205–39.
Pruitt, Dean G. Methods for resolving differences of interest: a theoretical analysis. *Journal of Social Issues,* 1972, 28, 133–54.
Scott, William G. *The management of conflict: appeal systems in organizations.* Homewood, Ill.: Dorsey, 1965.
Sennett, Richard. *The uses of disorder: personal identity and city life.* New York: Random House, 1970.
Sherif, M. Superordinate goals in the reduction of intergroup conflict. *American Journal of Sociology,* 1958, 3, 356–94.
Sigelman, Lee. An organizational analysis of news reporting. *American Journal of Sociology,* 1973, 79, 132–51.

Simon, Herbert A. *Administrative behavior: a study of decision-making processes in administrative organization.* New York: Macmillan, 1957.

Smith, Clagett. A comparative analysis of some conditions and consequences of intraorganizational conflict. *Administrative Science Quarterly,* 1966, *10,* 504–29.

Stagner, Ross. Corporate decision making: an empirical study. *Journal of Applied Psychology,* 1969, *53,* 1–13.

Stagner, Ross. Conflict in the executive suite. In Warren G. Bennis (Ed.), *American bureaucracy.* Chicago: Aldine, 1970. Pp. 85–95.

Stevens, C. M. *Strategy and collective bargaining negotiation.* New York: McGraw-Hill, 1963.

Tannenbaum, Arnold S., Kavcic, Bogdan, Rosner, Menachem, Vianello, Mino, and Wieser, Georg. *Hierarchy in organizations.* San Francisco: Jossey-Bass, 1974.

Thompson, Victor A. *Modern organization: a general theory.* New York: Knopf, 1961.

Toennies, Ferdinand. *Fundamental concepts of sociology.* (C. P. Loomis, trans.) New York: American Book Co., 1940.

Walker, Arthur H., and Lorsch, Jay W. Organizational choice: product versus function. *Harvard Business Review,* 1968, *46* (6), 129–38.

Walton, Richard E. Two strategies of social change and their dilemmas. In Warren G. Bennis, Kenneth D. Benne, and Robert Chin (Eds.), *The planning of change.* New York: Holt, Rinehart, and Winston, 1969. Pp. 167–76.

Walton, Richard E., and Dutton, John M. The management of interdepartmental conflict: a model and review. *Administrative Science Quarterly,* 1969, *14,* 73–84.

Walton, R. E., and R. B. McKersie. *A behavioral theory of labor negotiations.* New York: McGraw-Hill, 1965.

White, R. W. Motivation reconsidered: the concept of competence. *Psychological Review,* 1959, *66,* 297–333.

Whyte, William F. The social structure of the restaurant. *American Journal of Sociology,* 1949, *54,* 302–10.

Wildavsky, Aaron. *The politics of the budgetary process.* Boston: Little, Brown, 1964.

11

Control

INTRODUCTION

Once again we confront the dilemma of viewing organizations as rational tools and as open systems. The last chapter, "Power and Conflict," illustrates some of the processes that make organizations far more complex than the rational model indicates. And yet, that chapter suggests that complexities can be reduced through the application of rules and orders—the very substance of bureaucracies and other rational forms of organization. In the last chapter we said that interpersonal strife can be reduced in specific situations by . . . "the mediation of conflict by a third party, leading perhaps to the establishment of *rules and agreements* for equitable sharing. *By their impersonality, the rules so established may alleviate the more damaging, personal effects of conflict.*"

Various activities of organizational subunits must be coordinated and controlled somehow. Short of living in anarchy, we must accept constraints in our daily lives. The rational approach to management suggests that coordination be provided by constraints that are *external* to members of the organization. Rules, plans, and hierarchies of authority are imposed on the system to focus its energies on matters considered vital by top management. Alternatively, the natural (open) system model suggests that external constraints be minimized to enhance the system's flexibility and adaptability. Goals and means, it is argued, are most likely pursued when they are established *internally,* through the collaboration and participation of those affected by them.

Chapter Guide

1. We have taken something of an either/or position with respect to the rational and open system models thus far. We feel this is a pedagogical necessity. Is it also a valid fact of organizations or can the two views be combined successfully?
2. Are we for the most part internally or externally controlled in organizations and in our lives outside these institutions?

3.   Is internal control inherently superior to external control?
4.   What would it be like to live in a culture with few rules?
5.   If internal and external control are not mutually exclusive, how does one decide that one is more efficacious in a particular situation than the other?

INTERNAL VERSUS EXTERNAL CONTROL

These dilemmas may not be as troublesome as they appear at first glance. We frequently observe that contradictory schools of thought complement one another when studied at a level of aggregation that permits their integration. Rather than sift through the literature to separate "truth" from "error," we should search for an integrative model which lends order to the confusion found therein. A number of authors have attempted this approach recently (e.g., Filley and House, 1969; Hellriegel and Slocum, 1974; Kast and Rosenzweig, 1974). However, because of the paucity of germane research in the field, results tend to be modest. We will be equally modest in our expectations, but shall demonstrate the complementary qualities of the two views of organizations as they apply to coordination and control.

Planning

Control, it may be recalled from Chapter 9, was defined as obtaining desired behavior from another person. According to Kast and Rosenzweig: "The managerial system is concerned primarily with decision making for planning and controlling organizational endeavor" (1974, p. 355). A variety of models of the decision-making process are provided in the literature. Often they are elaborations of the general three-step process outlined by John Dewey (1910): (1) What is the problem? (2) What are the alternatives? (3) Which alternative is best?

Planning is a process wherein decisions regarding the future of the organization are made. Generally, we can differentiate between two major kinds of planning activities. On one hand, organizations engage in strategic planning, which, according to Ansoff and Brandenburg (1971), consists of establishing formal guidelines and constraints for the behavior of the organization and includes: (1) a search of the environment for potential threats and opportunities; (2) an analysis of these; (3) the selection of threats and opportunities to which the organization needs to respond; (4) planning and scheduling the implementation of responses; and (5) obtaining feedback on responses which can be used to improve future performance. Activities of this sort are

FIGURE 11–1
Pyramid of Business Policies

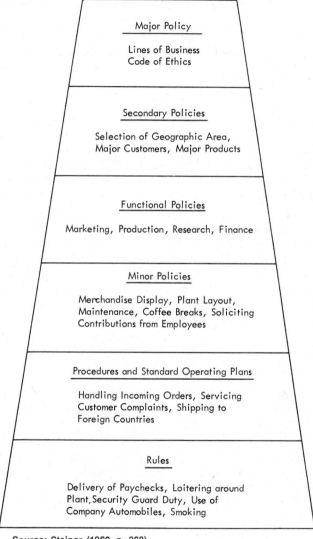

Source: Steiner (1969, p. 268).

included in the three uppermost cells of Steiner's Pyramid of Business Policies depicted in Figure 11–1.[1]

On the other hand, at lower levels of the organization we find plan-

---

[1] Strategic planning typically is viewed as a rational-hierarchical process in which means for attaining the goals of the larger organization become subgoals that are assigned to units at lower levels in the hierarchy.

ning used in coordinating task-related behaviors to make the means employed by the organization consistent with the ends it seeks. Such activities typically result in minor policies, operating procedures, and rules. It is this sort of planning we wish to investigate here. Rules, procedures, and clearly defined limits to authority and responsibility are characteristics of bureaucracies. We shall begin our investigation, then, with an elaboration of the concept of bureaucratic conflict that was introduced in the last chapter.

Bureaucratic Conflict

The formal hierarchy of authority provides a particular type of coordination of individuals, technological processes, and structural elements. Superiors can plan the activities of their subordinates and, by virtue of their authority, issue orders to set them in motion. Direct orders may be issued, but impersonal rules commonly evolve as means for controlling personnel. Unfortunately, this can lead to conflict.

Conflict can arise when subordinates perceive their superior attempting to exercise control over activities that are outside of legitimate or accepted areas. Similarly, superiors experience conflict when their attempts to control are thwarted and resisted by subordinates.

In large organizations, where leaders do not identify personally with subordinates, lower level personnel may find that their goals and aspirations are not considered in decision making. If the organization does not facilitate individual objectives, individuals will seek autonomy as a precondition for arranging their own need-fulfilling activities.

> The imposition of rules defines the authority relation more clearly and robs the subordinate of the autonomy provided by ambiguity. Replacing supervision with control by rules invariably narrows the subordinate's freedom of action, makes his behavior more predictable to others, and thus weakens his power position in the organization. Control over the conditions of one's own existence, if not over others', is highly valued in organizations, particularly in large organizations. The subordinate therefore perceives himself to be threatened by and in conflict with his superiors, who are attempting to decrease his autonomy (Pondy, 1967, pp. 314–15).

As Pondy sees it, subordinates resist attempts to control them and this resistance, being unpleasant for superiors, generates pressures toward the establishment of impersonal rules and routines. While this may reduce face-to-face conflict (but not necessarily the conflict, itself) and lead to fairly predictable behavior, it will also produce rigid behavior. Furthermore, Pondy reasons that: "Rigidity of behavior, which minimizes conflict in a stable environment, is a major source of conflict when adaptability is required" (1967, p. 315).[2]

---

[2] At the micro level of organizational functioning, Pondy sees leadership training and participative management as attempts to deal with vertical conflict. "In-

The Advantages of Rules and Operating Procedures

All types of organization have their advantages and disadvantages. Yet, bureaucracy has become a "whipping boy" in the literature of organizations and in our culture as well. There is a tendency to elaborate the disadvantages of bureaucracies while overlooking their positive aspects. Similarly, organic and participative organizational forms are advocated on the basis of the recognition they supposedly pay to the value and dignity of their members. The worth of a particular form of organization in a specific situation, however, is measured according to criteria that far exceed the attention given to member satisfaction (a system need).

One advocate of bureaucracy, Charles Perrow, argues that:

> After fifteen years of studying complex organizations, I have come to two conclusions that run counter to much of the organizational literature. The first is that the sins generally attributed to bureaucracy are either not sins at all or are consequences of the failure to bureaucratize sufficiently. In this respect, I will defend bureaucracy as the dominant principle of organization in our large, complex organizations. The second conclusion I have reached is that the extensive preoccupation with reforming, "humanizing," and decentralizing bureaucracies, while salutary, has served to obscure from organizational theorists the true nature of bureaucracy and has diverted us from assessing its impact upon society. The impact upon society in general is incalculably more important than the impact upon the members of a particular organization (Perrow, 1972, p. 6).[3]

In addition to pointing out that bureaucracies have not been judged adequately, Perrow suggests that they are superior to alternative forms of organization.

> . . . in my view, bureaucracy is a form of organization superior to all others we know or can hope to afford in the near and middle future; the chances of doing away with it or changing it are probably nonexistent in the West in this century. Thus, it is crucial to understand . . . not only how it mobilizes social resources for desirable ends, but also how it inevitably concentrates those forces in the hands of a few who are prone to use them for ends we do not approve of, for ends we are generally not aware of, and more frightening still, for ends we are led to accept because we are not in a position to conceive alternative ones (Perrow, 1972, p. 7).[4]

---

stead of minimizing dependence and increasing autonomy, leadership theorists have proposed minimizing conflicts by using personal persuasion and group pressures to bring subordinate goals more closely into line with the legitimate goals of the organization. They have prescribed solutions which decrease autonomy and increase dependence. By heightening the individual's involvement in the organization's activities, they have actually provided the basis for the intense personal conflict that characterizes intimate relations" (Pondy, 1967, p. 316). We shall examine this somewhat cynical view of participation below, for attempts to increase participation are pervasive in organizations today.

[3] From *Complex Organizations: A Critical Essay* by Charles Perrow. Copyright © 1972 by Scott, Foresman and Company. Reprinted by permission of the publisher.
[4] Ibid.

Rules and procedures are essential to bureaucracies because they are part of the structure that enables the organization to function effectively. In small groups, where individuals interact face-to-face with one another, coordination may be achieved informally. However, in larger organizations, where members are too numerous to interact directly, where turnover among members is significant, and where geographic distances between members mitigate against their interaction, such informal work relationships will not evolve. Instead, rules will be generated to facilitate coordination.

Rules are also useful because they restrict behavior. Only a limited portion of an individual's repertoire of behavior is appropriate in purposive organizations. In fact, some forms of behavior (e.g., social drinking) will impede organizational functioning if allowed on the job. Rules and regulations provide means of prohibiting these behaviors in the organization.

Complex problems can be rendered more simple through categorization. The routine aspects of a problem can be dealt with fairly automatically through the application of rules, thereby increasing the time and energy available for solving its more difficult aspects. For example, in writing a paper, we need not concern ourselves with selecting one of a large number of accepted footnote styles if the publisher rules that only a single style is acceptable. Footnote style, a matter of indifference to most authors, is settled, leaving more time for the substance of the paper.

Favoritism, nepotism, and discrimination on irrelevant grounds are inhibited by rules, according to Perrow.[5] Rules enable individuals to determine where they stand vis-à-vis organizational requirements and can help them organize their activities to benefit both themselves and the organization. In addition, rules protect and enhance the autonomy of subunits within the organization.

Rules are valuable in stabilizing a situation and protecting various kinds of practices, bargains, agreements, and payoffs. If they were permanent, problems would arise as the situations to which the rules were addressed changed. However, rules are changed too, but usually incrementally. Because of the complexity of organizations, drastic alterations of existing rules will "throw everything up for grabs" and create a crisis. So, we are saying that rules can be extremely useful and that one is well advised to proceed cautiously in trying to alter or eliminate them. According to Perrow:

---

[5] There are two sides to the question of nepotism, however, for the practice may be viewed as both rational and practical. Perrow admits that nepotism and favoritism may be vehicles for seeking personal rather than organizational imperatives. However, he goes on to suggest that the practices can produce a work force that is loyal. One's friends and relatives may not be the most efficient workers in the labor market, but when such relative disadvantages are slight they may be more than offset by the personal and organizational loyalties their employment engenders (pun intended, R.A.U.).

. . . they protect as well as restrict; coordinate as well as block; channel effort as well as limit it; permit universalism as well as provide sanctuary for the inept; maintain stability as well as retard change; permit diversity as well as restrict it. They constitute the organizational memory and the means for change (1972, p. 32).[6]

"Invisible" Rules

Some organizations, in which rules and procedures are not codified, give the impression of allowing far-ranging freedoms to their employees. However, Perrow (1972) suggests that such organizations can be more binding on employees than others, in which rules are made explicit. Although unwritten, rules exist within the organizational culture as norms, agreements, and accepted practices. On joining such an organization, new employees are likely to learn the rules only after transgressing them and suffering consequent sanctions. It is argued that a delineation of rules outlines the employees' areas of "freedom" and allows them to pursue their endeavors without suffering undue consequences that arise when "unwritten" restrictions are violated inadvertently.

In other situations, clearly-defined rules may be treated temporarily as if they do not exist. In theory, the superior in a bureaucracy will exert control over his or her subordinates and require them to follow regulations. In fact, Blau (1956) shows that supervisors frequently "play ball" with their subordinates, permitting infractions of numerous rules (e.g., no smoking rules). In using his or her discretion either to demand compliance or to permit violations of rules, the supervisor exercises what Blau terms "strategic leniency." Interestingly, the net outcome of strategic leniency is increased (rather than decreased) control over subordinates.

> Whereas the disciplinarian supervisor generally asserts his official prerogatives, the lenient and relaxed one does not. The latter attempts to take the wishes of his subordinates into account in arranging their work schedule, although he has the right to assign their work at his own discretion. Sometimes he goes to special trouble to accommodate a subordinate. Instead of issuing curt commands, he usually explains the reasons for his directives. He calls his subordinates by their first names and encourages their use of his first name (especially in democratically minded American organizations). When one of his subordinates gets into difficulties with management, he is apt to speak up for him and to defend him. These different actions have two things in common: the superior is not required to do them, and his subordinates welcome

---

[6] Ibid. In evaluating the impact of rules on organizational performance, we must be aware of "red herrings." Perrow (1972) suggests that rules are often treated as scapegoats for more basic organizational problems. It is a simple matter to demonstrate the conditions under which a particular rule is inappropriate. Frequently, though, such criticism is prompted, not by the shortcomings of rules (with which we are all familiar), but by the critic's dislike for the ends the rule seeks to achieve.

his doing them. Such conduct therefore creates social obligations. To repay the supervisor for past favors, and not to risk the cessation of similar favors in the future, subordinates voluntarily comply with many of his requests, including some they are not officially required to obey. By refraining from exercising his power of control whenever it is legitimate to do so, the bureaucratic superior establishes effective authority over subordinates, which enables him to control them much more effectively than otherwise would be possible (Blau and Meyer, 1971, p. 64).

We see, then, that some attempts to "democratize" bureaucracies can actually place greater controls on members than otherwise would exist. Where rules are made explicit and enforced routinely, control is said to be external. Control that arises from personal obligations is internal. Social obligations aside, internal controls can include professional norms and procedures, work-related values, intrinsic motivations, such as the need for achievement. The question arises, then, which is better and for whom—internal or external controls?

We submit that neither form of control is inherently superior to the other, but, when applied appropriately, they complement each other. Specialists and professionals seem the epitomes of employees whose work is regulated via internal controls. We shall examine the relationships of each to bureaucratic structures and then describe some of the techniques that appear useful in: (1) improving the "fit" between professional activities and the formal organization, and (2) increasing the internal control of nonprofessional employees—that is, "professionalizing" the work force.

Measuring Components of Bureaucracy

Before exploring the roles of professionals in bureaucracies, we need to examine bureaucratic organizations in slightly greater detail than was provided in Chapter 1. A good place to begin is with a now classic study of the dimensions of organizational structures conducted in the Birmingham, England, area by Pugh and associates (1968). A total of 64 structural measures was taken in each of 52 organizations in the research sample. The values obtained were compared across all organizations. One important conclusion was that measures of *specialization, standardization,* and *formalization* tend to co-vary (to increase or decrease together). Taken together, these three measures indicate the degree to which activities are structured. Hence, the combination is termed *structuring of activities.*

Specialization measures the degree to which labor is divided in organization. Standardization refers to established routines and procedures, such as those in personnel selection or promotion decisions. Formalization measures the degree to which rules, procedures, and instructions are codified in manuals and other documents.

A second important and apparently independent grouping of measures is termed the *concentration of authority.* Primarily, this factor comprises the extent of centralization—the degree to which authority for decision making is localized in a central, high level of line management. Specialization varies inversely with concentration of authority. Generally speaking, authority seems dispersed in organizations that employ relatively large numbers of specialists. A related finding shows that the percentage of employees involved directly in the work flow varies directly with concentration of authority. The greater the concentration of authority, the smaller the percentage of employees engaged in staff specialties and the greater the percentage of employees in line positions.

Relationships Between Centralization and Structuring of Activities

A number of studies (e.g., Blau and associates, 1966; Child, 1972) show a negative relationship between measures of centralization and structuring of activities; that is, organizations having centralized decision-making processes (in which top management tends to make most major decisions) have relatively few rules, standardized procedures, and specializations. Conversely, where the latter are relatively numerous, top management tends to delegate decision making to lower hierarchical levels.

In response to findings of still other studies that show the relationship between centralization and structuring of activities to be weak or nonexistent, Mansfield (1973) examined the effect of organizational size on the variables measured. He found that standardization, formalization, and specialization co-vary positively, but that each tends to vary inversely with centralization. His most interesting finding is that relationships between measures of specialization and centralization vary depending on the size of the organization studied.

A direct relationship between measures of specialization and centralization is found in relatively small centralized organizations, having

FIGURE 11–2
The Use of Specialists in Large and Small,
Centralized and Decentralized
Organizations

Size of Organization	Form of Organization	
	Centralized	*Decentralized*
Large	Few specialists	Many specialists
Small	Many specialists	Few specialists

about 150 employees on the average; that is to say, where control is concentrated in high, line-management positions, many specialists are employed, presumably to serve as advisers to decision makers. Small, decentralized organizations employ relatively fewer specialists.

In contrast, an inverse relationship is found between specialization and centralization in relatively large, centralized organizations employing over 6,000 personnel on an average. Where control is centralized, specialists are relatively few in number. Conversely, in large organizations having decentralized control, specialists are relatively numerous. It is suggested that specialists are used to advise line managers in handling problems brought about by the use of rules and regulations and the need to coordinate large, decentralized units. Finally, organizations that are medium-sized (that employ more than 150 and fewer than 6,000 employees on an average) generally show no significant relationship between measures of centralization and specialization.

Determinants of Structuring and Centralization

A more recent study by Pugh and associates (1969) describes the determinants of the factor *structuring of activities* that was isolated in the earlier study (Pugh, Hickson, Hinings, and Turner, 1968). From the original 52 organizations studied, numerous measures of "contextual variables" were taken. These variables may be summarized under the categories of origin, ownership and control, size, charter, technology, location, and dependence. Pugh and associates (1969) as well as others (Child, 1973; Reimann, 1973) show that the measures that constitute structuring of activities are related to the organization's size. These relationships also apply to the size of the parent organizations in the case of organizations that are not autonomous. Formalization is a substitute, as it were, for direct supervision (Gouldner, 1954). Concentration of authority seems most highly related to dependence on an external organization (Pugh et al., 1969). Dependent organizations (e.g., subsidiaries of larger organizations) tend to have centralized authority structures, but relatively little autonomy in decision making. In contrast, independent organizations have more autonomy to decentralize decision-making authority.

Khandwalla (1974) examined the effects of technology, vertical integration, and sophisticated managerial controls on the relationships among organizational size, structuring of activities, and centralization. In order to operate a "mass-production technology" (as defined by Woodward, 1965—see Chapter 4) efficiently, fluctuations in the environment must be buffered. One likely means to this end is vertical integration.[7] However, vertical integration leads to increased organizational

---

[7] Some forms of vertical integration are owning or controlling sources of raw materials, producing goods derived from what had previously been the organization's end products, retailing end products, and so on.

differentiation and consequently to delegation of authority (decentralization) which, in turn, is facilitated by the introduction of "sophisticated control mechanisms."

Khandwalla defines sophisticated management controls as control systems that require considerable information processing skills of managers employing them (e.g., statistical quality control systems, scheduling techniques, internal audit procedures, and the like).

Professionals and Bureaucracies

How do dimensions of bureaucracy, such as structuring of activities and concentration of authority, affect the work of professionals, whose orientations toward internal controls may conflict with external direction? Here the commonly assumed evils of bureaucracy come most into focus.

The issue of professionals in bureaucracies first surfaced in Talcott Parsons' (1947) discussion of Weber's concept of bureaucracy which, it will be recalled, described bureaucracies in terms of hierarchies of authority based on competence. Since superiors in the hierarchy may possess less *technical* competence than those below them, Parsons reasoned that bureaucratic structures contained an inherent source of conflict. The dependence of superiors on subordinates for technical advice is asymmetrical with status, authority, and other relationships. For example, in attempting to formulate personnel policies, the dean of a business school may come to depend upon, and be greatly influenced by, the advice of a junior faculty member in the department of organizational behavior. Differentiation between line and staff personnel arises, in part, to deal with this problem but does not alleviate it entirely.

Using the dimensions of bureaucracy described above, Hall (1968) explored relationships between professionals and this type of organization. He approximated the extent of professionalization of a variety of occupational roles by measuring the degrees to which incumbents of the various roles subscribed to the following professional values:[8]

1. The use of a professional organization (either a formal organization or an informal grouping of colleagues) as a major source of ideas and judgment of professional work.
2. A belief in service to the public, including the notion that the profession is indispensable and benefits both the public and the practitioner.
3. A belief in self-regulation which holds that fellow professionals are best qualified to judge professional work.

---

[8] The occupational roles included physicians, nurses, accountants, teachers, lawyers, social workers, stockbrokers, librarians, engineers, personnel managers, and advertising account executives.

4. A sense of calling or dedication to the field of professional endeavor —a dedication that is exercised even at the expense of material rewards.
5. Autonomy—the freedom to make decisions without direction or pressure from clients, the public, or the organization that employs the professional.

Extent of professionalization was compared to the degree of bureaucracy found in organizations employing various occupational roles. On the whole, Hall found bureaucratization inversely related to professionalization; for example, occupational roles in which members reported strong feelings of autonomy were found in organizations characterized by a relative absence of hierarchical authority, division of labor, rules, procedures, and impersonality. Conversely, practitioners who expressed weak feelings of autonomy were found in occupations that served more bureaucratic organizations. Negative correlations show that the existence of bureaucracy is found in the absence of professionalism and vice versa. One inference is that the two are incompatible, but this is not necessarily so, as we shall see.

While Hall found fairly systematic, negative relationships, it should be noted that none was of particularly great magnitude except the relationship between autonomy and bureaucracy. In the case of other aspects of professionalization, the relationships were not statistically significant. Therefore, Hall argues that the conflict assumed between bureaucracy and professionals may not be inherent at all. In fact, it may be that for a particular level of professionalization, a certain degree of bureaucratization is essential to the stability and control of organizational functioning.

Bureaucracy and Professionalism as Alternatives

For the moment, we shall leave this question of complementary roles and explore the possibility that organizations can employ bureaucracy and professionalism as *alternative* means for regulating and coordinating behavior. Both bureaucratic structures and professional orientations serve to organize, stabilize, and regularize the execution of organizational roles. Rules and procedures restrict and direct the behavior of employees. The same is true of professional norms, ethics, standards, and practices. In the latter case, however, restrictions are internalized. Within limits, an organization can employ either as a means of achieving control; for example, job enrichment, discussed in Chapter 6, provides a source of internal control for workers.

The limits that constrain choice seem fairly straightforward. In an organization employing professionals, excessive bureaucratization is likely to be dysfunctional. Conversely, the values, beliefs, attitudes, and motivations of nonprofessional workers will limit the efficacy of attempts to cause them to behave somewhat as professionals. In Chapter 6 we described the differences between the values of urban and rural blue-collar workers. External controls would seem less appropriate for the supervision of rural, blue-collar workers who subscribe to the Protestant ethic than for those who do not, and may, in fact, prove deleterious. Similar to the dedication of the professional, belief in the Protestant ethic is a form of internal control than can regularize work-related behavior within limits.

Be that as it may, Hall makes the point that in the choice of professional (or craft) standards, as opposed to organizational rules or procedures, the former is neither morally superior nor more efficacious than the latter.[9]

> Many analyses of the relationships between professionals and their employing organizations seem to imply that the professional standards are somehow better than those of the organizations. Unless there are available specific criteria of what the organization and the professionals are trying to accomplish, such an assumption is unwarranted (Hall, 1972, pp. 191–92).

For example, it has been noted in the area of health care that professional standards of medicine learned in a teaching hospital may be inappropriate in private general practice or in a community clinic. Treating a patient as an object and looking primarily for esoteric physical diseases may fit a professional model, but standards which emphasize responsiveness to the patient's expressed (and often psychological) problems may prove more appropriate (Duff and Hollingshead, 1968).

Bureaucracy in the Service of Professional Autonomy

From a study of physicians employed by three organizations that were, to varying degrees, bureaucratized, Engel (1969) found that bureaucracy was in some ways beneficial to professional autonomy. She studied physicians in solo and small group practices in which the bureaucratic elements of hierarchy, rules, and regulations were absent. In addition, she studied other physicians in moderately as well as highly bureaucratic organizations. The moderately bureaucratic setting was a privately owned, closed-panel medical organization. The highly bureaucratic organization was a governmental medical facility.

Engel examined professional autonomy with regard to innovation, individual responsibility, and communication as these affected clinical practice and research activities, the two major tasks of these bureaucracies. Physicians were asked whether they were able to alter a treatment

---

[9] For example, one must ask whether professionals, who ostensibly provide the means for solving organizational problems, actually employ an objective technology. In some instances, the prerogatives claimed by professionals serve vested interests rather than technological requirements. Freidson (1970) suggests that physicians sometimes refuse to explain their practices to patients in order to protect their monopoly on specialized knowledge.

procedure that was within their area of medical specialization, whether they could discharge a patient when they felt his or her treatment was completed, and whether they had access to all essential information concerning the patient. In the area of research, questions included matters of freedom to instigate research projects, the ability to determine the goals of research, and the extent to which new research techniques were discussed and evaluated by the physicians.

A comparison of the degrees of professional autonomy reported by physicians in the three different kinds of settings showed that autonomy was generally highest in the moderately bureaucratic organization and approximately equal in the nonbureaucratic and highly bureaucratic settings. Interestingly, this overall finding, which Engel expected and which will be explained below, did not hold for both clinical practice and research activities when examined separately. The highest degree of professional autonomy in research activities was found in the highly bureaucratic, government-owned facility. Examination of the data showed that very few rules were imposed on research activity by this organization. The bulk of the rules and regulations applied to clinical practice.

Engel explains the finding that high professional autonomy occurs in a moderately bureaucratic (as opposed to a nonbureaucratic or highly bureaucratic) setting by noting that bureaucracy can support and facilitate attainment of the professionals' goals. She suggests that autonomy is becoming less relevant to many professions. As the wealth of knowledge and professional specialization increase, so will interdependence among professionals, technicians, and other nonprofessionals. For example, many kinds of medical care cannot be obtained from physicians in solo or small group practice, but require the services of a large clinic or hospital where a variety of medical specialties, technical, and paramedical services are employed and where the appropriate supplies, equipment, and skills to operate equipment are available. In other words, large organizations can mobilize considerable resources for the professional by means of bureaucratic structures. While hierarchies of authority, rules, regulations, and the consequent requirement of organizational loyalty may have detrimental effects, these do not necessarily outweigh the advantage of being able to coordinate resources.

Matching Organizational Requirements with Professional Needs

In a study of 125 teachers, researchers, and administrative personnel employed by a small liberal arts college, Gouldner (1958) identified two major role orientations—*cosmopolitans* and *locals*. The cosmopolitan staff, as compared to the local staff, placed higher emphasis on the value of research as a source of job satisfaction, were more likely to feel that there were relatively few people in the college with whom they could share research interests, had more education, published more, were less loyal to the organization, were more likely to gain intellectual stimulation from outside sources, were less happy with their salaries, and were less rule oriented. In short, the cosmopolitan staff had standards derived from the profession, from outside the organization. Employees with local orientations identified more with the institution and its goals and regulations than did cosmopolitans.

There is some evidence that institutional loyalty and commitment to professional standards can be compatible in certain kinds of organizations (Thornton, 1970). Using a sample of nearly 400 teachers from eight Florida junior colleges, Thornton identified faculty members as cosmopolitans and locals.

A small negative correlation was found between the organizational and professional orientations; that is, if a teacher viewed external (organizational) control of teaching activities as desirable, he tended not to have a professional orientation. However, the incompatibility of these two orientations varied, for in some organizations individuals could accept external structuring and also display high professional commitment. This was true in organizations which gave special emphasis to: (1) professional performance criteria (e.g., recognizing research contributions in performance appraisals); (2) professional autonomy (e.g., using expertise as a basis for authority over students); and (3) professional supervision (e.g., using only professionally qualified staff to supervise other professionals). Apparently, organizations which attempt to structure the work of professionals need not confront them with a choice between organizational and professional commitment. As standards, regulations, and criteria within a bureaucracy approach and exemplify the norms and values of the professionals it employs, the two commitments will become congruent.

Having noted this, we must take a caution from Engel's study. There is a limit to the extent that professional organizations can be bureaucratized successfully. A relatively weak profession may permit professional and organizational congruence to be achieved by the domination of bureaucratic requirements over most of the professionals' activities. An alternative to this state of affairs is a relatively weak organizational structure that permits congruence to be achieved via domination by the profession. Such appears to have been the case in the studies of scientific laboratories reported by Miller (1967). Conflict was found between scientists and engineers, on the one hand, and the administrative hierarchy, on the other, when the former were located in departments that were part of the larger organization. Laboratories that were more or less autonomous evidenced a lack of conflict between professional and administrative staff.

Unprogrammed Coordination

A plausible explanation of Miller's finding is contained in Perrow's taxonomy of technological processes (see Chapter 4). Rules, regulations, procedures, programs, and the like are appropriate for tasks that have analyzable solutions and that vary within reasonable limits. All work roles contain tasks having these characteristics but some roles, such as those found in the professions, contain fewer than others. In the professional organization, the usefulness of bureaucracy is limited by the extent to which problems can only be solved using judgment or constructs.

However, the organization must be coordinated even in instances where planning, rules, procedures, and the like are inappropriate. In such cases unprogrammed coordination occurs. The importance of unprogrammed coordination in complex organizations is demonstrated by a study of ten Michigan community general hospitals by Georgopoulos and Mann (1962). A major aim of the study was to ascertain whether differences in the quality of patient care were associated with differences in the adequacy of coordination.

The study revealed that both programmed and unprogrammed coordination were related to the quality of patient care delivered, but that unprogrammed coordination was the more important of the two. As one might expect, unprogrammed coordination has many of the attributes discussed under informal organizations (Chapter 3) and organizational roles (Chapter 9). Georgopoulos and Mann refer to these attributes as "sharedness of expectations," "complementarity of expectations," and "cooperation."

THE LOCATION OF CONTROL IN ORGANIZATION DESIGN

Between Bureaucratic and Professional Organizations

There seem to be two basic design principles for adaptive systems such as organizations (Emery, 1974). These systems must contain redundancy either in the form of easily replaceable parts or in the form of parts that contain redundant functions. In the former case, one may design an organization to accommodate workers who perform very simple tasks and who may be replaced with a minimum of difficulty (e.g., assembly-line workers). In contrast, the design strategy of building potentially redundant functions into the parts is exemplified by professionalism, where, for instance, all attorneys are assumed to possess the same basic skills.

Following this logic, one will find resolution of the "rational-bureau-cratic—organic-open" system dilemma. To design adaptiveness into the system while avoiding sacrifices of operating efficiency and the lengthy process of professional education (as well as the possible scarcity of requisite intelligence, skill, and interest in the general population), Emery suggests the use of autonomous work groups such as those designed by the Tavistock Institute (Chapter 4). These seem to fall between the two different forms of organization (see Figure 11–3).

The groups consisted of individuals who were relatively similar in terms of status and skills—who, consequently, communicated freely and interchanged work roles as the job required. Viewed as a whole, the groups operated somewhat as professionals do, trying out different techniques and approaches to problems and being flexible as the need arose. In this regard, our discussion of sales representatives engaged in helping their colleagues deal with sales problems may be recalled (Chapter 3).

Rather than being completely autonomous on the one hand or directed by external, organizational controls on the other, the individual is controlled by the group of which he or she is a member. In this form of organization, participation may be full within the group, but it is bounded by existing external rules and policies which leave the individual something less than complete autonomy.

Location of Control as a Function of Information Processing Requirements

We have been careful thus far not to take an inflexible position regarding the "optimal" location of control, for this will vary. We shall now review a scheme for appropriately changing the locus in organizations as problem complexity changes.

Using a sample of 16 health and welfare agencies, Hage and Aiken (1969) studied relationships among centralization and formalization (as they are discussed above), task complexity (as measured by the

FIGURE 11–3
Forms of Organization and Individual Control and Participation

Type	*Bureaucratic*	*Group*	*Professional*
Locus of control of the individual	External (plans, schedules, rules, etc.)	Group (group norms, plans, rules, etc.)	Internal (individuals, professional standards, etc.)
Degree of participation by the individual	Low (centralized)	Bounded (varying degrees of participation depending on organizationally prescribed limits)	High (decentralized)

degree of professional training required of employees), and routineness of technology. They found that the more routine the technology, the greater the tendency toward centralized decision making and policy formulation, codified rules manuals, and job descriptions. Hage and Aiken also found that the more routine the technology, the less the average amount of professional training required of employees.

A related point comes from an analysis by Galbraith (1973). Building on Thompson's theory of organizations (1967) and a number of studies which examine predictability of organizational tasks, Galbraith concludes that task predictability is a primary determinant of organizational structure.[10] As tasks become more unpredictable, the amount of information that must be processed increases; for example, individuals engaged in uncertain tasks must communicate frequently in order to make the mutual adjustments that feedback from the task suggests.

> [The basic proposition is that] . . . the greater the uncertainty of the task, the greater the amount of information that has to be processed between decision makers during its execution. If the task is well understood prior to performing it, much of the activity can be preplanned. If it is not understood, then during the actual execution of the task more knowledge is acquired which leads to changes in resource allocations, schedules, and priorities. All these changes require information processing *during* task performance. Therefore, *the greater the task uncertainty, the greater the amount of information that must be processed among decision makers during task execution in order to achieve a given level of performance* (Galbraith, 1973, p. 4).

The amount of information processing required by task performance depends on three basic factors. The first is *task uncertainty* which arises because programs and routines for accomplishing the task are unavailable and because of the variability of the task itself (see Chapter 4). Second, information processing requirements increase with the *number of elements* involved in the decision-making process, as these are determined by (*a*) the size of the organization, (*b*) the complexity or diversity of occupations involved in decision making, and (*c*) the number of products or services produced. The third factor is *interdependence* among elements in the decision-making process. Changes in task performance in one department require changes in the work of other interdependent departments, and vice versa. For example, one can contrast a basic research laboratory in which scientists have autonomy to pursue different kinds of independent projects with a project development team. The latter is typified by the design of an aircraft, where armament development may run into difficulties, leading to increased weight. This will change the power requirements of the engine and perhaps the wing configuration, which will change still other elements such as control surfaces. These changes, in turn, may alter the constraints on armament.

---

[10] E.g., Burns and Stalker (1961), Woodward (1965), and Harvey (1968).

Mechanisms for Developing Information Processing Capacity

Galbraith (1973) provides a taxonomy of organization design strategies that seeks to balance information processing capacity with the requirements of the organization's tasks. The taxonomy answers the question: How does a large, functionally structured organization cope with information processing requirements that increase in response to increases in task uncertainty, interdependence, and the number of subunits engaged in task accomplishment?

The simplest way to coordinate interdependent departments is to (1) specify requisite actions in advance with plans, rules, and programs. The need for communication among departments will be reduced to the extent that planning adequately delineates each department's function. However, when the degree of problem complexity increases beyond the point where planning can cope with all contingencies, the organization will (2) resort to the use of its hierarchy of authority. Exceptions that cannot be planned for are referred to higher levels of management for resolution. Such *management by exception* is feasible so long as the exceptions are not of a magnitude that overloads the hierarchy with communications and decision making. When overload does occur, the organization generally turns to coordination that is achieved by (3) specifying goals and outputs (as opposed to planning specific activities that are means to these ends). At any one level of management, planning is concerned with the objectives of that level and not with specific means. The decentralization that is achieved by granting discretion in the choice of means to lower levels of the organization reduces the amount of information processed at higher levels. In addition, higher levels can differentiate the goals they establish for lower levels in order to reduce the interdependence of the latter. Galbraith provides the following example:

> An example of the way goals are used can be demonstrated by considering the design group responsible for an aircraft wing structure. The group's interdependence with other design groups is handled by technical specifications elaborating the points of attachment, forces transmitted at these points, centers of gravity, etc. The group also have a set of targets (not to be exceeded) for weight, design man-hours to be used, and a completion date. They are given minimum stress specifications below which they cannot design. The group then design the structures and assemblies which combine to form the wing. They need not communicate with any other design group on work-related matters if they and the interdependent groups are able to operate within the planned targets (1972, p. 58).

Increasing Capacity or Reducing Processing Requirements: A Dilemma

In the event that the three alternatives described above prove inadequate to the task of managing uncertainties, an additional series of

FIGURE 11–4
Organization Design Strategies

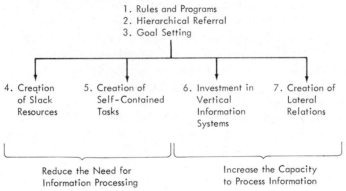

Source: Jay Galbraith, *Designing Complex Organizations*, 1973, Addison-Wesley, Reading, Mass.

strategies can be employed. According to Figure 11–4, management can create either (4) slack resources and (5) self-contained organizational units in an attempt to reduce the need for information processing or develop (6) vertical and (7) lateral systems to increase information processing capacity. Each strategy has inherent costs and advantages.

Organizational slack (4) can be created by delaying target or completion dates so that exceptions can be managed without straining the capacity of the organization, by relaxing budget and technical specifications to reduce the interdependence of various design groups, and by a number of similar tactics. The costs of organizational slack are measured in delayed delivery dates, backlogs of orders, inventory carrying costs, reduced standards of performance, and the like.

A second method of reducing task-required information processing is to modify the authority structure to allow greater *self-containment* (5) of subunits involved in the task. Interdependence is reduced by dividing the task into several smaller problems which are addressed by units having their own facilities and resources. An example is reorganization from a centralized functional structure to project management (see Chapter 2). In this example, information processing requirements are reduced by the delegation of decision-making authority to levels at which required information exists.

The costs of self-containment include the duplication of effort and resources that are inevitable when separate projects require separate personnel and equipment. Hence, economies of scale are reduced. In addition, project managers necessarily make decisions within all of the functional areas as they pertain to the project. Consequently, they must be generalists. Because of this the organization foregoes the depth of expertise enjoyed by specialists.

The development of what Galbraith calls *vertical information systems* (6) enables the organization to increase its information processing capacity to match the requirements of the tasks it encounters. Essentially, these systems provide reduced planning cycles. Once a plan is made, exceptions occur as the environment changes or as inadequacies in the plan, itself, are discovered. The older the plan becomes, the more exceptions arise. At some point, it will be easier for management to revise the original plan than to deal with increasing numbers of exceptions. Alternatively, by reducing the planning cycle (e.g., by planning monthly rather than quarterly) management will avoid many of the exceptions with which it would be faced otherwise. The costs associated with improving the vertical information system include increased numbers of staff specialists on the organization's payroll who are employed in the planning process as well as, perhaps, computers and various sophisticated peripheral data processing devices.

The capacity to process information can also be increased through the creation and improvement of *lateral relationships* (7). The simplest of these is direct contact between peers. Rather than send exceptions up the hierarchy for coordination by a superior, the manager can contact the unit with which he is interdependent and deal with the exception directly. This is similar to Likert's concept of linking pins discussed in Chapter 3. Obviously, one cost of this approach is the increased number of time-consuming interpersonal relationships that must be developed among colleagues. Somewhat more complicated is the creation of liaisons similar to those discussed in Chapter 10. These individuals are able to relieve management of some of the burden of coordination.

Another approach is the creation of task forces—temporary groups of full- or part-time members who serve as surrogates for higher levels of management. Task forces may achieve permanent status in the organization when the problems to which they are addressed are complex and enduring; for example, a functionally organized firm may designate representatives from each function to deal with coordination problems that arise with respect to a particular product.

It should be evident that we are closing the loop, so to speak. Galbraith's suggestions parallel those of Ansoff and Brandenburg (1971) presented in Chapter 2. Ansoff and Brandenburg address four criteria of organizational performance: (1) steady state efficiency, (2) operating responsiveness, (3) strategic responsiveness, and (4) structural responsiveness. Galbraith addresses the problem of managing increasing information and decision flows. One approach seems to verify the other. This is most evident in Galbraith's recommendation that extreme information processing requirements be met with a matrix form of organization. Here, the trade-off is strategic responsiveness gained at the expense of steady state efficiency and operating responsiveness.

From External to Internal Control

One way to interpret Galbraith's taxonomy is to observe the progression from external controls (rules, plans, and so on that are advocated for the coordination of relatively simple tasks) to increasingly internalized controls that are recommended for tasks of increasing complexity. Goal-setting provides subordinates with the autonomy to select their own means. Increasing slack resources increases lateral autonomy in the organization by decreasing interdependence between departments. The creation of self-contained tasks serves much the same purpose. Reducing the planning cycle causes the operating unit to become more responsive to feedback, since it is feedback in its various forms that suggests modifications to the plan. Finally, the establishment of lateral relationships places the responsibility for coordination of interdependencies in the departments, themselves, instead of with higher levels of management. This appears to pave the way for unprogrammed coordination as well as colleagual cooperation.

Implicit in Galbraith's taxonomy is the notion that internal control is increased as autonomy is expanded; for instance, commitment to a goal serves to control the choice and employment of means. The taxonomy also assumes that the individuals and groups to whom autonomy is extended are competent to exercise their discretion in the organization's interest. We will digress for a moment to review a management technique that makes one portion of the model (goal-setting) operational.

Management by Objectives

Management by objectives (MBO) can be traced to Peter Drucker's *The Practice of Management,* written in 1954. Drucker advises managers to work toward clear objectives which reflect and support those of their immediate superiors. Furthermore, he suggests that they work with their immediate superiors in establishing higher level objectives, enabling each manager to know and understand the goals of the organization and his superior as they are related to his own performance. With clearly defined objectives, the manager will be in a position to control his own performance and, thereby, able to achieve higher levels of motivation.

George Odiorne (1965) termed this philosophy "management by objectives" and provided systematic means for its implementation. His work emphasizes making objectives operational and specifying quantitative measures of progress toward their attainment. Working in pairs, each manager meets with each of his subordinates to agree on both the subordinate's objectives in the next time period and the means by which his progress will be evaluated at the end of the period in question. Used properly, MBO will include every manager, from the chief executive officer to the last line supervisor, in a dyad of this sort. Furthermore, it is each manager's responsibility under this system to help his subordinates meet their objectives.

At first glance, this appears the epitome of the rational view of organizations. In practice, MBO is compatible with the systems view as well. Goals other than those of the formal organization are included in the objective-setting process; for example, the subordinate and his or her boss may develop a program of objectives intended to result in the former's promotion within the organization. Thus, ways of meeting individual and system needs can be made congruent with the pursuit of organizational goals.

Research shows that specific goal-setting, knowledge of results, and participation enhance performance when goals are established at the proper level of difficulty, reasonable time limits are set, and sufficient energy is available for their attainment (Carroll and Tosi, 1973). Other studies (e.g., Carroll and Tosi, 1973; Meyer, Kay, and French, 1965; Raia, 1966), generally indicate that MBO results in improved planning, control, and motivation.

However, no system is without its faults. Raia (1966) reports managers' dissatisfactions with the paper work required by MBO and with the apparent overemphasis of quantitative measures. Some managers report attempts to "beat the system" by "fudging" reports. Other studies indicate that the benefits of MBO may deteriorate over time (Ivancevich, 1972). Rather than panaceas, techniques of this sort are remedies for organizational problems that occur in specific, limited circumstances. Abuses, failures, and unmet expectations are to be anticipated when they are applied "across the board."

Positive Reinforcement

In concluding this chapter, we shall comment briefly on one of the most unusual attempts to achieve control found in recent history of organizations—one that will add fuel to the debate over the "superiority" of internal versus external controls. In *Beyond Freedom and Dignity*, Skinner (1971) argues that freedom exists only as the "feeling of freedom." We are all controlled, but feel free when pursuing our own valued ends. We feel controlled (the absence of freedom) when avoiding punishment. In either event, we behave as we have learned (been conditioned) to behave. The professional's internal control was external at one point. The scholar was not born loving truth, but learned, or was taught to, as he became a scholar. Skinner states this more eloquently in his novel *Walden Two:* "A *laissez-faire* philosophy which trusts to the inherent goodness and wisdom of the common man is incompatible with the observed fact that men are made good or bad and wise or foolish by the environment in which they grow" (1970, p. 273).

Internal control is neither good nor bad. Means, such as discipline, and the ends they serve are to be evaluated in terms of the effects they produce ultimately. Animals can be conditioned to behave according to the desires of their trainers. At first, the desired behaviors are rewarded to establish consequences that are contingent upon their repetition. As the desired behaviors are repeated, the rewards are reduced and eventually eliminated as the learned behavior becomes "internalized."

Emery Air Freight is presently attempting to improve performance by applying this type of conditioning process to its work force (American Management Association, 1973). The "positive reinforcement program," as it is called, starts with an audit of performance to determine how well employees are doing. Where performance is found to warrant improvement, work standards are established by superiors. Following this, employees are required to maintain continuous records of their own performance in relation to the standards. These are submitted to superiors who recognize and praise specific improved performances and avoid censuring lesser efforts.

In theory, reinforcement comes in three stages. First, the superior gives frequent positive reinforcement based on the continuous feedback data he receives from subordinates, thus "shaping" their behavior. Later, reinforcement is given infrequently on an unpredictable schedule. Finally, supervisory reinforcement is reduced to a negligible level and feedback in the form of task accomplishment takes over as the major source of reward for the worker.

In practice, Emery has yet to achieve the stage envisioned where "natural" reinforcers replace those that are contrived. Supervisors have reduced the amount of recognition they give, but they continue to receive progress reports from their subordinates. Such reporting seems necessary to prevent decreases in productivity. It is argued that keeping progress reports and submitting them to supervisors augments the "natural" reinforcers—the satisfaction of having completed an assignment or of having given a fair day's work for a fair day's pay. This argument seems rather transparent, however, since submitting forms to supervisors implies evaluation and implicit disapprobation in the case of unfavorable reports.

Be that as it may, Emery Air Freight's positive reinforcement program seems to be quite successful so far. For instance, customer service standards have been 95 percent achieved, as opposed to 35 percent prior to the experiment. Through improvements such as this, the firm apparently has saved over $3 million in a three-year period (American Management Association, 1973).

There is something chilling and Orwellian about the use of behavior modification, perhaps because it appears overly manipulative. It could be argued that this entire book is about manipulation, but we are convinced that other means of control preserve more of the employee's options. For example, the participants in a job enrichment scheme or other form of reorganization are probably aware of their reactions to changes in the organization and are able to exercise whatever power they enjoy to comply with or resist them. This is not the case in behavior modification which generates forces the employee is not likely to understand. It may be that this approach is tainted unfairly by its origins.

Skinnerian systems of behavior modification were developed using subjects who had little control over their behavior. They were deviants who either lacked self-control or were deprived of control by the institutions to which they were committed. It would seem that behavior modification is suited to those whose control is weak and who cannot join coalitions which magnify their limited powers. It makes the assumption that the interests and values of the "behavior shaper" and the subject are congruent when such an assumption cannot be taken for granted. These kinds of reservations must be weighed against the fact that the technique does seem to work with normal subjects in industrial settings, who do not seem to have suffered any loss of moral responsibility as a result of their conditioning. It may be that we are all conditioned as Skinner suggests. Even the professional may be similar to the harem eunuch who is . . . "competent to do all but that which he should not do, and thus his loyalty is unquestioned" (Perrow, 1972, p. 17).

DISCUSSION QUESTIONS

1. Using the material studied to date, construct a plausible explanation of the failure of the Non-linear Systems experiment (Chapters 3 and 6).
2. Investigate the controls applied to college seniors in their major field and doctoral candidates writing dissertations. What major differences are apparent? How do you account for these differences?
3. Students are required to earn 120 semester hours credit in order to receive an undergraduate degree at many colleges. The student with 119½ hours credit cannot graduate. Where does the number 120 come from? What justifies this rule? What logic might produce a better rule? Can the logic used to determine a better rule be operationalized?
4. List some of the obvious internal and external controls that apply in your college or university? How were the external controls developed? How did you come to internalize the internal controls? To what extent will similar observations be valid about business firms? Hospitals? Governmental agencies?

REFERENCES

American Management Association. At Emery Air Freight: positive reinforcement boosts performance. *Organizational Dynamics*, 1973, 2, 3, 41–50.

Ansoff, H. I., and Brandenburg, R. G. A language for organizational design, Parts I and II. *Management Science*, 1971, B705–B731.

Blau, Peter M. *Bureaucracy in modern society.* New York: Random House, 1956.

Blau, Peter, Heyderbrand, Wolf F., and Stauffer, Robert. The structure of small bureaucracies. *American Sociological Review*, 1966, *31*, 179–91.

Blau, Peter M., and Meyer, Marshall. *Bureaucracy in modern society.* 2d ed. New York: Random House, 1971.

Burns, Tom, and Stalker, G. M. *The management of innovation.* London: Tavistock, 1961.

Carroll, Stephen J., and Tosi, Henry L. *Management by objectives: application and research.* New York: Macmillan, 1973.

Child, John. Organization structure and strategies of control: a replication of the Aston study. *Administrative Science Quarterly*, 1972, *17*, 163–77.

Child, John. Predicting and understanding organization structure. *Administrative Science Quarterly*, 1973, *18*, 168–85.

Dewey, John. *How we think.* Boston: D. C. Heath, 1910.

Drucker, Peter. *The practice of management.* New York: Harper & Bros., 1954.

Duff, Raymond S., and Hollingshead, August B. *Sickness and society.* New York: Harper & Row, 1968.

Emery, Fred E. Bureaucracy and beyond. *Organizational Dynamics*, 1974, *2*, 3–13.

Engel, Gloria V. The effect of bureaucracy on the professional autonomy of the physician. *Journal of Health and Social Behavior*, 1969, *10*, 30–41.

Filley, Alan C., and House, Robert J. *Managerial process and organizational behavior.* Glenview, Ill.: Scott, Foresman, 1969.

Freidson, Eliot. *Professional dominance: the social structure of medical care.* New York: Atherton, 1970.

Galbraith, Jay R. Organization design: an information processing view. In J. W. Lorsch and P. R. Lawrence (Eds.), *Organizational planning: cases and concepts.* Homewood, Ill.: Dorsey, 1972. Pp. 49–74.

Galbraith, Jay R. *Designing complex organizations.* Reading, Mass.: Addison-Wesley, 1973.

Georgopoulos, Basil S., and Mann, Floyd C. *The community general hospital.* New York: Macmillan, 1962.

Gouldner, Alvin W. *Patterns of industrial bureaucracy.* Glencoe, Ill.: Free Press, 1954.

Gouldner, Alvin W. Cosmopolitans and locals: toward an analysis of latent social roles. II. *Administrative Science Quarterly*, 1958, *2*, 444–80.

Hage, Jerald, and Aiken, Michael. Routine technology, social structure, and organizational goals. *Administrative Science Quarterly*, 1969, *14*, 366–77.

Hall, Richard H. Professionalization and bureaucratization. *American Sociological Review*, 1968, *33*, 92–104.

Hall, Richard H. *Organizations: structure and processes.* Englewood Cliffs, N.J.: Prentice-Hall, 1972.

Harvey, Edward. Technology and the structure of organizations. *American Sociological Review*, 1968, *33*, 247–59.

Hellriegel, Don, and Slocum, John W., Jr. *Management: a contingency approach.* Reading, Mass.: Addison-Wesley, 1974.

Ivancevich, John M. A longitudinal assessment of management by objectives. *Administrative Science Quarterly*, 1972, *17*, 126–38.

Kast, Fremont E., and Rosenzweig, James E. *Organization and management: a systems approach.* 2d ed. New York: McGraw-Hill, 1974.

Khandwalla, Pradip M. Mass output orientation of operations technology and organizational structure. *Administrative Science Quarterly,* 1974, *19,* 74–97.

Mansfield, Roger. Bureaucracy and centralization: an examination of organizational structure. *Administrative Science Quarterly,* 1973, *18,* 477–88.

Meyer, H. H., Kay, E., and French, J. R. P. Split roles in performance appraisal. *Harvard Business Review,* 1965, *43* (1), 123–29.

Miller, George A. Professionals in bureaucracy, alienation among industrial scientists and engineers. *American Sociological Review,* 1967, *32,* 755–68.

Odiorne, George S. *Management by objectives: a system of managerial leadership.* New York: Pitman, 1965.

Parsons, Talcott (Ed.). *Max Weber, the theory of social and economic organization.* (trans. A. Henderson and T. Parsons). New York: Free Press, 1947.

Perrow, Charles. *Complex organizations: a critical essay.* Glenview, Ill.: Scott, Foresman and Company, 1972.

Pondy, Louis R. Organizational conflict: concepts and models. *Administrative Science Quarterly,* 1967, *12,* 296–320.

Pugh, D. S., Hickson, D. J., Hinings, C. R., and Turner, C. Dimensions of organization structure. *Administrative Science Quarterly,* 1968, *13,* 65–105.

Pugh, D. S., Hickson, D. J., Hinings, C. R., and Turner, C. The context of organization structures. *Administrative Science Quarterly,* 1969, *14,* 91–114.

Raia, Anthony P. A second look at goals and controls. *California Management Review,* 1966, *8* (4), 49–58.

Reimann, Bernard C. On the dimensions of bureaucratic structure: an empirical reappraisal. *Administrative Science Quarterly,* 1973, *18,* 462–76.

Skinner, B. F. *Walden two.* Toronto: Macmillan, 1970.

Skinner, B. F. *Beyond freedom and dignity.* New York: Knopf, 1971.

Steiner, George A. *Top management planning.* New York: Macmillan, 1969.

Thompson, James D. *Organizations in action.* New York: McGraw-Hill, 1967.

Thornton, Russell. Organizational involvement and commitment to organization and profession. *Administrative Science Quarterly,* 1970, *15,* 417–26.

Woodward, John. *Industrial organization: theory and practice.* London: Oxford University Press, 1965.

12

Leadership

INTRODUCTION

Many contemporary, scientific observations of social organizations can also be found in the rich, archaic literature handed down to us throughout history. This is neither surprising nor a condemnation of the contemporary behavioral sciences. Sensitive and reasoned men and women throughout the ages have reflected upon the affairs of society and generalized from their experiences.

Leadership has posed questions for reflective minds throughout recorded history. Let us, then, look to history for a moment and consider the advice provided would-be leaders by the sage, but oft-maligned, Machiavelli in his book *The Prince* (1952, pp. 48–50):

> I say then that in new dominions, where there is a new prince, it is more or less easy to hold them, according to the greater or lesser ability of him who acquires them. And as the fact of a private individual becoming a prince presupposes either great ability or good fortune, it would appear that either of these things would in part mitigate many difficulties. Nevertheless those who have been less beholden to good fortune have maintained themselves best. The matter is also facilitated by the prince being obliged to reside personally in his territory, having no others. But to come to those who have become princes through their own merits and not by fortune, I regard as the greatest, Moses, Cyrus, Romulus, Theseus, and their like. And although one should not speak of Moses, he having merely carried out what was ordered him by God, still he deserves admiration, if only for that grace which made him worthy to speak with God. But regarding Cyrus and others who have acquired or founded kingdoms, they will all be found worthy of admiration; and if their particular actions and methods are examined they will not appear very different from those of Moses, although he had so great a Master. And in examining their life and deeds it will be seen that they owed nothing to fortune but the opportunity which gave them matter to be shaped into what form they thought fit; and without that opportunity their powers would have been wasted, and without their powers the opportunity would have come in vain.
>
> It was thus necessary that Moses should find the people of Israel slaves in Egypt and oppressed by the Egyptians, so that they were disposed to follow him in order to escape from their servitude. It was necessary that

Romulus should be unable to remain in Alba, and should have been exposed at his birth, in order that he might become King of Rome and founder of that nation. It was necessary that Cyrus should find the Persians discontented with the empire of the Medes, and the Medes weak and effeminate through long peace. Theseus could not have shown his abilities if he had not found the Athenians dispersed. These opportunities, therefore, gave these men their chance, and their own great qualities enabled them to profit by them, so as to ennoble their country and augment its fortunes.

Those who by the exercise of abilities such as these become princes, obtain their dominions with difficulty but retain them easily, and the difficulties which they have in acquiring their dominions arise in part from the new rules and regulations that they have to introduce in order to establish their position securely. It must be considered that there is nothing more difficult to carry out, nor more doubtful of success, nor more dangerous to handle, than to initiate a new order of things. For the reformer has enemies in all those who profit by the old order, and only lukewarm defenders in all those who would profit by the new order, this lukewarmness arising partly from fear of their adversaries, who have the laws in their favour; and partly from the incredulity of mankind, who do not truly believe in anything new until they have had actual experience of it. Thus it arises that on every opportunity for attacking the reformer, his opponents do so with the zeal of partisans, the others only defend him half-heartedly, so that between them he runs great danger. It is necessary, however, in order to investigate thoroughly this question, to examine whether these innovators are independent, or whether they depend upon others, that is to say, whether in order to carry out their designs they have to entreat or are able to compel. In the first case they invariably succeed ill, and accomplish nothing; but when they can depend on their own strength and are able to use force, they rarely fail. Thus it comes about that all armed prophets have conquered and unarmed ones failed; for besides what has been already said, the character of peoples varies, and it is easy to persuade them of a thing, but difficult to keep them in that persuasion. And so it is necessary to order things so that when they no longer believe, they can be made to believe by force.

Chapter Guide

Machiavelli observes that a prince's success in ruling new dominions is contingent upon both his ability to wield power effectively and the existence of an opportunistic situation. In Chapter 5 (Figure 5–3), we considered problems that arise when organizational members disagree on both the nature of the goals to which they should aspire and the means which will attain any of the goals in question.

1. What parallels exist in these two observations?
2. From what source(s) does a contemporary prince (executive) derive his powers?
3. Do you think that a man as brilliant as Machiavelli contradicted himself in suggesting that the followers who no longer believe ". . . can be made to believe by force"?

4. What forces are brought to bear on deviant members of democratic, participative organizations?

LEADER BEHAVIOR AND GROUP PERFORMANCE

Preliminary Definitions of Leadership

Leadership, as we use the term, refers to behavior (undertaken within the context of an organization) that influences the ways in which other organizational members behave. Leadership is usually thought of in terms of charisma, but we argue that a variety of behaviors, including authoritarianism, are appropriately considered under this rubric. As we shall discover, the efficacy of one managerial style as opposed to another varies according to the characteristics of the situation in which it is enacted.

Leadership can be defined to include the sources of influence that are "built into" a position in an organization's hierarchy. These include organizationally sanctioned rewards and punishments, authority, as well as referent and expert power (Katz and Kahn, 1966). However, some individuals seem to enjoy influence that exists over and above that provided by their role in the organization. We touched upon this notion in Chapter 5 by suggesting that individuals differ according to the skills they bring to bear on problems at various times.

While leadership may include the sources of power that are built into jobs, we will focus our attention on the "essence of leadership," i.e., those incremental sources of power that go beyond routine organizational functioning—that tap bases of power in excess of those organizationally decreed. Hall (1972) envisages leadership as the abilities to persuade other individuals and to be innovative in decision making. Obviously, if stewardship over the mechanical-functioning, routine activities in an organization is all that is required of a supervisor, precedents and existing structures will obviate the supervisor's need to innovate. As we shall see, this is sometimes the case. On the other hand, more ambiguous and less structured work situations necessitate defining novel problems, selecting appropriate solutions, and coordinating the activities of those responsible for enacting solutions. In this light, Bavelas (1960) defines leadership acts as those which help a group meet its objectives. Of particular importance among these activities are making choices and helping others to do so; especially in situations that help the group reach a desired state. In the most general terms, this sort of leadership consists of "uncertainty reduction," which entails making the kinds of choices that permit the organization to proceed toward its objectives despite various kinds of internal and external perturbations.

Some of the issues raised by the view of leadership sketched out here include:

1. The particular behaviors in which leaders typically engage.
2. The importance of personality, personal attributes, and skills in leadership situations.
3. The kinds of situations in which leaders (and particular leadership styles) are more or less effective.
4. The distribution of leadership functions throughout the organization and the effects of various distributions on organizational performance.
5. The special character of leadership in top management.

Two Factors in Leadership

In Chapter 6 we broached the subject of management style in terms of Blake and Mouton's (1970) managerial grid. The two dimensions postulated by the grid (concern for production and concern for people) are paralleled by findings from other studies of small group leaders, foremen, and other kinds of supervisors. One of these studies (Fleishman and Harris, 1962) examines the effects of two factors in leadership behavior which are called *consideration* and *initiating structure*. Consideration refers to behavior that increases mutual trust, respect, warmth, and rapport between the leader and his group. More than superficial friendliness, consideration emphasizes concern for the needs of group members, participative decision making, and two-way communications.

Thus defined, the degrees of consideration exhibited by foremen were compared to the grievance and turnover rates of their subordinates. As illustrated by Figure 12–1, turnover rate and the rate at which subordinates expressed grievances were found to diminish as the amount of consideration demonstrated by their foremen increased. However, this observation appears to be valid only within limits, for beyond a certain point, increased consideration was not found to affect grievance or turnover rates materially.

The second variable studied, initiating structure, was defined to include the foreman's behavior in assigning tasks, planning, deciding how things should be done, and pushing for productivity. Similar to Blake and Mouton's dimension, concern for production, initiating structure embodies overt emphasis on the achievement of organizational goals. As in the case of consideration, the degree to which different foremen used initiating structure was plotted against the average rates of grievance and turnover of their subordinates.

Figure 12–2 shows that turnover and grievance rates varied directly with the degree to which structure was initiated by foremen. Furthermore, as was the case above, this observation holds under limited

FIGURE 12–1
Relationships between Grievance and Turnover Rates and Consideration

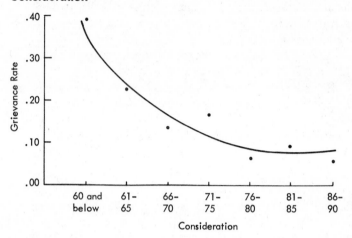

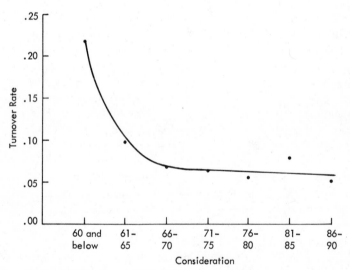

Source: Fleishman and Harris (1962, pp. 347–51).

conditions; beyond a certain point, decreases in initiating structure were not found to be accompanied by associated decreases in grievance or turnover rates.

When consideration and initiating structure were examined jointly (Figure 12–3), grievance rates were found to be highest for foremen

FIGURE 12–2
**Relationships between Grievance and Turnover Rates
and Initiating Structure**

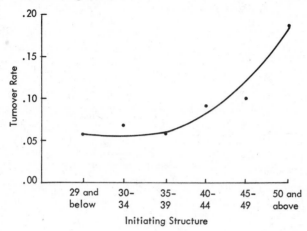

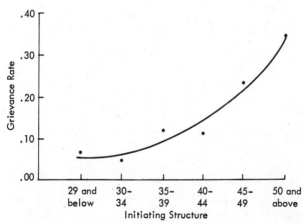

Source: Fleishman and Harris (1962, pp. 348–51).

FIGURE 12–3
The Combined Effects of Consideration
and Initiating Structure on Grievance
and Turnover Rates

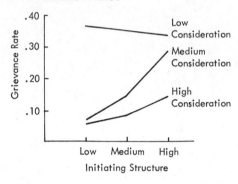

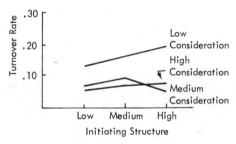

Source: Fleishman and Harris (1962, pp. 350–52).

low in consideration, regardless of whether they were ranked high or low on initiating structure. Similarly, supervisors ranked high on consideration produced low grievance rates despite differences in initiating structure. Foremen rated moderate in consideration and low on initiating structure produced relatively low grievance rates. However, for foremen rated moderately considerate, increases in initiating structure produced increases in grievance rates.

As was the case with grievances, it was found that foremen who were ranked relatively low on consideration experienced the highest employee turnover rates. Although the rate, in this case, varied directly with initiating structure, consideration seemed to be the overriding factor. Few differences in turnover rates were found to exist between foremen who were high and medium on consideration. Furthermore, meaningful differences were not found to accrue from changes in initiating structure exhibited by the latter two groups of foremen.

Other researchers have observed phenomena that appear similar to those described above: for example, Bales (1958) studied small discussion groups and found that influential group members (leaders) were rated relatively high on the dimensions of task ability and likability, which is to say that they were "task" leaders and "maintenance leaders." The leaders who performed task functions helped their groups to get on with their jobs. The maintenance leaders (who were sometimes the same individuals as the task leaders) appeared to be good at dealing with interpersonal tensions and conflicts and at helping to maintain individual satisfaction at levels that were high enough to ensure continued group functioning.

Initiating structure and consideration seem to be useful concepts for understanding some of the effects of different leader behaviors. We shall return to emphasize the importance of these factors, after reviewing some alternative approaches to leadership—including the leader trait approach and some more complex theories.

Leader Traits and Group Needs

Much of the early research on leadership focused on the personality characteristics and traits of leaders (Gibb, 1968). While some traits have been found more consistently among leaders than among others, the possession of these traits appears neither necessary nor sufficient to leadership. Dominance, intelligence, self-confidence, and empathy are often possessed by leaders, but they vary in importance according to the circumstances in which the leader finds himself; that is, one trait or another may be important depending on the goal sought by the group being led, the nature of the problems faced, the composition of the group, and so on.

A current view in the psychological literature is that leaders meet group needs. Furthermore, because different individuals may each contribute to fulfilling a particular group need, and because different needs may be met by different individuals, leadership is usually not confined to a single individual. It is useful to speak, rather, of "leadership functions" or of activities carried out by various individuals in order to facilitate the progress of the group and the fulfillment of its needs.

Four Theories of Leadership

A recent study (Mott, 1972) proposes four fairly general theories of leadership encompassing a number of specific investigations and particular findings. The first of these is Likert's System Four approach to management, which we have already discussed (Chapter 3). The three other theories to be discussed here are based on the work of Bowers and Seashore, Mann, and Katz and Kahn. Later in the chapter, we shall examine a still different and separate approach to leadership—that of Fiedler.

On the basis of an extensive review of leadership studies (including those of Fleishman and Harris [1962], Likert [1961], and others), Bowers and Seashore (1966) concluded that there are four basic dimensions of leadership: support, emphasis on goals, facilitation of interaction, and facilitation of work. *Support* is similar to "consideration" and to Likert's concept of supportive management. It is behavior that enhances someone else's feelings of personal worth and importance. We have already encountered *emphasis on goals* in Likert's System Four theory of management. This is the stimulation of enthusiasm for achieving high-performance levels. *Facilitation of interaction* involves encouraging group members to develop close, mutually satisfying relationships. Finally, *facilitation of work* is similar to Fleishman and Harris's dimension of initiating structure. It is behavior that promotes the attainment of goals through activities such as scheduling, planning, coordinating, and providing resources.

We have already proposed the view that requisite management skills and activities differ from one hierarchical level in the organization to another. The management of physical, human, and strategic resources receive different degrees of emphasis in lower, middle-, and top-management positions (see Chapter 6). Mann (1965) proposes a *skill mix* model of leadership that takes such differences into account. At lower organizational levels, *technical skills* (the ability to use pertinent knowledge, methods, techniques, and equipment in performing and directing work activities) are most important. Less important at lower levels are *human relations* skills (the ability to work effectively with people) and least important are *administrative skills* (the ability to plan, schedule work, make job assignments, monitor work flows, and coordinate work performed with the work of other units). Moving upward in the hierarchy, administrative skills increase in importance relative to the others. Human relations skills also increase in importance but, beyond middle management, they again become relatively less important. According to Mann's recent theorizing (Mott, 1972), a fourth requisite skill emerges at top-management levels—*institutional skill* (the ability to create and formulate policy, handle relationships with outside organizations, and manage the relationship of the organization's mission to the political, social, and economic environment).

A fourth theory of leadership, and one which is similar to Mann's in that it illustrates the appropriateness of different managerial behaviors at different levels of the organization, is the "three pattern" approach to leadership (Katz and Kahn, 1966). *Origination* (creating, changing, and eliminating structure), *interpolation* (supplementing and piecing out structure), and *administration* (using structure as it already exists) are management concerns of importance to top, middle, and lower levels in the hierarchy, respectively. Each of these three leadership patterns has both an affective and a cognitive component.[1]

The cognitive component of *origination* is found in the leader's "systematic perspective"—his awareness of the organization's relationship with its environment and of the interrelationships among subsystems within the organization—and in his ability to change or create new structures. The emotional component of *origination* is "charisma." This is the aura surrounding a leader that derives from his special gift for affecting individuals in an emotional way.

Interpolation, the managerial behavior thought to be appropriate at middle-management levels, has a "subsystem perspective" as its cognitive component. Middle managers need both an upward and downward orientation in order to implement policy directives emanating from above and to coordinate various interdependent subsystems. The middle manager must be a good problem solver and coordinator and be influential with both superiors and subordinates. The affective component of *interpolation* exists in the ability to integrate what sociologists have called "primary and secondary relationships." The manager must be able to establish warm human (primary) relations with employees and integrate them with the more impersonal (or secondary) organizational elements that exist outside of the primary work groups. He or she must integrate individual needs with organizational requirements.

The *administrative* pattern, which is appropriate at lower levels of management, has as its cognitive component the "technical knowledge" of a job and "knowledge of organizational roles." The affective component is "fairness" which enables rules to be applied equitably.

All four of these theories of leadership (Likert, Bowers and Seashore, Mann, and Katz and Kahn) were tested in a study of leadership effectiveness conducted in the Office of Administration at NASA headquarters in Washington (Butterfield, 1968; Mott, 1972). Twelve divisions of the Office of Administration (dealing with security standards, financial management, management information systems, personnel, transportation, and so on) and 28 branches within the divisions comprised the study population. Using a complex array of analytical techniques, Butterfield found that each of the theories had limited predictive power. Division effectiveness (measured according to Mott's questionnaire items described in Chapter 8) was generally predictable from the behavior of the division director, but branch (subunit) effectiveness could not be predicted from the behavior of heads of branches. It was not clear

---

[1] Note the similarity to the work of Bales (1958) wherein task and maintenance functions can be considered as, respectively, cognitive and affective in nature. Similar observations can be made about the dimensions of structure and consideration in the Fleishman and Harris (1962) study.

whether the criterion data used for branch-level analyses were improper, or whether the lack of findings was attributable to other causes.

Applying the skill mix theory at the division level, the best predictor of division effectiveness found was the degree to which human relations skills were utilized by division heads. Using the four-factor theory at this level, facilitation of work proved superior as a predictor to the other three. Application of the three-pattern theory demonstrated that integration and subsystem perspective correlated with effectiveness. Finally, of the components of System Four, supportive relationships was the best predictor. None of the four theories received complete validation in the study. Only some of the factors in a particular theory worked. Furthermore, taking all of the factors in a single theory simultaneously and comparing the theory in question to other theories so considered, none stood out as a superior predictor of effectiveness. Reviewing the variables that successfully predicted effectiveness, the familiar and simple *task* and *maintenance* factors account for most of the findings.

STRUCTURAL VARIABLES AND LEADER BEHAVIOR

Conditions and Intervening Variables in Leadership Processes

Comprehensive review of research undertaken to determine the roles that the two above-mentioned factors play in the leadership process shows that, taken singly or jointly, neither predicts leadership effectiveness consistently. A number of writers suggest that greater emphasis must be placed upon the conditions under which a leader operates, and that different leader behaviors will be differentially effective under different kinds of circumstances. As a theoretical model by Yukl (1971) suggests, some of these conditions may be intervening variables which can be controlled by the leader himself. These variables include subordinate motivation, task-role organization (job assignment and the technical quality of task decisions), and subordinate skill levels (which can be increased through training). In Yukl's model (Figure 12–4), leader consideration affects subordinate motivation directly while initiating structure affects motivation as well as task-role organization and subordinate skill levels. Yukl's model has a third leader variable termed "decision centralization" (or participation), which affects both motivation and task-role organization.

An important aspect of this model is the assumption that leadership behavior indirectly determines the effectiveness of the group as a whole by means of certain other, intervening variables which affect group performance directly. Study of these intervening variables should provide

FIGURE 12–4
A Multiple Linkage Model of Leader Effectiveness

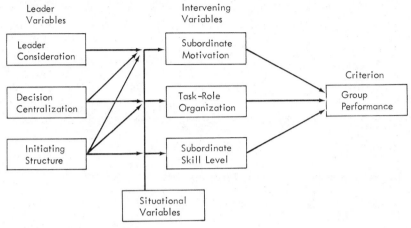

Source: Yukl (1971, p. 423).

us with information about the ways in which leadership behavior can be improved to increase the output of group members.

Yukl's first intervening variable is motivation. We have already seen how leader consideration can increase motivation to improve group performance and also (in Chapter 3) how decision decentralization or participation can affect motivation and coordination among various roles.

The skill level of subordinates may be improved through on-the-job instruction and training and through improved communications of task-relevant information. These are all elements of the component of leadership called initiating structure, and they explain how initiating structure affects group performance. Even highly motivated employees will not perform well if they lack prerequisite knowledge and skills.

Task-role organization refers to the efficient utilization of subordinates' skills in the pursuit of the group's assigned tasks. The adequacy of task-role organization depends upon how well job assignments and work-method selections are made. If jobs are highly specialized, if each job demands the exercise of different skills, and if there are differences in the skills possessed by subordinates, then decisions concerning job assignments will bear major consequences for group performance. When job assignments are poorly made, some workers will be underutilized while others will be unable to perform their jobs adequately. Decisions concerning the selection of work methods become important whenever tasks can be performed in a number of different ways, with some ways better than others.

We have indicated that leaders who are high on initiating structure will attempt to improve the efficiency of their groups, and if they have the proper organizing skills and technical knowledge, they will affect performance by means of task-role organization. In addition, however, subordinates' knowledge and skills of task-role organization can be utilized by means of participative decision making (in Yukl's model, decentralizing decisions). But where pressures exist to organize task roles quickly, participative decision making may be dysfunctional. In this event, unilateral or centralized decision making is advocated, assuming that the leaders possess the requisite knowledge and skills to do so.

Fiedler's "Favorableness" of the Situation for Leadership

Fiedler (1967) conducted an extensive program of research on the relative effectiveness of different leadership styles in different situations. He suggests that ". . . we must recognize that training people is at best difficult, costly, and time consuming. It is certainly easier to place people in a situation compatible with their natural leadership style than to force them to adapt to the demands of the job" (Fielder, 1965, p. 121). Executives should learn to recognize and diagnose group task situations in order to place their subordinates in jobs suited to their leadership styles. In addition, because appropriate placement is not always possible, Fielder (1967) suggests that organizations attempt to "engineer" jobs to fit the persons. All of these points have to do with the factors labeled "situational variables" in Yukl's model (Figure 12–4).

Fiedler found that the "favorableness" of the work situation will determine the effectiveness of a particular leadership style. Permissive (considerate) and authoritarian (controlling) styles of leadership are both effective, but each is effective in different kinds of work situations.

The "favorableness" of a work situation is defined in terms of three characteristics: the quality of leader-member relations, the extent to which the task is structured, and the extent of the leader's power. Of the three factors, leader-member relations is the most important, followed by task structure and power of the leader, respectively. The most favorable situation for a leader is one in which he or she enjoys good interpersonal relations with subordinates, supervises a highly structured task, and exercises considerable power over the group. The most unfavorable situation is described by poor leader-member relations, an unstructured task, and relatively little power vis-à-vis followers.

A considerable number of studies conducted in a variety of settings, including basketball teams, surveying parties, military combat groups, steel furnace crews, and boards of directors, show that the more directive and controlling leaders perform best when their group situation is either relatively unfavorable *or* relatively favorable, but not in-

FIGURE 12–5
How Style of Effective Leadership Varies with the Situation

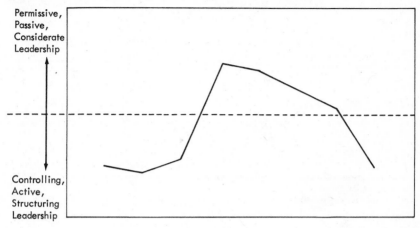

Leader–Member Relations	Good	Good	Good	Good	Poor	Poor	Poor	Poor
Task Structure	Structured		Unstructured		Structured		Unstructured	
Leader Position Power	Strong	Weak	Strong	Weak	Strong	Weak	Strong	Weak

Data below the midpoint of the vertical axis indicate that, under the circumstances described, task-controlling, managing leadership styles were more effective than permissive, nondirective, and human relations-oriented leadership styles. The opposite is true for situations in which data points occur above the midpoint.

Source: Fiedler (1967, p. 431).

between. In contrast, nondirective, human relations-oriented leaders are more effective in situations that are neither favorable nor unfavorable as defined here.

In more specific terms, the directive leaders performed best in basketball and surveying teams, and in open-hearth shops as well as (provided the leader was accepted by the group) in military combat crews and as company managers. In contrast, the nondirective leaders tended to perform best in decision- and policy-making teams and in groups having a creative task (provided that the group liked the leader or that the leader felt that the group was pleasant and free of tension).

Summarizing a large variety of different leadership studies, Filley and House (1969) provide specific conclusions about the conditions under which supportive leadership behavior is most effective. These conditions seem to parallel and amplify Fiedler's view. Supportive leadership is effective when:

1. Decisions are not routine in nature.
2. The information required for effecive decision making cannot be standardized or centralized.
3. Decisions need not be made rapidly, allowing time to involve subordinates in a participative decision-making process.

And when subordinates:

4. Feel a strong need for independence.
5. Regard their participation in decision making as legitimate.
6. See themselves as able to contribute to the decision-making process.
7. Are confident of their ability to work without the reassurance of close supervision (Filley and House, 1969, pp. 404–5).[2]

There seem to be several parallels here with the work of Fiedler, particularly regarding the degree of structure in tasks and also, to some degree, the relationships and differential needs of the leader and his or her subordinates.

The Path-Goal Theory of Leadership

A systematic treatment of leadership and its effects on Yukl's first intervening variable, motivation, has emerged in the "path-goal" theory (House and Mitchell, 1974). Building on the expectancy model of motivation, it emphasizes the leader's effects on subordinates' perceptions of personal and work goals and the "paths" leading to them (see also Evans, 1970, 1974; House, 1971; Nebeker and Mitchell, 1974). Leaders increase motivation by clarifying paths to subordinates' goals, and by strengthening and clarifying contingencies between subordinates' performance and valued outcomes. Motivation is also increased to the extent that the relationship between an individual's intention to perform and his actual performance is enhanced—by coaching and direction and even the removal of frustrating obstacles. Finally, the level of desired rewards may be manipulated directly; for example, by the superior increasing the amount of recognition he or she provides.

According to House and Mitchell (1974), two major classes of situational variables affect leadership. One is the nature of environmental demands determined by the task, the authority structure, and peer relations, all of which can affect motivation, clarify paths, and so on. The second class of variables concerns personal characteristics, especially individual differences in motivation. As one might expect from the discussion in Chapter 6, individuals predisposed to internal control are more satisfied with participative leadership. Also, individuals

---

[2] From *Managerial process and organizational behavior,* by Alan C. Filley and Robert J. House. Copyright © 1969 by Scott, Foresman and Company. Reprinted by permission of the publisher.

who perceive themselves to be competent to perform the required task are more satisfied with participative leadership than are those who are predisposed to external control or perceive their ability to be low.

The environment affects the relationships between leadership and subordinate motivation and satisfaction through its effects on the paths and goals and their outcomes for the individual. For example, subordinates performing ambiguous tasks are likely to prefer more directive leadership because such leaderships can facilitate goal achievement and achievement of related rewards. But in a structured task, the less directive the leadership the better. Since the path-goal relationship is already clear, directive leadership does not facilitate motivation or satisfaction.

While both environmental and personal characteristic variables moderate relationships between leader behavior and motivational and satisfaction outcomes, the environmental variables seem to have overriding importance (House and Mitchell, 1974). At lower levels of the organization, where tasks are routine, directive leadership may be preferred by relatively closed-minded, authoritarian individuals while nondirective leadership may be preferred by more open-minded, nonauthoritarian workers. At higher levels in the organization, where work is more nonroutine and ambiguous, directive leadership may be preferred by both authoritarian and nonauthoritarian subordinates. In other words, both the nature of the task and subordinate personality seem to determine the preferred kind of leadership, but task characteristics seem to have the greater effect.

In Chapter 3, we described Likert's suggestion that managers emphasize high-performance goals. The path-goal theory of leadership helps us understand how, and under what circumstances, such leadership behavior is effective. Leadership behavior which emphasizes achievement may affect subordinates' levels of aspiration vis-à-vis their tasks. Such emphasis is also likely to affect subordinates' confidence in their abilities and their perceptions of effort-performance probabilities (Chapter 6). Some confirmation of the theory is found in a study, described by House and Mitchell (1974), showing that for subordinates performing ambiguous, nonrepetitive tasks, there was a positive association between the leaders' emphasis on achievement and subordinates' expectancies that their efforts would lead to effective performances. But for subordinates performing more repetitive, less ambiguous tasks, leader emphasis on achievement did not seem to create higher expectancies that effort would lead to performance. Unfortunately, the possible effects of personality differences in the situation were not studied. (The same kind of qualification of Likert's emphasis on supportive management is found in House and Mitchell's review. In nine out of ten studies, subordinates were most satisfied with supportiveness *when they had to work on stressful and frustrating tasks.*)

A final example of the usefulness of the path-goal theory of leadership, provided by House and Mitchell, pertains to the effects of participative leadership. This kind of leadership may be expected to improve motivation in a number of ways, including helping subordinates (1) clarify path-goal contingencies (i.e., they learn about the organization by actually doing things and observing the results), and (2) select goals of higher value (because of the influence provided by participation). This increased motivation, together with the autonomy provided by participation, may be expected to lead to higher performance. There are, however, studies which show that some individuals prefer autonomy and self-control more than others (e.g., Vroom, 1959). Some individuals may prefer not to have autonomy, thus reducing the potential effects of participative leadership. Even more important, however, is the effect of the environment (i.e., the task) on the leadership-performance relationship. There is some evidence that in ambiguous and ego-involving tasks, subordinates prefer participative to nonparticipative leadership, regardless of their personality differences. But for repetitive and less ego-involving tasks, personality makes a difference—nonauthoritarian subordinates prefer participation more than authoritarian individuals.

While the path-goal approach to leadership is recent and largely untested, it is promising because it focuses on both the individual and his or her environment. The leader can be seen as mediating between the individual and the organization (its technology, structure, and goals). The leader can have important effects on the motivation of subordinates, in terms of the rewards and paths to rewards provided, and important effects on performance for the organization, by affecting the perceptions of contingencies that are important in motivation.

The Varying Effects of Leadership

In contrast to the preceding discussion of the effectiveness of leadership styles in different situations, a number of studies suggest that an even more significant question needs to be addressed. Namely, to what extent (or when) does leadership have any effect at all?

Earlier, in discussing the relationships between technology and structure proposed by Perrow (Chapter 4), we saw that coordination by feedback is appropriate for nonroutine technologies while coordination by planning is appropriate for routine technologies. This typology suggests that for highly structured technologies there is not much leeway for supervision or different supervisory styles.

In fact, no supervision at all may be appropriate in such highly structured technologies. A case in point is Woodward's (1965) study of technology, which shows that mass-production systems provide considerably more routinization and structure for management than do either batch or continuous process systems. The supervisor of a team performing batch production, as well as the supervisor of a maintenance crew for a continuous process technology, will have opportunities to affect the productivity of their workers, for better or worse, depending on the supervisory style used. This is in some contrast to the supervisor on the assembly line, where the task is so highly structured that his or her use of either a human relations style or a more directive approach to supervision makes relatively little difference to the productivity of the work unit.

Norms as well as technology may serve to structure the task (Mott, 1972). As indicated in Chapter 3, informal norms may produce just as much or more regularity in behavior as formal rules and regulations. Thus, a situation characterized by a restrictive normative structure (whether formal rules as in a bureaucracy or informal norms as in a work group) may be one in which different supervisory styles make little difference for the effectiveness of the group.

From his NASA study, Mott (1972) found that as one moves upward in the organizational hierarchy and as tasks become less structured, variations in leadership styles seem to have more effects (for better or worse) on the productivity of the division under study. Respondents in the study were asked whether their supervisors had any effect on their performance, and answers varied considerably according to the respondent's level in the organization. One third of the respondents low in the hierarchy (GS levels 1 to 7) agreed with the statement that supervisors have very little effect on the work they perform, in contrast to none of the respondents at high levels (GS level 12 or higher). That is, at lower GS levels, supervision's contribution to subordinates' performance was not as apparent as it was at higher levels. Those at lower levels felt the factors that *did* have an impact on their work included: (1) the stage at which work arrived, (2) whether or not it arrived on time, (3) the clarity of job requests, and (4) whether or not equipment was working properly. The individuals in question were performing highly structured and repetitive batch work, and their productivity depended primarily upon effective coordination, rather than upon the nature of their supervision. The supervisory behavior that they perceived as helpful included the application of technical skills, certain techniques of administration, fairness, and effective communication.

In contrast, respondents at the GS 12 or higher levels viewed supervision as important. They also mentioned a different set of supervisory skills. These consisted of task- and support-oriented skills which included the following: (1) good human relations skills, (2) willingness to stand up for subordinates with other higher level supervisors, (3) openness to employee influence in making decisions, (4) willingness to discuss work-related problems with employees, (5) the possession of authority adequate to their responsibility, and (6) good administrative and planning skills.

Generalizing from his findings, Mott (1972) suggests that the more closed a system is and the more it is routinized, the less effect leadership behavior has on the system's effectiveness. In the NASA study, respondents at higher organizational levels exercised their leadership within relatively unstructured (open) circumstances, while those at lower levels worked within systems that were more nearly closed. Mott goes on to suggest that leadership styles effective for higher level management are similar to those that are effective in the management of research laboratories, although the hierarchical positions of the managers and research directors may differ considerably. Both kinds of managerial endeavor occur within relatively open systems where feedback loops providing information for control purposes are long.

Mott also argues that the importance of leadership increases as the interdependence of tasks is increased. Unfortunately, this hypothesized relationship was not amenable to direct observation in his study. However, an indirect form of analysis did lend some support to the notion. The NASA divisions staffed by highly trained professionals, who were performing work which came from outside clients to whom they were assigned by the division director, experienced little need to share client information. In these divisions, supervisory behavior had little effect on performance. In contrast, leadership behavior was found to affect effectiveness in divisions wherein the work activities were closely interrelated.

Leadership in Changing Situations

Some factors affecting leadership effectiveness are restrictive in that they are not amenable to manipulation by the manager. However, awareness of their importance can enable managers to deal with them appropriately. A number of these factors concern change—changes in the situation of the group or organization.

The effects of crises on leadership have been studied in small groups (Hamblin, 1958). Each group in the study was assigned a complex task and allowed time to learn the rules under which the task was to be performed. After the groups were functioning smoothly, Hamblin exposed them to crisis situations in which the rules were changed radically. Leadership in the experimental groups was affected in two ways: (1) group members were more willing to follow a strong leader than a weak one, and (2) leaders who did not respond to the crisis rapidly and decisively were rejected and replaced by other leaders.

Occasionally, groups change leaders quite systematically as they move between situations that are alternatively crisis ridden and "normal." Shepard (1967) studied a World War II raiding unit that alternately operated as an organic system, with open interaction among all participants, and as a more mechanical system, with strict hierarchical command. In the organic system, leadership was widely shared when ideas and plans for upcoming raids were generated and as completed raids were reviewed and evaluated. However, during the execution of a raid, a strict command structure was followed, with leadership confined to the top of the hierarchy.

Time pressures and other forces that evoke a need for directive leadership, as opposed to more participatory forms of leadership, can be observed in organizations as complex as national governments. For example, the British rejected Chamberlain as the threat posed by Nazi Germany increased and turned to Churchill, only to turn away from their great war hero to Attlee when the crisis passed.

Mann (1965) describes how demands for supervision changed in an electrical utility during the introduction of an electronic data processing system. In addition, he found that the skills demonstrated by supervisors in six different power plants (which ranged from being new or in the process of being rebuilt to being obsolete and about to be retired) varied considerably according to the stage in the life cycle of each of their plants.

Lippitt and Schmidt (1967) view organizations as having different critical concerns and issues as they progress from origination to maturity, much as we recounted (in Chapter 5) the changing critical tasks performed over the history of a hospital studied by Perrow. Initially, the organization's members are concerned with creation and survival, while at later stages concern shifts to matters of stability, reputation, and to organizing, reviewing, and evaluating performance. Finally, as organizations mature, members become concerned with attaining organizational uniqueness, maintaining adaptability, and making contributions to society. According to the investigators, early stages of organizational growth require technical and administrative skills, while later stages require the exercise of human relations skills to a greater extent.

Leadership and Organizational Constraints

Organizational norms may severely constrain the use of a particular leadership style or changes in leadership behavior. Merei (1949) conducted an experiment on a large number of children's groups in which children identified as followers were placed together in special rooms. After these groups had sufficient time to function and to create their own rules, habits, and traditions, a child identified as a leader in previous settings was placed in each group. The leader, usually an older child who tended to give orders more often than he followed them and who tended to be imitated more often than he imitated others, was usually forced by the group to accept their traditions, as opposed to being able to lead the group. The leader's own proposals were either rejected by the group or accepted only after being made congruent with existing group traditions. Usually the leader was able to modify means that were employed by his group, but not the group's ends. Jay (1971) describes a similar attempt to change the organizational culture of an English school through the introduction of new teachers. They, too, were quickly absorbed by the school's normative structure or culture.

As Tannenbaum and Schmidt (1958) indicate, the supervisor must "fit" his behavior to the job at hand. The concept of "fit" implies that the leader must not only be "true" to himself and his personality, but also to subordinates in his work group. An elaboration of this thought is found in Hollander's (1958) work on *idiosyncrasy credits*. As the leader begins to conform to the norms of the group, he builds up idiosyncrasy credits with them. These credits allow him to behave idiosyncratically, and in so doing to lead the group in different and creative directions. A related finding is reported by Andrews (1967) from a study of two Mexican firms—one of which was highly achievement-oriented, progressive, and expansion-minded while the other was oriented more toward power relations. It was found that the most regularly promoted managers in both firms had power and achievement motives congruent with the values of the organization in which they were employed, but not necessarily with the formal goals of the organization. In short, the leader and the group may be viewed as engaging in an interpersonal process in which the leader may influence others in exchange for being influenced by them in some way. Fiedler's "favorableness" may be amenable to influence since the leader may not only initiate structure but also affect the interpersonal processes that occur with the structure (Hollander and Julian, 1969). Our description of the process of role-sending (Chapter 9) is quite relevant here, for the leader may attempt to influence followers' conceptions of their roles, as well as their expectations of his own behavior. The research described above seems to indicate that such attempts at influence by the leader are not always successful.

In a study of English hospitals, Revans (1964) demonstrates that one leader characteristic, authoritarianism, may be a system-wide phenomenon—as was evidenced by a situation in which student nurses were afraid to ask questions of their supervisors who, in turn, were reluctant to behave openly with other nurses or physicians. Revans suggests that open behavior by any individual is difficult in a climate characterized by anxiety and defensiveness. To ameliorate this system and the consequent anxiety and blocked communication it produced, Revans (1972) attempted to alter the behavior of top leadership in the hospital—senior nurses, physicians, and administrators. It was felt that to change the normative structure of the organization, the influence of those at the top of the hierarchy would be essential. In fact, in hospitals where the top leadership "bought" the action program, the system did seem to change, opening up and showing increased efficiency in patient care, even at the ward level (Revans, 1972).

Another study demonstrating the impact of relations across hierarchical levels was conducted by Fleishman (1953) who found that the leadership behavior of a supervisor was correlated with that of his boss. People who work for considerate superiors were reported more considerate of their own subordinates than were others who worked for less considerate individuals. A similar correlation was found for the dimension of leadership behavior we termed "initiating structure." The notion that organizational climate can constrain behavior is evidenced by the observation that supervisors tend to practice what they have learned in human relations training programs only when their own supervisors maintain a supportive climate. On returning from such training programs, foremen who work for supervisors low in consideration tend to revert to former patterns of behavior. Sykes (1962) found that supervisors trained in human relations became frustrated when top executives were unwilling to practice what they preached or had encouraged their subordinates to learn. Furthermore, the supervisors, who previously had been rated highly successful, became dissatisfied and, on occasion, left the organization because of their frustration.

In addition to a large number of *small group* studies which show that group members prefer leaders who show consideration, Pelz (1952) found in his studies of *organizations* that workers prefer supervisors who identify closely with higher levels of management. This does not imply that workers are indifferent to the amount of consideration that their supervisors give them. In addition to consideration, however, workers value the influence their supervisors enjoy in interactions with high levels of management. If the supervisor has good relations with his superiors, he will be able to supervise those under him in a more considerate fashion by virtue of his influence and ability to work at satisfying his subordinates' needs without interference from above.

While the scarcity of research findings in this general area prevents us from drawing definitive conclusions, it seems clear that the supervisor's influence and leadership style may be circumscribed both by normative structure in the organization and by general influence structures.

LEADER BEHAVIOR AND ORGANIZATIONAL PERFORMANCE

Top Management and Leadership

Perhaps we are being overly pessimistic in emphasizing the organizational constraints on leadership behavior. Most of the research cited has used lower and, occasionally, middle-level managers (as opposed to executives) as subjects. We have seen from Mott's research in NASA that the higher one moves in the organization, the greater difference leadership behavior can make for organizational effectiveness. However, the highest level of management studied by Mott consisted of division heads, who essentially performed staff functions and were considerably below the top-management level. This may explain, in part, why Katz and Kahn's three-pattern theory did not predict, in its entirety, the effectiveness of units at various levels of the organization. The best predictors in the Katz and Kahn theory were *subsystem perspective* and *integration*, both of which are second- or middle-level patterns. In Mann's skill mix theory, human relations skills were most effective in predicting unit effectiveness. These skills, too, are supposedly more important at middle levels of the organization than at higher or lower levels. Therefore, we conclude that neither of the two theories was tested completely since neither was applied to executives. Unfortunately, little exists in the way of systematic study of top-level management. Consequently, we are limited in our discourse to what are essentially case studies.

Top management is viewed as encompassing "institutional skills" (Mann), a "systematic viewpoint," and a "charismatic affective capability" (Katz and Kahn). Similarly, the primary functions of top management have been viewed as: (1) reducing uncertainty in turbulent environments and (2) making value judgments or acts of appreciation (McWhinney, 1968). These functions consist of perceiving reality and making value judgments that correspond to the cognitive and emotional components of top-level leadership seen by Katz and Kahn. Top management must be aware of the environment and of potential domains for the organization's activities (see Chapter 13) and must make value-laden decisions. Vickers (1965) has called the latter "appreciative decisions."

Selznick's Perspective of Institutional Leadership

These views of leadership at topmost levels of organizations are derived from the seminal work of Philip Selznick (1957). From Selznick's perspective, leadership entails dealing with organizations as "institutions" (see Chapter 1) and with the related phenomena of "organizational character" and "distinctive competence." Leadership at the top of an organization encourages the transformation of an "engineered" or technical arrangement of parts into a social organism, and, in these terms, consists of more than selecting means that can be applied efficiently toward given ends. Leadership consists of selecting ends and, second, selecting means that are both efficient and in keeping with these ends. Decisions related to attaining efficiency in operations are distinguished from more critical decisions that involve choices affecting the basic character of the enterprise. In addition to distinctive goals, organizations may come to have cultures, including values and ideologies, that are unique.[3]

We have viewed organizations, in part, as rational means toward goals—as technical instruments. These technical instruments are also social entities. Individual members and the organizations as a whole may (or may not) come to take on distinctive ways of making decisions and particular commitments to aims, methods, or clienteles. To some extent, these aspects of the organization can become ends in themselves, rather than remaining wholly rational, and therefore completely modifiable, elements of a technical instrument (Gouldner, 1959). The process whereby rational organizations become infused with values is termed "institutionalization" (Selznick, 1957). Institutional leadership assumes importance as the organization changes from a wholly rational instrument to a social institution.

The main responsibilities of leaders in top-management positions, therefore, are not found in technical, rational administration but rather in the creation and maintenance of organizational character and institutional integrity. In Selznick's view, integrity is achieved when organizational form and policy become congruent. A unity emerges in which social orientations imbue the organization so that all that is done reflects this orientation to one degree or another. The embodiment of organizational purpose with institutional character can, under favorable conditions, render the organization uniquely competent in its particular undertakings.

This transition from organization to institution goes on unconsciously and inevitably whenever leeway exists in the technical and rational system. Katz and Kahn and others argue that such leeway exists in all organizations by virtue of their openness and reliance on human members.

Leadership can provide conscious guidance of this transition from organization to institution. The history of the *New York Times* provides an example of a conscious effort of this sort. The ideals of objectivity and public instruction have been inculcated throughout the organization by means of staff selection and education, controlling the pace of work, managing relationships with advertisers, and defining the paper's role in relation to other newspapers.

An institutional perspective allows the manager to analyze existing and proposed procedures in terms of their expected or actual facilitation or hindrance of the enterprise's attempts to maintain and further its distinctive role and character. Some of the activities undertaken by

[3] Increasing efficiency in a inefficient organization may itself become a top-management goal that requires, for its realization, the exercise of creativity and choice and a reshaping of fundamental organizational perspective and relationships. But, this kind of decision regarding organizational efficiency should not be confused with routine, efficiency-related administrative decisions that are made in lower level, more rationalized units of the organization.

an organization may be considered neutral in this regard, but they are probably fewer than commonly thought. At the very least, an activity or technique can be considered neutral when it is suitable for a variety of institutions, while the most desirable activity or technique would be uniquely suited to the character of the enterprise.

As we saw in Chapter 5, organizations move through stages wherein different needs, problems, and environmental relations exist. Top management must examine the historical origins and the growth stages of the organization in order to determine whether organizational pressures to resist changes in basic character, as well as changes in particular procedures, personnel, and technologies, are appropriate to contemporary problems or if they are aftereffects of earlier situations. Yet, in so doing, management must recognize that basic character and organizational integrity cannot be changed wholly. In some cases, it may be better to start a new organization than to attempt drastic alterations of an old one.

Opportunism and Utopianism

Good leaders are known as much for the things they don't do as for what they actually do. Selznick suggests the importance of a leader avoiding *opportunism* and *utopianism*. Opportunism is the pursuit of immediate and short-run advantages in the absence of sufficient consideration of their ultimate consequences. Utopianism is the flight into abstractions and overgeneralizations that enables the leader to avoid limiting his or her aspirations according to the strengths, weaknesses, values, and aims of the organization.

To avoid opportunism, the leader must look to the long-run consequences of present advantages in order to conjecture the effects of present alternatives on the institution's future identity. This, of course, implies that leadership has attended to the prerequisite activities of goal-setting and mission definition, rather than letting the institution drift, whether through a laissez-faire policy or opportunistic maximization of short-run advantages.

The dangers in opportunism are: (1) that undertaking short-run, partial adaptations will affect the organization in such a way that in the long run there are unanticipated changes in its character, and (2) that the aggregation of opportunistic responses will not result in the attainment of long-range goals. Given the diffuseness of purposive leadership found in opportunism, organizational character may become attenuated or confused. According to Selznick, attenuation of character is found in tendencies toward vagueness, in abstraction of the organization's set of predispositions for distinctive competence, and in the consequent inability of this distinctive competence to influence the work of the staff and operating divisions. In actual practice, attenuation of character arises when the formulation of institutional goals is an after-thought or a way of rationalizing activities undertaken in the spirit of opportunism. Selznick describes an organization with a confused char-acter as one possessing a combination of unordered and disharmonious capabilities which render the organization incapable of acting with unity in any particular task.

Opportunism can also result from excessive adaptation to external pressures. Management needs to respond to external pressures, but it must limit its responses to demands that are potent threats to the or-ganization. Less severe pressures can be reduced through intervention, as is the case when the organization forms coalitions within the environ-ment to counteract these forces. An example (Chapter 5) is the uni-versity administrator who countered the pressures by an influential banker on his institution by appointing one of the banker's largest de-positors (who happened to be sympathetic to the administrator's posi-tion) to his advisory council.

Leadership must test the environment and ascertain the true strength of threats, rather than respond opportunistically to all and sundry. The lesser threats probably can be ignored without undue consequences. When adaptation to external pressures or opportunities comes to domi-nate an organization's strategic responses to the environment, the or-ganization ceases to be independent and, as a result, loses its unity and distinctive identity. Of course, sources of external pressure can be co-opted (see Chapter 13), but there is a difference between entering into such relationships consciously, bearing in mind the expected conse-quences on organizational integrity, and reacting blindly to external stimuli.

The danger of utopianism lies in the tendency for leaders to be se-duced by flights into abstractions and away from the necessity of mak-ing difficult and often disagreeable choices. In taking flight, they can avoid the critical functions and consequent psychological burdens of leadership. According to Selznick, one source of utopianism is the over-generalization of organizational purpose. The goal of "making a profit" can be stated so generally as to allow opportunistic reliance on quick re-turns, easy liquidation, and highly flexible tactics. These behaviors can be undertaken without regard for institutional responsibilities and spe-cific institutional purposes. To rely on overgeneralized purposes is, in fact, to rely on very little. Where the organization's mission has not been defined, decisions will still be made. However, in this event the criteria that enter the decision-making process will do so in an uncontrolled fashion. When this occurs, the organization will be threatened with the disintegration of its basic character.

Another form of utopianism is what Selznick calls the "retreat to technology"; the hope or belief that institutional problems will be re-solved through technological advances. The "retreat to technology" is known as the "technological fix" by environmentalists; it is the belief that advances in technology will alleviate the problems leading to over-population, pollution, and the like (See Meadows, Meadows, Randers, and Behrens, 1972). Another example is the tendency of soldiers (such as MacArthur) to advocate military solutions to problems that are in reality political in nature (as former President Truman and others saw it). Selznick terms this "adventurism"; the willingness to commit an organization as a whole, on the basis of some partial assessment of the situation, derived from limited professional or technical perspectives.

In short, responsible leadership attempts to operate between the extremes of utopianism and opportunism. It provides the organization with directions that are in keeping with the organization's basic character and limitations. It seeks to transcend mundane survival concerns by encouraging actions that promote the distinctive identity of the organization.

Leadership and Creativity

In addition to the reasoned conservatism that Selznick feels is a sine qua non of responsible leadership, he emphasizes a concern for organizational change and reconstruction. We alluded to this more creative side of top management earlier as "the institutional embodiment of purpose." Establishment of internal policy (the in-building of purpose) entails transforming individuals and groups from neutral, technical units into participants who have a particular set of capabilities, orientations, and commitments. Basically, this is an educational process in which the leader interprets the role and character of the enterprise and develops models through which other organizational members can gain the perspective of the organization as a whole.

There is, unfortunately, little research on this vital function of top management. Hollander and Julian (1969) advocate a reexamination of the Freudian concept of identification in which the leader serves as a conscience for group members and inculcates them with values and ideas. Hollander's research on voting behavior shows that agreement with the president on issues and views of conditions leads to loyal voting behavior; for example, regardless of the actual economic status of voters, if they agree and identify with the president's views on the economic prospects of the nation, they will continue to be loyal in their voting behaviors.

We should emphasize, however, that Selznick's description of the creation of internal policy and the education of organizational members has cognitive as well as emotional elements. The intent of the educational process is to orient members of the organization in such a way that their support of organizational policy has a basis in reason. This consists of more than mechanical or even authoritarian loyalty. Members who come to understand and embody institutional purposes (who intelligently assess long-run goals and the consequences of alternative choices available in the present) will be likely to abide by and support reasoned policy decisions.

Selznick speaks of the usefulness of elaborating and socially integrating these educational processes. A fairly explicit institutional philosophy may be developed which exemplifies the organization's ideals in a rather direct way. Clearly, this creative and constructive educational activity can be a vital aspect of leadership.

DISCUSSION QUESTIONS

1. Discuss the respective functions of leaders of assembly-line workers and members of a planning task force. What similarities and differences would you expect to find?
2. What personality traits do successful leaders hold in common?
3. Give examples of utopianism and opportunism. Is it possible for a leader to err in both extremes? How?
4. People frequently exercise leadership functions even though they lack the formal authority to do so. Can you provide examples of this phenomenon? Do the functions of these "informal leaders" differ from those of formal leaders?

REFERENCES

Andrews, J. D. W. The achievement motive and advancement in two types of organizations. *Journal of Personality and Social Psychology,* 1967, *6,* 163–69.

Bales, R. F. Task roles and social roles in problem-solving groups. In E. Maccoby, T. M. Newcomb, and E. L. Hartley (Eds.), *Readings in social psychology.* 3rd ed. New York: Holt, Rinehart and Winston, 1958. Pp. 437–47.

Bavelas, Alex. Leadership: man and function. *Administrative Science Quarterly,* 1960, *4,* 491–98.

Blake, R. R., and Mouton, J. S. *The managerial grid.* Houston: Gulf Publishing Co., 1970.

Bowers, David G., and Seashore, Stanley E. Predicting organizational effectiveness with a four-factor theory of leadership. *Administrative Science Quarterly,* 1966, *11,* 238–63.

Butterfield, Anthony. An integrative approach to the study of leadership effectiveness in organizations. Unpublished doctoral dissertation, University of Michigan, Ann Arbor, Mich., 1968.

Evans, M. G. The effects of supervisory behavior on the path-goal relationship. *Organizational Behavior and Human Performance,* 1970, *55,* 277–98.

Evans, M. G. Extensions of a path-goal theory of motivation. *Journal of Applied Psychology,* 1974, *59,* 172–78.

Fiedler, Fred E. Engineer the job to fit the manager. *Harvard Business Review,* 1965 (Sept.–Oct.), 115–122.

Fiedler, Fred E. A theory of leadership effectiveness. New York: McGraw-Hill, 1967.

Filley, Alan C., and House, Robert J. Managerial process and organizational behavior. Glenview, Ill.: Scott, Foresman and Company, 1969.

Fleishman, E. A. Leadership climate, human relations training, and supervisory behavior. Personnel Psychology, 1953, 6, 205–22.

Fleishman, Edwin A. (Ed.). Studies in personnel and industrial psychology. Homewood, Ill.: Dorsey, 1967.

Fleishman, Edward A., and Harris, Edwin F. Patterns of leadership behavior related to employee grievances and turnover. Personnel Psychology, 1962, 15 (Spring), 43–56.

Gibb, C. A. Leadership. In G. Lindzey and E. Aronson (Eds.), Handbook of social psychology. 2d ed. Vol. IV. Reading, Mass.: Addison-Wesley, 1968. Pp. 205–82.

Gouldner, Alvin W. Organizational analysis. In Robert K. Merton, Leonard Broom, and Leonard S. Cottrell, Jr. (Eds.), Sociology today. New York: Basic Books, 1959.

Hall, Richard H. Organizations: structure and process. Englewood Cliffs, N.J.: Prentice-Hall, 1972.

Hamblin, R. C. Leadership and crisis. Sociometry, 1958, 21, 322–35.

Hollander, E. P. Conformity, status, and idiosyncrasy credit. Psychological Review, 1958, 65, 117–27.

Hollander, E. P., and Julian, J. W. Contemporary trends in the analysis of leadership process. Psychological Bulletin, 1969, 71, 387–97.

House, Robert J. A path-goal theory of leader effectiveness. Administrative Science Quarterly, 1971, 16, 321–38.

House, Robert J., and Mitchell, Terence R. Path-goal theory of leadership. Journal of Contemporary Business, 1974, 3 (Autumn), 81–97.

Jay, Anthony. Corporation man. New York: Random House, 1971.

Katz, D., and Kahn, R. L. The social psychology of organizations. New York: Wiley, 1966.

Likert, R. New patterns of management. New York: McGraw-Hill, 1961.

Lippitt, G. L., and Schmidt, W. H. Crises in a developing organization. Harvard Business Review, 1967, 45, 102–12.

Machiavelli, Niccolò. The prince. New York: New American Library of World Literature, 1952.

McWhinney, William H. Organizational form, decision modalities and the environment. Human Relations, 1968, 21, 269–81.

Mann, F. C. Toward an understanding of the leadership role in formal organization. In R. Dubin, G. C. Homans, F. C. Mann, and D. C. Miller (Eds.), Leadership and productivity. San Francisco: Chandler, 1965. Pp. 68–103.

Meadows, Donella H., Meadows, Dennis L., Randers, Jorgen, and Behrens, William W. III. The limits to growth. New York: Universe Books, 1972.

Merei, F. Group leadership and institutionalization. Human Relations, 1949, 2, 23–29.

Mott, Paul E. The characteristics of effective organizations. New York: Harper, 1972.

Nebeker, D. M., and Mitchell, T. R. Leader behavior: an expectancy theory approach. Organizational Behavior and Human Performance, 1974, 11, 355–67.

Pelz, D. C. Influence: a key to effective leadership in the first-line supervisor. Personnel, 1952, 29, 209–17.

Revans, R. W. *Standards for morale: cause and effect in hospitals.* London: Oxford University Press, 1964.

Revans, R. W. (Ed.). *Communication, choice, and change.* London: Tavistock, 1972.

Selznick, P. *Leadership in administration.* Evanston, Ill.: Row & Peterson, 1957.

Shepard, H. A. Innovation-resisting and innovation-producing organizations. *Journal of Business,* 1967, *60,* 470–77.

Sykes, A. J. M. The effect of a supervisory training course in changing supervisors' perceptions and expectations of the role of management. *Human Relations,* 1962, *15,* 227–43.

Tannenbaum, R., and Schmidt, W. H. How to choose a leadership pattern. *Harvard Business Review,* 1958, *36,* 95–101.

Vickers, Geoffrey. *The art of judgment.* New York: Basic Books, 1965.

Vroom, Victor H. Some personality determinants of the effects of participation. *Journal of Abnormal and Social Psychology,* 159, *59,* 322–27.

Woodward, J. *Industrial organization: theory and practice.* New York: Oxford University Press, 1965.

Yukl, Gary. Toward a behavioral theory of leadership. *Organizational Behavior and Human Performance,* 1971, *6,* 414–40.

Case

Kingston Company[*]
R. Stuart-Kotze

The Kingston Company, located in Ontario, was a medium-sized manufacturing firm which made a line of machine parts and marketed them
to plants in the southeastern section of the province. Harold Kingston,
the president and majority shareholder in the company, held a Master of
Business Administration degree from an American university, and was
a vigorous supporter of the usefulness and value of a graduate business
education. As a result, he had on his staff a group of four young MBAs
to whom he referred as "the think group" or "the troubleshooters."

The four members of the group ranged in age from the youngest at
23 to the oldest at 35, with the two intermediate members being 27.
They were all from different universities and had different academic
backgrounds. Their areas of interest were marketing, organizational behavior, operations research, and finance. All had been hired simultaneously and placed together in the "think group" by Mr. Kingston because,
as he put it, "With their diverse knowledge and intelligence, they ought
to be able to solve any of this company's problems."

For their first month on the job, the "Big Four," as they became
known in the firm, familiarized themselves with the company's operations and employees. They spent a half-day every week in conference
with Mr. Kingston and his executive committee, discussing the goals
and objectives of the company, and going over the history of the major
policy decisions made by the firm over the years. While the process of
familiarization was a continuing one, the group decided after four weeks
that it had uncovered some of the firm's problems and that it would
begin to set out recommendations for the solution of these problems.

From the beginning, the members of the group had worked long

* This case was prepared by Professor R. Stuart-Kotze, for Acadia University as
a basis for class discussion.
    Distributed by the Intercollegiate Case Clearing House, Soldiers Field, Boston,
Mass. 02163. All rights reserved to the contributors. Printed in the U.S.A.

hours, and could usually be found in the office, well after the plant had closed, discussing their findings and trading opinions and ideas. The approach to problem solving which they adopted was to attack each problem as a group and to pool their ideas. This seemed to give a number of different slants to the problems, and many times helped clear away the bias which inevitably crept into each member's analysis.

Mike Norton, the finance specialist, and the youngest member of the group and Jim Thorne and Dave Knight, the operations research man and the behavioral management man, respectively, spent a lot of time together outside the work environment. They seemed to have similar interests, playing tennis and golf together, and generally having a keen interest in sports. They managed to get tickets together to watch the local professional football games, and ice-hockey tickets, etc. The fourth and oldest member of the group, Cy Gittinger, did not share these interests. The only "sports" he played were shuffleboard and croquet, and he didn't join the other three too often after work for a beer in a local bar, since he also abstained from alcohol.

The group, from the beginning, was purposely unstructured. All the members agreed to consider themselves equals. They occupied one large office, each having a desk in an opposite corner, with the middle of the room acting as a "common." Basic decisions were usually made with the four men pacing about in the open area, leaning against the walls and desks, and either squeezing or bouncing "worry balls" of a rubber-putty substance used for cleaning typewriters, off the walls. The atmosphere was completely informal, and the rest of the firm kidded the members of the group about the inordinately large amount of typewriter cleaner used in the room when there were no typewriters to be seen.

While consensus was not required, the group found that they were able to agree on a course of action most of the time. When they were unable to do so, they presented their differing opinions to Mr. Kingston, in whose hands the final decision rested. They acted in a purely staff capacity, and unless requested to help a particular manager and authorized to do so by Mr. Kingston, they confined their reports to the president and his executive committee. Reports were usually presented in written form, with all four members of the group present and contributing verbal support and summation.

The group realized that working in close contact would result in strained relations on occasion, and they agreed to attempt to express their feelings accurately and try to understand issues from the other members' point of view. Jokes about "happiness boys," "Junior Baruchs," "peddlers" and "formula babies" were bandied about, and each of the four made a conscious effort to see the biases introduced by his field of interest. Attempts at controlling the discussion and establishing a leadership position were handled by pointing out the behavior to the individual involved.

However, as the months passed, there seemed to be a growing uneasiness in the relationship between Norton, Thorne and Knight and the fourth member, Gittinger. The three brought their feelings out one day when they were playing golf. At the 19th hole, over a drink, Thorne commented on the amount of time Gittinger spent talking to Mr. Kingston in his office. They all spent a great deal of time out of their office talking to managers and workers all through the plant, gathering data on various problems, but, Thorne remarked, Gittinger seemed to confine his activities to the upper levels of management far more than the others did. The other two had made the same observation, but felt that it was really hard to put a finger on anything "wrong" about consulting with the president continually. They agreed that their fact-finding did not generally require as much time at higher levels as Gittinger was devoting, but when the point was brought up in subsequent discussion at the office, Cy explained that in order to get information from Mr. Kingston, he found an "indirect" approach, which entailed a certain amount of small talk, was most successful.

After the group had been functioning for ten months, Kingston called them into a meeting with his executive committee and went through an appraisal of their performance. He was, he said, tremendously pleased that his "think group" had performed so well, and he felt vindicated in his belief in the potency of applying the skills learned in graduate business school. His executives added their words of praise. Then Mr. Kingston brought up a suggestion he said he and Cy Gittinger had been discussing for the past month-and-a-half, to appoint one of the group members as a coordinator. The coordinator's job would be to form a liaison between Kingston and the executive committee on the one hand, and the group on the other, and also to guide the group, as a result of the closer ties of the coordinator with the management team, in establishing a set of priorities for different problem areas. When Kingston had finished describing the proposal, which, it seemed, met with his and the committee's approval, Jim Thorne remarked that this procedure seemed to be unnecessary in the light of the previous smooth functioning of the group, and began to explain that such a change would upset the structure and goals of the group. He was interrupted by Mr. Kingston who said he had an important engagement. "We'll leave the working out of all the details to you men," he said. "We don't want to impose anything on you, and we have all agreed that you should be the ones to work out just how this new plan can be implemented." At this point, the meeting ended.

As the group walked back to their office, Gittinger was the only one who talked. He wondered aloud who would be the most suitable man for the coordinator's job, and repeated Kingston's words, citing the advantages that would accrue to the company with the creation of such a position. Since it was 4:45 P.M., they all cleared their desks and left the plant together, splitting up outside to go home.

At 6:00 P.M., Thorne called Norton to ask him what he thought about the developments of the afternoon. The latter expressed surprise, anger, and resentment that the decision had been made without the consultation of the group, and remarked that Knight, to whom he had just been talking, felt the same way. The trio made arrangements to meet for dinner at their downtown athletic club at 7:00 P.M. that evening to discuss the situation.

section IV

Strategy

Chapter 13
  The Organization's Environment
Chapter 14
  Strategy Formulation

PREMISE

If either the rational or organic model of organizations was completely valid, the management of complex organizations would be less arduous than it is. However, as we have seen, neither model describes reality adequately for the simple reason that the two views are not mutually exclusive.

While we agree that social systems are open, we also argue that they are controlled, to some extent, by rational orderings of events and relationships. Beyond this, however, we suggest that the organization per se can be directed toward predetermined outcomes, and that instead of being at the mercy of events, the organization exerts some degree of control over its environment.

Here, we have come to the problem of organizational strategy. In the last chapter, we described how various leadership processes operate. In the next section we shall indicate how the directions of leadership are established. But, once again we shall find that strategy making, similar to other aspects of organizational behavior, is neither as rational nor as organic as one would suspect.

13

The Organization's Environment

INTRODUCTION

The past quarter century has given rise to unprecedented awareness of humanity's tenuous existence on a rather small planet. An increasing world population has magnified impact of people on the environment through the application of technology. We are now concerned with environmental problems that are aggravated daily.

But what do we mean by environment? Here is a term that is laced into discussions among business executives, physicians, economists, and naturalists; that is bandied about over coffee and cocktails; and that is part of the lexicon of roiling masses of grade school children. But what does it mean?

The common usage of the word is residual—environment means everything but the particular entity under study; for example, Thompson (1967) views the environment in terms of exogenous variables—the constraints and contingencies that are beyond the control of the organization. This is a valid, but not particularly useful, meaning. It leads us to contemplate nearly everything. Applied to its logical extreme, systems analysis tells us that everything is related systemically to everything else and that to understand one thing is to understand all things. Such understanding is beyond our ken.

The manager, therefore, must restrict his or her view of the organization's environment to a limited number of "important" systemic relations. Yet, even this is no easy task. Consider the auto maker's view of transactions between his industry and important segments of the environment.

Chapter Guide

According to the 1973 *Statistical Abstract of the United States*, 931,000 miles of designated federal-aid highway system existed in 1971. Eleven thousand miles of the system were completed that year at a cost of $4,788,000,000. Also that year Americans bought 18,300,000 new and used automobiles. About half of these were purchased with credit. The estimated cost of operating each new car for ten years exceeds $13,500. A sample of 430,000 vehicles shows that 30 percent of them were operated at speeds in excess of 65 m.p.h.—14 percent were driven faster than 70 m.p.h. Deaths due to motor vehicle accidents are estimated in excess of 52,000 for the 12-month period in question. (About 53,402 American casualties were suffered in all of World War I.) Polluting spills from vessels and transportation-related facilities released 8,991,000 gallons of oil and other substances into U.S. waters in 1971. About 800,000 Americans were employed in the manufacture of motor vehicles and equipment. So it goes.

1. What is the impact of financing 9 million automobiles bought in 1971? As we use credit for more and more of what we purchase, will financial institutions come to hold title, temporarily, to most of the durable goods in this country? How will they acquire the resources to do so?
2. How many acres of tillable land are consumed annually by road and highway construction? How many more highways can we afford in the face of worldwide food shortages?
3. What alternatives are there to a transportation system that kills 55,000 users a year? Is the average driver skillful enough to handle a car at speeds in excess of 60 m.p.h.?
4. What is the automobile's impact on society? How has it altered family life? How have shopping centers affected urban areas?
5. What new forms of competition will the automotive industry face in the next ten years? Public mass transportation? Turbine-powered cars? Rotary engines? Will the industry experience greater federal regulation?

These questions are a tiny fraction of the environmental concerns auto makers have. Yet, managers can respond to only a few of the myriad of concerns these questions represent. *How does management define its environment in terms of a limited number of vital concerns to which it must respond?*

IMPACT OF THE ENVIRONMENT

A Systems View of the Organization's Environment

We summarized Parson's (1960) description of the organization as three separate levels in Chapter 1. The technical level is concerned with efficient operation of the organization's technical process and is buffered from the environment as much as possible. The managerial level serves to articulate the technical levels with the environment on both the input and output sides. Finally, the institutional level attempts to relate the organization to its environment.

Emery and Trist (1965) elaborate on this notion in the following exhaustive matrix of relationships pertinent to an organization and its environment:

$$L_{11}, L_{12}$$
$$L_{21}, L_{22}$$

where: L represents some potentially lawful connection, the suffix 1 refers to the organization, and the suffix 2 refers to the environment.

L_{11} represents processes within the organization—interdependencies of internal units. Presumably, these would be observed most frequently in the technical level, which is isolated from the environment. L_{21} and L_{12} represent interdependencies between the organization and its environment. They refer to *input* and *output* processes, respectively. Finally, L_{22} represents interdependencies found within the environment that are independent of the organization in question.

Causal Texture of the Environment

Emery and Trist's deceptively elegant matrix directs our attention to the *evolution* of the environment. Changing and increasing interdependencies within the environment constitute its *causal texture*. For the most part, we have dealt with boundary problems in our previous discussions of transactions with the environment. We have been concerned primarily with input and output phenomena. Yet, as Emery and Trist tell us, suppliers and customers frequently are related independently of the focal organization. Other organizations are interrelated too, and these relationships affect the focal organization indirectly. Increasing interdependencies (causal texture) cause the environment to behave as a system. This is of crucial relevance to organizations.

Emery and Trist describe four types of causal texture, the simplest of which is the *placid, randomized environment*. Here, opportunities and threats are relatively unchanging and randomly distributed. The environment of a nomadic tribe is a crude illustration. The land over which they roam has changed little in the span of tribal memory. Food, shelter, beasts of prey, and other hazards do not change and are more or less randomly distributed. Under such conditions, there is no need to distinguish between tactics and strategy. The best strategy for the tribe is the perfection of "local" or tactical approaches to each situation as it arises. Furthermore, knowledge is accumulated through trial and error.

A second, more complicated form of environment is the *placid, clus-*

tered environment, in which objectives and threats are still relatively static, but are clustered rather than randomly distributed. Suppose that the tribe in our previous example gave up its nomadic existence to mine copper, which it bartered for food with a neighboring, agrarian village. While remaining unchanged, the opportunities and hazards facing the tribe now occur in clusters or, in our example, in copper mines. Strategy will now supersede tactics in importance. Search for new sources of copper must be undertaken prior to exhausting current supplies.

The next stage of environmental evolution is termed the *disturbed-reactive environment.* In addition to being placid and clustered, this environment includes the presence of one or more organizations in competition with the focal one. *Operations* become an adjunct to tactics and strategy. While strategy identifies an objective to be reached in the future and tactics implies short-term means to this objective, operations (a term used by German and Soviet military theorists) attempt to draw off the competition. Now the tribe is faced with competition from another copper producer. It is important to know the second tribe's strengths, weaknesses, intentions, and information sources. Our tribe may now be forced to think in terms of long-term contracts with customers, price and produce strategies, the threat of industrial espionage, and the like.

According to Emery and Trist, the present stage of evolution yields an environment containing *turbulent fields.* In the former stages, the focal organization rendered changes to its environment and reacted to changes caused by other organizations and unorganized entities with which it had direct contact (e.g., customers and competitors). In the turbulent environment we find changes that affect, but are independent of, the behavior of the focal organization. Our tribe, having forever abandoned its placid existence, is now an auto maker concerned with safety legislation, fuel shortages and consequent price increases, federal antipollution legislation, expected competition from public mass transportation facilities, rising expectations in the labor market, and a myriad of other problems.

Emery and Trist suggest that a number of trends contribute to the emergence of these dynamic forces in the environment. These include: (1) increasing interdependencies between the economic sector and other parts of the environment, (2) the increasing tempo of research and development activity, and (3) the increasing growth and complexity of organizations. As organizations achieve greater size, the environment comes to react to the largeness of these institutions per se.

Coping with Turbulence

The literature describes a number of means that organizations employ in dealing with environmental turbulence. Recognizing complexity, variability, and threat as attributes of turbulence, we find that some of these means have already been presented in other chapters. Galbraith's (1972) work was discussed in Chapter 11 in connection with complexity. Lawrence and Lorsch (1967) advocated organizational differentiation (and subsequent integration) as a means for dealing with complexity and variability (Chapter 4). Burns and Stalker's (1961) notion that organic structures are appropriate for dynamic environments was explored in the same chapter.

Terreberry (1968) suggests that the most important consequence of environmental evolution is the increase in the abilities of systems to learn and adapt to changing contingencies in their environments. She states that a system's ability to survive externally induced change in its transactional interdependencies is, in part, a function of diversity in the system's input and output interdependencies. The recent and rapid diversification in major industries is given as an illustration of this strategy. Flexible, decentralized decision making also facilitates adaptation. Most importantly, the system's perceptual and information-processing capacities affect adaptability. Terreberry suggests that the organization's ability to learn is enhanced by subsystems designed to: (1) provide advance information of impending changes in the environment, and (2) actively search for more advantageous input/output (L_{21}, L_{12}) relationships in the environment. Figure 13–1 reproduces the system model of organizations introduced in Chapter 8 in order to relate what may seem rather novel abstractions to earlier works in the field.

In some contrast, Emery and Trist suggest that the solution for orga-

FIGURE 13–1

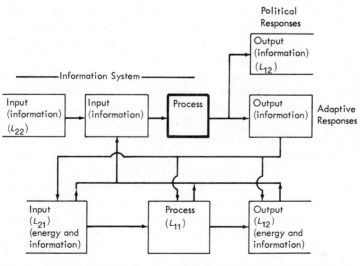

An Expanded View of the Organization as a System

nizations confronted by turbulent fields lies in the emergence of values that have overriding significance for all members of the field. Instead of strategies and tactics, values must regulate the behavior of organizations throughout the environmental field. This kind of overarching consensus may prove difficult to achieve through intentional, planned activity. However, a model presently exists in the form of professional associations. Possibly a study of these associations will yield suggestions for developing value consensus.

In addition, Emery and Trist advocate a form of "organizational matrix" in which cooperative relationships among member organizations are encouraged—partially through the embodiment of the values mentioned above. The consequent reduction of conflict and competition is expected to enhance the organizations' ability to cope with turbulence. However, Emery and Trist expect a generation or more to pass before such arrangements and values are institutionalized.

Organization Sets

We have discussed the environment in rather general terms. More specific means for coping with turbulence will be addressed in Chapter 14 on "Strategy Formulation." We shall turn our attention now to specific portions of the environment with which the focal organization has direct contact. In doing so it will be helpful to recall our discussion of role sets presented in Chapter 9, for a similar type of analysis applies here.

An *organization set* consists of organizations which interact with a particular, focal organization (Evan, 1966). These may provide inputs, accept outputs, or do both. The organization set functions in much the same way as a role set, in which role senders interact with and attempt to influence the focal role. These interactions take a number of forms. Goods, services, information, influence, and even personnel flow among members of an organizational set.

The interactions between organizations are usually conducted by boundary personnel, whose role sets include the boundary personnel of other organizations. For example, in addition to relating to members of his or her own production department, the purchasing agent must also interact with salespersons of supplier organizations.

Interorganizational relations develop for a number of different reasons. Some are based upon legislation and others on tradition. Occasionally, an organization develops new programs that overlap those of other organizations and require joint coordination; for example, internship programs require cooperation between the university and other organizations in the field. Alternatively, personnel may hold positions in several organizations, creating overlap, as is the case when professionals link their employers with professional organizations. Finally, most relations stem from reliance on a common pool of resources. Organizations frequently interact as they compete for (or cooperatively allocate) clients and customers, financial resources, raw materials, and the like.

One very simple way to analyze an organization set is to diagram it; for example, Hall (1972), concerned with the ways in which society attempts to control problem youths, diagrammed the organization set of a police department. Figure 13–2 diagrams this organization set in terms of the frequency of interaction between the focal organization and other elements of the set.

Analyses of this sort direct the manager's attention to the variety of interactions between his organization and others in the set, and cause him to inquire whether these relationships should be purposively coordinated and managed by his organization or reacted to in a passive way. They should cause the manager to ask whether his organization is designed to handle the relationships effectively. Should separate boundary

FIGURE 13–2
The Organization Set and Interaction Frequency

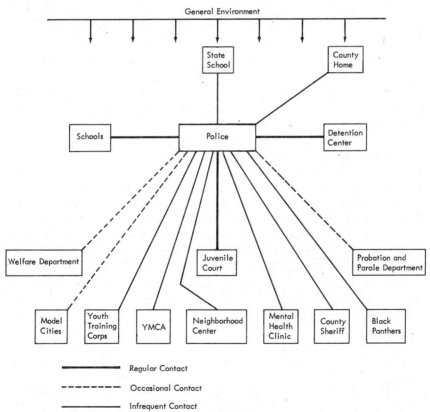

Source: Richard H. Hall, *Organizations, Structure and Process,* © 1972, p. 313. Reprinted by permission of Prentice-Hall, Inc., Englewood Cliffs, New Jersey.

roles be created for each different relationship? Should staffing and work load decisions be made on the basis of the number of relationships or their nature (e.g., cooperative or competitive)? Can formal procedures reduce the need for boundary personnel?

Evan (1972) suggests that three dimensions of the organization set are important to the focal organization: (1) size, (2) diversity, and (3) network configuration. Size refers to the number of organizations in the set. Diversity refers to the number of different functions performed by organizations in the set (e.g., manufacturing, health care delivery, consultation, legislation, and so on). Network configuration refers to the structure of interactions among members of the set. He lists as examples of the latter: (1) dyad (e.g., manufacturer-trade union); (2) a "wheel" network in which the focal organization interacts with numerous organizations that do not interact with one another (e.g., franchiser-franchisees); (3) an "all-channel" network in which each member can interact with each of the other members (e.g., an automobile dealer—National Automobile Dealers Association); and (4) a "chain" network in which the focal organization interacts with a member of the set which, in turn, interacts with a second member, which acts with a third, and so on (e.g., a coal-mining organization, a steelmaker, an automobile manufacturer, an automobile dealer).

A more sophisticated analysis of organization sets can be made by aggregating members of the set according to whether they relate to the input or output functions of the focal organization.[1] This approach, as applied to the Securities and Exchange Commission (SEC), is depicted in Figure 13–3. This figure can be interpreted as follows: Congress votes annual appropriations for the SEC; the president appoints its commissioners; the courts review some of its decisions, and it obtains information, personnel, and so on from numerous other agencies. The SEC's output set is extremely large, consisting of thousands of corporations issuing securities to be scrutinized, thousands of brokerage firms that sell these securities, 14 stock exchanges, and the National Association of Securities Dealers which regulates the conduct of corporations dealing in over-the-counter stock.

More complicated is the Interstate Commerce Commission (ICC) which has an input set similar to that of the SEC, but an output set consisting of approximately 17,000 common carriers which do not have self-regulatory agencies. Although several influential trade associations exist (e.g., American Association of Railroads), there is no organization to represent the consumers' interests.

In light of this, Evan suggests that the ICC's effective performance as

---

[1] Not easily diagrammed is the case where a portion of the organization set on the output side affects the input side. The following discussion of the ICC illustrates an instance in which organizations on the output side become sources of input as well. In other cases, organizations on the output side may affect organizations which, ultimately and indirectly, affect other members of the role set.

FIGURE 13–3
An Organization Set Analysis of the SEC

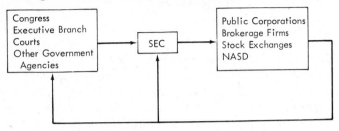

Source: Evan (1972, p. 193).

a regulatory agency is hampered by the tendency for organizations on the output side of the set to make significant *inputs* to the ICC. He states, for example, that:

> Further hampering effective regulation of the transportation industry is the ICC's extensive informal and formal contacts with industry. Notwithstanding the ICC Canons of Conduct prohibiting employees from engaging in any behavior which could affect their impartiality or adversely affect the confidence of the public in the integrity of the Commission, "industry regularly pays for luncheons, hotel rooms . . . , Commissioners and upper staff are commonly transported around at their convenience by corporate jets, private rail cars, and pleasure yachts." There are recurrent conferences between the ICC and seventeen organized groups representing the interests of the transportation industry, none of which represents consumers or the "public interest." Through these informal and formal contacts, members of the output-set become, in the course of time, members of the input-set, influencing information gathering as well as policy formation.
>
> Promoting this type of feedback effect is a frequent flow of ICC employees to industry. Of the last eleven Commissioners to leave the ICC, six became top executives of companies in the transportation industry, three became ICC practitioners, and two retired (Evan, 1972, p. 195).

Similar problems have been observed in other agencies; for example, the Food and Drug Administration, which regulates about 50,000 food manufacturing firms, over 1,000 pharmaceutical firms, and a number of trade and professional associations including the American Medical Association, has been criticized for the:

> subtle and potentially most dangerous aspect of the FDA setup . . . the well traveled, two-way street between industry and Washington. Men from the drug industry have gone on to FDA jobs and—more important —FDA specialists have gone on to lucrative executive jobs in industry. . . . It does not seem desirable to have in decision-making positions, scientists who are consciously or unconsciously always contemplating the possibility that their futures may be determined by their rapport with industry (Mintz, 1965, p. 177).

REACTION AND PROACTION

Organizations, Society, and the Physical Environment

The foregoing discussion of organization sets causes us to step back from the problem and search for a more useful definition of the environment than the "residual" one mentioned earlier. Our point of view is that environmental problems are organizational problems more frequently than societal or biological/geological ones. The scarcity of raw materials, such as crude oil, is not so much a "problem" of the physical environment as it is a problem of misallocation by individuals and organizations. While there is a fixed, short supply of such raw materials, the problem is not how to increase nature's supply, obviously, but how to use it more efficiently and, ultimately, how to develop substitutes.

Similarly, social problems confronting organizations may evolve from the activities of other organizations rather than from independent societal trends. The significant environment of organizations is probably other organizations rather than society. According to Perrow:

> Society is adaptive to organizations, to the large, powerful organizations controlled by a few, often overlapping, leaders. To see these organizations as adaptive to a "turbulent," dynamic, ever changing environment is to indulge in fantasy. The environment of most powerful organizations is well controlled by them, quite stable, and made up of other organizations with similar interests, or ones they control (1972, p. 199).[2]

Following this reasoning, we can attribute part of the crude oil shortage to the collaboration of OPEC nations, part to the interaction of oil, auto producing, and highway construction firms who all stand to benefit mutually as petroleum usage is increased, part to federal legislation that serves the interests of these organizations, part to our own energy consumption habits that have been encouraged through advertising, and so on. We agree with Perrow that large organizations affect society and the physical environment to a greater extent than the latter two affect the former in industrialized nations. For this reason, we shall continue our investigation of interorganizational relationships as they constitute the environment of the focal organization.

Organizational Prestige Sets

A different type of organization set is discussed by Caplow (1964), who views *prestige sets* as comprising organizations of the same type

---

[2] From *Complex Organizations: A Critical Essay* by Charles Perrow. Copyright © 1972 by Scott, Foresman and Company. Reprinted by permission of the publisher.

which engage in similar activities that are deemed important by the organizations concerned and which view themselves as a set. "The sociology departments of major universities constitute a set. So do the Protestant churches in a small city, the baseball teams in the American League, the teenagers' clubs at a settlement house, or the leading manufacturers of electrical equipment" (Caplow, 1964, p. 201).

A consequence of this type of set is the emergence of a prestige order. Members of certain sociology departments see their departments as higher or lower in prestige than other departments, and so do members of certain churches, baseball teams, manufacturing organizations, and the like. While complete consensus on rank orderings usually is lacking (members of an organization are prone to exaggerate the prestige of their own organization relative to that of others), a general consensus can be found. This consensus is also apparent to individuals who do not belong to organizations in the set.

High rank in the prestige set is useful in a number of ways. Prestige constitutes a source of power (Thompson, 1967) that can be used to influence the behavior of lower members of the set. High-ranking members establish standards (which they can achieve readily) that ultimately become the standards by which lesser members are judged.[3] Prestige facilitates recruitment of new personnel, since a new recruit will be compensated, in part, by the prestige and social stature conferred by his or her employment. By the same token, prestige can be used to "pay" others for needed resources, such as grants and contracts, and constitutes a competitive advantage over lower members of the set.

A number of studies indicate that organizations in prestige sets are linked together informally by exchanges of personnel, just as the FDA is linked to the industry it regulates. Gross (1970) reports that among the top 20 sociology departments in this country, 86 percent of the faculty members received their Ph.D.s from one of the 20 departments, leaving only 14 percent with degrees from universities having lesser ranked departments. Looking at the top 5 departments, he finds that 73 percent of the faculty members are alumni of 1 of the 5, 21 percent are alumni of the next 15 departments in the top 20, while only 6 percent come from lesser ranked doctoral programs.

Comparable exchanges of executives may occur among firms in certain industries, and Pfeffer and Leblebici (1973) argue that it is mutually advantageous to interlock firms in the same industry. Stabilized interaction patterns yield a reduction in uncertainty which enables the organizations to behave more rationally and efficiently. Perrow makes a similar observation:

---

[3] One is reminded of the philosophy of Friedrich Neitzsche. ". . . [T]he judgment of *good* does not originate with those to whom the good has been done. Rather it was the "good" themselves, that is to say the noble, mighty, highly placed, and high-minded who decreed themselves and their actions to be good. . . . (Nietzsche, 1956).

Standard Oil and Shell may compete at the intersection of two highways, but they do not compete in the numerous areas where their
interests are critical, such as foreign policy, tax laws, import quotas,
governmental funding of research and development, highway expansion, internal combustion engines, pollution restrictions, and so on. Nor
do they have a particularly turbulent relationship to other powerful
organizations such as the auto companies, the highway construction
firms, the Department of Defense, the Department of Transportation,
the State Department, the major financial institutions. (Perrow, 1972,
pp. 199–200)[4]

Pfeffer and Leblebici find that exchange of personnel is related to the
number of firms in an industry (and to the concentration in the industry). Where many firms compete, it is difficult for managers to
"disburse" themselves to each other's firms. The study of top executives
of 5 firms within each of 20 major industries shows that, where an
industry comprises relatively few firms, executives are more likely to
have: (1) had their last job in the same industry, (2) undergone a
large number of job changes, and (3) experienced a relatively shorter
average tenure in the company before obtaining the chief executive
position than is the case when the industry contains many firms.[5]

Now, exchanges of personnel, whether among members of the organization set or between the former and "feeder organizations" are expected to lead to similarities among these institutions. However, a more
important set of dynamics contributes to these similarities. According
to Caplow (1964), members of a prestige set come to resemble one
another because:

> . . . each organization in a set functions as a partial model to those
> below it while continuously imitating those above. The leading organiza-
> tion in any set . . . comes to be regarded as the embodiment of the
> pattern. Since other organizations in the set lose prestige by deviating
> from the procedures of the leading organization, the latter may exercise
> an influence over its followers and competitors that at times approaches
> outright control (p. 206).

Influence such as this can be used to further either innovation or
conformity. At one extreme, a top organization in the set may be extremely innovative and other members will follow suit. At the other
extreme, conservativism may be viewed as a hallmark of organizational
prestige. Be that as it may, it has been argued that innovations are
usually introduced by organizations in the middle of the hierarchy and,
if successful, are adopted later by higher and lower ranking members
of the set.

---

[4] From *Complex Organizations: A Critical Essay* by Charles Perrow. Copyright ©
1972 by Scott, Foresman and Company. Reprinted by permission of the publisher.

[5] In industries comprising very few firms (e.g., two) the level of job changes was
low, argued Pfeffer and Leblebici (1973) because ". . . uncertainty was reduced
easily with such tactics as price leadership and the development of stable patterns
of expectations without communication" (pp. 452–53).

Innovations are, it appears, less likely to be introduced by organizations at the peak of a set since they have little to gain and much to lose from extensive tampering with existing and heretofore successful processes. One might speculate that the steam- or battery-powered automobile, solely needed to reduce air pollution, will be introduced by either a small automobile manufacturer or, more likely, by American Motors or the Chrysler Corporation, rather than by . . . the most successful automobile manufacturers (Tausky, 1970, p. 161).

There is a dearth of research in the area, but it would seem that personnel flows among members of the prestige sets reinforce the effects on innovation discussed here. Innovation results from intellectual ferment and the clash of ideas. As organizations become like one another, as personnel are exchanged, intellectual ferment is likely to diminish. Where people think alike and serve the same purposes, disagreements leading to innovation are likely to become muted.

Preserving Rationality

According to Thompson (1967), organizations attempt to behave rationally despite their openness to environmental uncertainty. Several techniques are appropriate to this end: namely, *buffering, smoothing,* and *anticipating* (adapting to environmental changes that cannot be buffered or smoothed). Ideally, the organization's input and output flow at continuous, constant rates. This is rarely possible, and a similar effect is achieved by buffering and smoothing:

> Buffering on the input side is illustrated by the stockpiling of materials and supplies acquired in an irregular market, and their steady insertion into the production process. Preventive maintenance, whereby machines or equipment are repaired on a scheduled basis, thus minimizing surprise, is another example of buffering by the input component. The recruitment of dissimilar personnel and their conversion into reliable performers through training or indoctrination is another; it is most dramatically illustrated by basic training or boot camp in military organizations. . . .
> Buffering on the output side of long-linked technologies usually takes the form of maintaining warehouse inventories and items in transit or in distributor inventories, which permits the technical core to produce at a constant rate, but distribution to fluctuate with market conditions.
> . . . Whereas buffering absorbs environmental fluctuations, smoothing or leveling involves attempts to reduce fluctuations in the environment. Utility firms—electric, gas, water, or telephone—may offer inducements to those who use their services during "trough" periods, or charge premiums to those who contribute to "peaking." Retailing organizations faced with seasonal or other fluctuations in demand, may offer inducements in the form of special promotions or sales during slow periods. Transportation organizations such as airlines may offer special reduced fare rates on light days or during slow seasons.
> Organizations pointed toward emergencies, such as fire departments,

attempt to level the need for their services by activities designed to
prevent emergencies, and by emphasis on early detection so that demand is not allowed to grow to the point that would overtax the capacity
of the organization. Hospitals accomplish some smoothing through the
scheduling of nonemergency admissions (Thompson, 1967, pp. 20–21).[6]

Where neither buffering nor smoothing is sufficient to the task of
protecting the technical core from variations in input or demand for
output, the organization can preserve the rationality of its functioning
by treating environmental fluctuations as constraints and adapting accordingly. According to Thompson:

> The manufacturing firm which can correctly forecast demand for a
> particular time period can thereby plan or schedule operations of its
> technical core at a steady rate during that period. Any changes in
> technical operations due to changes in the environment can be made at
> the end of the period on the basis of forecasts for the next period.
> Organizations often learn that some environmental fluctuations are
> patterned, and in these cases forecasting and adjustment appear almost
> automatic. The post office knows, for example, that in large commercial
> centers large volumes of business mail are posted at the end of the
> business day, when secretaries leave offices. . . . It can . . . antici-
> pate heavy demand during November and December, thus allowing its
> input components lead time in acquiring additional resources. Banks
> likewise learn that local conditions and customs result in peak loads at
> predictable times during the day and week, and can schedule their
> operations to meet these shifts (Thompson, 1967, p. 22).[7]

Finally, when none of the three techniques proves effective, organizations resort to rationing.

> Rationing is most easily seen in organizations pointed toward emer-
> gencies, such as hospitals. Even in nonemergency situations hospitals
> may ration beds to physicians by establishing priority systems for non-
> emergency admissions. In emergencies, such as community disasters,
> hospitals may ration pharmaceutical dosages or nursing services by
> dilution—by assigning a fixed number of nurses to a larger patient
> population. . . . Teachers and caseworkers in social welfare organiza-
> tions may ration effort by accepting only a portion of those seeking
> service, or if not empowered to exercise such discretion, may concen-
> trate their energies on the more challenging cases or on those which
> appear most likely to yield satisfactory outcomes. . . . But rationing is
> not a device reserved for therapeutic organizations. The post office may
> assign priority to first-class mail, attending to lesser classes only when
> the priority task is completed. Manufacturers of suddenly popular items
> may ration allotments to wholesalers or dealers, and if inputs are
> scarce, may assign priorities to alternative uses of those resources.
> Libraries may ration book loans, acquisitions, and search efforts
> (Thompson, 1967, p. 23).[8]

---

[6] From *Organizations in Action* by James D. Thompson. Copyright 1967, McGraw-
Hill Book Company. Used with permission of McGraw-Hill Book Company.

[7] Ibid.

[8] Ibid.

Domains

Although we discussed domain consensus at some length earlier (Chapter 5), the topic deserves further mention as still another facet of the organization's environment. Each organization is based on the application of a particular technology which is the means to specific ends, and each organization in an industry must find a niche and establish boundaries around that part of the total industry effort for which it will take initiative. Organizations compete with one another to be sure, but the establishment of domain consensus provides a shared understanding of the delimited areas in which particular organizations will take their competitive stances within the industry; for example, the competitive arenas of motorcycle manufacturers are fairly evident. The serious rider who tours long distances will be attracted to BMW or Harley-Davidson. Each has unique characteristics that set it apart from the other. The BMW will appeal to the more conservative rider, for instance. Individuals wanting motorcycles for basic, "around-town" transportation are likely to purchase Hondas, Suzukis, or Yamahas. Some enthusiasts are loyal to four-stroke machines and, consequently, to Honda. Those who like two-cycle engines will find substantial differences between Suzuki and Yamaha machines. The really serious street rider will probably own a Triumph rather than one of the three above. Finally, dirt and competition bikers look to manufacturers such as Bultaco and Husqvarna for their machines. Although they may seem in competition for a large, unsegmented market, these firms exert the bulk of their competitive efforts in unique market segments.

The establishment of a domain is a matter of consensus according to Thompson (1967). It is one thing to lay claim to a domain and another thing to have it recognized and accepted by others. "Domain consensus defines a set of expectations both for members of an organization and for others with whom they interact, about what the organization will and will not do. It provides, although imperfectly, an image of the organization's role in a larger system, which in turn serves as a guide for the ordering of action in certain directions and not in others" (Thompson, 1967, p. 29). We can postulate (in terms of Emery and Trist's matrix of organizations) that domain consensus incorporates a series of unwritten agreements that reduce uncertainty in the environment by delimiting the areas in which rivalry and competition take place.

Other Bases for Exchange

The notion of domain seems useful in understanding interchanges between organizations and environments, but we must be careful to take the domain as problematic and to view this as an empirical question.

In this regard, Terreberry (1968) suggests that such legitimation of organizational activities is a difficult matter to measure. Just as one may raise the question of how much consensus is needed for a norm to exist, one may ask how much agreement is necessary in order that a niche for the organization is legitimated. Perrow (1972) points out that illegitimate organizations such as the Mafia may flourish, nevertheless. This suggests that there are a variety of values and forms of legitimation existing in society. What is legitimate and acceptable to one group may be unacceptable or a matter of indifference to another group. Thus, the whole area of social responsibility is fraught with disagreements about what is or is not "in the public interest." Similarly, Perrow describes how some business executives seek accommodations between organizations which are viewed by some, but not all, segments of the environment as illegitimate or immoral. Examples include cases of price fixing as well as cartels, industrial espionage, and bribery.

It seems that the existence of a domain with a wide and clear consensus would facilitate relations between an organization and its environment, but functional interactions between organizations and their environments may occur with profit in the absence of such normative support (i.e., an amoral relationship) or even in the presence of positive disapproval (i.e., an immoral relationship).

Autonomy and Dependency

Regardless of whether we examine sets or domains, we observe that transactions between organizations contribute to their dependencies. A manufacturing organization that depends on a single, large supplier or customer will become dependent and subject to its influence. Organizations that maintain diversity in their suppliers and customers remain more autonomous.

The nature of interorganizational relations, as well as their number, determine these dependencies. Organizations wishing to preserve their autonomy (as do most) seek the kinds of exchange relationships that limit dependency. All other things being equal, exchange based on bargaining (low external control) will be preferable to exchange resulting from coalition (high external control). Figure 13–4 suggests the range of relationships from which organizations may choose. According to Klongan and associates (1972), relationships tend to progress from low interdependency (awareness) to high interdependency (co-optation, coalition, or written agreements) although this progression is entered into reluctantly.[9]

---

[9] This excludes interactions and interdependencies over which the organization has little or no control, for example, interdependencies that are legislated. See Hall et al. (1973).

FIGURE 13–4
A Range of Interorganizational Relationships

1. *Awareness:*
   As far as you know is there (name of other organization) in this (state, area, or county)?

2. *Acquaintance:*
   Are you acquainted with the director or person in charge of (contact organization)?

3. *Interaction:*
   Have you met with the director of (contact organization) any time during the past year to discuss the activities of your respective organizations?

4. *Information exchange:*
   Is your organization on (contact organizations) mailing list to receive newsletters, annual reports or other information? OR: Is (contact organization) on your organization's mailing list to receive any of your newsletters, annual reports or other information releases?

5. *Resource exchange (bargaining):*
   Has your organization shared, loaned or provided resources such as meeting rooms, personnel, equipment or funds to (contact organization) at any time during the last three years? OR: Has (contact organization) shared, loaned or provided resources such as meeting rooms, personnel, equipment, or funds to your organization at any time during the last three years?

6. *Overlapping boards or councils (co-optation):*
   Does anyone from your organization or (contact organization) including staff, board members or members serve on boards, councils or committees of the other organization?

7. *Joint programs (coalition):*
   Within the last three years has your organization worked jointly in planning and implementing any specific programs or activities with (contact organization)?

8. *Written agreements:*
   Does your organization have any written agreements with (contact organization) pertaining to personnel commitments, client referrals, procedures for working together or other joint activities?

Source: Klongan et al. (1972, p. 8–9).

Managing Interdependence

We have dealt with two major strategies for coping with environmental uncertainties thus far: (1) adaptation to the environment and (2) isolation from the environment through buffering. In addition, organizations can be proactive, taking advantage of interdependencies that flow from exchange relationships.

Dependence is proportional to the extent the organization needs its suppliers and customers. There are ways of distorting customers' and suppliers' perceptions of the extent to which these needs exist; for example, management may play down the importance of a major supplier in attempting to lessen the latter's perception of the former's dependence. Alternatively, the organization may alter its structure, technology, or goals in order to reduce its dependency on a particular resource. Thus, we used reduced speed limits, lowered thermostat settings, and car pools to reduce our dependence on the OPEC alliance.

The availability of alternative resources (or markets) also affects dependency. By diversifying suppliers and customers, the organization avoids granting unwarranted power to any one of them in particular. Applied to consumer interests, this logic gave rise to existing antitrust legislation.

Another vehicle for maintaining independence is the quest for prestige. "Acquiring prestige is the 'cheapest' way of acquiring power" (Thompson, 1967). The status associated with supplying or purchasing from a prestigious organization can be a quid pro quo unlikely to be sacrificed through attempts at domination.

Finally, we come to direct, but costly, approaches to reducing dependency. Thompson (1967) suggests that organizations can seek power over those on whom they depend. Strategies for achieving this end are termed *contracting, co-opting,* and *coalescing.*

Contracting refers to negotiating agreements to exchange resources. Labor-management bargaining that results in a contract is an example. However, contracting may also be informal as in the case of an "understanding" between a university and a prospective donor regarding the naming of a building or awarding of an honorary degree. Informal contracts can have a specific life or they may be open-ended. In the latter case, long-standing exchange relationships frequently give rise to norms which eventually replace the informal contract.

Co-optation occurs when members of an organization are absorbed into the top leadership, policy-making structure of the focal organization so as to avoid threats to the focal organization. Selznick (1949) describes a classic case of co-optation in which the Tennessee Valley Authority absorbed strong centers of influence and opposition in the valley in order to facilitate its objectives in the valley as well as its relationships with the Congress, which was antagonistic toward its "socialistic" experiments.

Co-optation, however, is a double-edged sword. More than contracting, it may lead to constraints on the organization's leadership and policy-making functions; for example, Selznick reports that "the T.V.A. commitments to its agricultural constituents resulted in a fractional alignment involving unanticipated consequences for its role on the national scene." The authority, for instance, attempted to exclude the soil conservation service from the valley area because the American Farm Bureau Federation opposed the situation as a co-opted element.

"This resulted in the politically paradoxical situation that the intimately New Deal T.V.A. failed to support agencies with which it shared a political communion, and aligned itself with the enemies of those agencies."

A relatively weak organization may deal with environmental dependency by forming a coalition or merging with other dependent organizations (see, e.g., Pfeffer, 1972a). For instance, numerous small businesses may combine their purchasing activities in order to increase their power vis-à-vis suppliers. This strategy involves an obvious trade-off, however, for power is gained at the expense of mutual interdependence among coalition members.

Finally, an organization that has difficulty dealing with one sector of its environment may seek power over the remaining sectors. According to Thompson:

> The business firm constrained by an impoverished market, as during a recession, finds it urgent to have power to curtail the rate and price of inputs provided by supply elements of the task environment. To the extent that it has power, it may renegotiate contractual arrangements. If the firm is also constrained by large fixed costs, as in heavy industries, . . . [we] would predict that the organization will seek power to curtail the flow of labor inputs. It is in such industries that wage payments typically are in hourly or piece rates, and firms are not committed to fixed salaries or guaranteed annual wages (Thompson, 1967, p. 37).[10]

Environment, Technology, and Organizational Design

According to Thompson (1967), organizations that are subject to the norms of rationality attempt to control or limit environmental uncertainty by employing design strategies determined by the organization's technology. Three major classes of technology are envisaged: (1) *long-linked*, (2) *mediating*, and (3) *intensive*.

Long-linked technology is epitomized by the assembly line that produces a single product. The process involves activities occurring in a fixed sequence. Function N follows M and function O follows N. Suppose that the organization in question performs functions I through Q. Presumably, functions A through H and R through Z are performed by suppliers and customers, respectively. Rather than suffer the independence of these other organizations, the focal organization can integrate its activities vertically, subsuming functions of suppliers and, perhaps, middlemen. This is in contrast to the diversification strategy mentioned earlier which is termed *horizontal integration*.

Vertical integration reduces uncertainties in long-linked technologies. Chandler (1962) describes how American oil firms, which began as refining operations, integrated forward into distribution and marketing and backward into crude oil production and transportation. Alcoa simi-

---

10 From *Organizations in Action* by James D. Thompson. Copyright 1967, McGraw-Hill Book Company. Used with permission of McGraw-Hill Book Company.

larly moved from aluminum production to bauxite mining on one hand and the manufacture and marketing of finished products on the other. Thompson gives a more recent example of this strategy:

> With the recent shrinkage of profit margins, which led to renewed emphasis on rationality norms, major meat packers have moved backward behind the livestock auction markets to establish contractual relationships with livestock feeders. By owning the livestock and feed, and contracting to have livestock fed, the packers can control the flow of animals into slaughterhouses and can calculate their costs in advance, both of which are serious contingencies when packers depend on irregular volume and fluctuating prices in auction markets (Thompson, 1967, p. 41).[11]

The most severe limitation to vertical integration is dispersion of sources of input and output. Basic steel producers, according to Thompson, are prevented from integrating forward into manufacturing because of the myriad of products that are fabricated from steel. Similarly, because of diversity in its product lines, Sears is unable to move backward into the manufacture of all its supplies.

Mediating technologies link clients or customers, who wish to be otherwise unrelated, for the purpose of exchange. Commercial banks employ a mediating technology in linking depositors to borrowers. Similarly, telephone companies and post offices link parties who wish to communicate. Employment agencies link job seekers to recruiters. Independence of sorts is achieved by increasing the number of transactions handled, either by increasing the population served or by saturating a given market. A single, large depositor may come to influence a banker (as was illustrated in Chapter 5). A large number of relatively small depositors is less likely to do so, given their heterogeneity of interests, lack of organization, and the like.

Intensive technologies generally incorporate the client and seek to alter his or her behavior. Hospitals operate intensive technologies. The patients become involved directly in the medical technology which is applied in a form suggested by information taken directly from the patients and their responses to earlier applications of technology. For example, although all hospitals possess the technology to perform glucose tolerance tests, these are not applied routinely, but only when the patient's behavior suggests that diabetes may be a cause of his or her suffering. The client is both the source of information (feedback) which directs the application of technology and a willing participant in the technological process.

Universities also employ an intensive technology. The student becomes part of the system that attempts to inculcate values and attitudes, as well as skills and knowledge. To the extent that instruction is personalized, the application of technology is controlled via feedback.

---

[11] Ibid.

In situations of this sort, environmental uncertainty is reduced to the extent that clients become subservient to the organization that serves them. Hospitals demand "obedience" of patients, and universities have numerous constraints for their students. In extreme cases, the organization places its boundaries completely around the "client" as is the case in prisons, mental hospitals, and monasteries. These have been termed *total institutions* by Goffman (1961).

Top Management and the Environment

For the most part, we have provided a relatively abstract, organizational, level analysis of the organization in relation to its environment. In fact, individual employees in various boundary roles interact with members of other organizations to implement strategies such as buffering and cooperation.

As we indicated in Chapter 1, top management often plays an institutional role, relating the organization to the environment which comprises not only similar organizations but also dissimilar organizations and perhaps even religious, educational, and military institutions and the like. Also, in Chapter 12 we described top management's responsibilities for making valuing decisions and maintaining the organization's character and identity vis-à-vis the environment. Top leadership must also implement various strategies (the formulation of strategy will be discussed in the next chapter), using many of the procedures for conflict-management discussed in Chapter 10. The discussion of bargaining conflict in that chapter is especially useful in understanding interactions with other organizations, since these organizations often are engaged in conflict over scarce resources. The discussion of coalition-formation and negotiations between subgroupings over the goals of the organization (Chapter 5), as well as the discussion of systems conflict in Chapter 10 are also useful in understanding environmental relations, especially the behavior of leaders of organizations that are joined in close (often formal), economic or political relations. The behavior of the top administrator in a local YMCA—in relation to other Ys in the local association, and in relation to the national organization (which is a confederation) is one example (Zald, 1970), as is the behavior of the top management of a subsidiary in relation to the parent firm, and vice versa.

Organizational Intelligence

An important aspect of leadership, and of boundary positions generally, concerns gathering information (or "intelligence"), which enables buffering, co-opting threatening rivals, and so on, to be performed efficiently and effectively. Top leadership, so to speak, is at the apex of an organizational hierarchy to which information from boundary positions flows. Additional information is obtained from the contacts of top managers themselves—as they go about their role of relating their organization to others—and is supplemented by staff inputs from planning departments (including futurologists—see Chapter 19).

Inherent characteristics of organizational hierarchies may preclude accurate intelligence gathering. Subordinates are dependent on superiors for raises and promotions and thus may feel compelled to bias upward communication of the situation as they see it. Because most organizations are pyramidal in structure, competition for limited positions and associated rewards may ensue, often with the information-restricting characteristics of bargaining conflicts (Chapter 10). Top management, recognizing the endemic nature of such conflict, may make use of it and encourage advocacy of different and competing positions, so that alternative views of the environment and alternative strategies are developed (see Chapter 14).

Wilensky (1967), for example, describes how President Kennedy relied on the CIA for information on the internal situation in Cuba before the Bay of Pigs invasion. One might expect that, to the extent the CIA had a positive interest in the invasion, its assessment of the situation might have been biased, leading to predictions of a general uprising when the small invasion force of exiles landed. In contrast, if the Department of State, Army Intelligence, and the like, as well as the CIA had been relied on for intelligence, the differential biases and competition between the intelligence services might have provided several alternative views, which when weighed, could have led to a more accurate assessment of the situation.

Boards of Directors

Boards of directors or trustees sometimes are selected for their expertise in a particular industry or field of endeavor and for their ability to keep abreast of developments in the organization's environment. Board members also are selected for their ability to provide resources—for their potential influence on the environment. In Chapter 5, we described how trustees initially were important in the determination of a hospital's goals because they were able to (or had contacts who could) provide financial resources that were needed as the hospital was starting up. Pfeffer (1973) studied some 57 boards in a variety of hospitals, and showed that voluntary, community hospitals tended to have larger boards than Veterans Administration hospitals. Voluntary hospitals need community support (in terms of finances and also in terms of patients). The larger the board, the greater the support provided or mediated by board members. VA hospitals depend on the government for funds and have a designated source of patients. Thus, a smaller board, comprising members with administrative expertise, is utilized. In general, one might say that board members are likely to be selected according to the degree the organization is dependent on the environment for various inputs (see also Pfeffer, 1972b; Zald, 1967, 1969).

In addition, as we have seen, the organization's environment often includes organizations and constituencies that are threats to the effectiveness and survival of the organization. For example, a local school board, usually elected by voters in a school district, may pose a threat to the school superintendent and his administrators (Kerr, 1964). However, school board members often are easily co-opted. Because they lack expertise in education (e.g., regarding curriculum and the like), administrators are sometimes able to control the flow of information to board members and thus, mold their views or premises (Chapter 11). As a result, board members are socialized to support the administration's views. Also, because the members often do not represent an organized group (constituency), they are free to modify their views and behavior along the lines suggested by the information provided by the administration. The result of these processes is, as Kerr indicates, that the school board comes to legitimate the administration's policies, rather than represent the community to the school administration. The latter, when questioned regarding various policies, can point to the duly elected representatives who have "set" policy for the school system.

The significance of the presence or absence of an organized constituency is shown in a study (Rubin, 1972) of a board's failure to deal with a threatening environment—groups concerned with the busing issue. Working class and lower middle-class members of a San Francisco Bay area community formed an "umbrella" organization to fight the liberal-oriented school board, which planned to bus black children into neighboring white schools. In contrast to the usual voter disinterest between school board elections, this issue, being emotional and reflecting major differences in values, engendered continued interest. In addition, the ambivalence of the school board in implementing busing (over some three years) allowed the community to organize, and eventually elect conservative school board members who ousted the superintendent, suspended the integration plan, and implemented a token plan agreeable to its constituencies.

Community Power Structure

Sociological studies of "community power structure" help explain the role of the board member, or any organizational member, who relates the organization to the local community. Hunter's (1953) classic study of Atlanta, as well as other early studies, showed a structure comprising an elite of business leaders who single-mindedly preserved the city's institutions in their own image. This view has given way to a more complex and pluralistic view of the power structure of communities. A study of New Haven (Dahl, 1961), for example, shows that a large number of individuals have power, depending on the particular issue, with the dynamics of power and the interfaces of groups being important.

While recent studies of community power structures often reveal them to be complex and pluralistic, communities differ, and organizational strategies should vary appropriately. The dispersion of power in a community is found (Aiken, 1970) to be associated with: (1) location in the North, (2) a high degree of absentee ownership, (3) heterogeneous populations, and (4) lower socioeconomic status populations. Cities with more concentrated power structures were found outside the North, had lower absentee ownership, and so on.

The concentration or dispersion of community power seems relevant for understanding effective mobilization of community efforts to deal with problems; for example, Aiken found that mobilization (e.g., obtaining external resources for the community) was associated with decentralized power. It may be that initiation of new organizations or new organizational efforts (akin to the problem or creativity) is facilitated by decentralized power, while developing actions or bringing initial actions to a successful, high level of impact (akin to the problem of implementation) is facilitated by centralized power structures. (We shall discuss these different stages of change further in Chapter 15.) Apparently reflecting the latter point is Turk's (1973) finding, in a study of the 130 largest U.S. cities, that successful formation of hospital councils and antipoverty networks was associated with the existence of organizational linkages—through a high degree of municipal governmental organization and through a large population of voluntary organizations.[12]

Power in Boundary Roles

A final emphasis on the role of power in organizational-environmental relations is provided by a study of industrial salesmen (Pruden and Reese, 1972). This study indicates how the external and internal power of boundary personnel can be related, and how both seem necessary for effective performance (our earlier descriptions of power in the goal-setting process, in Chapter 5, should also be recalled).

---

[12] Power relations in the community have been found to extend to the nation as a whole in Domhoff's (1967, 1970) studies of the "higher circles"—the American upper class. Domhoff investigated the social registers of large American cities such as New York, New Orleans, and San Francisco, and found that there were many overlaps in membership and, as other studies have shown, also high levels of membership on corporate boards of directors, foundations, certain universities, and so on. From an extensive investigation, Domhoff concludes that there is a ruling circle of upper class individuals who dominate industry, government, and other important institutions in this country. This is a relatively closed circle, and entrants are only admitted after a considerable period of socialization during which their values become congruent with those of the ruling circle. If such a ruling circle does exist, then its values, and the power behind these values, appear to be an important aspect of the environment to be taken into account by the top leadership of an organization.

Pruden and Reese studied a sample of 91 outside salesmen, employed by a national producer and distributor of wood products to sell a broad line of building materials to retail, contractor, and industrial users throughout the nation. These customers are powerfully situated in the role set of the salesmen, because they can choose among competing salesmen, all of whom deal with relatively undifferentiated products. Pruden and Reese found that salesman "performance" was associated with the salesman's "identification" with the customer; that is, there was a perception of considerable similarity between the high-performing salesman and his customers, and he tended to know his customers not only as business acquaintances, but also as friends.

Pruden and Reese argue that salesmen are effective to the extent they have power in a number of areas. Compared to low-performers, the higher performing salesmen had greater authority over inside salesmen and procedures for the collection of credit, and greater influence over delivery time. Power and authority apparently enabled the successful salesmen to protect their familiarity with customers, to modify irritating behavior of inside salesmen, and to control the very crucial (for the building industry particularly) variable of delivery time, and thereby differentiate themselves from competing suppliers. Salesmen apparently are able to use their power to increase discretion over certain functions, ones that are essential to consummating transactions between the organization and the customer (i.e., credit, delivery, price, and product functions). At the same time, power is used by the salesman to build up good relationships with customers, giving him some leverage, then, in the exchange between organization and customer. By offering one's friendship and a modicum of control over important elements of the seller's organization, the salesman is able to offer a good exchange for the buyer's willingness to purchase. Ideally, such relationships are regularized with time, and the organization can depend on such environmental linkages and perform more effectively.[13]

The Residual Meaning

We have argued that the environment to which organizations respond consists of other organizations. To an extent this position is viable—but only to a limited extent. Lest we appear to indulge in sleight of mouth, our omissions must be acknowledged.

There is no doubt that other portions of the environment (exclusive of organizations) affect and are responded to by organizations. Yet, it is impossible to write a chapter, or even a book, about "Everything Except the Focal Organization and Its Effects on the Focal Organization." We have omitted much in the hope of providing a lucid analysis of that

---

[13] See also the study of the "political economy" of organizations (Walmsley and Zald, 1973; Zald, 1970).

portion of the environment which accounts for a significant amount of the variance observed.

In cataloging our sins of omission, please add organizational responses that are essentially nonrational. Attending to the norm of organizational rationality, we have ignored responses to the environment such as denial and rationalization. Hopefully, the gist of these phenomena has been presented elsewhere in a form that translates easily from individual to organizational responses. With this, we shall close Pandora's box, as it were, and proceed to the more manageable topic of strategy.

DISCUSSION QUESTIONS

1. In what ways has the environment of higher education changed over the past 25 years? How have colleges and universities responded to these changes?
2. How have colleges and universities attempted to influence the environment?
3. What business schools would you list in an organizational prestige set? What evidence can you find that such sets exist?
4. To what other organizations is your college or university related. What are the implications of these relationships?
5. What sort of technology does an institution of higher learning employ: long-linked, mediating, intensive, or some combination of these?

REFERENCES

Aiken, Michael. The distribution of community power: structural bases and social consequences. In Michael Aiken and Paul E. Mott (Eds.), *The structure of community power.* New York: Random House, 1970. Pp. 487–525.

Brooks, Harvey, and Bowers, Raymond. The assessment of technology. *Scientific American*, 1961, 222, 2, 13–21.

Burns, T., and Stalker, G. M. *The management of innovation.* London: Tavistock, 1961.

Caplow, Theodore. *Principles of organization.* New York: Harcourt Brace Jovanovich, Inc., 1964.

Chandler, Alfred D., Jr. *Strategy and structure.* Cambridge, Mass.: M.I.T. Press, 1962.

Dahl, Robert A. *Who governs?* New Haven, Conn.: Yale University Press, 1961.

Domhoff, William G. *Who rules America?* Englewood Cliffs, N.J.: Prentice-Hall, 1967.

Domhoff, William G. *The higher circles.* New York: Random House, 1970.

Emery, F. W., and Trist, E. L. The causal texture of organizational environment. *Human Relations*, 1965, *18*, 21–31.

Evan, William M. The organization-set: toward a theory of interorganizational relations. In J. D. Thompson (Ed.), *Approaches to organizational design.* Pittsburgh: University of Pittsburgh Press, 1966. Pp. 173–91.

Evan, William M. An organization-set model of interorganizational relations. In Matthew Tuite (Ed.), *Interorganizational decisionmaking.* Chicago: Aldine, 1972. Pp. 181–200.

Galbraith, Jay R. Organization designs: an information processing view. In J. W. Lorsch and P. R. Lawrence (Eds.), *Organizational planning: cases and concepts.* Homewood, Ill.: Dorsey, 1972. Pp. 49–74.

Goffman, Erving. *Asylums.* Garden City, N.Y.: Anchor Books, 1961.

Gross, George R. The organization set: a study of sociology departments. *The American Sociologist,* 1970, 5, 25–29.

Hall, Richard H. *Organizations: structure and process.* Englewood Cliffs, N.J.: Prentice-Hall, 1972.

Hall, Richard H., Clark, John P., Giordano, Peggy, Halpert, Burton, Johnson, Paul V., Van Roekel, Martha, and Choi, Thomas. Interorganizational relationships. Paper presented at American Sociological Association meetings, New York, August 1973.

Hunter, Floyd. *Community power structure.* Chapel Hill, N.C.: University of North Carolina Press, 1953.

Kerr, Norman D. The school board as an agency of legitimation. *Sociology of Education,* 1964, 38, 34–59.

Klongan, Gerald E., Paulson, Steven, and Rogers, David. Measurement of interorganizational relations: a deterministic model. Paper presented at American Sociological Association meetings, New Orleans, August 1972.

Lawrence, Paul R., and Lorsch, Jay W. *Organization and environment.* Boston: Harvard University, Graduate School of Business Administration, 1967.

Meier, Richard L. Communication overload. *Administrative Science Quarterly,* 1963, 7, 521–44.

Mintz, Morton. *The therapeutic nightmare.* Boston: Houghton Mifflin, 1965.

Nietzsche, Frederich. *The birth of tragedy and the genealogy of morals.* Garden City, N.Y.: Doubleday, 1956.

Parsons, Talcott. *Structure and process in modern societies.* Glencoe, Ill.: Free Press, 1960.

Perrow, Charles. *Organizational analysis: a sociological view.* Belmont, Calif.: Wadsworth, 1970.

Perrow, Charles. *Complex organizations: a critical essay.* Glenview, Ill.: Scott, Foresman and Company, 1972.

Pfeffer, Jeffrey. Merger as a response to organizational interdependence. *Administrative Science Quarterly,* 1972, 17, 382–94. (a)

Pfeffer, Jeffrey. Size and composition of corporate boards of directors: the organization and its environment. *Administrative Science Quarterly,* 1972, 17, 218–28 (b)

Pfeffer, Jeffrey. Size, composition, and function of hospital boards of directors: a study of organization-environment linkage. *Administrative Science Quarterly,* 1973, 18, 349–64.

Pfeffer, Jeffrey, and Leblebici, Huseyin. Executive recruitment and the development of interfirm organizations. *Administrative Science Quarterly,* 1973, 18, 449–61.

Pruden, Henry O., and Reese, Richard M. Interorganizational role-set relations and the performance and satisfaction of industrial salesmen. *Administrative Science Quarterly,* 1972, 17, 601–9.

Rubin, Lillian B. *Busing and backlash: white against white in an urban school district.* Berkeley, Calif.: University of California Press, 1972.

Selznick, Philip. *TVA and the grass roots.* Berkeley, Calif.: University of California Press, 1949.

Tausky, Curt. *Work organizations: major theoretical perspectives.* Itaska, Ill.: F. E. Peacock, 1970.

Terreberry, Shirley. The evolution of organizational environments. *Administrative Science Quarterly*, 1968, *12*, 590–613.

Thompson, James D. *Organizations in action*. New York: McGraw-Hill Book Company, 1967.

Turk, Herman. Comparative urban structure from an interorganizational perspective. *Administrative Science Quarterly*, 1973, *18*, 37–55.

Walmsley, Gary L., and Zald, Mayer N. *The political economy of public organizations*. Lexington, Mass.: D. C. Heath, 1973.

Wilensky, Harold L. *Organizational intelligence*. New York: Basic Books, 1967.

Zald, Mayer N. Urban differentiation, characteristics of boards of directors and organizational effectiveness. *American Journal of Sociology*, 1967, *73*, 261–72.

Zald, Mayer N. The power and function of boards of directors: a theoretical synthesis. *American Journal of Sociology*, 1969, *75*, 97–111.

Zald, Mayer N. *Organizational change: the political economy of the YMCA*. Chicago: University of Chicago Press, 1970.

14

Strategy Formulation

INTRODUCTION

Earlier we suggested that many models of decision-making processes are elaborations of John Dewey's (1971) three-step process: (1) What is the problem? (2) What are the alternatives? (3) Which alternative is best? These models are valid only to the extent that: (1) the problem is well defined, (2) all feasible alternatives are known, and (3) the consequences of each alternative are certain and couched in terms that allow comparison with the consequences of all other alternatives. These conditions may obtain in closed systems (such as some technologies), but are lacking in most other managerial situations. The further we move from the organization's technical core, the less the decision-making process resembles Dewey's model.

March and Simon (1958) describe the decision-making process in more complex terms in their classic *Organizations*. (1) The first adequate alternative is sought (satisficing), rather than the best one (maximizing). As they point out, organizational life is extremely complex, and problem solving a time-consuming process. In light of this, searching the haystack for a needle sharp enough to sew with may be better than persevering after the sharpest needle in the haystack. (2) Alternatives are discovered sequentially and their consequences are analyzed in this order. Search for alternatives is concluded when the first satisfactory solution is found. (3) Organizations deal with problems sequentially since relatively few parts of the organization are adaptive at any one time.

Dewey's model is ultimately rational. The March and Simon model describes *bounded rationality*. Lacking the capacity to deal with all relevant aspects of a problem and lacking the knowledge to see them all clearly, people are forced to limit their search and to base their decisions on crude analogues of reality. Humans are not irrational, but *intendedly rational* in the absence of the wherewithal to follow Dewey's advice.

Chapter Guide

The choice of a college major is a strategic choice. Having made this choice, the decision to attend one college rather than another is tactical.

403

1. Try to recall the decision process that led you to choose a particular undergraduate major. What alternatives did you consider? What did you know about the consequences of the various alternatives? How did you choose one alternative?
2. From how many college admissions offers did you choose? What did you know about each of the colleges? What information led you to choose one college over another?
3. Review these two decision processes. Are they similar or dissimilar? Why?

MODELS OF DECISION MAKING

Strategy

Strategy refers to the means that enable the organization to attain its goals in the environment. Organizational goals are decided by various processes including leadership (Chapers 5 and 12). Strategy refers to the means by which objectives are achieved. A firm may strive for profits by aggressive marketing of new products or by efficient production and price competition in the marketplace. A hospital may provide health care by collaborating with other organizations in a broad network of referrals and contracts or it may attempt to be comprehensive and self-contained. Occasionally, the term *policy* is used in the same context. Because they are concerned with the organization's relations with its environment, strategy or policy decisions emanate from the *institutional* level of the organization (Chapter 1).

Glueck (1972) gives the following example of corporate strategy:

> Consider a medium-sized manufacturer of clothing. In this firm 60 to 70 percent of its business is with the military. The firm's executives are satisfied with the profit margin, but fear military cutbacks if and when the U.S. can extract itself from Vietnam and avoid similar encounters. What to do? The other 30 percent of its business involves the manufacture of private label shirts and slacks for a large retailer. One corporate strategy would be to shift a portion of its profitable but vulnerable military business (let's say 20 percent over a 2-year period) to other business. But to what?
>
> The first strategy would be to aggressively develop its private label business with other retailers. This may not please its one customer, however, but this strategy requires little increase in organization (perhaps addition of only one salesman), no new financing for equipment, little new knowledge of the business, and so on.
>
> A second strategy might be to stay in the same business, but market men's shirts and slacks under the firm's own label. It also may involve developing new fashion concepts which in turn requires new machin-

ery, designers, and so forth. It also requires advertising, a sales force, new pricing techniques, and so forth. So, a *corporate strategy* is an integrated functional plan in response to a problem perceived to be thrust upon the company by the environment or in response to initiations of the corporation to change the impact the company wishes to have on the environment. The strategic plan is carefully thought out through consideration of the major implications to the company's move in the following areas: marketing, operations, finance, management, personnel, and so forth (p. 183).

Some authors take issue with definitions that treat strategy as a plan or an explicit set of guidelines developed in advance of the activities they seek to direct. Mintzberg (1972), for instance, argues that this view limits our focus to abstract, normative aspects of the phenomenon. He suggests that we study strategy as *a pattern in a stream of significant decisions*. This definition can be clarified with a simple example. Early in his presidency, Richard Nixon made a number of decisions that appeared to enhance Republican voting support in the South. The press labeled these decisions Nixon's "southern strategy." In Mintzberg's terms, the implication is ". . . simply that, in spite of the fact that Nixon never announced such a strategy, there appeared to be a pattern in his decisions" (1972, p. 90). Using Mintzberg's perspective, our focus will be directed to the process through which strategy is formulated and to its continuous nature.

Strategy and Planning

How does strategy making differ from the planning described at the beginning of Chapter 12? In a book on planning and control systems, Anthony (1965) differentiates between two kinds of planning, one primarily concerned with the ongoing administration of the organization and the other with policy formulation, goal-setting, and top-management planning.[1] The latter is referred to as "strategic planning" and is defined as "the process of deciding on objectives of the organization, on changes in these objectives, on the resources used to obtain these objectives, and

---

[1] The term "long-range planning" is used variously in literature but often refers to what Anthony terms management control. Despite the concern of long-range planning with future events, it is generally a relatively routine activity:

"A five-year plan usually is a projection of the costs and revenues that are anticipated under policies and programs *already approved*, rather than a device for consideration of, and decision on, new policies and programs. The five-year plan reflects strategic decisions already taken; it is not the essence of the process of making new decisions. The procedures used in preparing a five-year plan are in many respects the same as those used in preparing an annual budget. Indeed, in companies in which long-range planning is most successful, the annual budget is simply the first year of the five-year plan. In some companies, the so-called five-year plan is nothing more than a mechanical extrapolation of current data, with no reflection of management decisions and judgment; such an exercise is virtually worthless" (Anthony, 1965, pp. 57–58).

Organizations: Behavior, Design, and Change

on the policies that are to govern the acquisition, use, and disposition of these resources" (p. 16). Planning concerned with ongoing administration of the organization is termed "management control" and is defined as "the process by which managers assure that resources are obtained and used effectively and efficiently in the accomplishment of the organization's objectives" (p. 17).

In terms of the distinction between institutional, managerial, and technical levels of the organization, we see that strategic planning activities take place primarily at the institutional level, and management control activities at the managerial level. Management control consists primarily of interpreting institutional decisions and using them as guidelines for various boundary-passing (input-output) activities. Figure 14–1 provides examples of activities found at the two different levels. Activities required by strategic planning are complex, unstructured, and nonroutine, as opposed to management control activities, which tend to be simpler and more routine.

FIGURE 14–1
Examples of Activities in a Business Organization

Strategic planning	Management control
Choosing company objectives	Formulating budgets
Planning the organization	Planning staff levels
Setting personnel policies	Formulating personnel practices
Setting financial policies	Working capital planning
Setting marketing policies	Formulating advertising programs
Setting research policies	Deciding on research projects
Choosing new product lines	Choosing product improvements
Acquiring a new division	Deciding on plant rearrangement
Deciding on non-routine capital expenditures	Deciding on routine capital expenditures
	Formulating decision rules for operational control
	Measuring, appraising, and improving management performance

Source: Anthony (1965, p. 19).

Strategy Formulation: The Normative Approach

Mintzberg (1967) identifies two basic approaches to strategy making and likens them to the biblical portrayal of creation on one hand and Darwin's theory of evolution on the other. The "biblical" approach to strategy is normative and rational. It describes how strategy *ought* to develop by following the systematic steps advocated by some decision theorists. Glueck (1972) suggests that once the organization's goals and objectives are established, the following steps are appropriate: (1) appraisal of the company's status in terms of strengths and weaknesses, (2) the generation of a set of alternative strategies consistent with the strengths and weaknesses, and (3) selection of the best alternative. Ansoff's (1965) approach is similar.

Unfortunately, there is little empirical research on normative approaches to strategy formulation. For one thing, it is extremely difficult to develop samples and control groups of similar, representative organizations. For another, until recently few firms had special planning departments or made use of formal strategic planning systems (Ringbakk, 1969). Indeed, as Hofer (1973) indicates, most studies of the normative approach to strategic planning have investigated the planning process itself, rather than the relationships between various processes and organizational performance. Rather than describing the effectiveness of different forms of strategy making, these studies tell us how to make the process more rational.

Descriptive Studies

However, several studies have begun to describe and relate the use of strategic planning to organizational performance. Thune and House (1970) studied 36 firms and found that companies with formalized, companywide, long-range planning systems were more successful, according to five criteria of financial performance, than companies without these systems. These findings obtained for firms in the drug, chemical, and machinery industries, but not for those in steel, oil, or food processing. Ansoff and colleagues (1970) investigated relationships between formal planning for acquisitions and subsequent improvement in financial performance. Approximately 30 percent of the firms studied engaged in formal acquisitions planning and were found to be more successful than the remainder of the sample. However, these findings are limited to acquisitions planning as opposed to the broader activity of strategic planning. Vancil (1970), on the other hand, studied the accuracy of long-range planning and found no relationship between the accuracy with which sales revenues were projected and the firm's rate of return on investment.

In the most comprehensive study to date, Rue and Fulmer (1973) examined 386 organizations in an attempt to relate planning to financial performance. Interestingly, at the time of the study, the majority of firms having five-year plans had engaged in the planning process for only five years or less. Using four different performance criteria (sales growth, growth in earnings, earnings to sales ratio, and return on investment), Rue and Fulmer found no straightforward relationship between the completeness of long-range planning and performance. In the service industries, nonplanners outperformed planners in all cases. Planners outperformed nonplanners in the durable goods industries. According to the authors: "Obviously, such variables as timing, luck, and the immeasurable quality of 'overall managerial competence' have a more direct relationship to a firm's performance success than the formality of its long-range planning activity" (Rue and Fulmer, 1973, p. 72).

Unfortunately, matters can be complicated still further. Despite Thune and House's (1970) finding that planning is related to performance in certain industries, it is not clear that planning caused the improvement noted. Improved performance may lead to subsequent initiation of long-range planning, as Thune and House (1970) found for firms in the food and petroleum industries. It is also quite possible that some third factor, a causal variable, contributes both to improved performance and to the installation of planning systems; for example, changes in top management may (1) cause increases in performance and (2) introduce various new management techniques, such as strategic planning. Although these factors may be associated, neither is necessarily the cause of the other. Finally, numerous other factors contribute to performance. Schoeffler and colleagues (1974) found that 37 factors accounted for 80 percent of the variation in profitability in a study of more than 600 firms. Thune and House conclude:

> . . . we have speculated that firms engaged in formal planning also use more sophisticated methods for organization design and analysis; managerial selection, development, and compensation; and administrative control. Thus, it is most likely that formal planning is a characteristic of a well-managed firm than the single cause of successful economic performance (Thune and House, 1970, p. 87).

Strategy Formulation: The Disjointed Incremental Approach

The second approach to strategy making, the evolutionary approach, has been termed *disjointed incrementalism*—a term borrowed from political scientists who deem it descriptive of the way policies are actually formulated in our democratic society (Braybrooke and Lindblom, 1963; Lindblom, 1965). However, in addition to being descriptive, disjointed incrementalism is viewed by some as the way in which such decisions ought to be made. In large measure, this argument is offered in the belief that the normative (rational) approach is infeasible. The rational approach assumes a decision maker who is nearly omniscient and omnipotent. In reality, decisions of the sort described here frequently are made by groups of intendedly rational satisficers who cannot agree on objectives and priorities that are complex, interrelated, and have no clear implications for "self-interest." Furthermore, no single individual has sufficient power to ensure that the chosen alternative(s) will be properly implemented (Bauer, 1968; Friedman and Hudson, 1974; Schoettle, 1968).

If there is no simple problem statement; no single decision-making unit with a single set of interests, values, and goals; no way to calculate the rank ordering of alternatives; and no assurance that chosen alternatives will be implemented, how are policy and strategy decisions made? Essentially, strategy is a matter of tactics and of starting with specifics and "muddling through" (Lindblom, 1965). Braybrooke and Lindblom's disjointed incrementalism has been summarized as follows:

1. Choices are made at the margin of the status quo ("the politically feasible").
2. A restricted variety of policy alternatives are considered in a social system, those which differ from existing policies only incrementally.
3. Only analyses of incremental differences in consequences are considered.
4. Means and ends are intermingled. Ends adjust to means, as well as means to ends.
5. Identification and evaluation of alternatives is fragmented, taking place at a large number of disjointed points in the social system.
6. Identification of policy alternatives occurs in response to emergent problems rather than being the result of a positive search for meeting a preconceived set of goals (Guth, 1973, p. 5).

Disjointed incrementalism may be illustrated by decision making on budgets (Wildavsky, 1964; Wildavsky and Hammond, 1965). Generally, the current budget of an agency or organizational unit is taken as given, and what are closely examined are changes at the margin. Since there would be considerable uncertainty about consequences of major changes in the budget (such as removing several items completely or adding major new items), examination of the consequences of marginal increments is made instead. Decisions are made not on the whole package, but, rather, according to incremental changes and their implications for the interests and values of other units politically involved with the unit whose budget is being considered.

Budgetary changes may be approved as much for the means or activities proposed as for the objectives which these means are intended to facilitate. Decisions are not made rationally in terms of selecting objectives and choosing the best means toward those objectives. The budgeted activities may be acceptable to decision makers for quite different reasons, and, given the agreement on the budgeted activities, the ends will have to adjust to the means.

Because organizations generally lack sufficient time and expertise, the full range of alternatives to existing policy is rarely considered. Only if a major budgetary change is proposed are time and effort expended in evaluation and explicit decision making. Moreover, this search occurs in response to proposals, and sequentially proposal by proposal, rather than being comprehensive, synoptic, and rational with regard to the objectives of the unit being budgeted.

A Contingency Approach

Throughout this book we have tried to demonstrate that two-valued (either/or) orientations invariably are replaced by contingency approaches. No less is true of strategy making. There is no single, best way to formulate strategy. Newman (1971) argues that strategy is determined by the "outlook," the environment and the organization's relation to it. Once formed, strategy dictates technology, which, in turn determines structure, as Perrow argues (Chapter 4). A routine technology requires comprehensive, detailed, operational planning, while a nonroutine technology can be served by planning that covers the "main points" and not the details. If management structures (e.g., operational planning, leading, organizing) are contingent on technology and strategy in this manner, an efficient fit will have been achieved. However, not only does structure result from strategy, but also (as indicated by the feedback arrow in Figure 14–2) the appropriate technology and management structure affect strategy (Chandler, 1962), making some strategies easier to implement than others. "Adjustments in planning, leading, and controlling, as well as organizing, are often needed to execute a new strategy; and integration of these sub-processes into a total *management design* is vital" (Newman, 1971, p. 66).

An extension of this approach is provided by Kast and Rosenzweig (1973) who categorize organizations according to their location on a continuum ranging from "closed/stable/mechanistic" at one extreme to "open/organic/adaptive" at the other. As illustrated in Figure 14–3, this approach suggests that organizations residing in placid environments are well served by the rational approach to strategic decision

FIGURE 14–2
A Contingency View of Strategy Formulation

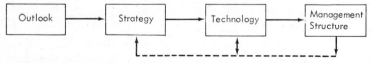

Source: Newman (1971, p. 61).

making, while those in turbulent environments are better served by disjointed incrementalism. Kast and Rosenzweig see the "closed" organization as having: (1) a single, clear-cut set of goals; (2) a goal-setting process that resides solely with top management; (3) a decision-making apparatus that is autocratic, programmed, and computational; and (4) an information system that supplies primarily quantitative data. These characteristics seem to fit the rational planning process. In contrast, they describe the "open" organization as a system having: (1) multiple goal sets determined by the need to satisfy numerous constraints; (2) lower level personnel involved in goal-setting processes; (3) decision-making processes that are satisficing, heuristic, and grounded in disjointed incrementalism; and (4) information flows comprising qualitative data.

At this point, we must caution against embracing the contingency model wholeheartedly. In the words of Kast and Rosenzweig: "Hypotheses about these relationships have not been proven via substantial empirical research [and] in fact, it is doubtful whether or not they can ever be proven conclusively" (Kast and Rosenzweig, 1973, p. 319). We would like to be somewhat "incremental" ourselves for this reason. The contingency models describe extremes which some organizations may experience, but these models do not deal adequately, in this case, with the world faced by most organizations. We would like to suggest that the average manager works somewhere between "open" and "closed" systems; placid and turbulent environments; and rational and disjointed incremental planning processes. An environment falling between these extremes may merely set broad perimeters within which the organization must operate if it is to succeed.

For one thing, organizations have a degree of choice over the environment in which they operate (Child, 1972); for example, one strategic choice confronting management may be whether to enter a growing market or a mature one. Similarly, choice concerning geographic location enables management to select from alternative labor sources and taxation policies. Second, organizations can exert considerable degrees of control over their environment. Galbraith's (1967) discussion of the *technostructure* and its ability to manipulate and create demand for its products is an example of this point. Finally, as we noted earlier, organizations exert political influence. Given sufficient political leverage, an organization can survive and even prosper regardless of whether it fits the requirements of the contingency model or whether its stated objectives are achieved.

Values

On the basis of both observation and systematic studies of top management in business organizations, Guth and Tagiuri (1965) con-

FIGURE 14–3

A Conceptual Model of Contingency Views of Organization and Management

Systems and Their Key Dimensions	Characteristics of Organizational Systems	
	Closed/Stable/ Mechanistic	*Open/Adaptive/Organic*
Environmental Suprasystem		
General nature	Placid	Turbulent
Predictability	Certain, determinate	Uncertain, indeterminate
Degree of environmental influence on organization	Low	High
Control of task environment by organization	High	Low
Technology	Stable	Dynamic
Input	Homogeneous	Heterogeneous
Boundary relationships	Relatively closed. Limited to few participants (sales, purchasing, etc.). Fixed and well defined	Relatively open. Many participants have external relationships. Varied and not clearly defined
Organization means for interfacing with environment	Routine, standardized procedures	Nonroutine, flexible arrangements
Interorganizational relationships	Few organizations and/or organization types with well-defined, fixed relationships	Many diverse organizations with changing relationships
Overall Organizational System		
Boundary	Relatively closed	Relatively open
Goal structure	Organization as a single goal maximizer	Organization as a searching, adapting, learning system which continually adjusts its multiple goals and aspirations
Predictability of actions	Relatively certain, determinate	Relatively uncertain, indeterminate
Decision-making processes	Programmable, computational	Nonprogrammable, judgmental
Organization emphasis	On performance	On problem solving
Goals and Values		
Organizational goals in general	Efficient performance, stability, maintenance	Effective problem solving, innovation, growth
Pervasive values	Efficiency, predictability, security, risk aversion	Effectiveness, adaptability, responsiveness, risk taking
Ideological orientation	Undimensional and dualism	Multidimensional and relativism

FIGURE 14–3 (continued)

	Characteristics of Organizational Systems	
Systems and Their Key Dimensions	Closed/Stable/ Mechanistic	Open/Adaptive/Organic
• • •	• • •	• • •
Managerial System		
General nature	Hierarchical structure of control, authority, and communications; combination of independent, static components	A network structure of control, authority, and communications; co-alignment of interdependent, dynamic components
Specificity of managerial role	High	Low
Problem solving	Algorithmic, systematic, optimizing models	Heuristic, "disjointed incrementalism," satisficing models
Decision-making techniques	Autocratic, programmed, computational	Participative, nonprogrammed, judgmental
Information flow	Quantitative data	Qualitative data
Content of communications	Decisions and instructions	Advice and information
Planning process	Repetitive, fixed, and specific	Changing, flexible, and general
Planning horizon	Short term	Long term
Types of plans	Standing plans, specific policies	Single-use plans, general policies
Control structure	Hierarchic, specific, short term. External control of participants	Reciprocal, general, long term. Self-control of participants
Control process	Control through impersonal means (rules, regulations, e.g.)	Control through interpersonal contacts (suggestion, persuasion, e.g.)
Position-based authority	High	Low
Knowledge-based authority	Low	High
Formality of authority	High	Low
Degree of professionalization	Low	High
Reaction to individual differences	Disallow, or at best tolerate	Recognize and value
Means of conflict resolution	Resolved by superior (refer to "book") Compromise and smoothing Keep below the surface	Resolved by group ("situation ethics") Confrontation Bring out in open
Management development	Orientation and training to fit the organization	Personal growth leading to organizational adjustments

Source: Abstracted from Kast and Rosenzweig (1973, pp. 315–18).

clude that "personal values are important determinants in the choice of corporate strategies" (p. 123). As used here values mean conceptions of what is valued or desirable, lying somewhere between very general, positive attitudes and a philosophy toward life. Values are quite basic and are generally taken for granted unless questioned or challenged. They may be viewed as a part of personality, acquired early in life from the socialization practices of parents and, to a lesser extent, from peers and schooling. Values are inculcated by one's society, subculture, and family through systematic applications of sanctions and models. Because they are infrequently verbalized and pervasive, we typically do not become aware of our values until faced with a strange set of values or a value conflict.

The values studied by Guth and Tagiuri were measured by the Allport, Vernon, and Lindzey *Study of Values* (1960) which is based on Spranger's (1928) six types of men.

Edward Spranger concluded a study of values in 1928 by postulating that there are six basic attitudes which men can hold toward life. All six attitudes or tendencies are present in all men, but this varies among persons to the extent that some of them predominate, while others play less potent roles in the individual personality. To describe these tendencies Spranger used the technique of imagining six individuals, each of whom possessed a different attitude to the exclusion of the other five. Thus, the types of men to which we will refer are, in Spranger's words, ". . . only a fiction and never found in reality." Yet, he states that where one attitude dominates all others in an individual's psychological make-up, the individual's personality will approximate the appropriate fictional type. Spranger's types of men, then, are as follows:

The *theoretic* man is a lover of knowledge whose sole passions are to seek objective knowledge, to solve problems, to formulate correct equations and to learn. He feels that all solutions to the world's problems will arise from increases in the general level of education—that education is the only road to progress.

The *economic* man appears as a fictional businessman who, to all else in life, prefers those things which are useful. He sees nothing wrong with destroying a beautiful (but useless) landscape to construct a paper mill. He sees men in economic terms, as producers and consumers, and is consequently unlikely to sacrifice himself for others. His ethos, as manifested in the Protestant Ethic, is characterized by thrift, industry, efficiency, order and reliability.

Whereas the theoretic man sees nature as an orderly system, the *aesthetic* man views nature with affinity as a living entity of quasi-mythological stature. He feels that the *pure* being of aesthetic objects is destroyed when either usefulness or theory is ascribed to them. To this extent he feels that political and economic activities are necessary, but subordinate to the art of living.

What beauty is to the aesthetic man, love is to the *social* man. Humanity, being the carrier of love becomes the object of love. Nothing expresses the concept as well as: "From each according to his ability; to each according to his need."

The *political* man is consumed with a will to dominate others, a driving force to be on the top rather than on the bottom. He sees knowledge as power and wealth as the means to control others, and is willing to sacrifice his constituents, as in war, in order to maintain his degree of political control.

The *religious* man, finally, relates to an ultimate value which is not of this world. His sole passion is to find the highest value which surrounds the world and soul; a state we refer to as the state of grace (Ullrich, 1970, p. 6).

The Study of Values scale has a total of 240 points and is scored so that an average response yields 40 points for each value. Administration of the scale to high-level U.S. executives attending an advanced management program at the Harvard Business School (Tagiuri, 1965) yielded the average value profile in Table 14–1.

We see that these executives are high on economic and political values, as one might expect, and also on theoretical values, for, as Tagiuri indicates, the high-level executive needs to have some theories in order to sift through details and abstract what is going on in the organization.

The influence of values on corporate strategy may be seen in the following case:

> In early 1961 the four top executives of U.S. Research, Inc. (disguised name), a large research and development company with a high proportion of its business in government work, were considering possible strategies for the future. Three major alternatives had been identified:
>
> (1) Attempt to triple, over the next three to five years, the company's volume of business by broadening its base of research "products" and thus capturing a larger share of the then growing government expenditures for space exploration.
>
> (2) Aim for the same growth objective, but achieve it through the development of commercially exploitable hardware products generated in the research activity.
>
> (3) Aim for a slower rate of growth, continuing the business along the lines in which it had achieved its present position.
>
> The president, convinced that each top executive of the company needed to be personally committed to the strategy finally chosen, held a number of meetings directed at achieving consensus on one of the alternatives. The meetings proved fruitless. All three possibilities were

TABLE 14–1

Value	Score
Economic	45
Theoretical	44
Political	44
Religious	39
Aesthetic	35
Social	33
Total	240

strongly favored by one or more of the officers, each of whom justified his choice as the only "objectively" feasible alternative.

The president believed, on the basis of the evidence available, that all three alternatives were equally feasible. It occurred to him that further progress might be made in achieving a personal commitment from each manager if attention were focused on the relationship of the managers themselves to the nature of the alternatives. Using knowledge about *personal values,* he was able to identify differences between himself and the other three top officers which seemed to account for their choices among the strategic alternatives:

The vice president who favored the first alternative—tripling the volume of business through broadening the company's base of research products—was seen by the president as having the values of a business-man-scientist whose involvement in the company was motivated by a desire to earn as much money as possible while at the same time being associated with the intellectual stimulation of a research "atmosphere." He wanted the company to grow rapidly and become more profitable, but he also wanted it to remain exclusively a research company.

The vice president who favored rapid growth through the development of commercially exploitable hardware products was seen by the president as having the value orientation of a businessman whose involvement with the company was predominantly motivated by an interest in economic progress as measured by growth and profitability. Rapid growth and increased profitability for the company were his prime interests, along with efficiency and orderliness in the company's day-to-day operations. . . .

The third vice president, favoring continuation of the present activity aimed at achieving a slower rate of growth, was seen by the president as having the values of a scientist who joined the company with the principal objective of working on research projects with practical applicability. This vice president viewed the possibility of getting into commercial production with alarm, believing such activity would disturb the company's research climate. In addition, he believed that substantial company growth in any field might lead to bureaucratic organizational practices also potentially inimical to creative research.

The president saw *his own* values as an almost equally balanced combination of economic, scientific, and human-relations concerns. His involvement in the company reflected not only economic and scientific objectives, but also an interest in working closely and productively with a tightly knit group of men who were all personally involved in the company's efforts.

On the basis of these insights, the president switched from favoring the first alternative to favoring a modification of the third alternative, which called for attempting to double the company's growth in the next five years through continuing the business along the lines in which it had achieved its present position. He believed this new alternative matched the values of the *group* of top executives better than any of the three previously identified alternatives (Guth and Tagiuri, 1965, pp. 123–24).

In one of the few studies of the effect of values on a number of organizations, Hage and Dewar (1973) examined the value of change among top people in 16 health and welfare organizations providing rehabilitation services. A five-item scale of values favorable to change was administered to the staff of these organizations. Hage and Dewar were interested to see whether the values of (a) the leader (executive director) alone, (b) the "formal elite" (executive director and department heads), (c) the "behavioral elite" (the leader and all staff members who reported that they participated in decisions about policy, programs, personnel, and promotions—clearly critical or strategic decisions), or (d) the "entire staff" would best predict actual subsequent change in the organization over the following three years.

Change was measured in terms of addition of new programs (such as a stroke clinic for a rehabilitation agency or a program for unwed mothers in an agency that had never handled these clients before). Expansion of or change in existing programs were not considered a change. The study sought to answer the question: Whose values determine strategic decision making (inferred) and subsequent implementation of decided-upon strategic changes?

The leader's values, or course, did predict the amount of change. What was rather interesting, however, was that the "behavioral elite" predicted even better. Those of the "formal elite" predicted less well and the values of the entire staff not at all. One might conclude that a general predisposition favoring change is not sufficient for creating change, nor is the valuing of change by formally designated top staff. The values of the leader and the behavioral elite (corresponding to what Thompson [1967] terms the "dominant coalition") seem to affect the implementation of strategy.

Processes of Strategy Formulation

Strategy formulation is more than the cognitive or intellectual exercise emphasized so often in management literature. This decision making is embedded within social processes. According to Bower (1970):

> [We focus on] those strategic moves which direct an organization's critical resources toward perceived opportunities in a changing environment. . . . [We are at once concerned with the] (1) intellectual activities of perception, analysis, and choice which often are subsumed under the rubric "decision making," (2) social process of implementing formulated policies by means of organizational structure, systems of measurement and allocation, and systems for reward and punishment, and finally (3) the dynamic process of revising policy as changes in organizational resources and the environment change the context of the original policy problem (pp. 7–8).[2]

An illustration of the usefulness of this general approach is found in a recent study by Allison (1971) which describes the U.S. govern-

---

[2] From *Managing the Resource Allocation Process: A Study of Corporate Planning and Investment*, by Joseph L. Bower (Boston: Division of Research, Harvard Business School, 1970), pp. 7–8.

ment's strategy formulation process during the Cuban missile crisis. Three different models are used to describe different factors of the process. Model 1 views the American and Russian governments as unitary actors seeking to determine each other's strategies and objectives, much as two opponents in a colossal, macabre chess match. Khrushchev had told Robert Frost several months earlier that the American people were "too liberal to fight," and emplacement of the missiles was a test by Russia of the U.S. and Kennedy's intentions to stand fast. This analysis is in keeping with the rational approach and is useful in studying organizations as complex as nation-states. It assumes that members of a particular nation-state share common values, beliefs, and ideologies that establish the parameters within which actual policy decisions will be made—that serve as constraints to the processes described by the second and third models.

The predictive power of the first model is simple to demonstrate in theory. A common American value is the desirability of separating church and state. Suppose that the government were approached by a religious leader with the suggestion that his sect be given official recognition. Predictably, the government would respond as a single individual. This is not so much because decisions are made by a single individual, but because all parties to the decision act within a common frame of reference, in this case within a shared value.

Model 2 views strategy as an organizational output which can be inferred from past performance. Organizational constraints, procedures, and routines yield outcomes that are similar to past outcomes produced by the organization in question. Thus, when U–2 flights over Cuba showed that missile installations were being laid out in readily identifiable, trapezoidal patterns, the patterns were compared to those observed in Russian missile sites and found to be identical. Presumably, faced with a novel situation, Russia responded with the application of routine procedures. Similarly, one could presume its Cuban strategy to be an extension of past strategies.

Model 3 views the problem of strategic choice in much the same way that we viewed goal selection in Chapter 5. Coalitions, trade-offs, and the like complicate the process. Focusing on distributions of formal and informal power (e.g., influence, persuasion, bargaining), Model 3 examines the roles of individuals and groups in the strategy formulation process. Applied to the Cuban missile crisis, the model draws our attention to President Kennedy's role. Apparently predisposed to agree with the military, who were in favor of firm military action in response to the missile sites, Kennedy was swayed by the opinions of his brother and other influential members whom he perceived to be on "his side." The latter, of course, favored the military blockade which was established eventually.

All three models—the rational "unitary actor," "organizational output," and "political maneuvering models," provide some "truth" about how strategy is made by nations and by organizations.

Coalitions in Strategy Formulation

Factors entering into strategy formulation in complex organizations exceed the comprehension of the individual chief executive. No single individual is likely to comprehend adequately the organization's structure, technology, goal sets, personnel, and environment and their interrelationships and contingencies. Thus, the executive must depend on others in the decision-making process. Participants in this process form what Thompson (1967) calls the *dominant coalition*—those who act together by pooling their separate knowledge and separate sources of power.

Recalling Thompson and Tuden's (1959) analysis of goals and means as determinants of organization design (Chapter 5), we argue that complete agreement among coalition members on the outcomes of means is rare in complex organizations in changing environments. For this reason, strategic decisions are made judgmentally. Those who make these judgments are important to the organization since they reduce uncertainty which,.if unchecked, will impair the rational functioning of the technical core. Thompson suggests: "The more numerous the areas in which the organization must rely on the judgmental decision strategy, the larger the dominant coalition" (1967, p. 136). The dominant coalition must co-opt those groups or individuals upon which it is dependent, so as to amass sufficient power to control decision premises and the functioning of the organization.

We have presented a static view of the dominant coalition but, as Thompson suggests: "a coalition inevitably is *in process*" (1967, p. 138). Because each member enjoys information that is vital to the others, all are interdependent. The interdependence is not equally distributed, however, for the knowledge, influence, and consequent power of one member may be greater than that of another. Other differences between members accrue in different ways. Some members may be recalcitrant, having outcome preferences that are idiosyncratic and different from those of the majority of coalition members. Some members may hold boundary positions in the organization and represent the outcome preferences of external bodies in addition to those of the focal organization. Other members have *cosmopolitan* orientations that conflict with the preferences of *locals* (Chapter 11).

These observations cast a melancholy pall over the expectation that dominant coalitions can achieve internal coordination. Seemingly, according to the terms used in Chapter 5, compromise (bargaining) decision making is necessary as well as judgmental decision making. The problem is resolved, however, through the creation of an *inner circle* which conducts the business of the coalition (Thompson, 1967). Out of disagreement, conflict, confusion, and frustration a small group is formed by election, appointment, or self-selection.[3] There is a smaller coalition within the dominant coalition. Only a small group of individuals, who meet face-to-face, can deal with the uncertainties and disagreements inherent in the strategy formulation process. According to Thompson, the larger dominant coalition is limited in its problem-solving activity to judgmental strategies. Sheer numbers of participants mitigate against the success of compromise strategies. The inner circle, however, is small enough to pursue negotiation and bargaining strategies that lead to compromise. In the inner circle, individuals can get to know each other well enough so that normative structure, tacit communication, and other subtle processes of compromise may be used (Chapter 11).

At first glance, the dominant coalition may appear to make decisions and reconcile differences among members. According to Thompson, what appears as decision-making behavior is more likely the ratification of decisions made by the inner circle. Thompson points to curriculum revision processes as an example. Changing a curriculum alters each faculty member's work load, subjects taught, and perhaps even career opportunities, not to mention outcomes for students and the university as a whole. Such changes cannot be achieved by the faculty acting as a whole, but are determined in advance by an individual or small group which proceeds to influence the remaining members of the faculty so that general agreement is reached eventually. Consequently, the faculty votes as a whole to ratify the change, but as a "rubber stamp" rather than a decision-making body. At least, this is what happens when the inner circle does its "homework" effectively.

Rational or Natural System Model for Strategy?

According to Thompson (1967), organizations tend to reflect the rational orientation imposed by their technical cores, where efficiency and the reduction of uncertainty are emphasized. Nevertheless, the natural-system model is more applicable to subsystems that are in direct contact with the environment—those that must deal with uncertainties and contingencies as they import resources, export products and services, and develop political support. As suggested in Chapter 1, these subsystems comprise the managerial level of the organization.

Members of the managerial level must cope with both environmental uncertainty and the steady state requirements of the technical core. They are coordinated in these activities by members of the institutional level. Top executives and their staff coordinate and integrate the activities

---

[3] Where the inner circle is self-appointed, its activities may be covert—hidden from the remainder of the dominant coalition.

of departments in the managerial level so that each group makes the concessions essential to effective organizational performance. Leaders of these critical units usually are members of the dominant coalition and it is their interaction, as managed by top executives, which determines strategy.

This view of organizations is clearly a departure from the rational view that holds strategy making to be an executive function. Petit (1972) argues that:

> . . . the middle technical managers attempt to persuade executives to adopt policies designed to achieve technical rationality and middle environmental managers do the same on behalf of uncertainty avoidance. The executives develop corporate strategies that balance these policies. This reverses the cause-and-effect relationships in the [rational] model. Policies are the causes rather than the effects of corporate strategy (Petit, 1972, p. 106).[4]

This "bottom-up" analysis of strategy formulation suggests that middle-level managers influence top executives to adopt policies that are favorable to their respective subsystems. Carried to an extreme, this will give way to suboptimization. It is top management's responsibility to see that this does not occur by managing the conflict that emerges between different coalition members as they attempt to pursue subsystem ends at the expense of system goals.

Obviously, strategy formulation is not entirely a "bottom-up" proposition; rather, it is influenced by lower participants in the organization. In Petit's view, top management maintains a responsibility for determining what the organization must do in order to survive as an institution. We submit that top management undertakes appreciative decisions and displays the form of leadership behavior described by Selznick (Chapter 12). Strategy formulation, then, consists, in part, of balancing the demands of the technical core with environmental pressures via institutional leadership.

DECISION MAKING AS A PROCESS

The Strategic Decision Process

Mintzberg and associates (1973) provide a plausible model of the strategic decision-making process. They characterize strategic problems as being novel, complex, open-ended, and ambiguous. Rarely do decision makers have more than a vague idea of the problem or how it will be evaluated once it is developed. Fitting the textbook description

---

[4] The term, policy, is used here to suggest a class of decisions that serve as precedents for similar decisions as routine responses to reoccurring problems.

of decision making under uncertainty, the problem of strategic decision making comprises ambiguity where literally nothing is known with certainty.

Mintzberg and associates directed teams of students who studied organizations for periods ranging from three to six months. The students sought to identify strategic decisions, to describe them, and to program their development. Twenty-five strategic decisions were identified. Typically, the decision-making processes spanned relatively long periods of time. While a third of the decisions required less than a year, another third spanned one to three years, and the remaining third took three years or more. More than half of the resulting decisions yielded "custom-developed" solutions, a quarter relied on existing programs, and the remaining quarter generated "customized modifications" to existing programs. The decisions included an airline choosing a new type of aircraft, the hiring of a star radio announcer, a hospital instituting a new and controversial form of treatment, and a consulting firm negotiating a merger after losing its major client.

Mintzberg and associates identified the structure of strategic decision making. Classical models, such as Dewey's, do not describe the observed process whereby decisions are achieved. The former models are sequential, whereas Mintzberg observed an iterative process. Certain elements of the decision-making process are recycled time and again while others are combined. This phenomenon is described by Witte (1972):

> We believe that human beings cannot gather information without in some way simultaneously developing alternatives. They cannot avoid evaluating these alternatives immediately, and in doing this are forced to a decision. This is a package of operations, and the succession of these packages over time constitutes the total decision-making process (p. 180).

Identification Phase

The decision-making process described in this study begins with the *identification* phase which comprises *recognition* that strategic action is required and a *diagnosis* of the situation in which action is to occur (see Figure 14–4). Somehow or other, from the continuous bombardment of data which they receive, managers identify situations requiring decisions and mobilize resources to deal with them. However, ". . . unlike programmed decisions, strategic decisions do not typically present themselves to managers in automatic or convenient ways" (Mintzberg, Rasinghani, and Theoret, 1973, p. 13).

Apparently, problems, crises, and opportunities are recognized by means of a threshold phenomenon. From the plethora of data received by managers, certain unique kinds of information exceed a threshold of perception and galvanize strategic responses. From the work of Pounds

FIGURE 14–4
A General Model of the Strategic Decision Process

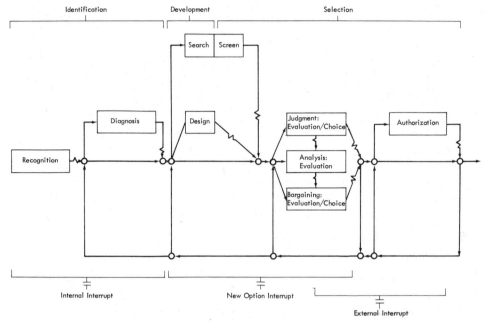

Source: Adapted from Mintzberg et al. (1973, p. 46).

(1969), we deduce that these thresholds may be exceeded when information deviates from uniformity. Managers may look for deviations from the expected by employing any of five comparative "models":

1. Historical (comparison of current data with past trends).
2. Planning (comparison of current data with projected trends).
3. Extraorganizational (comparisons with other organizations).
4. Other people's (comparisons with the expectations of others).
5. Scientific (comparisons with theoretical predictions).

Crises are recognized apparently by the perception of a single stimulus, as are opportunities which the organization can exploit. Problems, though, seem to be recognized only after repeated stimuli are generated. This observation may be explained by management's reluctance to act on problems when solutions are not readily available. For crises and opportunities, this reluctance is obviated by necessity in the case of the former and desire for gain in the case of the latter. Mintzberg and colleagues suggest that, when faced with a crisis, the manager's threshold of perception increases for stimuli generated by opportunities or problems, rendering their recognition less likely and causing the manager to behave reactively instead of proactively. Conversely, managers confronted by minor problems and relatively light work loads have lower thresholds for problems and, particularly, opportunities. These managers enjoy the prerequisites to proactive behavior.

The diagnostic phase of the identification process serves to define and structure the situation. Stimuli and cause-and-effect relationships are clarified in attempting to place the issue within a conceptual framework. However, these activities vary according to the nature of the issue at hand. Mintzberg and associates find that opportunities, serious problems, and crises generate a lower incidence of diagnostic activity than do milder problems. Apparently, opportunities do not require extensive investigation, because response is not mandatory. Crises and very serious problems displace formal diagnostic techniques by virtue of their immediacy. In any event, the diagnostic phase is seldom reiterated. In contrast to later phases of the decision-making process, where reiteration is common, diagnostic procedures are almost never repeated and, consequently, initial diagnoses are rarely revised.

Development Phase

After identification comes *development,* the heart of the entire decision-making process and recipient of the bulk of available time and effort. The *search* and *design* procedures that constitute the development phase are differentiated in that the former are used to find ready-made solutions (existing programs) while the latter seek custom-tailored solutions or modifications of existing programs.

Search activities generally precede design efforts. First, existing solutions are sought for their relevance to the situation at hand. Even when existing programs are found lacking, search provides a useful service by reducing design alternatives and, perhaps, identifying existing programs that can be rendered appropriate by modification.

The design phase, itself, is extremely complex, consisting of interrelated, nested subdecisions which are iterative. Furthermore, each subdecision contains its own search and design activities. The decision maker starts out with a vague image of an ideal solution. Different elements of the "roughhewn" solution are refined by reiterations of nested cycles of search and design activities until a workable solution takes form. "The organization continually clarifies, redefines, and modifies, groping its way along, gradually building a solution brick by brick without really knowing what it will look like until it is completed" (Mintzberg et al., 1973, p. 20).

Design activities generally yield a single solution in situations requiring customized responses. The design of custom-made solutions seems so expensive that only one can be made. Alternatively, a single innovation may exhaust the creative capacities of decision makers. Finally, it may be that psychological closure prohibits the exploration of further alternatives. Conversely, search generally produces any number of ready-made solutions owing, perhaps, to the slight costs entailed by search and alternative generation. Modified solutions, in which moderate custom-design efforts are invested, fall somewhere between the two extremes. Typically, two solutions are generated, one of which is ultimately rejected in the subsequent selection phases of decision making.

Selection Phase

Viewed from a rational perspective, *selection* ought to follow identification and development. However, in some cases, subdecisions resulting from development activities are evaluated and subjected to selection prior to the conclusion of the total development phase. Thus, selection may occur any number of times throughout the decision-making process.

Selection, itself, is a multistage, iterative process. The three basic programs within the selection phase, *screening, evaluation/choice,* and *authorization,* may be applied sequentially. Alternatively, each of the three steps may be multistaged or nested. In sequential selection, screening is used to reduce alternatives to a feasible number. Evaluation then identifies the best alternative, which is chosen and authorized for implementation. Alternatively, the selection phase can be nested, with alternatives evaluated in toto, next evaluated in more detail, and then subjected to intense scrutiny. At each step, alternatives can be eliminated as they fail to meet successively rigorous criteria.

Mintzberg and associates generally found that screening is not very evident in the strategic decision processes studied, presumably because it is implicit in the search process. As ready-made alternatives are found, they are screened and the infeasible are eliminated without further ado.

In analyzing the *evaluation/choice* phase of the process, Mintzberg and associates utilize portions of the decision-making topology of Thompson and Tuden (1959): *judgment* (a single individual making choices), bargaining (selection by a group of individuals, having conflicting goals and using individual judgments), and *analysis* (computation—a systematic evaluation of relevant data). Judgment is utilized, Mintzberg found, when decision situations are characterized by centralized responsibility, a lack of rigorous data, and relatively urgent time pressures. When forced to exercise judgment, managers frequently rely on surrogate criteria. For example, one organization in the study chose IBM equipment because of the company's reputation. Analytic (computational) problem solving would have begun by comparing specific, competing data processing devices with the organization's information processing requirements. Bargaining is found to be common, appearing in half of the strategic decision-making processes studied. Computational decision strategies are found in larger business organizations, especially where strategy is contingent upon technical considerations.

The final phase of the process, *authorization*, consists of approval by top management, the board of directors, or those vitally concerned with strategy decisions—often because they have the authority to commit or withhold resources. Typically, the authorization process is a binary one in which proposed decisions are either accepted or rejected. Even when accepted, the decision may be subject to further iterations of authorization at even higher organizational levels.

> The authorization decision is a difficult one because the time for it is typically limited; because at this level the decision must be considered in the light of other strategic decisions and overall resource constraints (Mintzberg, 1973, p. 87); because outside political forces are often brought to bear on the decision at the point of authorization; and because the authorizers generally lack the knowledge that the developers (and sponsors) of the solution have. This last point is, in fact, a chief problem in capital budgeting as well as in less formal (*ad hoc*) types of authorization—the choices are made by people who often do not fully comprehend the proposals presented them. Hence, in authorization the comparative ignorance of the manager is coupled with the inherent bias (commitment) of the sponsor (Carter, 1971; Pettigrew, 1972). This explains why empirical studies of capital budgeting have shown it to be a somewhat distorted, political process, far less analytical than the normative literature suggests (Bower, 1970, Carter, 1971a, 1971b). (Mintzberg et al., 1973, p. 26.)

The Complexity of Strategic Decision Processes

The strategic decision process as a whole is described by Mintzberg and associates in terms of 12 elements. In addition to the three central phases of the process (identification, development, and selection), there are three sets of parallel processes (decision control, communication, and political processes) and six special, "dynamic factors" which distinguish strategic decision processes from other decision processes (interrupts, scheduling delays, feedback delays, and timing delays and speedups, comprehension cycles, and failure recycles). Only a small portion of this additional complexity is shown in Figure 14–4.

The three parallel processes (which are not shown in Figure 14–4) occur throughout the decision-making process. *Decision control processes* consist of "meta-decision making"—decision making about the decision process itself. Included are planning the planning process and allocating resources to implement it, as well as choosing appropriate programs within the decision sequence. *Decision communication processes* are also parallel in the sense that they exist throughout the decision process. They consist of exploration, investigation, and dissemination. Finally, there are *political processes* during decision making, usually in the form of bargaining among those having control over choices. There may be disputes over whether to recognize the issue in the first place. Another common example is bargaining between the organization and outsiders who may have been ignored during the development and who disagree with the proposed solution.

The remaining six elements consist of dynamic factors which are characteristic and distinguishing features of strategic decision processes. *Interrupts* consist of unexpected constraints that may cause delays, and often force an organization to cycle back to the development phase. The three most common types are shown in the model. *Internal* (political) interrupts occur in the identification phase, when there is disagreement about the existence of problems requiring decisions. Mintzberg states that

> Such interrupts come from within the organization, and lead to cycling in the recognition program (to resolve the disagreement by bargaining or persuasion), to delays (until the resistance subsides), or to political design (to remove the resistance). . . . *external* interrupts (constraints or political resistance) [arise] during the selection phase, where outside forces block the selection of a fully-developed solution. These interrupts typically lead to modification in the design (to bring it in line with the difficulty encountered), to complete redevelopment of a new solution (if the solution appears to be unacceptable), or to bargaining (to confront the resistance directly). . . . *new option* interrupts . . . typically occur late in development or during the evaluation/choice program. These lead the process either back to design (to elaborate or modify the new option) or directly to evaluation/choice to select or reject it immediately (Mintzberg et al., 1973, p. 47).

Scheduling delays may occur between every step of the decision process because top managers, extremely pressed for time, must turn their attention to other matters. *Feedback delays* occur because the decision maker must await the results of previous actions. *Timing delays and speedups* occur because a manager purposefully acts to take advantage of special circumstances.

Comprehension cycles occur in the process when issues are complex and require time to be understood. This cycling may facilitate recognition of the issue. In design activities there may be nested cycling of design and search processes in which solutions are developed. Finally, there are *failure recycles* in which the decision maker is faced with no acceptable solutions and must either delay until one appears or, ultimately, end the decision process. More commonly, it was found that organizations faced with failure in finding or designing an acceptable solution recycled back to development activity. Mintzberg and colleagues conclude that: "given the failure of a solution, the decision maker first tries to branch to remove a constraint and thereby make it acceptable; if that is infeasible, he tries to recycle to the development phase to modify the solution but maintain its basic parameters; if that is not possible, he tries to develop a whole new solution; finally, if resources will not permit this, or if he meets with continued failure, the decision maker will try to change his criteria to make a previously unacceptable solution acceptable" (p. 45).

Manifestations of this complexity are provided in the example and in Figure 14–5:

> . . . a small manufacturing firm was faced with a series of pressures indicating that its plant was obsolete. A proposal to sell the building was developed (design), and a real estate agent then contacted (search), but no buyers were found. It was then realized that the city might expropriate the land (interrupt), and an agent was hired to negotiate a good price should such an eventuality occur. Meanwhile, a neighboring firm moved out, and their adjoining parking lot was acquired to provide room for expansion or increase the expropriation value of the property (evaluation/choice). At the same time, the firm employed architects to investigate two alternatives, but rejected both proposals as too expensive (evaluation/choice), and attention was then focused on moving. Three alternative sites were found (search) and employees were polled and road networks investigated (evaluation). One area proved to be the most desirable, and when an existing facility was found there at a good price (search), it was identified as a favorite candidate and purchased (evaluation/choice). The company planned the modification of the building (design), and commenced the alteration. Two months later, however, the government expropriated at the same time both the old plant and the new, and gave the firm a short time to vacate (interrupt). Now the firm faced a crisis. It did, however, have a considerable source of funds from the expropriation, and could now consider buying land and building a new plant. Only one area was investigated, and a suitable site was located (search). The firm now obtained rezoning sanctions from the municipal government, a mortgage from

FIGURE 14–5
A Dynamic Design Decision Process (Facilities)
A New Plant for a Small Firm

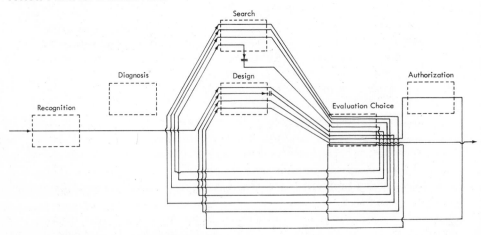

Source: Mintzberg et al. (1973, Figure 11).

the bank (design), and the assurance that this property would not be expropriated (authorization). The site was purchased (evaluation/ choice), the engineering department, in consultation with the architect, prepared building plans, layouts, etc. (design), and the plans were finalized quickly and efficiently (evaluation/choice). To summarize, what started as a basic design decision process reverted to a dynamic design process because of a governmental interrupt (Mintzberg et al., 1973, p. 57–58).

The Behavior of Strategy Makers

What little empirical evidence we have seems to corroborate the picture presented of strategy making as an ongoing process rather than the creation of a rational plan. Wrapp (1967), reporting on participant observation from consulting relationships, suggests that "good" managers (those able to move their organizations significantly toward the goals they have set) behave as follows:

> . . . good managers don't make policy decisions . . . rather, they give their organizations a sense of direction, and they are masters of developing opportunities . . . the successful general manager does not spell out detailed objectives for his organization . . . he seldom makes forthright statements of policy . . . he is an opportunist, and he tends to muddle through problems—although he muddles with a purpose. He enmeshes himself in many operating matters and does not limit himself to "the big picture" (p. 91).

As Wrapp sees it, the good manager is not a "prime mover":

> The successful manager is sensitive to the power structure in the organization. In considering any major current proposal, he can plot the position of the various individuals and units in the organization on a scale ranging from complete, outspoken support down to determined, sometimes bitter, and oftentimes well-cloaked opposition. In the middle of the scale is an area of comparative indifference. Usually, several aspects of a proposal will fall into this area, and *here is where he knows he can operate.* He assesses the depth and nature of the blocs in the organization. His perception permits him to move through what I call *corridors* of comparative indifference. He seldom challenges when a corridor is blocked, preferring to pause until it has opened up.
>
> Related to this particular skill is his ability to recognize the need for a few trial-balloon launchers in the organization. He knows that the organization will tolerate only a certain number of proposals which emanate from the apex of the pyramid. . . . As the day-to-day operating decisions are made, and as proposals are responded to both by individuals and by groups, he perceives more clearly where the corridors of comparative indifference are. He takes action accordingly (p. 93–94).

Another skill found in the successful general managers studied by Wrapp was the "art of imprecision." These managers knew how to satisfy their subordinates as well as the public and stockholders clamoring for statements on objectives, by making very general and imprecise announcements such as "growth and profit." While the managers do have objectives, they do not get committed publicly to a specific set of objectives, since such specific objectives could constrain the organization when it needs, as it will, to change direction. The successful manager seldom makes a forthright statement of policy despite claims of management textbooks that well-defined policies are essential to a well-run organization. The spelling out of detailed written objectives, as in management by objectives, is really only useful at lower levels of management.

And as Wrapp sees it, it is impossible to communicate objectives to the entire organization anyway. Organizational members will perceive the statements differently, according to their various positions in the organization. Wrapp suggests that objectives for the organization can only be communicated over time by means of consistency or a pattern in the operating decisions. He reminds us that decisions linked to actions are more meaningful than mere words.

The most important skill Wrapp found in his effective managers was "muddling with a purpose":

> The successful manager in my observation, recognizes the futility of trying to push total packages or programs through the organization. He is willing to take less than total acceptance in order to achieve modest progress toward his goals. Avoiding debates on principles, he tries to piece together particles that may appear to be incidentals into a program that moves at least part of the way toward his objectives. His attitude is based on optimism and persistence. Over and over he says to himself, "There must be some parts of this proposal on which we can capitalize" (1967, pp. 95–96).

Wrapp describes an example of muddling through with a purpose:

> A division manager had set as one of his objectives, at the start of a year, an improvement in product quality. At the end of the year, in reviewing his progress toward this objective, he could identify three significant events which had brought about a perceptible improvement.
>
> First, the head of the quality control group, a veteran manager who was doing only an adequate job, asked early in the year for assignment to a new research group. This opportunity permitted the division manager to install a promising young engineer in this key spot.
>
> A few months later, opportunity number two came along. The personnel department proposed a continuous program of checking the effectiveness of training methods for new employees. The proposal was acceptable to the manufacturing group. The division manager's only contribution was to suggest that the program should include a heavy emphasis on employees' attitudes toward quality.
>
> Then a third opportunity arose when one of the division's best customers discovered that the wrong material had been used for a large lot of parts. The heat generated by this complaint made it possible to institute a completely new system of procedures for inspecting and testing raw materials.

As the division manager reviewed the year's progress on product quality, these were the three most important developments. None of them could have been predicted at the start of the year, but he was quick to see the potential in each as it popped up in the day-to-day operating routines (1967, p. 96).

Wrapp's description of strategy making is corroborated by Mintzberg (1973), who studied the chief executives of five relatively large organizations (a consulting firm, a consumer goods manufacturer, a technology firm, a hospital, and a school system), by recording their activities during one week of intensive observation. He found the great responsibilities of chief executives forced them to adopt immense work loads:

> . . . they seldom stop working. Their evening activities are usually work related, and they seldom appear able to put their concern for their work aside. During office hours, the pace of work is hectic and, should free time become available, an ever-present pile of mail or an eager subordinate will quickly usurp it. This is not a job for reflection and relaxation (Mintzberg, 1973, p. 24).

Furthermore, the chief executive's work is discontinuous, fragmented, and full of variety. Significant issues were interspersed with trivial ones. Half of all activities were completed in less than nine minutes. The realities of the job, then, encourage the manager to "make decisions abruptly, to maintain the hectic pace, to avoid wasting time" (p. 25).

Chief executives typically are not planners, not contemplative and abstract thinkers, because of the great pace of work and its discontinuous nature. In addition, Mintzberg feels that they gravitate toward, and prefer, hectic, concrete work styles. Mintzberg's study shows that the chief executives gave little attention to routine operating reports, participated in few regularly scheduled meetings, and almost never took part in general, abstract discussion. ". . . (t)he job breeds adaptive information manipulators, men who work in an environment of stimulus-response and who prefer live action . . . [the typical chief executive] becomes conditioned by his pace and workload. He tries to keep all his activities brief, actively encouraging interruption in his work in order to maintain the rapid pace and the flow of information . . ." (Mintzberg, 1973, pp. 24–25).

This descriptive study of top managers' work conforms to our view of the strategy maker as a participant in a complex process rather than as a comprehensive, rational planner. As Wrapp points out so well, the top manager is motivated to participate in many operating situations (although not necessarily in making operating decisions) so that he can obtain needed information and avail himself of opportunities to influence subordinates as are required by the complex process of strategy making.

In a prescriptive addendum to his report, Mintzberg suggests that the manager (engaged in the complex and frantic activities described above) must gain control of time. The effective top manager apparently does this by taking advantage of what he is obligated to do in any event.

> . . . success derives from turning to their own advantage those things they must do. The shrewd top manager treats the chaos of a crisis as an opportunity to make some necessary changes. A mutiny in a department may be the opportunity to effect a needed reorganization; a drop in sales is a chance to overcome opposition to the dropping of old product lines. He uses a ceremonial speech as an opportunity to lobby for a cause; every time he meets a subordinate, no matter what the reason, he encourages him in his work; and every time he must meet an outsider, he tries to extract some useful information" (Mintzberg, 1973, p. 28).

Strategic Management

Clearly, strategy consists of more than the formulation of a strategic plan, or any other formal, static product such as an environmental forecast or listing of marketing and production options. In contrast, as Gerstner (1972) suggests it is ". . . fundamentally a creative process. It cannot be programmed or systematized" (p. 6). We would add, however, that engaging in planning and undertaking the strategic exercises offered by management consultants can be a valuable educational exercise, sensitizing managers to the problem of strategy, helping them to think abstractly, to conceptualize, and to model the systematic relations between organizational goals and objectives, environmental threats and opportunities, and organizational strengths and weaknesses. The danger, as discussed in Chapter 10, is that the specific plans thus developed may displace the more diffuse management activity needed to create an organizational strategy. Recognition is now given to this danger by the increased emphasis on "strategic management" rather than "strategic planning" (Ansoff, Declérck, and Hayes, 1973).

Some of the most recent research on business organizations reflects this changing emphasis. Rather than determine whether strategic planning makes a difference in performance, researchers are relating different strategies to different levels of profitability. Hofer (1974), in reviewing this research suggests that "firms perform best by relating all their product/market activities to some distinctive competence and/or common theme" (p. 8). Rumelt (1974) found that among the 246 companies listed in the *Fortune 500* in 1949, 1959, and 1969, firms which were vertically integrated or which engaged in unrelated businesses were the poorest performers, for example. The best performers were somewhat diversified, but related all of their activities to some central skill or strength. Similarly, Gutman's (1964) study of manufacturing firms with high rates of growth showed that they concentrated on a few segments of the industries in which they competed.

Some successful business strategies seem to center around the notion of maintaining a strong market share. Chevalier (1972), studying cookie manufacturers, cement producers, and the automobile industry, emphasizes: (a) domination of market segments in which the firm operates, (b) divestment in market segments where the share is small, and (c) dominance in a small market (rather than being a follower in a larger market). Similarly, Fruhan (1972) reports how, in the grocery business, National Tea and a number of other firms attempted to get a "toehold" in many markets (cities) nationwide, while Winn-Dixie aimed at market depth in a limited area, the Southeast. The latter strategy has been shown to be related to higher profits. Obviously, it is the strategy, not the type of planning process used, that is important.

Dissonance Reduction, and the Intractability of Managers

Managers are risk takers and those who make strategy decisions bear the greatest risks. There is abundant evidence that strategy decisions do not emerge from neat, scientific inquiry, but from judgments and bargains formulated from data that are anything but well understood. The need to make strategy decisions is unavoidable. As the world changes, organizations must change. But managers who make these changes can commit millions of dollars and man-hours to activities designed under conditions of overwhelming uncertainty.

In strategy formulations, especially as portrayed by Mintzberg and associates, an accepted diagnosis of the problem may be less accurate than those rejected, for all the manager knows—or, the solution accepted may be inferior to the alternative rejected—and this is a source of *cognitive dissonance.*

In everyday terms, cognitive dissonance arises when our perceptions do not "fit"; for example, imagine an individual faced with a choice of attending either of two universities, each as attractive as the other for all the prospective student knows. Although the individual may waiver, agonize, and fret, he or she eventually chooses one over the other. This is where cognitive dissonance sets in, for there is a basic incongruity in rejecting an alternative as attractive as the one selected. Festinger (1957) explains that such dissonance is "uncomfortable" and is normally reduced by the individual. For instance, he or she may revise earlier opinions of the rejected university to make it seem inferior to the other. This can occur in the absence of additional information, and may be nothing more than self-delusion. Alternatively, the individual can seek additional selective information that confirms the decision. Other mechanisms can be employed as well. The point is that eventually dissonance will be reduced to the extent that the choice *appears* rational.

Such is also true of managers. Mintzberg and associates suggest that the typical manager enters the decision situation in a relatively unbiased state. "In effect, he is out to get what he can, and will choose any alternative that provides a lot of something, anything, reasonable" (Mintzberg et al., 1973, p. 33). But having made a choice, the manager must reduce the dissonance generated by alternatives foregone. Corroborating Soelberg (1967), Mintzberg and associates suggest that there is a "confirmation" process in which the implicit choice is subsequently rationalized. Having been rationalized, the choice is announced as a decision. It is no wonder, suggest Mintzberg and associates, that a manager often is not open to suggestions and "reason" once a decision has been made (announced). Having completed the difficult task of forging choice from ambiguity, he has ". . . created the reality in which he will work," rendering it extremely difficult for him to alter his position.

DISCUSSION QUESTIONS

1. How do strategic decisions differ from tactical decisions? Give examples of each.
2. In what sense is the choice of a college major a strategic decision?
3. Can you identify strategic decisions made by your college or university within the past five years? What makes these stand out as strategic decisions?
4. List some examples of disjointed incrementalism.
5. Give some everyday examples of cognitive dissonance and postdecision dissonance reduction.

REFERENCES

Allison, Graham T. *Essence of decision: explaining the Cuban missile crisis.* Boston: Little, Brown, 1971.
Allport, G. W., Vernon, P. E., and Lindzey, G. *A study of values.* Boston: Houghton Mifflin, 1960.
Ansoff, H. Igor. *Corporate strategy.* Harmandsworth, Eng.: Penguin, 1965.
Ansoff, H. Igor, Avner, Jay, Brandenburg, Richard G., Portner, Fred E., and Radosevich, Ray. Does planning pay? The effect of planning on success of acquisition in American firms. *Long Range Planning,* 1970, *3* (2), 2–7.
Ansoff, H. Igor, Declerck, Roger P., and Hayes, Robert L. From strategic planning to strategic management. Paper presented at the International Conference on Strategic Management, Nashville, Tenn., Vanderbilt University, May 1973.
Anthony, Robert N. *Planning and control systems; a framework for analysis.* Boston: Division of Research, Harvard Business School, 1965.
Asch, Solomon. *Social psychology.* Englewood Cliffs, N.J.: Prentice-Hall, 1952.
Bauer, Raymond A. The study of policy formation. In R. A. Bauer and K. G. Gergen (Eds.), *The study of policy formation.* New York: Free Press, 1968. Pp. 1–26.

Bower, Joseph L. *Managing the resource allocation process.* Boston: Harvard University, Graduate School of Business Administration, Division of Research, 1970.

Braybrooke, David, and Lindblom, Charles E. *A strategy of decision.* New York: Free Press, 1963.

Carter, E. Eugene. Project evaluations and firm decisions. *The Journal of Management Studies,* 1971, *8,* 253–79. (a)

Carter, E. Eugene. The behavioral theory of the firm and top level corporate decisions. *Administrative Science Quarterly,* 1971, *16,* 413–28. (b)

Chandler, Alfred D., Jr. *Strategy and structure: chapters in the history of the American industrial enterprise.* Cambridge, Mass.: M.I.T. Press, 1962.

Chevalier, F. The strategy spectre behind your market share. *European Business,* 1972 (34) (Summer), 63–72.

Child, John. Organizational structure, environment and performance: the role of strategic choice. *Sociology,* 1972, *6,* 2–22.

Dewey, John. *How we think.* Chicago: Henry Regnery, 1971.

Festinger, Leon. *A theory of cognitive dissonance.* Evanston, Ill.: Row, Peterson, 1957.

Friedman, John, and Hudson, Barclay. Knowledge and action: a guide to planning theory. *American Institute of Planners Journal,* 1974, *40,* 2–16.

Fruhan, William W., Jr. Pyrrhic victories in fights for market share. *Harvard Business Review,* 1972, *50*(5), 100–7.

Galbraith, John Kenneth. *The new industrial state.* Boston: Houghton Mifflin, 1967.

Gerstner, Louis V., Jr. Can strategic planning pay off? *Business Horizons,* 1972, *15*(6), 5–16.

Glueck, William F. *Business policy: strategy formation and management action.* New York: McGraw-Hill, 1972.

Guth, William D. Toward a social system theory of corporate strategy. Proceedings of the 16th Annual Midwest Management Conference, Academy of Management, Midwest Division, April 1973.

Guth, William D., and Tagiuri, Renato. Personal values and corporate strategy. *Harvard Business Review,* 1965, *43*(5), 123–32.

Gutman, Peter M. Strategies for growth. *California Management Review,* 1964, *6*(4), (Summer), 31–36.

Hage, Jerald, and Dewar, Robert. Elite values versus organizational structure in predicting innovation. *Administrative Science Quarterly,* 1973, *18,* 279–90.

Heider, Fritz. Attitudes and cognitive orientation. *Journal of Psychology,* 1946, *21,* 107–12.

Hofer, Charles W. Some preliminary research on patterns of strategic behavior. Proceedings, Academy of Management, Division of Business Policy and Planning, 33rd Annual Meeting, Boston, August 1973. Pp. 46–54.

Hofer, Charles W. Research on a contingency theory of strategic behavior: issues and methods. Paper given at Academy of Management Meetings, Seattle, August 1974.

Kast, Fremont E., and Rosenzweig, James E. *Contingency views of organization and management.* Chicago: Science Research Associates, 1973.

Lindblom, Charles E. *The intelligence of democracy: decision-making through adjustment.* New York: Free Press, 1965.

March, James G., and Simon, Herbert A. *Organizations.* New York: Wiley, 1958.

Mintzberg, Henry. The science of strategy-making. *Industrial Management Review*, 1967, *8*, 71–81.

Mintzberg, Henry. Research on strategy-making. Proceedings, Academy of Management, 32nd Annual Meeting, Minneapolis, Minn., August 13–16, 1972. Pp. 90–94.

Mintzberg, Henry. A new look at the chief executive's job. *Organizational Dynamics*, 1973, *1*(3), 20–30.

Mintzberg, Henry, Rasinghani, D., and Theoret, A. The structure of "unstructured" decision process. Montreal: McGill University, Faculty of Management Working Paper, 1973.

Newman, William H. Strategy and management structure. *Journal of Business Policy*, 1971, 2, 56–66.

Petit, Thomas A. Systems problems of organizations and business policy. Proceedings, Academy of Management, 32nd Annual Meeting, Minneapolis, Minn., August 13–16, 1972. Pp. 103–7.

Pettigrew, Andrew M. Information control as a power source. *Sociology*, 1972, 6, 187–204.

Pounds, William F. The process of problem finding. *Industrial Management Review*, 1969, *11*, 1–19.

Ringbakk, K. A. Long range planning in major U.S. companies. *Long Range Planning*, 1969, 2(2), (December), 46–57.

Robinson, John P., and Shaver, Phillip R. *Measures of social psychological attitudes*. Ann Arbor, Mich.: University of Michigan, Institute for Social Research, Survey Research Center, 1969.

Rue, Leslie W., and Fulmer, Robert M. Is long-range planning profitable? Proceedings, Academy of Management, 33rd Annual Meeting, Boston, August 1973. Pp. 66–73.

Rumelt, Richard P. *Strategy, structure, and economic performance*. Boston: Harvard University Press, 1974.

Schoeffler, Sidney, Buzzell, Robert D., and Heany, Donald F. Impact of strategic planning on profit performance. *Harvard Business Review*, 1974, 52(2), 137–45.

Schoettle, Enid C. B. The state of the art in policy studies. In R. A. Bauer and K. G. Gergen (Eds.), *The study of policy formation*. New York: Free Press, 1968. Pp. 149–79.

Soelberg, P. O. Unprogrammed Decision Making, *Industrial Management Review*, 1967, 8(2), (Spring), 19–29.

Spranger, E. *Types of men*. Halle (Saale): Max Niemeyer Verlag, 1928.

Tagiuri, Renato. Value orientations and the relationships of managers and scientists. *Administrative Science Quarterly*, 1965, *10*, 39–51.

Thompson, James D. *Organizations in action*. New York: McGraw-Hill, 1967.

Thompson, James D., and Tuden, Arthur. Strategies and processes of organizational decision. In James D. Thompson et al. (Eds.), *Comparative studies in administration*. Pittsburgh: University of Pittsburgh Press, 1959.

Thune, Stanley S., and House, Robert J. Where long range planning pays off. *Business Horizons*, 1970, *13*(4) (August), 81–87.

Ullrich, R. A. Changing values and American industry. *Business and society*. 1970, 2, 56–61.

Vancil, Richard F. The accuracy of long range planning. *Harvard Business Review*, 1970, 48(5), 98–101.

Wildavsky, Aaron. *The politics of the budgetary process*. Boston: Little, Brown, 1964.

Wildavsky, Aaron, and Hammond, Arthur. Comprehensive versus incremental budgeting in the department of agriculture. *Administrative Science Quarterly*, 1965, *10*, 321–46.

Witte, Eberhard. Field research on complex decision-making processes—the phase theorem. *International Studies of Management and Organization*, 1972, 2, 156–82.

Wrapp, Edward H. Good managers don't make policy decisions. *Harvard Business Review*, 1967, 45(5), 91–99.

Case

Walnut Avenue Church[*]
R. W. Ackerman

Harry Tillotson, Moderator of the Walnut Avenue Church, was uncertain about what he should do next to help resolve a problem that had deeply divided his congregation. The difficulty, which began when lightning severely damaged the church's historic steeple in September, had by the following January come to involve in Mr. Tillotson's mind some fundamental questions concerning how and for what purpose the church was to govern its affairs. The following . . . pages include first a description of Walnut Avenue Church and second a summary of the events surrounding the steeple episode.

Walnut Avenue Church

Walnut Avenue Church was Congregational in polity and tradition and located in the downtown section of a middle-sized industrial city on the outskirts of Philadelphia. The church, dating back to colonial times, had a membership of 900 of whom approximately 400 were active members. As is typical of most churches in this sociological situation, its membership had gradually been declining over the past several decades as people moved to surrounding suburban areas. Walnut Avenue Church had remained, however, feeling it had a ministry to the city and its people and was highly regarded in church and lay circles as a responsible and dedicated institution.

The congregation was highly diverse in age and interests. About half the church family were older people, many having children who had grown and left the city. There were only a few families in the 30 to 50 age bracket with growing children. Slightly less than half the congrega-

---

[*] Names and places have been disguised.

This case was prepared as a basis for class discussion rather than to illustrate either effective or ineffective handling of an administrative situation.

tion were younger people, both single and married, in college and working, many of them related to the universities located nearby. The youth education program was modest in size.

Between annual meetings, the church was governed by the Prudential Committee, composed of the chairmen of standing committees, the entire Board of Deacons, the Treasurer, Secretary, two members elected at large, and the Moderator, who acted as chairman. Members of all committees including designated chairmen were placed for election by the Nominating Committee before the congregation at the annual meeting. The elections were not contested and there had rarely been a dissenting vote. Mr. Tillotson, in his six years as Moderator, had confined his role to assembling the agenda and chairing meetings of the congregation and the Prudential Committee.

The Prudential Committee approved the budget before it was submitted to the congregation for final ratification. In recent years the church had had to strain to maintain its level of activities though it was fortunate to have a small endowment to ease the impact of fluctuations in pledging. The fund-raising and investment management functions were handled by the Finance and Property Committee, which also had responsibility for the church building. Over time this committee had come to view itself as responsible for the "secular affairs" of the church —those matters involving money and physical assets.

During the past several years, the Mission and Community Committee had expanded its activities beyond making contributions to traditional charitable and denominational agencies and participated in social action programs of various kinds, sometimes involving modest expenditures of funds. On one occasion the committee asked for and received approval from a special meeting of the congregation of a resolution expressing support and concern for the Black community during disturbances in a nearby ghetto area. The resolution was sent to the mayor and referred to in the press. The committee, and especially its chairman, had subsequently drawn strong criticism from some in the parish who felt the use of the resolution to be "quasi-political" and hence inappropriate.

The Church Steeple

On a Friday night in September lightning struck the steeple igniting a fire which caused severe structural damage.

The following morning the Finance and Property Committee meet in emergency session. They concluded that an architect should be engaged immediately to ascertain the extent of the damage and the probable cost of repairs. Three days later the architect reported that emergency measures were necessary to ensure that the steeple would not collapse on the next windy day. He also informed the committee that these measures, costing about $1,000, were not sufficient, and that either the steeple should be taken down or completely rebuilt at a cost he thought would run about $40,000. After some discussion, the committee told the architect to proceed with the emergency work and that Fred Thornton, chairman of the committee, would contact him about further steps to be taken. After the architect left, the committee, without dissent, agreed that the steeple ought to be rebuilt and a special gift campaign should be organized to raise money to cover the cost.

At a special meeting of the Prudential Committee the following week, Fred Thornton traced what had happened and presented its recommendation to rebuild the steeple. The response was immediate.

"In a time like this, with all the poverty and problems in the city, and world refugees and war and all, how can we justify this much money on a steeple which has no function even for us?" asked Danny Cranston, chairman of the Mission and Community Committee.

"Because," replied Fred Thornton, "if we don't fix it, it will fall down, and if we take it down, who will know this is a church?"

An elderly gentleman, Richard Gilroy, a loyal churchman and substantial giver, then offered to contribute a neon lighted cross, to go atop the repaired steeple so that the whole neighborhood would see the church identified by this radiant symbol.

Though there were no immediate remarks expressing negative feelings about the cross, several scowls from members implied to Mr. Tillotson a twofold problem. How could one stand out against the cross without hurting Mr. Gilroy, and if his gift were refused, would it jeopardize his sizable pledge, which was almost 10 percent of the entire budget? However, Henrietta Gibson, a deacon, came to his support, saying, "This church is the church of my childhood, and I want the steeple to stay on. I know there are many others who feel the same way about it. The Finance and Property Committee voted unanimously to fix the steeple and if Mr. Gilroy wants to put a cross up there, we ought to go along."

Carlotta Carlyle, another deacon, who said she had joined the church because she thought it could work to bring changes in society, was aghast at this, and literally shouted to the meeting, "The world is going to pot, and we sit here discussing spending money on a steeple. It seems to me we have our priorities turned upside down. Jesus sent the church out to minister to mankind, not to make monuments out of our buildings."

The moderator, by now ill at ease, suggested a subsequent meeting because it was now already 11:00 P.M. Mr. Thornton indicated that he felt his committee ought to secure a detailed estimate of the cost of rebuilding. Wallace Berry, chairman of the Music and Arts Committee, then said that since the bells were a part of the music program, his committee ought to be represented. After some discussion, this latter suggestion was put aside on the ground that the matter could best be handled by Finance and Property at this stage. Mr. Berry was encouraged, however, to secure the views of his committee before the next Prudential Committee meeting.

During the ensuing month Reverend Anderson, who had kept his opinions on the matter to himself, preached on the virtues of compassion, forgiveness, acceptance and brotherly love, and reconciliation. He also began to visit the Messrs. Tillotson and Thornton to try to reach an accommodation that would not split the church. Mr. Thornton had urged him to pave the way for conciliation in his preaching. He had also been heard to say, "These ministers don't know anything about money and bricks and real estate values; they ought to stick to spiritual matters." He further implied that as a friend of Richard Gilroy, he thought that if the steeple didn't get fixed, and the cross was refused, Gilroy might very well withdraw his membership and pledge.

By the end of October, when a second meeting of the Prudential Committee was called, the Finance and Property Committee had secured estimates from three builders and after much consultation settled on one for $50,000. Although the estimates were roughly comparable in price (the others were $46,400 and $53,000), the choice was complicated by the great many factors to be considered—design, finish, etc. The recommendation was put in a motion to the Prudential Committee including the neon cross at an additional cost of $3,500.

In the following debate, Wallace Berry noted that while his committee, in a 3–2 vote (with two members absent), was in favor of retaining the steeple and the bells, he personally opposed it and was uncertain how to vote on the motion. One deacon responded by saying, "I think this whole thing is getting out of hand. Let's let those who want to have the steeple replaced raise the money among themselves and leave the rest of us out of it."

Another member answered, "But that is no way for a Christian community to behave—we must learn to work and worship together!"

Eventually the motion was brought to a vote. It lost 11 to 9 with Reverend Anderson abstaining. A resolution was then passed respectfully declining Mr. Gilroy's gift but thanking him for his generosity and thoughtfulness.

Through Christmas the atmosphere was tense. The Finance and Property Committee refused to do anything at all in the way of arranging for the removal of the steeple. Reverend Anderson, bearing the brunt of well-intentioned but often harsh criticism from some parishioners, began to feel isolated and alone.

Finally, in mid-January, Mr. Tillotson was informed that a meeting of the congregation was being called by a group of parishioners including several on the Finance and Property Committee to consider a motion having the effect of reversing the Prudential Committee vote. Should this motion carry, a second one was to be made requesting that the

EXHIBIT 1
Organization Chart

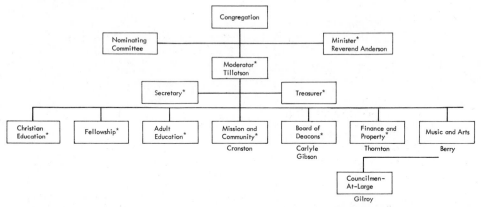

* Members of Prudential Committee. Including nine deacons and Reverend Anderson, there were 21 people on the committee.

Moderator appoint a committee on governance to consider changes in the bylaws that would have the effect of involving the congregation more directly in the decision-making process in the church.

It was in this situation that Mr. Tillotson pondered over the nature of the church's purpose and what, if anything, he could do to help resolve Walnut Avenue Church's current dilemma.

PREPARATION QUESTIONS

1. How well do you think the steeple incident has been handled?
2. What should the congregation do about the steeple?
3. What responsibilities does the Prudential Committee have in resolving the problem?
4. What responsibility do individual committees have in resolving it?
5. How should Wallace Berry have voted?
6. Was the Finance and Property Committee justified in not acting to have the steeple removed after the December Prudential Committee meeting?
7. Should the organization structure be changed by amending the bylaws? How, in broad terms?
8. What should Harry Tillotson do at the end of the case?

section V
Changing the Organization

PREMISE

As we look at our society, we cannot help but sense frustration. So many aspects of contemporary life could be improved! We seem to possess the means with which to change for the better, and surely there are ends upon which we all agree. Why, then, are improvements so long in coming?

We have made modest suggestions for improving organizations throughout our text. These range from the "trivial" (changing relationships between people) to the "monumental" (changing an organization's technology or goals). However, we have not yet dealt systematically with the problems encountered in introducing even trivial changes to organizations. The problems associated with changing complex organizations together with tentative solutions for these problems constitute the substance of our final chapters.

15

Introduction to Organizational Change

INTRODUCTION

Throughout preceding sections of this text we have suggested changes that can improve organizational performance when applied under appropriate circumstances. However, it is one thing to understand the nature of desirable changes and quite another to know how to make them. Introducing successful organizational change is an extremely difficult task—one that requires a great breadth of knowledge and skill. We have devoted the remaining section of our text to the study of change processes for this reason.

We indicated that strategic change, in theory, is an organizational response made in anticipation of substantial environmental changes. We also attempted to provide convincing evidence that the process of strategic change is less rational and more political than is sometimes thought. The evidence also compels us to assume that strategic changes are more often reactions to discontinuities in the environment than anticipations of such changes. For reasons to be investigated in this section, individuals and organizations seem to adhere to the status quo, even after changing circumstances render such behavior inappropriate. It sometimes appears as if organizations forestall needed adaptations until impending crises force the issue.

For example, consider the plight of higher education in America today. As the last member of the post-World War II baby boom receives a sheepskin, the wave of young adults for whom existing educational facilities were expanded will have passed through the system. Although many schools experienced increased enrollments in 1975 because of the high rate of unemployment, we can predict with near certainty that the number of 18 year olds applying for admission to colleges and universities will decline over the next decade. This trend is elaborated in the following *Time* article:

The Student Shortage

For graduating high school seniors, the once-traditional spring/ summer struggle to get into college—any college—appears to have gone

445

the way of the draft and campus demonstrations. With fall sessions at some schools only weeks away, the National Association of College Admissions Counselors reported last week that there are still about 500,000 openings for freshmen and transfer students at colleges and universities across the country. The figures mark the second straight year of declining college enrollments. California alone has at least 40,000 vacancies. Even in New England, some 25,000 places are going begging, although the area's Ivy League and other prestigious schools can still pick and choose as much as they please.

Officials attribute the decline to a number of factors. The 1970s have brought both the close of the postwar baby boom that swelled the ranks of college-age youth in the 1960s and the end of the Viet Nam conflict, which drove many young people to seek shelter on campus from the Selective Service. Vocational schools are becoming more popular, while fewer parents are willing or able to cope with rising college costs (the current annual average at private four-year schools: $3,504).

Many institutions, especially state colleges, overexpanded in the 1960s. They now find themselves underutilized. Says Nancy Barber of the Western Interstate Commission on Higher Education: "Colleges will have to find other ways to put their facilities to use. Hopefully there will be more recruitment of the poor, minorities and the elderly" (*Time*, 1974, p. 86).[1]

Chapter Guide

1. Although estimates vary, it is common to hear that 200 to 300 colleges and universities will close their doors within the next decade. Do you think that this form of societal divestment will be the result of strategy or merely a reaction to circumstances?

2. What are the goals of a university? Do you think that present goals can be met if institutions of higher learning change their recruiting strategies to attract large numbers of elderly students?

3. Is it desirable to change the purposes of universities, if this is essential to keep them from closing?

4. It appears that large numbers of students from the OPEC nations will be sent abroad for their education as a result of the imbalance between existing educational facilities in these nations and their demands for advanced skills. How many American universities, faced with extinction, will react to this environmental change by catering to the implied demand?

5. Suppose that a university decides to become an international center of learning in order to serve large numbers of students from OPEC and other nations. What basic changes will be required? How will faculty members, students, board of trust members, and alumni and other supporters respond to these changes? How would you implement these changes?

[1] Reprinted by permission from *Time*, The Weekly Newsmagazine. Copyright Time Inc.

DETERMINANTS OF ORGANIZATIONAL CHANGE

Some Determinants of Change in Organizations

As our discussion of change phenomena unfolds, it will become evident that most work in the area comes from psychologists, whose studies emphasize the behavior of individuals in organizations. Equally important, from our point of view, is the study of the organization as a whole. The major, systematic sociological study of this sort is the work of Hage and Aiken (1970), to which we shall devote a considerable part of this chapter.

Hage and Aiken are concerned with the rate at which organizations change themselves and the factors that determine this rate of change. Why is it that some organizations are quick to adopt even untested ideas while others are slow to implement changes that have withstood the test of time? Although General Motors and Ford faced comparable circumstances during the 1920s, the former developed a number of new products while the latter did not. Why do organizations with the same general objectives and comparable environments seem to differ in terms of the rate at which they change themselves? This is the question addressed by Hage and Aiken.

The focus of their study is *program change,* which they define as the addition of new services or products. Please bear in mind that these were the only kinds of changes studied and that, furthermore, the ultimate success or failure of these change efforts was not considered.

Hage and Aiken look to seven organizational aspects for determinants of organizational change: (1) degree of complexity, (2) centralization, (3) formalization, (4) stratification, (5) production, (6) efficiency, and (7) job satisfaction. These particular aspects were selected because they were well studied in the literature and found to be related in one way or another to the rate of program change. Other aspects were considered but discarded when found to be more or less unimportant in determining the rate of change in organizations.

We shall take each of these aspects in turn and examine evidence that suggests its relationship to the change process. Much of this evidence comes from Hage and Aiken's survey of 16 welfare agencies which provided services in the areas of physical rehabilitation, mental rehabilitation, or psychiatry.

Complexity

Complexity refers to (1) the extent of knowledge and skill required of occupational roles and (2) their diversity. Professional organizations and organizations employing many different kinds of professions are highly complex. One way to measure complexity is to determine the *number* of different occupations within an organization that require specialized knowledge and skills. An organization can be considered complex when it employs numerous kinds of knowledge and skills (occupations) and when these occupations require sophistication in their respective knowledge and skill areas. A general hospital is a complex organization. Typically, members of 50 different occupational groups will appear on the wards in the course of 24 hours. One will find a variety of kinds of nurses (having different amounts and kinds of training), dieticians, X-ray technologists, laboratory technologists, a variety of physicians of different specialities, occupational therapists, orthopedic therapists, medical social workers, psychiatric social workers, chaplains, ward clerks, housekeepers, janitors, engineers, various kinds of administrators, and others.

Organizations employing professionals of a single kind (or a few kinds) are less complex. An elementary school is of moderate complexity. Relatively few occupations are employed, and required levels of knowledge and skills within occupations are relatively modest. At the low end of the scale of complexity, one finds organizations such as automobile factories which employ a relatively homogeneous, unskilled, and unknowledgeable work force.

Hage and Aiken measured complexity in their sample of welfare agencies in terms of the number of occupational specialties employed, the length of professional training required by each specialty, and the extent of employees' involvement in professional societies and activities. It was found that the greater the complexity, the greater the rate of program change. The rationale for this relationship seems clear. In addition to their formal training, professionals engage in constant study to remain abreast of advances in their respective fields. Acquisition of new knowledge paves the way for change. Professionals may work themselves into new professions eventually. Alternatively, they may recognize the need for new kinds of professionals who can aid in the pursuit of their objectives. Social psychologists are results of the first kind of change, and media specialists who support faculty teaching are results of the latter. The professional's service ideal also contributes to the high rate of change in complex organizations. To be of service implies seeking the best ways to meet client needs. Obviously, improvements to existing service delivery practices frequently take the form of program changes.

Centralization

Centralization (Chapter 10) is a measure of the distribution of power within the organization. According to Hage and Aiken, the fewer the occupations participating in decision making and the fewer the areas of decision making in which they are involved, the more centralized the organization.

Hage and Aiken find that the higher the organization's degree of centralization, the lower its rate of program change. As used here, program change refers more to the initiation of change than to its implementation. An explanation of this finding is that a centralized organization, with power concentrated in a few individuals, tends toward the status quo because their power enables them to protect their own interests and to veto changes that are likely to threaten them. Michel's Iron Law of Oligarchy describes the situation well.

In a decentralized organization, where decision-making power is more widespread, a variety of different views will emerge from different occupational groups having access to the decision in question. This variety of opinion can lead to conflict, but also to successful resolution of conflict and to problem solving. In any event, decentralization appears to facilitate the initiation of new programs and techniques, which are proposed as solutions to various organizational problems. Hage and Aiken suggest that these organizations will be slow to implement the changes initiated. In a decentralized organization, it takes time for suggested changes in products and services to receive approval of all individuals party to the decision to implement them. A centralized organization may produce fewer new ideas, but once an idea is put forth its implementation is fairly straightforward. Lines of communication are clear and direct. The route to top management for ultimate approval or disapproval is traveled quickly. Nevertheless, in the long run, it is likely that the decentralized organization will experience more initiation of change and a greater number of actual program changes than the centralized organization. This, in fact, is what Hage and Aiken found in their study of welfare agencies.

Formalization

Formalization represents the extent to which jobs are governed by rules and specific guidelines. It may be recalled that this aspect of organization is typical of bureaucracies. Measures of formalization can be attempted in a number of ways. One may count the number of rules that apply to *jobs*, as these are found in formal job descriptions, rules manuals, or staff handbooks. In fact, the mere existence of such documents suggests a relatively high degree of formalization. Alternatively, one may count the number of rules and regulations that operate in the *organization* as a whole. These may be codified or unwritten as in the case of norms.

As one would expect, Hage and Aiken found that the greater the degree of formalization, the lower the rate of program change. Rules and norms restrict not only behavior, but also thinking, creativity, and initiative. They discourage search for better ways of doing things. Furthermore, they rigidify the organization and promote homogeneity among its various units. Thus, implementation of change is made difficult, since even a minor change may impact on extensive portions of the organization. Rules, regulations, job descriptions, and the like serve to stabilize an organization's behavior—to make it reliable and predictable. Obviously, they mitigate against change.

A recent study of the Teacher Corps, however, provides an instance where formalization (as well as centralization) can facilitate change (Corwin, 1972). The aim of the Teacher Corps is to promote educational reforms in low-income schools through innovative teacher training programs, based on teaching interns and university support. Corwin found that in the 42 schools studied, innovations (such as team teaching, introduction of black history, and mixed-age grouping) were associated with the organizational control exerted by the schools. Those with centralized decision-making procedures, stress on rules and procedures, and emphasis on pupil discipline were schools which innovated.

The contrast with the Hage and Aiken study is explained by the observation that implementation, not initiation of innovations, was studied in these organizations. While the universities and interns provided ideas, the administrators and their staff selected and implemented them. In this kind of situation, formalization and centralization facilitate change. In this situation teachers *had to change* the way they were teaching. Rather than "tacking on" a new program in addition to ongoing programs, a fairly simple matter for Hage and Aiken's professionals, top administration was responsible for selecting innovations and then seeing that they were implemented properly. A centralized administration with control of resources and the ability to formulate and enforce rules and regulations was able to enforce and also to *help* the process of innovation. (See also Gross, Giacquinta, and Bernstein [1971] for further evidence, and Wilson [1966], Zaltman et al. [1973] for a similar argument.) In sum, where emphasis is on implementation rather than initiation of innovations, centralization and formalization may be assets.

For each of the above—complexity, centralization, and formalization—Hage and Aiken found evidence in both the research literature and their own study regarding relationships with program change. Several further aspects of organizations discussed below, however, receive less support from the literature and the study, and they are to be viewed somewhat more tentatively as determinants of organizational change.

Stratification

Rewards are distributed fairly equally among members in some organizations and differentially in others. Stratification is a measure of this phenomenon. When some employees receive higher salaries, greater status, and more fringe benefits than others, their organization is said to be highly stratified. A second dimension of stratification concerns mobility between different parts of the organization. An organization is *not* considered highly stratified when employees are free to move vertically and horizontally among jobs, even when the rewards associated with these jobs differ markedly. Barriers to mobility (advancement), as well as heterogeneity in rewards, contribute to stratification.

According to Hage and Aiken, the greater the degree of stratification, the lower the rate of program change. Here again the Iron Law of Oligarchy seems to apply. Where rewards are distributed unequally, those receiving the largest share resist changes that threaten their advantage. Now, one might argue that differences in rewards will motivate individuals at lower levels of the organization to work their way up in the hierarchy, and that, consequently, they will seek improvements over the status quo to gain recognition that eventually will result in promotion. While this may occur, suggestions for change will be muted to the extent that they are perceived as criticisms of higher level employees. Thus, advocacy of change is undertaken reluctantly.

In general, high stratification discourages accurate upward communication. Lower level employees tend to tell their superiors what the latter want to hear. It has been argued that much of the distorted information in the Vietnam War was attributable to this phenomenon. Inflated body counts were reported because they were met with approbation by superiors. What evidence there is suggests that stratification blocks interaction and communication and, therefore, retards not only the initiation of change, but also its implementation.

Production

As used by Hage and Aiken, production measures organizational emphasis on *volume* of output rather than *quality*. The number of units produced (or clients served) varies from one organization to another. Some automobile manufacturers engage in mass production of cars just as large state universities offer their services to a large number of students. These can be contrasted with manufacturers of limited production cars (e.g., Jensen, Jaguar, Shelby-Cobra) and small, private universities that employ low student-faculty ratios.

Hage and Aiken argue that the higher the volume of production, the lower the rate of program change. Their rationale is that emphasis on speed of production and volume, rather than on quality and control, leads management to resist interruptions of the productive process such as program changes are likely to entail. High-volume production enables the realization of economies of scale. Steady state efficiency becomes valued more than operating or strategic responsiveness (Chapter 2).

Success attained in operating the implied kind of technology will miti- gate further against change. It is difficult to argue in favor of altering a system that produces satisfactory results.

Organizations with these characteristics can be contrasted with others emphasizing quality of production. The latter orientation will direct management's attention toward standards—toward means for improv- ing production standards or, at least, for preventing their deterioration. Research and development activities will be directed toward product (or service) improvement. These improvements are often found in the form of program changes.

Efficiency

The sixth variable studied, efficiency, measures the relative cost of producing the organization's product or service. Some organizations are more concerned with costs than others; for example, research institutes are generally less concerned with operating efficiently than are the or- ganizations that apply knowledge generated by the former.

A review of the literature provides some evidence that the greater the emphasis on efficiency, the lower the rate of program change. As Hage and Aiken suggest, new programs incur additional costs, some of which are unpredictable. Additional costs, especially those which are uncer- tain and, thus, uncontrollable, are unattractive to managers whose ori- entations are toward cost reduction and operating efficiencies. Of course, some innovations are sought as a means toward cost reduction. Neces- sity is the handmaiden of discovery, as we say, and problems having high associated costs may lead to innovations directed toward their im- provement. A close examination of such innovations, however, suggests that costs are *not* reduced in many cases. The application of computer technology to "paper work" problems is a common example of innova- tion that does not necessarily improve costs. Furthermore, cost-cutting innovations seem to be rarer than other kinds aimed at improving quality or providing hitherto unavailable services. In short, the efficiency-seeking organization is likely to play a "wait and see" game—to be a follower rather than an innovator in its industry.

Job Satisfaction

The final variable studied by Hage and Aiken is job satisfaction. Over- all job satisfaction is usually assumed to be related to satisfaction with a variety of specific factors such as pay, fellow workers, supervision, working conditions, and the like.[2] One index of job satisfaction is rate of employee turnover. Dissatisfied employees tend to leave their organi- zations in search of better jobs.

---

[2] The nature of this relationship, though, is anything but clear. See, for example, Wanous and Lawler (1972).

Hage and Aiken found a moderate relationship between job satisfaction and the rate of program change. The more satisfaction, the greater the rate of change. Apparently, satisfied employees become committed to their organizations. This commitment entails a desire to improve organizational effectiveness and a willingness to explore new ideas and try out the suggestions of others.

Systemic Qualities of the Variables Studied

Hage and Aiken's most important point is that the seven variables and rate of program change seem interrelated. In static organizations the rate of program change is low and *all* of the seven variables seem to be configured to contribute to organizational stability. Organizations that do not change their programs frequently also seem typified by high degrees of (1) centralization, (2) formalization, (3) stratification, and (4) emphasis on high-volume production, and (5) efficiency and low degrees of (6) complexity and (7) job satisfaction.

In other words, these seven characteristics are *systemic qualities* of organizations. If one variable changes, the others tend to change as well in directions that are compatible with the change in the first. Hage and Aiken carry this analysis further. First, they argue that dynamic and static organizations arise in different kinds of environments. The dynamic organization arises in an unstable environment and the static organization in one that is stable. This analysis is useful since it enables us to anticipate changes in an organization based on our perceptions of changes in its environment. Second, Hage and Aiken suggest that changes in certain variables induce conforming changes in the remaining variables. A dynamic organization is most likely created by increases in its *complexity*. Alternatively, an organization can be rendered more stable by increasing its degree of *centralization*. These two observations provide us with "levers," as it were, with which managers can attempt to move their organizations in desired directions.

Before examining the characteristics of static and dynamic organizations in greater detail, we are compelled to emphasize that neither kind is superior to the other. In general, it is appropriate to view the organization's degree of change propensity in terms of its adequacy in meeting environmental demands. Therefore, it is important to understand how both kinds of organization evolve, since it may be necessary for management to move the organization first in one direction and then in the other as its environment changes.

Dynamic Organizations

As the knowledge employed by an organization increases in quantity, complexity, and diversity, it becomes increasingly difficult for a few top managers to maintain a monopoly on power. As organizations become knowledge intensive, they make decisions on the basis of the combined inputs from experts and specialists. *Complexity* seems to require decentralization of power to make or influence decisions. Furthermore, as we noted in Chapter 11, experts and specialists seem to work best on a relatively informal basis. Gaining external control of professional activities is difficult, if not at times impossible. Generally, professionals require freedom sufficient to deal with problems that cannot be programmed in any simple fashion with rules, regulations, job descriptions, or plans. Knowledge-based organizations tend to rely on the quality of their professionals' training to control their behavior and ensure adequate job performance rather than on rules or programs. In consequence, the relative absence of rules and programs together with the associated distribution of decision-making power foster horizontal as well as vertical communication. Reliance on others for help in the coordination and execution of one's own tasks fosters teamwork and tends to diminish status differences among interrelated occupations. In other words, stratification is reduced.

As we saw earlier, highly trained employees may emphasize quality and service to the client as opposed to efficiency, "cutting corners," or cost reduction. Finally, highly trained employees (whose training is utilized in their occupations) seem to derive more satisfaction from their jobs than do employees possessing and using lesser skills. This may result from their power to demand or negotiate better, more satisfying conditions of work. In general, then, it seems that although each of the variables can affect the others, *complexity* is of paramount importance in determining the dynamic properties of the organizational system.

Static Organizations

Let us turn now to static organizations. The less complex an organization, the more it depends on unskilled employees who perform simple, specialized tasks. Similarly, these organizations do not depend on the knowledge and training of such employees to the extent indicated above. Such organizations tend to be highly *centralized*. Centralization (control from the top) implies that behavior in the rest of the organization is controlled via formalization, the use of job descriptions, rules manuals, evaluation systems, records, and the like. Also flowing from centralization is stratification—differences in rewards and low mobility in the organization.

The general policies of such organizations are likely to stress quantity of production and efficiency. As we indicated earlier, quantity is a less costly criterion of effectiveness than quality, which may require continual changes in the productive processes. Finally, external control, inequality of rewards, simple-minded jobs, and poor working conditions are likely to affect employee satisfaction adversely. In short, the qualities mentioned are likely to conform to one another in static organizations. Apparently, the critical factor among these is centralization, which seems to affect the others directly.

Stable and Dynamic Environments

Hage and Aiken suggest that the environment becomes unstable (dynamic) as a result of increases in knowledge. Growth in knowledge can affect both the demand for products and services and the technologies used to produce them. As knowledge increases, new products become available and the demand for older products diminishes. Thus, demand fluctuates. When this happens, the organization must adapt accordingly, seeking innovations to replace services and products for which demand is waning and installing technologies capable of producing them.

Changes in technology sometimes require the addition of new occupations spawned by the technology itself; for example, consider the number of computer programmers and systems engineers employed today and recall that these occupations were not found in businesses, governmental agencies, or hospitals 30 years ago. Major organizational changes have resulted from the introduction of computer technology which, in turn, resulted from acquisition of knowledge in the information sciences. In summary, this suggests that environmental instability stems from increased knowledge which, in turn, requires organizations to become more complex. As we have suggested, increased complexity produces corresponding changes in other organizational qualities which allow the organization to become more change propensive.

This can be contrasted with a relatively stable environment in which organizations experience constant or steadily changing (predictable) demand for their products and services. Since knowledge develops slowly, technology changes gradually. Under these conditions, there is little need to launch new programs to produce new products or services, nor is there need to introduce new technologies and occupations. In a stable environment, organizations can pursue the modus operandi suggested by the rational school of thought (Chapter 1). When goals are clear (e.g., market share in an unchanging market) and when means toward the achievement of these goals are stable (e.g., technology), the organization can centralize and structure itself to produce as efficiently as possible. From this follow the other characteristics of stable organizations, including low rates of program change.

Diversification

The environment can encourage or force diversification in a number of ways, and diversification is another way in which complexity is increased; for example, governments may force diversification through antitrust proceedings. Declining markets may encourage similar changes, although more subtly. As indicated at the beginning of this chapter, colleges are seeking to diversify their services in the face of declining student populations. Competition may produce similar effects. Hage and Aiken suggest that the steel industry's response to erosion of its markets by such materials as glass, aluminum, and plastic was intensification of its research and development efforts in search of diversified steel products.

The important point is that diversification increases organizational complexity. The addition of products and services requires employment of additional occupations which add to complexity. As we have noted, increases in complexity are likely to affect change propensity through the remaining variables. Diversification also seems to encourage decentralization. Problems of coordination increase as heterogeneous elements are added to the organization. The resulting overload of top management is ameliorated when decentralized profit centers are established (Chapter 11). These centers are responsive to local circumstances and free top management's time for matters of strategic concern.

Similar to the effects of diversification are those of interorganizational programs. When organizations collaborate to produce a product or service, different occupational groups may be brought into contact. It follows that the creation of joint programs can increase organizational complexity.

Scientific Management

A number of variables in addition to the seven identified by Hage and Aiken seem to affect the organization's propensity to change. The first of these might be termed *rationalism*, as exemplified by scientific management (Chapter 1). Victor Thompson (1969) suggests that application of scientific management techniques may hinder the organization's propensity to change.

Bureaucracy is a rational form of organization emphasizing formal rules and a hierarchy of authority which can be ascended by only the most competent employees. The higher one rises in the organization, the greater the rewards and power one enjoys. Scientific management contributes a second dimension of rationality to bureaucracy—economic rationality, which Hage and Aiken term *efficiency*. Going beyond structural arrangements, scientific management addresses problems of efficiency in decision making. Formulas and programs are sought to provide optimal solutions to problems of middle and top management as well as to those of shop floor employees which were studied in Taylor's early work.

The so-called Planning, Programming, and Budgeting System (PPBS) of control developed by the Department of Defense under Secretary McNamara is a modern elaboration of Taylor's line of thought. Under this system, the organization identifies its goals and objectives, elaborates various means for their attainment, and estimates the results to be expected from each alternative for each dollar spent over a period of, perhaps, several years. If all costs and benefits are measured for all feasible alternatives, an optimal arrangement will be found, and the organization will be enabled to plan its activities accordingly. This logic presumes that organizational effectiveness is a function of rational management.

Thompson's point is that even when such approaches to management work, they are liable to have drastic effects on the organization's propensity to change. Furthermore, there are many situations in which the approaches will not work at all. Most organizational problems include human factors which cannot be measured adequately, and, therefore, cannot be entered into a formula. Another area of difficulty concerns goals. Most organizations pursue multiple goals. The optimal strategy to achieve one goal (supposing it can be identified) may prove detrimental to the attainment of a second, equally important, goal. Yet, it is impossible to consider these goals simultaneously—to determine an indifference schedule that permits identification of trade-offs of progress toward one goal at the expense of another—given the present state of the art.

An obvious example is found in the American government which pursues the following goals among others: national security; an adequate (if not affluent) standard of living for all; justice; and equality. Unfortunately, there is no calculus for determining the point at which we should trade increments in standards of living for increases in national security. For such problems, rational methods have not been devised, and the application of existing techniques may produce results that are misleading.

In fact, we find that PPBS has been a failure of sorts (Hoos, 1972). It has not worked well when transferred from the Department of Defense to other departments. One might even question its degree of success in defense. Vietnam provides a tragic example of the limitations of such rational approaches. True to the principles of scientific management, we sought the "biggest bang for the buck" in Vietnam. Studies of "kill ratios" were conducted to determine the amount of destruction wrought by different weapons systems. Records were maintained on the tonnage of bombs dropped on North Vietnam and the Ho Chi Minh Trail. These data were "plugged" into formulas devised to allow the United States to pursue an effective war effort.

Such rational approaches tend to ignore the human element, presumably because they are imprecise and difficult to incorporate. Thus, an inverse relationship was assumed between enemy morale and tonnage of bombs dropped. In light of evidence developed during World War II, the opposite assumption would seem more appropriate. A major finding of that war was that the tonnage of bombs dropped on German cities was positively related to the morale of residents of the cities (United States Strategic Bombing Survey, 1947). Only when the tonnage of bombs approached extreme amounts did morale begin to decline.

This limitation of bombing is noted in Speer's (1971) book, which details the ways in which Germans overcame most of the effects of bombing. Only late in the war, when precision bombing stopped production in certain aircraft factories and petroleum refineries, did morale deteriorate. Until that time, morale was unaffected and even improved by bombing and seemed to compensate for the material inconveniences wrought by destruction.

Similarly, the Ho Chi Minh Trail continued to operate efficiently despite numerous bomber attacks. The morale of the North Vietnamese, an imponderable to PPBS, presumably remained unaffected. When important variables are left out of an organization's decision-making process, the organization cannot react appropriately to negative feedback. Such organizations cannot adapt to the environment successfully. In short, overreliance on rationalism, or any other managerial viewpoint that excludes attention to important variables, impedes appropriate organizational change.

Organizational Affluence

Another factor that seems to contribute to change propensity is the organization's affluence. Organizations having large amounts of money seem to innovate more than those constrained by lack of funds. As Hage and Aiken suggest, money is essential to the developmnet of new programs and techniques. Yet, their survey did *not* show that affluence caused innovation. They asked heads of the welfare agencies studied what they would do if additional funds became available. Responses varied considerably. Some agency heads indicated they would expand existing services to increase the number of clients served or reduce the staff's case load. Quantity in the former case and quality in the latter were emphasized. Other agency heads said they would use additional funds to add new programs or services. Hage and Aiken infer from these findings that affluence is a necessary, but not sufficient, condition for innovation and change.

Other research shows that affluence, or *organizational slack* (Cyert and March, 1963), bears a low, positive relationship to innovation (Mohr, 1969; Rosner, 1967). This relationship may arise in part through the indirect effect of affluence on other variables, which affect innovation. According to Wilson (1966), these other variables include some of those studied by Hage and Aiken. Wilson suggests that organizations, such as railroads or gold-mining firms, which suffer from a scarcity of resources, tend to suppress conflict, maintain hierarchical controls, and proclaim the supremacy of certain explicit organizational goals. More affluent organizations tend to avoid conflict, relax hierarchical controls, proliferate new products and processes, and engage in the elaboration of vaguely defined goals.

Two folk sayings attempt to resolve this problem of innovation and affluence. First, necessity is said "to be the mother of invention." However, it appears that necessity often makes for hierarchical controls and concerns for costs and efficiency. These concerns, in turn, appear related to a low rate of program change or innovation.

The other saying is that "the devil makes work for idle hands." Organizational affluence may lead to relaxation of hierarchical controls, greater decentralization, and less formalization and stratification. These changes, in turn, are conducive to organizational change. But, not all change is good. Let us give the devil his due!

"Everyday" Change

Thus far, we have dealt with change as if it were an extraordinary event for organizations. Of course, change is everpresent. The organization is never the same from one month to the next. A useful way to visualize the manager's job was presented in Chapter 14. While he or she does have general goals and strategies, the manager usually reacts to events, attempting, for example, to maintain production despite problems of absenteeism, material shortages, line imbalances, and the like. The manager makes "changes" by dealing with these everyday problems.

Another source of everyday change not readily apparent is turnover of personnel. Each change in staffing provides new human inputs to the organization (attitudes, motivations, expectations regarding norms, and so on). To some extent newcomers will be socialized to conform to the requirements of the organization, but it is also true that they can affect and come to change the organization, since each individual is a role sender as well as a recipient of sent roles.

McNeil and Thompson (1971) refer to "regeneration of organizations"—a measure of personnel change akin to the half-life of radioactive elements. Examining faculty records at two universities, during the middle and late 1960s, they find a half-life of about four to five years; i.e., at the end of four or five years, oldtimers are matched by newcomers. For one university, which had a growth rate (i.e., increase in faculty size) of 26 percent, the half-life was about five years, for the other, which had a greater rate of growth (42 percent), the half-life was reached in four years or less.

The significance of regeneration arises in part because of the need to socialize newcomers. If the half-life is too short, the socialization process may require excessive organizational effort. High rates of turnover in typing pools, or on assembly lines, require that time be spent inducting and socializing members. In many cases, management may not devote sufficient time to the socialization processes, but socialization will take place anyway—through the efforts of peers, with the possible result that undesirable norms will be inculcated.

McNeil and Thompson suggest that regeneration may be especially disruptive if it outpaces the normal production process. If a bachelor's degree takes four years and the half-life of the faculty is three years, then students will become the oldtimers watching the faculty come and go. To the extent that the school utilizes an intensive technology (Chapter 13) to socialize students into certain attitudes and values, a high rate of faculty turnover will render it ineffective.

On the other hand, a high rate of regeneration offers some advantages—primarily for the achievement of organizational flexibility. In discussing individual motivation and attitudes, we emphasized the difficulties involved in changing behavior. Instead of requiring veterans to "unlearn" old behavior and attitudes, one can hire newcomers having desired predispositions. It is said that science progresses in major steps (as from the Aristotelian-Ptolemian Tradition to the Copernican view of the universe) not so much by persuading the old guard to see the "truth," but rather by replacing the old guard with a new generation which has grown up accepting the new view as natural (Kuhn, 1957).

This aspect of organizational regeneration is significant in leadership succession. New leaders commonly ensure that their accession is accompanied by major organizational regeneration by replacing existing personnel, adding to existing personnel, or both. This tactic is useful if the new leader is to have an impact on the organization, for, as we saw in Chapter 12, leaders by themselves do not always find that they can lead and influence the organization more than the organization leads them.

Growth

At a number of points in the text, we allude to organization growth, a seemingly ubiquitous phenomenon. Its apparent pervasiveness renders this phenomenon a source of "everyday" change. Perhaps organization growth is ubiquitous because it has been viewed, until very recent times, as either an end or a means to other ends. In Western industrial society, growth seems to be valued as a symbol of achievement and success. Where organizational effectiveness is especially hard to measure, as in nonprofit organizations, attained size has been employed as a surrogate criterion measure. Starbuck (1965) lists a number of different goals for which organizational growth constitutes either the means for achievement or a side effect of such achievement. Individuals may be motivated by the desire for adventure and risk—they may wish to gamble on new activities and to expand the organization; they may desire the prestige, power, and job security that comes from managing large numbers of people; and they may desire higher salaries. Research shows that salaries of top executives sometimes are not correlated with profit, but with sales volume (Roberts, 1956, 1959). Starbuck suggests, further, that increased size results from the manager's desire for stable jobs and an organization which has a high probability of survival, leading to diversification, the wherewithall to affect the environment, and large amounts of "slack." Finally, organizational growth is pursued as a means to increase profits by reducing costs (economies of scale), and increasing revenues (through sales volume).

Consequence of Growth

In Chapter 10, we saw that one apparent consequence of growth is increased structuring of the organization; for example, as indicated by formalization. Starbuck suggests that members of new organizations are committed to the organizations' goals. These are primary relations focusing on goals, to use our terminology of Chapter 10, while means are less sacrosanct. This comes to be less true as the organization ages and increases in size. With organizational growth, individuals transfer their commitments from goals to means and social structure. This is because: (a) friendships and interpersonal loyalties spring up; (b) the organization itself tries to create loyalty to its structure, rather than to specific goals or products; and (c) individuals with such loyalties tend to move into central, policy-making positions. Weber describes this general process in terms of the "routinization of charisma" (Demerath and Hammond, 1969; Weber, 1947). When a new, charismatic leader passes from the scene (and even before), personal and emotional bonds between organizational members are replaced by less emotional ties which are supported by structure—by rules, norms, and other aspects of formalization. The disciples create a church, as it were, to replace the leader and hold the organization together.

The formalization accompanying growth and the associated gain in flexibility with regard to goals (compared to inflexibility regarding survival) might be viewed as undesirable, but there is a positive side to formalization as we indicated in Chapter 11.[3] Formalization may result from organizational learning (Starbuck, 1965). The organization learns

---

[3] Hall, Haas, and Johnson (1967) suggest that increasing size may lead to increasing formalization, if the technology is routine (e.g., mass production). If it is not, growth may lead to the use of more professionals, in which case additional formalization may not result. However, if the increase in size comes about in the administrative component of the organization, then formalization probably will increase (Meyer, 1968).

to ignore unimportant problems as it develops causal models that indicate critical variables. Trivial, reoccurring problems are assigned routine solutions. The young organization requires intense loyalty to goals and must select its members carefully, according to their attitudes, motivations, and potential internal controls. The older, more formalized organization can be more rational, divesting goals when they have been achieved or when the environment changes, and less careful in selecting members, since the external controls in the structure can be relied upon.

However, formalization alone may not be adequate to deal with the added complexity in the growing organization. A general research finding is that larger organizations tend to have lower morale as well as higher absenteeism, turnover, and accident rates. The study of role stress by Kahn et al. (Chapter 6) showed role stress to increase with size, leveling off in organizations of 5,000 or more members. A nationwide survey of hospitals similarly found pressures on individuals and tensions between groups increase with organizational size (Wieland, 1965).

Even the turmoil in the 1960s among university students has been attributed in part to organizational (university) growth and associated increases in formalization (Scott and El-Assal, 1969):

> In becoming large, high quality, and heterogeneous, many schools had to expand and to formalize their administrative structures in order to coordinate large diverse numbers of communication activities and people in the massive educational enterprises of teaching, research, and public service. Accordingly, they expanded their administrative staff personnel such as vice-presidents, deans, associate deans, department chairmen, associate department chairmen, administrative assistants, secretaries, executive secretaries, clerks, clerical helpers, and consultants. Simultaneously, they formalized and routinized their administrative procedures in order to coordinate and to regulate the granting of examinations, of degrees, of stipends, of scholarships, research on human subjects, teaching and research facilities, housing, extracurricular organizations, teaching schedules, speakers, sports activities, and hiring, termination, promotion and evaluation of personnel (p. 708).

As a trade-off, of course, the large, bureaucratic university, or similar organization, offers its members resources and security, as well as freedom, as we saw in Chapter 11. A move to decentralized units (such as residential colleges) within the larger organization may provide a way to avoid these dilemmas so that such trade-offs become unnecessary.

Organizational Life Cycles

Related to growth are phenomena associated with aging. Lippitt and Schmidt (1967) described six stages of organizational development which are based on their consulting experience with organizations:

1. Creating a new organization.
2. Surviving as a viable system.

3. Gaining stability.
4. Gaining reputation and developing pride.
5. Achieving uniqueness and adaptability.
6. Contributing to society.

Of major concern in the first stage, organizational creation, are planning and decision making regarding resources and manpower risked, and in the second stage, the sacrifices to be made in terms of deferred activities. The third stage, achievement of stability, is concerned with organizing members and leading them to accept and enforce discipline (see also Sarason, 1972). Lippitt and Schmidt provide the following description of problems encountered at this stage, including those of formalization, described above:

> As an organization grows, the original leaders undergo varying degrees of trauma in surrendering personal leadership; the expanding hierarchy breeds factions and results in complicated politics; the maintenance of records becomes ever more burdensome; and there is a certain loss of freedom. It becomes hard to decide between further development, with concomitant stability and resilience, and the retention of close relationships and control.
>
> In the birth stage, there is excitement in creation and challenge in survival. The youthful stage is far less dramatic; the organization is accommodating itself to its environment and adjusting its internal operations. Here is where the concept of what we have called a sociotechnical system becomes *functional*.
>
> As the outside pressures (e.g., market uncertainties, creditors demands) on such a system diminish, the internal defects become more evident. Interpersonal or intergroup tensions which could be overlooked in the early stage now clamor for attention. Differing expectations of the founders, managers, and workers are freely expressed. Compensation for sacrifices made earlier is demanded in the struggle to distribute recognition, rewards, and profits. Motivation is complicated by the conflicts between short-term personal gain and long-term organizational gain. Management faces problems of training and retraining personnel, developing a team spirit, stabilizing a core clientele, and developing a long-range plan.
>
> Willingness to accept and enforce discipline means recognizing that expansion is not synonymous with success, that larger gross sales may not mean larger net profit. It also involves the wisdom required to avoid overcommitment of resources; this is a time for solidifying gains before launching into larger arenas of action (1967, p. 106).

Thus, we see that in the normal course of growing, the organization generates internal forces that make change inevitable.

Two Stages of Organizational Change

Having begun this survey of change with a study of organization structures and characteristics that facilitate or hinder change, we have reviewed many of the elements of the contingency model of organizations. The evidence presented suggests that organizations configured according to the rational, mechanical model do not facilitate change as readily as those configured after the natural-system or organic model. However, at several points we suggested that organizational character-istics, such as centralization, have differential effects on the rate of program change, depending on whether the change process is in the initiation stage or the implementation stage. This point must be ampli-fied, for identification of the different stages in the process of organiza-tion change is essential to understanding the nature of change.

Most conceptualizations of change can be simplified as follows: Ini-tially there is a process of creativity or idea formulation and subsequently there is a process of gaining acceptance of these ideas from key in-dividuals and the organization generally. Much of the literature dealing with the first half of this sequence has a cognitive, rational emphasis. The focus is on communication—on getting new information to the right individuals. Chin and Benne (1969) term this the "rational" strat-egy for change. Examples of this literature concern the "diffusion" or acceptance of new drugs among physicians (Coleman, Katz and Menzel, 1966). These studies identify opinion leaders—key individuals who keep abreast of innovations and who disseminate this information to fol-lowers in their profession. (Katz and Lazarsfeld, 1955).

The second half of the change sequence, dealing with implementa-tion, is addressed by a somewhat different body of literature—the "planned change" literature which is concerned with emotional and structural problems involved in changing the behavior of individuals in organizations (Benne, Bennis, and Chin, 1969). This literature empha-sizes that communication of ideas is necessary, but not sufficient, to the change process. Resistance to change and the multitude of problems en-countered in changing individuals and their informal structures must be overcome.

The distinction between the rational-cognitive view of change and the emotional-structural approach is greatly oversimplified and overgeneral-ized here, but serves a useful purpose in reminding us that, in the rather underresearched field of organizational change, basic assumptions and perspectives are very important and somewhat controversial. Below, we shall cite literature from both perspectives, but our emphasis will be on the emotional-structural approach to change, especially in Chapter 16 on "Organizational Development." In the remainder of this chapter we shall take a primarily rational-cognitive view of dilemmas in the process of change.

DILEMMAS IN THE PROCESS OF CHANGE

Determining the Need for Change

Hage and Aiken (1970) view the change process as comprising four different stages: (1) determining the need for change, (2) initiation, (3) implementation, and (4) routinization.[4] During the first stage, the organization becomes aware of problems that suggest the inadequacy of the status quo. Perhaps goals are not being met as adequately as in prior periods, or as projected by forecasts. In any event, perception of a gap between desired and actual performance initiates the process of organizational change.

An external consultant might think of this as the diagnostic phase of the process. However, from management's point of view, this term is not exactly appropriate. Most organizations have ongoing surveillance and monitoring procedures as well as programs for gathering information in nonroutine situations. Identification of gaps between actual and intended performance is a routine activity. When interpreted according to the theories, constructs, or paradigms employed by management, these gaps suggest both the sources of problems and tentative remedies for them.

An interesting question at this stage concerns the extent of consensus about the need to change. Need for change is indicated by the perception of gaps between intended and actual performance, as we have said. But we have also said that organizations typically pursue a number of goals which occasionally are in conflict. Goals and shorter run objectives constitute statements of intended performance. Depending on the goals most salient to managers and the validity with which performance toward them can be measured, conflicts may arise due to different perceptions of the need for change. The processes by which these perceptions are communicated to top management as well as the negotiation and compromise strategies that lead to consensus should interest us here. Unfortunately, these aspects of the change process have received little attention from behavioral scientists, perhaps because they occur so early in the change process that they precede the scientists' interventions. One description of the process is provided in Chapter 14. A modified rational theory of perception of the need for organizational change is found in March and Simon (1958) and, more recently, in Downs (1967). The interested student may wish to pursue these theories for a view of how the first stage of the change process would look if managers behaved "rationally."

One dilemma facing management during the early part of the change

---

[4] Hage and Aiken term the first stage "evaluation." We have changed their terminology since we use the term in a different sense elsewhere.

process is whether to engage in a large-scale or modest change effort. Modest changes are relatively simple to make and bear proportionate risks. Large-scale changes are more difficult to bring about, more costly, and riskier, although more likely to remedy serious problems. One way to analyze the magnitude of a change effort is in terms of its depth of intervention (Downs, 1967). Relatively shallow structural changes modify a limited portion of the organization; for instance, a university may create a new associate dean's position in its school of business in response to administrative overload. A deeper change affects the organization's rules for decision making. At this level, the university in our example may alter the formula by which funds are allocated to its various schools. Still deeper are changes in the organization's structural arrangements for making and enforcing rules. This depth of change would be observed in a university that granted students a vote in decisions to tenure faculty members. Finally, the deepest level of change modifies the purposes of the organization, and would be found in a university that divested its traditional goals to become a training center.

Different managers and consultants have different predilections for shallow and deep changes. Some will prefer to operate at shallow levels while others will be attracted to more dramatic efforts. Similarly, different individuals will entertain different theories of organizational behavior and change. These will give rise to contrasting opinions of the ends and means of change efforts. Please bear in mind that these differences are based on attitudes and predilections as well as on objective scientific experience. Thus, a series of dilemmas can arise. We shall introduce some of these dilemmas in the present chapter and attempt to elucidate them throughout the remainder of the text.

Initiation of Change

The initiation stage of the change process arises when it is decided that change is necessary and when one alternative solution is perceived to be more desirable than competing alternatives. At this stage, management must decide *who* is to conduct the remainder of the change process. Should the organization employ external consultants or rely on the talents of its own employees? Using insiders is preferable if management wishes to avoid major disruptions. However, because of existing obligations, loyalties, preconceptions, vested interests, and the like, insiders may find themselves unable to bring about major changes. The opposite is true of outsiders, of course, who can bring new ideas and directions for change to the organization, but who are likely to create conflict and resistance in the process.

A second dilemma concerns the source of financial support for the change effort. Use of existing resources will curtail other planned or ongoing activities. Thus, reallocation of a fixed budget is likely to en-

gender conflict or at best a lack of whole-hearted cooperation from segments of the organization adversely affected. Going outside the organization for financial support will create dependency on the source of
funding. The various arrangements described by James Thompson
(1967) are relevant here: namely, cooptation and cooperation. The form
of dependency experienced will depend on the nature of the arrangement; for example, a bank loan will be accompanied by the bank's insis-
tence on safeguards such as limitations on the organization's activities,
the right to certain kinds of surveillance, and the right to specific reports.

The need to identify the starting point for a change program gives
rise to another series of dilemmas. An organization contemplating
changes in its branch offices has a choice of targets for its initial change
attempts. Should the parent organization begin the change program in
units that are weak or powerful? Should it begin with independent units
or those that are linked with other units? Should integrated, cohesive
units be selected, or should the program begin with personnel who are
not so closely knit?

A stronger effort is required to change powerful, integrated, or cohesive units than to achieve the same initial results with those that are
relatively weak, independent, or fragmented. However, the long-run
effectiveness of the change program may be enhancd by starting with
units having the former characteristics. Powerful and cohesive units
may serve as models for others. The latter may follow the lead of the
former to the extent that changes will be emulated. Interrelated units
must remain compatible. A change in one unit will create pressures in
the others to change accordingly. Where this is the case, change tends
to be diffused throughout the organization more readily.

The degree of risk inherent in the intended change is an important
factor in the decision to select a particular starting point. If the change
is modest and experience suggests that attendant risks are slight, it is
probably well to begin with the more difficult units. When the change
program is envisaged to be difficult or portending substantial risks, it is
appropriate to begin with a pilot project in a unit separate from the
others and weak enough to offer minimal resistance to change. Having
demonstrated the effectiveness of change in the pilot unit, management
can turn its efforts to more difficult areas of the organization.

Implementation of Change

Top management tends to operate on its own, without involving
others, throughout the first two stages of the change process. In the implementation stage, lower level personnel must become involved as well.
Awareness of a need for change and exploration of alternative courses
of action tend to disrupt (unfreeze) top management's habitual ways of
thinking and acting. We shall examine the phenomenon of "unfreezing"

habitual behavior in Chapter 18. At this point, it is important to note that lower level participants must be "unfrozen" as well.

Habits, rules, structures, and procedures contribute to organizational stability. The more stable the organization, the more readily its steady state activities can be predicted and controlled. This situation can be described as one of equilibrium. Hage and Aiken note that the implementation of change increases organizational disequilibrium. At this point, more of the staff have become "unfrozen." In the utopian world of the rational school of thought, this is the point at which a plan for change is implemented, behavior refrozen, and equilibrium reestablished. In actual practice, we find this stage to be a prolonged period of "muddling through."

Management cannot make complete plans for change. For one thing, they lack a science of organizational change. For another, they lack vital, detailed information residing at lower levels of the organization. Furthermore, intended changes may be resisted by various personnel. When organizational objectives and the self-interest of participants conflict, employees appear perverse, unpredictable, and stubborn. The behavioral sciences are inexact. We cannot predict all responses to change accurately. As these and other shortcomings compound the situation, mistakes are made. Thus, the change process must proceed gradually, using feedback to correct mistakes and accommodate unforeseen contingencies. The organization must be unfrozen for the initiation of change and *remain* unfrozen for the duration of the change.

Hage and Aiken note that conflict is prone to arise during the implementation stage. Units undergoing change or newly created by change frequently demand additional resources, authority, and changes in rules. However, these demands can affect other units adversely. Resources may be taken directly (or indirectly) from the budgets of other units. Changed rules may impede their functioning. Newly acquired authority may encroach on established "turfs." If top management does not accede to legitimate demands of this sort, the change effort may die on the vine. It it does accede, it may disrupt the organization and possibly limit its effectiveness.

A related dilemma concerns the extent to which change programs should be made participative. Should all parties affected be allowed to participate, as human relations practitioners suggest? An expected result of such participation is increased commitment to the process. Another expected outcome is that participants will express their desires and change the program to suit their own ends, possibly hindering or curtailing those of top management. Cooperation is bought at the price of alterations to the change program envisaged. Alternatively, the integrity of the change effort may be maintained at the cost of resistance to change and conflict.

Top management may decide to make structural changes unilaterally, expecting that, in the long run, interpersonal conflicts and adverse attitudes will die out—that eventually behavior will conform to new structural arrangements. Alternatively, behavioral scientists may be brought into the organization to alter behavior prior to making structural changes. Changing people is costly, risky, and occasionally subject to question on ethical grounds. However, appropriate changes may facilitate intended structural modifications.

Another dilemma arises in attempting to decide whether to use a highly structured or unstructured change effort. On the one hand, management can plan changes in considerable detail beforehand and then proceed to implement its plan systematically. On the other hand, it may be decided that planning is infeasible, or too costly. In this event, change will be implemented and coordinated by feedback. The advantage of planning is that it provides a degree of security when it can be done effectively. Contingencies are foreseen, costs projected, and pitfalls, hopefully, avoided. Management can determine its progress by comparing actual to planned results at any point in time. Anxieties of those responsible for implementation may be reduced to the extent that the direction of the effort is foreseen. The existence of a plan, similar to the existence of rules, may reduce potential for interpersonal conflict (Chapter 10).

However, flexibility is lost in the process. In relatively deep change efforts containing risk and uncertainty, mistakes in the initial planning effort are difficult to correct. The mere existence of a detailed plan may cause those charged with its implementation to become relatively insensitive to feedback. Accomplishment will be measured in terms of executing the plan rather than in terms of the achievement of objectives which may entail modifying what has been planned.

Routinization of Change

A problem arising in both the implementation and routinization stages concerns identifying the point at which changes will be consolidated. One strategy is to prolong the unfrozen state and to work numerous changes simultaneously—to move from one change to the next without attempting to freeze behavior. The alternative strategy is to consolidate each change as it is accomplished. An advantage of the latter approach is that management can devote its attention to other portions of the organization without worrying about backsliding in previously changed units. This outcome may be offset by the very attributes that make it seem advantageous. Interdependent units must remain compatible despite changes undergone. We may find that a change in unit 2 requires modification of unit 1. If unit 1 was previously changed and refrozen, it must be unfrozen, changed, and refrozen once again if resistance to change is to be overcome. At the extreme, the situation becomes expensive, frustrating, and baroque.

This may be contrasted with the strategy of leaving change efforts unfrozen temporarily. As change proceeds in one unit, interdependencies will affect other, unfrozen units influencing them to change appropriately and reinforcing them for these responses. In fact, the situation can be mutually reinforcing. Changes made in the second unit reinforce and stabilize those made in the first. The problem with this approach is that it disperses the attentions of management across numerous units. Although the total change effort may be substantial, the effort directed to any one unit may be meager.

The timing of efforts to consolidate changes is contingent upon the degree to which changes have been completed. Ideally, consolidation occurs after the gap between intended and actual performance is eliminated. In reality, it may be impossible to measure this gap precisely. Alternatively, the gap may have shrunk as a result of organizational change, but not completely. In this case, the question arises whether major or minor effort is required to complete the process. Continued major effort is costly and time consuming. Oftentimes, the costs of change are salient while the benefits are not. Time and money spent, conflict and anxiety suffered, and inefficiency and confusion endured are readily identified with attempts to change organizations. Benefits, such as improved morale, are intangible. Improvements such as organizational growth and survival are remote in time from changes intended to cause them. In short, when costs are more apparent than benefits, change efforts may be terminated prematurely.

Resistance to Change

As the manager contemplates and initiates change in the organization, one theme is likely to emerge time and again—resistance to the change process. These reactions have been emphasized in the psychological literature, perhaps overly so (Gross et al., 1971), but "resistance to change" is a major problem that can develop at any point in the change process. As Gross indicates, there is little research on the actual process of change or overcoming associated resistance to change. For this reason, we are forced to rely primarily on the day-to-day experience of change agents, who work with management to bring about organizational change.

The organization member's response to change depends on his perception of the proposed change and, of course, on the effects he[5] thinks the change will have on his needs and aspirations (Mann and Neff,

---

[5] As stated previously, the common pronoun "he" refers to persons of either sex and is not intended to be masculine or feminine.

1961). If he experiences ambiguity, the individual may engage in search behavior which may appear as resistance from the perspective of those initiating change. Also related to search behavior are the individual's perception of his ability to control the situation and his general trust in those in charge of proposed changes (see Figure 15–1). Ambiguity may not lead to resistance if the individual is permitted a degree of control over his destiny, as is the case when he is encouraged to participate in the change process. Participation in the planning phases of change, of course, provides not only the opportunity for control, but also clarity about the nature of the intended change. Trust also affects the degree to which the individual views prospective changes positively. Mann and Neff suggest that information, participation, and the organizational culture determine the individual's perception of a proposed change by operating through the mediating viables of ambiguity, control, and trust. Participation is useful in overcoming resistance to change because of its potential to increase the accuracy of perceptions and extent of control, and to reduce ambiguity. However, trust may or may not in-

FIGURE 15–1
A Model for Understanding an Individual's Response to Change

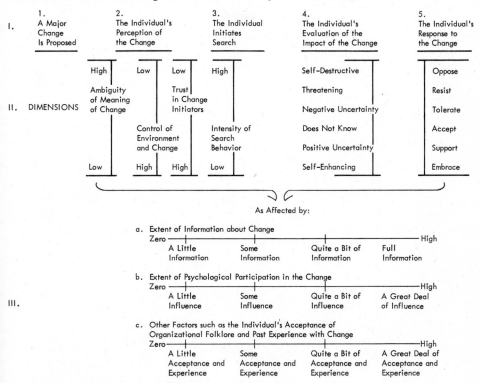

Source: Mann and Neff (1961, p. 69).

crease, depending on what is observed in the act of participation. The individual's perception of participation as a facade, used to increase manipulation (see Chapter 10), or as an opportunity openly granted, with openly stated risks and trade-offs, is likely to affect trust.

This is basically a rational model in which individuals respond to change situations by considering the implications and acting in their self-interests. Ambiguities and anxieties enter into the model by coloring perceptions. It is assumed that individuals react either positively or negatively, depending on how the change is presented. Sometimes, however, we can expect to find individuals with basic predispositions toward change—who view either change or the status quo as an end in itself (Barnes, 1967).

If the individual perceives change to be compatible with his or her personal goals, and management concurs in this estimate, there are few problems. However, if the individual's perception is inaccurate (e.g., if he or she sees change as compatible when it is not), management will need to clarify the situation even though the individual's resistance may increase as a result. If management were to deliberately mislead employees, the longer-range effects on trust and acceptance of future changes (even those clearly within the individual's interest) would be costly.

When management experiences resistance from individuals who perceive changes to be incompatible with their goals, even when management's view is to the contrary, increased communication is also advised, although the climate of trust may be such that perceptions of negative implications of change cannot be altered. Mann and Neff suggest that management emphasize its *actions* when these are compatible with individual goals, and that the proposed change be differentiated from other, past changes.

When individuals see change as incompatible with their goals and management concurs in this view, then, Mann and Neff suggest, management must review the objectives of the change and either alter them or proceed with the original change program (assuming that the wherewithal to overcome resistance is available, and that the various costs of change do not outweigh its benefits).

Sometimes, management is uncertain about the effects of a proposed change. Here the offer of employee participation may be in order. When employees are involved in decisions concerning change, its implications for both management and employees become clearer.

In general, then, Mann and Neff suggest that the management of change can be improved by giving those affected more information and allowing them to participate in the change process. While these are useful suggestions, we shall explore change phenomena in greater depth, developing more detailed, specific approaches to organizational change.

Dilemmas in Perspective

Throughout this chapter we have raised major issues without resolving them. As we move into more detailed analyses of change phenomena, we shall address them as best we can. Be forewarned, however, that science cannot provide precise resolutions for these issues. Yet, every organization faces them at one time or another, resolves them in one way or another, and continues to play its role in society. This is an area in which theory lags practice. Thus, we shall pursue these few remaining chapters cautiously, treading, as it were, the frontiers of knowledge.

DISCUSSION QUESTIONS

1. We have discussed numerous attributes that facilitate or hinder change in organizations. Using these attributes, formulate organizational designs appropriate to stable and dynamic environments.
2. How do these designs compare to those discussed in Chapter 2?
3. Should all organizations be made change propensive. Why?
4. Changes in the university's environment include decreases in student demand for higher education and increases in the numbers of candidates for faculty positions. What organizational responses may be appropriate under these circumstances? What forms of resistance are to be expected when these responses are made? What dilemmas are raised by alternative responses?

REFERENCES

Barnes, Louis B. Organizational change and field experimental methods. In V. H. Vroom (Ed.), *Methods of organizational research*. Pittsburgh: University of Pittsburgh Press, 1967.

Benne, Kenneth D., Bennis, Warren G., and Chin, Robert (Eds.). *The planning of change*. 2d ed. New York: Holt, Rinehart and Winston, 1969.

Chin, Robert, and Benne, Kenneth D. General strategies for effecting changes in human systems. In W. G. Bennis, K. D. Benne, and R. Chin (Eds.), *The planning of change*. 2d ed. New York: Holt, Rinehart and Winston, 1969. Pp. 32–59.

Coleman, James S., Katz, Elihu, and Menzel, Herbert. *Medical innovation: a diffusion study*. Indianapolis: Bobbs-Merrill, 1966.

Corwin, Ronald G. Strategies for organizational innovation: an empirical comparison. *American Sociological Review*, 1972, 37, 441–54.

Cyert, Richard M., and March, James G. *A behavioral theory of the firm*. Englewood Cliffs, N.J.: Prentice-Hall, 1963.

Demerath, N. J., III, and Hammond, Phillip E. *Religion in social context: tradition and transition*. New York: Random House, 1969.

Downs, Anthony. *Inside bureaucracy*. Boston: Little, Brown, 1967.

Gross, Neal, Giacquinta, Joseph B., and Bernstein, Marilyn. *Implementing organizational innovations: a sociological analysis of planned educational change*. New York: Basic Books, 1971.

Hage, Jerald, and Aiken, Michael. *Social change in complex organizations.* New York: Random House, 1970.

Hall, Richard H., Haas, J. Eugene, and Johnson, Norman J. Organizational size, complexity, and formalization. *American Sociological Review,* 1967, 32, 903–12.

Hoos, Ida R. *Systems analysis in public policy: a critique.* Berkeley, Calif.: University of California Press, 1972.

Katz, Elihu, and Lazarsfeld, Paul F. *Personal influence: the part played by people in the flow of mass communications.* Glencoe, Ill.: Free Press, 1955.

Kuhn, Thomas S. *The Copernican revolution.* Cambridge, Mass.: Harvard University Press, 1957.

Lippitt, Gordon L., and Schmidt, Warren H. Crises in a developing organization. *Harvard Business Review,* 1967, 45(6) (November–December), 102–12.

Mann, Floyd C., and Neff, Franklin W. *Managing major change in organizations.* Ann Arbor, Mich.: Foundation for Research on Human Behavior, 1961.

March, James G., and Simon, Herbert A. *Organizations.* New York: Wiley, 1958.

McNeil, Kenneth, and Thompson, James D. The regeneration of social organizations. *American Journal of Sociology,* 1971, 36, 624–37.

Meyer, Marshall W. Automation and bureaucratic structure. *American Journal of Sociology,* 1968, 74, 256–64.

Mohr, Lawrence. Determinants of innovation in organizations. *American Political Science Review,* 1969, 63, 111–26.

Roberts, D. R. A general theory of executive cooperation based on statistically tested proportions. *Quarterly Journal of Economics,* 1956, 20, 270–94.

Roberts, D. R. *Executive cooperation.* Glencoe, Ill.: Free Press, 1959.

Rosener, Marvin M. Economic determinants of organizational innovation. *Administrative Science Quarterly,* 1967, 12, 614–25.

Sarason, Seymour B. *The creation of settings and the future societies.* San Francisco: Jossey-Bass, 1972.

Scott, Joseph W., and El-Assal, Mohamed. Multiversity, university size, university quality and student protest: an empirical study, *American Sociological Review,* 1969, 34, 708.

Speer, Albert. *Inside the Third Reich.* New York: Avon, 1971.

Starbuck, W. H. Organizational growth and development. In J. G. March (Ed.), *Handbook of organizations,* Chicago: Rand McNally, 1965. Pp. 451–533.

Thompson, James D. *Organizations in action.* New York: McGraw-Hill, 1967.

Thompson, Victor A. *Bureaucracy and innovation.* University, Ala.: University of Alabama Press, 1969.

Time. The student shortage. *Time,* 1974, 104(3) (July 15), 86.

United States Strategic Bombing Survey. *The effects of strategic bombing on German morale, Vol. 1.* Washington, D.C.: Government Printing Office, 1947.

Wanous, John P., and Lawler, Edward E., III. Measurement and meaning of job satisfaction. *Journal of Applied Psychology.* 1972, 56, 95–105.

Weber, Max. *The theory of social and economic organization.* (Trans. A. M. Henderson and Talcott Parsons). New York: Free Press, 1947.

Wieland, George F. *Organizational complexity and coordination.* Unpublished doctoral dissertation, University of Michigan, 1965.

Wilson, James Q. Innovation in organization: notes toward a theory. In J. D. Thompson (Ed.), *Approaches to organizational design*. Pittsburgh: University of Pittsburgh Press, 1966. Pp. 193–218.

Zaltman, Gerald, Duncan, Robert, and Holbek, Jonny. *Innovations and organizations*. New York: Wiley, 1973.

16

Organizational Development

INTRODUCTION

Social change is difficult to achieve, even within relatively small social units. For about 25 years scholars and practitioners have explored various techniques for changing organizations. The name usually given to these activities is *organizational development* (or OD). The field is new and, as we shall see, controversial. Change strategies range from job enrichment schemes (Chapter 6), which are relatively straightforward and readily understood, to marathon encounter groups, which are difficult to describe and produce results that are uncertain at best.

Typical of much of the work in organizational development is laboratory training (or T-groups, sensitivity training, or human relation labs as they are sometimes called). For this reason, we shall begin with a summary of T-group activities and then move on to other, less controversial practices.

Beliefs about the efficacy of T-groups tend to be polarized even among behavioral scientists. You have probably been exposed to some of the continuing debate over whether T-groups are dangerous. Note the extreme views taken by the two scientists quoted below.

> 1. Now for the argument that the laboratory program can hurt people and is, therefore, dangerous. The facts of life are that people are being hurt everyday. I do not know of any laboratory program that did, or could, create for people as much tension as they are experiencing in their everyday work relationships.
>
> It is true that laboratory education does require people to take risks. But does anyone know of any learning that truly leads to growth which does not involve some pain and cost? The value of laboratory education is that it keeps out people who want to learn "cheaply" and it provides the others with control over how much they wish to learn and what they want to pay for it (Argyris, 1970, p. 330).
>
> 2. Our study did find group experiences damaging to 8 percent of those who began the groups, a figure which most people would not consider "safe." The ghost, in short, is not at all laid to rest. It appears that previous studies of encounter groups, and the claims of practitioners, tend to minimize negative effects. This minimization seems explained by limited follow-up contact with members after the group, insufficiently

careful attention to the existence of negative outcomes during the group, and ideological rejection of "negative effects" as a meaningful concept (Lieberman, Yalom, and Miles, 1973, p. 426).[1]

Chapter Guide

1. What are your beliefs concerning T-groups? What scientific facts can you marshal in support of these beliefs?
2. As we shall see, T-groups and similar change strategies attempt to produce "deep" changes within participants. How deep is it necessary to go in order to change organizational behavior?
3. Job enrichment, as described in Chapter 6, is considered to be a change strategy by some OD practitioners. Yet, as we have seen, its applicability seems to be limited to certain kinds of workers and work situations. Do you think this is true for all change techniques? If so, how does one go about matching the appropriate change techniques to the problems at hand?

TRAINING GROUPS IN ORGANIZATIONAL DEVELOPMENT

Controversies in Organizational Development

Some of the most controversial work in the field of organizational change falls under the rubric of organizational development. Many current practices are unquestionably sound, having withstood scientific inquiry and produced demonstrable positive results. Other practices have polarized the opinions of both managers and members of the academic community because of their inherent risks and uncertain payoffs. Magnusen (1973), for example, concludes:

> If OD is to become a respectable applied profession, greater attention must be given to the integration of theory and practice. Despite a few select efforts, the area has no tradition of adding knowledge cumulatively or keeping a balanced perspective on change strategies. Little interest has been shown in long-term projects to evaluate the development of organizations over time and searching questions have been raised about how to train competent practitioners (p. 81).

Practitioners range in ability from those who have dedicated years to the development of professional competence to individuals whose claims to competence are based on having attended a few three-week training programs. At the extreme, one finds practitioners whose quali-

---

1 From *Encounter Groups: First Facts,* by Morton A. Lieberman, Irvin D. Yalom, Matthew B. Mills, © 1973 by Morton A. Lieberman, Irvin D. Yalom, and Matthew B. Miles, Basic Books, Inc., Publishers, New York.

fications appear to consist of little more than their self-confidence.[2] Similarly, the techniques employed range from sensitivity training and encounter groups with their attendant risks (Lieberman et al., 1973) to relatively bland exercises such as the managerial grid described in Chapter 6. Within this context of uncertainty, debate, and polarized beliefs, we shall attempt to describe and evaluate some of the major OD techniques currently practiced.

Characteristics of Organizational Development

There are many definitions of OD and its basic nature. Friedlander and Brown (1974) speak of OD as "a method for facilitating change and development in people (e.g., styles, values, skills), in technology (e.g., greater simplicity, complexity), and in organizational processes and structures (e.g., relationships, roles)" (p. 314). Beckhard (1969) also sees OD as having a broad purview, being "an effort (1) *planned*, (2) *organization-wide*, and (3) *managed* from the top, to (4) increase *organization effectiveness* and *health* through (5) *planned interventions* in the organization's 'processes' using *behavioral-science* knowledge" (p. 9).

Warren Bennis (1969) describes OD as an educational strategy intended to bring about planned organizational change. While numerous strategies (techniques) are advocated, all are related in that they seek organizational change through changes in "people" variables such as values, attitudes, interpersonal relations, and organizational climate. This is in contrast to some of the change strategies described earlier that deal with structure, technology, and the physical environment. The primary focus on "people" variables arises because those who developed and presently work in the field are, for the most part, psychologists. To these people, the individual and small group aspects of a situation are most readily understood and appear most amenable to change.

The second basic characteristic of OD, according to Bennis, is that it attempts to solve *problems* that are experienced by members of the organization. The changes sought are not advocated by an outside consultant. Rather, they are in response to needs felt within the organization. As examples of problems typically addressed by OD, Bennis cites communications problems, intergroup conflicts, leadership issues, questions of identity, problems of satisfactions and inducements to work, and questions about organizational effectiveness.

A third characteristic of OD is its reliance on educational strategies emphasizing *experienced behavior*. Data feedback, sensitivity training,

---

[2] Sashkin *et al.* (1973) suggest ". . . doubtless there are as many incompetents and quacks in the field of OD as there are in the fields of medicine and psychotherapy" (p. 192).

confrontation meetings, and other kinds of experiential learning methods are used to generate publicly shared data and experiences upon which the organization can plan and act.

A fourth characteristic is that change agents are, for the most part, *external* to the client system. Bennis argues that an external change agent can be more objective than an employee in his assessment of an organization. Furthermore, he can affect the power structure in ways that are unavailable to internal change agents.

A fifth essential aspect of OD is the *collaborative* relationship between the change agent and the client system. Bennis defines collaboration as comprising mutual trust, joint determination of goals and means, and high total influence.

The sixth point is that change agents share a *social philosophy* (or a set of values) about the world in general and especially about organizations. Practitioners tend to believe that realization of these values will lead to the development of more humane, democratic, and efficient systems.

Normative Goals in Organizational Development

The values of change agents in OD stem from the so-called *humanistic psychology,* and are in contrast with those arising from the Protestant ethic (e.g., rationality, task orientation, and so on). According to Bennis, goals arising from these values include the following:

1. The improvement of interpersonal competence.
2. The reinforcement of values that legitimize feelings and emotions.
3. The increased understanding of behavior in groups.
4. The development of more effective work groups and team management.
5. The development of more effective methods of conflict resolution; namely, replacing bureaucratic methods with more open approaches.
6. The transition from rational to organic systems.

Process Consultation

Schein (1969) emphasizes the role of *process* in organizational development programs; that is, the change agent studies organizational processes (ways of behaving) in order to help his client become more aware of the way in which he[3] behaves and affects others. It is this awareness and understanding that enables the client to improve the effectiveness of his organization.

Schein argues that studying interpersonal and group events enables

---

[3] It has been stated previously that the common pronoun "he" refers to persons of either sex and is not intended to be masculine or feminine.

the change agent to help the manager define his own problems and decide what further help he needs. The *process consultant,* as Schein terms the change agent, examines work flows, interpersonal relations, communications, intergroup relations, and the like and *works with* managers in diagnosing problems and the processes from which they arise. Schein feels that the consultant can seldom learn enough about the client organization to know which improvements are best for the particular group of people involved, given their unique traditions, histories, and personalities. The process consultant's job is to help the manager help himself—to help him diagnose his own problems, generate alternatives, and select a solution that is suited to his own unique circumstances. As a result, clients also become aware of potentials for group conflict, anxieties that may prevent or distort communication, unspoken organizational assumptions and beliefs, consequences of various managerial styles, and of alternative ways of communicating, providing leadership, and inducing communication and cooperation among individuals and groups.

Schein suggests that process consultation be contrasted with two alternative models: (1) the consultant as *expert advice giver* and (2) *patient-physician* model. In the first model, the client defines his needs in terms of knowledge or services that are lacking and engages a consultant to provide them. This assumes that the client can diagnose his needs accurately, communicate them effectively, and identify change agents who are competent to deliver the appropriate information and services. Furthermore, the model assumes a known cause and effect relationship between the consultant's activities and the elimination of the problem to which they are addressed. These are tenuous assumptions that can lead the client to purchase consultations that ultimately prove unsatisfactory. Many consultants' reports gather dust in some forgotten file because they are not what the client wanted. Even worse, consultants can generate unnecessary conflict between groups that will benefit or suffer losses if the recommended action is undertaken. Furthermore, where recommended actions are inconsistent with the organization's culture, progress may be fleeting and changes reversed over time. For these reasons, Schein advocates collaboration between change agents and clients wherein the client system learns to diagnose and remedy its own problems.

In the second model (patient-physician), the client hires consultants who diagnose the organization's ills and recommend a program of "therapy." Difficulties arise when individuals and departments resent and resist the consultants' probing or reject the diagnosis or therapy. Again, Schein's advocacy of process consultation is based on his belief that collaboration in diagnosis and problem solving will alleviate the causes of these difficulties.

As Schein sees it, the change agent must pass on *skills* and *values,* not knowledge. He helps the organization learn about its processes and the problems they generate and how to solve these problems using internal, rather than external, resources.

Schein's view of OD provides an amplification of the philosophy of practitioners in general. However, we shall now examine some of the more common practices in detail.

Structuring Interventions

Much of the practice of OD is based on knowledge and experience built up by consultants and passed on orally rather than in written journal articles. Of course, there is a great deal of literature now, especially in the *Journal of Applied Behavioral Science*, but the real "nuts-and-bolts" techniques of OD are hard to describe, varying as they do from practitioner to practitioner. French and Bell (1973) provide a useful list of the basic principles, or "secrets" as they put it, of structuring an OD intervention. The ideal intervention is structured according to the following principles:

1. The relevant people (those affected by the problem) are there.
2. It is (*a*) problem oriented or opportunity oriented and (*b*) oriented to the problems and opportunities generated by the clients themselves.
3. The goal is clear and the way to reach the goal is clear.
4. There is a high probability of successful goal attainment.
5. It contains both experience-based learning and conceptual/cognitive/theoretical-based learning.
6. Individuals are "freed up" rather than anxious or defensive.
7. The participants learn both how to solve a particular problem and "learn how to learn" at the same time.
8. Individuals can learn about both *task* and *process*.
9. Individuals are engaged as whole persons, not segmented persons. (Abstracted from French and Bell, 1973, pp. 99–101.)

Training Groups

Laboratory training groups (or T-groups and sensitivity training groups as they are called) have been one of the most common elements of organizational development efforts. Rush (1969) gives evidence of the widespread use of T-groups in noting that a 1968 study of some 240 companies indicated that one-third used sensitivity training.

The Objectives of Training Groups

T-groups have been used for a quarter of a century, ever since the National Education Association joined the Research Center for Group Dynamics of the University of Michigan in holding experimental laboratories at Bethel, Maine. These laboratories were designed to teach the processes involved in social change. As the name *sensitivity training* implies, contemporary laboratories are designed to make participants more sensitive to: (1) their own behavior; (2) their conscious and unconscious motivations; (3) the ways in which their own behavior is perceived by, and affects, others; (4) the behavior of others and its underlying motivations; and (5) the processes that help and hinder group functioning.

Sensitivity training differs from other educational endeavors in that it is not designed primarily as an intellectual exchange between the teacher and learners. Rather, the group's behavior, including members' emotional responses, is the subject of study. Actual behavior in face-to-face interactions constitutes the process from which learning occurs. It is claimed that sensitivity training works by making participants aware of the determinants of group and individual behavior. This awareness, furthermore, paves the way for improvements in the participant's control of his or her own behavior and interaction with others.

The Setting and Role of the Trainer

T-groups are usually conducted in settings remote from the participants' organizations—where distractions and props such as habitual roles, furniture arrangements, various kinds of technologies, books, reports, and the like are absent. It is claimed that a setting of this sort allows the participants to involve themselves totally (physically, intellectually, and emotionally) in the task of studying their behavior in the group.

T-groups are normally led by trainers who neither lecture nor engage in typical leadership functions, but serve instead as observers and nondirective resource persons.[4] After the usual 10 or 15 persons have gathered in the group setting, the trainer may give a brief introduction, stating the group's task. Typically, the introduction is bland and rather uninformative and suggests merely that participants will engage in learning about the behavior of individuals in groups. There is no agenda and nothing else to structure the group. The trainer generally retires to the "sidelines" without instructing participants further.

Task-oriented managers who are accustomed to meeting for specific purposes become rather frustrated in a situation that lacks both structure and assigned roles. Groups begin in a number of ways. Some start with a lengthy silence which is broken by an individual attempting to structure the task of the group. Other groups begin when a member introduces himself or herself to the group and invites others to do likewise. In some cases, conflict arises when several participants vie for the leadership role. Frustration also develops as participants attempt to

[4] Audio tapes that serve as surrogates for the leader are currently available as well.

deal with the lack of agenda. Some group members become anxious, some hostile, others apathetic.

At some point, the trainer will comment that the group has already begun to learn—that members are behaving and reacting to each other's behavior. He or she may articulate some of the feelings and behavior observed. At any point, he may ask participants to examine what is occurring. Occasional pointed questions help members become aware of the dynamics of the group's behavior.

With the help of the trainer, group members learn to speak their minds and express their feelings. Openness and honesty are encouraged. Norms of trust, openness, and helpfulness emerge as participants report how they perceive and react to behavior in the group.

It is also claimed that participants learn about the dynamics of group behavior and individual behavior within groups in this manner. Furthermore, self-understanding and the opportunity to "work through" feelings and experiment with new, more appropriate behaviors are considered attributes of training groups.

Research on the Effectiveness of Training Groups

Until recently, little scientific research has been directed toward the evaluation of training groups. Organizational development is a field in which theory has followed practice. Two major arguments are advanced by practitioners in refuting the applicability of the scientific method to the study of OD techniques (Lieberman et al., 1973). First, it is argued that the phenomena encountered are so complex that meaningful research designs are beyond our present research technology. Alternatively, it is argued that the scientific method has nothing relevant to contribute to OD, which deals in perceptions and emotions rather than with factual data. Of course, it may also be that the anti-intellectual spirit of the OD movement serves as a barrier to research—that it constitutes a reaction against the authority of science.

Several reviews of research on sensitivity training have appeared, however (Campbell and Dunnette, 1970; Campbell, Dunnette, Lawler, and Weick, 1970; House, 1967). Campbell and associates suggest that 30 to 40 percent of trained individuals are reported to exhibit some sort of perceptible change. Typically, changes are perceived by colleagues in terms of increased sensitivity, more openness to communication, and increased flexibility in role behavior. It should be mentioned that most of these studies lack control groups. Furthermore, the raters usually know who has attended a T-group and who has not, and thus a bias may creep in. Furthermore, Campbell and associates emphasize that while the individual's behavior may change, it is not clear that these changes lead to better job performance. In fact, one study (Underwood, 1965) shows that trainees display more positive changes (rated in terms of effects on job performance) than controls, but also more negative changes.

A major study of the effects of T-groups (and encounter groups in general) on individuals was published in 1973 (Lieberman et al., 1973). In this research, 210 student volunteers were assigned to 18 encounter groups and 69 students were assigned to a control group. Sixteen leaders were chosen to conduct the experimental groups and were, in the words of Lieberman and colleagues, ". . . highly experienced group leaders [who] were uniformly esteemed by their colleagues as representing the best of their approach" (p. 11). These 16 leaders represented nine major approaches to encounter groups.[5] Two additional groups used a leaderless approach based on audio tape recordings.

Measures were developed to record educational and therapeutic outcomes of the semester-long experiment and were administered prior to the experiment, immediately after its conclusion, and again six months later. The researchers conclude that at the termination of the encounter groups one third of the participants benefited from them, a little over one third experienced no change at all, and the remainder suffered negative consequences. Six months later, three quarters of those experiencing positive outcomes maintained such learning. A similar decline applies to those who experienced negative outcomes. About 10 percent of the participants were found to be "late bloomers" who experienced positive outcomes six months after the experiment, but these came only from the group that had previously experienced no change in either direction from the encounter sessions. One conclusion that can be drawn from these observations, as we shall see, is that while the odds of attaining personal benefits from group experiences are slightly better than one in three, the associated risks are considerable.

Lieberman and colleagues (1973) describe the participants who experienced negative outcomes as ". . . dropping out of the group for psychological reasons, making negative changes, or experiencing psychological decompensation" (p. 129). Of these, some were found to be *casualties*. "By definition a casualty had a negative psychological reaction that was both enduring and, to the best of our judgment, *a direct result of their encounter group experience*[6] (Lieberman et al., 1973, p. 147). Although the measure was conservative, and likely to err on the positive side, the casualty rate was found to approach 10 percent—a rate that, to the authors, ". . . is alarming and unacceptable in an endeavor calculated to foster positive growth" (p. 193).

If the overall picture regarding the effects of encounter groups is as grim as Lieberman and colleagues suggest, why does enthusiasm for

---

[5] These approaches consist of T-groups, gestalt therapy, transactional analysis, personal growth labs, synanon, psychodrama, marathon, psychoanalytically oriented groups, and Esalen eclectic.

[6] Italics from original source.

sensitivity training continue to flourish? We can suggest several possible reasons. First, groups that are composed of strangers disband when training concludes. In the absence of a systematic follow-up of participants, casualties are unlikely to come to the attention of practitioners. Second, some trainers reject medical definitions of psychological injury and view psychological decompensation as a necessary step in the process of personal growth. This bias is couched in the jargon as: "You need to get sicker before you can get better." "In some quarters this approaches the advocacy of psychotic experience as a desideratum of personal growth" (Lieberman et al., 1973, p. 168). Third, trainers may overestimate their contributions to the group. In the research cited here, trainers estimated that 90 percent of the participants gained some form of benefit, or three times the number found by Lieberman et al. Finally, participants themselves generally experience brief, but intense, emotional episodes that seem particularly meaningful at the time. These perceptions, when shared with the trainer, may serve as reinforcement.

Training Groups and Organizational Change

Suppose that a manager undergoes positive changes as a result of his T-group experiences. We must ask how effectively these changes are utilized "back home" to improve organizational performance. Much of the criticism of T-groups centers around this question of whether or not changes in the manager's behavior transfer to his work role and improve his performance on the job.

The returned T-group veteran frequently is unable to articulate what he has experienced and how he has changed for the better. This inability to communicate affects the manager's ability to enlist the cooperation of other employees in behaving differently (i.e., more appropriately). Furthermore, it probably signifies the manager's inability to maintain whatever changes he or she achieved. To the extent that the individual is unable to think about what has happened and how he is different, he may lack control over his changed potentialities.

Even when this is not the case, the T-group veteran will still have difficulty applying newly learned modes of behavior. Because members of organizations are interdependent and have roles and jobs that interact with other roles, any change in the returned manager's behavior will be upsetting to others unless they, too, change their expectations of him or her and alter their own behavior accordingly. This criticism is particularly apt where the manager's organization is bureaucratic, having rigid definitions of roles, fixed distributions of power, and great status differences among various levels in the organizational hierarchy.

Several remedies for this problem have been suggested. The earlier T-groups were *stranger labs* in which members of different organizations came together. In this way, members of the same organization could have T-group experiences without feeling inhibited by the presence of co-workers. It was felt that members of an organizational unit who attended stranger labs would probably have had very similar experiences which would serve as the basis for transferring newly learned behavior to their organization.

More recently, T-groups have been designed to include members of the same organization who are not co-workers. These so-called *cousins* or *diagonal-slice* labs comprise members who have experience with a single organization in common. In contrast to *family labs*, which are attended by co-workers, the cousins labs are unlikely to be inhibiting. Yet, they would seem to be more effective in producing organizational change than stranger labs by virtue of the commonality of their membership. There seems to be a trade-off between family labs and stranger labs: the easier it is to join in and behave differently in an uninhibited manner, the harder it will be to transfer the newly learned behavior back to the workplace, and vice versa.

Research on Training Groups and Organizational Change

Again, we are faced with a situation in which proponents and critics of the T-group movement voice strong, sometimes extravagant claims in the absence of comprehensive research data. The one major study of the effect of T-group training on organizational effectiveness, however, leads us to side with those who view T-groups unfavorably.

Bowers (1971, 1973) examined the effects of four OD practices on over 14,000 respondents in 23 organizations. Most of the organizations remained in the Bowers' study for at least two years. Subjects included both white- and blue-collar workers from a variety of industries.

The four OD practices examined in the study were: (1) T-groups, (2) interpersonal process consultation, which is similar to Schein's process consultation described earlier, (3) task process consultation, which focuses on task or work objectives and the interpersonal relations associated with their attainment, and (4) survey feedback, the topic of our next chapter. In addition, two control groups consisted of one which received no treatment whatsoever and a second ("data handback") in which members were sent tabulated survey data in envelopes.

Pre- and postsurveys were undertaken to measure changes in 16 indices of organizational behavior. These included measures of organizational climate,[7] managerial leadership, peer leadership, group processes, and employee satisfaction. Many of these correspond to the measures used by Likert in his studies (Chapter 3). It was found that the survey feedback technique was associated with significant improve-

---

[7] Organizational climate entailed such measures as the importance of human resources, communications flow, motivational climate, decision-making practices, and influence at lower organizational levels.

ments on almost all of the measures. Interpersonal process consultation was associated with improvements on about half of the measures. In contrast, task process consultation, no treatment, data handback, and laboratory training were associated with little, or negative, change.

Criticisms of OD

Despite a number of negative features (among which are included anti-intellectualism, overselling of results, and overemphasis on conflict) we find that OD is not wholly without merit. Strauss (1973), a long-time observer and sometime critic of "human relations," suggests that:

> . . . compared to traditional management training, OD is generally more meaningful, certainly leads to far more involvement, and clearly runs less risk of being excessively stressful. Despite the difficulties of research, it is now reasonably clear that *under some circumstances* OD can lead to lasting organizational gain (p. 16).

In addition to asking what conditions are prerequisite to positive outcomes from OD (conditions described, in part, in Chapter 17), one must ask about the comparative efficacy of OD, as opposed to alternative approaches to change, and also about the relative costs of such alternative efforts. Strauss, for example, suggests that ". . . it is often better to change the organization so that ordinary people can function well within it rather than to try to change the people themselves. Thus, I sympathize with those who believe that the purpose of OD should be to induce managers to step back, not just to reexamine their interpersonal relations and emotions, but to take a fresh look at the organization as a whole, its goals, and its relationship to its environment" (pp. 17–18). As we emphasize throughout this book, organizations comprise not only people but also technology, structure, goals, management systems, and strategies. Attempts to improve organizations should consider all of these.

Critics of organizational development also question whether the aims of changing people espoused by practitioners are always matters of choice. For example, Levinson (Sashkin et al., 1973) is critical of OD's reliance on confrontation techniques and advocates more thorough diagnostic processes which can suggest alternative change strategies. "Organizations indeed have changed significantly as a result of other (non-OD) consultants' interventions, as a result of supportive efforts without confrontation, and with many other devices . . . this is not to say that I think confrontation is by definition bad, but only that it must be a technique of choice based on diagnosis" (p. 203).

Strauss (1973) asks,

> If, as one authority on the subject insists, OD turns out . . . better decision-makers, would equal results be obtained from programs speci-

fically designed to improve decision making (such as Kepner-Tregoe)? Dalton and Korman both argue that OD's key objective should be to raise self-confidence and esteem. If so, perhaps the answer is to provide training directly designed to alter levels of aspiration and aggressiveness —such as "rational training," the various programs designed by McClelland and Miner, or those packaged under the title of "Behavior Reinforcement" (p. 18).

In the long run, answers to questions regarding the relative efficacy of different approaches to organizational change will be provided by comparative research. Such research must deal with generic variables (the basic differences in these various approaches), and it is to several such generic variables that we now turn.

ALTERNATIVE OD STRATEGIES

The Consultant-Trainer Role

One way of viewing the problems associated with changing behavior is in terms of its cognitive and emotional components (Wieland and Leigh, 1971). As used here, cognitive refers to the aspect of a problem that is amenable to logic and rationality, to intellectual approaches. The emotional component is based on feelings, attitudes, and emotional reactions.

Some organizational problems may be essentially cognitive, requiring information for their solution. Clients may be ignorant and a simple provision of information or correction of misinformation may be all that is required of the consultant. Even if the problem is one of conflicting beliefs rather than ignorance, the change agent is likely to find that the communication of better information or expert opinion can serve to reorganize these beliefs. At the very least, it can be argued that this kind of change is easier to bring about than changes in people's feelings.

We sometimes believe that people are so rational that if one provides reasons for behaving differently they will do so, or if one supplies more and better information they will make better decisions. Emotions, feelings, and attitudes are not developed rationally or logically. Behavior and decisions based on emotions, therefore, are not likely to be altered by appeals to logic or reason. One's aversions toward snakes and spiders, for example, are not likely to be altered by knowledge that these are generally useful creatures, nor is one's behavior toward these creatures likely to change.

Emotions and feelings are difficult to change, but once altered they may become stable. Furthermore, it is believed that overt behavior is more closely linked to feelings and emotions than to ideas or thoughts.

This is the reason psychoanalysts lead their patients to reexperience the emotional situations and stimuli that are sources of their apparent maladjusted behavior. By relearning emotionally, the patient comes to behave more adaptively.

Because of the phenomena described here, Seashore and Van Egmond (1959) advocate that the roles of expert advice giver and group trainer be combined. This combination they term the *consultant-trainer role.* The expert portion of the role enables the consultant to diagnose organizational problems and to make sure that important issues are raised. This, of course, does not always happen in T-groups. The training portion of the role enables the consultant to pass on the attitudes, values, and behavioral skills that are essential changes in OD.

Depth of Intervention

Viewed one way, the consultant-trainer role seems to combine two extremes. Harrison (1970) labels attempts to change a person's values (that are central to his or her sense of self) as *deep change strategies.* *Shallow change strategies* are those more formal and public attempts to change ideas, technologies, and the like. The operations research analyst, in redesigning tasks and roles to fit a rational model, uses shallow strategies. Psychological readjustments do not enter into his design for change. The Seashore-Van Egmond approach may be viewed as an attempt to combine deep and shallow kinds of change.

Harrison, though, argues that the depth of intervention ought to be as shallow as the problem permits. Intervention strategies can be arrayed on a continuum of depth. The choice of a particular change strategy will be determined by two criteria: (1) the depth to which one must go to locate information that must be exchanged in order to improve organizational performance, and (2) the level of intervention that is acceptable to the client.

At the shallow end of the continuum of change strategies one finds *cognitive and rational* problem-solving techniques such as those used in operations research, managerial accounting, and the like.

Somewhat deeper are the practices of *industrial psychology,* which include methods for employee selection, placement, and appraisal. Here the focus is on individual performance as it can be predicted by education, work experience, biographical data, personality characteristics, and other dimensions that are measured, but not changed. Using these kinds of measurements, industrial psychologists advise management on hiring, promotion, and dismissal decisions. Other change strategies at a comparable level include job enrichment and management by objectives. In neither case is personality change sought.

A still deeper, *instrumental* or "work style," approach to change is exemplified by the Blake and Mouton (1970) *managerial grid* described in Chapter 6. Using a two-dimensional rating scale, managers rate themselves and their colleagues on their orientations toward people and production. By analyzing their own ratings and those given them by others, managers are helped to alter their managerial styles, attitudes, and work-related behavior. Some managers are encouraged to give more emphasis to productivity, others to attend more to the needs of employees, and still others to increase their emphases of both. These changes in emphasis are manifested in increased delegation of authority, enhanced concern for employees' needs, better planning, and increased use of feedback in the control and support of subordinates. Change at this instrumental level is deeper than interventions made using MBO and similar techniques. Job enrichment and MBO alter task-related behavior and the objectives to which it is addressed. The Blake and Mouton approach (1964) attempts to change attitudes and social orientations as well, but only insofar as these are instrumental to effective task performance.

The next level down, according to Harrison, deals with *interpersonal relations* and is exemplified by some of the so-called human relations training programs. These change strategies bring to light the feelings, attitudes, and perceptions that individuals have about one another. The focus here is not only on instrumental behavior, but also on the quality of interpersonal experiences. T-group sessions which emphasize trust, openness, and authentic behavior are designed to produce changes at this level.

Finally, Harrison cites *intrapersonal analysis* as the deepest level at which change is commonly sought. Psychoanalysis is an example in which the patient's attitudes, values, and conflicts concerning his ability to function effectively, his identity, and existence are examined. Some of the most extreme T-groups operate at this level, such as marathon groups which probe to the very basis of the individual's psychological makeup.

Depth of Intervention and Client Dependency

Harrison suggests that the deeper change strategies make the client *dependent* upon the change agent. As we have indicated, deep changes are *difficult* to bring about and carry considerable risks for the client. Furthermore, it is hard for the client to *transfer* the benefits of these change efforts to other members of the organization.

If a change effort is shallow, the change agent will be able to teach his or her practices to the client; for example, when a consultant employs an operations research technique to solve a problem, the client will gain some understanding of the technique and its applications. In fact, should the client wish, he or she can learn to solve such problems and teach others what has been learned. At deeper levels, change efforts are less readily communicated. It is difficult for a trainer to explain what a T-group is going to be like to potential participants. Even after experiencing a T-group, the clients will be at a loss to explain what has happened to them. Furthermore, they may have trouble imagining themselves ever acquiring the skills to train others. The T-group experience does not equip participants to act as trainers.

Because of this, clients tend to become dependent on consultants using deep change strategies. This, of course, has its consequences. Dependency is costly since the consultant's role cannot be reduced as clients learn the consultant's skills. Furthermore, change will spread slowly in the organization. Unlike shallow change attempts, which can "snowball" as clients begin to impart their newly gained knowledge to others in the organization, deep change generally is limited to those who participate in exercises with the consultant. In general, dependence makes it difficult for the consultant and client to terminate their relationship. Clients may find they are "hooked" on the help of the change agent. As a result of this dependency, the change agent comes to have considerable power—the ability to exert influence—over his or her client. Being unable to provide, let alone understand, the process through which help is given, the client must depend upon, and even accept strong influence from, the change agent.

At this point, the reasoning behind one of Harrison's criteria for determining the depth of intervention should be apparent. Because "costs" increase with the depth of change sought, one ought to go no deeper than necessary. Ideally, the client and consultant will examine the situation in which changes are sought and agree on an appropriate depth of intervention; for example, it may be found that bottlenecks in the work flow can be eliminated by the applications of methodologies from operations research or industrial engineering. Morale and productivity may be improved through the introduction of job enrichment schemes. Sources of conflict may be ameliorated through redesign of work roles. Each of these change efforts, although relatively shallow, may be sufficient for the problem to which it is addressed and may spare the organization the costs of deeper efforts.

The second criterion states that the depth of intervention should be limited by its acceptability. According to Harrison, the consultant must investigate the client system's norms, values, fears, and resistance to deep interventions. The consultant will need to ask: Do the clients resist discussing their management styles, personalities, or innermost feelings? How much of this sort of information can be discussed, examined, and acted upon legitimately? This varies considerably from one organization to another and among individuals within a single organization. It is particularly important for the change agent to ascertain whether there are group or organizational norms that are likely to be violated by a deep intervention strategy. For example, if there is a norm that one should refrain from discussing personal matters at work (such as one's feelings about the boss or the personalities of co-workers), then one would assume that deep strategies such as T-groups will effectively violate the norm.

Deep Intervention Strategies and Social Norms

Because deep change strategies tend to make clients dependent on consultants, the latter are able to exert influence on the former; that is, the change agent can utilize power over the client to overcome organizational norms. Despite the existence of a norm of the sort described above, the T-group trainer can establish norms to the contrary. However, Harrison suggests that in doing this, the trainer is likely to become counterproductive. While the change agent may have considerable power vis-à-vis individuals and small groups, he or she does not have such power over the organization as a whole. In the larger organization, established norms are more powerful. Thus, individuals leaving the sheltered T-group setting will revert to their former behavior once their newly learned attempts to reveal their feelings and change the feelings of others are met with sanctions or organization-wide norms to the contrary.

Harrison describes how change agents working at the interpersonal and deeper levels tend to adopt a resistance-oriented approach to change. Some consultants seem to take pride in confrontation, in dramatically violating organizational norms, and in pressuring organizational members into departing from them. He cites the marathon T-group as a case in point wherein the irritability and fatigue that attend prolonged contact and lack of sleep move participants to deal with one another more emotionally, personally, and spontaneously than they would normally.

Harrison's point is substantiated by the study of encounter groups by Lieberman and colleagues (1973) cited above. It was found that the type of group technology (sensitivity training, gestalt therapy, transactional analysis, marathons, etc.) did not affect the individual outcomes achieved. In fact, what went on in the groups of the same type was usually not very similar, and groups supposedly of a different type often had fairly similar processes and outcomes.

What did make a difference in terms of outcomes, and especially casualty rates, was the behavior of the leader. Leaders who "pushed" the individual participants (regardless of the readiness of participants to confront their problems and deal with the perceptions of the group) produced high casualty rates. In Harrison's terms, a deep, resistance-oriented approach tended to produce a high casualty rate.

The practice of inducing clients to behave in ways of which they would not approve otherwise is subject to question on ethical grounds

In addition, Harrison judges it to be ineffective since existing organizational norms will tend to reverse changes attained in this fashion.

This problem may be likened to that of the community developer in an underdeveloped nation who, by virtue of his or her personal influence over certain villagers, succeeds in convincing them to dig a well or build a school which, upon the developer's departure, quickly falls into disuse. In situations such as this, the change agent fails to integrate "improvements" into the social structure of day-to-day life. Although successful in solving an immediate problem (or perhaps in removing a symptom of a more basic problem), the community developer fails. In order to succeed, he or she must develop new norms supporting the use and maintenance of the improvements and overcome existing norms that impede this progress. In the absence of the latter activities, community development may even be counterproductive to the extent that it discourages future projects of a similar nature.

If the change agent is to work at a level of intervention that is deeper than organizational norms permit, he (or she) must create new norms, and this is no easy task. It is better, Harrison suggests, to establish the level of intervention at the *level of the system's felt need for changes.* Certain problems of communities and organizations are given high, conscious priorities by their members. Individuals and groups generally are willing to invest time and energy in dealing with these felt needs. Conversely, needs that are experienced solely by the outside consultant (experienced because of the consultant's values or his power to achieve specific kinds of changes) are unlikely to spur the cooperation of the community or organization. In short, the consultant must take the role of collaborator in the client's attempts to solve problems that are important to him, and, in so doing, mobilize existing motivations.

Here, then, we have summarized the reasoning behind Harrison's second criterion for choosing an intervention strategy: intervene no deeper than the level at which the client desires change. In attempting to meet this criterion, the change agent will examine the norms of the organization to determine whether they will legitimize the depth of intervention he is considering. Furthermore, he will devise change strategies that are clearly relevant to the consciously felt needs of the organization's members.

The Consultant's Dilemma

Unfortunately, it appears that these two criteria can be contradictory when applied in practice. The first criterion suggests intervention at a level deep enough to obtain information with which to diagnose the problem and subsequently rectify it. This level is sometimes deeper than the level at which an individual or a group is willing to invest energy and resources. Harrison refers to this discrepancy as the *consultant's dilemma.*

Ideally, the dilemma is resolved by intervening first at a level that generates support from organizational norms, the power structure, and the felt needs of members. As time passes and the consultant gains trust and support from within the organization, he or she can begin to intervene at deeper levels—levels at which particularly important forces may be operating. This, however, is no simple matter to accomplish. To quote Harrison:

> I believe we should always avoid moving deeper at a pace which outstrips a client system's willingness to subject itself to exposure, dependency, and threat. . . . [I]f the dominant response of organization members indicates that an intervention violates system norms, . . . then one has intervened too deeply and should pull back to a level at which organization members are more ready to invest their own energy in the change process. This point of view is thus in opposition to that which sees negative reactions primarily as indications of resistances which are to be brought out into the open, confronted, and worked through as a central part of the intervention process (Harrison, 1970, p. 199).[8]

In short, Harrison encourages consultants to accept the client's felt needs and problems and to work on them at the level where the client can serve as a confident and willing collaborator. He generalizes from his own experience that the level of intervention most likely to permit collaboration and feelings of legitimacy falls somewhere between interventions at an instrumental level and those at the interpersonal relations level. Deeper levels of intervention are likely to produce hostility, passivity, and dependence in clients.

In Harrison's words:

> If I intervene directly at the level of interpersonal relationships, I can be sure that some members, and often the whole group, will react with anxiety, passive resistance, and low or negative commitment to the change process. Furthermore, they express their resistance in terms of norms and values regarding the appropriateness or legitimacy of dealing at this level. They say things like; "It isn't right to force people's feelings about one another out into the open"; "I don't see what this has to do with improving organizational effectiveness"; "People are being encouraged to say things which are better left unsaid."
>
> If I then switch to a strategy which focuses on decision making, delegation of authority, information exchange, and other instrumental questions, these complaints about illegitimacy and the inappropriateness of the intervention are usually sharply reduced. This does not mean that the clients are necessarily comfortable or free from anxiety in the discussions, nor does it mean that strong negative feelings may not be expressed about one another's behavior. What is different is that the clients are more likely to *work with* instead of *against* me, to feel and express

---

8 From "Choosing the Depth of Organizational Intervention" by Roger Harrison, *Journal of Applied Behavioral Science*, 1970, 6, 181–202. NTL Institute Publications. Reproduced by special permission.

some sense of ownership in the change process, and to see many more possibilities for carrying it on among themselves in the absence of the consultant (Harrison, 1970, pp. 200–1).[9]

In light of the controversy which surrounds some techniques of organizational development, the risks to which clients are sometimes exposed by practitioners, and the uncertain results, we generally subscribe to Harrison's conclusions and guidelines. His argument does not completely solve the dilemma he posits, though. The problems of an organization very often rest at levels deeper than the client is willing to go. But Harrison argues that to stay at the more shallow level, where collaboration is feasible, is in the long run, more productive than moving to deeper strategies.

However, even if relatively deep interventions are found to be somewhat effective, we must still consider questions of values and ethics prior to advocating their use. For example, how shall we weigh the right to privacy and respect for the desires of others in our decision to impose deep change techniques to solve organizational problems? Can we ignore the rights of participants and subject them to problem-solving methods of questionable efficacy?

As we see it, organizational development, broadly conceived, must utilize flexible approaches that allow the consultant to produce both cognitive and emotional changes which are linked together by the problem's solutions. Depth of intervention should be limited by the informed consent of participants and by the practitioner's competence to deal effectively with the psychological and social forces released by such practices. Above all, we advocate caution in the face of uncertainty.

DISCUSSION QUESTIONS

1. Despite research evidence that casts serious doubt on the efficacy of T-groups, many T-group participants are enthusiastic about their experiences, claiming to have benefited greatly from them. Why do you think this happens?
2. Some critics claim that OD is characterized by an anti-intellectual bias. What is the basis for this observation? Is the observation valid? Does the observation, if valid, constitute a criticism?
3. What ethical issues arise in the application of deep change strategies?
4. What are the major limitations of shallow change strategies?

REFERENCES

Argyris, C. T-groups for organizational effectiveness. In G. W. Dalton, P. R. Lawrence, and L. E. Greiner (Eds.), *Organizational change and development.* Homewood, Ill.: Irwin, 1970.
Bennis, Warren G. *Organization development: its nature, origins, and prospects.* Reading, Mass.: Addison-Wesley, 1969.

---

[9] Ibid.

Beckhard, Richard. *Organization development: strategies and models.* Reading, Mass.: Addison-Wesley, 1969.

Blake, R. R., and Mouton, J. S. *The Managerial Grid.* Houston, Tex.: Gulf Publishing, 1970.

Blake, R. R., Mouton, J. S., and Sloma, R. L. The union-management intergroup laboratory: strategy for resolving intergroup conflict. *Journal of Applied Behavioral Science,* 1965, *1*, 25–27.

Blake, R. R., Shepard, H. A., and Mouton, J. S. *Managing intergroup conflict in industry.* Houston: Gulf Publishing, 1964.

Bowers, David G. Development techniques and organizational climate: an evaluation of comparative importance of two potential forces for organizational change. Technical Report. Office of Naval Research, 1971.

Bowers, David G. OD techniques and their results in 23 organizations: the Michigan ICL study. *Journal of Applied Behavioral Science,* 1973, *9,* 21–43.

Campbell, John P., and Dunnette, Marvin D. Effectiveness of T-group experiences in managerial training and development. *Psychological Bulletin,* 1970, *70,* 73–104.

Campbell, John P., Dunnette, Marvin D., Lawler, Edward E., III, and Weick, Karl E., Jr. *Managerial behavior, performance and effectiveness.* New York: McGraw-Hill, 1970.

French, Wendell L., and Bell, Cecil H., Jr. *Organization development: behavioral science interventions for organization improvement.* Englewood Cliffs, N.J.: Prentice-Hall, 1973.

Friedlander, Frank, and Brown, Dave L. Organization development. *Annual Review of Psychology,* 1974, *25,* 313–41.

Harrison, Roger. Choosing the depth of organizational intervention. *Journal of Applied Behavioral Science,* 1970, *6,* 181–202. NTL Institute Publications.

House, R. J. T-group education and leadership effectiveness: a review of the empirical literature and a critical evaluation. *Personnel Psychology,* 1967, *20,* 1–32.

Lieberman, M. A., Yalom, I. D., and Miles, M. B. *Encounter groups: first facts.* New York: Basic Books, 1973.

Magnusen, Karl. Perspectives on organizational design and development. Research Paper No. 21, Graduate School of Business, Columbia University (May 1973).

Rush, Harold M. F. *Behavioral science: concepts and management application.* New York: National Industrial Conference Board, 1969.

Sashkin, Marshall, Burke, W. Warner, and Levinson, Harry. Organization development pro and con. *Professional Psychology,* 1973, *4,* 187–208.

Schein, Edgar H. *Process consultation: its role in organization development.* Reading, Mass.: Addison-Wesley, 1969.

Seashore, Charles, and Van Egmond, Elmer. The consultant-trainer role in working directly with a total staff. *Journal of Social Issues,* 1959, *15,* 36–42.

Strauss, George. Organization development: credits and debits. *Organization Dynamics,* 1973 (Winter), 2–19.

Underwood, W. J. Evaluation of laboratory method training. *Training Directors Journal,* 1965, *19* (5), 34–50.

Wieland, George F., and Leigh, Hilary. *Changing hospitals: a report on the hospital internal communications project.* London: Tavistock, 1971.

17

The Survey Feedback
Approach to Organizational
Development

INTRODUCTION

The results of the Bowers' (1973) study reported in the last chapter, as well as our own experiences, suggest that the survey feedback technique is one of organizational development's most promising approaches to organizational change. As we have said, the field is rife with controversy. Techniques often have been developed in the absence of sound empirical support and theoretical understandings. Admittedly, this is as true of survey feedback as it is of other techniques. Yet, available evidence moves us to a tentative conclusion that this technique is superior to others on a number of counts: (1) its efficacy in improving organizational performance is indicated by empirical studies (e.g., Bowers, 1973; and Mann, 1957); (2) its flexible technique lends itself to shallow applications that expose participants to relatively few risks; and (3) it is readily learned by clients and need not cause dependency on the practitioner. Given these opinions, we advocate use of the technique and shall present it in some detail for the reader's consideration.

Most organizations have used surveys of one sort or another for many years. Yet, as we shall see, it is not the survey, but how it is used, that determines its effectiveness in facilitating productive organizational change. By way of example, we have summarized the history of a survey questionnaire used in a graduate school.

In response to apparent student dissatisfaction, the associate dean of the graduate school devised a questionnaire to assess student opinions of the curriculum. This instrument included 26 items, most of which were Likert scales similar to those described in Chapter 3. The entire student body received the questionnaire, and over 90 percent responded. Responses were disparate. In some cases the data were bimodal, but in most cases, responses seemed to be random.

A ten-page report of the data and inferences was distributed to all faculty and students, who met separately to discuss the findings and explore ways to improve the situation. As planned, a "town meeting" followed in which the two groups shared their perceptions and advocated specific remedies. The following is reproduced from the associate dean's diary which was kept to record this attempt at organizational change:

> The rate at which students are coming to see me with problems and concerns has increased since I sent out the questionnaire. I suspect that I have (in so doing) indicated a willingness to listen on (behalf) of the school.

Dissatisfactions similar to those prompting the initial survey moved a new crop of students to begin designing their own instrument the following year. After consultation with the associate dean, they decided to use a slightly modified version of the original instrument to obtain comparative data. Data obtained with the resulting 21 item questionnaire were summarized and discussed in a 29 page report submitted to a standing committee for curriculum revision which comprised faculty members and students. This report followed the format of the previous year and contained similar data and conclusions. Specifically, responses again were disparate.

A survey was not conducted the following year, but two years later a new student group approached the associate dean with a proposal that student opinion be solicited on numerous curriculum matters. Rejecting earlier instruments for their lack of specificity, the student group devised a questionnaire of 176 items. Their entire class was polled and response was better than 85 percent. Once again, disparate data were found in the 260 page computer printout that was submitted as a report to the associate dean.

Chapter Guide

1. Both the questionnaire and the uses of the resulting data varied over the years. What assumptions do you think prompted these changes?
2. The increased contact with students noted by the associate dean was felt to be a direct outcome of the survey. What other unforeseen outcomes may result from the use of surveys?
3. Of the approaches undertaken in each of the years, which is superior? Why? Are there better approaches to the problem than the ones used?

THE SURVEY FEEDBACK TECHNIQUE

Surveys in General

Surveys consisting of interviews or questionnaires have enjoyed widespread use in organizations as sources of information on internal functioning. It is a rare employee who has not responded to at least one survey of his or her morale, feelings, attitudes, beliefs, or opinions. The rationale for conducting organizational surveys—whether they are conducted by outside consultants or in-house staff such as personnel specialists—is to assemble information that will aid management in diagnosing problems and selecting remedies for them.

Be that as it may, problems with survey procedures frequently limit their usefulness to management. As Katz and Kahn (1966) indicate, top management occasionally feels that it has done the right thing just by authorizing a survey; for example, Perrow (1972) cites that Hawthorne studies and notes that at one point:

> A large number of personnel—some 300 or so—were employed to wander about the plant encouraging workers to tell them their complaints in confidence. Management did not act upon the complaints (they were not even told of them), but the workers supposedly felt much better after having blown off steam and having concluded that management was interested (Perrow, 1972, p. 100).[1]

In cases such as this, findings are likely to be filed away in the personnel office and forgotten. In other cases, top management routes findings to subordinates unaccompanied by directives for their use. If the survey results are read by the subordinates (which is problematic in some cases), selective inattention possibly will distort their meaning. All of us have a tendency to select information that is congruent with our current views and beliefs and to disregard findings that are contrary and indicate a need for change. When this happens, the usefulness of the survey is diminished.

When survey results are not utilized, the organization may suffer harm above and beyond the waste of time. A survey's immediate effect may be somewhat positive; respondents sometimes experience mild catharsis in expressing their attitudes and feelings. But in responding, employees may be led to expect that survey information, including their own statements, will be used to rectify the problems and unpleasant situations they describe. These employees may become cynical, if not angry, about management's motives in instigating the survey. One can make a strong case that it is better to "let sleeping dogs lie" and not conduct a survey than it is to raise expectations inadvertently and leave them unfulfilled.

Surveys and Overlapping Groups

Mann (1957) developed a procedure for group discussion of survey results which attempts to put the information to good use. Survey data provide the basis for discussion and analysis in appropriate *organiza-*

---

[1] From *Complex Organizations: A Critical Essay* by Charles Perrow. Copyright © 1972 by Scott, Foresman and Company. Reprinted by permission of the publisher.

tional families throughout the organization under survey. Organizational family refers to a supervisor and all employees reporting to him directly. This is no different than the linking pin organizational structure advocated by Likert (1967) in Chapter 3. Many employees belong to two families: those in which they are superior to subordinates and those in which they are subordinate to their bosses. Hence, the organizational structure comprises overlapping family groups.

Mann takes advantage of the hierarchical character of organizations by starting the feedback process with the top organizational family: namely, the president and vice presidents. In this initial meeting, the consultant helps the group discuss and interpret survey data. Following this, a series of feedback discussions are held at the next organizational level. In these meetings, each vice president meets with the department heads who normally report to him. This is followed by a third set of meetings between department heads and their subordinates, and so on, down to the organizational families comprising foremen and shop floor workers.

Reliance on organizational families attempts to produce cohesive work groups having the characteristics and attributes discussed in Chapter 3. In addition, the technique draws on a phenomenon noted by Lewin (1952) in a now famous experiment. This experiment suggested that individuals taking part in a decision were more likely to execute the agreed course of action than were those who were not involved directly in the decision-making process. This phenomenon is incorporated in the survey feedback technique; for example, a vice president participates with the president in discussing the survey results in the initial feedback meeting. In addition to discussing the nature of the findings, the group plans the kind of feedback to be used at the next level down. Because each vice president participates in a comparable discussion with his peers and chiefs, he[2] is exposed to a model for conducting the discussion in which he, as a superior, meets with his subordinates. According to the logic of the argument, having participated in planning the feedback session with subordinates, the vice president will be committed to its execution, even in the event that the survey team is unavailable to help and support him.

Tailoring Data to Hierarchical Levels

The nature of survey data presented for discussion will vary depending on the group's status in the organizational hierarchy. Data must be of direct relevance to the group in which it is studied; for example, a branch chief meeting with his department heads will be given company-

---

[2] It has been stated previously that the common pronoun "he" is not intended to be masculine or feminine but simply "human."

wide totals for employee attitudes and breakdowns for the various branches including his own. In addition, data pertinent to the branch in question will be broken down further according to the specific departments represented at the meeting. Thus, each participant will be provided sufficient information to compare: (1) branch performance with overall company performance, (2) branch performance with that of other branches according to the dimensions measured by the survey, and (3) relative standings of departments within the branch. Similiar procedures will be followed throughout the organization. For instance, the individual department head will next meet with supervisors under him to discuss department standing vis-à-vis other departments in the branch as well as each supervisor's standing vis-à-vis his peers.

Comparison and discussion of the data for this hypothetical meeting may indicate that members of one department are more dissatisfied with their jobs (and with supervision in particular) than are members of other departments. The objective data upon which discussion is based may confirm vague feelings that previously existed in the absence of objective evidence. Alternatively, the data may indicate that job satisfaction is high and, in so doing, lay to rest contrary rumors. Either outcome is potentially beneficial to the organization, insofar as the survey findings are valid.

In either event, members of the group are likely to contribute their own observations as they attempt to understand the objective data. In so doing, they may reveal further areas in need of attention. By defining the data according to its own experience, the group will define the problem in terms to which it can respond. The next step for the group is to plan a program of change that will modify dissatisfying situations.

According to Mann, one important aspect of the survey feedback technique is the objective atmosphere it creates. Use of survey data (facts and figures), together with emphasis on task orientation, lends a degree of rationality to issues that are usually clouded by emotionalism.

The use of organizational families for these rational, task-oriented discussions is important because members possess not only relevant information to supplement the data but also solutions to problems brought to light by the survey.

The technique attempts to solve problems at their locus in the organization. Top levels of management lack detailed information for solving complex problems at lower levels in the organization. By the same token, lower level personnel cannot be expected to cope adequately with the problems of top management. The disaggregation of survey data allows pertinent information to be routed to the parts of the organization that can understand and respond to it. The technique involves the "right" people in both diagnosing and solving the problem. As we have said, individuals who have participated in planning a solution usually are committed to implementing the course of action on which they have decided.

Prerequisites to Survey Feedback

Mann suggests that certain conditions must be met if the survey feedback method is to operate effectively. As mentioned above, an objective, task-oriented climate must be maintained. Second, each organizational family must be allowed discretion to consider the implications of findings for its own organizational level. While each group plans the feedback for the next lower group, planning must allow leeway for the lower group to add its own observations to the data. Similarly, each group must be given prerogatives to implement changes at its level, as these are suggested by analysis of the data. The latter point is a delicate one, for changes made by a group at one organizational level cannot be so pervasive that they preclude discretionary action at lower levels. Rather, groups are advised to work at one level as broadly as possible, leaving specific details that affect subordinates to their discretion.[3]

Meeting these prerequisites enhances the likelihood that members of organizational families at each level will perceive genuine opportunities to participate in decision making and become involved in and committed to the process. In the absence of discretion, discussion of survey results will be perfunctory. Employees will view the feedback and discussion process as a mere sham.

An account by Hall (1966) of an application of the survey feedback technique in a university setting illustrates the points made above. The individuals conducting a survey of the university's staff were researchers, not consultants, and apparently lacked the power to establish the proper prerequisites. Specifically, the researchers failed to secure top management's commitment to provide feedback and to allow discretion for change to lower organizational levels. Instead, top managers resisted delegation and sought to act on the findings themselves.

Hall was sucessful in pressing for divisionwide meetings, but these were overly large and inadequate to the task of problem solving. Hall's recommendation that organizational family meetings be held was generally ignored. Middle managers did not seem to perceive themselves as members of overlapping groups; since they were not involved in planning the meetings they were to lead (by virture of the absence of former meetings in which they were subordinates), they generally were unprepared and uninvolved in the process. Furthermore, these managers seemed somewhat anxious about the survey in the first place. The combined result was that meetings were not held. Needless to say, organizational changes did not eventuate from survey findings.

---

[3] See also Bass (1970).

Two-way Reporting

An early experiment by Mann (1957) demonstrates the technique's superiority compared to simple surveys in producing organizational change. A branch of a large electrical utility used survey findings; four departments were involved in survey feedback while two others received survey data in the absence of feedback and discussion sessions. A follow-up survey conducted a year and a half later indicated considerable changes and improvements had accrued in the four departments using the technique. Comparable progress was not indicated by surveys of the two departments that merely received survey data.

Generally speaking, these findings indicate that survey feedback is effective in resolving problems brought to light by survey results. In addition, the experiment suggests that the feedback process may improve interpersonal functioning within the organization—specifically, communication and understanding among managers, their peers, and subordinates. Further analysis of findings from the four experimental departments led Mann to conclude that departments that had achieved the greatest change were those that held the most meetings and involved the most employees in these meetings.

In addition to highlighting the importance of participation, Mann's study illustrates the importance of reporting the results of feedback sessions to higher levels of management. For example, when a department had found satisfactory answers to some of its problems and was ready to make specific recommendations, the department head reported back up the line, presenting his findings at a subsequent meeting of his peers and superior. In this meeting, the department head was able to report on matters to be resolved within the department and also on problems that seemed to stem from conditions over which the branch, or perhaps top management, exercised some authority. Similar meetings followed in which branch managers met with their superior for the same purposes.

This two-way reporting is useful in several ways. First of all, it establishes the accountability of organizational family groups to other, higher level groups. Results of the survey cannot be ignored or "buried," but must be acted upon and these actions reported to groups of higher level managers. In some cases the report back will consist merely of additional questions raised by the survey data and, perhaps, requests for additional information. Even in this event, the outcome can lend direction to the change activities of higher level managers by indicating that existing problems or alternative solutions are inadequately defined.

In addition, the managers who know that they will eventually report back to a group comprising of their peers and superiors will be moved to "touch all of the bases"—to involve, rather than bypass, significant employees in the problem-solving and change processes. This can be quite important, given the propensity of some managers to act unilaterally rather than to take time to seek the cooperation and opinions of others.

THE SURVEY FEEDBACK PROCESS

The Consultant's Role in Survey Feedback

Mann and Likert (1960) argue that if survey results are to be used effectively, managers must *understand* the results and their implications *and incorporate this information with existing attitudes and behavior.* In order to be effective in producing change, survey results must produce more than cognitive learning. In order to make use of new cognitive experiences people must alter their attitudes and feelings. We have noted (Chapter 14 and elsewhere) that problem solving, especially in ambiguous situations, necessitates a psychological structuring of reality and, to some extent, psychological closure. Hence, altering people's information base will not necessarily alter their perception of reality, attendant feelings and attitudes, or consequent behavior. This problem is overcome to some extent by involvement in data feedback and problem-solving sessions. Participation fosters emotional involvement with the problem, the data that describe it, and other members of the problem-solving group. Emotional involvement is instrumental in changing perceptions, attitudes, and motivations. By participating in feedback sessions, the members can translate survey data into terms that are meaningful to them. Furthermore, the ideas of the group, to which they have contributed, are more likely to be transcribed into practice than are the suggestions of outside experts.

Mann and Likert contend that participation must start at the outset of a survey project. Consultation with top executives provides their views of major organizational problems and the kinds of data they desire of the study. This information, in turn, serves as a basis for the survey design. Other members throughout the organizational hierarchy must also be given the opportunity to learn the purposes of the survey and to suggest problems and data to be investigated.

At the conclusion of the survey, participation continues via the feedback and discussion activities of organizational families. In fact, Mann and Likert make it a rule that no report containing recommendations based solely on their own analysis of data will be given to the client. Instead, they present data in preliminary form and involve members of the client organization in interpreting the data and deciding on specific courses of action.

By disaggregating the data according to its relevance to managers at different levels in the hierarchy, functional areas, and geographic locations, the consultants match their input to the interests of the groups with which they work. The more relevant the survey results, the more likely they are to elicit the interest and motivation of management. Also note that the consultant serves as a model when he or she participates in interpreting and acting on survey findings. Hopefully, managers will engage in similar behavior as they work with organizational families at the next lower hierarchical level.

When conducted effectively, the survey feedback technique improves the "fit" between the formal and informal aspects of the organization. Small group dynamics can be aligned with formal organizational authority. The survey process begins at the top of the organization and, thus, carries with it the authority of top management. Each organizational family includes a member of management from the next higher level in the chain of command who can lend legitimacy and authority to the decisions and activities of subordinates. Involvement of line management in the process is essential. Line managers, rather than staff, generally have the authority to implement changes. Finally, the linking pins that bridge the membership of contiguous organizational families facilitate complementary decisions. They serve to relate the decisions taken by one group of managers to those at successively lower levels.

Use of organizational families brings a number of favorable attributes to the problem-solving process. Individual group members are able to contribute a wide range of experience to the definition and solution of problems. Furthermore, since these groups contain overlapping membership, matters of authority and higher level responsibility can be incorporated into the group's actions. Problems emerging from survey activities become public and, therefore, amenable to the contributions of numerous other individuals in the organization. This contrasts notably to the normal modus operandi wherein problems are handled in confidence by one, or a few, individuals who may be ignorant of potential support available from others. Finally, as we have seen, a group decision based on general, public commitment has a potent effect on the behavior of the individual, whether or not he or she is a member of the group in question.

Several other points guide the consultant's role in the survey feedback process. Feedback on performance can be motivating and cause the individual to raise his or her aspirations for future performance. Similarly, knowledge of results is essential to the learning process. A program of repeated surveys and feedback sessions can foster organizational learning that leads to productive change, increased motivation, and more effective organizational behavior in general.

Mann and Likert caution the consultant against the temptation of playing expert. Faced with difficult problems, clients naturally seek expert advice. However, the consultant's job is to help clients develop their own solutions, for their participation and consequent learning, not the consultant's advice, set the stage for productive change.

Timing and pacing are also important. In some situations survey results turn out to be disconfirming, quite dissimilar to the client's expectations. Caution is essential when this occurs, as clients must be allowed to establish the tempo. As Harrison suggests (Chapter 15), management must be allowed to limit the rate and depth of organizational change to levels where they can work comfortably and effectively. However, it is the discrepancy, or mildly disconfirming nature of the information compared to what was expected, that is the source of motivation for change (Bowers and Franklin, 1972).

The consultant's presentation of survey findings should be made within a positive group setting. Favorable results should be emphasized as well as those that indicate problems. Furthermore, when dealing with negative findings, emphasis shoud be on means for improving these shortcomings, rather than on the shortcomings themselves.

Surveys are not easily designed. Although a wealth of literature has been written on the subject, the design of questionnaires and interviews that produce valid, reliable data is a demanding task—the success of which cannot be guaranteed a priori. Even carefully designed surveys contain misleading questions and omit important data. Clients frequently question the accuracy of data and the validity of procedures. These questions should be handled objectively. Examination of other relevant information such as organizational records is useful in cases such as this. However, rigid defense of the survey's accuracy can only serve to arouse client resistance.[4]

A Model for Diagnosis with Surveys

Likert (1967) remarks that surveys often are no more informative than fever charts and are of limited value in improving an organization. We shall explore this analogy in some detail, since it provides some major implications about the ways in which surveys ought to be designed and conducted.

Physicians need two kinds of information to diagnose illness. They need general information about health and pathology, stemming from research on bodily conditions and relationships between symptoms and

---

[4] Something can be said for using ambiguous, although valid, data. Wieland (1971) found unclear survey data to be more effective in creating attitude changes among hospital managers than unambiguous data. If the data were clear, managers tended to look at survey results and conclude: "Right! Here is the answer!" Provided more ambiguous data, managers tended to discuss them with others, puzzling over the findings with consultants and colleagues. In the course of these discussions, the managers learned about one another and, with the help of the consultant, formed cooperative working groups. These changes led to changes in the attitudes some managers had about one another and other members of the organization. In some cases, the process beginning with ambiguous data led to new patterns of work and cooperation.

diseases. The second kind of information they need is obtained from appropriate measurements taken from the patient at a particular point in time.

Managers face an analogous problem when attempting to diagnose organizational problems. First of all, they need to understand the fundamental nature of the system: the ways in which the parts function (e.g., make adaptive responses to the environment). Second, they need diagnostic measures of the organization's internal state and functioning at a particular point in time. The problem is that many survey efforts focus on the measurement of *end-result* variables such as absenteeism and turnover rather than on causal variables.

End-result variables provide after-the-fact kinds of information. They are similar to the patient's fever which may result from a variety of conditions (e.g., any one of a number of bacteria causing infection). What the physician needs to learn is the cause of the fever; namely, the type of bacteria causing the infection and, thus, the fever. To attempt to reduce the fever without knowing the infection's source is an ineffectual approach to medicine. Similarly, treating organizational symptoms often fails to cure the source of the problem.

Likert recommends measurement of *causal* and *intervening* variables that provide information on the internal state of the organization and the causes of problems (as evidenced by end-result variables). For example, he suggests that participative decision making, a causal variable, improves communications, reciprocal influence, confidence, and trust. These intervening variables in turn lead to end-result variables, such as reduced absenteeism and turnover and increased productivity. To measure only absenteeism and productivity would be futile. What management needs to know is the relationships among intervening and causal variables and end states. Ignorance of these relationships renders effective organizational change problematic at best. However, even when such relationships are known, attention limited to end-result variables (e.g., horses running out of the barn) is likely to tell us that a problem has occurred (e.g., someone left the barn door open). Measurement of causal and intervening variables will more likely call management's attention to potential problems and the need for preventive action.

Likert describes how surveys focusing on end-result measures are used in System Two firms (Chapter 3). Such organizations tend to specify the processes of management and to assign specific, limited objectives to managers. Standard procedures and achievement of designed objectives are emphasized. Knowing that their performance is evaluated according to these end-result measures, managers attempt to "look good" in these terms. Typically, managers are told that end-result productivity should be accompanied by favorable employee attitudes, which are also end results.

Such firms have a veneer of human relations concerns that masks serious shortcomings. As we have indicated, knowing about employee attitudes and work patterns will not necessarily describe the organization's problems. Management will attempt to treat symptoms—to "look good" on survey measures—when survey data do not represent a model of organizational functioning. Unfortunately, applying salve to symptoms, as it were, may only make matters worse. Unable to come to grips with basic problems, management will appear ill-informed and ineffectual to employees.

Likert contrasts this approach to problem solving with what he calls System Four management. The latter design recognizes major causal and intervening variables in organizations. In System Four organizations employees are provided information on major variables with which they can guide their decisions and behavior to accomplish, not only the specific goals they set for themselves, but also the broad objectives they have helped set for the organization as a whole. Likert's (1967) work contains a comprehensive listing of assumed causal and intervening variables to which System Four managers respond.

Diagnosis Using a Systems Perspective

Ackoff (1970) arrives at conclusions similar to those of Likert, but from a different perspective—that of a management scientist. Ackoff contends that understanding the organization as a system (i.e., in terms of causal and intervening variables) is the sine qua non of effective managerial decision making. Such understanding forces the realization that system goals cannot be set until their means have been specified. We have already referred to the interdependency of ends and means in our discusion of incrementalism in strategy formulation (Chapter 14).

Failing to recognize this aspect of systems, management may resort to relatively ineffectual planning philosophies such as satisficing or optimizing (Chapter 5). Satisficing tends to be conservative. Moreover, ". . . it seldom increases understanding of either the system being planned for or the planning process itself" (Ackoff, 1970, p. 9). Optimizing tends to ignore goals that defy quantification, and does not account for the structure of the organization. According to Ackoff, a system view of organizations gives rise to a third planning philosophy, "adaptivizing." Ackoff provides the following example to differentiate between the optimizing and adaptivizing approaches to planning:

> Consider [a] company that produces a raw material used in more than 3,000 different forms. Of these about 10 percent accounted for all of the profits and most of the volume of business. Small orders for the remaining large number of small-volume unprofitable items led to frequent disruptions of production schedules, which were geared for long, continuous production runs of the high-volume profitable items.

Marketing management refused to drop the small-volume unprofitable items from the company's product line or to raise their prices even to cover cost because—it argued—this would antagonize those customers who were also heavy consumers of the high-volume profitable items and would run the risk of losing them.

An optimizer's approach to this problem consisted of constructing a model of the production-inventory-sales system and deriving from it a way of scheduling the production line to meet the demand on it—a way that minimized the sum of the production, inventory, and shortage costs. The improvements yielded were significant but small.

An adaptivizer took a different approach. He found that by eliminating 4 percent of the least profitable items from the product line he could reduce production costs and increase profits by an amount equal to the improvement the optimizer had obtained. Therefore, he concentrated on the marketing, not the production, system. He found that salesmen were given a base salary plus a percentage of the dollar value of their sales. This led him to design a new salesman incentive plan. It was profit (rather than volume) oriented; it paid no commission on sales of unprofitable items and higher commissions than before on profitable ones. The plan was so designed that, if salesmen continued to sell the same mix of items as they had before, their earnings would not change. In the first year of this plan's operation sales of about half the unprofitable items in the product line virtually stopped, and sales of the profitable items increased significantly.

The optimizing planner generally takes the system structure for granted and seeks a course of action that best solves the problem. The adaptive planner, on the other hand, tries to change the system in such a way that more efficient behavior follows "naturally" (Ackoff, 1970, pp. 19–20).[5]

Ackoff argues that planners should concern themselves less with evaluating alternatives than with understanding the system and, in so doing, inventing new alternatives. An understanding of the system tends to expose areas of misunderstanding and ignorance that prevented recognition of desirable goals and policies in the past. New alternatives thus exposed may be so superior to previous alternatives that comparative evaluation is rendered unnecessary. As Ackoff suggests:

The key to both creating and evaluating courses of action and policies lies in *understanding* the system involved; that is, in the ability to *explain* its behavior, not merely to predict it. One may be able to predict the behavior of a system without being able to explain it, for example, by extrapolating from its past behavior. The ability to explain, however, necessarily involves the ability to predict. More important, it provides a basis for redesigning the system in some fundamental way so as either to eliminate problems or significantly improve effectiveness.

Research, which involves at least some limited experimentation, is usually required to develop understanding of most systems or even significant parts of them. The management scientist normally embodies his understanding, once acquired, in a model of the system involved;

that is, in symbolic representations. . . . Such models can be used both to evaluate and innovate, but innovation generally requires broader understanding: the ability to explain and perceive the interrelatedness of parts of the system (Ackoff, 1970, pp. 43–44).[6]

The research process to which Ackoff refers is difficult to implement successfully. Many of the constraints on such processes are self-imposed. Premise-setting as a mechanism of social control (Chapter 10) as well as the organization's culture (Chapter 9) tend to obscure management's understanding of the organization as a system. However, the research process itself can remove these constraints ultimately through activities akin to the survey feedback technique. Ackoff advocates that research-planning task groups comprise line managers as well as planning specialists from a variety of management service groups. Such arrangements facilitate the dissemination of information about the organization when managers and staff planners are rotated back to their respective departments. Ackoff also suggests that task group participants meet with other managers in the context of multilevel "planning review boards" which are similar to Likert's overlapping, linking-pin groups described in Chapter 3.

Why Survey Feedback Works

Most of our tentative conclusions about the way survey feedback works are based on Bowers' (1973) research cited in Chapter 16. A more detailed review of his work will shed additional light on the subject. Please recall that Bowers studied the effectiveness of various OD techniques in 23 organizations. His findings indicate survey feedback to be more effective in producing organizational change than the other techniques studied.

The OD techniques examined in Bowers' study can be arrayed according to a number of dimensions; for example, they differ according to what Harrison (1972) terms depth of intervention (Chapter 16). At the extremes, both "deep" (T-group) and "shallow" (data handback) strategies were employed. Survey feedback appears to lie somewhere between these extremes, which may account for its effectiveness.

Bowers also directs our attention to the temporal dimensions of the change processes studied. Laboratory training focuses participants' attention on experienced behavior that occurs in the "here and now." Interpersonal and task process consultation are somewhat similar in this regard. In contrast, survey feedback deals with "then and there" data as well as immediate perceptions (Bowers and Franklin, 1972). Thus, a variety of organizational characteristics such as roles, regulations, policies, and technologies as well as immediate interpersonal reactions are explored and evaluated.

---

[6] Ibid.

Three other dimensions can be used to differentiate survey feedback from other techniques studied. Bowers identifies these as: (1) extensiveness of coverage, (2) extent of "unfreezing," and (3) relevance. Regarding extensiveness of coverage, it is apparent that survey feedback is the only technique in which change activities "fan out" into the organization. Survey data are disseminated throughout the organization and problem-solving activities are assigned to various appropriate levels in the organization. Moreover, the feedback format employed by the technique produces information about the organization which most members are anxious to see and act on.

"Unfreezing" is a term that describes the initial phase in change processes. We shall examine this concept below (Chapter 18) in some detail. For the present, we will merely suggest that various parts of a system must be loosened up (unfrozen) before they can be modified or rearranged. One way to unfreeze an organization is to present members with data that disconfirm existing perceptions of the organization. Sensitivity training may have powerful unfreezing effects in a small group. However, survey feedback tabulations are more likely to contain disconfirming information about the organization per se. Furthermore, such tabulations may be more pursuasive than feedback within sensitivity training or other small groups. The former comprise aggregated perceptions of fairly large numbers of people, and are permanent records that can be considered from time to time, whereas the latter usually are verbalized observations of a single individual. In short, survey tabulations may be harder to disregard than interpersonal communications and, thus, more effective in preparing an *organization* for change.

The final dimension to be discussed, relevance, refers to the degree of "fit" between the OD technique employed and the manner in which the organization normally functions. Analyses of day-to-day problems usually are based on data obtained from the organization's information systems (e.g., production statistics, grievance rates, sales records, and the like). Thus, as Bowers observes:

> Against this background, it perhaps seems quite natural to launch a problem-solving discussion of "people" issues from a base of tabulated, quantitative data whose accuracy is attested by an outside expert (just as the other data with which they work come from the comptroller, the quality control department, or the production control office). Alternative treatments, of a process consultation or laboratory training variety, may seem, on the other hand, to be a bit peculiar. They are asked to accept the observations of an outsider who, they may feel, knows neither them, their business, nor their problems, and to accept them in off-the-top-of-the-head format, rather than in the more customary form of tabulated data.
>
> Thus a credibility gap may ensue. It may also be enlarged by some of the change agent's more confronting interventions. It may be, for example, that a change agent who spends most of his work time in a confrontation mode becomes somewhat jaded, such that what, to client

group members, is terribly confronting—just barely within tolerable limits—is to him a "cop-out," whereas what to him is confronting is to them an outrageous assault upon propriety (Bowers, 1971, p. 34).

Client Perceptions of OD Techniques

Bowers' observation that organizational members did not view the various OD techniques as particularly important elements of the change process is particularly interesting. Where survey feedback was used, individuals acknowledged the occurrence of change and viewed survey tabulations as useful. However, credit for the resulting change often was given to organizational members themselves—not the technique employed. Similar observations are reported for the other OD techniques. Bowers' interpretations of these observations are reproduced below:

> In fact, some anecdotal evidence would suggest that client reactions were connected more to the personality and style of the change agent than to what he accomplished. In certain instances, the change agent played, as Interpersonal Process Consultant, a lower key, more ambiguous role; despite the fact that, in those sites, one could usually point to significant improvements in leadership behavior in the organization as a whole, the months toward the close of the project, and those immediately following its termination, often resulted in blame-fixing upon him as one reason for what was perceived to have been a non-success. In other instances, the change agent responsible for the intervention strategy was, in personal style, more active and charismatic. Despite an overall pattern of little change, anecdotal evidence suggests that he is highly regarded, that he is seen as having been responsible for much constructive change. In still other instances, especially those focusing around Laboratory Training, enthusiasm waxed greatly at the moment, but rapidly waned to indifference or disillusionment shortly afterward.
>
> Although far from constituting convincing evidence, these bits of anecdotal information certainly suggest the possibility that client system affect is whimsical and no reliable measure of what has really changed. Client system affection may be both useful and necessary for continuation of projects and contracts, just as disaffection is a rather reliable precursor of their cancellation, but they may bear little or no relationship to real accomplishment (Bowers, 1971, pp. 31–32).

This anecdotal evidence suggests a source of much of the present-day confusion about the relative effectiveness of different OD techniques. In the absence of rigorous, experimental evidence, managers and OD practitioners have used client attitudes as surrogate measures of contributions toward organizational improvement—attitudes which may be unrelated to the actual effectiveness of the technique employed.

DISCUSSION QUESTIONS

1. Suppose that an organization decided to survey employee morale and work-related attitudes. What model(s) would serve as a basis for the survey instrument? How valid are these models?

2. Using the Bates Company case found at the end of Section I, describe some possible uses of the survey feedback technique. How would you go about implementing a project of this sort? What data would you collect? How would you tabulate the data? What employee groups would you form? What data would they receive? To whom would they report?
3. What difficulties would you expect to encounter in a project of this sort?
4. We have observed that a change technique may be effective when it is consistent with the organization's norms and culture in general. What are the norms, values, and other manifestations of culture in your school? What change techniques would be appropriate for this institution?

REFERENCES

Ackoff, Russell L. *A concept of corporate planning.* New York: John Wiley & Sons, Inc., 1970.
Bass, Bernard M. When planning for others. *Journal of Applied Behavioral Science,* 1970, 6, 151–71.
Bowers, David G. Development techniques and organizational change: an overview of results from the Michigan Inter-Company Longitudinal Study. Technical Report, Office of Naval Research, 1971.
Bowers, David G. OD techniques and their results in 23 organizations: the Michigan ICL Study. *Journal of Applied Behavioral Science,* 1973, 9, 21–43. NTL Institute Publications.
Bowers, David G., and Franklin, Jerome L. Survey-guided development: using human resources measurement in organizational change. *Journal of Contemporary Business,* 1972, 1 (3) (Summer), 43–55.
Hall, Richard H. The applied sociologist and organizational sociology. In A. B. Shostak (Ed.), *Sociology in action: case studies in social problems and directed social change.* Homewood, Ill.: Dorsey, 1966. Pp. 33–38.
Harrison, Roger. Role negotiation: a tough minded approach to team development. In W. W. Burke and H. A. Hornstein (Eds.), *The social technology of organization development.* Washington, D.C.: NTL Learning Resources Corp., 1972. Pp. 84–96.
Katz, Daniel, and Kahn, Robert L. *The social psychology of organizations.* New York: Wiley, 1966.
Lewin, K. Group decision and social change. In G. E. Swanson, T. M. Newcomb, and E. L. Hartley (Eds.), *Readings in social psychology.* New York: Holt, 1952. Pp. 459–73.
Likert, Rensis. *The human organization: its management and value.* New York: McGraw-Hill, 1967.
Mann, Floyd C. Studying and creating change: a means to understanding social organization. In C. M. Arensberg et al. (Eds.), *Research in industrial human relations.* New York: Harper, 1957. Pp. 146–67.
Mann, Floyd, and Likert, Rensis. The need for research on the communication of research results. In R. N. Adams and J. J. Preiss (Eds.), *Human organization research: field relations and techniques.* Homewood, Ill.: Dorsey, 1960. Pp. 57–66.
Perrow, Charles. *Complex organizations: a critical essay.* Glenview, Ill.: Scott, Foresman, 1972.
Wieland, George F. Evaluation report. In G. F. Wieland and H. Leigh (Eds.), *Changing hospitals.* London: Tavistock, 1971. Pp. 211–401.

18

The Process of Change in Organizations

INTRODUCTION

One of the foundations of classical economic thought is the assumption that each individual will act in his or her own best interest if allowed sufficient freedom of behavior. In the aggregate, individuals' pursuits of their self-interests contribute to the well-being of society. Thus, the capitalistic system is guided by an *invisible hand:* enlightened self-interest. Or, so it was thought by Adam Smith.

Much of the classical thought contained in Smith's germinal work has been replaced by contemporary economic theory. Unfortunately, belief in the individual's ability to act in his or her self-interest lingers on in one form or another. Management tends to diagnose many problems as products of poor communications, and assumes that workers will cooperate with their supervisors once they understand such cooperation to be in their eventual self-interest. Carried to the level of policy formulation, this assumption suggests that the availability of programs designed to enhance the well-being of participants is sufficient to engage their interest and cooperation.

For reasons to be investigated in this chapter, people often do not act in their own best interests. In some cases this seeming perversity has its roots in personality disorders or other forms of pathology. In other cases, perhaps the vast majority, the individual is simply unable to implement the kinds of change that will improve his or her lot. For example, consider the following:

> . . . as surely as we can say that people shape their environments, we can also state that people's environments, in turn, shape their behavior. A vivid example of the latter phenomenon is provided by Guest (1962). Of his research with automobile workers, he remarks:
>
> > "One theme expressed as often as any other concerned the hopelessness of making any plans for the future or having any strong aspirations whatever. . . ."

The following interview data which support Guest's observation do not seem to have come from the men who have never had ambitions, but from men who have come to the pathetic realization that their previous ambitions are irrelevant to their foreseeable futures.

"I don't know. I've been there for fourteen years and I haven't accomplished a thing."

"I'll be on the (assembly) line fifteen years in July and I think I can last another fifteen, if I take care of myself. Then I'll get a job off the line . . . maybe a sweeper's job. Wouldn't that be something, to end my years at [plant Y] in a blaze of glory as a sweeper?" (Ullrich, 1972, p. 153)

Chapter Guide

1. The sources of the dissatisfaction expressed in Guest's quotations should be apparent from what we have said in other chapters. What forces keep the individuals experiencing these dissatisfactions from seeking better jobs?
2. Have you been in dissatisfying situations that you were unable to improve or leave? What kept you in these situations? What made you want to leave? What kept you from altering the situation?
3. Think of a situation you would like to change. Can you change it? What resistance to change must be overcome? Why does the situation remain as it is?

THEORETICAL VIEWS OF CHANGE PROCESSES

Behavioral Equilibrium

Lewin's (1952) *unfreezing-changing-refreezing* model provides a useful vehicle for understanding change processes. According to this model, behavior is determined by the net effect of an elaborate set of contemporaneous forces. A crude analogy, if you will, likens these forces to fields of magnetic flux within which an iron particle is trapped. In some configurations of flux, the particle will move. In all static configurations, it will eventually come to rest at a point where each force on the particle is met by an equal and opposite force.

It is helpful to view behavior in terms of analogous forces. Theoretically, we can postulate forces that move individuals to change their behaviors, but we must also recognize similar forces that resist deviations from habit or the *status quo*. Some of these forces emanate within the individual and include needs, attitudes, feelings, and habits. Others flow from second and third parties who respond to the focal individual's behavior with rewards or punishments.

The focal individual experience these forces as he or she perceives them. While perceptions may be valid or not, Lewin argues that they are real to the individual, who responds to them regardless of their actuality; that is, imagined threat is experienced as realistically as actual threat and is responded to accordingly. Thus, the forces described by Lewin are psychological forces.

It is probably impossible to comprehend all of the forces acting on an individual in a unique situation. No wonder human behavior seems unpredictable. Yet, we admit that behavior is fairly predictable within reasonable limits. This is most often true when dealing with groups of individuals whose norms are well understood. The study of group dynamics follows Lewin's early work. Particularly, studies of group norms and group pressures follow his original theoretical directions. We shall examine Lewin's work in terms of group work norms and behavior. For this purpose, we shall define norm and norm-following behavior, respectively, as: (1) a set of expectations for behavior held by group members and (2) the fairly regular behavior resulting from these expectations and the positive and negative sanctions used for their enforcement.

Lewin's model can be applied to a group norm specifying level of worker productivity. Where such norms exist, the individual's behavior will conform fairly closely since deviations in either direction may be met with negative sanctions. Yet, there are forces on the individual that, by themselves, would cause him to deviate in one or the other direction.

First, group pressures limit deviation in either direction. Slight deviations are met with mild sanctions, such as half-joking, half-critical comments from fellow workers. Major deviations evoke more severe sanctions; for instance, the informal group leader may rebuke the offending worker, other group members may threaten action, and, ultimately, physical violence may erupt. The latter sanction is a rare, but not unknown, penalty for violating important group norms.

Several motives can cause a work group to establish and maintain norms such as the one discussed here. First, output above the norm is likely to signal to management that it has established unrealistically low output requirements. One likely consequence is that the requirements will be restudied with the result that workers eventually find themselves working harder for the same hourly wage. This can be especially threatening to older members of the work group who would have difficulty keeping a faster pace of work. Output below the norm is also sure to attract management's attention. A consequence to be anticipated in this event is increased pressure from supervision. Our discussion of psychological work contracts in Chapter 6 suggests that interaction with management in any form may be undesirable from the workers' point of view.

We have looked at two kinds of forces limiting deviation from the norm and serving to maintain behavioral equilibrium. In addition to forces emanating from the work group are those solely within the individual; for example, fatigue serves to limit the individual worker's rate of productivity. Counteracting this force to some extent are psychological forces that stem from the need for achievement or the Protestant ethic. Work-related aspirations, anxieties about the state of the economy and employment security, and pressures and inducements applied by the organization may also enter into the balance.

According to Lewin, the net effects of these forces are stabilized behavior and social equilibrium. However, the resulting equilibrium is dynamic rather than static and, thus, is termed *quasi-stationary equilibrium*. It is dynamic in the sense that it can be altered by a number of possible changes in the balance of forces.

Unfreezing Behavior

For convenience, Lewin terms forces hindering movement from the existing equilibrium *restraining forces*. Opposing forces which direct behavior away from the status quo are called *driving forces*. Now, in order to cause change, one must upset the balance of driving and restraining forces; that is, *unfreeze* the quasi-stationary equilibrium. There are, of course, three ways to unfreeze the situation: (1) increase the driving forces, (2) decrease the restraining forces, or (3) accomplish some combination of the first two strategies. We shall examine these change strategies in order.

Driving forces can be increased through manipulation of positive and negative incentives; for example, management may inform the work force of impending layoffs that can be avoided only by increases in employee productivity. Alternatively, an incentive payment scheme can be implemented. The success of neither approach is guaranteed. In the first case, workers are led to fear that their present level of productivity will result in punishment in the form of unemployment. Even so, they may think that in yielding to these pressures they will encourage management to seek further changes in the same manner. In the second case, workers may fear that increased productivity motivated by incentive payments will lead management to restudy the job (Whyte, 1955). Both attempts appear to produce additional restraining forces inadvertently.

Thus, increasing driving forces can produce or increase restraining forces, especially as movement is made away from the previous equilibrium. In the event that the increased driving forces are of sufficient magnitude to overcome existing and newly created restraining forces (which is not true in all cases), behavior may reach a state of equilibrium at a new level. Whether or not a new equilibrium level is reached, the individual will experience greater tension. This occurs because both driving and restraining forces have been increased. Were this not the case, behavior would change endlessly in the direction of the driving forces. Obviously, this cannot occur, for fatigue, if nothing else, will restrain behavior ultimately.

Increased tension of this sort creates additional dynamic potentialities in the situation, which imply greater instability and unpredictability. A minor fluctuation in one of the major driving or restraining forces may create widely fluctuating behavior. Large forces are not maintained effortlessly and are more likely to change than are smaller forces. This produces a tendency toward instability. In psychological terms, the individual experiencing pressures from two directions is in a conflict situation. He or she will expend considerable energy monitoring the conflicting pressures and making tentative moves, first in one direction, then in the other.

Because of this, it appears more reasonable to unfreeze behavior by removing restraining forces. In the previous examples, we described restraining forces arising from labor's distrust of management. To continue the example, we note that these forces can be reduced by assurances that such distrust is unfounded. This may, of course, require effort over and above giving assurances. Trust between workers and management must be established, possibly by some tangible evidence that such restraining forces are unwarranted. Other avenues of progress include redesigning work to reduce worker fatigue, reformulating group norms, and so on.

In the event that management is successful in reducing or removing certain restraining forces, existing driving forces may be sufficient to change behavior in the desired direction; that is, forces already in the situation, such as need for achievement, can drive performance higher and in so doing unfreeze the situation. Furthermore, the new equilibrium will contain less tension since a smaller set of opposing forces results.

From this observation, we find the two major advantages of the second change strategy over the first. First, it takes less effort to remove forces than to add them. Adding driving forces may create opposing restraining forces. Thus, further driving forces may be needed. Reducing restraining forces permits existing forces to effect change. Second, given the same degree of change, the latter strategy produces a more psychologically healthy and, in managerial terms, more controllable situation than does the former. This occurs because the reduction in forces yields lower tension, more stability, and greater predictability.

The third strategy, increasing driving forces while reducing restraining forces, is probably the most advantageous of the three. The addition of driving forces can provide further impetus for change in the desired direction. Furthermore, the unfreezing effect may be more pronounced as positive motivations are increased. Theoretically, the increased tension experienced at the new equilibrium may be justified by the arousal of positive motivation. Not all tension is undesirable or unpleasant.

Changing Behavior

The second stage in Lewin's model is the *changing stage* which we have already begun to discuss. Unfreezing sometimes elicits change as the addition and reduction of forces drive behavior away from the initial point of equilibrium. However, this is not always the case. Despite a reasoned alteration of the force field, new forces may come into play as existing ones are manipulated. We might think of this in terms of people's willingness to tolerate uncertainty and ambiguity rather than move in directions they do not wish to travel.

When unfreezing does not produce adequate change, management is left with the task of analyzing and reshaping the force field. Returning to our former example, we may find that production has increased somewhat but is limited by employee fatigue. Management will deal with this restraining force, perhaps by redesigning the job or employing superior equipment. These actions, in turn, can evoke additional restraining forces. We resist change "in principle" because it can lead to unanticipated consequences and requires additional effort. Thus, the change process must be supported by psychological as well as material improvements. In our example, workers will need assurances that change will not work to their detriment.

Refreezing Behavior

Typically, behavioral changes gained even through the expenditure of considerable resources and effort dissipate over time; for example, the manager whose attitudes and behavior have changed as a result of recent management development activities may return to old habits shortly after his or her return to the organization from the classroom. This occurs when the *refreezing stage* of the change process has been dealt with inadequately.

Following change, a new quasi-stationary equilibrium must be established by an appropriate, balanced configuration of driving and restraining forces. The unfreezing and change stages of the process usually are facilitated by psychological support and inducements applied by the change agent. These forces tend to disappear once change has been accomplished and management loses interest in the problem, assuming that its remedy has been found. Indeed, the maintenance of these forces over the long run may prove infeasible. Yet, as they are removed they must be replaced by other forces if the new equilibrium is to be maintained. Failing this, behavior may return to its former state.

Change programs are likely to be accompanied by something akin to the "Hawthorne effect" arising from the attentions of management and other novel influences that may disappear once the process of change appears to have been completed. The refreezing stage is advocated in recognition of this phenomenon. Basically, this stage consists of the systematic replacement of temporary forces with more permanent ones. In some cases, the technique used to create change can be continued as a vehicle for its maintenance; for example, if the change program was structured around the survey feedback technique, the same technique can be employed to investigate problems and performance arising from the new equilibrium point. In other cases, it may suffice to formalize the changed situation through revisions of rules, regulations, and procedures. These activities can lend organizational authority as well as legitimate sanctions to the new state of equilibrium and, thus, maintain it temporarily until norms evolve to sustain it in a more permanent fashion.

Change and the Larger Organization

Thus far we have restricted our view of the change process to individuals and small groups. Lewin's model can also be applied to problems of organizational change—to the diffusion of change from one group to another, and from subsystem to subsystem throughout the organization. If one subsystem is unfrozen and changed, other related parts of the system will be affected. Furthermore, the effect of subsystem A on adjacent subsystem B is likely to produce a countereffect wherein B affects A. We noted the managers' tendencies to revert to habitual behavior on reentering their organization following management development activities. This may be due, in part, to their inability to sustain newly learned attitudes and behaviors as members of subsystems that expect their former behavior of them. Specifically, the returning manager's altered behavior affects his or her group and, perhaps, other adjacent groups as well. But, these subsystems have not undergone corresponding changes that would enable them to incorporate the manager's newly acquired behavior successfully. Consequently, they fail to reinforce this behavior and, in some cases, sanction against it. These acts can shift his or her behavior back to its prior form.

Similarly, changed work groups can experience frictions with other groups with which they no longer "fit"; for example, our workers, who now produce at a higher rate, pass their increased output downstream to other groups in the productive process. These interdependent groups, feeling pressured by increased supplies of work in process, may react adversely, having been inadvertently unfrozen. Whyte (1955) describes a change program that was curtailed by this phenomenon. Employees working at one station of a production line were encouraged to organize their own work and to enrich their jobs by combining delimited individual tasks into a group operation. The increased motivation thus tapped caused an increase in productivity. However, the increased productivity of one group entered the work flow of the next group in the process. Unfortunately, the second group could not be reorganized as the first had been to handle the increased work required of them. In Lewin's terms, the second group became unfrozen by the output of the first. Restraining forces in the situation prevented them from adapting to the new driving forces (increased work in process inventories). Ultimately, they were successful in resisting change, and the experiment with the first group was discontinued.

Of course, pressures and discomfort experienced by adjacent subsystems can provide an entree for the change agent as he[1] attempts to move his change effort through the organization. His potential to help with uncomfortable, unsettling problems can elicit cooperation from other subsystems, paving the way for additional changes that are congruent with changes made in the initial subsystem. Furthermore, by decreasing the resistances of adjacent subsystems, refreezing (maintenance of change) in the initial subsystem is enhanced.

A Process for Consultants

The intervention of a consultant complicates the change process somewhat. Lippitt and colleagues' (1958) amplification of Lewin's model clarifies the role of the consultant as he aids his client in bringing about organizational change.[2] The first of seven phases in the change process described by Lippitt is *the development of a need for change* and is the essence of Lewin's unfreezing stage. The second phase, *the establishment of a change relationship,* creates the basis for all subsequent phases of the change process. The third through fifth phases have to do with change itself; phase three is *the clarification of the client system's problems,* phase four is *the examination of alternative means and ends and the choice of those to be implemented,* and phase five is *the transformation of intentions into actual change efforts.* The sixth phase concerns *the generalization and stabilization of change* and is comparable to the refreezing stage of the Lewin model. Peculiar to the consultant's role in the change process, the seventh phase directs effort toward *ending the relationship.* This phase is essential since dependence on the consultant throughout the change process must be dissipated prior to his departure if change is to be permanent.

---

1 As previously noted, the common pronoun "he" refers to persons of either sex.

2 This model is based on a great variety of observations of work by consultants with individuals, groups, organizations, and communities, and is a distillation of what seems to be effective in helping the client to change.

Developing a Need for Change

Stress or disruption within a system or between the system and its environment must be translated into actual problem awareness (desire for change) before the process of organizational change can begin. Oddly enough, this does not occur naturally in all cases. In some instances, management is unaware of existing problems. In other cases, awareness has not advanced to a level at which problems are conceptualized and, thus, meaningfully viewed as needing (and amenable to) change; for example, existing problems can be seen as inevitable. Alternatively, they may be viewed as being prohibitively expensive to correct. However, even when awareness of problems is accompanied by knowledge of potential sources of help, an additional form of resistance must be overcome. Seeking help is admitting to failure, in a sense. It admits to problems beyond the capabilities of management.

Now, it is quite likely that these elements in the first phase of the change process will be resolved in the absence of a consultant. Even so, the change agents may find that the problems they are asked to address are symptomatic of others of which management is unaware. In this instance, the change agents will eventually work at several phases in the process concurrently, progressing on one problem and developing the need for change on others.

Establishing Change Relationships

Initial relationships between the consultant and client serve as levers for subsequent change in the organization. For this reason, the second phase can be critical to the consultant's role in the process of planned change. First impressions are important. Consultants, as professionals, must be competent and trustworthy. Furthermore, they must *appear* so to members of the client organization. The change agents must convey evidence of their skills and knowledge and the ability to employ them successfully. At the same time, they should appear similar to clients—as people who will understand their roles and problems and respect their organization's needs and values.

A critical element of the second phase is *clarification* of the consultant's relationship to the client. Each party must learn of the effort and participation expected by the other. This is admittedly difficult, coming as it does before a thorough diagnosis of the organization's problems. The change agent must communicate realistic, though general, goals for the change program as well as a realistic assessment of the effort that will be demanded of his or her client. The issue of depth of intervention should also be raised at this point to establish joint norms regarding appropriate and inappropriate areas in which to pursue change.

Because organizations comprise a variety of subsystems, the change agents need to clarify their relationship vis-à-vis each subsystem with which they will work. Although this cannot be accomplished in any detail at this preliminary stage, the consultants will at least "touch base" with important sources of power. In light of the tentative nature of arrangements at this point in the change process, the consultant and client may agree to a "shake down" period of finite duration, giving both parties an option to withdraw from the relationship should this appear warranted by events of the trial period.

Clarifying the Problem

The substance of this phase of the change process will be determined by techniques employed by the consultant. One format will be used for survey feedback approaches while other formats will accompany techniques such as MBO. In general, the format will be collaborative regardless of the particular techniques employed. The client possesses information which the consultant needs. The consultant has a range of diagnostic skills that can aid the client. Wherever possible, we advocate that the consultant help the client learn these diagnostic skills so that collaboration can occur. For instance, using the survey feedback technique, the client may be called upon to design and implement means for data collection and analysis with the help of the consultant (see e.g., Wieland and Leigh, 1971).

The diagnostic phase also serves to unfreeze further the client's organization. Analysis of data may show that problems are more numerous and more threatening than had been expected. The need for change may be seen as more pervasive or as affecting more subsystems than was originally thought. At this point, the change agent may guide the process of diagnosis to prevent the client from becoming overly impressed with his or her problems, fatalistic about them, or convinced that their solution can only be achieved by experts such as the consultant. Numerous problems can be brought to light by the diagnostic phase. Balance is achieved as alternative change strategies are considered for each problem as it is brought to light. Rather than an inventory of problems lacking solutions, the process yields an assortment of problems in various stages of resolution as management considers alternative actions and definite intentions to change in specified ways (Lippitt et al., 1958).

Choosing from Alternatives

At this point, the fourth phase has begun. Evaluation and choice are cognitive, rational processes, ostensibly. As we saw in Chapter 14 on

"Strategy Formulation," the actual process is likely to deviate from these expectations to one degree or another. Satisficing behavior may supersede optimization by necessity. One or at most two custom-made solutions may be considered rather than a broad array of feasible alternatives.

Equally important as the cognitive aspects of alternative selection is a motivational process accompanying this phase of the process, for at this point the organization must marshal commitment to act and carry out the programs of change selected. This is accomplished in large measure by the collaborative nature of the change process as the client develops commitment to the solution he or she helped design.

Transforming Intentions into Change Efforts

As we indicated earlier, many client-consultant relationships terminate at the conclusion of the previous phase when alternatives are selected and described in report form. This is unfortunate when it occurs, for the present phase is at the heart of the change process, so to speak. It is at this point that the consultant's expertise can be critical to the entire process of change. As we indicated in discussing Lewin's model, the change agent's expertise can be of value in aligning an adequate configuration of forces and maintaining a favorable imbalance in the force field throughout the change period. In a sense, the consultant helps the client progress through a series of cycles in the change process in which: (1) preliminary moves are made, (2) gains are consolidated and compared to desired outcomes, and (3) depending on the nature of this comparison, further consolidation is effected or further changes are sought.

Stabilizing Change

The sixth phase of the process concerns diffusion of change throughout the client organization. As we indicated in our discussion of Lewin's model, a change in one subsystem often necessitates corresponding changes in adjacent subsystems. In helping the client achieve this, the consultant serves a second purpose; namely, providing an external and fairly objective evaluation of progress. Added to the client's own evaluation, the consultant's opinion can provide reinforcement for the efforts and results obtained.

Stabilization can also be achieved as the consultant helps the client diffuse change to adjacent subsystems. As converts to a better way of life reinforce their own conversions by proselytizing new converts, so do managers reinforce their newly learned skills and behaviors by helping others acquire them.

Ending the Relationship

When change is realized and stabilized, the consultant's role has been discharged. To the extent the change agent involved the client in participation and transferred his or her skills to the client's organization, difficulties in terminating the client-consultant will have been reduced. Be that as it may, they still may be substantial. By seeking expert help, the client began a process through which he became dependent, although perhaps not as dependent as he might have been had the consultant behaved differently. The consultant attempts to reduce this dependence as the change program draws to completion. If he has been successful in transferring skills to the client's organization, the problem may entail little more than reinforcing the client's confidence by demonstrating his competence.

DESCRIPTIVE VIEWS OF CHANGE PROCESSES

Descriptive Studies of Change Processes

March and Simon's (1958) observation that people rarely achieve the degree of rationality to which they aspire is reinforced throughout the literature in organizational behavior. We are not surprised, then, to find discrepancies between normative and descriptive views of organizational change. It appears that the clinical rationality described in Lippitt's work represents a model for organizational change that is rarely, if ever, achieved.

Greiner (1967) began a descriptive study of the change process by identifying relatively successful and unsuccessful planned change programs in complex organizations. The former numbered 11 and the latter 7. The 11 successful change programs included Blake and Mouton's managerial grid study of a factory (Blake and Mouton, 1964), Guest's (1962) study of a factory, Jaques' (1951) study of Glacier Metal, Rice's (1958) Ahmedabad experiment discussed in Chapter 4, and Seashore and Bower's (1963) implementation of Likert's System Four Management. Each of the 18 change programs dealt with substantial, complex changes that were monitored by systematic, objective evaluation. Greiner (1967) found that successful programs seemed to consist of identifiable sequences of steps undertaken in the following order.

Problem Recognition

Successful change programs were found in organizations whose top management was under considerable pressure to change. Furthermore, pressures emanated both from the environment and from within the organization. In contrast, unsuccessful change programs were launched in response to pressures originating either internally or externally *but not both*.

Furthermore, it should be emphasized that these pressures were quite serious from top management's point of view. Typical sources of external pressure were stockholder discontent, decreasing sales volumes, and breakthroughs by competitors. Internal pressures emanated from strikes, low worker productivity, rising costs, and interdepartmental conflict. Greiner emphasizes the probable significance of the simultaneous existence of internal and environmental pressures. Pressure from one source or the other, by itself, can be rationalized as temporary or even inconsequential, as is likely to happen, for instance, when low employee morale is accompanied by high profits. Such rationalization is less likely when the two are experienced together. If Greiner's observations are valid, one is led to question whether the consultant alone will be able to develop a need for change.

Search for Solutions

The second stage observed in successful change programs involves top management's search for solutions. Presumably, success at this stage precludes the next stage. In any event, we postulate that problem-solving activities of top management are approximated by our discussion of strategic decision making in Chapter 14. However, these activities do not arise automatically in response to problems. Even under severe pressure, management may rationalize its problems by blaming them on the union, government, or other entities over which they lack control.

Arrival of a Change Agent

Failing to react successfully to pressures, management will seek out (or have thrust upon them) the services of an outsider, known for his or her ability to improve organizational functioning. Sometimes organizations in dire straits find their top management replaced by a "man of the hour." More frequently, existing management employs a consultant. The newcomer's position is advantageous. Having no vested interests in the organization or historical loyalties to one manager or another, he can provide a relatively objective appraisal of the organization. Furthermore, his reputation (or "aura") as a change agent will provide leverage to influence top management's behavior.

Commitment of Top Management

The fourth stage involves the newcomer's attempts to commit top management to one change strategy or another. Dealing with top management appears to be critical to success, since changes are most likely to come about if the organization's power structure is behind them. In successful change programs, the newcomer encourages top management to examine past practices and current problems. He encourages the power structure to suspend temporarily its preconceptions and accustomed ways of viewing problems. In this vein, management is led to original perceptions of the causes of organizational behavior.

Collaboration

Successful change efforts tend to involve the head of the organization and the immediate subordinates in extensive reexaminations of past practices and current problems. After having secured the collaboration and support of top management, fact-finding and problem-solving discussions are begun in lower levels of the organization. Top-management support is important at this stage, since it enables subordinates to view their own efforts as legitimate, having the backing of important people in the organization. Greiner (1967) suggests that subordinates have evidence that top management is willing to change, since they are involved in the diagnosis and change efforts. They have evidence that important problems are being acknowledged and faced up to and furthermore that ideas from lower levels are being valued by upper levels.

Creativity

At some point, management may become convinced that its problems, as they have been redefined, defy solution using available techniques. Here, the change agent's function is to provide new ideas and methods for developing solutions. Management is generally involved in learning and practicing new forms of behavior that permit creative problem solving. As unique solutions are generated, top management's commitment increases. Greiner notes that none of the less successful change programs reached this particular stage of development. The seeds of failure, sown in previous stages, grow into severe resistance to change prior to this. As this occurs, top management usually gives up or regroups for another effort.

Reality Testing

Solutions developed in the previous stage are tested on a pilot basis to determine their efficacy. This is observed in successful change efforts prior to attempts to broaden the scope of change to larger problems and the entire organization. Difficulties are nearly inevitable in the pilot run. Rather than presenting problems, they serve as opportunities to modify solutions and enhance their effectiveness.

Diffusion

Following pilot testing, adequate solutions are introduced on a larger scale. With each successful implementation, management support grows and the change is gradually absorbed into the organization's way of life. This final phase of the change process seems identical to our prior discussions of diffusion and reinforcement of change.

Greiner's findings may be disturbing to some students of organizational change, for they contradict the ideologies of some organizational development theorists. Some writers advocate "democratic," grass-roots change strategies that bring about change by first involving lower level members of the organization. Clearly, Greiner's findings do not provide empirical support for such a belief. Other scholars make much of the change agent's ability to cause change—to move the organization in anticipation of problems rather than in reaction to them. Yet, Greiner suggests that awesome pressures, perhaps near calamities, must arise before management will consider changing their organization substantially. We also observe in Greiner's work an emphasis on formal authority as a prerequisite to change. This too runs contrary to schools of thought emphasizing organizationwide collaboration in the absence of formal sanctions. As we said at the start of this section, the field of OD is rife with controversy and based on ideology as well as fact. The field is relatively young compared with others. For these reasons, we suggest that the material presented here be viewed as a description of the state of the art, rather than as a set of normative prescriptions.

Group Change versus Organizational Change

Our preceding discussions of change have not adequately dealt with problems of changing organizations as systems. Advocates of organizational development techniques, such as T-groups, primarily emphasize changing individuals, increasing their potentials to behave appropriately. As we indicated in Chapter 15, the evidence that these changes result in more effective organizational functioning is mixed.

Other techniques such as the survey feedback approach make explicit use of formal organizational structures (hierarchies of authority and power) to facilitate change in organizational families. Yet, the primary focus is improvement of personal and role relationships within small groupings. The specific changes realized using this technique may

vary from one group to another and may add up to an overall improvement or even major changes in organizational functioning, but the
specific improvement must be viewed as a consequence of the technique,
not its stated objective. The technique does not specify a priori the nature
of the change to be rendered to the system. Furthermore, such changes
may fall short of needed, systemwide improvements; for example, an
organization decentralized by profit centers and organized within profit
centers by function is likely to retain this form following an OD intervention despite its inadequacy. Obviously, there are occasions that call
for radical alterations of goals, technology, and formal structure in
addition to improvements in interpersonal and intergroup relations.

An Example of Organizational Change

The most common approach to organizationwide change is to change
the organization itself directly, by changing its structure, technology,
people, and perhaps even goals according to some predetermined plan
for accomplishing specified outcomes. Top management may plan and
organize mergers, reorganizations of existing structures, or divestments
of existing programs, for example.

Rigorous scientific study of this kind of organizational change is
rare. Especially rare are applications of experimental methodologies
to the change phenomenon. This is understandable, given the magnitude
of the phenomenon and its complexity. One example of this sort of research is Morse and Reimer's (1956) study of a large insurance company which modified its authority and decision-making structures.

The objective of the experiment was to alter role structures with
respect to decision making and related activities, to give employees at
lower hierarchical levels adequate power and authority to conduct more
of the organization's work. It was felt that the human relations approach, with its emphasis of group involvement and participatory management, would prove inadequate unless the groups to which it was
applied were given authority to make decisions and power to implement them. Hence, the human relations approach was augmented with
a planned change in the organization's power structure which was to be
accomplished through decentralization.

General support for this change strategy was found in a study by
Pelz (1952), who noted the conditions under which human relations
training tended to be effective or ineffective. The success of such training, that is, its usefulness to the trainee's organization, seemed to be
influenced directly by the trainee's power and authority within his organization. Trainees having sufficient authority and power were able
to delegate decisions to their subordinates and to back these decisions
in the larger organization. Those in weaker positions were unable to

provide subordinates with the breadth of responsibility participatory decision making requires.

To alter existing patterns of authority and responsibility, the experimenters then worked with top management to restructure the firm's production department. The intent of this change was to give rank-and-file employees the wherewithall to discharge not only their previous functions, but also those of first-line supervision. In turn, first-line personnel were to assume responsibility for running the division. Displaced by foremen, division managers were made responsible for their department. Finally, the department head was to assume some of the executive vice president's functions, specifically, the coordination of the production department and other departments.

Thus, the change program entailed moving authority and responsibility for decision making downward in the hierarchy, not only at lower levels, as is done, for instance, in some job enrichment schemes, but at upper levels of the organization as well. In contrast to individual or group changes, the experiment encompassed systematic changes in the organization's structure from the shop floor to the department head. The latter kind of change is more likely to endure the passage of time since changes to individuals and groups that do not cause subsequent adjustments in the remainder of the organization are likely to be reversed.

Elements of Organizational Change

Katz and Kahn argue that although organizational characteristics are difficult to change since so much must be changed in the process, it is important to alter these characteristics directly. Failing to do so may incur even greater costs and effort in the long run as unchanged elements of the system exert pressure on changed elements to revert to their former states.

Now, this does not mean that acting on systemic variables precludes the use of individual and group change techniques. In fact, they are used, although they are not the foci of change. Rather than individual or group behavior, interdependent structural aspects of the organization are selected as targets of the change effort. Management may become convinced of the efficacy of structural changes through participation in surveys or group sessions, but the intent of these activities will not be to change managers' attitudes about themselves or others, but to change their understanding of the relationships between systemic variables and organizational performance.

In the present study, this was accomplished by providing the executive vice president with survey results indicating that higher producing sections in the firm were less closely supervised and more involved in decision making than were lower producing sections. For instance, clerks in the higher producing sections helped one another in addition to discharging their own duties. Similarly, supervisors of higher producing clerks gave them more freedom within their own tasks.

Employees at various levels of the organization were prepared for the anticipated change by involvement in group discussions. These discussion sessions attempted to prepare supervisors for their new roles as well. As the discussions progressed, intended structural changes were introduced as official policy changes, which were presented and explained to employees by the executive vice president, himself. Finally, group decision making was implemented as the firm's routine mode of operation for rank-and-file and supervisory employees.

Results of the Organizational Change

As these changes were introduced, a second, unrelated group of employees was selected as a control. The control group received the opposite treatment, more or less. Further centralization was implemented. Measures of morale and productivity were taken in both the experimental and control groups before and after the experiment. The experimental manipulations were, in fact, successful in changing the intended systemic variables. Clerical work groups in the decentralized unit made decisions on matters that were important to them, such as recess periods, the handling of tardiness, and work methods and processes. In the control group, all decisions were made by management, and most were made at least one level above first-line supervision.

The results were generally as expected. Self-actualization, as measured in the study, increased among employees in the decentralized unit and decreased under centralization.[3] Relations with supervisors improved under the decentralized program and deteriorated in the control group. Unfortunately, measures of productivity left something to be desired. Only clerical time and costs could be measured against throughput of work. Both groups showed significant increases in productivity in terms of the clerical costs associated with output. However, the centralized unit achieved greater productivity than the experimental unit. Morse and Reimer explain this finding by observing that employees in the centralized unit experienced more dissatisfaction than their counterparts in the experimental unit. Consequently, greater labor turnover was also experienced. However, new personnel were not hired to replace those who terminated their employment. Rather, the work was distributed among fewer remaining employees. Since the work flow was nearly constant, the reduction in the work force decreased clerical

---

[3] Given the lack of evidence that a need for self-actualization exists, we question what actually was measured (see Chapter 6).

cost per unit of work. It can also be argued that since measurement was made shortly after the change, productivity measures may have noted short-run effects that would not have lasted over the long run.

Katz and Kahn (1966) also observe that the rate of work flow was nearly constant for both groups. This implies that the cooperative group spirit engendered in the decentralized group could not be expressed fully in terms of increased productivity without disrupting the group. Under these conditions, increasing group productivity would have required decreasing the group's size. Specifically, clerks would have had to declare one or more of their number redundant and request that they be transferred to another group. This is a difficult step for a cohesive group to take.

A more general explanation of the decentralized group's failure to realize greater productivity is that human relations programs may be inappropriate for certain technologies such as assembly lines and other routine functions such as the clerks performed. According to theorists such as Perrow (1970), productivity results from effective organization achieved when structure and technology are matched appropriately (Chapter 4). Yet, this raises additional questions. One may introduce participative management and other human relations techniques for reasons other than the attainment of optimal productivity. As we noted, productivity in the experimental unit exceeded its prior level. We may be satisfied with this outcome and not seek ultimate performance provided we value gains in employee satisfaction and the dignity of work as well. As indicated in Chapter 5, productivity is but one of the criteria to be used in assessing organizational performance.

The point of reviewing this experiment is not so much to evaluate its end results as it is to explore organizationwide change attained by altering basic structural variables. To continue in this vein, we shall review a second example to indicate the great variety of activities required in changing an organization.

Reorganizing

Service unit management (SUM), a relatively new structural design for hospitals, brings a manager into the wards to work with nurses, ward orderlies, housekeepers, and clerks. Problems encountered introducing SUM together with the arrangement's operating characteristics were examined by a multidisciplinary research team. The team focused its attention on eight hospitals employing SUM and, in addition, conducted a nationwide survey of hospitals. Their work is described by Jelinek, Munson, and Smith (1971).

Advocates of SUM claim it addresses two major problems in hospitals. First, the continuing shortage of nurses is aggravated by the amount of administrative and supervisory work required of them, which removes them from activities for which they are trained—direct patient care. In fact, the more skilled the nurse—the greater his or her training and experience—the greater the likelihood that he or she will be assigned administrative and supervisory duties. This leaves patient care to the less skilled and inexperienced. Second, most nurses are not trained managers. Therefore, it would seem reasonable to separate professional and managerial activities and assign the latter to those uniquely qualified to discharge them.

The role of the service unit manager was designed to subsume managerial functions on the hospital ward and consequently free nurses' time for patient care. In addition, cost savings were anticipated. Presumably, the service unit manager would assign some of nursing's unskilled tasks to less skilled personnel under his or her supervision. Furthermore, the management orientation of the service unit manager was expected to be more effective in reducing costs than the more professional orientations of nurses. The reorganization was expected to increase the work satisfaction of various personnel on the ward. Nurses, freed from "paper shuffling," would have opportunity to exercise more of their professional skills and, presumably, increase their satisfaction in the process. Finally, the manager's training was expected to result in better quality supervision and fewer related employee dissatisfactions.

Typical service unit managers order equipment and supplies from various hospital departments. Similarly, they schedule required maintenance service for the ward. They supervise the ward clerk, who answers phones, greets visitors, schedules appointments, and maintains patient records. They coordinate requests for charts and records, lab and X-ray information, and supervise the various clerical activities that arise from these and associated tasks. Other activities of the service unit managers include coordinating food, laundry, and housekeeping services on the ward. Supervision of patient transportation frequently is delegated to the managers as well as patient feeding.

There are two common procedures for locating the service unit manager in the organizational structure. In both cases he or she enjoys status equal to that of the head nurse, or the senior nurse on the ward. In one case, both the head nurse and the manager are located in the nursing division and report to the director of nursing who, in turn, is subordinate to the hospital administrator. In the second case, the head nurse is subordinate to the director of nursing. The manager, though, reports directly to the hospital administrator. Another variation is found in the number of units or wards managed. Typically, these range from one to three (the latter comprising about 80 beds). Further variations occur across shifts. In some hospitals, service unit managers are employed around the clock. In others, the manager's responsibilities revert to the head nurse between the hours of 5:00 P.M. and 8:00 A.M. Obviously, these and related variations must be decided upon prior to implementation of this form of management.

Introducing Structural Change

Major problems arise as changes of the magnitude described here are introduced to the organization's traditional structure. As Smith (1971) and Jelinek and colleagues (1971) indicate, organizational change creates problems at numerous levels in the hierarchy. At the *individual level,* the manager must be particularly concerned with employees' feelings of security. He or she will need to anticipate potential reactions of head nurses, who may view their administrative skills as having been rendered obsolete and their status as having diminished accordingly. At the extreme, ambiguities arising from the transition period and attendant insecurities may lead to personality conflicts, to disruptions, and to staff turnover.

New patterns or relationships will be created at the *unit level* by the creation of the service unit manager's position. Existing patterns of interaction and status will be altered. Left to themselves, these alterations may produce undesirable consequences; for example, the head nurse may use the time she once spent on administrative matters to supervise licensed practical nurses more closely. This change in the relationship between superior and subordinate may result in a decrease in the latter's job satisfaction.

Problems also arise at the *system level.* The service unit manager will replace the head nurse as liaison with other hospital units. Consequently, relations between nursing and other departments will change. In addition, the service unit manager will need to forge new relations with other units in order to discharge his or her boundary role.

It is possible to eliminate the causes of some of these problems in the planning phase of the change effort. The process whereby unfreezing is achieved and motivations mobilized can be structured to minimize resistance and anxiety. Here, of course, the whole area of participation in planning is relevant. Individuals who will be most involved and affected can participate in planning for change. Those whose involvement will be merely tangential ought to have the opportunity to provide input. Finally, various other individuals will need to be kept informed, at least.

Training can also pave the way for change. The study in question showed lack of training to be a source of serious problems—especially in the case of the service unit manager. When he or she was inadequately trained for the tasks associated with the role, nurses and others were reluctant to relinquish their control and pass their authority on to the newcomer. Where justified, this concern implied the service unit manager's striving for undeserved status. The training advocated here should focus on the development of interpersonal skills as well as technical competence. If he or she is sensitive to potential conflict areas and competent to deal with them, the service unit manager will be free to perform the technical aspects of the job more easily. This is equally true for the head nurse and ward staff.

Phases of Change Processes—Development of the Role

According to Smith (1971), the change process can be divided into three phases, each concerning problems relevant to the three levels discussed above. The first phase concerns *development of the role,* the second *unit integration,* and the third *system integration.*

Problems facing the head nurse are acute, since he or she must not only learn a new role, but unlearn an old one as well. The former role consisted of stabilized sets of role expectations together with skills and attitudes consistent with the former. This integrated set of skills, attitudes, and behaviors is disrupted by the change, and the nurse will be required to learn new responses to events on the ward.

Smith suggests three approaches to preparing the head nurse (as well as other nursing personnel) for the anticipated changes. First, they can be made aware of the problems associated with role changes—the need to unlearn and suppress old behaviors before new behaviors can be learned. Second, they can be provided emotional support throughout the period of transition. Admittedly, this is difficult, but at the very least, nurses should be provided opportunities to express their feelings and be reinforced as they demonstrate progress in adapting to their new roles. Third, and most important, is to provide the nurses with role models which they can emulate. It is not enough to inform them of tasks that will no longer be required and to assume that they will use their free time effectively. What is required is a model, or description, of the new role—one that is integrated and makes sense in terms of the nurses' training, skills, and function in the hospital.

Please note that other case studies indicate the importance (and usual lack) of role models and support in moving into new roles. New educational programs, for example, may attempt to change the teacher's role from lecturer to resource person. Teachers can be unfrozen by learning the shortcomings of the lecture method and of the possible harm it does as it creates dependency in the student. Teachers can be persuaded to adopt new roles, but these experiments frequently meet with failure. If the new role is not clearly defined, the teacher will not *know how* to be a resource person. If adequate training in the role is not provided, the teacher will lack the *skills* of a resource person. Even when these are provided, the teacher will need additional resources in the form of materials and supplies as well as psychological support.

Unit Integration

As progress is made in the first stage (as roles are learned), new problems come to the foreground. In the second phase of the change process one finds inter-role conflict. What was formerly a single role (head nurse) has now become two separate roles (head nurse and service unit manager). Other individuals must therefore reorganize their roles vis-à-vis the two major changes. This is descriptive of the integration phase.

Smith describes how the new arrangement (the creation of roles that are highly interdependent and physically close) creates potential for conflict. Role conflict emerges as individuals solve the problems of learning their new roles. Power plays are symptomatic of role conflict. Typically, management and nursing will seek influence higher up in the organization, to pressure the rival group to conform to specific role expectations; for instance, management may court the hospital administrator's support in laying claim to an area of authority that is also claimed by nursing. Distrusting one another, the two groups resort to power plays, defensiveness, and rigidity, rather than confront the disagreement directly. Such cooperation may be perceived as a sign of weakness and subservient status.

The change agent must be aware of the potential for role conflict and, in this situation, reinforce the individuals' perceptions of equal status. It is particularly important that role overload be avoided at this point in the change process. Overload is likely to heighten the intensity of existing conflict. Excessive work-related demands cause the individual to suffer tension and frustration which frequently lead to aggression and aggravate difficulties in interpersonal relations. Furthermore, excessive tasks absorb organizational slack which could have been used to explore and remedy sources of conflict.

Another potential source of conflict is found in differences between the nurses' and managers' roles. The orientation of the nurses' role is professional while the manager's is efficiency-seeking. Thus, managers are likely to value stability as a means to steady state efficiency, while nurses value flexibility as the sine qua non—individualizing health care according to the patient's needs. The change agent may alleviate this source of conflict by devising performance measures that evaluate the ward as a total entity, as opposed to constructing separate measures of management's and nursing's performance. Thus, attention is focused on a superordinate goal. Pressures to suboptimize performance are reduced to the extent that incumbents of each role perceive cooperation as essential to goal attainment.

System Integration

The third phase of the change process, system integration, becomes salient as problems encountered in unit integration are stabilized. At this point, the manager finds himself caught between the demands of nursing (which he has come to view as legitimate in the second phase) and those of other departments such as housekeeping, dietetics, or the lab. Typically, these departments do not adapt automatically to changes on the ward. According to Smith, their unresponsiveness has its roots in their ability to maintain the status quo without suffering undue consequences; for example, lab employees can continue old ways of behaving toward people on the ward. They will still contact nurses when problems arise with respect to a patient's test, rather than follow the new lines of communication. Consequences of this behavior will be borne on the ward, but not in the lab. Thus, even after relationships and roles are established on the ward, they will be threatened by elements of the system that have not articulated with these novel roles.

This is probably the lowest point in the change process. The act of solving problems on the ward level has created new problems elsewhere in the hospital, which impede the service unit manager's effectiveness. One possible remedy for problems of system integration is the temporary assignment of an assistant administrator to oversee relationships between service unit management and the various ancillary departments. A second remedy is to establish a task force, comprising department heads and representatives of service unit management, to establish guidelines for interaction. Either way, formal authority is brought to bear in one form or another on recalcitrant department members.

It is entirely possible that problems arising in the third stage of the change process may never be solved. Alternatively, it may be that as one set of problems is resolved another is created. Hospitals, indeed, all complex organizations, are systems. Changes to one part of a system must be met with adaptation in the remainder of the system for interdependencies to remain viable. Furthermore, each of these changes is temporary in the sense that each can be altered by feedback and adaptation. Thus, phase three may never come to an end. As radical as this notion may seem when made explicit, we suggest that it is one with which most of us are familiar and comfortable. Organizations and societies are never freed of their problems by acts of humans or nature. Rather, they alleviate the severity of those most intolerable and, in so doing, create new ones.

Evaluation of the Change Effort

Of final interest is whether the introduction of service unit management improved patient care and reduced its costs in the eight hospitals surveyed. It turns out that the quality of nursing and nonnursing patient care improved overall. However, there is no evidence that the change reduced personnel costs. Job satisfaction increased for both professional and nonprofessional employees. One might conjecture that because of this labor turnover will be reduced, constituting one form of cost reduction.

One interesting finding is that while the change provided head nurses more time to devote to improving the quality of patient care, the greatest improvements were made by nonprofessionals. Nurses generally failed to take full advantage of the opportunities provided by the service unit management system. This may have been due to the failure of many of the hospitals to provide adequate training and support for nurses whose roles changed. In short, one major conclusion of the present study is that service unit management is productive but can be made even more productive if sufficient attention is paid to the implementation of the nurses' role. Obviously, there is more to changing an organization than changing its structure, and that is what this book has been about.

Sequencing Changes in Technology, Structure, and People

The outline of the second section of this text provides a useful framework within which attempts at planned organizational change can be analyzed. Since technology, structure, people, and the like are interdependent, a change in one may require changes in the others. Observing this phenomenon, one is led to wonder whether there is an optimal sequence of organizational changes; that is, whether it is better to permit people to adapt to a change in the formal structure of their organization, or whether structural changes should follow change efforts focusing on employee behavior.

We have described numerous ways of changing organizations at various points throughout the text. Beginning with the rational view of organizations, we examined alternative formal structures. Major structural changes are found in reorganizations (e.g., from a functional structure to a decentralized divisional structure or a matrix organization). The service unit management program in hospitals is another example.

Technological change can include applications of scientific management, work measurement techniques, time and motion study, job classification schemes, and various industrial engineering techniques. Operations research seems similar to these, but appears to be more applicable to managerial tasks (e.g., selecting media in an advertising agency, controlling inventories, and scheduling production runs).

Now we are led to ask, what are the relationships between these structural and technological approaches to organizational change and the behavioral approaches described in Chapters 16 and 17? Structural and technological changes often have been implemented without concern for people variables; for example, when reorganization follows a decision to implement a more appropriate formal structure, employees are moved to "new sets of boxes" on the organizational chart. Similarly, when technological changes follow the determination of more efficient production methods, tasks are reassigned to employees accordingly. These are oversimplifications, of course. Training programs and "shakedown" periods are employed frequently. Furthermore, a change in structure or technology often is "sold" to lower level staff. However, these practices suggest that attempts to change structure (or technology) precede attempts to change people.

The Tavistock study of the change to the longwall mining system (Chapter 4) is a case in point. However, the sequence did not operate as planned, and the technology did not "take." Structural and people change had to proceed apace with a redesign of the technology. We might say that it was necessary to match the social system to the technological system.

Here, we are developing a loose and informal argument for a contingency approach to organizational change. The notion of "fit" (Chapter 6) is appropriate in this regard. Yet, there is an argument to the contrary—that external, unilateral change efforts involving technology or structure may be cheaper. If they are sufficient in and of themselves, they can be used alone. Furthermore, it can be argued that attempts to change people often do not work. Even when they do work, their effects may be unpredictable.

On the one hand, we note problems in change attempts such as those reported in the Tavistock study. On the other hand, we can refer to countless structural and technological changes (e.g., installation of computer systems) that were not accompanied by the application of behavioral science techniques. While the debate goes on, we profess to have no answer to these arguments at this time.

Postscript

Introduction of service unit management seems a relatively modest change, particularly when the substance of the change is viewed in the context of the hospital, an extremely complex organization. And yet, as Smith indicates, even as simple a change as the addition of one individual to the ward structure must accommodate complex social and technical interdependence that comprise the organization.

We have tried to unravel these interrelationships and to examine each in its context in the organization. Yet, we have only scratched the surface in doing so. Each chapter of this text represents a field of inquiry in which scientists and scholars pursue their careers. We hope we have been fair and accurate in reporting and integrating the fruits of these labors and that in so doing we have given you something of value, of use in your careers in a complex and changing society.

DISCUSSION QUESTIONS

1. Can Lewin's force field analysis of behavioral change be used as a tool for problem solving in organizations? How?
2. What are the limitations of the force field analysis?
3. The force field analysis is an analogy to physical systems. What are some limitations of all such analogies?
4. Identify some of the interdependencies that exist between your school and other parts of the university. How would these be affected by a hypothetical change in your school's modus operandi?

REFERENCES

Blake, R. R., and Mouton, J. S. with Barnes, L. B. and Greiner, L. E. Breakthrough in organization development. *Harvard Business Review*, 1964, 42 (6), 133–55.

Greiner, Larry E. Patterns of organizational change. *Harvard Business Review*, 1967, 45 (3) (May–June), 119–30.

Guest, Robert Henry. *Organizational change: the effect of successful leadership.* Homewood, Ill.: Irwin, 1962.

Jaques, Elliot. *The changing culture of a factory.* London: Tavistock, 1951.

Jelinek, Richard C., Munson, Fred, and Smith, Robert L. *SUM (Service Unit Management): an organizational approach to improved patient care.* Battle Creek, Mich.: W. K. Kellogg Foundation, 1971.

Katz, Daniel, and Kahn, Robert L. *The social psychology of organizations.* New York: Wiley, 1966.

Lewin, Kurt. Group decision and social change. In G. E. Swanson, T. M. Newcomb, and E. L. Hartley (Eds.), *Readings in social psychology.* Rev. ed. New York: Holt, 1952. Pp. 459–73.

Lippitt, Ronald, Watson, Jeanne, and Westley, Bruce. *The dynamics of planned change.* New York: Harcourt, Brace & World, 1958.

March, James, and Simson, Herbert. *Organizations.* New York: Wiley, 1958.

Morse, Nancy, and Reimer, E. The experimental change of a major organizational variable. *Journal of Abnormal and Social Psychology,* 1956, 52, 120–29.

Pelz, Donald C. Influence: a key to effective leadership in first-line supervision. *Personnel,* 1952, 29, 205–17.

Perrow, Charles. *Organizational analysis: a sociological view.* Belmont, Calif.: Wadsworth, 1970.

Rice, Albert K. *Productivity and social organization: the Ahmedabad experiment.* London: Tavistock, 1958.

Seashore, Stanley E., and Bowers, David G. *Changing the structure and functioning of an organization.* Monograph No. 33. Ann Arbor, Mich.: Survey Research Center, 1963.

Smith, Robert L. Management of change. In Jelinek et al., *SUM,* Battle Creek, Mich.: W. K. Kellogg Foundation, 1971. Pp. 57–78.

Ullrich, Robert A. *A theoretical model of human behavior in organizations: an eclectic approach.* Morristown, N.J.: General Learning Press, 1972.

Whyte, William F. *Money and motivation.* New York: Harper & Bros., 1955.

Wieland, George F., and Leigh, Hilary. *Changing hospitals.* London: Tavistock, 1971.

19

The Future: Some Ways of Thinking

INTRODUCTION

What will life be like 5, 10, or, say, 25 years from now? How will organizations change? How much of what we have covered in this text will be relevant in ten years?

Looking into the future—once the pastime of wool-gatherers and the occupation of science fiction writers and occultists—is now an accepted and lucrative trade. According to one estimate, one out of every five firms in the *Fortune* "500" employs futurologists of one sort or another (Gallese, 1975). Major works in the area of futurology are reported in the popular press and scientific journals. As the rate of change in society increases, futurology may rival history as a source of inspiration and direction, or so it seems.

Our intent in this concluding chapter is not to lay out the various utopias and horrors that futurology presents as alternative futures, but to review the bases of these predictions, to examine some of their limitations, and to suggest the use of "genotypic" variables in forecasts of this sort. In essence, we shall present some ways of thinking about forecasts and their use in organizations. One way to begin is to examine the premises—the hidden assumptions—upon which works of this sort are based. What follows is the preface to a research proposal written by one of the authors some years ago. What assumptions are made about the future?

> Educators have always tried to prepare their students for "tomorrow." But technology and society have undergone such rapid changes in the last third of this century that the tasks of the teacher, and the student, have never been more complex. Moreover, our colleagues the world over have begun to resurrect and revise Parson Malthus' gloomy prophecy. Resource depletion, pollution, and unchecked population growth are expected to contribute to a world-encompassing catastrophy by the middle of the next century. The discovery of additional resources and increments to existing technology will not ward off the impending disaster, they tell us, but will merely postpone or, in some cases, hasten

its eventuality. The only remaining hope for contemporary society lies in our being able to alter our values and ways of living. We must husband our remaining resources and produce services in place of numerous consumer durable and semi-durable goods. We must limit population growth and learn to desire national growth along dimensions other than economic stature. We will need to develop and learn to value the abilities to ration, recycle, and ephemeralize. In short, we will need to produce a society which bears a symbiotic relationship to its environment and is both satisfying to its members and supportive of their personal growth. From what has been reported to date, one is led to imagine that art, philosophy, psychology, and the life sciences will guide and direct the application of physical and engineering sciences in this symbiotic society. But our various learning disciplines do not seem to be supplying the proper responses to the challenges of Today and Tomorrow (Ullrich, Experimental Learning Community, 1971).

Chapter Guide

1. What are the author's assumptions about the role of technology in the solution of future problems? What are possible sources of these assumptions?
2. In what sense must values change to accommodate the future? Have the author's values colored the premises of his argument? Is it possible to make value free forecasts?
3. If you were to write a comparable paragraph about the future, how would it differ from the one presented above?
4. How could a college respond to the problems raised by the author? Would you advocate making these organizational responses? What difficulties might arise if these responses were to be implemented?

MAJOR APPROACHES TO FUTUROLOGY

The Inevitability of Mishap

In 1964, Slater and Bennis published a paper entitled "Democracy is Inevitable" in which they predicted the coming demise of bureaucracy. Unsuited to the demands of contemporary society, bureaucracy would be made obsolete by new organizational forms based on humanistic-democratic ideals. Bennis' subsequent experience, however, led him to recant in a follow-up article entitled "A Funny Thing Happened on the Way to the Future" (Bennis, 1970a). This denouement is instructive, since it parallels the fate of many such forecasts and illustrates the origins of their inaccuracy.

As Slater and Bennis saw it, bureaucracy could not endure the pressures building in society. Applications of human relations techniques, System Four Management, and the like would relieve some of these pressures, but bureaucratic structures inherently were ill-equipped to survive the rapid growth of science and technology and unable to adapt to increasingly turbulent environments. Bennis' many years of experience as a leading OD practitioner led him to conclude that bureaucracies were unable to meet changing human needs as well. For these reasons, he expected bureaucratic structures to be replaced by ". . . adaptive, problem-solving, temporary systems of diverse specialists, linked together by co-ordinating and task evaluating specialists in an organic flux . . ." (Bennis, 1970b, p. 14).

As a high-level university administrator, Bennis had the opportunity to implement organizational forms of the type he advocated. This experience gave rise to his doubts expressed in the second paper. Specifically, he admits that the democracy of the small group does not transfer readily to the large-scale organization which comprises subsystems having differing interests. Moreover, he suggests that the earlier paper underplayed power of all types, and emphasized the management of conflict while ignoring the strategy of conflict. His most recent writings continue to reflect doubt that large-scale organizations can be made more democratic. In fact, he wonders aloud whether complex organizations such as the university are governable at all.

Recent enthusiasm for utopian organizations such as communes provides another example of prediction gone wrong. A tremendous upwelling of interest among young people led to the creation of thousands of these organizations during the late 60s and early 70s. Concomitant were predictions that the "counterculture" values of these organizations' founders would soon characterize most of Western society (see, e.g., Roszak, 1969). The process through which this would occur became known as the "greening of America" (Reich, 1971).

As these predictions were being made, Peter Drucker (1971) noted the imminent demise of the counterculture. He suggested that the upwelling of emphasis on humanistic values was caused by demographic factors which were soon to change and, in so doing, dissipate the counterculture. Although many people assumed that young people would retain these values as they moved into later stages of adulthood, Drucker pointed out that the demographic characteristics of the situation were unique and temporary. From 1948 to 1953 the number of babies born rose by nearly 50 percent. Consequently, the percentage of the population in the 17-year-old group increased proportionately from 1965 to 1970. In addition, because of low birthrates during the Great Depression and World War II, the sudden increase of postwar births caused the center of gravity of the U.S. population to shift from the 35 to 40 age group in 1960 to the 17-year-old age group in 1965. Thus, each 17-year-old group was larger than the previous one for the next seven years. Because this age group marks the transition from family control to self- or peer-control, it played a critical role in the development of the counterculture. As Drucker indicates, it has been the age of rebellion for centuries.

Because the baby boom crested in 1955, 17-year-olds are becoming less numerous and are having less effect on societal values. In fact, the 1960-67 "baby bust" will decrease the numbers of 17-year-olds even further in the period 1977 to 1984. Drucker interprets this to mean that youth will have even less influence in society in the future. If we assume that the most numerous group in society has the most impact on its values, we can expect 21 to 35 year olds to shape the course of history over the next 15 years. According to Drucker, this group will be concerned primarily with concrete problems, not addicted to causes, intoxicated with ideas, or in search of identity. His view, from the vantage point of 1971, is that the values of these individuals will concern jobs, economic performance, and productivity.

While population dynamics cannot explain all of the psychology or economics of the future, Drucker seems to have made a case for viewing demographics as a factor of some importance. Not to incorporate such genotypic variables in forecasts is to invite mishap, as we have just seen.

Genotypic Variables in the Social System

One problem with the kinds of prognostications cited above is that they often are based on projections, or extrapolations, of short-term trends for phenotypic (superficial) variables. To improve the accuracy of prediction, we must identify genotypic (basic) variables *and* their relationships to the system for which predictions are sought (Emery, 1967). We shall investigate the nature and importance of several genotypic variables later in this chapter. For the moment, we shall focus on the degree to which various approaches to futurology emphasize societal ends and the means of achieving those ends.

Approaches to Futurology

The major approaches to futurology can be categorized according to two dimensions: (1) specification of system goals and (2) specification of strategies or means. First, futurologies differ according to whether they define or specify the social goals and values that are desired. Often futurologists take their own values for granted, neglecting to specify them and ignoring those of others; for example, the dominant technological, materialistic values in our society are implicitly accepted without conscious choice. Second, futurologists may specify and delineate the means or strategies to achieve their values, or they may neglect the problem of change strategies, perhaps in favor of the value question. This categorization scheme is depicted in Figure 19–1. *Surprise-free*

FIGURE 19–1
Orientations of Futurology

System Means Specified	*System Goals Specified*	
	No	*Yes*
Yes	Surprise-free (Toffler)	Strategy-Formulation (Etzioni)
No	Crisis (Meadows)	Valve-critical (Reich)

Source: Adapted from Hake (1973, p. 6).

futurology, the most common form of futurology, does not specify the goals or values desired of the system in question. It does accept and extend current, usually materialistic and technological, strategies into the future, thereby yielding "surprise-free" futures. Reduced to its simplest form, this approach to forecasting takes the system where it seems to be headed. Writers such as Bell (1960, 1973), Kahn and Wiener (1967), and Toffler (1970) tend to see mankind converging on a single future, a "post-industrial society," which is determined by the continuation of past trends. The directions of the engines of change —economic growth and technological development—are easily plotted, and the derived expectations often have been validated. For example, Ayres (1969) has stated: ". . . if the envelope curves for macro-variables representing the state of the art of a given technology show a definite trend, there already exists an internal dynamics which tends to continue the trend more or less straight ahead (on the appropriate scale) until some constraint is reached" (pp. 114–15).

The limitations of surprise-free forecasting are numerous. We may not wish to go where society seems to be headed. What alternative ends are available to us? How are we to select from among possible alternative futures? How are we to change society to reach a preferred alternative?

In contrast to the emphasis on current, existing societal strategies, the *crisis futurologists* have indicated that we may not achieve the surprise-free future plotted for us. There are limits to growth because "space-ship earth" is a closed system—resources are finite. This approach to futurology has provided a useful criticism of the emphasis on current materialistic, technological, and growth-oriented strategies, but it suffers from the same limited view of possible societal values and a negativistic approach to strategies. If measures for avoiding catastrophe are suggested, they generally consist of more of the same techno-logical answers, but better, more efficient ones: Population control, re-cycling, conservation, pollution control, and the like. The main thrust of this approach is a negative one; that current strategies will not work. Little attention is given to social or political strategies. As Hake (1973) suggests, the approach demonstrates political naïvete about the imple-mentation of any technological reforms that might be proposed.

A third school of futurology rests on dissatisfactions with present societal values and goals. These *value-critical futurologists* focus on alternative values and goals and the need to go beyond our current predominant values. The problem is that means to desired ends are not considered. As Hake (1973) suggests "New social ideals do not in themselves create a new society. Idealistic utopian thinking, divorced from the action of social groups, is no more viable as a creator of change than . . . technological determinism. . . ." (p. 7). Thus, while Reich (1971) advocates the "greening of America" he does not examine the workings of our society to determine whether and how such ends are attainable.

The limitations of futurology noted above can be overcome in theory by an approach akin to *strategy formulation* (Chapter 14). This ap-proach attempts to specify alternative goals and values for society as well as the means by which these can be achieved. There is an emphasis on the process by which both ends and means jointly, can be more clearly articulated. Etzioni's *The Active Society* (1968) is an example of this approach to futurology.

Unfortunately, there are limits to what we can expect from social strategy formulation. In the world system, everything is related to every-thing else. Political and social factors affect technological and eco-nomic factors and vice versa. These interrelations are too numerous and complex to be understood in their entirety, and the result is a very imper-fect forecasting technique. Yet, this approach probably holds more promise than the others. As Hake indicates: "We cannot know the future, but we can know alternative possibilities and the means of their attainment and we can act to produce one or another of these concrete utopias" (1973, p. 7).

It is interesting to note that when we assume both consensus regard-ing goals and the knowledge with which to select appropriate means, forecasting and planning become inseparable. Social strategy formula-tion, similar to organizational strategic planning, may seem to imply omnipotence. As we saw in Chapter 14, though, this is hardly the case. We do not mean to imply that either perfect knowledge of the system or complete consensus regarding goals is ever attained. Rather, we have described an approach to planning and futurology that allows muddling through to take on purpose.

SOME GENOTYPIC ORGANIZATIONAL VARIABLES TO CONSIDER

Many reports of futurologists omit analysis of organizational variables. To our way of thinking this is unfortunate, for prediction must include some notion of the limits to organizational capabilities and responsiveness. For this reason, we shall describe organizational phenomena that may circumscribe the alternatives available to society.

Rationality in Organizational Life

Rationality, the conscious marshaling of the most efficient means toward organizational ends, is critical to Weber's description of bureaucracy. In these terms, the coming "death of bureaucracy" touted by Bennis and others is far from imminent, for rationality of the technical core (Thompson, 1967) increases with the complexity of technological processes. As technologies become more complex, we can expect organizations to become more rational. Protecting the rationality of the technological core from environmental and human uncertainty may constitute a prime organizational problem in the future.

While this may sound contradictory in the face of growing interest in the human relations movement, we agree with Scott (1969) that OD, job enlargement, and the like often are based on values similar to those espoused in Taylor's scientific management. Viewed from one perspective, the human relations movement is merely the behavioral scientist's approach to management science. Observing a credibility gap between the pronouncements of the human relations movement and the goals of its various programs, Scott remarks that management generally installs human relations projects where they are consistent with economic values; that is, with better, more efficient functioning of personnel. Thus, OD and other practices serve as intended means to even greater organizational efficiency, productivity, and rationality.

As rationality increases and at the same time the environment becomes more complex, management's problems are magnified. In Chapter 13 we discussed buffering, smoothing, anticipating, rationing, exchange, acquiring prestige, and more direct uses of power as ways of dealing with uncertainty. Strategic planning (Chapter 14), as well as planned change (especially Chapters 16–18), are also useful in this regard. However, as problems become more acute, more drastic steps may become appropriate.

One apparent response has been for organizational roles to become increasingly specified and segmental, or fragmented. Thompson's

(1973) scenario of organizations in the year 2000 illustrates this. In the year 2000 plus or minus 10 years we are likely to work for more than one organization. Technical "reps" employed by private contractors to work with government personnel, as well as university professors who pursue research funded by external agencies, are prototypes of tomorrow's workers according to Thompson. Please note that the kinds of role conflict described in Chapter 9 are likely to be intensified by these kinds of arrangements. Second, organizations (including managers and clientele) are likely to be located in widespread, changing networks, as are present-day firms that subcontract parts of various projects from the federal government. In this case, interorganizational relations such as those described in Chapter 13 are likely to become more important in day-to-day organizational functioning. Finally, Thompson suggests that individuals and organizations will cease to work under unitary authority systems. He cites the war on polio as an example which:

> . . . involved the activities of 3,100 local chapters, each of which raised funds through solicitations by volunteers, with 50 percent of those funds to be retained locally for treatment of local polio victims. But it motivated the pooling of the remaining 50 percent nationally, both as insurance against local outbreaks which might overrun local funds and for research and education purposes. In 20 years the Foundation spent $315 million on patient care, $55 million on research and $33 million on fellowships and scholarships . . . (1973, pp. 330–31).

The Limits to Rationality

At this point we must ask whether the average person will be able to survive the fragmentation of his work role that results when such drastic attempts to increase rationality are made. While the increased tempo of change and the temporary character of relationships may provide the individual greater freedom and opportunity (see, e.g., Bennis and Slater, 1968), his ability to adapt, let alone stay in control of the situation, will be taxed severely. At present we have limited, but compelling, evidence that excessive life changes produce somatic illness and psychological distress (Moss, 1973).

Taking a larger perspective, it would seem that increasing rationalization can destroy the organization per se. The essence of organization is the dedication of its parts to some ultimate purpose. Excessive rationality questions everything with an eye to efficiency. Nothing is held sacred. Everyone is assumed ultimately flexible, adaptable, and malleable. We wonder how the ultimately rational organization can be coordinated to act with unity of purpose. We suspect that organizational character (Chapter 12) and trust are dissipated by fragmentation and excessive change.

Values as Genotypic Variables

In Chapter 1 we described organizations as social systems. Such systems are part of the culture in which they reside and reflect society's norms and values as well as those idiosyncratic to the organizations. As used here, value is defined as: ". . . an enduring belief that a specific mode of conduct or end-state of existence is personally or socially preferable to an opposite or converse mode of conduct or end-state of existence" (Rokeach, 1973, p. 5). Many social scientists have taken a Marxian or substructural view of society—that values are determined by technology and other basic aspects of society. According to Marx, whether one owns the means of production or not determines one's ideology. We argue, however, along with superstructure theorists, that values affect the substructure to some degree—for example, that, the rise of Protestantism facilitated the growth of capitalism through its emphasis on the individual, work as a spiritual calling, and wealth as an index of spiritual standing.

McClelland (1961, 1971), for example, shows that the basic motivations that characterize societies can change over time. Studying the appearance of achievement-related themes in children's literature, for instance, he notes that increases in the frequency of achievement-related themes are paralleled by increases in economic activity some 20 years later, when those for whom the literature was intended are well established in the work force. Commenting on a study of the United States which covered the period 1800–1950, McClelland observes:

> Thus, if higher n Achievement is producing more technological innovations from people who have it, indexes reflecting these two factors should be closely associated in time and both should precede general increases in economic productivity. Such seems clearly to be the case so far as the United States is concerned . . . (1961, p. 151).

The little evidence we have to date causes some observers to comment on an apparent decline in values related to work and achievement in America. A provocative study by Miner (1971), for instance, indicates that levels of competitive motivation, positive attitudes toward authority, willingness to accept administrative responsibility, and the desirability of assuming masculine roles have declined among college students between 1960–61 and 1966–69. Miner argues that these changes result from markedly different child-rearing practices in vogue when the respective groups of students were children. If these observations as well as McClelland's reasoning are valid, there are major consequences for management in the near future.

Along with pessimism about worker motivation, some observers suggest reason to be pessimistic about man's intentions toward other men. The problem is that each individual is basically self-interested, and, left to his own devices, will use his power for self-aggrandizement. There will be "war of all against all." This Hobbesean problem can only be solved by formal, contractual relations which protect individuals from unbridled acts of self-interest. Carried to its logical conclusion, this view leads to pluralism as a way of protecting individuals and society against the tyranny of an elite (Scott, 1969).

We may, in fact, be moving into a period in which the effects of power motivation are in ascendance (McClelland, 1975). This observation corresponds to the Hobbesean view of human nature, suggesting approaches to management that protect organizations and organizational members from one another. Yet, these are gloomy predictions that do not fit our own desires and values, and move us to seek more satisfying alternative futures.

The Emergence of Common Values as Means for Organizational Control

As we indicated in Chapter 13, Emery (1967) suggests that the problem of responding appropriately to an unpredictable environment can be remedied by ". . . the emergence of values which have an overriding significance for all members of the field" (p. 228). Rules such as the Ten Commandments help us to act in ways consistent with far-reaching goals, even when we cannot discern the ramifying consequences of our acts because of the situation's complexity. Hierarchies of values help us avoid conflicts in selecting from among alternative possibilities.[1] Assuming that such values can help simplify complex situations, Emery suggests that we need to select appropriate values and find ways to reinforce them in society.

In Chapter 11 we discussed two basic approaches to organizational design. In the first approach, organizational survival is enhanced by strengthening and elaborating external control mechanisms. Redundancy is created by using redundant parts. Coordination is achieved by dispensing with ineffective parts. Reliability is enhanced through increased specialization, thus reducing the cost of any part that may be dispensed with at a later time. Emery likens this approach to an ant colony.

The alternative approach is based on redundancy of functions within the individual. Able to perform numerous functions, individuals substitute for one another as the task requires. The control mechanism for this system is internal to the parts. Thus, each member of a surgical team

---

[1] By hierarchy of values we mean value system. Theoretically, we esteem all values (e.g., truth, wisdom, love, freedom). However, if we prefer one value to another, a rank ordering, or value system will result. This raises a knotty problem. While all values may be thought worthwhile by all people, all value systems are not equally attractive. If society chooses to reinforce certain values, as Emery (1967) suggests, rank orderings—that is, value systems—will change. Rokeach (1973) finds that different value systems predispose individuals to behave differently. This is a relatively new area of study, and little is known for certain. However, Rokeach's work leads us to ask whether altering value systems in organizations or society will produce unintended and perhaps undesirable behaviors?

internalizes the welfare of the patient and need not be supervised closely.

Of the two, Emery finds the latter approach to be more congruent with Western values (e.g., respect for the individual). Throughout the text we have provided evidence that internalized control is feasible in contemporary organizations (e.g., System Four, autonomous work groups, job enrichment, and so on). However, we have also indicated possible limitations of such schemes.

Values in the Design of Future Organizations

Emery predicts that the structure of future organizations will include matrices of interorganizational relationships akin to Thompson's networks. However, he only hints at how value congruence within these networks can be achieved. His use of the professional association as a prototype is not an altogether happy example of interorganizational value consensus, given the dissension and self-serving tendencies within some professions (see, e.g., Freidson, 1970). Perhaps our discussion of bargaining in Chapter 10 is useful here. It may be recalled that tacit communication and informal negotiation are enhanced by conditions that allow normative structure to evolve. Similarly, socialization processes akin to those discussed in Chapter 10 may be developed within organizational groupings. Be that as it may, the road to Emery's future is by no means clear.

Reprise

It may seem that we are overly pessimistic about future changes in organizational life. Our pessimism stems from an attempt to counterbalance the mass of literature that predicts technological cornucopias and idyllic social arrangements to come. While we have no dread of the future, we do not look ahead for utopias. Although we do have means to control some aspects of future society through forecasting and planning, they are not without limits.

We have much to learn before societywide programs of planning become feasible and compatible with our individualistic values (Friedman, 1973; Michael, 1973; Schon, 1971). Yet, some progress has been made. Corporate programs such as those used by General Electric are promising. GE's strategic planning incorporates technological and economic forecasting and also social and political projections (Wilson, 1974). These activities suggest the development of appropriate technologies for futurology and planning. Hopefully, similar efforts in other sectors of the economy will combine eventually to provide us with more control over where we are going. In any event, we suspect that, despite future challenges to our managerial capability, the rational attributes of organizational functioning first described by Weber and Taylor (Chapter 1) will survive.

DISCUSSION QUESTIONS

1. One rarely hears values such as honesty, reliability, and industry extolled. Have values been deemphasized in our society? If so, what are the implications for organizations?
2. Is it always the fault of the forecaster that his forecast turns out wrong?
3. What is your scenario of organizational life in the year 2000?

REFERENCES

Ayres, Robert U. *Technological forecasting and long-range planning.* New York: McGraw-Hill, 1969.

Bell, Daniel. *The end of ideology.* Glencoe, Ill.: Free Press, 1960.

Bell, Daniel. *The coming of post-industrial society: a venture in social forecasting.* New York: Basic Books, 1973.

Bennis, Warren G. A funny thing happened on the way to the future. *American Psychologist,* 1970 (a), 25, 595–608.

Bennis, Warren G. Beyond bureaucracy. In Warren G. Bennis (Ed.), *American Bureaucracy.* Chicago: Aldine, 1970 (b). Pp. 3–16.

Bennis, Warren G., and Slater, Philip E. *The temporary society.* New York: Harper & Row, 1968.

Drucker, Peter F. The surprising seventies. *Harper's Magazine,* 1971, 243 (1454) (July), 35–39.

Ehrlich, Paul R., and Ehrlich, Anne H. *Population, resources, environment.* San Francisco: W. H. Freeman, 1970.

Emery, F. E. The next thirty years: concepts, methods, and anticipations. *Human Relations,* 1967, 20, 199–236.

Etzioni, Amitai. *The active society.* New York: Free Press, 1968.

Freidson, Eliot. *Profession of medicine.* New York: Dodd, Mead, 1970.

Friedman, John. *Retracking America: a theory of transactive planning.* Garden City, N.Y.: Anchor Books, 1973.

Fuller, R. B. *Utopia or oblivion: the prospects for humanity.* New York: Bantam, 1969.

Galese, Liz Roman. The soothsayers: more companies use 'futurists' to discern what is lying ahead. *The Wall Street Journal,* 1975 (March 31), 1, 10.

Hake, Barry. Values, technology and the future. *Futures Conditional,* 1973, *1*(6) (June), 6–7.

Kahn, Herman, and Wiener, Anthony J. *The year 2000: a framework for speculation on the next thirty years.* New York: Macmillan, 1967.

McClelland, David C. *The achieving society.* Princeton, N.J.: Van Nostrand, 1961.

McClelland, David C. *Motivational trends in society.* Morristown, N.J.: General Learning Press, 1971.

McClelland, David C. Love and power: the psychological signals of war. *Psychology Today,* 1975, 8(8) (January), 44–48.

Meadows, Donella H., Meadows, Dennis L., Randers, Jorgen, and Behrens, William W., III. *The limits to growth.* New York: Universe Books, 1972.

Michael, Donald, N. *On learning to plan—and planning to learn.* San Francisco: Jossey-Bass, 1973.

Miner, John B. Changes in student attitudes toward bureaucratic role prescriptions during the 1960s. *Administrative Science Quarterly,* 1971, *16,* 351–64.

Moss, Gordon E. *Illness, immunity, and social interaction: the dynamics of biosocial resonation.* New York: Wiley, 1973.

Reich, Charles. *The greening of America,* New York: Bantam Books, 1971.

Rokeach, Milton. *The nature of human values.* New York: Free Press, 1973.

Roszak, Theodore. *The making of a counter culture.* Garden City, N.Y.: Doubleday, 1969.

Schon, Donald A. *Beyond the stable state.* London: Maurice Temple Smith, 1971.

Scott, William G. Organization government: the prospects for a truly participative system. *Public Administration Review,* 1969, *29,* 5, 43–53.

Slater, Philip E., and Bennis, Warren G. Democracy is inevitable. *Harvard Business Review,* 1964, *42* (2), 51–59.

Thompson, James D. *Organizations in action.* New York: McGraw-Hill, 1967.

Thompson, James D. Society's frontiers for organizing activities. *Public Administration Review,* 1973, *33,* 327–35.

Toffler, Alvin. *Future Shock.* New York: Random House, 1970.

Wilson, Ian H. Socio-political forecasting: a new dimension to strategic planning. *Michigian Business Review,* 1974, *26*(4) (July), 15–25.

Case

A Consultant's Working Paper*
J. W. Lorsch and P. H. Thompson

MEMORANDUM

To: Scott Morgan and Gary Skeen
From: Bill Murdock
Subject: Education Innovations, Inc.

After our discussion of the situation at EII, I decided to write up some concrete proposals which we can discuss at our next meeting.

EII presents a complex picture of a dynamic group of ex-academics and professionals struggling to create a profitable business in a highly uncertain (but presently abundant) environment dominated by government contracts. The issues, as I see them, are:

1. Organizational. What problems exist, what "ideal" remedies might be suggested?
2. Personalities, Power, and Philosophy. What are the dynamics of power, and the values of the individuals as they interrelate which will constrain implementation of the "ideal" organizational solutions?
3. Internal Changes. What efforts have the company made to address its problems, and with what success?
4. Implementation. There are clearly high and low priority needs, as well as more or less amenable problems. How can some of the less amenable problems be shifted to the more amenable category? How can remedies be carried out and in what manner is a remedy indeed feasible, and at what cost? I shall discuss each of these areas in turn.

Organizational Problems

With its origins, both technological and directorial, in academe, its back turned on its confining bureaucracy and its goals autonomous social innovation, the successive granting of five contracts and a foundation grant has led to the meteoric growth of EII from 12 employees (3 directors) and $75,000 in sales to 115 employees (5 directors, 60 professionals) and over $1.5 million in sales in three years.

At the present time EII must accomplish four tasks in order to be successful:

1. *Winning contracts,* which requires maintaining external contracts, generating innovative ideas, listing "name" personnel on contract bids, and writing appropriate yet imaginative proposals.

   This activity is at present the firm's strongest area, largely due to the efforts of Menschel and Cohen. However, if EII is to remain successful at winning contracts, delivery must be made on current projects.

2. *Staffing* is also essential, since the assignment of certain personnel is promised in contract proposals. If key people are listed on a contract proposal, they must be available to do the work.

3. *Completion of projects,* with appropriate attention to quality of project work, is necessary to ensure future business. Cost is not too important since most projects are cost plus fixed fee, but quality and time deadlines are important. EII is at present quite lax about this aspect of contract work.

4. *Adequate financing* must be secured, since the company has cash flow problems due to undercapitalization and the delay in government payment. Furthermore, the dependence on government funds will always contribute to problems of stability.

An additional aspect of EII operations is that these four major activities must be related to each other. A flow chart of the current contract development process shows a lack of continuity:

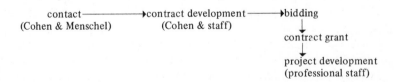

Contract development is not matched to internal resource availability nor to any policy of overall development either technological, resource based, or ideological. Decisions are arbitrary and unilateral. No procedures exist for integrating the various stages in the process. Projects are not executed by contracting agencies. Finally, there is a lack of integration of field offices and headquarters.

Staffing problems have occurred because professional staff members are recurited for specific projects and they are interested in particular areas. Their salaries are above average but their major incentive lies in the opportunity to do innovative work of social value; the problem is that EII's best people are interested in innovation and development rather than performance. Furthermore, the professionals are very mobile and able to find other work, so EII has relatively little power over them.

Personalities, Power and Philosophy

The predominant values of people in the organization are expressed in commitments to self, ideas, freedom, and society. Linzner is the only senior professional who feels constrained by responsibility to the company. There is a major ideological conflict between societal and profit goals, at least as articulated by the staff. However, my guess is that this is more a function of sloppy thinking than of real conflict. Ambiguity and uncertainty are seen as conducive (though causing chaos), while structure is seen as confining. Some of this mess is creative, some sloppy, and some a clear result of a power struggle at the top level. As a result of this deliberate ambiguity, there are no clear-cut and agreed goals regarding company direction, administration, identity, and decision making. Essentially EII is a group of individual playing a series of more or less responsible games.

Conflict is evident in the division of ownership shares, in the failure to develop coherent goals, in the bypassing of the board by Menschel, in Cohen's ignoring his responsibilities. The order of the hierarchy at the top appears to be first Menschel, then Cohen (both of whose sources of power lie in the critical value to the company of their external contacts), then Linzner, and finally Franklin and Miller, who have so little power that they appear to be directed into staff jobs. Linzner acknowledges that the only power he has to make things happen comes from de facto situations. The allocation of shares is merely symbolic of an attempt to make demonstrable their relative positions—and they cannot agree whether the basis should be money contributed, energy spent, etc. This confusion—exacerbated by the board's failing to distinguish board roles from executive roles, possibly deliberately because of the power implications—is clearly at the root of the company's problems. Each decision (contract development, hiring of personnel) becomes a test of who has control and a means to retain or increase power. This situation is complicated by the fact that the professionals cannot be manipulated easily because of their salable skills. Nor do any of the principals really have to continue if the business becomes uncongenial, so there is little incentive for them to modify gratifying behavior (including the playing of power games).

Other personality-related problems exist because Cohen is a freewheeler, Menschel likes to be in charge, and Linzner has a strong sense of responsibility. This impulsivity must be harnessed to company goals. Each person concentrates on the area that gives him power. (The only area that requires some procedures—finance—is the only area which is not sensitive to control issues because of governmental constraints. And, ironically, this area is overcontrolled.) The modeling supplied by the top brass is seen in the behavior of the professionals, who feel entitled to be in on everything. There is no real organizational leadership or coherent identity for the company.

A major problem resulting from these circumstances is a failure to develop or plan administrative structures and mechanisms appropriate to rapid growth and autonomous staff, highly dispersed, and which would still be responsive to the necessary constraints of finance and operating while seeking a more diverse and stable base.

Internal Changes

EII has made four changes in response to its awareness of certain problems. An examination of these changes is quite revealing.

1. *Hiring Canlis.* Originally the position of assistant to the president was defined to carry some potential power, but the job was later redefined into powerlessness.
2. *Thursday Afternoon Committee.* No attempt was made to determine if the membership or the activities of this committee were appropriate to its goals. Menschel and Cohen, whose presence should have been critical, were absent. The only significant accomplishment of this group was a training program.
3. *Administrative Service Groups.* This group replaced Miller, executive vice president, who was then shifted into project work. Formation of the Administrative Services Group, while recognizing a necessary staff function, was not a real examination of power issues.
4. *Linzner/Menschel Switch.* This move represents a recognition that Menschel really has more power than Linzner. However, it is still unclear how the switch will make the organization more effective.

Solutions and Implementation

In this section I have included a rough organization chart for the present organization (Exhibit 1) and a chart for the proposed organization (Exhibit 2).

EII must clarify company goals and then design an appropriate organizational structure. Exhibit 2 shows a proposed organization chart,

EXHIBIT 1
Approximate Organization Chart

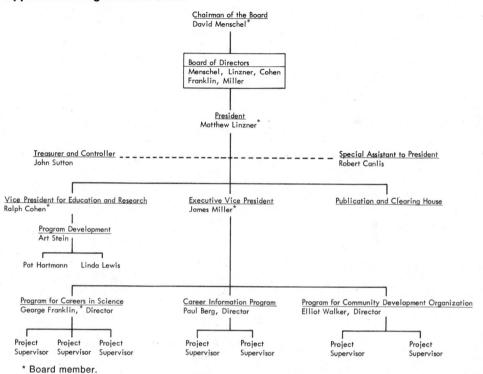

* Board member.

which is a first step in a necessary clarification of organizational relationships. I think that the desired organizational changes include:

A. A distinction between board and executive roles. While executives may be board members, they should clearly distinguish their activities in each role.

B. Long-range planning, to determine trends in technology and funding, and to aid decision making on such contract issues as development, staffing, financing, etc.

C. Research and development applications of social and behavioral knowledge pertinent to contracts in the education and public policy domain, and to stimulate the use of such technology in new and ongoing contracts.

D. Contract Development Team. After the initial contact for a new contract, this team would be formed to marshal the appropriate company resource to make a decision on whether or not to bid and to generate ideas for the bid. The team members would include (1) the program director, (2) the director of long-range planning (early

EXHIBIT 2
Proposed Organization Chart

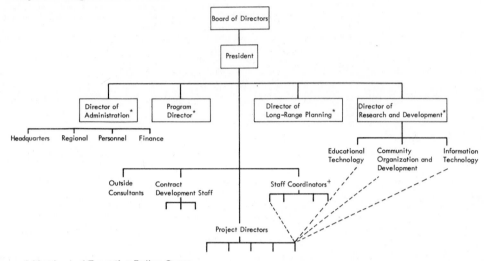

* Members of Executive Policy Group.
† Staff Coordinators maintain liaison between program director, and project personnel, and recommend shifts of personnel in order to optimize allocations of expertise over entire program.

stages only), (3) one of the contrast development staff members (the group of three currently under Cohen), (4) one or two members of R&D, (5) a staff coordinator (see Exhibit 2), and (6) the potential project director. It is important to get a candidate for project director in on the early stages of the contract development so he will have a thorough knowledge of the project and be committed to seeing it through to completion. One guideline on contract development might be not to bid if no one is willing to be project director.

E. Assignment of Personnel. The project director will draw from R&D and the consulting staff to form project teams. Staff members could work on more than one project. Coordinators would be responsible for regional and technological staff. The project director would have line responsibility for the project and to the client.

F. The project directors would handle recruiting and selection of personnel, with approval of the program director and the personnel director. Compensation and evaluation would be handled by project directors, with overall coordination being the responsibility of the program director so as to maintain some uniformity in the company. Definite career paths should be identified which would allow increasing autonomy and opportunity for innovative activities.

G. Project Evaluation. The program director and his staff would develop a control system enabling them to monitor the progress of each project. In addition, periodic reviews of the projects would be made by the executive policy group.

Can the company make these necessary changes with the current personnel? It seems doubtful. Who is necessary? It is unclear—Cohen and Menschel have the contacts, Linzner makes it run, their relationships are probably not amenable to direct confrontation, and Cohen and Menschel will not be amenable to diminished power (besides, they like playing around). I have listed three possible approaches to implementation of our recommendation.

1. *Nonthreatening Slow Approach.* Suggest to the board that there are several aspects of EII operations that require new procedures. The board might appoint task forces to examine problems and recommend solutions. We would initially point out areas that are not politically sensitive.

Some nonthreatening areas might include:

a. Communication and coordination between headquarters and field offices.
b. Hiring and compensation policies for clerical workers. The assumption behind this approach is that success in handling these problems would give task force members confidence and experience as well as possible methods for approaching more difficult and controversial problems, such as development of procedures for selecting contracts to bid on, etc.

2. *Confrontation.* In a meeting with the full board we could point out that the company has a number of serious problems (use interview data and perhaps even an attitude survey to substantiate such an assertion) and that these problems will continue and perhaps increase unless the board begins to resolve its conflicts and clarify power relationships in the organization. Until the power struggle can be resolved at the top it would be a waste of time to institute changes at a lower level. In the confrontation meeting we would help the board to identify areas of conflict and to confront each other on those issues (such as the procedures for deciding which contracts to accept) until they arrive at an acceptable solution. There is a certain amount of risk in this strategy but the board members are highly educated men and they like to think of themselves as reasonable, so they might respond to this approach.

3. *Challenge the Board to Develop an Innovative Organization.* This approach emphasizes the positive aspects of the organization. The board likes to develop innovative and creative solutions to difficult social problems. Therefore, we could challenge them to be equally creative in developing an innovative and exciting organization. The

challenge is to create a clear company identity or image as well as an organization where people can be given (1) a great deal of autonomy and freedom to generate their own programs, and (2) the encouragement to see the programs through to completion. If the board seems willing to accept that challenge, then we could indicate the areas that an organization of this type should be concerned about, i.e., winning contracts, staffing projects, completing projects, financing, etc., and we could stress the importance of relating these tasks to each other.

I can see arguments pro and con for all three of these approaches. The slow approach is less risky and it may begin to solve some of the company's problems, but how much time does this company have? The confrontation approach is faster but more risky. Are the board members prepared to confront each other on these difficult issues when they haven't been willing to do so before? And what if some of the top people leave? Finally, if we use the challenge approach, what do we do if they are not interested in the challenge? I would like to get your reactions on this problem as soon as possible so we can begin to develop our strategy in detail.

Index

Index

This book has been set in 9 point Primer, leaded 3 points, and 8 point Primer, leaded 2 points. Section numbers are 24 point (large) Melior Italic and 30 point Melior Italic and section titles are 24 point (small) Melior Italic. Chapter numbers are 60 point Bernhard Modern Bold and chapter titles are 24 point (small) Melior. The size of the type page is 27 by 46½ picas.